ANCIENT NEAR EASTERN STUDIES

SUPPLEMENT 42

ANCIENT NEAR EASTERN STUDIES

SUPPLEMENT 42

ACROSS THE BORDER: LATE BRONZE-IRON AGE RELATIONS BETWEEN SYRIA AND ANATOLIA

Proceedings of a Symposium held at the Research Center of Anatolian Studies, Koç University, Istanbul May 31–June 1, 2010

Edited by

K. Aslıhan YENER

PEETERS
LEUVEN – PARIS – WALPOLE, MA.
2013

Series Editors: Antonio Sagona and Claudia Sagona

A catalogue record for this book is available from the Library of Congress.

ISBN 978-90-429-2715-5
D/2013/0602/52

Cover illustration: Stone sculptures showing Katuwas from Carchemish (left) facing Taita, king of Palastin, from Aleppo (right). After Mazzoni, this volume.

PRINTED IN BELGIUM

Peeters N.V., Warotstraat 50, B-3020 Herent

CONTENTS

Introduction: Imperial Demise and Forging Emergent Kingdoms 1
K. A. YENER

SECTION A:
EXCAVATIONS IN LEVANTINE TURKEY
AND LEVANTINE SYRIA

Chapter 1
New Excavations at Alalakh: The 14th–12th Centuries BC 11
K. A. YENER

Chapter 2
The Late Bronze Age Fortresses at Alalakh: Architecture and Identity in Mediterranean Exchange Systems 37
M. AKAR

Chapter 3
Tayinat in the Early Iron Age 61
T. P. HARRISON

Chapter 4
Chatal Höyük in the Amuq: Material Culture and Architecture during the Passage from the Late Bronze Age to the Early Iron Age 89
M. PUCCI

Chapter 5
The Crisis of Qatna at the Beginning of the Late Bronze Age II and the Iron Age II Settlement Revival. A Regional Trajectory towards the Collapse of the Late Bronze Age Palace System in the Northern Levant 113
D. MORANDI BONACOSSI

Chapter 6
Shedding New Light on the Elusive Late Bronze and Early Iron Ages at Tell 'Acharneh (Syria) 147
M. FORTIN and L. COOPER

Chapter 7
Sabuniye: A Late Bronze-Iron Age Port Settlement on the Northeastern Mediterranean Coast 173
H. PAMIR

Chapter 8
A Re-evaluation of the Late Bronze to Early Iron Age Transitional Period: Stratigraphic Sequence and Plain Ware of Tarsus-Gözlükule 195
S. YALÇIN

Chapter 9
Exploring Sirkeli Höyük in the Late Bronze Age and its Interregional Connections 213
E. KOZAL

Chapter 10
The Transition from the Late Bronze Age to the Early Iron Age at Tell Afis, Syria (phases VII-III) 227
F. VENTURI

SECTION B:
EXCAVATIONS IN EASTERN TURKEY
AND EASTERN SYRIA

Chapter 11
Across Assyria's Northern Frontier: Tell Fekheriye at the End of the Late Bronze Age 263
P. V. BARTL and D. BONATZ

Chapter 12
Between the Mušku and the Aramaeans: The Early History of Guzana/Tell Halaf 293
M. NOVÁK

Chapter 13
Some Implications of Revised C14 and Dendrochronological Dating for the "Late Bronze Levels" at Tille Höyük on the Euphrates 311
G. D. SUMMERS

Chapter 14
The Late Bronze Age to Early Iron Age Transition: A Perspective from the Upper Tigris River 329
T. MATNEY

Chapter 15
Neo-Hittite Melid: Continuity or Discontinuity? 349
M. FRANGIPANE and M. LIVERANI

Chapter 16
Pottery as an Indicator of Changing Interregional Relations in the Upper Euphrates Valley. The Case of the Late Bronze-Iron Age Assemblages from Arslantepe/Malatya 373
F. MANUELLI

Chapter 17
New Excavations at the Late Bronze Age and Iron Age Site of Gre Amer on the Garzan River, Batman Province 393
G. PULHAN and S. R. BLAYLOCK

SECTION C:
FUNERARY PRACTICES, TEXTS AND THE ARTS

Chapter 18
Funerary Practices and Society at the Late Bronze-Iron Age Transition. A View from Tell Shiukh Fawqâni and Tell an-Nasriyah (Syria) 423
A. TENU

Chapter 19
Working Ivory in Syria and Anatolia during the Late Bronze-Iron Age . . . 449
A. CAUBET

Chapter 20
Arts and Cross-Cultural Communication in the Early 1st Millennium: The Syro-Anatolian Contact 465
S. MAZZONI

Chapter 21
The Luwian Inscriptions from the Temple of the Storm-God of Aleppo . . 493
J. D. HAWKINS

Chapter 22
Qadesh, Sea-Peoples, and Anatolian-Levantine Interactions. 501
K. STROBEL

Chapter 23
An Amulet with the Names of Ramesses II from the Roman Baths at Ankara 539
H. PEKER

INTRODUCTION
IMPERIAL DEMISE AND FORGING EMERGENT KINGDOMS

K. Aslıhan YENER
Koç University
Department of Archaeology and History of Art
Rumelifeneri Yolu
Sarıyer, 34450 Istanbul, Turkey
And
University of Chicago
Oriental Institute
1155 East 58th Street
Chicago, Illinois 60637, USA
E-mail: ayener@ku.edu.tr
akyener12@gmail.com

ABSTRACT

One of the most intriguing issues facing archaeologists working in the second millennium BC is the collapse of Late Bronze Age empires and the rise of the smaller principalities known as the Iron Age kingdoms. Some of these kingdoms retain vestiges of the previous Hittite, Middle Assyrian, and Mitannian cultures while others represent an ethnic diversity of newly emerging centers of power. These decentralized kingdoms stretch from Cilicia to the Tigris River and are situated on both sides of the modern border of Syria and Turkey. Theories about the cause of this period of upheaval and political transition have variously blamed everything from catastrophic environmental change or earthquake to internal dynastic struggles or marauding bands of "Sea Peoples" and other mass migrations. The purpose of this conference was to bring together researchers from both sides of the Turkish-Syrian border for a new assessment of the Late Bronze-Early Iron Age transition.[*]

* I would like to warmly acknowledge and thank three Koç institutions for making this conference possible: the Dean, Sami Gülgöz, Department of Archaeology and the History of Art at Koç University, the Koç University Research Center for Anatolian Civilizations (RCAC), and the Pera Museum. There are numerous students, personnel, faculty, and administrators who generously donated time, funding, and energy to make this symposium possible, and I would like to express my sincere gratitude for their efforts. I sincerely thank Mara Horowitz, Murat Akar and David Hawkins for reading, adding to, and commenting on this manuscript; all mistakes are my own.

INTRODUCTION

The collapse of the Late Bronze Age empires of the Near East and Anatolia and the subsequent rise of smaller, independent Iron Age kingdoms is a crucial juncture in ancient history. Modern political realities across the border between Turkey and Syria have unfortunately minimized the flow of scholarly information about this important transitional period. The 'Across the Border' symposium, held at the Research Center for Anatolian Civilizations (RCAC) in Istanbul from May 31–June 1, 2010 and jointly sponsored by the Department of Archaeology and the History of Art at Koç University, underscored the need for sharing and comparing archaeological data from new as well as established excavations. This chapter gives an introduction to the topic of cross-border investigations in the Late Bronze and early Iron Ages, as well as the author's contribution to the conference from the ongoing excavations at Tell Atchana.

The landscape through which the modern border of Turkey and Syria runs is a diverse one.[1] In the east, the upper Khabur River drains the rugged mountains of southeastern Anatolia through a grassland with sufficient rainfall for dry farming. The upper Euphrates River likewise emerges from the highlands along the modern border and proceeds southeast through temperate steppe into the drier Mesopotamian zone. A mosaic of hills and small plains lies west of the Euphrates, a fractured landscape with bare rocky hills and fertile river valleys. At the western terminus of the modern border, the fertile and prosperous Amuq Valley lies adjacent to the Amanus Mountains and the Mediterranean Sea.

These areas, though today separated by a political boundary, were once united in a series of evolving nation-states and empires of both local and foreign origin. Due to their location at the intersection of Anatolia, the Levant, and Mesopotamia, the modern Turkey-Syria borderlands have a long history of dynamic sociocultural interactions. The river valleys of the Euphrates and its tributaries served as pathways from the plains to the highlands. The Amuq has long been used as a crossroads owing to its unique position. Valleys open to the Amuq plain from the four cardinal directions, providing natural highways into Anatolia via the Maraş plain to the north, into Cilicia via the Belen Pass to the west, into Mesopotamia via the Aleppo region to the east, south to Canaan via the upper Orontes valley (part of the north-south African rift zone), and out to the Mediterranean via the Orontes delta.

The modern border cuts through the territories of a number of Bronze and Iron Age political entities whose academic investigations have suffered as a result. Each participant at the 'Across the Border' symposium presented new results from instrumental analyses, ceramic sequences, and environmental research, which have augmented the discussions about interconnectedness between regions of modern Turkey and Syria and

[1] See figure 1, chapter 1 and map, this chapter.

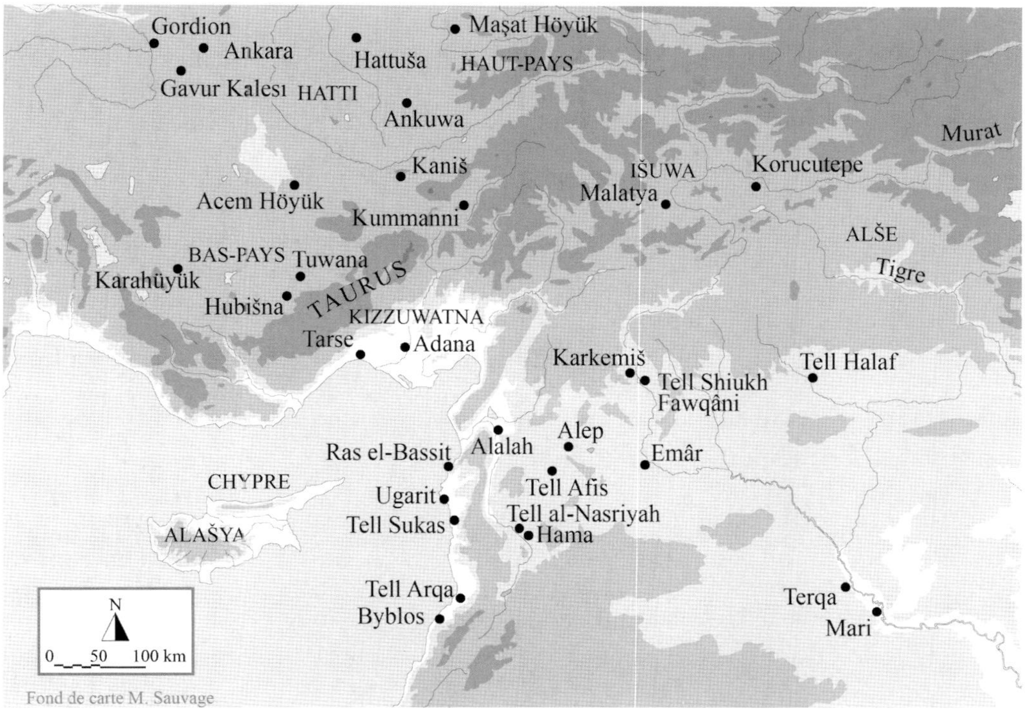

provided crucial archaeological context for the structural collapse at the end of the Late Bronze Age. Participants also gave special attention to significant new understandings of chronology stemming from their recent excavations and reassessments of stratigraphy. The discovery and translation of new inscriptions from Aleppo, Tell Tayinat, and elsewhere have also helped elucidate the political history of the Iron Age 'Neo-Hittite' kingdoms of Syria and southern Anatolia before the eventual rise of the next great socio-political juggernaut, the Neo-Assyrian Empire in the 9th century BC.

The transition from the Late Bronze Age to the Iron Age in the late second millennium BC has found voice and attention in several recent conferences.[2] As the results of renewed excavations at the sites of important urban centers in Anatolia and Syria, many of which had been left dormant for over half a century, become available, scholarly conceptions of this transition have become much more nuanced. Furthermore, an increase in archaeological and paleo-environmental survey has greatly enhanced traditional site-specific excavations by embedding the research into regional studies of the hinterlands of central settlements. New climatic data, derived from sediment cores throughout the Near East and Anatolia, has provided evidence to reconstruct the paleo-environment and its many fluctuations and allowed for new hypotheses about provisioning, or failing to provision, these populations.

[2] Bachhuber and Roberts 2009; Hawkins 2009; Harrison 2008, 2009a, 2009b, Venturi 2010.

In a recent publication, Rohling and his colleagues[3] state that "the Late Bronze Age-Early Iron Age transition in the eastern Mediterranean about 1200–900 BC coincided with one of the interglacial Holocene Rapid Climate Changes (RCC event) as documented in about 50 globally distributed climate proxy records." Other studies in Syria[4] confirm these data, which indicate the development of steppe/desert conditions with a 3° C change of temperature, transforming the coastal lowlands into a desert-like environment incapable of adequate food production. Such RCC impacts would necessarily have had dramatic historical consequences in this region, a topic worthy of exploring more carefully despite reluctance towards evoking environmental determinism. The proliferation of such environmental information for the Bronze and Iron Ages, especially in Syria and recently in Turkey, provides context to the fluid and dynamic social conditions at work during this time frame.

As queried recently by Robert McCormick Adams,[5] what role did the imperial ambitions of the Hittite, Mitanni, and Middle Assyrian Empires play in the subsequent formation of post-collapse kingdoms and the coming of the Iron Age, including iron as a technological breakthrough? Adams rightly notes that "transformative impulses" came from a diversity of directions, including the environment and, especially, social institutions, and sociocultural relations. The Late Bronze imperial players were Hittite Anatolia, Mitanni and Middle Assyrian Syria, and New Kingdom Egypt, all of which were engaged in a global political struggle during this period. Numerous other ethnic and sociopolitical entities in the region, both local and immigrant, formed the tapestry upon which the imperial ambitions of these larger polities were embroidered and served as the raw materials from which the Iron Age kingdoms were subsequently formed. The West Semitic populations of Ugarit, the Amurru of west-central Syria, and the related Amorite peoples of Mukish (Amuq), Aleppo, and the central Orontes valley, all were caught between dueling empires in the Late Bronze Age.[6] Hurrian-speakers from the east and Luwian-speakers from the west had begun to settle along a line from Cilicia to the Euphrates already in the LBI and increasing through to the Iron Age. Aegean material culture as early as the MB[7] well through the Iron Age[8] levels across Cilicia and the Amuq could suggest immigration or contact with regions further west.

In order to address these research priorities, the 'Across the Border' conference brought together scholars from a wide range of specializations and areas of research, beginning with the Late Bronze Age and continuing into the early Iron Age. The

[3] Rohling et al. 2009, p. 2.
[4] Kaniewski 2010.
[5] Adams 2000.
[6] von Dassow 2008.
[7] Most notably the Aegean related iconography on seals and frescoes of Alalakh from the MB level VII Palace.
[8] Harrison 2010.

relationship between the Late Bronze II Hittite Empire, a quintessential expansionist state in Anatolia, and its powerful Syrian rivals, the Mitanni in LBI-IIa and Middle Assyrians in LBIIb, was addressed in the presentation of the Boğazköy (Hattusha) excavations by Andreas Schachner. Two papers by Aslıhan Yener and Murat Akar (this volume) focused on recent efforts to fine-tune the stratigraphy and chronology of Late Bronze Tell Atchana (Alalakh), a site located on the political fault line between the Hittite and Mitanni imperial spheres and which had formerly provided the anchor for the so-called "middle chronologies." New excavations at Tell Fakheriye on the Khabur headwaters by Dominik Bonatz and Peter Bartl (this volume) have revealed the long-lost Late Bronze Age Mitanni capital, Washukanni, of which Alalakh was a vassal during the time of Kings Idrimi and Barattarna.

The Middle Kingdom Hittites and the prelude to empire were represented by papers from Aygül Suel on the excavations at Ortaköy, Hittite Shapinuwa, in north-central Anatolia, as well as Ekin Kozal on Sirkeli in Cilicia (this volume) and Karl Stroebel (this volume) on the 'Sea Peoples.' Hatice Pamir (this volume) described new excavations at the Late Bronze/Iron Age port city, Sabuniye, on the delta of the Orontes River, and Annie Caubet (this volume) focused on the more famous port city, Ugarit, and its ivories. Nicolo Marchetti's paper discussed the region around Islahiye in the LBA, while Marina Pucci (this volume) described her new work on the unpublished Bronze and Iron Age materials from Chatal Höyük in the Amuq Valley. Lynn Swartz Dodd reported on the intensive surface survey in the Amuq and in the crop fields of Alalakh, revealing the first indication of a lower town from late in the Bronze Age city's history.

The transition from the Late Bronze to the early Iron Age was illuminated by the ceramic sequences presented by Daniele Morandi-Bonacossi at Qatna (this volume). Departing from the perspective of ceramic sequences, Aline Tenu (this volume) reported on the changes in burial practices at Tell Shiukh Fawqâni and Tell an-Nasriyah in Syria.

Michel Fortin (this volume) contributed with an assessment of excavations at Tell 'Acharneh, ancient Tunip. A massive basalt pedestal block with Luwian inscriptions was reported by Ali Dinçol and Belkıs Dinçol which was unearthed in the scarp of Siçanlı Höyük near Demirköprü in the Amuq by a group of geologists, headed by Altunel,[9] investigating the Dead Sea Transform fault. More evidence for the link between the Turkish province of Hatay and northern Syria in the early Iron Age was provided by Kay Kohlmeyer from the Citadel of Aleppo where new excavations unearthed a temple to the Storm God dating to the Hittite Empire period (Late Bronze Age). The temple was rebuilt in the Neo-Hittite period with reliefs and Luwian

[9] Altunel et al. 2009, Akyüz et al. 2006.

inscriptions mentioning the Kingdom of Walistin/Palistin, thought to be centered at Tell Tayinat in the Amuq Valley, and its ruler, King Taita.[10]

Timothy Harrison has updated the chronology of the Luwian inscriptions previously found at Tayinat based on new stratigraphic work (this volume). The Kingdom of Walistin/Palistin is again mentioned in these inscriptions. Newly uncovered Neo-Assyrian tablets and a temple at Tell Tayinat illustrate the change from local to imperial hegemony in the later Iron Age. Another new discovery related to the powerful yet poorly-known Iron Age kingdom of Walistin/Palistin comes from the Turkish Mediterranean coast at Arsuz (ancient Rhosus). Two massive Iron Age basalt stelae with Luwian inscriptions make reference to this kingdom, with the spelling 'Walistin', and a certain Suppiluliuma (a name with royal Hittite Bronze Age heritage) was identified as the king of this country by Ali and Belkıs Dinçol. David Hawkins (this volume) has incorporated all of this exciting information into a comprehensive history of a rather large Iron Age kingdom that once stretched along the borders of modern Turkey and Syria from the Mediterranean to the Euphrates. The diversity attested in the country of Walistin/Palistin, and the possibility of new ethnic arrivals during the Iron Age, are in keeping with the long history of dynamic and fluid population movements through the Hatay-Aleppo region.

Four papers presented information on the Iron Age in the less well-known eastern borderlands of Turkey and Syria. AMS radiocarbon dating and dendro-chronological reassessments opened new possibilities in understanding the processes of change in the transition from the Late Bronze Age to the Iron Age in this region. Geoffrey Summers at Tille on the Euphrates (this volume) has reported new assessments in chronology based on radiocarbon dates during these transitional periods. Tim Matney on the Upper Tigris reported on the excavations of Ziyaret Tepe in the Ilısu Dam project, identified as Middle Assyrian Tushhan. He explored the possibility of decentralized Aramaean polities forming in the region during periods of Neo-Assyrian weakness (this volume).

Mirko Novak (this volume) reported on renewed excavations at Tell Halaf (Guzana), where new ceramic evidence suggests an influx of Anatolians in the early Iron Age. Gül Pulhan and Stuart Blaylock have presented new finds on the peripheries of the Hittite and Hurro-Mitannian Empires at the salvage site of Gre Amer near Batman (this volume). Further north, Mario Liverani and Marcella Frangipane reported on the reactivation of work at the Late Bronze/ Iron Age levels at Arslantepe (this volume) and the finding of relief-decorated stelae. The history of this important site near Malatya is given additional chronological support by Federico Manuelli (this volume), who has presented details of the ceramic repertoire as well as the the stratigraphy and architecture of the Iron Age levels.

[10] Hawkins 2009; Kohlmeyer 2009.

Stefania Mazzoni (this volume) contributed a paper on the continuity of Imperial Hittite artistic styles, sculptural traditions, and relief decoration on orthostats from the Iron Age. Fabrizio Venturi presented an important paper on the Bronze Age-Iron Age transition at Tell Afis on the basis of the ceramic sequence (this volume). The research by Remzi Yağcı at Soli in Cilicia (Que) introduced the Neo-Assyrian destructions there. Hartmut Kühne, who gave a rousing and perceptive final presentation during the Iron Age session on Tuesday, summed up the state of research in the Khabur region of Syria during the late second and early first millennia BC.[11]

Bibliography

ADAMS, R. M.
2000 "Accelerated Technological Change in Archaeology and Ancient History," in *Cultural Evolution: Contemporary Viewpoints*, edited by G. M. Feinman and L. Manzanilla, pp. 95–119. New York: Plenum.
AKYÜZ, S. H. et al.
2006 "Historical Earthquake Activity on the Northern Part of the Dead Sea Fault Zone, Southern Turkey," *Tectonophysics* 426: 281–293.
ALTUNEL, E. et al.
2009 "Archaeological Sites (Tell and Road) offset by the Dead Sea Fault in the Amik Basin, Southern Turkey," *Geophysical Journal International* 179: 1313–1329.
BACHHUBER, C. S. and ROBERTS, R. G.
2009 *Forces of Transformation*. Oxford: Oxbow Books.
HARRISON, T. P.
2008 *Cyprus, the Sea Peoples and the Eastern Mediterranean: Regional Perspectives of Continuity and Change*. Toronto: Canadian Institute for Mediterranean Studies.
2009a "Lifting the Veil on a "Dark Age": Ta'yinat and the North Orontes Valley during the Early Iron Age," in *Exploring the Longue Durée: Essays in Honor of Lawrence E. Stager*, edited by J. D. Schloen, pp. 171–84. Winona Lake, IN: Eisenbrauns.
2009b "Neo-Hittites in the "Land of Palistin": Renewed Investigations at Tell Ta'yinat on the Plain of Antioch," *Near Eastern Archaeology* 72: 174–189.
HAWKINS, J. D.
2009 "Cilicia, the Amuq, and Aleppo: New Light in a Dark Age," *Near Eastern Archaeology* 72: 164–173.
KANIEWSKI, D. et al.
2010 "Late second–early first millennium BC abrupt climate changes in coastal Syria and their possible significance for the history of the Eastern Mediterranean," *Quaternary Research* 74: 207–215.
KOHLMEYER, K.
2009 "Temple to the Storm God at Aleppo during the Late Bronze and Early Iron Ages," *Near Eastern Archaeology* 72: 190–202.

[11] One paper by Peker on the new finds of a Ramses II amulet not presented at the conference was included in this volume.

ROHLING, E. J. et al.
2009 "Holocene climate variability in the eastern Mediterranean, and the end of the Bronze Age," in *Forces of Transformation*, edited by C. S. Bachhuber and R. G. Roberts. Oxford: Oxbow Books.

VENTURI, F. ed.
2010 *Societies in Transition: Evolutionary Processes in the Northern Levant between Late Bronze Age II and Early Iron Age. Papers presented on the occasion of the 20th anniversary of the new excavations at Tell Afis*. Bologna: CLUEB.

VON DASSOW, E. M.
2008 *State and Society in the Late Bronze Age: Alalah under the Mittani Empire.* Studies on the Civilization and Culture of Nuzi and the Hurrians 17. Bethesda: CDL Press.

Section A

EXCAVATIONS IN LEVANTINE TURKEY AND LEVANTINE SYRIA

CHAPTER 1

NEW EXCAVATIONS AT ALALAKH: THE 14TH–12TH CENTURIES BC

K. Aslıhan YENER
Koç University
Department of Archaeology and History of Art
Rumelifeneri Yolu
Sarıyer, 34450 Istanbul, Turkey
And
University of Chicago
Oriental Institute
1155 East 58th Street
Chicago, Illinois 60637, USA
E-mail: ayener@ku.edu.tr
akyener12@gmail.com

ABSTRACT

Recent research at the site of Tell Atchana, ancient Alalakh, has clarified the history of the city in the Late Bronze (LB) II and Early Iron I periods. While it was previously thought that the city was continuously inhabited from c.2000 BC to about 1190 BC, new excavations are suggesting that most if not all of the city was abandoned around 1300–1290 BC while only the temple and perhaps its immediate surroundings continued to be used in the mid-13th *century. After a period of abandonment, the site was reoccupied briefly c.1140 BC by a group that utilized a combination of local Bronze Age-derived wares, LH IIIC-Middle Developed ware, and Handmade Burnished Ware. This paper details the new findings and begins to reconstruct the historical narrative of this important site in the LBII-Iron I.*

INTRODUCTION

This chapter focuses on the latest phases in the history of Tell Atchana-Alalakh and the continuing research[1] that addresses the questions of Late Bronze collapse and the early Iron Age establishment of the important 'Neo-Hittite' kingdom of Walistin/ Palistin. Alalakh, though not among the largest cities of the ancient Near East and

[1] After the close of the conference and the subsequent 2010 and 2011 excavation seasons at Alalakh, new information emerged about the hitherto unknown early Iron Age at this site.

Anatolia, is nevertheless of preeminent importance both to archaeology and in the ancient world due to both its long history of excavation and its natural strategic position and abundant natural resources. Located at the southern edge of the Amuq Valley on the major westward bend of the Orontes River, Alalakh was once the capital of the small Bronze Age state of Mukish (**Fig. 1**).

The political history and cultural dynamics of the second millennium BC are encapsulated in the archaeological sequences of Tell Atchana which, unlike most tell sites, dates exclusively to the Middle and Late Bronze Ages (2000–1200 BC, Middle Chronology) and the early Iron Age (c.1200–1000 BC in the Amuq sequence). Finds such as the multi-lingual palace archives with texts in Akkadian, Hittite, and Sumerian, some of which contain Luwian and Hurrian names, reflect a multi-ethnic population at this Amorite capital. Previous excavations have recovered a sequence of palaces and temples, replete with imported luxury goods, which reveal Alalakh to be a capital city with a lively international discourse and shared artistic styles with the greater cosmopolitan world of the ancient Near East, Anatolia, the Aegean, and Egypt.

The establishment of a standard chronology for Atchana based on a fine-grained relational stratigraphy, dendrochronology, radiocarbon sampling, ceramic seriation, and textual data has taken precedence in the new round of excavations. The preliminary results of this collaborative effort have suggested that the levels as defined by Woolley, while broadly correct, are nevertheless in need of some revision, especially in the Levels IV-I. The new excavations have also paid particular attention to dating the final cessation of habitation at Atchana in concert with efforts by the Canadian team at neighboring Tell Tayinat to find the earliest Iron Age settlement there. New evidence has complicated the once-neat scheme of the Atchana and Tayinat mounds, each serving in turn as the capital city of the region from the Early Bronze through Iron II periods while the other mound lay uninhabited. Newly excavated sequences from several parts of the site are strongly suggesting that Atchana's final phase of widespread Bronze Age habitation ended by around 1300 BC with the exception of the temple area, and that most of the site lay deserted throughout the 13th century with a resettlement sometime in the mid-12th century, the Iron Age.

Previous interpretations of Alalakh: unsolved mysteries

Tell Atchana was originally excavated by Sir Leonard Woolley from 1936–39, and after World War II from 1946–49, for the British Museum and Oxford University.[2] Woolley's publications, particularly his 1955 volume on Alalakh, have been widely used as a source for further study in the past 60 years. While in many ways ahead of

[2] Woolley 1955 for references to earlier preliminary reports.

his time in terms of archaeological methodology, Woolley's work, nevertheless, left a number of gaps and uncertainties in the documented history of ancient Alalakh. It is especially unfortunate that despite 60 years of scholarship based on Woolley's findings, surprisingly little consensus exists on the second millennium BC chronology of Alalakh (see **Fig. 2**), impeding attempts at inter-site and cross-cultural research.[3]

The new round of research at Tell Atchana began in 2000 under the direction of the author now sponsored by Koç University in Istanbul. Seven seasons of excavation have been completed from 2003–2010,[4] exploring areas both within and beyond the zone previously explored by Woolley. Thirty-six new trenches (see **Fig. 3**), sixteen borings, and two exploratory sections have been excavated on the site in addition to extensive field survey and geophysical exploration. After an exhaustive correlation of the new excavation results with Woolley's stratigraphy, a new phasing system is in preparation that is based on the numbers assigned by Woolley using Roman numerals, but written in Arabic numerals to be clear where we have independently phased a new context or rephased a Woolley context. The numbers assigned to major phases remains the same; e.g. Level VII Palace is now Level 7, and Level IV Palace is now Level 4. In the discussion below, the designation "local phase" refers to the stratigraphy in the individual squares (excavations units) that begin with the number 1 at the top of each sequence, whereas "Period" refers to the site-wide sequence. The identifications given to various structures by Woolley, such as 'Hittite Fortress,' are distinguished by quotation marks.

Woolley Excavations and Phasing

Based on his excavation campaigns and the chronological information available at the time, Woolley developed a narrative for his stratigraphic assessment of Alalakh using the successive rebuilding phases of the palace and temple precinct at the north end of the tell as a master sequence.[5] Woolley's sequence for the latest levels of Alalakh was as follows (see **Fig. 4**, left): Palace Level IV[6] (the 'Niqme-pa Palace') was destroyed around 1400 BC and the 'Castle' area was subsequently re-used in a poorly-documented period also labeled Level IV. This 'Castle re-use IV' ended in a burning around 1370 BC, which Woolley attributed to the Hittite king Suppiluliuma I.

[3] See now radiocarbon dates for the second millennium in Bruins 2010, Ramsey et al. 2010; Heinemeier et al. 2009; Manning and Kromer 2011 articles on the dating of the Santorini explosion.

[4] Yener 2005, 2010, in prep., with Murat Akar as senior field supervisor.

[5] Woolley 1955, p. 399.

[6] This is the so-called Niqmepa palace, although it may have been built by Idrimi and used by Niqmepa and Ilimilmma; see arguments according to texts by von Dassow 2008.

Immediately thereafter, a massive mud-brick 'Military or Hittite Fortress' (now, Northern Fortress[7]) was constructed, Level III. According to Woolley, this fortress was renovated around 1350 BC ('Fortress' Level II) before being abandoned when the area was rebuilt around 1273 BC (Level I). Woolley believed that the "Sea Peoples" had destroyed Alalakh Level I around 1190 BC. A nebulous 'Level O' dating to c.1140 BC was added to the sequence when it became clear that there were poorly preserved remains above Level I, after an abandonment phase that had a very short lifespan. To arrive at these dates, Woolley considered information from textual sources, ceramic imports, and other chronologically sensitive artifacts such as Egyptian scarabs, all combined with his observations about the character and duration of his excavated levels. In the half-century elapsed since Woolley's final publication, significant advances in chronological and material studies have been made that, in combination with the new excavations at Tell Atchana, allow for a re-assessment of the site's dating and historical narrative.

ALALAKH LEVELS IV-II: NEW EXCAVATIONS IN THE PALACE AREA

The history of Alalakh between c.1400 (Level IV Palace destruction) and its eventual abandonment is one of the most poorly understood yet vitally important parts of the city's past. The major textual record of Alalakh ends with the destruction of the Level IV palace,[8] with the possible exception of the statue of Idrimi whose date and context are uncertain. In order to clarify the stratigraphy and chronology of Woolley's work in the palace precinct, new squares were established cross-cutting Woolley's massive excavation trench in the Royal Precinct (now 'Area 1'). Standing architecture from the Woolley project was digitally mapped to aid in the stratigraphic re-study, and the new squares were placed in contact with the extant buildings. These new squares have enabled us to produce a fresh profile of the Woolley excavation and to proceed to lower levels in the palace area. Ultimately the aim was to provide a corrective for Woolley's broadly-defined levels and chronology.

The first task in researching the LB II sequence in Area 1 was to clearly define what constitutes 'Level IV.' Woolley defined Level IV as the 'Niqme-pa Palace,' a large wing built over the previous palace (Level VB) at a somewhat different angle but still integrated into the surrounding architecture, which remained in use. However, he stipulated that the stratigraphy of the area was complex and the various interlinked structures not co-synchronous:

[7] The subject of LBIIA fortresses at Alalakh has been addressed by M. Akar 2012 in his doctoral dissertation; see also this volume.

[8] See von Dassow 2008 for a clear contextualization of Woolley's post-Level IV tablets.

> "Although it is convenient to call the building [Castle] Level IV it is not literally correct. In our stratification-sequence Level IV was correlated with the palace of Niqme-pa as the principal monument of the period, and this is not only justified by the emergence in the palace period of types of pottery which are not found earlier and by the disappearance of types characteristic of Level V, but has the further advantage of giving a fixed date for the beginning of Level IV and associating it with political history."[9]

Given that the extensive 'Palace' and 'Castle' complex labeled Level VB by Woolley were still in use in IV when the 'Niqme-pa Palace' wing was built, and given the quite different nature of the stratigraphy being recovered from new excavations beneath the 'Palace VB' wing, it is perhaps more natural to consider the entire palace/castle complex VB/IV as a distinct phase, that is, Level 4 in the new phasing. One system currently being considered (see **Fig. 4 center, right**) is to label the 'VB Castle and Palace' Level 4a and the 'Niqme-pa Palace' wing Level 4b. These assessments will depend on future results in the palace area and to some extent on the results of the excavations in the succeeding phases such as those provided by the section cut in Square 32.54.

A Section Cut through Levels O-IV

Important chronological and stratigraphic correctives to Woolley's problematic analysis of the LB II and early Iron Age were provided by Square 32.54 (**Fig. 4b**),[10] which was intended to re-examine the phases between the Level IV Palace and the final cessation of settlement at Alalakh. The section articulates with the 'Saray Gate' attached to the Level IV 'Niqme-pa Palace' and 'Castle' and can therefore be directly connected to Woolley's stratigraphy. It is located in what would have been the 'Castle' building. The section clearly shows a badly burnt context [phase 2d] with mudbrick collapse over a floor that extends along wall foundations connected to the standing remains of Woolley's 'Saray Gate.' Phase 2d can therefore be correlated with the 'Niqme-pa Palace' and its destruction (dated c.1400 in Middle Chronology). Two graves, one of an infant and one of an adult, were found dug into the burnt level once the following levels had been removed, suggesting that the burials were placed into the rubble before the succeeding phase was built.

What follows local phase 2d are three rebuildings of the 'Castle' based on the same plan and reusing old walls as foundations for new (local phases 2c, 2b, 2a). None of them have evidence for burning or other destruction. Unfortunately the excavated area in association with this section was disturbed by Woolley's cut and the subsequent erosion of 60 years, limiting the usefulness of the small horizontal exposures recovered so far. The plans for 2012 field season include widening the exposures to recover more significant and undisturbed contexts in these phases.

[9] Woolley 1955, p. 156.
[10] Yener et al. in prep., see Akar chap. 2 Fig. 6.

Following phase 2a, the construction of the Level II 'Fortress' is clearly visible. The Fortress also used the older walls as foundations but added deep v-shaped trenches (noted by Woolley) filled with mudbrick. The casemate spaces of the 'Fortress' platform were often placed above preexisting rooms that were then filled with rubble. The 'Fortress' can be clearly seen to have had only one phase, that is, Level II. In the area of the section cut, the remnants of the 'Fortress' are standing to a height of nearly two meters and disappear into a subsequent deposit of weathered mudbrick and soil. There is no evidence of a 'Level I' in this area. The weathering deposit is overlain by structures from the Iron II, as detailed below.

The lack of a 'Fortress III' in the 32.54 section cut is significant, but it should be remembered that Woolley excavated a huge area including that lying above the ruins of the 'IV Palace' and might well have encountered something there that did not extend to the 'Castle' area, adjacent though it is. If there were a structure predating Level II in that area, it might have been contemporary with local phase 2a 'Castle' rebuilding. Because Woolley removed all the overburden in the relevant area, there is no way to revisit this problem via excavation.

Implications for the LB IIa Sequence of Alalakh

Based on the section in 32.54, the sequence of levels in post-'Palace IV' Atchana may be given a preliminary reassessment. Beginning the consideration with Level IV, Woolley believed that certain alterations in the 'Castle IV' post-dated the 'Palace IV' destruction and represented a period when the heirs of Idrimi's dynasty struggled out a living adjacent to the ruins of the old palace before the arrival of the Hittite King Suppiluliuma caused the entire area to be rebuilt in a fortress in Level III. Our section of these phases reveals that Woolley's work is not replicable in this part of Area 1. There is no evidence for a 'Fortress' III, only the 'Fortress' Level II built on the foundations of earlier structures of quite different character.

Between the fire of Palace IV and the construction of Fortress II are seen three re-buildings of the 'Castle' that can be interpreted several ways. One possibility (see **Fig. 4, right**) is that local phases 2c and perhaps 2b correspond with the post-destruction rebuilding of the 'Castle IV' that Woolley described, to end at perhaps 1370 BC, and that phase 2a is yet another re-rebuilding that was mistakenly called 'Fortress III' by Woolley.

A second solution (**Fig. 4, center**) is to place Woolley's IV 'Castle re-use' contemporary with 'Palace IV' on the grounds that there is evidence for only one burning episode in the section of 32.45 and it seems to clearly correlate with that of 'Palace IV.' Local phases 2c-a would then occupy the time between the 'Palace IV' destruction (c.1400 BC) and the construction of Fortress II (post-1344 BC, if it is attributable to Suppiluliuma I), and constitute a newly defined Level 3 of significant duration. Until further fieldwork is completed, this dilemma, not to mention the exact dating of these phases beyond a general assignment to the 14th century BC, cannot be resolved.

ALALAKH LEVEL I AND THE ELUSIVE 13TH CENTURY BC

In order to reconsider the final Bronze Age habitation of Alalakh, Level I, it is necessary to first decouple the various areas of excavation reported by Woolley for that phase: the 'Temple', 'Fort', and 'Private Houses.' None of these areas was unambiguously integrated with the others, meaning that they may not have been contemporary or co-terminous. The 'Fort' and 'Private Houses' at least were built on top of the massive foundation of the Level II 'Fortress,' giving them a common strata. The 'Temple' sequence is entirely detached.

Woolley correctly recognized that the Level II 'Fortress' and 'Private Houses' were dated to the second half of the 14th century, but unfortunately he had already decided that Alalakh Level I was destroyed by the "Sea Peoples" and therefore chose the presumed date of destruction based on the narrative of Ramesses IV. That left him with a need for Level I to extend from about 1300 to 1190 BC, the date of Ramesses' great battle in the Nile delta. In the end, Woolley compromised by moving the end of Level II forward to 1275 BC, disregarding the ceramic evidence that the Level I 'Houses' also dated to the end of the 14th century. He also disregarded the fact that while his Level I 'Houses' contained at most two subphases of remodeling, the Level I 'Temple' contained at least three and possibly four subphases.

While no traces of Level I have yet been encountered in the new exposures in Woolley's cut, a reassessment of the material culture of all those contexts assigned to Level I from that area have yielded interesting results. Recent radiocarbon dates[11] from new squares in Area 1 (southwest) (43.54) and Area 4 (64.72 and 64.82) support the dating of all the final phases of habitation, (local phases 1–4 in these squares equivalent to Levels III–I), to the fourteenth century BC (**Fig. 5**), and the material culture is identical to that coming from the Level I 'Private Houses' of Area 1. The final phase of occupation in Areas 1 (southwest) 2, 3 and 4, located just below the modern plough zone in all cases, displays the same combination of Nuzi and Mycenaean (LH IIIA: 2) imports (**Fig. 6: 8, 9–10**). Cypriot imports remain common in all levels alongside a strong local ceramic tradition.

In addition to the foreign components characterizing the uppermost phases of settlement across the tell, certain locally-made features distinguish these levels from their predecessors.[12] Whereas from Periods 6–3 the most significant foreign influence on

[11] Radiocarbon dating performed by the Vienna Environmental Research Accelerator (VERA), Universität Wien, Vienna; courtesy, Eva Marie Wild and Manfred Bietak and Sturt Manning at the Wiener Laboratory in Cornell in collaboration with the Oxford laboratory.

[12] Horowitz in prep.

local pottery had been Mitannian (**Fig. 6: 2**), beginning in Period 2 a number of innovations appear that may be traced to Hittite cultural practices. One of these is the use of miniature votive vessels (**Fig. 6: 3–5**) and pointed juglets (**Fig. 6: 6**) very similar to those which were found in ritual pools at Hattusha.[13] Furthermore, bronze weapons, especially ceremonial ones related to particular deities such as the stormgod, show strong relationships with the Hittite Empire.[14] New ceramic forms such as the ring stand and pilgrim flask, first introduced in Levels IV or III, also become common at this time (**Fig. 6: 1, 7a–b**). It is still uncertain whether Late Helladic IIIB and Cypriot White Slip II-late ceramics occur at the site.[15]

Evidence for the 13th century BC at Atchana is slight and comes only from Woolley's Level I 'Temple' sequence with its subphases (Ia, Ib, Ic, and the Annex).[16] In a significant shift, the Level Ia 'Temple' disregarded the plan of the preceding Level II 'Temple' and was laid out with an ostentatious entryway flanked by a pair of basalt lions in the Hurrian style and flanked by stone orthostats. In a subsequent remodeling of the entryway (Level Ib), an orthostat with Hittite-style carvings and inscriptions was found re-used as part of the steps. This stone depicts Tudhaliya, a Hittite described as 'prince' [REX.FILIUS] and 'chief charioteer' [MAGNUS.AURIGA] alongside a female figure, possibly a Hittite princess [REX.FILIA] and interpreted as Tudhaliya's wife (the inscription is badly eroded).[17]

The dating of the Level Ia-b 'Temple' has been suggested by a number of historical synchronisms. The treaty text CTH 63 mentions a Tudhaliya as contemporary with Mursili II and in a context suggesting that he is on a par with the rulers of Aleppo and Carchemish; it has been argued that this Tudhaliya was the governor of Mukish at that time (Mursili II, c.1320–1295 BC).[18] If this is the same Tudhaliya depicted on the orthostat re-used in Alalakh 'Temple' Ib, it helps to situate the Level Ia 'Temple' to the latter part of the 14th century.

The subsequent addition of an 'annex' and the continuation of the 'Temple' in Level 1c are also difficult to phase properly[19] yet the presence of two biconvex Hittite seals, one of which belongs to Paluwa, 'prince' [REX.FILIUS] and 'country lord'

[13] Glatz 2009.

[14] Yener 2011.

[15] Woolley's identification of LHIIIB ceramics is uncertain; these finds have been re-studied by Robert Koehl and reassigned to LHIIIA: 2 date, despite his original hesitation in Koehl 2005.

[16] Woolley 1955, p. 82–89.

[17] Niedorf 2002, pp. 521–522, see also Guterbock 1954; Niedorf 2008; de Martino 2009, 2010 for updates on the Tudhaliya stele which now is thought not to be Tudhaliya IV.

[18] Niedorf 2002, p. 522.

[19] Fink 2010 restudied the Temple sequence and suggested a rephasing of the annex in particular to post-Temple Ic; see Akar (unpublished Ph.D., Florence University 2012) for critical discussion of Fink's speculations.

[REGIO.DOMINUS] has been stylistically dated to the 13th century BC.[20] The political history of the 13th century BC with regard to Alalakh and Mukish is also accessible from textual sources and seals from a variety of contemporary sites, but unfortunately none of them specify whether there is still a settlement on the Atchana mound itself or whether the Hittite governance was based at another location. Of particular relevance is a letter (RS 20.03) from Alalakh to neighboring Ugarit. The letter originates from 'prince [DUMU.LUGAL] Shukur-Teshub' and his letter to King Ammishtamru of Ugarit (c.1260–30 BC) is reportedly written in a style specific to Mukish.[21] There are no texts or seals of a Shukur-Teshub yet discovered at Atchana.

If the ceramic and radiocarbon evidence are taken together, they seem to indicate that the uppermost known habitation level of Alalakh (Level I), whether in the palace area or across the city, is dated to the end of the 14th century BC while the 'Temple' continued in use into the 13th century. It may be hypothesized that the city of Alalakh was subjected to a major disruption around 1300 BC[22] that resulted in the abandonment of the majority of the site. Given the descriptions of mass deportations by Mursili II[23] of other sites in northwestern Syria (e.g. Tunip) in the period c.1310–1295 BC, it is possible that such a fate befell a rebellious Alalakh as well.

The governance of the kingdom of Mukish, apparently reduced to an annexed territory in the reign of Mursili II (given the presence of Tudhaliya the 'country lord'), still seems to have been in the vicinity of Atchana at least in the first half of the 13th century if the seal of the 'country lord' Paluwa is any indication. Neither Alalakh nor Mukish is mentioned as a Hittite ally on the Kadesh inscriptions of Ramesses II, describing the Hittite army that faced the Egyptians in 1274 BC, though Ugarit, Aleppo, Mitanni, Carchemish, and Kizzuwatna all appear.[24] However, Atchana is not the only mound with indications of 13th century BC Hittite presence. From Tell Tayinat stratums XIV–XV come three biconvex seals in the

[20] Woolley 1955, p. 266 catalogue states the seal stems from Level I-II; pl. 67, no. 155; see Singer 2000, p. 70 for Paluwa.

[21] Niedorf 2002; Nougayrol et al. 1968 (Ug. V, no. 26); this is a rare occurrence of the name 'Alalakh.' I thank Alfonzo Archi and Itamar Singer for discussing this with me. Mursili continues his father Suppililiuma's policy of punishing Mukish/Alalakh for its lack of cooperation by ceding part of its southern lands to collaborating Ugarit. Mukish ceases to exist as a separate kingdom and is annexed to Hatti, ruled by a Hittite governor; see Singer 1999 for references; von Dassow 2008, pp. 216–217; interestingly Mukish is mentioned as a "city" during this and earlier periods in Alalakh and other texts. For example, Level IV Text Alt 350 notes distributions of sheep from two cities, Alalakh and Mukish, suggesting that Mukish was a separate site in the vicinity.

[22] Richter 2005 and 2008 for this chaotic time and the view from the Qatna texts.

[23] Hoffner 2002, p. 61–64; Alparslan 2006.

[24] Bryce 2005.

style of the 13th century,[25] one bearing the name Armaziti [A4314] which might be equated with a powerful individual known from the court of Hattušili III[26] (reg. 1267–1237). The name 'Armaziti' also appears on a tablet fragment from Alalakh although its find place is not secure.[27] While the find-spots of the Tayinat biconvex seals may be secondary, they suggest a possible Hittite administrative complex on Tayinat in the second half of the 13th century BC. The team at Tell Tayinat is currently investigating these issues.

Alalakh level O: the early Iron Age

The surprise finding of the Atchana 2007 season, further excavated in 2011, was multiple phases dating to the Iron I and II periods on one of the few surviving unexcavated sections at the northern end of the site (Squares 32.52/42), beginning just 10–20cm below the modern surface (historically plough zone, but more recently used as the parking lot adjacent to Woolley's dig-house). The earliest of these, dating to the 12th century BC, consisted of a thin strata of ephemeral surface deposits containing Late Helladic IIIC Middle 'Developed' ware[28] (**Fig.** 7) and possibly Handmade Burnished Ware as well. The bulk of the ceramics consisted of local Iron Age wares with strong continuity from the Late Bronze Age, including plain wheel-made ware, red slipped ware, local geometric and banded painted ware, and shell-tempered cookware. These deposits were partly disturbed by the corner of a large mud brick building that is provisionally dated to the mid-Iron II period (Amuq O, c.950-750 BC). This is the first time that Iron II remains have been identified on Atchana, and the study of this material is ongoing. It is also the first time that LH IIIC-Middle "Developed" ware has been identified anywhere in the Amuq, and it thus falls at the poorly known boundary of what Braidwood defined as Amuq M/Judaidah VI (LBA) and Amuq N/Judaidah V (Iron I), which Swift dated at c.1150 BC due to the lack of LH IIIC-Early (then called LH IIIC1a) at any of the Amuq sites.[29] Neither Tell Tayinat nor Chatal Höyük has yet confirmed the presence of LH IIIC-Early or Middle 'Developed' wares, or Handmade Burnished Ware, among their collections.[30]

[25] Gorny 1993, but cf. Meyer 2008; the reuse of 13th century Hittite biconvex seals in Iron Age contexts seems to have caused some confusion over the exact manufacturing period of the type. I thank M.Horowitz for this reference.

[26] Singer 1999, p. 685; Imparati 1988.

[27] von Dassow 2005, p. 64; see also Helft 2010, p. 60.

[28] Personal communication R. Koehl, who with M. Horowitz identified the Iron Age assemblage at Alalakh and will be publishing a comprehensive report on these materials and their contexts.

[29] Braidwood 1937 for phasing; Swift 1958, p. 117.

[30] M. Pucci, personal communication. I would like to thank Dr Pucci for viewing the Alalakh material and sharing her knowledge of Chatal Höyük with us. See also M. Pucci, this volume, and Pucci 2010.

The newly discovered ceramic assemblages are quite distinct from the evidence cited by Woolley for Level O being a "Sea People" resettlement of Alalakh, though ironically it amounts to much the same thing, namely, a localized and short-lived (LH IIIC Late does not occur on Atchana though it is typical of Tell Tayinat) reuse of the site in the mid-12th century BC. Woolley presented a single scarab (AT/37/47) found in a grave dug into the Level I 'Private Houses' (Grave ATG/37/2) as evidence for a date for Level O in the later 12th century (c.1140 BC), identifying the scarab's cartouche as belonging to Ramses VI.[31] However, Prof. Robert Ritner (Oriental Institute, Chicago) has recently reexamined this scarab and identifies it as belonging to the pharaoh Amenhotep III of the mid-14th century.[32] Assuming the scarab was contemporary or more likely slightly earlier than the time in which it was buried, the grave (likely Level I) should date to the later 14th century BC. Woolley's scarab thus actually provides more evidence for the current hypothesis that Woolley's 'Private Houses' and in fact most of Alalakh's Level I dates to the end of the 14th century BC. Woolley himself noted that most of the graves found dug into his Level I 'Private Houses' from above contained LH IIIB pottery, now re-identified as LH IIIA:2/IIIB:1 and thus, the Level I 'Houses' could not be the final phase of LB occupation at the site.

The newly-discovered 12th century phase at Atchana has prompted a re-examination of Woolley's evidence for other structures post-dating Level IC, namely, two fragmentary structures labeled Level OA–B and a possible Level O reconstruction of the Ishtar temple described as being a large stone foundation running above the northeast wall of the Level I temple and the Annex, with traces of associated cement floors. This structure was built above a one meter deep deposit of soil and rubble indicating some period of abandonment, and it cannot currently be said whether it is in fact a temple or what period it might date to.[33] The two fragmentary structures above and partly cutting the northwest side of House 38/B are likewise undated by any associated artifact. Now that an Iron II structure and 12th century surfaces have been identified in the vicinity, the possibility exists that these fragmentary remains could date to anything from the later 13th century onwards. Work in the upcoming field seasons at Tell Atchana will be dedicated to disentangling and phasing the post-Bronze Age phases of this important site and examining the relationship with the Neo-Hittite capital city on neighboring Tell Tayinat.

[31] See Woolley 1955, plate 66: no. 131.

[32] Professor Ritner (pers. comm. 2010) writes "it is clear to me that the piece cannot be Ramses VI, whose cartouche should be '*Nb-maat-Ra, mri-Amon*.' It is possible that the text reads *Neb-maat-Ra*, but there is no room for the needed *mri-Amon* ("beloved of Amon") epithet. This changes the scarab from Ramses VI to the similarly-named Amenhotep III (IF the traces really are a *nb*-basket under the seated Maat goddess)...I suspect that Woolley chose the later *Nb-maat-Ra* to fit his expected chronology." Professor Ritner will be republishing the Alalakh hieroglyphic scarabs with updated information. See earlier redating by Kitchen 1982, p. 88.

[33] Woolley 1955, pp. 89, 197 see also pp. 170–171, Fig. 69.

Environmental studies

The findings of intermittent settlement on Atchana in the 13th-12th centuries BC have very important implications about the nature of the Atchana-Tell Tayinat relationship. The two sites are separated by a mere 700m and might easily have once been separate neighborhoods of the same urban complex (i.e. the same city), initially settled in different periods with the location of the ruler's palace and administrative center periodically moving from one mound to the other.[34] Confirmation for this hypothesis awaits full-scale environmental studies; however, preliminary results have yielded important new evidence.

Ongoing fieldwork including geophysical survey and sediment borings initiated by Dr Derek Ryter of the USGS determined several important changes in the immediate landscape of Alalakh since the Bronze Age. Ryter's preliminary soundings determined that the Orontes River once wrapped around three-quarters of the site. Middle Bronze Age Simple Ware sherds from the east side of the mound of these borings suggested a Bronze Age date for this river channel.

The integration of a river into a larger political unit is very similar to the Tigris River channel/canal and its relationship to the mounds of Nebi Yunus and Kuyuncuk at Iron Age Nineveh (**Fig. 8**). The discovery of this extinct bend of the Orontes River around the site suggests that the odd elongated shape of the city mound of Alalakh may have been due to the existence of an underlying natural levy formed by river deposits. It is also possible that the elaborate Level VII gate excavated by Woolley was in fact a "water gate" leading directly to the river.[35] This new assessment also gives more credence to the theory that the Orontes was important for transportation in the Bronze Age. Indeed even in the early twentieth century before extensive damming in Syria, the Orontes was certainly much more conducive to transport than today (**Fig. 9**).

The results of the borings also provide supporting evidence for the existence of a lower town to the southwest of the Atchana mound, a hypothesis that had emerged during intensive survey on the west side of Tell Atchana in 2009. This would make the city much larger than originally thought. While there is evidence that the off-mound virgin ground level is obscured by at least seven meters of post-Bronze Age sedimentary deposit, the presence of fresh ceramic material dating to LBII on the modern field surface west of the tell seems to indicate that a lower portion of the mound exists there, buried only very shallowly by later sediments.

[34] Given its proximity, Alalakh/Alakhtum, Mukish, Walistin/Palistin and Kunulua may have been perceived as one and the same urban complex by other state polities. The Iron II building at Alalakh confirms the contemporeneity of both sites

[35] See Yener 2005, fig. 4.27.

New evidence from Tell Tayinat[36] suggests a subsequent shift in the river's course from its Bronze Age bend around Atchana and the formation of a lake at a critical transitional time, the beginning of the Iron Age in the early 12th century BC. While rivers in flat terrain such as the Amuq Valley often change their courses, the sedimentary cores from around Tayinat suggest a more radical alteration of the landscape: the mound was surrounded by standing water at that time, apparently subsuming much of the existing Orontes riverbed and turning Tayinat as well as the small mound Tayinat al-Sugir in between into islands while Atchana became a lakeside mound. Any settlement along the banks of the river between the two mounds (now buried beneath up to 7m of alluvium) would have been drowned.

Such a dramatic change in the landscape suggests that a climatic shift brought a period of much greater precipitation in the early Iron Age. Prior attempts by the AVRP survey[37] at reconstructing contemporary climate conditions from sedimentary cores in the Amuq Valley were unsuccessful since the conditions at the coring sites were not conducive to pollen preservation. Current information on the history of the Amuq Valley landscape and climate comes from Tony Wilkinson's[38] fine-grained geoarchaeological studies of the area for the AVRP survey. Wilkinson's work presents a portrait of a dynamic, constantly changing environment; from the expansion of Lake Antioch (Amik Gölü) in the Chalcolithic period, to its diverse dry periods, inundations, and interludes with a mosaic of ponds, marshes, rivers, and meadows.

The changing aquatic features of the landscape have important implications for understanding the periodic and apparently cyclical settlement and abandonment of Alalakh and Tayinat. The Amuq Valley was created by tectonic uplift blocking passage for regional rivers to the Mediterranean, and receives runoff from a very large and well-watered catchment area. On the plain, dry land was and still is a precarious circumstance; as recently as 2002 when the Orontes dam in Syria burst after heavy rains, Atchana became an island. Both the Atchana and Tayinat teams are currently investigating the fluctuations of Amuq Valley lake levels and river courses during the Late Bronze and early Iron Ages in the hopes of understanding what role climate and environmental circumstances may have played in the historical narrative of these important sites.

Conclusions

Changing the 'conventional wisdom' of a long-published site like Atchana is never an easy task. The site has been discussed so long and frequently in the literature that it has become part of an overarching historical narrative of the ancient Near East regardless of the many acknowledged uncertainties about Woolley's work. Today the history of

36 Batiuk 2007, Batiuk, Harrison and Pavlich 2005.
37 Yener 2000, 2005.
38 Wilkinson 1998, 1999, 2000, 2002; Wilkinson et al. 2001.

Alalakh in the LB II and early Iron Age is still in the process of being recovered. Ongoing work on chronology, material culture, city landscapes, and environmental changes are beginning to form a coherent picture of a small Amorite city that dared to play a hard game of territorial checkers with its larger imperial neighbors, and ultimately lost both independence and apparently, the right to continue living on Tell Atchana.

Evidence for the missing 13th century is still being sought, both off-mound and on Tell Tayinat. Ongoing research will help elucidate the final end of the Hittite imperial period in the Amuq Valley and the foundation of the Iron Age kingdom of Walistin/Palistin.[39] What is certain is that despite the collapse of empires, many fluid and dynamic forms of exchange, from trade in commodities to art and ideas, perhaps even religious practices, as well as technological knowledge continued to flourish between Anatolia, Syria, and intermediate areas such as the Amuq in the Iron Age. It is within this context that the changing human landscape of this corner of the northeastern Mediterranean, from the Late Bronze Age empires to the Iron Age kingdoms, begins to make sense.

BIBLIOGRAPHY

AKAR, MURAT
2012 "The Late Bronze Age II City of Alalakh and Its Social Context in the Northern Levant: A Re-Examination of the Post-Level IV Stratigraphic Sequence (I-III) based on New Excavation Results (2003–2010)." Unpublished Ph.D., Florence University.

ALPARSLAN, M.
2006 "II. Murşili ve Dönemi," [The Period of Murşili II]. Unpublished Ph.D. dissertation. Istanbul University.

BATIUK, S.
2007 "Ancient Landscapes of the Amuq: Geoarchaeological Surveys of the Amuq Valley, 1999–2006," *Journal of the Canadian Society for Mesopotamian Studies* 2: 51–57.

BATIUK, S., HARRISON, T. P. and PAVLISH, L.
2005 "The Ta'yinat Survey, 1999–2002," in *The Amuq Valley Regional Projects. Vol. I: Surveys in the Plain of Antioch and Orontes Delta, Turkey, 1995-2002*, edited by K. A. Yener, pp. 153–169. Chicago: Oriental Institute Press.

BRAIDWOOD, R. J.
1937 *Mounds in the Plain of Antioch: An Archaeological Survey.* Oriental Institute Publications 48. Chicago: University of Chicago Press.

BRUINS, H. J.
2010 "Dating Pharaonic Egypt," *Science* 328: 1489–1490.

FINK, A. S.
2010 *Late Bronze Age Tell Atchana (Alalakh): Stratigraphy, Chronology, History.* BAR International Series 2120. Oxford: Archaeopress Publishers of British Archaeological Reports.

[39] Harrison 2009, 2010.

GLATZ, C.
2009 "Empire as network: Spheres of material interaction in Late Bronze Age Anatolia," *Journal of Anthropological Archaeology* 28(2): 127–141.
GORNY, R.
1993 "The Biconvex Seals of Alişar Höyük," *Anatolian Studies* 43: 163–191.
HARRISON, T. P.
2009 "Neo-Hittites in the "Land of Palistin:" Renewed Investigations at Tell Ta'yinat on the Plain of Antioch," *Near Eastern Archaeology* 72: 174–189.
2010 "Late Bronze Age/Early Iron Age Transition in North Orontes Valley," in *Socities in Transition. Evolutionary Processes in Northern Levant between Late Bronze Age II and Early Iron Age, Papers Presented on the Occasion of the 20th Anniversary of the New Excavation in Tell Afis, Bologna, 15th November 2007,* Studi e Testi Orientali 9, Serie Archeologica 2, edited by F. Venturi, pp. 83–102. Bologna: CLUEB.
HEINEMEIER, J., FRIEDRICH, W. L. and WARBURTON, D. eds.
2009 *Time's up!: Dating the Minoan Eruption of Santorini: Acts of the Minoan Eruption Chronology Workshop, Sandbjerg November 2007.* Athens: The Danish Institute at Athens.
HELFT, S.
2010 "Patterns of Exchange/Patterns of Power: A New Archaeology of the Hittite Empire." Unpublished dissertation, University of Pennsylvania.
HOFFNER, H. A.
2002 "The Treatment and Long-Term Use of Persons Captured in Battle according to the Maşat Texts," in *Recent Developments in Hittite Archaeology and History: Papers in Memory of Hans G. Güterbock*, edited by K. A. Yener and H. A. Hoffner, pp. 61–72. Winona Lake: Eisenbrauns.
HOROWITZ, M. T.
In prep. "The Evolution of Plain Ware Ceramics at the Regional Capital of Alalakh in the Second Millennium BC".
IMPARATI, F.
1988 "Armaziti: attivita di un personaggio nel tardo imperio ittita," in *Studi di Storia e di Filologia Anatolica Dedicati a Giovanni Pugliese Carratelli*, pp. 79–94. Florence: Elite.
KITCHEN, K. A.
1982 "An Egyptian New Kingdom Scarab from Alalakh," *Levant* 14: 88.
KOEHL, R. B.
2005 "Preliminary Observations on the Unpublished Mycenaean Pottery from Woolley's Dig-House at Tell Atchana (Ancient Alalakh)," *Aegaeum* 25: 415–422.
MANNING, S. W. and KROMER, B.
2011 "Radiocarbon Dating Archaeological Samples in the Eastern Mediterranean, 1730 to 1480 BC: Further Exploring the Atmospheric Radiocarbon Calibration Record and the Archaeological Implications," *Archaeometry* 53: 413–439.
DE MARTINO, S.
2009 "Anatolia after the Collapse of the Hittite Empire," in *From the Aegean to the Adriatic: Social Organisations, Modes of Exchange and Interaction in Postpalatial Times (12th-11th BC)*, edited by E. Borgna and P. C. Guida, pp. 21–28. Roma: Edizioni Quasar.
2010 "Symbols of Power in the Late Hittite Kingdom," in *Pax Hethitica: studies on the Hittites and their neighbours in honour of Itamar Singer*, edited by Y. Cohen, A. Gilan, J. L. Miller, and I. Singer, pp. 87–95. Wiesbaden: Harrassowitz.

McClellan, T. L.
1989 "The Chronology and Ceramic Assemblages of Alalakh," in A. Leonard, Jr. and B. B. Williams ed., *Essays in Ancient Civilization Presented Helene J. Kantor*, SAOC 47, pp. 181–212. Chicago: University of Chicago Press.

Meyer, J.-W.
2008 *Die eisenzeitlichen Stempelsiegal aus dem 'Amuq-Gebiet: Ein Beitrag zur Ikonographie altorientalischer Siegelbilder.* Friburg: Academic Press.

Niedorf, C.
2002 "Ein Hethitisches Breiffragment aus Alalakh", in *Ex Mesopotamia et Syria Lux*, AOAT 281, edited by O. Loretz, K. Metzler and H. Schardig. Münster: Ugarit Verlag.
2008 *Die mittelbabylonischen Rechtsurkunden aus Alalaḫ (Schicht IV).* Münster: Ugarit-Verlag.

Nougayrol, J., Laroche, E., Virolleaud, C. and Schaeffer C. F. A.
1968 *Ugaritica* 5. *Nouveaux texts accadiens, hourrites et ugaritiques des Archives et Bibliothèques privées d'Ugarit, commentaries des texts historiques,* Mission de Ras Shamra 16. Paris: Imprimerie Nationale.

Pucci, M.
2010 "The Chatal Höyük Publication Project: a work in progress," *Proceedings of the 6th International Congress on the Archaeology of the Ancient Near East, vol. 2,* edited by P. Matthiae et al., pp. 567–580. Wiesbaden: Harassowitz.

Ramsey, C. B. et al.
2010 "Radiocarbon-Based Chronology for Dynastic Egypt," *Science* 328: 1554–1557.

Richter, T.
2005 "Qatna in the Late Bronze Age," in *General studies and excavations at Nuzi 11/1,* edited by D. I. Owen and G. Wilhelm, pp. 109–126. Bethesda, Md: CDL Press.
2008 "Šuppiluliuma I. in Syrien. Der 'Einjährige Feldzug' und seine Folgen," in *Ḫattuša - Boğazköy: das Hethiterreich im Spannungsfeld des Alten Orients; 6. Internationales Colloquium der Deutschen Orient-Gesellschaft, 22. - 24. März 2006, Würzburg*; Colloquien der Deutschen Orient-Gesellschaft, Band 6, edited by G. Wilhelm, pp. 173–203. Wiesbaden: Harrassowitz.

Singer, I.
1999 "A Political History of Ugarit," in *Handbook of Ugaritic Studies*, edited by W. G. E. Watson and N. Wyatt, pp. 603–733. Leiden: Brill.
2000 "A New Hittite Letter from Emar," in *Landscapes. Territories, Frontiers and Horizons in the Ancient Near East. Papers presented to the XLIV Rencontre Assyriologique Internationale, Venezia, 7-11 July 1997. Part II: Geography and Cultural Landscapes*, edited by L. Milano et al., pp. 65–72. Padova.
2010 *Societies in Transition: Evolutionary Processes in the Northern Levant between Late Bronze Age II and Early Iron Age. Papers presented on the occasion of the 20th anniversary of the new excavations at Tell Afis.* Bologna: CLUEB.

Swift, G. F., Jr.
1958 "The Pottery of the 'Amuq, Phases K to O, and Its Historical Relationships." Unpublished Ph.D. Dissertation. University of Chicago.

von Dassow, E. M.
2008 *State and Society in the Late Bronze Age: Alalah under the Mittani Empire*, Studies on the Civilization and Culture of Nuzi and the Hurrians 17. Bethesda: CDL Press.

2005 "Archives of Alalah IV in Archaeological Context," *Bulletin of the American Schools of Oriental Research* 338: 1-69.

WILKINSON, T. J.

1998 "The History of the Lake of Antioch: A Preliminary Note," in *Festschrift for Michael Astour*, edited by R. Averbeck, pp. 557–576. Bethesda, Md.: CDL Press.

1999 "Holocene Valley Fills of Southern Turkey and Northwestern Syria: Recent Geoarchaeological Contributions," *Quaternary Science Reviews* 18: 555–571.

2000 "Geoarchaeology of the Amuq Plain," *American Journal of Archaeology* 105: 1–51.

2002 "Archaeological Survey in the Amuq Valley, Tell Atchana, The Oriental Institute 2001–2002," *Annual Report of the Oriental Institute 2001–2002*, pp. 20–23. Chicago: University Press.

WILKINSON, T. J. et al.

2001 "The Geoarchaeology of a Lake Basin: Spatial and Chronological Patterning of Sedimentation in the Amuq Plain, Turkey," in *Recherches en Archéométrie*, edited by M. Fortin, pp. 211–226. Quebec: Laval University.

WOOLLEY, L.

1955 *Alalakh: an account of the excavations at Tell Atchana in the Hatay, 1937-1949.* Oxford: Printed at the University Press for the Society of Antiquaries.

YENER, K. A.

2005 *The Amuq Valley Regional Projects, vol. 1: Surveys in the Plain of Antioch and Orontes Delta, Turkey, 1995–2002*, 1st ed., Chicago: University of Chicago Press.

2010 *Tell Atchana, Ancient Alalakh, a Bronze Age Capital in the Amuq Valley, Turkey. Volume I: The 2003–2004 Excavation Seasons*. Istanbul: Koç University Press.

2011 "Hittite Metals at the Frontier: A Three Spiked Battle Ax from Alalakh," in *Metallury: Understanding How, Learning Why. Studies in Honor of James D. Muhly*, edited by S. Ferrence and P. Betancourt. Philadelphia: INSTAP Press.

YENER, K. A., AKAR, M., HOROWITZ, M. eds.

in prep *Tell Atchana, Ancient Alalakh. Volume 2: The Late Bronze Age City.* Istanbul: Koç Universitesi Yayınları.

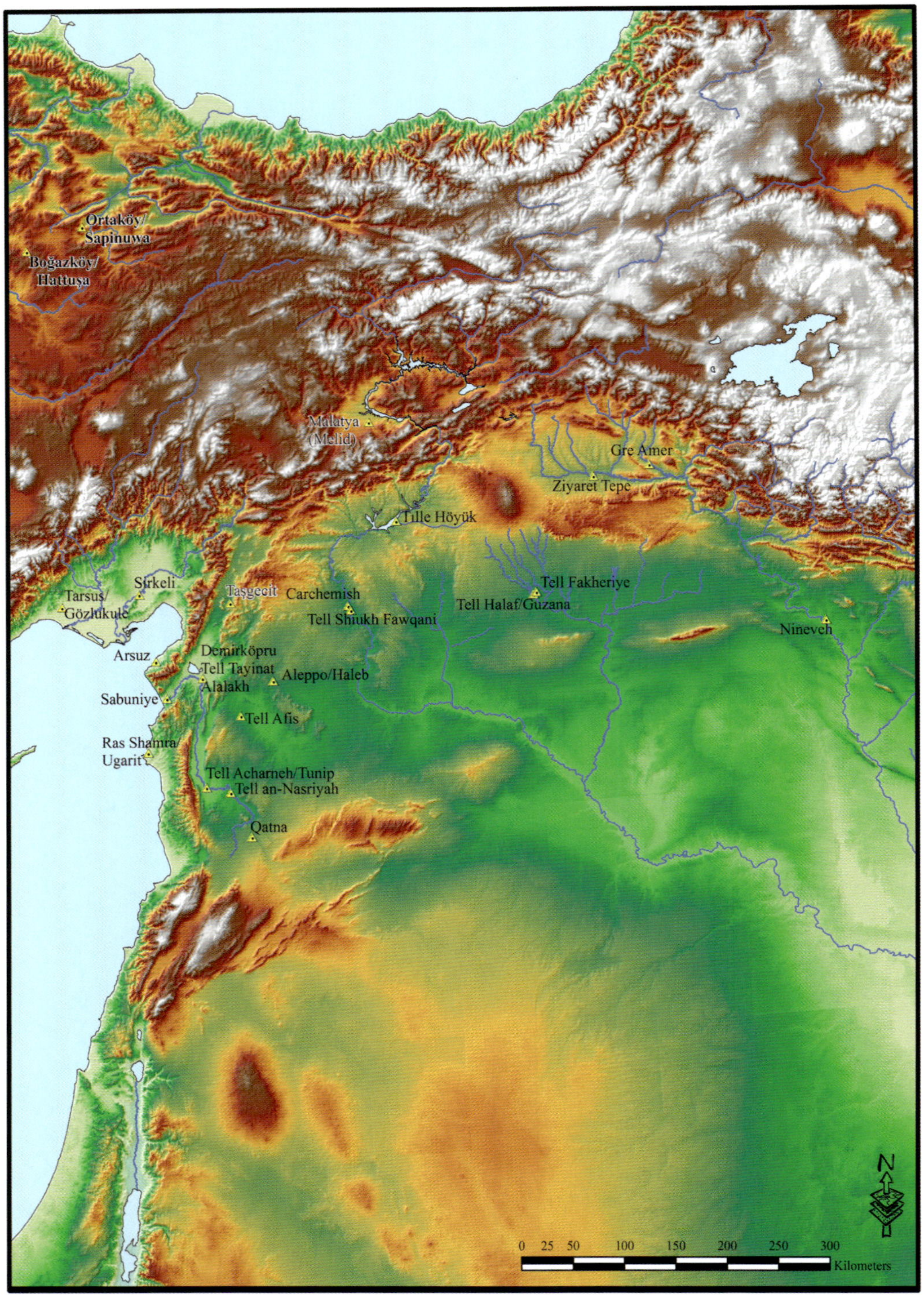

Fig. 1 Map of the Turkish-Syrian borderlands. M. Akar, S. Batiuk.

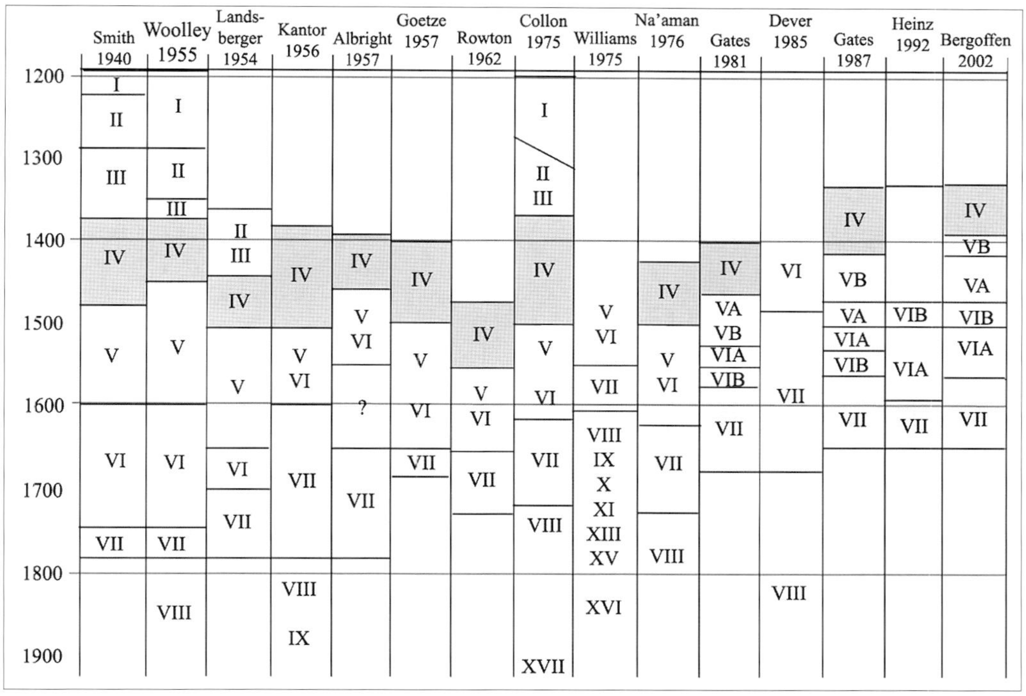

Fig. 2 Chart with previous and current chronologies for Tell Atchana, modified from McClellan 1989; M. Horowitz.

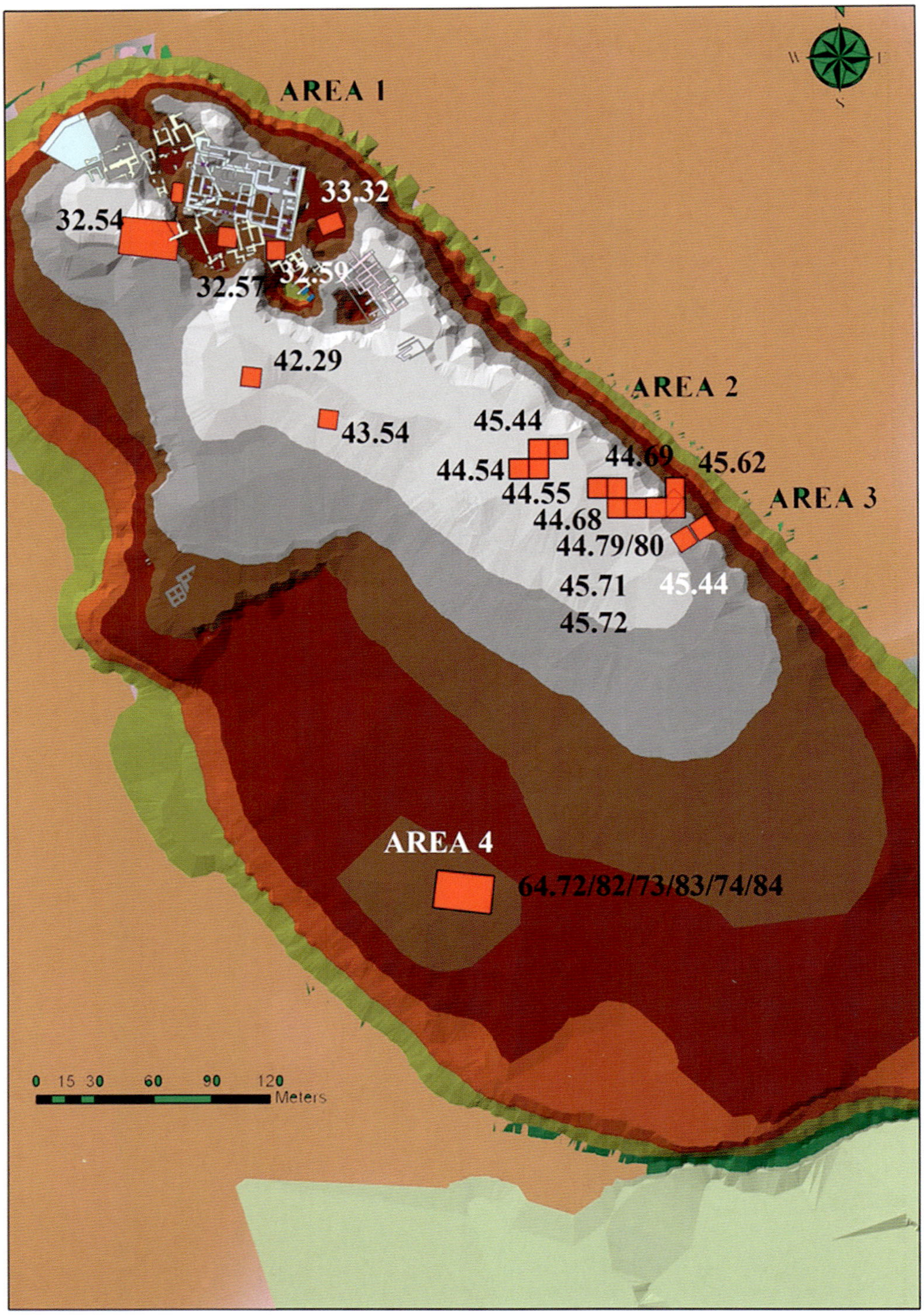

Fig. 3 Plan of Tell Atchana with excavation areas, architecture, 2003–2010 seasons. M. Akar.

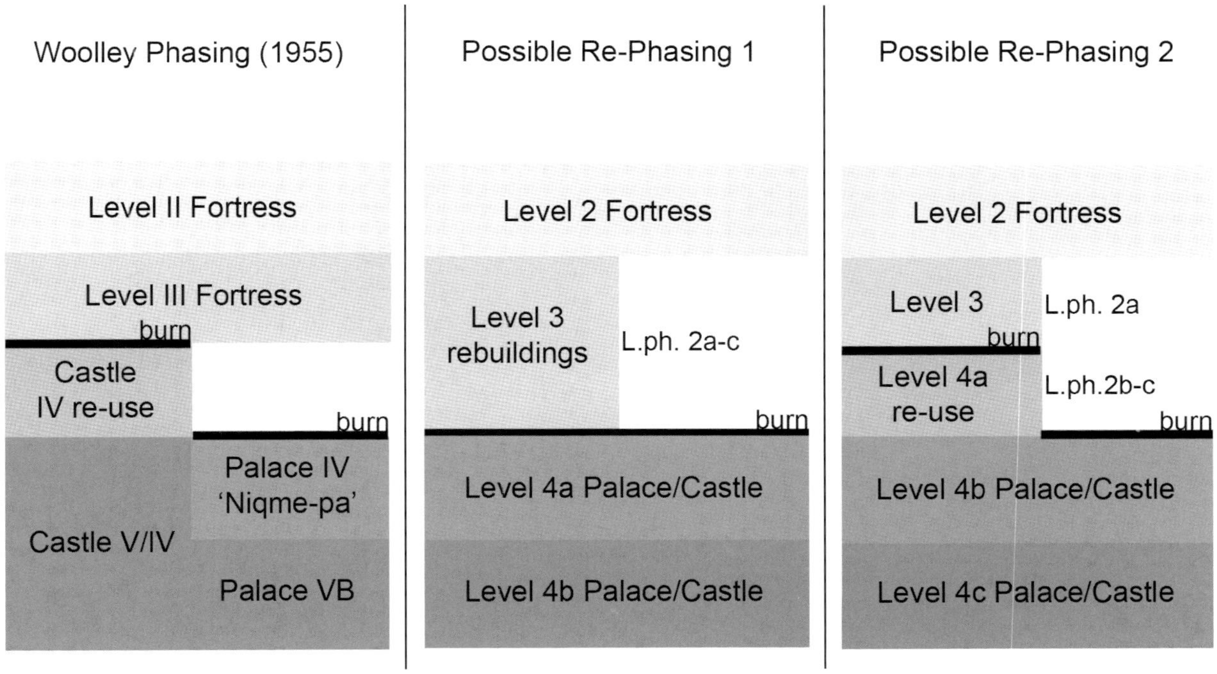

Fig. 4 Chart of Woolley and Yener phasing of Levels IV-I

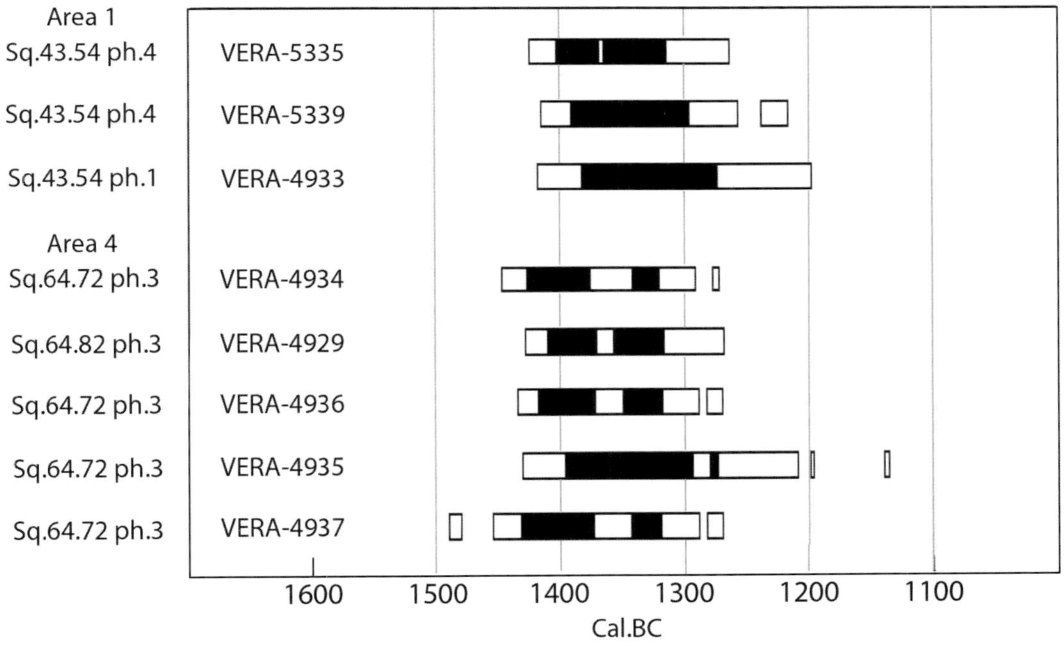

Fig. 5 Radiocarbon results from three LBII sequences.
AT6362, VERA-4933: 3045+-40; AT10147, VERA-5335: 3075+-35;
AT12229, VERA-5339: 3055+-35; AT8038, VERA-4935: 3060+-45;
AT7759. VERA-4929: 3085+-35; AT6761, VERA-4936: 3095+-35;
AT8035, VERA-4934: 3105+-35; AT6755, VERA-4937: 3110+-40.
Chart, M. Horowitz.

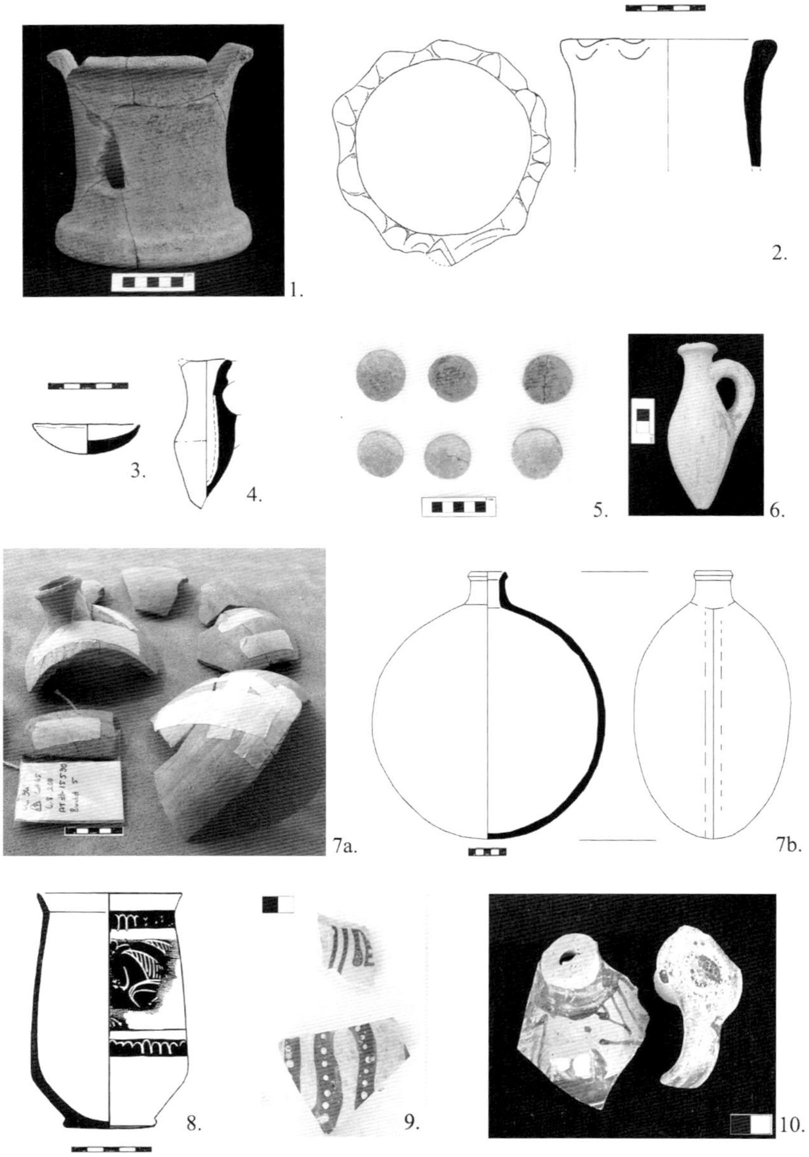

Fig. 6 Typical LBIIA ceramics from Tell Atchana.
1. Fenestrated stand, AT12546, 2009. M. Akar.
2. 'Flowerpot' stand, AT5913.902, 2008. S. Hawley.
3. Miniature open vessel, AT7185, 2007. Ö. Yarma.
4. Miniature closed vessel, AT3524, 2007. Ö. Yarma.
5. Miniature open vessels, AT4198.1-6, 2008. M. Akar.
6. Pointed Juglet, AT10331, 2009. M. Akar.
7. a,b: Lentoid Flask, AT15590, 2011. M. Horowitz.
8. Nuzi Ware cylindrical goblet, A04-20, 2004. B. Craddock.
9. Mycenaean LH IIIA-2 fragments, AT7166, 2008. M. Horowitz.
10. Mycenaean LH IIIA-2 fragment, AT10170, 2009. M. Horowitz.

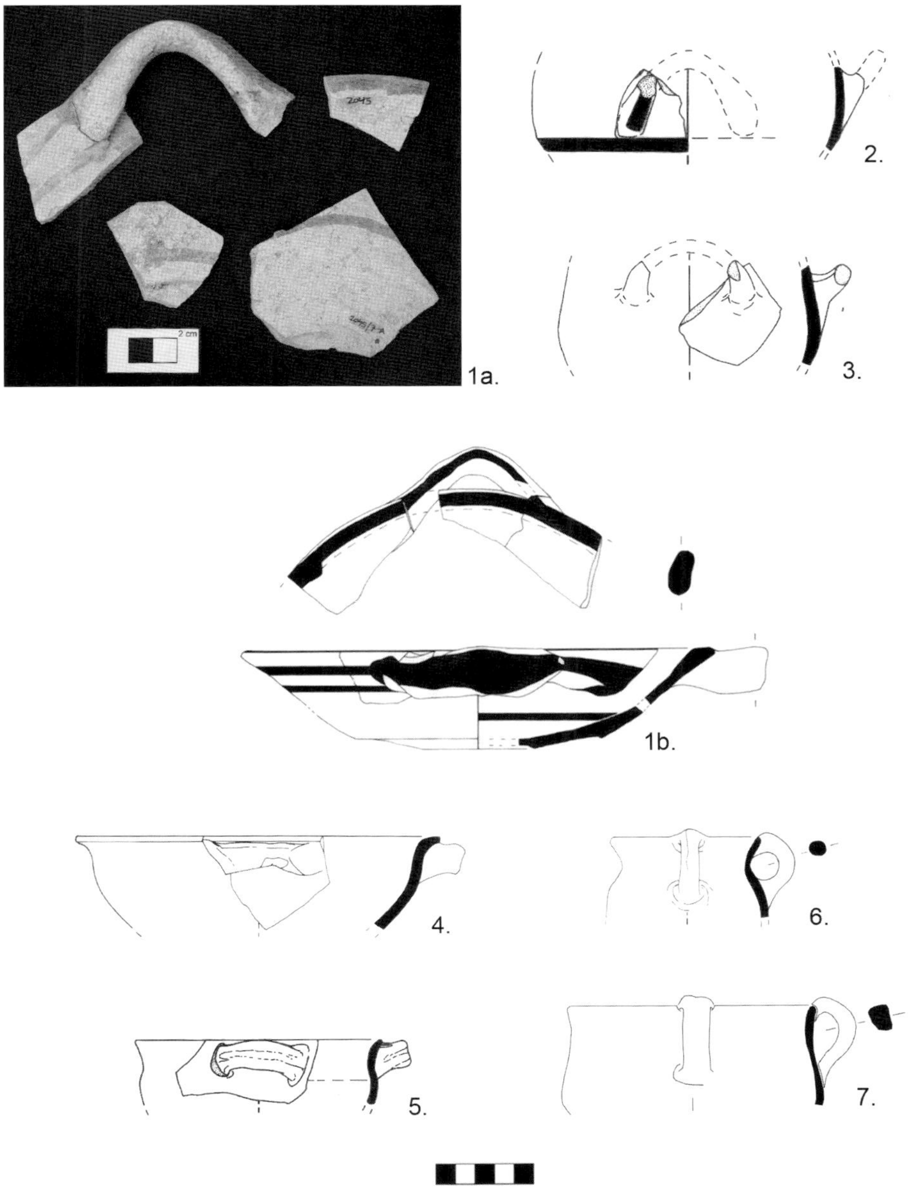

Fig. 7 Early Iron Age ceramics from Tell Atchana.
1. a,b: LH IIIC Basin, AT2045.7, 2007/2011. M. Akar, E. Arauz.
2. LH IIIC Deep bowl, AT11932.1, 2011. E. Arauz.
3. LH IIIC Deep bowl, AT11144.2, 2011. E. Arauz.
4. LH IIIC Shallow angular bowl, AT14942.1, 2011. E. Arauz.
5. LH IIIC Shallow angular bowl, AT11176.2, 2011. E. Arauz.
6. LH IIIC Cookpot, AT11114.3, 2011. E. Arauz.
7. LH IIIC Kylix, AT11134.3, 2011. E. Arauz.

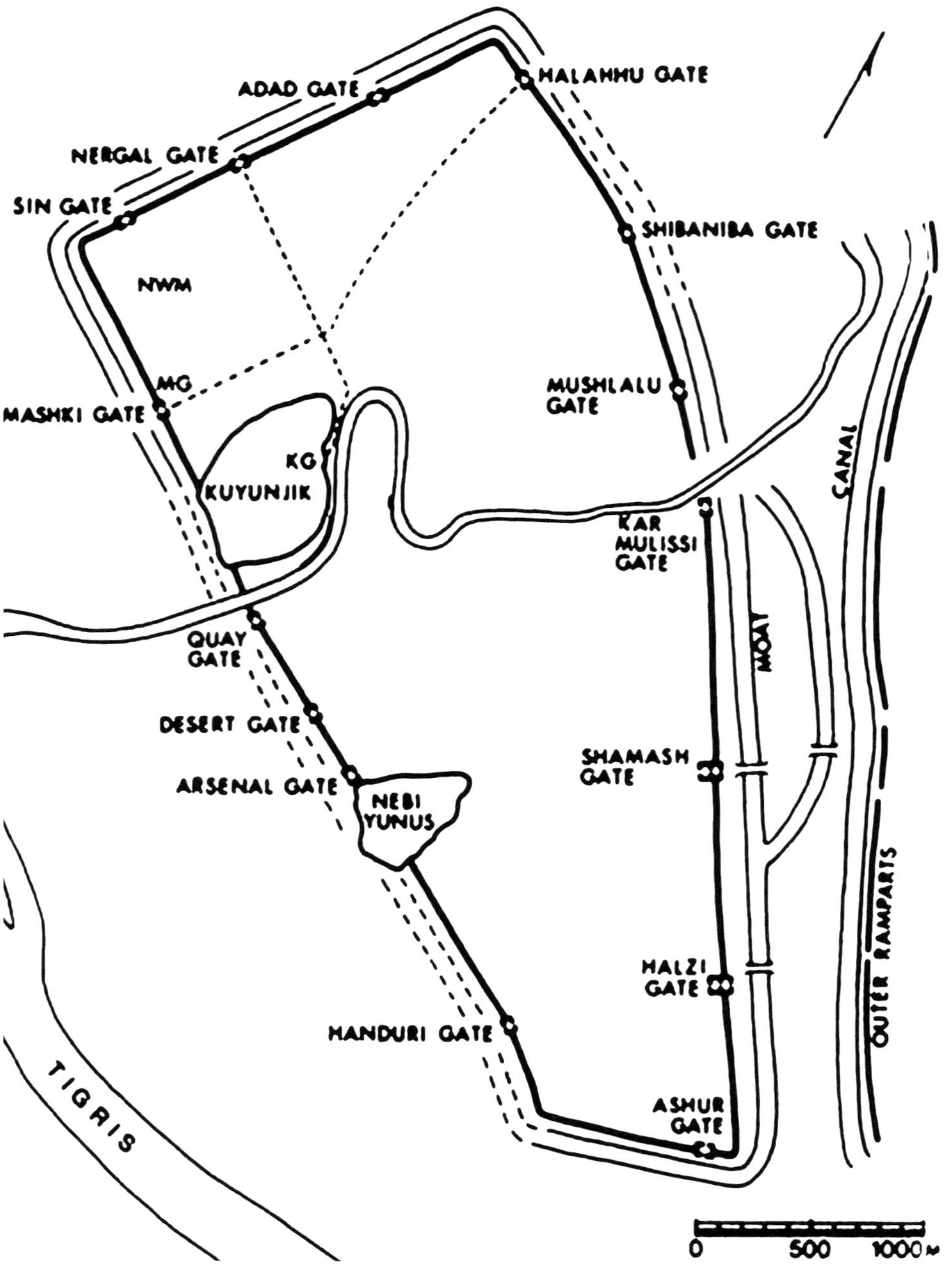

Fig. 8 Iron Age Nineveh depicting the mounds of Nebi Yunus and Kuyuncuk and a branch of the Tigris River.

Fig. 9 Photo taken in the early twentieth century depicting the Orontes River at Antakya.

CHAPTER 2

THE LATE BRONZE AGE FORTRESSES AT ALALAKH: ARCHITECTURE AND IDENTITY IN MEDITERRANEAN EXCHANGE SYSTEMS

Murat AKAR
Tell Atchana/Alalakh Excavation, Senior Field Supervisor.
Director, Koç University Archaeology Laboratory,
Istanbul, Turkey
E-mail: makar@ku.edu.tr.

ABSTRACT

This paper focuses on the military architecture of Tell Atchana (ancient Alalakh), the capital city of the Kingdom of Mukish, located in the Turkish province of Hatay. Based on the results of the renewed excavations, the exposure of 14th century BC fortress type buildings in its southern and northern extremities offer information about the military character of the city in its final levels and reflects its political and economic organization. The significance of Late Bronze Age commerciality and interaction patterns are not only visible in the material culture but also evident in the monumental scale architecture and in the case of Alalakh, is embedded into the concept of militaristic use of space in the contiguous time span of a shift in supremacy.

INTRODUCTION

In the heartland of the kingdom of Mukish, Alalakh is located at the passageway between great empires; its unique location is a buffer zone that interconnected with numerous regions which increased the potentials of a hybrid social community that evolved in this particular landscape. Following the same structural organization of Middle Bronze Age regional state kingdoms of the Levant, the transformative and imperialistic impulses of the subsequent Late Bronze Age empires had a dramatic impact on the structural organization of its capital city Alalakh.[1] Being sensitive to political and economic changes and by controlling the major land and sea networks between Anatolia and the Syrian plain, the role of this marginal territorial kingdom has always been of great interest to understand the dynamics of international and cross cultural interactions between distinct civilizations. An overview is presented here of

[1] Yener 2006, p. 373; see also Sinopoli 1994 and Glatz 2009 for the archaeology of empires.

the two recently excavated monumental fortress complexes at Alalakh and in keeping with the title and theme of this workshop, the comparative study explores the meaning of Alalakh's Late Bronze Age architecture in its international setting by going further across the borders to touch on the boundaries of Egypt (**Fig. 1**).

Current evidence from the Levant has already indicated the globalized stage of this period and its impact on the formation of Bronze Age urban centers.[2] At Alalakh this is visible in intra-site patterns, including monumental architecture and the variety of imported products. On a regional scale, this globalism is reflected in the accumulation of centers in close proximity to major commercial routes.[3] Starting from the Middle Bronze Age onwards, Anatolia and the Levant seem to have witnessed extensive exploitation of its resources, which flowed through connected sea and land routes. This kind of interdependency and the importance of commercial exchange combined with the political and socio-economic structure of the region, should be seen as the major reason behind the expansion of Late Bronze Age empires. This control of routes and nodal centers was pivotal to imperial policies.[4] From this perspective, substituting the terms *isolated* as meaning being surrounded by the mountain ranges and *globalized* as being on the nodal point of land and sea networks, the Amuq Valley can be qualified as a promising zone for investigating the political and social structure of the Eastern Mediterranean Bronze Age.[5] Alalakh, as a leader in this network within its regional setting, has provided a significant amount of information regarding the trends in material culture and the way cityscapes were formed under neighboring imperialistic policies. The excavations conducted at the site not only allowed the understanding of its own structural and regional organization, but since it was a periphery of the Hittite and Mitanni empires in the Late Bronze Age, it reflects the strategies of these core centers as well.[6]

The results from the excavations at Tell Atchana allow a unique opportunity to understand the multifaceted conditions of Late Bronze Age exchange systems.[7] The LBIIa (c. 1400–1300 BC) levels of the site document the rise of complex commercial and political dynamics where traces of 'globalization' from an Eastern Mediterranean perspective seem to characterize the general nature of the settlement. Evidence for cross-cultural harmony is already evident in Middle Bronze Age contexts, where Minoan-style wall paintings and seal impressions were found in the Level VII palace.[8] This multi-cultural integration reached its peak in the 15th–14th centuries BC when Mitannian, Hittite, Cypriot, and Mycenaean products became widely distributed in

[2] Feldman 2006.
[3] Akar 2009; for a detailed analysis of the settlement patterns of Amuq see also Casana 2003, 2009.
[4] Akar 2009; see also Sherratt and Sherratt 1991 for Late Bronze Age exchange systems.
[5] Akar 2012, p. 6.
[6] Yener 2010, p. 2.
[7] Woolley 1955; see also Yener 2005, 2010.
[8] Woolley 1955, pp. 228–234; see also Niemeier 1991; Collon 1994.

Alalakh's palatial and residential contexts.[9] Apart from the available artifact and ceramic data, I believe that the study of the architecture and the urban organization of Alalakh can define and further add to our understanding of the patterns of the social and political interactions in the Late Bronze Age.

The northern fortress (Woolley, Level III-II Fortress)

Sir Leonard Woolley's 1955 publication of Alalakh has provided some important information targeting the fortification systems of Levels III-II. However, there are a number of discrepancies regarding their stratigraphic relations between the earlier and later levels.[10] Textual evidence from several sources indicated that Mukish was under the control of Hittite governors in the mid-14th century BC.[11] The exposure by Woolley of an administrative fortress-type complex[12] constructed above the ruins of the Level IV palace would appear to be the architectural manifestation of this historical event in the archaeological record (**Fig. 2 and Fig. 3**).

Woolley noted the diverse architectural approaches in the fortress construction project. The thickness of the walls, the casemate chambers, and the overall plan is completely different from any of the other fortified buildings that had been excavated at the site.[13] Even though the structure itself is lacking secure floor contexts, the attribution of this building to the Hittites is mainly based on partial data collection from the location. There are some Hittite tablets claimed to be found in Level III-II contexts but they are stratigraphically not secure.[14] A number of artifacts from these levels were suggested to be consistent with Anatolian styles.[15] Yener also proposed that the Level II temple had Anatolian elements in its architectural style.[16] Several artifacts from Level I have also been used to define Hittite presence at the settlement. For example, the Tudhaliya relief was found face down, used as a staircase pavement in the annex of the Level I temple.[17] Woolley proposed that this was a way of showing disrespect for the Hittite authorities and therefore must date to a period after the end of the Hittite control over the site. The available data led him to conclude that Levels III-II represented the period of Hittite control of the site, and he identified the major

[9] Yener 2008; 2011; see also Gates 1981; Bergoffen 2005; Kozal 2010; Koehl 2005, 2010.

[10] Yener 2005; see also Batiuk and Burke 2005; Fink 2008, 2010; Akar 2012.

[11] Klengel 1992, p. 119; see also Niedorf 2002; Astour 1969, 1972; Beckman 1999.

[12] Woolley 1955, pp. 166–170. The fortress is monumental in scale with an approximate dimension of 80 x 80 meters.

[13] There are no other identical buildings excavated from both the Woolley and Yener expeditions at the site.

[14] For a discussion on the post Level IV tablets found in the royal precinct see von Dassow 2008.

[15] For a list and discussion of the artifacts from the Woolley excavations with Anatolian origin see Helft 2009. See also Yener 2005; 2011.

[16] Yener 2005, p. 111.

[17] Woolley 1955, p. 86.

architectural construction project as *the Hittite fortress of Alalakh.*[18] Unfortunately, the building and its stratigraphic sequence is only described in three pages and not provided with visual documentation (except one photograph and a general plan of the building).[19] Based on the size of this structure, however, one should note that it is one of the most well-organized and largest scale construction projects that was ever undertaken at the site.

Archaeological levels identified by Woolley at Tell Atchana are linked to historical events, which is often problematic. The synchronisms of textual evidence with architectural data were in some cases satisfactory in describing destruction deposits, which is best exemplified by the textual attribution of the demolition of the Level VII city to Hattushili I.[20] However, these linkages do not fully explain the historical events that followed and more specifically, the way in which the city regenerated after its collapse. Additionally, for the LBII levels, Woolley's publications gave a sense of sudden change at the site following the destruction of the Level IV palace. Unfortunately, these alleged historical events which followed were not correctly defined in terms of archaeological deposition.

After Woolley's final publication of the site stratigraphy and chronology, extensive literature was penned by various scholars to understand the chronological, historical and cultural linkages between Alalakh and the other contemporary major civilizations of the Near East.[21] These scholars have made significant efforts to re-examine Alalakh's stratigraphic sequence by reevaluating pottery typology, epigraphic information, and architectural data. All of these studies have been successful in pointing out the discrepancies in the excavation data, and each scholar has proposed their own chronological sequences, as well as reconstructions of the ancient cityscape.

To further the confusion, in the final Woolley publication, the chapters were organized by levels within the functional attributions of the architecture. Each architectural unit (palaces, temples, fortifications) had been stratigraphically assessed within their own relative sequence and linkages to stratigraphic levels with other areas of the site were established later. This is one of the major reasons for the problematic state of Woolley's stratigraphic attributions. Before the initiation of a large scale excavation project, the Yener expedition focused on this particular problem. Through detailed examination of all of the published plans, an effort was made to visualize all these separate plans based on their assigned levels given by Woolley. The GIS study of

[18] Woolley 1955, p. 166.

[19] The major reason for the limited documentation is no doubt the absence of small finds from its associated contexts. A few artifacts were associated with the fortress however, the value of these stratigraphic attributions are questioned in this article and by Yener (this volume).

[20] Woolley 1955, pp. 91–106; see also Landsberger 1954; Klengel 1992; Bryce 2005.

[21] There are extensive numbers of publications dedicated to Alalakh studies. For a major discussion on site stratigraphy, see references in Stein 1997; Yener 2005; Fink 2008, 2010. For the revision of site stratigraphy based on new archaeological data see Akar 2012 and Yener (this volume).

Alalakh's spatial data suggested relationships between buildings that had not been put forward before and gave the opportunity to get a sense of the way the capital functioned spatially. It also revealed that some of the major buildings were stratigraphically and spatially assigned to the wrong levels.[22] These observations can be identified, but cannot be proven definitively since, with the exception of the standing ruins of the Level IV and the Level VII palace and the gate complex, much of the architecture no longer exists. The 2002 section cleaning undertaken in the Temple Deep Sounding showed that the stratigraphy of the tell was much more complicated than initially expected, and that it should not be used as an agenda to solve the problems concerning the stratigraphy of the entire site.[23]

Following this pre-excavation comprehensive work, a recent study by Fink analyzed the problems encountered with mapping the architectural levels in the Woolley excavations. By going through some of the unpublished photographs in the collections of UCL and pointing out several more possible discrepancies in Woolley's data, Fink presented evidence that the post Level IV sequence of the site should be revised. In conclusion, Fink proposed his own stratigraphic sequence for the site.[24] Unfortunately such studies are erroneous and frequently misleading, since their foundations were already initially weakened, as they are based on the limitations of the original excavation data. Fink's stratigraphic revision of Alalakh's site sequence could not be accomplished without conducting new systematic excavations that can then be linked to the data produced by Woolley's excavations.

From this perspective, the renewed Yener excavations at the site have dedicated the last six years of fieldwork to understanding the stratigraphic sequence of the palatial district. Eight excavation squares were located in an E-W orientation in the royal district of Alalakh, Area 1. One excavation square was located in the courtyard of the Level VII palace and another at the Level IV palace courtyard. While these two units were successful in exploring the pre-Level IV palace sequence, six squares located in front of Woolley's old dig house, at the western edge of his excavation area, added extensive amount of information regarding the poorly understood post-Level IV sequence. Conducting wide horizontal excavations over six squares, the continuation of the now renamed, Northern Fortress was exposed, adding another 20 × 30 m of the structure to what had previously been excavated (**Fig. 4 and Fig. 5**).

The vertical excavation soundings in Square 32.54 in the east provided the possibility to re-investigate the stratigraphic relationship between the Level IV palace and the so-called Level III-II (Northern) Fortress. With the last excavation campaign in 2010, the western portion of the Level IV castle and the gate complex (*serai gate*) was finally

[22] Yener 2005; see also Batiuk and Burke 2005; Fink 2008; 2010.

[23] Woolley 1955, pp. 5–90; see also Batiuk and Horowitz 2010.

[24] Fink 2010, p. 2. The erroneous stratigraphical attributions presented by Fink are not discussed in this paper. See Akar 2012 for the criticism of Fink's conclusions.

exposed in this square.[25] The succeeding levels show that the remains of the Level IV city were re-used; the walls were erected with mud bricks, which had survived the destruction of the Level IV city. Several floor levels and changes in the building plan indicate that the site was not rebuilt but followed immediately after the collapse of the Level IV administrative control. Rather, it went through a period of decline followed by regeneration. More in depth analysis of these building levels and its contribution to our understanding of the chronology and stratigraphy of Alalakh is presented elsewhere.[26] What can now be understood, however, is that the Northern Fortress, contrary to Woolley's initial understanding, did not have two levels (Woolley suggested that the fortress was re-modified in Level II after its original construction in Level III); rather, it is of a single solid construction that occupied the entire palatial district.

Woolley stated that "the construction must date from the time of our Level III and the walls were re-used, with floors at a higher level, in the Level II period."[27] However, neither his text nor the architectural plans give any information of these proposed modifications.[28] Examining the stratigraphic relationships with earlier levels, one can understand why he assumed that the fortress had two phases. In the west section of our new Square 32.54, it is clearly seen that the Northern Fortress was erected on top of earlier building levels with the walls running in the same orientation. The builders of the Northern Fortress carefully planned the steps of its construction and the earlier remains were used as part of the foundation to support the weight of the building. The Northern Fortress extended towards the west and sat on top of the Level IV Castle which followed the same orientation. This process is particularly due to the desirability of using the old standing walls as part of the foundation. The rooms of the earlier building levels were deliberately filled with mud bricks and rubble. Therefore, due to this type construction technique, much of the assemblages got mixed and lost their inherent chronological value (**Fig. 6**).

Construction techniques

Based on our architectural examination, the construction of the building can be divided into the following three different sections: the foundation trench, the foundation platform and the standing walls.

[25] Yener (this volume); see also Akar 2012.
[26] Akar 2012 on the post Level IV stratigraphy of Alalakh as part of the PhD Dissertation at the University of Florence.
[27] Woolley 1955, p. 167.
[28] Woolley 1955, p. 167.

1. *The Foundation Trench*

The foundation trench cut into the rooms and open spaces of the earlier levels and has a very peculiar character. Looking at the west section of Square 32.54 that descended into the courtyard of the Level IV palace, it can be seen that mud bricks were used to fill up this very large foundation trench. The walls of earlier levels were deliberately left intact and served a supporting function. The open spaces were filled with mud bricks. Once the foundation was filled, the mud bricks of the platform extended on both sides of the trench and became wider than the foundation. This is what Woolley referred as a "v-shaped foundation" in his publication.[29] This peculiar construction technique is only observed in this fortress complex (**Fig. 6**).

Although his interpretation is correct in that the walls became much larger than the foundations, the misinterpretation arose mainly from the way the building was conceived. The deliberate packing of mud bricks and rubble in between the designated spaces indicates that the greatest effort was given to the construction of a platform. When one looks at the plan of the building, it can easily be noted that there are no passages or doorways between the chambers. The rubble and brick packing indicates that they were not designed to be in use as storage areas, rather the construction is more akin to a casemate system.[30] Examining the old plans, one also notes that some of these spaces are much larger than others, creating a visual appearance of a courtyard or large rooms. However, rather than seeing these "rooms" of different uses or functions, it is better to see them as artifacts of a combination of ancient topography and the availability of old standing remains that were incorporated into the construction. This is substantiated by Woolley, who notes that "..the width of the brick work increasing with the slope of the sides of the trench as it rose; but, as the trench was not cut to the full width intended for the walls of the superstructure, when the ground level was reached the next course of bricks was laid overlapping the course below and resting on the soil on either side of the trench..."[31]

2. *The Foundation Platform*

On top of the foundation trench, the building expanded into a much wider space, and the superstructure became larger than the foundation trench. Looking at the foundation platform, which reaches up more than 2m in height, one can understand the nature of the settlement at the time of this structure. The difference in elevation of the Royal Precinct from the rest of the settlement owes its formation to this

[29] Woolley 1955, p. 167.

[30] The term casemate is conventionally used to define the spaces filled in between the walls but *caisson* is the right architectural term due to their non-inhabited solely architectural character and function.

[31] Woolley 1955, p. 167.

particular construction method. In other words, the builders of the fortress artificially raised the building area. This could intentionally reflect the style of the Hittite overlords, who constructed their capital in defensive northern Anatolian rock outcrops, but were now adapting to the flat plain of the Amuq Valley. It should also be noted that apart from the concerns about security, to a certain extent this must have also included a level of symbolism where the architecture itself was used as an indicator of power, raised up over this newly dominated landscape.

3. *The Standing Walls*

Above the platform no sign was observed of a floor level. Woolley claimed that the storage compartments with floor levels which were exposed in the southeast were part of the fortress. However, judging from the general plan of the building as well as looking at the single photograph[32] published in his 1955 publication, it is clear that these compartment units belong to the modification phases of the Level IV castle, and *not* to the Level III Fortress. Both the size and the orientation of this section fit into the earlier Level IV Castle complex. Consequently, if the reassignment of these storage compartments to the earlier palace (Castle) is correct, then the artifacts and other finds should also be reassigned to an earlier phase. It can also be observed from this single photograph that the elevation of this spot is much lower than the foundation platform. Woolley tried to argue that the elevation differences were possible terracing, but this idea contradicts the very way the fortress was constructed. The standing remains support the suggestion that a significant effort was given to the creation of a large, one-level platform.

Since none of the floor levels or the superstructure has survived from this Northern Fortress construction, two interpretations can be proposed. The construction of a large scale complex must have required a high number of craftsman and a significant amount of time. The absence of any remains from the superstructure may indicate that the final construction of the building may never have been accomplished.[33] A second option is to suggest that the Level I builders were responsible for the flattening of any extant architecture.[34] Although one should assume that such large mud brick buildings are meant to survive for generations of occupation with modest repairs and modifications, the complete demolition or disappearance of this fortress is a rather extraordinary reconstruction.

[32] Woolley 1955, p. 168, pl. 33.

[33] This interpretation was first put forward by Dr. Ekin Kozal in one of our discussions at Tell Atchana.

[34] Woolley 1955, p. 170.

THE SOUTHERN FORTRESS

In an effort to understand Alalakh's greater cityscape and stratigraphy, new excavation squares were initiated in 2006 on an elevated rise in the southwestern part of the tell. The excavations in six squares measuring 10 x 10 meters revealed another fortress structure which, based on ceramic parallels, is believed to be roughly contemporary with the Northern Fortress.[35] Resembling the architectural style that was attested to in the northern part of the tell, this second fortress did not have a foundation trench or a platform; rather, it was reinforced by double walls with casemate chambers (**Fig. 2 and Fig.** 7). A street system, which ran along the exterior line of the wall and bounded possibly by a type of enclosure system, was erected with the Southern Fortress itself forming part of the fortification system.[36] This fortress was of a solid mud brick construction with no stone foundations and from a technological point of view, does share some similarities with the Northern Fortress. When the earlier levels were reached by removing the exterior wall of the Southern Fortress, it was clearly visible that the fortress was built in the same orientation as the earlier building level. The much thinner, mud brick walls of the earlier complex were incorporated into the construction of the foundations for the wider walls of the later fortress. Casemate chambers were carefully distributed throughout the foundations, resulting in keeping the remains of the old structures intact within the areas corresponding to these chambers. Furthermore, the rubble of the earlier building levels was used as the earth packing in the casemate chambers.[37]

The Northern and Southern Fortresses at Alalakh fit into the chronological period of the political dominance of the Hittites at the site and in the region. Several artifacts and reliefs recovered in other contexts from the Woolley excavations provided evidence of Hittite occupation; however, the exact nature of the expansion of the Hittite occupation into the kingdom of Mukish was never fully understood. The excavations conducted from 2006 onwards in a North-South strip along the western line of the tell are starting to produce very promising results that help to elucidate the nature of this expansion. From the material perspective, a major part of the pottery assemblage fits into the plain monochrome ware horizon (also known as drab ware) or, as a better definition, into the North Central Anatolian pottery traditions.[38] Miniature cups and vessels found roughly 50 meters from the Northern Fortress in Square 43.54 are identical to the ones discovered at Hattusha in the Temple Pools.[39] A ceremonial Hittite

[35] Akar 2012, p. 182; see also Horowitz in prep.

[36] The magnetometry survey spotted some anomalies along the western edge of the site where it looks like the street system follows the line of the fortification wall; a similar type of construction that is observed in the 14th century B.C Yümüktepe contexts, Jean 2006.

[37] Akar 2012, pp. 182–194.

[38] Glatz 2009.

[39] Yener 2008, p. 295, fig 7; see also Neve 1993, p. 28.

axe[40] is another unique find that adds to the Anatolian corpus of artifacts from Alalakh.

Even though it may be early to give any definite statement about intra-site settlement patterns, it is possible to suggest that the final levels of the site are characterized by major construction projects rather than a decline. The excavation of these two fortresses and the domestic units excavated in the Royal Precinct also indicates that the late 14th-early 13th century BC contexts do not provide any signs of destruction; instead, more of a pattern of planned abandonment is observed. These new constructions give the indication of a heavily fortified city, rather than an impoverished ruin. The final study of the appearance and distribution of the pottery assemblages will ultimately enable us to define the extent and nature of this LBIIa city. As already proposed by Yener in this volume, the Bronze Age occupation at the site ends at the beginning of the 13th century BC.[41]

The evidence of large scale construction and fortification systems connects well with the geo-archaeological research conducted around the site. Boring with mechanical drill-work conducted in 2009 implied that a river ran along the NE face of the site and suggested the possibility of a lower city extending at the southwestern side of the mound. Based on the proposed environmental reconstruction, it seems like the fortresses were located at the western and southwestern portions of the site where there was no natural protection by the river. Thus it was heavily defended with a line of fortification walls with fortresses at regular intervals (**Fig. 2**).[42]

The exchange of technology

The Late Bronze Age witnessed a period of globalism where primary concepts such as trade and exchange dynamics were only a minor representative of this interconnected time period. The interactions between cities, regions or empires were more complex than we have thought and the relationships were not always direct and visible in the way that we expected. I believe that an understanding of architecture can be used as a powerful tool for reconstructing sociopolitical interactions and for deciphering the symbols and ideologies imprinted in the construction of monumental architecture.[43] When we try to look at all these achievements characterizing the mid-14th century BC construction projects, several issues need to be addressed from a technological and political standpoint. Even though mud brick as a construction medium is widely attested all over the ancient Near East, the way it has been manipulated in the

40 Yener 2011.
41 See Yener (this volume).
42 The geoarchaeological research is conducted by Derek Ryter from the USGS. See Yener (this volume).
43 Ullmann 2010; see also Burke 2004.

construction of these buildings may well have specific cultural distinctions. With the rich cedar and stone sources of the Amanus Mountains and basaltic rock outcrops of the Hassa region, the availability and usage of heavy timber framework and large basalt and limestone blocks are the key architectural features of the Level VII and Level IV palaces of Alalakh,[44] but are not characteristic of post-Level IV construction. So what event forced and/or inspired the builders of these fortresses to switch to a rather different type of architectural practice?

Comparative research suggests the possibility of Egyptian influence, where apart from some monumental complexes, everything is achieved with sun-dried mud bricks.[45] The idea of establishing isolated 'fortress' type structures is a common concept and defines the military technology that Egyptians advanced from the Old Kingdom onwards to protect the borders of their kingdom. Egypt's long interest in Nubian gold mines and their effort to keep the southern boundary of the Kingdom protected from attacks contributed to a significant amount of technological knowledge accumulated from the construction of their isolated fortress structures. They formed the main element of defensive principles in Egyptian military architecture. All the Egyptian fortresses were constructed with mud bricks, altering the surrounding landscape dramatically with their massiveness. In the flat Egyptian deserts or the narrow rocky valleys of the upper Nile, these structures would have been defined as landmarks that state the imperial might of the Egyptian Pharaoh.

Egyptian fortresses were located in all the strategic routes that connected Egypt with Eastern Mediterranean traffic. Information about the Middle Kingdom Egyptian military architecture and defense strategies were achieved by the investigation of a series of fortresses located between the first and second cataracts of the Nile. Many Egyptian fortresses would have been located in the Israeli and Palestinian coastal route in the 'Ways of Horus' in the New Kingdom that would have defined the strategies applied to secure the borders from Hittite and Syro-Mitanni intrusions.

The Middle Kingdom fortresses of Egypt characterized the standard principles of defense architecture which continued to be in use in the New Kingdom.[46] These strikingly, are the closest parallels for the Alalakh Northern Fortress; in particular, the foundation platform resembles the Delta site, Tell el Dab'a, ancient Avaris.[47] The post-Hyksos construction project at the royal district in the Tuthmoside period has two important buildings. Palace G and the smaller Palace F were constructed over the

[44] Woolley 1955, pp. 91–131.

[45] Contemporary monumental architectural traditions from the heartland of Mitanni are excluded from this comparative research. Wider exposures at sites like Tell Fekheriyeh (see Bonatz and Bartl this volume) will eventually improve our understanding of the international styles in Late Bronze Age monumental architecture in the future.

[46] See fortress of Buhen as an example of Middle Kingdom fortress in Egypt, Emery et al. 1979; Hamblin 2006.

[47] Bietak 2006, 2007; see also Bietak et al. 2007.

ruins of the Hyksos city. Both of these palace-fortress type structures were raised seven meters above the ground level by the construction of substantial mud brick platforms (**Fig. 8**).[48] The superstructure did not survive in Palace F, however, the pottery from the casemate chambers filled with rubble includes late Hyksos period material and thus provides a *terminus post quem* for the end of Hyksos occupation and the beginning of the Egyptian XVIIIth dynasty.[49] What has been identified as the administrative fortress complex was built in the same manner as the Alalakh Northern Fortress. By constructing a substantial mud brick platform, the building at Avaris was elevated above the ground level and a ramp system was built to provide access to the building.[50] The use of platforms physically and symbolically sealed the unfortunate days of the city under foreign rulers. The erection of the platform not only symbolized the power of the Pharaoh but seems to have been intended to erase an epoch from its history. This intriguing piece of evidence is further supported by other examples of the Egyptian type fortresses excavated along the Israeli and Palestinian coast.

Recently dated to the end of 13th century BC, a fortress structure measuring 20 × 20 meters was excavated at Deir el-Balah Stratum VII,[51] which is one of the Egyptian garrisons located on the Ways of Horus, 13 km southwest of Gaza in the southern coastal plain. Only the foundations were preserved in this fortress, and no floor levels were traced (**Fig. 9**). Another fortress discovered at Beth Shan Level VII[52] had the same technological approach in its construction with substantial platforms (**Fig. 10**). Another example comes from the site of Tell Borg where a fosse was intentionally filled to erect a new fortress during the reign of Thutmosis III or Amenhotep III.[53] The intentional filling of the fosse and the raising of the foundation platform are unique architectural features of these complexes. A much later example comes from the Saite period (664–525 BC) of Egypt in the east Delta plain. At site T.21, a similar construction technique is attested on a massive scale.[54] Since the Delta water table was very high, Oren suggested that the shafts and hallows or casemates were intentionally filled with debris to counteract dampness and provide proper drainage. He also pointed out that hollowed compartments were required to relieve the pressure created by masses of brick work.

Mitannians, Hittites, Assyrians and Egyptian were the major players of the Late Bronze Age when the struggle between empires ultimately played a significant role in the development of imperial strategies and responses to warfare and political stress.

[48] Both of these buildings were constructed over 7m high platforms. Ramps were used to access to the buildings. This is an identical construction technique with the Northern Fortress of Alalakh.

[49] Bietak 2006, 2007.

[50] Bietak 2007, p. 288; see also Bietak et al. 2007.

[51] Killebrew et al. 2006; see also Dothan 1987.

[52] Mazar 2003.

[53] Hoffmeier 2006, p. 14; see also Hoffmeier and Abd El-Maksoud 2003.

[54] Oren 1984.

But at the same time, the interconnected nature of the landscape might have also provoked an imperial competition between different parties. The administrative fortress type structures were not only achieved with military concerns in mind, but they were the three-dimensional representations of imperial power. The Northern Fortress itself seems to have been intended to be a symbol of the Hittite authority at Mukish; however, one can hardly find a correlation with the Anatolian style of military organization in the construction of these building complexes from a technological point of view. While the organization of the Southern Fortress, separated by a street system from the city fortifications, does share the same arrangement as the Hittite defense systems of Hattusha at Büyükkale[55] or Yümüktepe Hittite Levels VII-V,[56] this is not strong evidence for suggesting a Hittite identity to these structures. Then how do all these technological parallels fit into the political relations of the Late Bronze Age kingdoms and what was the mechanism of interaction? Various modes of gift exchanges and continuous warfare and power relations played between empires characterized the interaction between the different kingdoms in the Late Bronze Age.

In his 1983 article, Zaccagnini stated that according to textual evidence, the level of gift exchange was not only limited to luxury items and/or raw materials but also included the exchange of skilled craftsmen. There are several texts of Hittite kings requesting craftsman and physicians from Egypt. Working under Egyptian palatial organization, these skilled craftsmen, masons, and physicians were sent to serve the Hittite King.[57] In the reign of Suppiluliuma I, Hittite relations with Egypt were fluctuating. Not only do we have the attestation of gift exchanges but even the attempted establishment of deeper ties through the intended marriage of the son of Suppililuma I with the widowed Queen of Egypt, which clearly attests to the level of this interaction. The mutual relationship with Egypt was ended following the assassination Zannanza, son of Suppiluliuma, on his way to Egypt to marry the young widowed queen.[58] In Suppiluliuma's revenge campaigns, many Egyptian prisoners of war were believed to be brought back to Hittite-occupied territories.[59] One may also consider that these Egyptian prisoners had different skills and were forced to work in the construction programs in the frontier settlements of the Hittite empire, such as Alalakh.

These are two direct possibilities that are based on hypothetical historical reconstruction of the time period. But these all together may not be the reason for observing Egyptian type of elements in Alalakh's fortress construction programs. Technology and knowledge exchange between interconnected empires of the Late Bronze may have occurred over the *longue durée* and is difficult to trace in the archaeological

[55] Mielke 2011.
[56] Jean 2006, p. 313.
[57] Zaccagnini 1983, p. 250.
[58] Bryce 2003, pp. 178–189.
[59] Bryce 2005, p. 183.

record. However, one should not neglect the high level of technological advancement that Egypt established and its likely role in the development of similar types of architecture in the Near East.

Practical concerns also need to be considered in the understanding of the uniqueness of the fortress construction program at Alalakh. During the reign of territorial empires, alternative architectural solutions would have been investigated to accomplish the various construction projects that would have secured the conquered land of Mukish. If architecture is the combined reflection of the landscape and the indigenous culture that creates it, then the alterations in the technological approaches can be seen as an agenda used to define the changes in the political setting.[60] Yet the core Hittite landscape of the Halys River basin is a radically different landscape than the Kingdom of Mukish, centered on the Amuq Plain. The limited availability of stone, the flatness of the plain, and the absence of natural protection would have been the primary concerns of the Hittite engineers. In his dissertation, Ullmann[61] investigated the close relationship between Hittite landscape and its symbolic and functional meaning in Hittite culture. He correctly points out that Hittites were people of the highlands and they had a different understanding and perception of the landscape that surrounded them, which formed the cultural landscape of Anatolia in the Middle and Late Bronze Ages. Mukish in the late 14th century was not their landscape, and Hittite management of this terrain must have required a process of adaptation.

The Hittite presence in the Amuq was not isolated to the Late Bronze Age. The Hittite military campaigns in the region were successful from Hattushili I onwards. Over the course of the LBI and LBIIa, the Hittites probably sacked, destroyed, and ruled the same city at least twice and were probably well aware of the weaknesses of the indigenous fortification systems. It was Suppiluliuma I who looked for solid architectural as well as political foundations in the newly conquered landscape of the kingdom of Mukish. The large scale construction projects beginning in the late 14th century contexts at Alalakh can be indicative of such structural re-organization. Even though the fortresses share the concept of Hittite imperialism, technologically they are neither Anatolian nor Syrian products. The convincing parallels with Egyptian type fortresses indicate the possibility that a technological knowledge transfer might have occurred from Egypt to Hatti.

Conclusions

In examining the fortresses at Alalakh, one could easily argue and could likely expand the argument into a much larger ancient Near Eastern setting. Several comparative

[60] Akar 2012.
[61] Ulmann 2010.

architectural practices can be suggested from different areas of the Near East, in particular Mesopotamia. But the limits of this comparative particular research are set within the socio-economic interaction of the Late Bronze Age empires of the Eastern Mediterranean. The discovery of the Uluburun shipwreck[62] shed light on the complex exchange and trade systems, and the Amarna[63] letters provided a glimpse of the political interactions that occurred between the interconnected empires and kingdoms of the Late Bronze Age. In this broader sense, it is not surprising to evaluate the possibility that foreign elements in Alalakh's defensive architecture can be linked with what I refer to as Egyptian technology. The definition of this Egyptian characteristic can be seen as problematic to attest, since most of the Egyptian fortresses excavated are not from the core center of the empire but were found in its periphery. Yet the knowledge that was accumulated by the Egyptian architects working in the peripheries of the kingdom seem to have created a particular technological approach that manifests itself in the way the defensive architecture was formed under the demands of imperialistic policies. Thus the Late Bronze Age did not only witness an 'international style' in the concept of material culture[64] but also in the concept of architecture and its local adaptation by different cultures. At Alalakh the adaptation of Egyptian construction principles that are visible in the fortresses would have served both for the security of periphery and the representation of Hittite imperial power.

Bibliography

AKAR, M.

2009 "The Role of Harbour Towns in the Re-Urbanization of the Northern Levant in the Middle Bronze Age: Perspectives from Cilicia and the Amuq Plain of Hatay," in *ArchAtlas, February 2010, Edition 4*, http://www.archatlas.org/workshop09/works09-akar.php (accessed: 22 February 2011).

2012 "The Late Bronze Age II City of Alalakh and Its Social Context in the Northern Levant: A Re-Examination of the Post-Level IV Stratigraphic Sequence (I–III) based on New Excavation Results (2003–2010)." Unpublished Ph.D Diss. Florence University.

ASTOUR, M. C.

1969 "The Partition of the Confederacy of Mukis-Nuhasse-Nii by Suppiluliuma: A study in the Political Geography of the Amarna Age," *Orientalia* 38: 338–414.

1972 "Harrusilis, Halab, and Hanigalbat," *Journal of Near Eastern Studies* 31: 102-9.

BATIUK, S. D. and BURKE, A. A.

2005 "The Tell Atchana Mapping and GIS Project," in *The Amuq Valley Regional Projects. Vol. 1, Surveys in the Plain of Antioch and Orontes Delta, Turkey, 1995-2002*, Oriental Institute Publications 131, edited by K. A. Yener, pp. 145–152. Chicago: University of Chicago Press.

[62] Pulak 1998.
[63] Moran 1992.
[64] Feldman 2006.

BATIUK, S. D. and HOROWITZ, M.
2010 "Temple Deep Sounding Investigations 2001-2006," in *Tell Atchana, Ancient Alalakh. Volume 1: 2003–2004 Excavation Seasons*, edited by K. A.Yener, pp. 161–168. İstanbul: Koç University Press.
BECKMAN, G. M.
1999 *Hittite Diplomatic Texts*, Writings from the Ancient World. Atlanta: GA Scholars Press.
BERGOFFEN, C. J.
2005 *The Cypriot Bronze Age Pottery from Sir Leonard Woolley's Excavations at Alalakh (Tell Atchana)*, Contributions to the Chronology of the Eastern Mediterranean 5. Wien: Verlag der Österreichischen Akademie der Wissenschaften.
BIETAK, M.
2006 "Egypt and the Aegean: Cultural Convergence in a Thutmoside Palace at Avaris," in *Hatshepsut. From Queen to Pharaoh, Exhibition Catalogue of the Metropolitan Museum of Art, New York in 2006*, edited by C. H. Roehring, pp. 135–143. New York.
2007 "Bronze Age Paintings in the Levant: Chronological and Cultural Considerations," in *The Synchronization of Civilizations in the Eastern Mediterranean in the Second Millennium BC (vol. III), Proceedings of the SCIEM 2000-Euro Conference, Vienna, 2nd of May – 7th of May 2003*, Contributions to the Chronology of the Eastern Mediterranean, edited by M. Bietak and H. Hunger, pp. 269–300. Wien: Verlag der Österreichischen Akademie der Wissenschaften.
BIETAK, M., MARINATOS, N. and PALYVOU, C.
2007 *Taureador Scenes in Tell el- Dab'a (Avaris) and Knossos*. Wien: Verlag der Österreichischen Akademie der Wissenschaften.
BRYCE, T.
2003 *Letters of the Great Kings of the Ancient Near East*. London: Routledge.
2005 *The Kingdom of Hittites*. Oxford: Clarendon Press.
BURKE, A. A.
2004 "The Architecture of Defense: Fortified Settlement of the Levant during the Middle Bronze Age." Unpublished Ph.D Dissertation University of Chicago.
CASANA, J.
2003 "From Alalakh to Antioch: Settlement, Land, Use, and Environmental Change in the Amuq Valley of Southern Turkey." Unpublished PhD Diss. University of Chicago.
2009 "Alalakh and the Archaeological Landscape of Mukish: The Political Geography and Population of a Late Bronze Age Kingdom," *Bulletin of the American School of Oriental Research* 352: 7–37.
COLLON, D.
1994 "Bull-Leaping in Syria," *Egypt and the Levant* 4: 81–88.
DOTHAN, T.
1987 "The Impact of Egypt on Canaan during the 18th and 19th Dynasties in the Light of the Excavations at Deir el-Balah," in *Egypt, Israel, Sinai: Archaeological and Historical Relationships in the Biblical Period*, edited by A. F. Rainey. Tel Aviv: Tel Aviv University Press.
EMERY, W. B., SMITH, H. S and MILLARD, A.
1979 *The Fortress of Buhen: The Archaeological Report (Excavations at Buhen 1)*. London: Egypt Exploration Society.
FELDMAN, M. H.
2006 *Diplomacy by Design: Luxury Arts and an 'International Style' in the Ancient Near East, 1400–1200 BCE*. Chicago: University of Chicago Press.

FINK, A. S.
2008 "Where was the Statue of İdrimi actually found? The Later Temples of Tell Atchana," *Ugarit-Forschungen* 39: 162–245.
2010 *Late Bronze Age Tell Atchana (Alalakh): Stratigraphy, Chronology, History*. BAR International Series 2120. Oxford: Archaeopress Publishers of British Archaeological Reports.

GATES, M. H.
1981 *Alalakh Levels VI and V: A Chronological Reassessment*, Syro-Mesopotamian Studies 4/2. Undena, Malibu.

GLATZ, C.
2009 "Empire as network: Spheres of material interaction in Late Bronze Age Anatolia," *Journal of Anthropological Archaeology* 28(2): 127–141.

HAMBLIN, W. J.
2006 *Warfare in the Ancient Near East to 1600 BC: Holy Warriors at the Dawn of History*. London: Routledge.

HELFT, S.
2010 "Patterns of Exchange/Patterns of Power: A New Archaeology of the Hittite Empire." Unpublished Ph.D Dissertation University of Pennsylvania.

HOFFMEIER, J. K.
2006 ""The Walls of the Ruler" in Egyptian Literature and the Archaeological Record: Investigating Egypt's Eastern Frontier in the Bronze Age," *Bulletin of the American Schools of Oriental Research* 343: 1–20.

HOFFMEIER, J. K. and ABD EL-MAKSOUD, M.
2003 "A New Military Site on 'The Ways of Horus': Tell el-Borg 1999–2001: A Preliminary Report," *The Journal of Egyptian Archaeology* 89: 169–97.

HOROWITZ, M.
In prep *The Evolution of Plain Ware Ceramics at the Regional Capital of Alalakh in the Second Millennium BC.*

JEAN, É.
2006 "The Hittites at Mersin Yümüktepe: Old Problems and New Directions," in *Structuring and Dating in Hittite Archaeology*, edited by D. P. Mielke, U. D. Schoop and J. Seeher, pp. 311–332. İstanbul: Ege Yayınları.

KILLEBREW, A. E., GOLDBERG, P. and ROSEN, A. M.
2006 "Deir el-Balah: A Geological, Archaeological, and Historical Reassessment of an Egyptianizing 13th and 12th Century B.C.E. Center," *Bulletin of the American Schools of Oriental Research* 343: 97–119.

KLENGEL, H.
1992 *Syria: 3000 to 300 B.C.: a Handbook of Political History*. Berlin: Akademie Verlag.

KOEHL, R. B.
2005 "Preliminary Observations on the Unpublished Mycenaean Pottery from Woolley's Dig-House at Tell Atchana (Ancient Alalakh)," *Aegaeum* 25: 415–422.
2010 "Mycenaean Pottery," in *Tell Atchana, Ancient Alalakh. Volume 1: 2003–2004 Excavation Seasons*, edited by K. A. Yener, pp. 81–82. İstanbul: Koç University Press.

KOZAL, E.
2010 "Cypriot Pottery," in *Tell Atchana, Ancient Alalakh. Volume 1: 2003–2004 Excavation Seasons*, edited by K. A. Yener, pp. 67–80. İstanbul: Koç University Press.

LANDSBERGER, B.
1954 "Assyrische Königsliste und Dunkles Zeitalter," *Journal of Cuneiform Studies* 8: 31–45.

Mazar, A.
1994 "Four Thousand Years of History at Tel Beth-Shean," *Qadmoniot* 27: 66–83.

MIELKE, D. P.
2011 "Hittite Cities: Looking for a Concept," in *Insights into Hittite History and Archaeology*, edited by H. Genz and D. P. Mielke, pp. 153–194. Leuven: Peeters.

MORAN, W. L.
1992 *The Amarna Letters*. Baltimore: Johns Hopkins University Press.

NEVE, P.
1993 *Hattusa, Stadt der Götter und Tempel.* Mainz am Rhein: von Zabern.

NIEDORF, C.
2002 "Ein Hethitisches Breiffragment aus Alalakh," in *Ex Mesopotamia et Syria Lux*, AOAT 281, edited by O. Loretz, K. Metzler and H. Schardig. Münster: Ugarit Verlag.

NIEMEIER, W.-D.
1991 "Minoan Artisans Travelling Overseas: The Alalakh Frescoes and the Painted Plaster Floor at Tel Kabri (Western Galilee)," *Aegaeum* 7: 189–201.

OREN, E. D.
1984 "Migdol: A New Fortress on the Edge of the Eastern Nile Delta," *Bulletin of the American Schools of Oriental Research* 256: 7–44.

SHERRATT, S. and SHERRATT, A.
1991 "From Luxuries to Commodities: The Nature of the Mediterranean Bronze Age Trading Systems," in *Bronze Age in the Mediterranean*, edited by N. H. Gale, pp. 351–386. Jonsered: Åström.

SINOPOLI, C. M.
1994 "The Archaeology of Empires," *Annual Review of Anthropology* 23: 159–80.

STEIN, D. L.
1997 "Alalakh," in *Oxford Encyclopedia of the Ancient Near East*, edited by E. Meyers. Oxford: Oxford University.

ULLMANN, L.
2010 "Movement and the Making of Place in the Hittite Landscape." Unpublished PhD Diss. Columbia University.

PULAK, C.
1998 "The Uluburun Shipwreck: An Overview," *The International Journal of Nautical Archaeology* 27: 188–224.

VON DASSOW, E. M.
2008 *State and Society in the Late Bronze Age: Alalah under the Mittani Empire*, Studies on the Civilization and Culture of Nuzi and the Hurrians 17. Bethesda: CDL Press.

WOOLLEY, L.
1955 *Alalakh: an account of the excavations at Tell Atchana in the Hatay, 1937–1949.* Oxford: Printed at the University Press for the Society of Antiquaries.

YENER, K. A., ed.
2005 *The Amuq Valley regional projects. Vol. 1, Surveys in the Plain of Antioch and Orontes Delta, Turkey, 1995–2002*, Oriental Institute Publications 131. Chicago: University of Chicago Press.
2010 *Tell Atchana, Ancient Alalakh. Volume 1: 2003–2004 Excavation Seasons.* İstanbul: Koç University Press.

YENER, K. A.

2005 "Introduction, Alalakh Spatial Organization: Augmenting the Architectural Layout of Levels VII-0, Conclusions and Future Objectives, Appendix B," in *The Amuq Valley Regional Projects. Volume 1. Surveys from the Years 1995–2002*, edited by K. A. Yener. Chicago: Oriental Institute Press.

2006 "Transformative Impulses in Late Bronze Age Technology: A Case Study from the Amuq Valley, Southern Turkey," in *Settlement and Society: Essays Dedicated to Robert McCormick Adams*, edited by E. Stone, pp. 360–385. Los Angeles: Cotsen Institute of Archaeology at UCLA.

2008 "Tell Aççana Hőyűk'te Bulunan Miken Boğa Atlama Krateri," in *Festschrift for Muhibbe Darga*, edited by E. Konyar. İstanbul: Koç Vakfı Yayınları.

2009 "Alalakh, Aççana Höyük 2007 Kazı Çalışmaları," *Kazı Sonuçları Toplantısı* 30: 285–296.

2010 "Introduction," in *Tell Atchana, Ancient Alalakh. Volume 1: 2003–2004 Excavation Seasons*, edited by K. A. Yener, pp. 1–9. Istanbul: Koç University Press.

2011 "Hittite Metals at the Frontier: A Three Spiked Battle Ax from Alalakh," in *Metallurgy: Understanding How, Learning Why. Studies in Honor of James D. Muhly*, edited by S. Ferrence and P. Betancourt. Philadelphia: INSTAP Press.

ZACCAGNINI, C.

1983 "Patterns of Mobility among Ancient Near Eastern Craftsmen," *Journal of Near Eastern Studies* 42: 245–64.

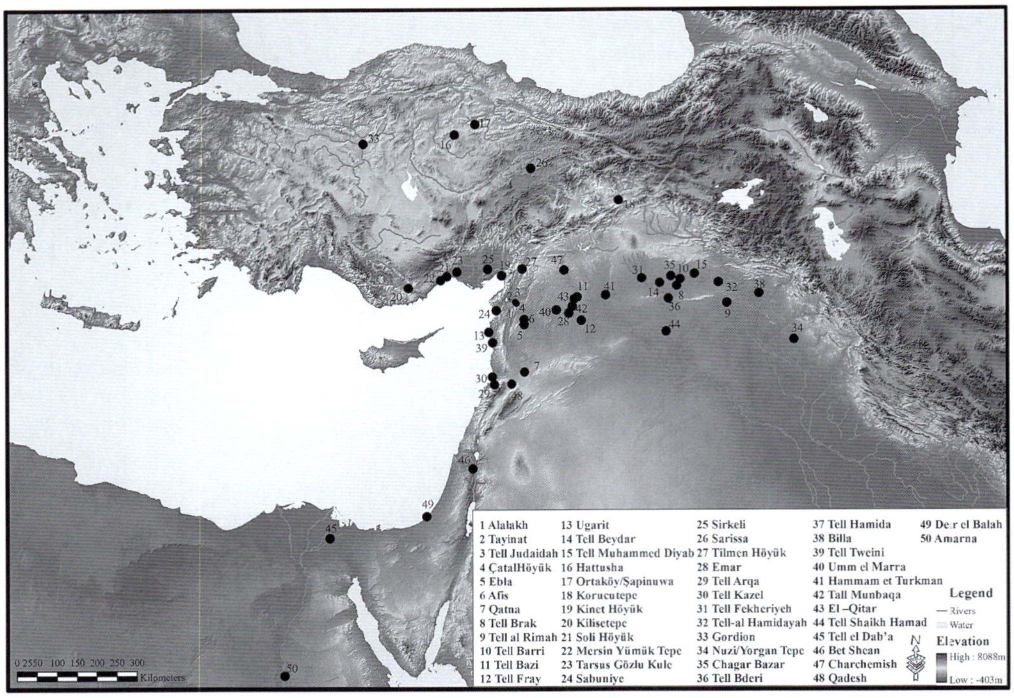

Fig. 1 Map of Anatolia and the Near East with sites mentioned in the text (courtesy of S. Batiuk).

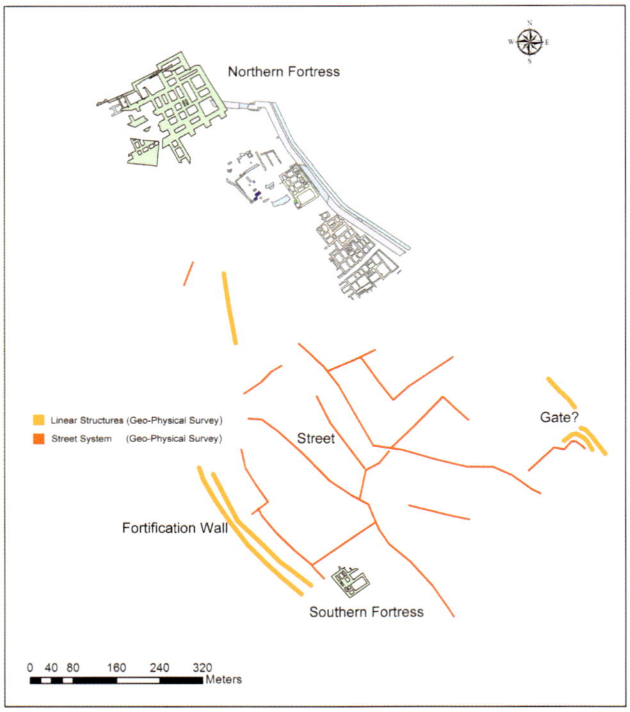

Fig. 2 Fortresses of Tell Atchana/Ancient Alalakh in relation to Woolley's excavation and magnetometry survey results (Drawn by Murat Akar).

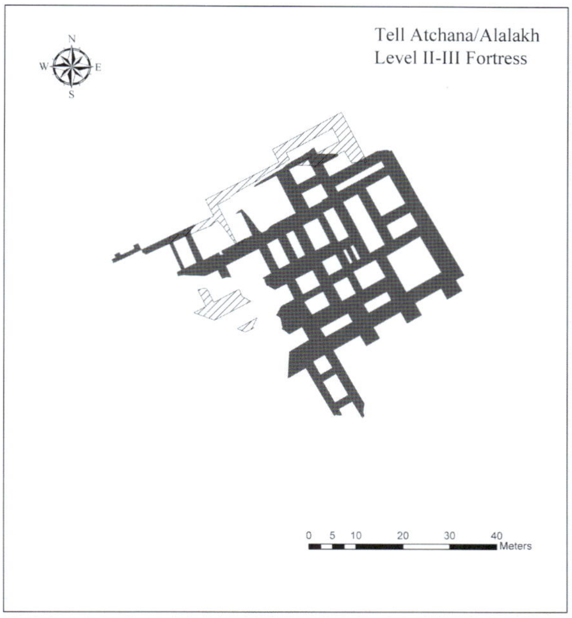

Fig. 3 Plan of the Northern Fortress (Level II-III) redrawn after Woolley 1955 (Drawn by Murat Akar).

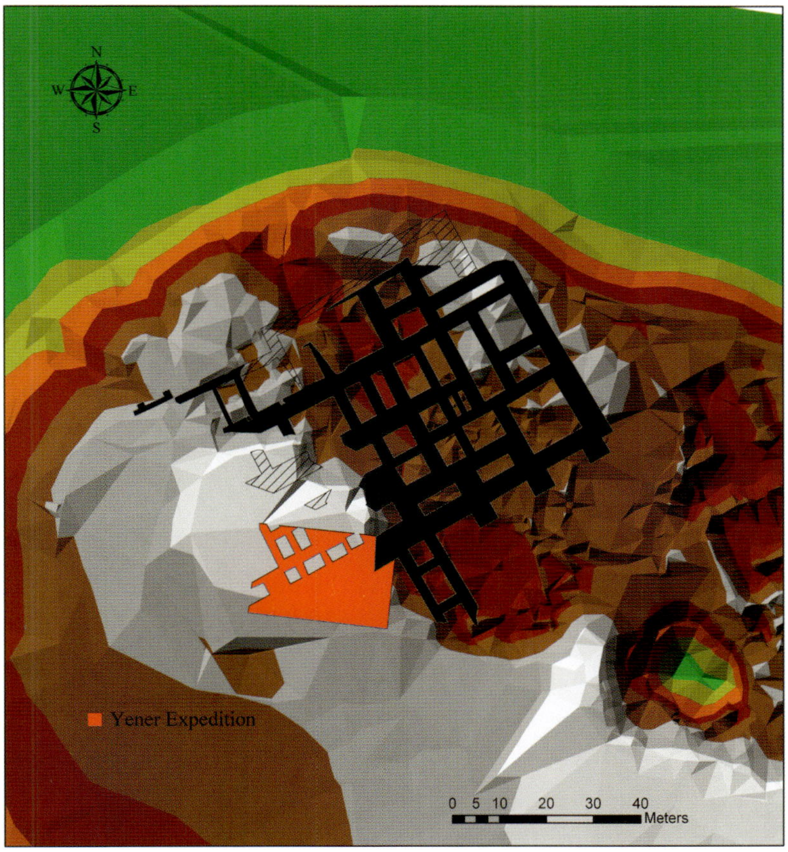

Fig. 4 Plan of the Northern Fortress including the new excavation areas (Drawn by Murat Akar).

Fig. 5 Aerial View of the Northern Fortress (Photograph by Murat Akar).

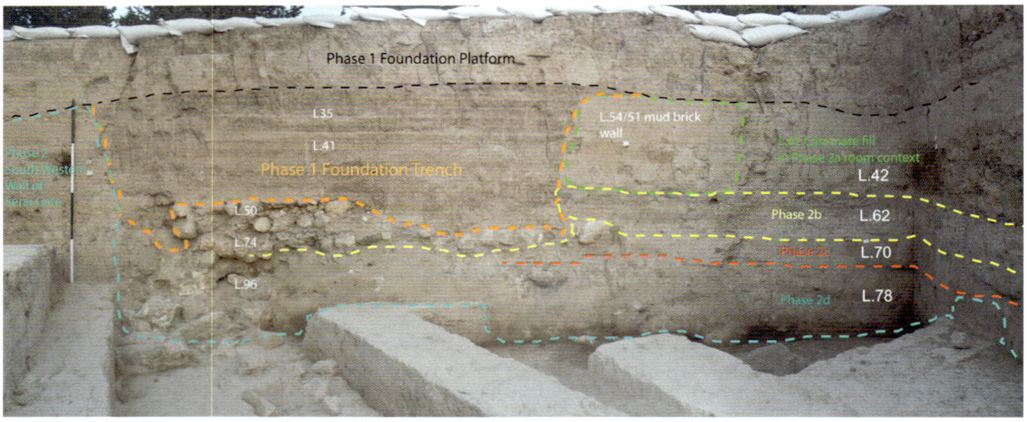

Fig. 6 West Section of square 32.54 (Photograph by Murat Akar).

Fig. 7 Aerial View of the Southern Fortress (Photograph by Murat Akar).

Fig. 8 Palaces of Tel el Dab'a, Ancient Avaris. After Bietak 2006, fig 3.

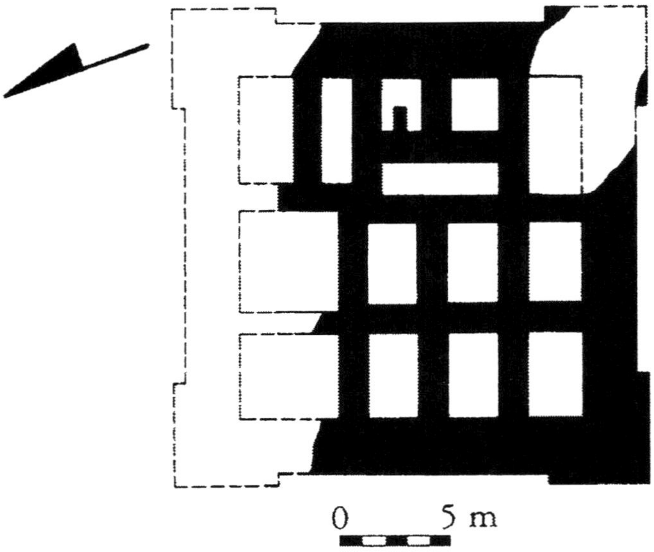

Fig. 9 Egyptian Type Administrative Complex (Stratum VII). After Killebrew et al. 2006:116.

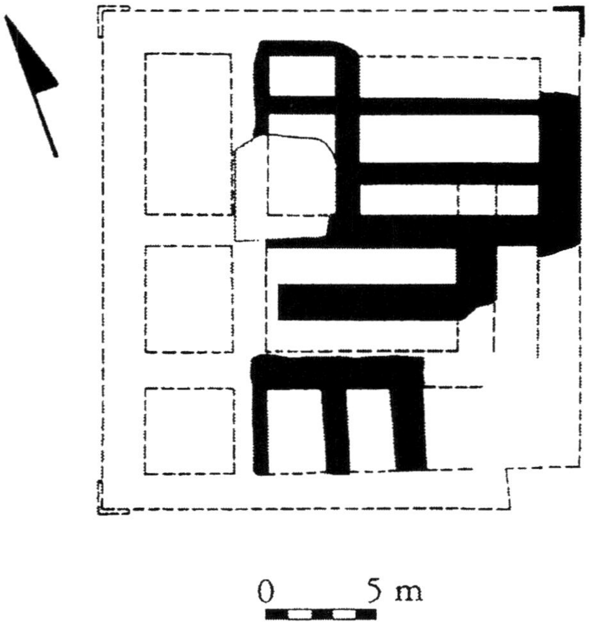

Fig. 10 Egyptian Type Administrative Complex at Beth Shean (Late Level VII). After Mazar 1994: 80.

CHAPTER 3

TAYINAT IN THE EARLY IRON AGE

Timothy P. HARRISON
Department of Near and Middle Eastern Civilizations
University of Toronto
4 Bancroft Avenue
Toronto, ON, M5S 1C1, Canada
E-mail: tim.harrison@utoronto.ca

INTRODUCTION

It is now widely acknowledged that the Early Iron Age (ca. 1200–900 BCE) constituted a fundamentally formative era in the development of the Syro-Hittite states of the first millennium BCE. While it may be true that this era, the 'Dark Age' of Homeric lore, was characterized by cultural devolution, political fragmentation and ethnic strife, there is also growing evidence of cultural and political continuity. As now chronicled by numerous scholars, ongoing archaeological excavations and an ever-expanding corpus of epigraphic discoveries portray a complex historical experience.

In this paper, I will review the evidence from the North Orontes Valley during this formative period. The evidence indicates the emergence of a powerful regional state, possibly an appanage survival of the Hittite Empire's collapse, centered at Tell Tayinat, and comprised of an intriguing amalgam of Aegean, Anatolian (or Luwian) and Bronze Age West Syrian cultural traditions. As I will attempt to demonstrate, the archaeological record points to the foundation of a new settlement at Tayinat in the Early Iron Age, either co-terminus with, or immediately following, the destruction or abandonment of nearby Tell Atchana (ancient Alalakh). Although our investigations are still ongoing, and the results presented here therefore preliminary, when combined with the mounting epigraphic record, the emerging picture of this formative 'Dark Age' is of a considerably more complex historical process than previously imagined, marked by both continuity and change.

THE EARLY IRON AGE EPIGRAPHIC RECORD

The discovery of the Temple of the Storm-God on the Aleppo citadel has played a pivotal role in transforming our understanding of the historical developments of the

Early Iron Age in the region.[1] In the course of restoring the citadel's standing medieval monuments, the German-Syrian expedition uncovered the north wall of a large building, comprised of twenty-six stunning, carved-stone reliefs. This discovery, in turn, led to the excavation of the east wall of the complex, revealing in the center the magnificently carved representation of the Storm-God of Aleppo facing a human figure, with both flanked by alternating false windows and bull-men. Most importantly, an intact, 11-line Hieroglyphic Luwian inscription (ALEPPO 6) emerges from the human figure's mouth. The inscription begins with the figure's name, followed by his titles, placed between his raised right arm and face, with the remainder running on behind him and continuing across the doubly rebated slab behind him. In content, the inscription is a relatively conventional temple dedication; its unique importance is found in the name, titles and country of the human figure:

> I (am) King Taita, the Hero, the Ruler of [the land of] Palistin
> For my lord the Halabean Storm-God I honoured the image...[2]

Subsequent excavations unearthed the south entrance of the temple, revealing the relief figures of a fish-man and lion, and broken figures of a sphinx and a second lion, the latter two bearing parts of a second, fragmentary inscription (ALEPPO 7) that also references Taita, but also — most intriguingly — Karkamiš and Egypt.[3]

These dramatic epigraphic discoveries in the Temple of the Storm-God on the Aleppo citadel preserve virtually the entire historical record we have for Taita. Yet, it has become increasingly clear that he was an important historical figure during the formative centuries of the Early Iron Age (ca. 1200–900 BCE), and in some ways he has come to symbolize the revolution underway in our understanding of this period.

Although excavations of the Aleppo temple are ongoing, Hawkins has made a number of observations with potentially significant historical implications, based on the epigraphic finds, in particular regarding the prospect of an Early Iron Age polity associated with the 'Land of Palistin'. Hawkins dates the inscriptions to ca. 1100–1000 BCE, based on the paleography of the script and the iconography of the associated reliefs, and he has drawn attention to the similarity between the name and title of its author and three previously known fragmentary Hieroglyphic Luwian inscriptions.[4] Two of these inscriptions were found on stelae discovered in secondary contexts in the villages of Meharde and Sheizar, located near Qalʿat al-Mudiq, northwest of Hama. The former bears a female figure on its obverse, identified as the "Divine Queen of the Land," and the second is a funerary stela for a certain Kupapiyas, the wife of

[1] For preliminary reports, see Kohlmeyer 2009; also Kohlmeyer 2000; and Gonnella et al. 2005.
[2] For translation, see Hawkins 2011; and broader historical context, Hawkins 2009, pp. 169–172.
[3] Hawkins 2011, pp. 48–49.
[4] Hawkins 2009, pp. 169–170.

Taita.[5] Both inscriptions refer to Taitaas 'Hero, of the land of WaDAsatini,' which Hawkins argues represents a variant of the PaDAsatini/Palistin renderings on the Aleppo inscriptions. Most recently, he has raised the possibility that there existed two Taitas: the first associated with the Aleppo inscriptions, and their 'Palistin' rendering, and the second corresponding to the Meharde and Sheizar references to 'Walistin', with both rulers covering a time span sometime in the eleventh to early tenth centuries BCE.[6]

The third reference was recorded on a fragmentary Hieroglyphic Luwian inscription recovered during the Syrian-Hittite Expedition's excavations in the 1930s at Tell Tayinat (specifically Tell Tayinat Inscription 1, fragments 3–5, 1.1).[7] Unfortunately, the surviving hieroglyphic fragments do not actually mention Taita, but instead refer to a certain Halparuntiyas, who also appears to have ruled 'the land of WaDAsatini.' Hawkins, following Gelb,[8] has noted the similarity to Qalparunda, and has raised the possibility that he may be the same Patinean ruler said to have paid tribute to Shalmaneser III in 857 and 853 BCE.[9]

In addition, two Hieroglyphic Luwian stelae were recently discovered near the resort town of Arsuz, south of Iskenderun and west of the Amanus Mountains.[10] The Arsuz inscriptions preserve an autobiographical statement from a certain Suppilulimma, 'the Hero, ruler of WaDAsatini, and son of King Manana.' They also make reference to the city/land of Adana, and to a campaign against the 'land of Hiyawa' (ancient Cilicia). Suppiluliuma and his father Manana must predate the earliest previously known Patinean king, Lubarnas, encountered by Ashurnasirpal II during his raid through the region in 870 BCE, placing their rule in the early 9th or 10 centuries BCE, at the very latest, and the two possible Taitas, presumably, still earlier in the 10th, or the 11th century, as Hawkins has proposed.

In this context, mention should be made of Steitler's recent suggestion that the biblical Toi, King of Hamath (II Samuel 8: 9–10; I Chronicles 18: 9–10), whose son, Joram, is said to have formed an alliance with the Israelite King David, was in fact Taita, based on the etymology of the two names.[11] According to Steitler, Taita, or Toi, installed his son as ruler (or viceroy) of the Hamath district within his larger Palistinian kingdom, a Luwian practice dating back to the Hittite Empire period. If Steitler's linguistic arguments are accepted, they would provide an independent source dating the reign of at least one of the Taitas to the late 11th–early 10th centuries BCE.

[5] For translation, see Hawkins 2000, pp. 415–419.
[6] Hawkins 2011, p. 51.
[7] Hawkins 2000, pp. 365–367.
[8] Gelb 1939, p. 39.
[9] Hawkins 2000, pp. 365–366.
[10] Dinçol 2010.
[11] Steitler 2010.

Finally, and perhaps most intriguingly, Hawkins has proposed that the 'Palistin' ethnicon shares an etymology with the *Peleset* mentioned in the Medinet Habu reliefs of Sea Peoples fame,[12] and thus presumably also shares a common ethnic, if not historical, association. As has been noted by others,[13] the *Peleset* are the only Sea Peoples named in the Medinet Habu reliefs who receive a geographical designation, specifically the "Land of the Peleset," a reference which occurs in several of the accounts of Ramesses III's battles against the Sea Peoples, including his repulsion of their attempted invasion of Egypt in his eighth regnal year (ca. 1175 BCE).

Although there remains some uncertainty regarding the provenance and dating of this growing corpus of Luwian inscriptions, as Hawkins has observed,[14] they collectively infer the existence of an Early Iron Age kingdom of considerable size and influence, apparently encompassing an area that extended east as far as Aleppo, west across the Amanus Mountains to the bay of Iskenderun, and south as far as the Middle Orontes Valley northwest of Hama. It is worth noting the close correspondence between this territorial extent and the combined territories of the Late Bronze Age vassal kingdoms of Mukiš, Niya and Nuhašše, which were consolidated under the control of Aleppo during Šuppiluliuma I's administrative reorganization of the region in the late 14th century.[15]

Early Iron Age Tayinat

Tell Tayinat is located at the northern bend of the Orontes River, some 700 m northwest of Tell Atchana (ancient Alalakh), its Bronze Age sister settlement. Tayinat was the scene of large-scale excavations between 1935 and 1938, conducted by the University of Chicago's Syrian-Hittite Expedition. The Chicago excavations focused primarily on the Iron II and III levels at Tayinat, which they delineated into five discrete architectural phases, or Building Periods.[16] However, traces of the Early Iron Age (their Amuq Phase N), primarily in the form of residual pottery, were encountered in virtually all of their trenches on the site's upper mound (**Fig. 1**).

Following preliminary surface surveys conducted between 1999 and 2002,[17] the Tayinat Archaeological Project (TAP) reinitiated excavations at Tell Tayinat with a brief two-week exploratory season in 2004. These investigations were expanded to full-scale excavations in 2005, and have continued on an annual basis since.[18] As with the Syrian-Hittite Expedition's investigations, Early Iron Age remains have been

12 Hawkins 2009, pp. 171–172.
13 See summary in Kahn 2011.
14 Hawkins 2009, pp. 169–171; 2011, pp. 51–52.
15 See further in Harrison 2009b, p. 174.
16 For a summary of the Chicago excavations, see Haines 1971.
17 See further in Batiuk et al. 2005.
18 For yearly reports, see Harrison 2006; 2007; 2008; 2009a; 2010; 2011.

encountered in all the TAP excavation areas, or fields, that have reached pre-Iron II levels. The most substantive exposures have been achieved in Fields 1, 2 and 4 (see **Fig. 2**). What follows represents a summary of the excavated results achieved to date in these three respective areas.

Field 1

Field 1 is located in the center of the upper mound, on the southern edge of the Syrian-Hittite Expedition's West Central Area excavations (**Fig. 2**). The Field 1 excavations were initiated in order to link the renewed TAP investigations with their earlier work. The Field 1 excavations were launched as part of a two-week exploratory sounding in 2004, and in 2005 expanded to the current four 10x10 m squares. To date, the excavations have succeeded in delineating nine superimposed architectural phases, or Field Phases (FP), with the primary sequence dating to the 12th–11th centuries BCE, or the Iron IA period (FPs 3–6), and the late third millennium BCE, or EB IVB (FPs 7–9).[19]

The earliest Iron Age settlement excavated to date (FP 6) was comprised primarily of a series of large storage 'silos,' and lay directly atop remains dating to the late third millennium BCE (specifically Amuq Phase J; **Fig. 3**). Smaller pits interspersed between these larger installations contained concentrations of non-perforated, cylindrical clay loom weights and other artifacts associated with textile production.

A number of poorly preserved wall segments and storage silos were assigned to the subsequent FP 5 (**Fig. 3**). The FP 5 remains were unfortunately disturbed by later activities associated with a number of phases, including construction activities during FP 4 (Iron I) and FP 2 (Iron II), and pitting activity during FP 3 (Iron I). Nevertheless, the surfaces and soil layers associated with FP 5, and in particular the ashy deposits removed from the silo-like storage pits, produced a wealth of faunal and botanical evidence. In addition, a carbon sample from a sealed context in this field phase has produced a radiocarbon date of 2910 $\pm$ 50 BP (or a calibrated date of 1115 BCE).

FP 5 was sealed by a substantial cultural layer, FP 4, which included the best preserved architectural remains found in the Iron I sequence (**Fig. 3**), most notably a small rectilinear structure in the northern part of the field. The walls from this phase were built using a distinctive 'header and stretcher' construction technique. Deep foundation trenches were excavated into the surrounding soil matrix, and packed with mud bricks to support the free-standing superstructure. Although generally well-preserved, the remains of FP 4 appeared to have been heavily damaged by the leveling that occurred during construction of the foundations and sub-structures of

[19] For a more thorough presentation of the Iron IA sequence in Field 1, see Harrison et al. forthcoming.

the later Iron Age temple (or Building II) associated with FP 2, and by extensive pitting activity during the intermediate FP 3.

FP 3, the final phase in the Iron IA sequence, formed a somewhat enigmatic phase, inserted between FPs 2 and 4. It was represented primarily by substantial pitting activity, best exemplified by two large ashy pits in the northwestern part of the field, the former of which was sealed in turn by a slightly concave-shaped plastered installation. No walls or other free-standing structures were assigned to this phase.

The four-phase Iron IA sequence delineated in Field 1 appears to correlate well with the Early Iron Age sequences uncovered at other sites in the region. In the Amuq Plain, for example, the Syrian-Hittite Expedition's excavations at Chatal Höyük identified four architectural phases dating to the Iron I (collectively, their Phase IV, or Amuq Phase N), while the excavations at Tell Judaidah identified three discrete phases (Levels 11–9, or collectively Phase V).[20] Elsewhere in the region, the Tell Afis excavations have also produced four Early Iron I levels, their Phases Va [=Levels 9c–b], IVc [=Level 9a], IVb [=Level 8b], and IVa [=Level 8a].[21] In contrast to the Tayinat sequence, however, the Early Iron I levels at Afis form part of a longer sequence that spans the Late Bronze II/Early Iron Age transition. Stratified sequences spanning the LB II/Early Iron I have also been excavated at Ras el-Bassit and Ras Ibn Hani,[22] and at Tell Kazel,[23] with the Early Iron I levels at the latter two sites producing significant quantities of Late Helladic IIIC pottery.

Late Helladic III Pottery[24]

The Iron I levels in Field 1 have produced large quantities of LH IIIC pottery. Although analysis of this material is still in its early stages, it is clear that LH IIIC wares formed the dominant potting tradition during FPs 6 through 3. The assemblage includes a wide spectrum of forms, motifs and fabrics, and is characterized by non-standardized production. Shallow rounded bowls and deeper bell-shaped bowls, or skyphoi, are the most common vessel types in the assemblage (see **Fig. 4**). The deep bowls are equipped typically with close-set horizontal handles, usually with a painted band applied along the handle, a ring base, and are decorated with horizontal, painted bands and linear motifs on the exterior, and only rarely bear monochrome (solidly painted) interiors. Two fabric color combinations predominate: red painted decorations on a pinkish fabric (RoP), and black painted decorations on a buff, white fabric (BoW). Deep bowls were also well-represented at Chatal Höyük and Tell Judaidah, with thirty-five examples recorded by the Syrian-Hittite Expedition, and grouped

[20] Haines 1971, pp. 2–5, 27–28.
[21] Venturi 2007, pp. 137–149, 301.
[22] du Piêd 2008.
[23] Capet 2008.
[24] This section summarizes the analysis of the LH IIIC pottery conducted by B. Janeway.

according to three decorative schemes.[25] More recently, decorated deep bowls have been found at nearby Tell Gindaris[26] and Tell Atchana.[27] The assemblage also includes other Aegean bowl types, such as shallow angular bowls and one-handled conical bowls. Other painted wares commonly found in the Field 1 assemblage include carinated kraters, amphoroid kraters, possibly bell kraters, and neck-handled amphorae, their handles typically decorated with dangling hooks, and spouted jars,[28] referred to as feeding bottles in the southern Levantine tradition.[29]

The LH IIIC tradition appears to have enjoyed widespread distribution in the North Orontes Valley. In addition to its predominance at Tell Tayinat, LH IIIC pottery has been reported by the AVRP survey at eighteen other sites in the valley,[30] and according to Swift was overwhelmingly dominant in the Phase N assemblages excavated by the Syrian-Hittite Expedition.[31] Largely (though not exclusively) the product of local manufacture,[32] the unique formal and stylistic features of the LH IIIC pottery preserved in the Early Iron Age levels at Tell Tayinat, and in the North Orontes Valley more generally, reflect the local, idiosyncratic character of this distinctive potting tradition, and reinforce the regionalized and heterogeneous nature of its development throughout the eastern Mediterranean. As a result, not surprisingly, there is as yet no clear consensus regarding its chronological development, although there have been numerous attempts to do so.[33] Nevertheless, over the course of the Iron I, the developmental trajectory experienced in the North Orontes Valley clearly witnessed the gradual eclipse of LH IIIC, and its eventual replacement in the Late Iron I/Early Iron II by the Red Slipped Burnished Ware tradition, a trend that has also been observed elsewhere in the region.[34]

Local Plain Ware[35]

The Local Plain Wares, or Hittite Monochrome Ware (HMW), are wheelmade and tempered with sand and lime inclusions, and occasionally with mica or chaff. Their color ranges from pink to pale brown and a smaller number of vessels have a reddish tinge. The surface treatment is minimal, in most cases restricted to a simple

[25] Swift 1958, pp. 66, figs. 19–21; see also Pucci in this issue.
[26] Sürenhagen 1999.
[27] Yener in this issue.
[28] Eight spouted jars are reported to have been recovered by the Syrian-Hittite Expedition; see Swift 1958, p. 68, fig. 25.
[29] Dothan and Zuckerman 2004, pp. 24, 26, 28, fig. 30; Dothan et al. 2006, p. 87, fig. 3.25:13.
[30] Verstraete and Wilkinson 2000, pp. 188–189.
[31] Swift 1958, p. 64.
[32] The Iron I levels in Field 1 have also produced a few isolated sherds of imported Myc IIIB and Cypriot White Slipped Ware.
[33] Summarized conveniently in Dothan and Zuckerman 2004, pp. 2–3.
[34] See Venturi 2007, pp. 297–300; Janeway 2008, pp. 136–137. Pucci this issue.
[35] The following descriptions of the Tayinat local wares summarize analysis conducted by E. Ünlü.

smoothing of the surface. Most vessels are well fired with no dark cores. The typical vessel types in this ware category are plates and shallow bowls, deep bowls, kraters and jars (**Fig.** 5).

The HMW tradition is best represented in FP 6, and then continues in diminishing quantities into FP 5 and the later phases of the Iron I in Field 1. In the earliest levels of FP 6, the LB II Plain Ware tradition dominates the pottery assemblage, while the LHIIIC, although extant, is not the dominant potting tradition. This trend is reversed in FP 5, with LHIIIC pottery becoming the dominant ware.

Since FPs 6–5 are the earliest Iron I occupational phases thus far attested at Tayinat, this suggests that the LB II HMW potting tradition continued even after the settlement shift had occurred between Atchana and Tayinat. This continuity also strengthens the possibility that both settlements were occupied contemporaneously for at least part of the transition. The persistence of the HMW potting tradition, following the collapse of the Hittite political and administrative center at Hattuša, has also been reported at other sites in the region, including the capital Hattuša itself,[36] Kilise Tepe,[37] Mersin-Yumuktepe,[38] Tarsus-Gözlükule,[39] Norşuntepe,[40] and Lidar Höyük.[41]

Local Painted Wares

In the terminal stages of the Late Bronze Age, specifically the LB IIB, local potting industries in the Syro-Anatolian region revived a painted decorative tradition common during the Middle Bronze and Late Bronze I, and reported at sites ranging from Cilicia to northwest Syria and the northern Levant. In central Anatolia, a painted tradition, but in an exclusively handmade ware, appears already in the late 13th–early 12th centuries BCE.[42]

The Tayinat Local Painted Ware shares the same fabric texture as the Plain Ware and it also exhibits similar surface treatment, although lightly burnished external surfaces are encountered more frequently due to the painted application, which required a smooth vessel surface. The paint ranges in color from red to brown, and the decorative design is restricted to geometric motifs, with the most frequent patterns comprised of hatched triangles, parallel straight lines, and wavy lines framed by parallel lines. Some of the Local Painted Ware forms, such as the krater, find parallels in the Anatolian Late Bronze Age repertoire.

[36] Schoop 2003, p. 172; Genz 2003, p. 181.
[37] Hansen and Postgate 2007, p. 344.
[38] Sevin and Köroğlu 2004, p. 80.
[39] Goldman 1956, p. 203; Hanfmann 1963, p. 70; Yalçın this issue.
[40] Müller 2005, p. 109 and Korbel 1985, fig. 74.
[41] Müller 1999, p. 123 and Müller 2005, p. 124.
[42] Genz 2003.

The Tayinat Local Painted Wares seem to continue the earlier LB I painted tradition of the region, as represented at Tarsus-Gözlükule[43] and Sirkeli Höyük,[44] but also encountered during the LB II at neighboring Tell Atchana.[45] Genz has more recently proposed that this painted tradition appeared in central Anatolia following the collapse of the Hittite ruling dynasty at Hattuša.[46]

Shell-Tempered Cooking Ware

Shell constituted the main tempering agent used in cooking ware. The shell-tempered fabric is coarse, and was used in the production of large, closed vessels. Frequent mottling on their exterior surfaces suggests these vessels were used for cooking. The use of crushed shell as a tempering agent for cooking pots has a long tradition both in the Amuq, as attested at Tell Atchana since LB I,[47] and in Cilicia, as encountered at Tarsus-Gözlükule from at least the LB I. The Tayinat shell-tempered ware continued this tradition throughout all phases of Iron IA. In the earliest phases of the Iron IA, the shapes consist of closed, often two-handled pots, with a ridge running along the exterior of the rim, and then become more varied in form in the later phases of Iron IA.

Slipped and Burnished Ware

Slipped and Burnished Ware is present in small quantities in the FPs 6 and 5 assemblages. The Slipped and Burnished Ware forms have a red slip, and are varyingly burnished, from lustrous to dull; a few examples of white, cream-slipped surface treatment also occur. The fabric ranges from fine to medium-course in texture, and is fired to a red, oxidized core. However, some vessels exhibit a sharply different, finer fabric, fired to a pale yellow/brown color. A similar fabric occurs in the LB II assemblage at Tarsus-Gözlükule.[48]

The Slipped and Burnished Ware at Tayinat continues a Late Bronze Hittite Empire period potting tradition, and includes Hittite transport amphora, a particularly common central highland Anatolian form. These transport amphorae are also found in the Late Bronze Age levels at neighboring Tell Atchana,[49]and in the LB IIA levels of Tarsus-Gözlükule.[50] At Tayinat, they occur primarily in FPs 6 and 5. The finer fabric vessels belong to the Red Lustrous Wheelmade Ware (RLW-w) class, and at Tayinat are best represented by spindle bottles.

43 Goldman 1956, figs. 313 and 380.
44 Haider 1999, figs. 29, 31.
45 M. Horowitz, personal communication.
46 Genz 2005, p. 82.
47 M. Horowitz, personal communication.
48 Goldman 1956, p. 203.
49 Woolley 1955, plate CXI.39.
50 Goldman 1956, fig. 385.1191.

Gray Ware

Gray Ware is indigenous to northwest Anatolia, as attested at Troy throughout the Late Bronze Age and well into the Early Iron Age levels, following the destruction horizon of VIIa.[51] Gray Ware has also been found throughout the eastern Mediterranean, albeit in limited amounts and primarily at coastal sites, where it typically occurs in terminal Late Bronze Age levels or post-destruction contexts.[52]

The Tayinat Gray Wares have a very fine fabric texture, and were fired in a reducing environment, resulting in a grayish black fabric and surface color. The vessels are generally highly burnished. Although the application of the incised decoration is careless, it accentuates the sharp profiles of the vessels. Found in relatively small, but significant numbers, the range of forms include carinated bowls, small jars, juglets, and cups with simple rims and high vertical handles.

Tan Ware

The Tayinat excavations thus far have produced only one recognized example of Tan Ware, another distinctive northwest Anatolian pottery tradition, and the leading ware type in the LB II/EIA levels at Troy, where it accounts for up to 70 % of the Level VIIa assemblage.[53] Tan Ware does not have a wide distribution in the eastern Mediterranean.

Loom weights[54]

The Field 1 excavations thus far have produced more than two hundred and fifty non-perforated, cylindrical unbaked clay loom weights. Variously described as spools or spool weights,[55] these distinctive indicators of weaving activity are commonly found in LH IIIC levels at sites throughout the Aegean, most notably at Mycenae and Tiryns.[56] More recently, they have been recognized in Early Iron Age levels at an increasing number of Levantine sites, generally in association with LH IIIC pottery.[57]

The non-perforated, cylindrical unbaked clay loom weights from Tell Tayinat occur almost exclusively in Iron I contexts. These items have been found in a wide variety of sizes, ranging from 3 to 14 cm in length, and weighing between 30 and 770 gm. Generally speaking, two size ranges predominate: a smaller size averaging 7–8 cm in length, and weighing approximately 170–180 gm, and a larger size

[51] Becks 2003, p. 49.
[52] Allen 1991, p. 152; Allen 1994, p. 40–41.
[53] Blegen et al. 1958, p. 23.
[54] Analysis of the Early Iron Age textile industry has been conducted by D. Lumb.
[55] Stager 1998, p. 346; Rahmstorf 2003, pp. 397–400.
[56] Rahmstorf 2003, pp. 397, 400–2; 2008, pp. 59–73.
[57] Stager 1998, p. 346; Rahmstorf 2003, pp. 403–406.

averaging 10–12 cm in length and 550–560 gm in weight. Significantly, chronological variation in loom weight size is evident at Tell Tayinat, with larger heavier loom weights appearing in the earliest FPs, and smaller, lighter examples occurring in the later phases.

Variation in the shape of cylindrical non-perforated loom weights has also been noted. Despite some degree of individual variation, two forms typically occur: 1) cylindrical forms with straight sides and rounded ends, and 2) examples with a distinct hourglass shape with a tapered mid-section and flattened ends. Many examples of this second type have a single notable indentation approximately 1 cm in diameter on one end. Chronological developments in shape do not seem to be evident in the Tayinat assemblage, with examples of both dominant forms occurring in a range of sizes and during all phases of the Iron I. In addition, suggested developments in the quality of manufacture that have been noted at other sites in the region, namely at Tell Afis,[58] are not evident in the Tayinat data. Specifically, a shift from unbaked clay cylinders towards fired clay cylinders over time has not been noted. A majority of the non-perforated loom weights at Tayinat are unbaked. However, low-fired examples are present in small numbers throughout the Iron I, and examples that appear to have been accidentally burned occasionally occur.

The Field 1 loom weights typically have been found in caches, sometimes of twenty or more, deposited in pits, although isolated examples have also occurred. The Syrian-Hittite Expedition also uncovered a cache of these distinctive loom weights at Chatal Höyük, although apparently in an early Phase O context (Room T81, Level 5b).[59] It is now generally accepted that the warp-weighted loom was reintroduced to the eastern Mediterranean during the Early Iron Age,[60] providing further support for a non-local origin of this weaving technology. Cylindrical loom weights become less frequent towards the end of the Iron I at Tell Tayinat, and are eventually replaced entirely by round, doughnut-shaped centrally-perforated stone loom weights, mirroring the similar decline in the presence of LH IIIC pottery.

Spindle Whorls

In addition to loom weights, the Field 1 excavations have uncovered numerous spindle whorls, attesting to the attendant thread-making activities associated with textile production at the site. In total, more than 200 spindle whorls have been recovered from the field 1 excavations to date. Two main categories can be distinguished: 1) whorls deliberately fashioned for the purpose of spinning, of which just over 100 have been found, and 2) perforated sherd-discs manufactured from re-used pot sherds,

[58] Cecchini 2000, p. 219.
[59] Haines 1971, pl. 16B.
[60] Cecchini 2000, p. 213; 2011, p. 195.

either body or base sherds. A majority of the deliberately fashioned whorls are typically carved out of stone, with a number of ceramic examples also represented; bone and wooden spindle whorls have not been recovered. The spindle whorls are primarily conical or truncated conical in shape, with a smaller number of bi-conical forms. The whorls vary in weight between 7 and 65 gm, with an average weight of 28 gm. Reused pot sherds tend to be lighter, varying between 2 to 44 gm, with an average of 14 gm. Stone spindle whorls are manufactured primarily from green serpentine, a common rock found in the Amanus Mountains, but a breccia-like stone was also used. Several of the stone spindle whorls exhibit finely carved decorations.

Miscellaneous Small Finds

The Iron I levels in Field 1 have produced a wealth of other cultural remains, including a number of miscellaneous small finds, figurines and potters marks in particular, of possible Aegean derivation. The Field 1 excavations have also produced extensive botanical and faunal records, the latter of which may reflect western culinary practices.[61]

Contrastingly, a clay bulla, originating from FP 6c, the earliest Iron I phase in Field 1, preserves a seal impression from a circular seal similar to known Hittite seals and seal impressions. The center of the seal contains a series of Hieroglyphic Luwian signs, including an oval sign with vertical markings that resembles the god sign (DEUS). A second sign does not match any discernable Hieroglyphic Luwian sign, but could conceivably be a /la/ or a /li/.[62]

Field 2

The Syrian-Hittite Expedition achieved limited exposures of two large structures, identified as Buildings XIII and XIV, beneath the floors and walls of buildings assigned to the Second Building Period complex in the West Central Area, this latter complex dated by the excavators to the late 9th and 8th centuries (ca. 825–720 BCE).[63] Similar to the Second Building Period, Buildings XIII and XIV appear to have formed part of a large complex oriented around a central courtyard.

Although only the sub-floor structural foundations of Building XIII were found intact, its general outline was reasonably clear, betraying the unmistakable characteristics of a *bit hilani*. The building was roughly rectangular in shape, measuring approximately 28 × 35 m, and was entered from the south through what appears to have been a porticoed entrance, with a series of side rooms arranged around a long,

[61] For a more thorough description of this material, see Harrison et al. forthcoming; also Lipovitch 2008.
[62] T. van den Hout, personal communication.
[63] Haines 1971, p. 66.

rectangular central room, presumably the main reception hall.[64] The building's foundations were formed by deeply cut, vertically-faced trenches filled with unbaked brick, a distinctive construction technique also used in many of the other monumental buildings of the West Central Area.[65]

Building XIV, though only partially excavated, appears to have been considerably larger than Building XIII. As with Building XIII, very little of its superstructure was found intact, and the excavators therefore were unable to reconstruct a coherent plan of the complex, nor identify its function.[66] However, they did assemble a composite outline of the architectural remains they encountered that gives some indication of its enormous size,[67] which they estimate to have been at least 49 × 95 m. A number of isolated architectural finds also appear to belong to this First Building Period complex, including at least two enormous column bases, found out of context stratigraphically above Buildings XIII and XIV, and possibly as many as three lion-headed orthostats, found reused in the walls of buildings assigned to the Second Building Period.[68]

In 2005, excavations were initiated to the north of Field 1 in the vicinity of Building I. The primary objectives of the excavations in this area, identified as Field 2 (**Fig. 2**), were to determine whether anything remained of Building I, and then to excavate the earlier levels associated with Building XIV and thereby better establish the stratigraphic relationships between these two structures.

The 2005 excavations, limited to a 10 × 10 m area, proceeded to uncover a series of large mudbrick walls immediately below the modern plow zone. In 2006, two 10 × 10 m squares were opened to the south and east, linking Fields 1 and 2, and in 2007 three additional squares to the east and north. The 2006 and 2007 seasons also revealed a series of substantial walls which, together with the 2005 remains, appeared to form part of a single monumental structure (**Fig. 6**). The walls averaged more than 3 m in width, and form a tight grid pattern of small rooms, none of which were equipped with entryways. Probes were excavated in the corners of two of these rooms, and reached a depth of more than 3 m before uncovering the bottoms of their walls. Unfortunately, no internal surfaces or floors corresponding to the use-phase of the complex were identified, although a number of earlier surfaces cut by the walls were encountered. Clearly the foundations of an enormous structure, our excavations suggest that the Field 2 walls very probably formed part of the southeastern corner of Building XIV (**Fig. 7**).

[64] Haines 1971, pp. 38–39.
[65] Braidwood and Braidwood 1960, p. 13.
[66] Haines 1971, pp. 39–40.
[67] See Haines 1971, pl. 95.
[68] For more detailed descriptions of this material, see Harrison 2009b, pp. 177–178.

In 2007, excavations were initiated to the east of this structure in an effort to find surfaces that might have sealed against the eastern exterior of the building. These excavations revealed a stone pavement, which in turn sealed a densely packed sherd-strewn surface, comprised predominantly of Red Slipped Burnished Ware (or Iron II) pottery. Unfortunately, the Syrian-Hittite Expedition had trenched along the exterior face of the wall, effectively obliterating any stratigraphic connections that might have existed between these surfaces and the wall. Despite the stratigraphic break, and the lack of internal surfaces, the pottery associated with this monumental structure suggests a Late Iron I/Early Iron II date (ca. 10th–early 9th centuries BCE) for the complex.

The TAP investigations have also begun to shed more light on the depositional history of the numerous Hieroglyphic Luwian fragments recovered during the course of the Syrian-Hittite Expedition's excavations, in part due to the discovery of additional fragments with the resumption of excavations.[69] These fragments, and those of the Chicago expedition, cluster tightly around Building XIV. The extraordinary size of its walls, the monumental column bases and carved orthostats possibly associated with it, and the rich epigraphic record concentrated in its vicinity, unquestionably mark this structure as an important building. Moreover, although further excavations and analysis are needed, its apparent date and relative stratigraphic position within the Early Iron Age sequence at Tayinat also raises the prospect that Building XIV might have been constructed as part of the elite residential area of the rulers of the Land of Palistin.

Field 4[70]

An Early Iron Age metal workshop was uncovered in Field 4, located along the western flank of the upper mound (**Fig. 2**). The workshop can be divided into three rooms. A southern room consisted of a semi-circular installation with a mudbrick platform built on top of a layer of sherds, bones and cobble-sized stones. The installation measured 2.3 × 1.2 m, and was covered by a layer of ash. In the northern room, five ash deposits, each about 50 cm in diameter, formed an 'L-shaped' pattern in the southwest corner of the room. The deposits were spaced approximately 75 cm from the center of each deposit; a trail of ash was also detected in the northeast corner of the room. A concentration of slag cakes was found deposited in a semi-circle in the southwest corner of the third room. Significant amounts of slag, copper and iron fragments, and tuyère and crucible fragments were recovered from each of the rooms. The workshop was dated to the Iron IA period based on the associated pottery, most notably the presence of LH IIIC.

[69] For a more thorough description of this material, see Harrison 2009b, p. 179; 2009c, p. 179.
[70] This section summarizes the ongoing analysis of the Early Iron Age metal workshop by J. Roames.

Metallurgy

Ten iron and twelve copper artifacts of identifiable form were found in the metal workshop, including weaponry (projectile points and armor scales), tools (needles and a nail), and jewelry (pins, a ring and a fibula). In addition to the identifiable metal artifacts, numerous scraps of iron and copper fragments were recovered. Preliminary X-Ray Fluorescence (XRF) analysis on two of these copper fragments indicates that the copper was alloyed with high amounts of tin.[71]

XRF analysis of the slag further indicates that both bronze and iron were being worked in the same rooms. Four of the slag samples analyzed were determined to come from bronze-working, and two were determined to come from iron-working. Hearth bottom slag cakes associated with iron smithing were among the quantities of slag recovered. Two sizes of iron slag cakes were identified: (1) concavo-convex shapes, approximately 6 cm in diameter and 1 cm in thickness, and (2) plano-convex shapes, with diameters over 10 cm and thicknesses of 3 cm. Future work will try to determine whether these discrete types of iron slag cakes represent different iron-working processes, such as forging and secondary smithing. Additionally, flake hammerscale from iron smithing was recovered from the northern room. Consequently, a 20 × 20 cm fine grid was set up in this room, and each find grid sampled. Magnets were then used to recover the hammer scale flakes from each of the collected soil samples.

The slag analysis indicates that iron smithing, copper smelting and copper alloying all occurred in the workshop, and that both iron and bronze were worked in all three rooms. While there was some separation of certain features within these rooms, there was no clear separation between the iron-working and bronze-working remains.

Additionally, approximately 100 tuyère fragments were recovered from the metal workshop, some of which were part of the same tuyère. The tuyères grouped into round and square types, based on their cross-sections. Their bore holes are generally 0.6 to 1.0 cm, unless the back-end is preserved, in which case the inner diameter starts at about 2 cm and then tapers down. Outer diameters or widths are mostly in the range of 2.5 to 5 cm, but can reach as much as 8 cm. Although the tuyères recovered from the metal workshops discovered at the southern Levantine sites of Tell Beth-Shemesh and Tell Hammeh were square,[72] round tuyères have been found alongside square tuyères in the workshop at Tell es-Safi.[73] The longest preserved Tayinat tuyère, at approximately 15 cm, was elbow-shaped. In addition to tuyère fragments, the refractory materials included both crucible and furnace fragments. It was often difficult to distinguish between these fragments, but the preservation of

[71] See Roames 2011.
[72] Veldhuijzen 2009.
[73] Eliyahu-Behar et al. 2012, p. 261.

complete rims with slag adhering to their rim interiors was interpreted as indication they were crucible remains.

The analysis completed to date on the remains recovered from the Early Iron Age metal workshop at Tayinat permits a number of important observations. In particular, the analytical results point to the existence of a non-specialized metal workshop involved in the production of both iron and copper goods of a variety of types. Iron smithing occurred alongside the melting and mixing of copper and tin. A wide variety of activities were carried out in this small workshop, with no discrete areas devoted to any particular specialized activity. Thus, it appears, at least in the Tayinat workshop, that early iron-workers were also bronze-workers, and that craft specialization had not yet fully separated these two activities in the Early Iron Age, or more specifically the Iron IA (or 12th century BCE). Furthermore, the variety of goods produced indicates that these metalworkers were producing utilitarian and prestige goods made from both metals.

Early Iron Age Tayinat and the 'Land of Palistin/Walistin'

Though the specific historical circumstances continue to remain elusive, the accumulating archaeological and epigraphic evidence point ever more confidently to the existence of a powerful — even if ephemeral — Early Iron Age kingdom, with its royal city centered in the North Orontes Valley at Tell Tayinat. Ruled by a line of kings with traditional Hittite names, and very possibly with direct ancestral links to the Hittite royal dynasty, this Early Iron Age polity intriguingly also preserves an identity, or name, the 'Land of Palistin/Walistin,' with possible roots in the migratory movements that marked the end of the Bronze Age so famously portrayed on the walls of the mortuary temple of Ramesses III at Medinet Habu. This heterogeneity is mirrored in the material cultural diversity exhibited in the archaeological record of Early Iron Age Tayinat which, as we have seen, portrays an intriguing amalgam of Aegean, Anatolian (or Luwian) and Bronze Age West Syrian cultural traditions.

The emergence of Palistin/Walistin as a regional power also appears to have coincided with a decisive settlement shift in the North Orontes Valley. While the existing survey data indicate significant levels of settlement continuity during the transition from the Late Bronze to the Early Iron Age,[74] there is also evidence of change, attested perhaps most revealingly in the shift of the primary settlement in the valley from Tell Atchana (ancient Alalakh) to nearby Tayinat.[75] Whether the terminal Late Bronze Age

[74] For more on these settlement trends, see Harrison 2009b, pp. 175–176.

[75] Yener has now raised the provocative possibility that Atchana and Tayinat were in fact part of a single, two-mounded mega site, with a mobile central administration, during this period; see this issue.

settlement at Alalakh was destroyed or abandoned remains unclear, but the renewed excavations at Tayinat have now demonstrated conclusively that it was resettled in the Early Iron I (either early 12th century, or possibly the late 13th century BCE), after an eight-century hiatus corresponding to the period of Alalakh's ascendancy. Moreover, the Taita reliefs in the Storm-God temple in Aleppo suggest that Palistin/Walistin had eclipsed Aleppo as the dominant regional power by the eleventh century, shifting the locus of power west to the North Orontes Valley. By the ninth century, Tayinat had emerged as the royal city of Kunulua, capital of the Neo-Hittite Kingdom of Patina (or alternatively Unqi), though its political fortunes had waned. Caught in the geopolitical contest between the greatpowers of the Iron Age, it would eventually lose its independence altogether to the Assyrians in the latter part of the eighth century.

Acknowledgements

The Tayinat Archaeological Project has received research grants and financial support from the Social Sciences and Humanities Research Council of Canada, the Institute for Aegean Prehistory (INSTAP), and the University of Toronto, for which we are deeply grateful. I wish also to thank the Directorate of Cultural Heritage and Museums of Turkey, which has graciously awarded the research permits necessary to conduct each of our excavation seasons, the landowners who have generously permitted us to work on their land, and our project staff, whose dedicated efforts have ensured the successful results of each field season.

Bibliography

Allen, S. H.

1991 "Late Bronze Age Grey Wares in Cyprus," in *Cypriot Ceramics: Reading the Prehistoric Record*, edited by J. A. Barlow, D. L. Bolger and B. Kling, pp. 151–167. Philadelphia: University Museum of Archaeology and Anthropology.

1994 "Trojan Grey Ware at Tel Miqne-Ekron," *Bulletin of the American Schools of Oriental Research* 293: 39–51.

Batiuk, S., Harrison, T. P. and Pavlish, L.

2005 "The Ta'yinat Survey, 1999–2002," in *The Amuq Valley Regional Projects. Vol. 1: Surveys in the Plain of Antioch and Orontes Delta, Turkey, 1995–2002*, Oriental Institute Publications 131, edited by K. A. Yener, pp. 171–192. Chicago: Oriental Institute of the University of Chicago.

Becks, R.

2003 "Troia VII: Transition from the Late Bronze to the Early Iron Age," in *Identifying Changes: the Transition from Bronze to Iron Ages in Anatolia and its Neighbouring Regions*, edited by B. Fischer, H. Genz, E. Jean and K. Köroğlu, pp. 41–53. Istanbul: Ege Yayınları.

Blegen, C. W., Boulter, C. G., Caskey, J. L. and Rawson, M.

1958 *Troy: Excavations Conducted by the University of Cincinnati, 1932–1938, Vol. 4: Settlements VIIa, VIIb, and VIII*. Princeton: Princeton University.

BRAIDWOOD, R. J. and BRAIDWOOD, L. S.
1960 *Excavations in the Plain of Antioch I: The Earlier Assemblages: Phases A–J* Oriental Institute Publications 61. Chicago: University of Chicago Press.

CAPET, E.
2008 "Les peuples des céramiques "barbares" à Tell Kazel (Syrie)," *Scripta Mediterranea* 27–28: 187–207.

CECCHINI, S. M.
2000 "The Textile Industry in Northern Syria During the Iron Age According to the Evidence of the Tell Afis Excavations," in *Essays on Syria in the Iron Age*, edited by G. Bunnens, Ancient Near Eastern Studies Supplement 7, pp. 211–233. Leuven: Peeters.
2011 "Loomweights and the Textile Industry in North Syria in the Early Iron Age," in *On Cooking Pots, Drinking Cups, Loomweights and Ethnicity in Bronze Age Cyprus and Neighbouring Regions; An International Archaeological Symposium Held in Nicosia, November 6th–7th 2010*, edited by V. Karageorghis and O. Kouka, pp. 195–202. Nicosia: The A.G. Leventis Foundation.

DINÇOL, A.
2010 "Two New Inscribed Storm-God Stelae from Arsuz (Iskenderun) and the Base from Demirköprü (Jisr-el Hadid IV)." Paper presented at the symposium on *Across the Border: Late Bronze-Iron Age Relations Between Syria and Anatolia*, Koç University, May 31-June 1, 2010.

DOTHAN, T. and ZUCKERMAN, A.
2004 "A Preliminary Study of the Mycenaean IIIC:1 Pottery Assemblages from Tel Miqne-Ekron and Ashdod,"*Bulletin of the American Schools of Oriental Research* 333: 1–54.

DOTHAN, T., GITIN, S. and ZUCKERMAN, A.
2006 "The Pottery: Canaanite and Philistine Traditions and Cypriote and Aegean Imports," in *Tel Miqne-Ekron Excavations 1995–1996: Field INE East Slope Iron AgeI (Early PhilistinePeriod)*, Final Field Report Series 8, edited by M. Meehl, T. Dothan, and S. Gitin. Jerusalem: W.F. Albright Institute of Archaeological Research and Institute of Archaeology, Hebrew University of Jerusalem.

DU PIÊD, L.
2008 "The Early Iron Age in the Northern Levant: Continuity and Change in the Pottery Assemblages from Ras el-Bassit and Ras Ibn Hani," *Scripta Mediterranea* 27–28: 161–85.

ELIYAHU-BAHER, A., YAHALOM-MACK, N., SHILSTEIN, S., ZUCKERMAN, A., SHAFER-ELLIOT, C., MAEIR, A., BOARETTO, E., FINKELSTEIN, I. and WEINER, S.
2012 "Iron and Bronze Production in Iron IIA Philistia: New Evidence from Tell es-Safi/Gath, Israel," *Journal of Archaeological Science* 39: 255–267.

GELB, I. J.
1939 *Hittite Hieroglyphic Monuments*. Oriental Institute Publications 45. Chicago: University of Chicago Press.

GENZ, H.
2003 "The Early Iron Age in Central Anatolia," in *Identifying Changes: the Transition from Bronze to Iron Ages in Anatolia and its Neighbouring Regions*, edited by B. Fischer, H. Genz, E. Jean and K. Köroğlu, pp. 179–191. Istanbul: Ege Yayınları.
2005 "Thoughts on the Origin of the Iron Age Pottery Traditions in Central Anatolia," in *Anatolian Iron Ages 5*, edited by A. Çilingiroğlu and G. Darbyshire, pp. 75–84. London: British Institute at Ankara.

GOLDMAN, H.
1956 *Excavations at Gözlü Kule, Tarsus. From the Neolithic through the Bronze Age. Vol II.* Princeton: Princeton University.

GONNELLA, J., KHAYYATA, W., and KOHLMEYER, K.
2005 *Die Zitadelle von Aleppo und der Tempel des Wettergottes.* Münster: Rhema.

HAIDER, P. W.
1999 "Sirkeli Höyük 1997. Zur Stratigraphie und Geschichte am Sirkeli Höyük," *Istanbuler Mitteilungen* 49: 118–140.

HAINES, R. C.
1971 *Excavations in the Plain of Antioch II: The Structural Remains of the Later Phases: Chatal Hoyuk, Tell al-Judaidah, and Tell Ta'yinat*, Oriental Institute Publications 92. Chicago: University of Chicago Press.

HANFMANN, G. M. A.
1963 "The Iron Age Pottery of Tarsus," in *Excavations at Gözlü Kule, Tarsus III*, edited by H. Goldman, pp. 18–332. Princeton: Princeton University.

HANSEN, C., and POSTGATE, N.
2007 "Pottery from Level III–II," in *Excavations at Kilise Tepe, 1994–98: From Bronze Age to Byzantine in Western Cilicia*, edited by N. Postgate and D. Thomas, pp. 329–370. London: British Institute at Ankara.

HARRISON, T. P.
2006 "2004 Yılı Tayinat Höyük Kazıları,"*Kazı Sonuçları Toplantısı* 27: 353–362.
2007 "Neo-Hittites in the North Orontes Valley: Recent Investigations at Tell Ta'yinat," *Journal of the Canadian Society for Mesopotamian Studies* 2: 59–68.
2008 "Tayinat Höyük Kazıları,"*Kazı Sonuçları Toplantısı* 29/2: 85–98.
2009a "Tayinat Höyük Kazıları, 2006–2007,"*Kazı Sonuçları Toplantısı* 30/2: 503–520.
2009b "Lifting the Veil on a 'Dark Age': Ta'yinat and the North Orontes Valley during the Early Iron Age," in *Exploring the Longue Durée: Essays in Honor of Lawrence E. Stager*, edited by J. D. Schloen, pp. 171–184. Winona Lake, IN: Eisenbrauns.
2009c "Neo-Hittites in the 'Land of Palistin': Renewed Investigations at Tell Ta'yinat on the Plain of Antioch," *Near Eastern Archaeology* 72: 174–189.
2010 "Tayinat Höyük Kazıları, 2008,"*Kazı Sonuçları Toplantısı* 31/3: 491–504.
2011 "Tayinat Höyük Kazıları, 2009,"*Kazı Sonuçları Toplantısı* 32/3: 368–384.

HARRISON, T. P. et al.
Forthcoming "Shifting Networks and Community Identity at Tell Tayinat in the Iron IA (ca. 12th–mid 11th Cent. BCE)."

HAWKINS, J. D.
2000 *Corpus of Hieroglyphic Luwian Inscriptions.* Berlin: Walter de Gruyter.
2009 "Cilicia, the Amuq and Aleppo: New Light in a Dark Age," *Near Eastern Archaeology* 72: 164–173.
2011 "The Inscriptions of the Aleppo Temple," *Anatolian Studies* 61: 35–54.

JANEWAY, B.
2008 "The Nature and Extent of Aegean Contact at Tell Ta'yinat and Vicinity in the Early Iron Age: Evidence of the Sea Peoples?" *Scripta Mediterranea* 27–28: 123–146.

KAHN, D.
2011 "The Campaign of Ramesses III against Philistia," *Journal of Ancient Egyptian Interconnections* 3: 1–11.
KOHLMEYER, K.
2000 *Der Tempel des Wettergottes von Aleppo*. Münster: Rhema.
2009 "The Temple of the Storm-God in Aleppo during the Late Bronze and Early Iron Ages," *Near Eastern Archaeology* 72: 190–202.
KORBEL, G.
1985 *Die spätbronzezeitliche Keramik von Norşuntepe*, Institut für Bauen und Planen in Entwicklungsländern Mitteilungen 4. Hannover: Institut für Bauen und Planen in Entwicklungsländern.
LIPOVITCH, D.
2008 "Modeling a Mycenaean Menu: Can Aegean Populations be defined in Near Eastern Contexts based on their diet?" *Scripta Mediterranea* 27–28: 147–159.
MÜLLER, U.
1999 "Die eisenzeitliche Stratigraphie von Lidar Höyük,"*Anatolian Studies* 49: 123–131.
2005 "Norşun Tepe and Lidar Höyük. Two examples for Cultural Change during the Early Iron Age," in *Anatolian Iron Ages 5*, edited by A. Çilingiroğlu and G. Darbyshire, pp. 107–114. London: British Institute at Ankara.
RAHMSTORF, L.
2003 "Clay Spools from Tiryns and Other Contemporary Sites: An Indication of Foreign Influence in LH IIIC?" in *The Periphery of the Mycenaean World. 2nd International Interdisciplinary Colloquium, 26-30 September, Lamia 1999*, edited by N. Kyparissi-Apostolika and M. Papakonstantinou, pp. 397–415. Athens: Aohna.
2008 *Kleinfunde aus Tiryns. Terrakotta, Stein, Bein und Glas/Fayence vornehmlic aus der Spätbronzezeit*. Wiesbaden: Reichert Verlag.
ROAMES, J.
2011 "The Early Iron Age metal workshop at Tell Tayinat, Turkey," in *MRS Proceedings 1319: Material Issues in Art and Archaeology IX*. Cambridge: Cambridge University Press.
SCHOOP, U.-D.
2003 "Pottery Traditions of the Later Hittite Empire: Problems of Definition," in *Identifying Changes: the Transition from Bronze to Iron Ages in Anatolia and its Neighbouring Regions*, edited by B. Fischer, H. Genz, E. Jean and K. Köroğlu, pp. 167–178. Istanbul: Ege Yayınları.
SEVIN, V. and KÖROĞLU, K.
2004 "Late Bronze Age at Yumuktepe: New Evidence from Step-Trench South," in *Mersin-Yumuktepe: A Reappraisal*, edited by I. Caneva and V. Sevin, pp. 73–83. Lecce: Dipartimento di Beni Culturali Universita degli Studi.
STAGER, L.
1998 "The Impact of the Sea Peoples," in *The Archaeology of Society in the Holy Land*, edited by T. Levy, pp. 332–348. Leicester: University of Leicester Press.
STEITLER, C.
2010 "The Biblical King Toi of Hamath and the Late Hittite State 'P/Walas(a)tin'," *Biblische Notizen* 146: 81–99.
SÜRENHAGEN, D.
1999 "Tell Gindaris and the Western Afrin Valley," *AAAS* 43: 159–167.

SWIFT, G. F.
1958 "The Pottery of the 'Amuq, Phases K to O, and It Historical Relationships." Unpublished Ph.D. Dissertation, University of Chicago.

VELDHUIJZEN, H. A.
2009 "Hip to be Square: How Tuyères shaped the Hammeh Iron Production," in *Modesty and Patience: Archaeological Studies and Memories in Honour of Nabil Qadi "Abu Salim,"* edited by H. G. Gebel, Z. Kafafi, and O. Al-Ghul. Berlin: Yarmouk University.

VENTURI, F.
2007 *La Siria nell'età delle trasformazioni (XIII-X sec. a.C.). Nuovi contribute dallo scavo di Tell Afis*. Bologna: CLUEB.

VERSTRAETE, J. and WILKINSON, T. J.
2000 "The Amuq Regional Archaeological Survey," *American Journal of Archaeology* 104: 179–192.

WOOLLEY, L.
1955 *Alalakh: An Account of the Excavations at Tell Atchana in the Hatay, 1937–1949*, Reports of the Research Committee of the Society of Antiquaries of London 18. London: Society of Antiquaries.

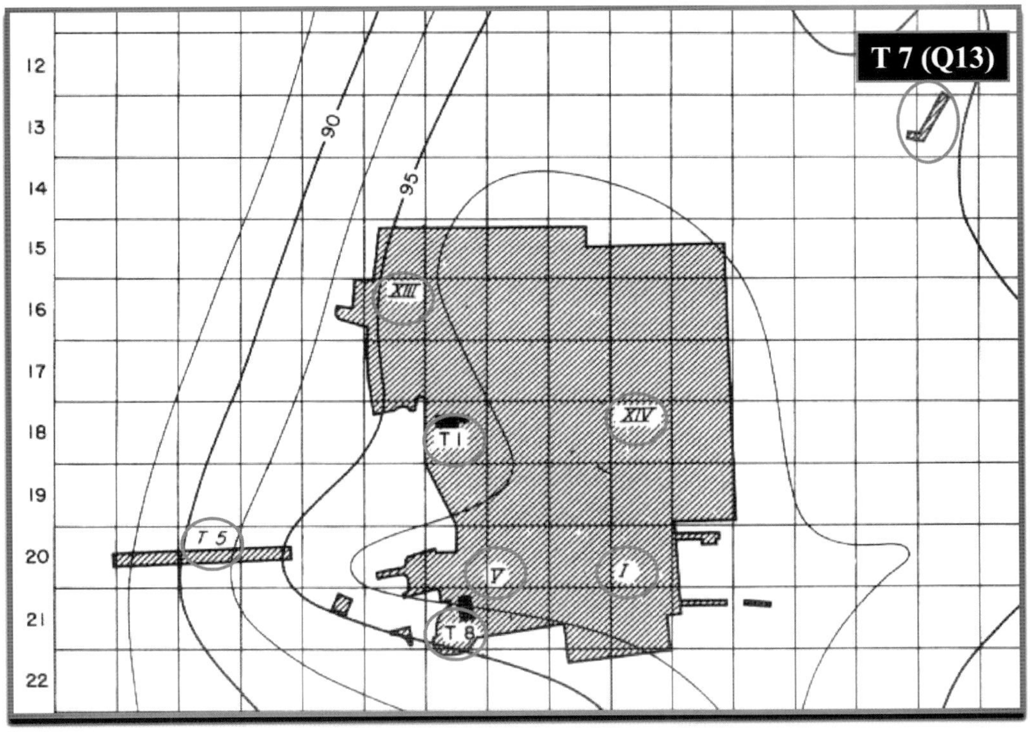

Fig. 1 Contour map of Tell Tayinat showing the Syrian-Hittite Expedition excavation areas that produced traces of Early Iron Age (Phase N) settlement (adapted from Haines 1971: pl. 93).

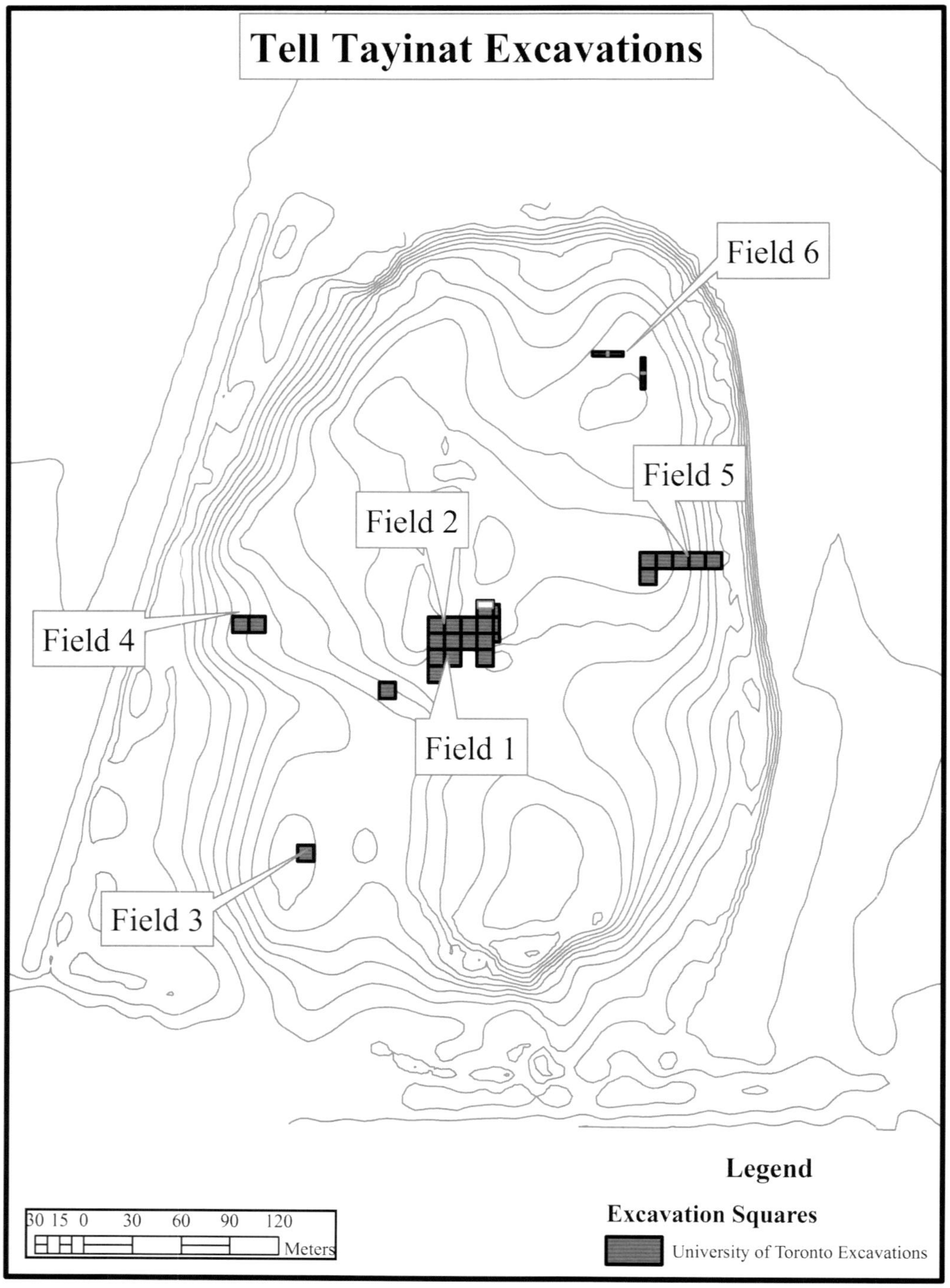

Fig. 2 Contour map of Tell Tayinat showing the principal TAP excavation areas (created by S. Batiuk).

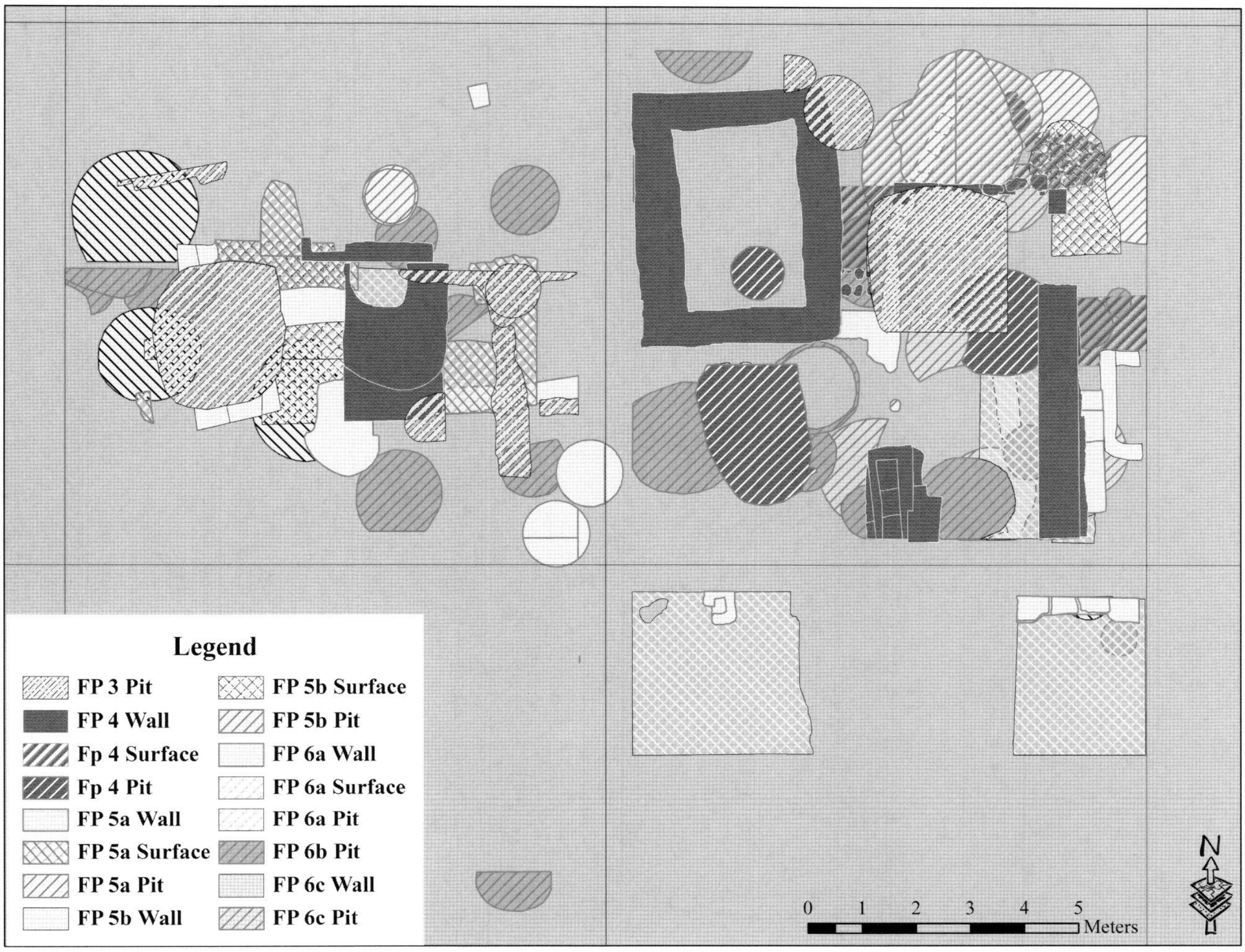

Fig. 3 Composite plan of the Early Iron Age architecture in Field 1 (created by S. Batiuk).

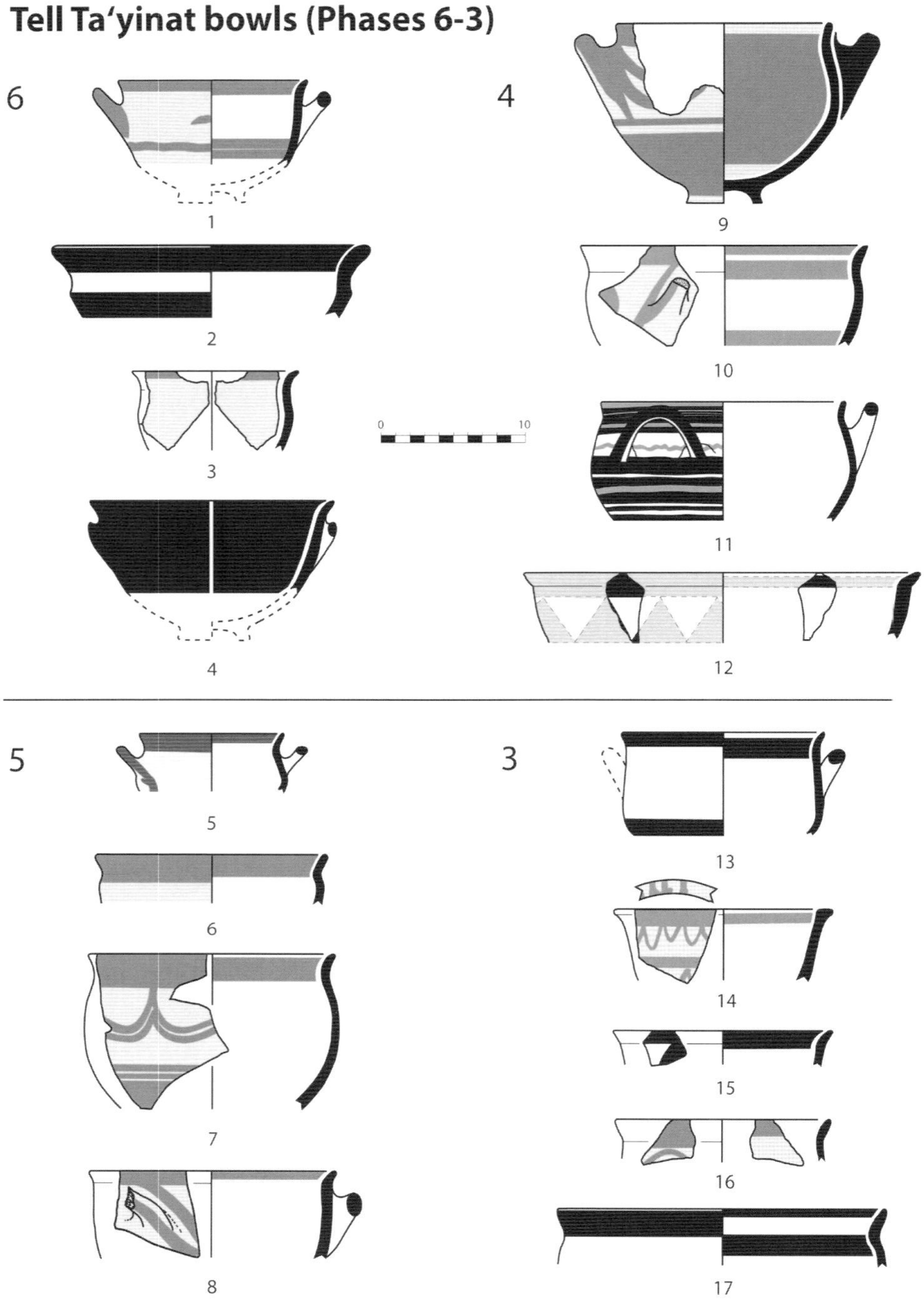

Fig. 4 Late Helladic IIIC pottery from Field 1 (drawn by B. Janeway).

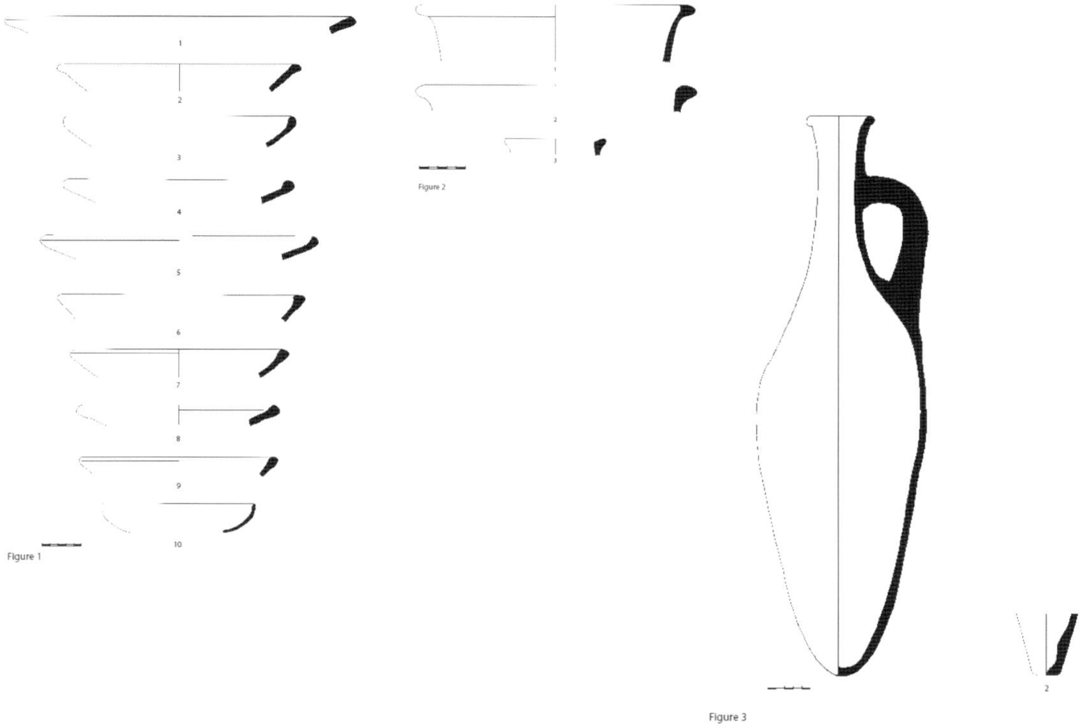

Fig. 5 Local Wares from Field 1 (drawn by E. Ünlü).

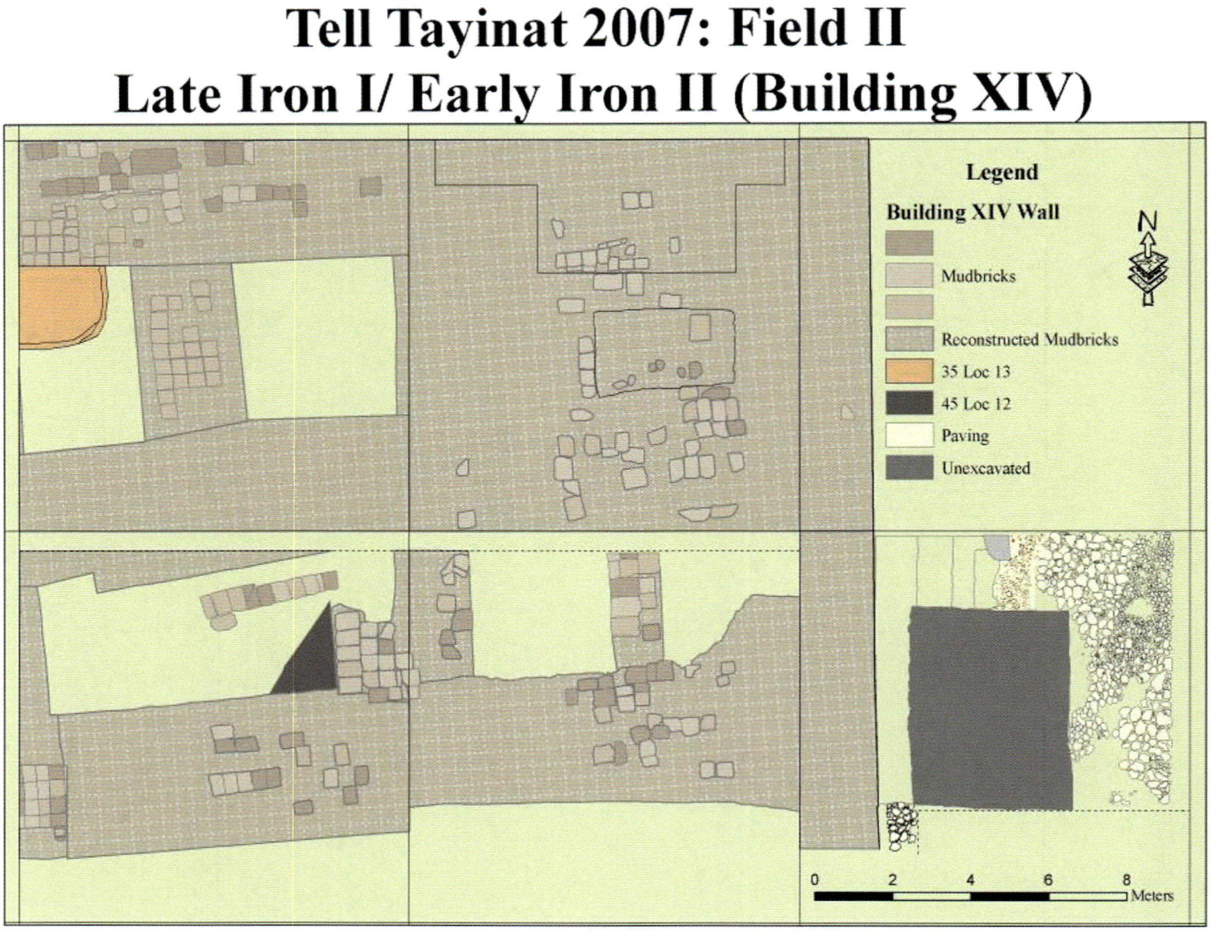

Fig. 6 Plan of Field II architecture in Field 2 (created by S. Batiuk).

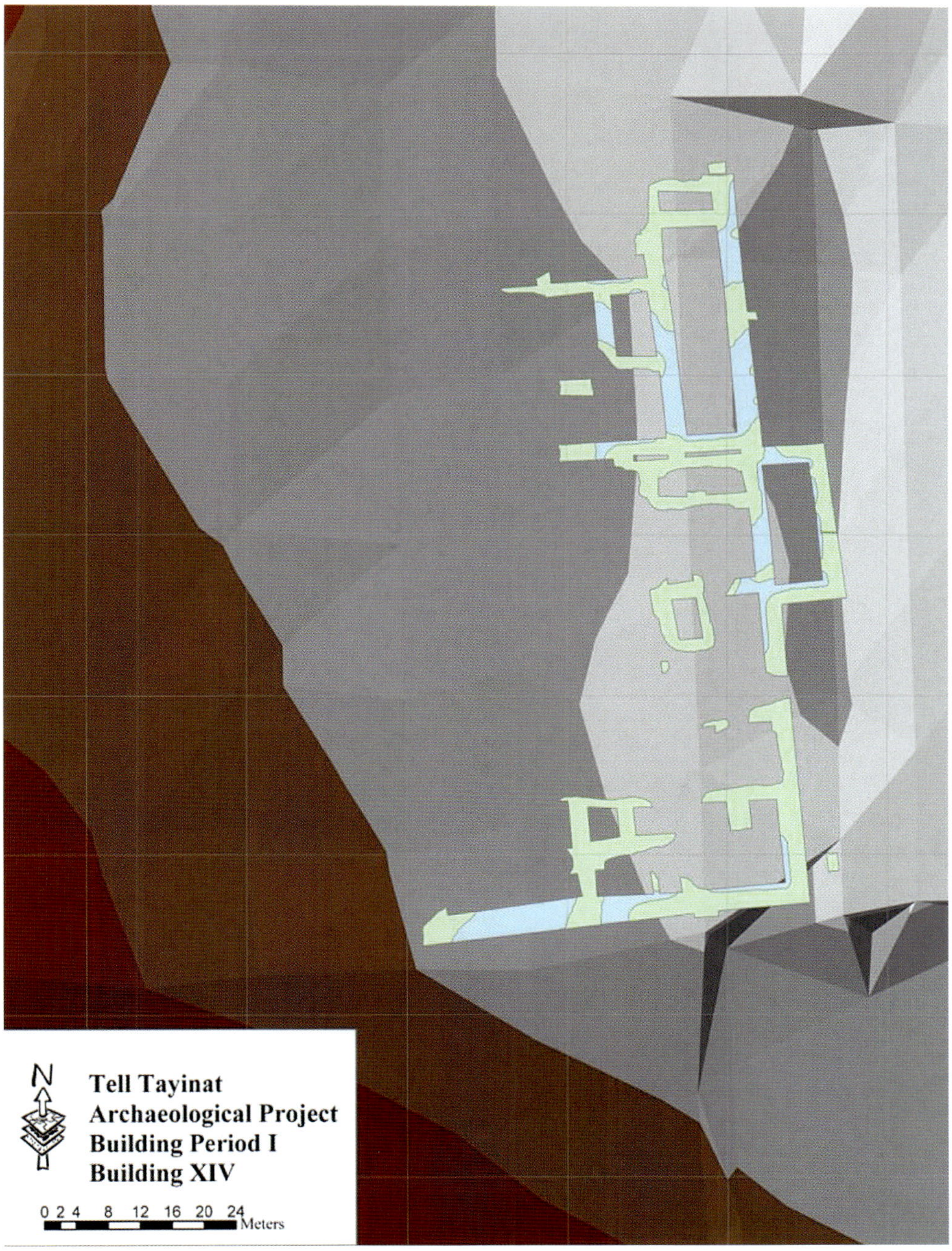

Fig. 7 Plan of Building XIV remains (created by S. Batiuk).

CHAPTER 4

CHATAL HÖYÜK IN THE AMUQ: MATERIAL CULTURE AND ARCHITECTURE DURING THE PASSAGE FROM THE LATE BRONZE AGE TO THE EARLY IRON AGE

Marina PUCCI
Freie Universität Berlin
Institut für Vorderasiatische Altertumskunde
Hüttenweg 7
14195 Berlin, Germany
E-mail: mpucci@zedat.fu-berlin.de

Abstract

The analysis of the results of the excavation carried out at the site of Chatal Höyük in the Amuq plain during the 1930s by the Oriental Institute of Chicago has yielded further data on the passage from the LBA to the EIA in this region, i.e. from Amuq phase M to Amuq phase N. The architectural remains show both a discontinuity in one part of the settlement during phase M and a strong continuity in the passage from phase M to N. On the other hand, however, the material culture, especially the pottery points to a stark change at the end of phase M, changing from a local standardized, possibly Anatolian influenced repertoire during phase M, to a strong Late Helladic IIIC influenced assemblage during phase N. These changes in the material culture seem to indicate not only a change of the sphere of influence in Iron Age pottery production, but also the incorporation of foreign elements, which together with a lack of strong local standardized production suggest a new eclectic phase.[1]

Introduction: the Excavations in the Plain of Antioch and chronology of the Amuq phases

It is always a very difficult task to interpret archaeological remains as evidence of political change, especially for very complex historical periods such as the end of the second and the beginning of the first millennium in the Near East. This task becomes

[1] I owe my gratitude to Prof. Aslihan Yener, not only for having organized this congress but also because in 2001 she offered me to work on the Chatal Höyük materials at the Oriental Institute Museum. The project has been financed by the Shelby White-Leon Levy Foundation. Many thanks are due to Dr. F. Venturi for his frequent suggestions and input.

even greater when, as is the case here, the analysed archaeological evidence is linked to excavations carried out in the 1930s, i.e. using older digging methods and when this evidence is available, only through two sets of sources, that is, small finds and pottery in museums and notes and documents left by archaeologists. Nevertheless, both the archaeological materials (pottery sherds and small finds) and the written documents from the excavations at the site of Chatal Höyük in the Amuq region provide such a complex and complete bulk of sources for analysing the archaeological evidence during this period, that one must necessarily take these excavations into account when analysing the Late Bronze and Iron Ages in northern Syria and southeastern Anatolia.[2]

While the forthcoming final publication of all materials from the excavations by the Oriental Institute at the site of Chatal Höyük will provide all the data on pottery and small finds, the main aim of this contribution is to point out the chronological sequence of the architectural levels at the site and its dates according to the pottery and to emphasize those elements, which may suggest a political or social change during the passage from the Late Bronze Age to the Early Iron Age.[3]

Since 1944 and mainly with their publication in 1960 and 1971, a sequence of cultural phases identified by letters (A is the most ancient) defines the regional chronology in the Amuq plain.[4] The features of the cultural phases were based on both the stratigraphic sequence at Tell al Judaidah and on the pottery assemblages from the Amuq survey. While the materials of the earlier phases (A–J) have been fully published, those of the later phases (L–T), although they represent the largest assemblage, have only been sketched out in short papers.[5] These publications provided only an overview of the criteria used in distinguishing the phases, criteria which had already become evident during the excavations.[6] According to these principles and to the terminology used in the phasing sequence, it is possible to identify Amuq phase M with the Late Bronze Age, Amuq phase N with the Iron Age I, and Amuq phase O with Iron Ages II and III. Considering that this paper is based upon data from a single settlement in the Amuq region, only the regional terminology (Amuq Phases M–O) is employed here, discarding the general archaeological terminology of the Late Bronze Age and Iron Ages.[7]

[2] For the Amuq excavations and survey cf. McEwan 1937; Braidwood 1937; Braidwood and Braidwood 1960; Haines 1971. The survey has been resumed under the directorship of A. Yener, cf. Yener (ed.) 2005.

[3] The final publication of the analysis of materials from Chatal Höyük is currently in review.

[4] Braidwood 1937; Krogman 1949; Braidwood and Braidwood 1960; Haines 1971.

[5] Swift 1958; Gevirtz 1967; Levenson 1973; Meyer 2008.

[6] The first appearance of the Amuq phases (with Roman numerals) was in Braidwood 1937, while its first appearance with letters was in a short table in Krogman 1949.

[7] A general archaeological periodization is employed for a very large geographical area and the criteria employed to distinguish Iron Age I, II and III are sometimes different from area to area (e.g. the fine periodization used in Palestine does not have a direct correspondence in the north Syrian/southwest Anatolian area), Lehmann 2008; Gilboa and Sharon 2003.

Using Braidwood's regional division of phases also necessitates keeping the main distinguishing criteria to identify these phases, which have been used during the research analysis as the basis for generally assigning the assemblages to the phases. According to Braidwood's publication[8] "Spindle Bottles, Cypriot milk bowls, White-on-Black (or -Red) painted Wares of Hurrian tradition" characterized the Phase M assemblage, "Sub-Mycenaean or Late Helladic IV wares" identify phase N, while "Red-slipped and Burnished series, bichrome painted series, which copies Sub-Mycenaean and Cypriot motifs" are typical of Phase O.[9] Swift in 1954 adopted these criteria and on the basis only of complete vessels attempted to date the phases and link them to the Alalakh (Tell Atchana) sequence.

Using these criteria, it became possible to chronologically assign the archaeological contexts of the assemblages (or "structural levels"), while their stratigraphic vertical position and their archaeological features (such as architecture and earth fill) provided further information on a more detailed vertical sequence.[10] The following paragraphs provide a general overview of the pottery and architectural remains from phases M and N, highlighting only those areas where both phases were excavated and the period of passage from the one phase to the other.

Phase M: Architecture and Material Culture

The earliest archaeological contexts excavated on the mound belong to phase M[11] and were identified in two areas (II and IV). While the trench in Area V was very small and consequently the remains found in it were few and slightly confused from a stratigraphic point of view,[12] the trench in Area II was large enough to indicate a clear stratigraphic sequence during phase M, so that it has been possible to archaeologically distinguish a late from a middle phase M and consequently present their assemblages accordingly.[13] The archaeological context of the most ancient level in Area II (II_12) consists of a single building with two narrow rectangular rooms and a larger square one (**Fig. 1.2**). The floors of this structure were never reached, however, the burnt earth fill in the small rooms contained several whole vessels (including four storage

[8] Braidwood 1937, Table 1. Cultural Periods VI, V, IV become respectively, Phases M, N, and O.

[9] I expunged some features, which Braidwood noted in his table 1. These are no longer distinctive for each phase. Moreover, some terms are retained here, which are no longer in use such as "painted wares of Hurrian tradition," indicating Nuzi/Atchana ware.

[10] The assemblages were collected by locus; each locus was then grouped by structural level.

[11] Older materials were collected from the so-called "small base cuts" at the foot of the hill and were published in Braidwood and Braidwood 1960.

[12] Although the trench was very small archaeologists left the walls intact as they were excavating to lower levels, cf. Haines 1971, pl. 15.

[13] This distinction is based on the vertical stratigraphy. The sequence in this area is also published in Pucci 2010, however, in the last period it has been possible to point out a mistake in the assemblage assignation so that the sequence presented here should be considered as definitive.

jars), which not only suggests that the two rooms were used for storage but also that the structure was abandoned after its destruction.

The pottery assemblage consists of a large majority of simple ware sherds, in particular, conical platters with squared or incurving rims (**Fig. 2.1**, **2.2**, **Fig. 6.4**),[14] conical bowls with triangular (**Fig. 2.6**) or thickened internal rims (**Fig. 2.3**), and narrow bowls with internal angular rims (**Fig. 2.14**).[15] Necked jars with simple rims and globular walls (**Fig. 2.13**) and single-handled storage jugs with piriform bodies (**Fig. 3.7**)[16] are the most common closed containers found in this assemblage. Indented rim shapes used probably in large bi-conical narrow bowls recur twice (in a simple ware bowl and on a painted piece),[17] while cooking pots with short collars and triangular (similar to **Fig. 2.17**) or triangular and pressed (**Fig. 2.15**) rims are very frequent in the assemblage.

The fabric and surface treatment of the conical platters differ greatly; the surfaces range from pale brown self-slip, some black burnished examples, and light reddish brown ones. The ware is orange/pink with a central grey core on approximately one third of the platters, while in the remaining ones is uniform pale brown.[18] The fabric of the kraters and bowls is mostly light, reddish brown. Chaff temper is used on approximately half of the assemblage, while crushed shells are employed on the large majority of the cooking pots.

The uniform dimensions (the diameters ranging from 200 to 300 mm), the high number (this shape is 75 % of the whole simple ware production), and the extremely similar shapes of these conical platters seem to suggest a standardized production. The simple ware bi-conical krater (A26968) is similar to the large kraters at Afis VIb and Vb, although a bottom perforation seems to suggest a different function; also, the single handled piriform jars (**Fig. 3.7**) find comparisons with the large jars from Afis Vb.[19]

The painted pottery class represents 11 % of the whole assemblage and consists of simple or bi-conical bowls with geometric decorations on the shoulder (vertical or oblique lines forming triangles, cf. **Fig. 2.16**) and of cylindrical bowls with horizontals bands.[20] Generally speaking, this assemblage is very similar to the painted examples

[14] Inventory number are indicated in the plates with A##### numbers for the Oriental Institute Museum numbers and a-/b-/e-#### numbers for those in the Antakya Archaeological Museum in Turkey .

[15] The terminology employed for the descriptions of pottery parts follows Hendrix et al. 1997

[16] The number b-2881 indicates eight similar jars found in the same room in level II_12. Only one (b-2881/008) is shown in **Fig. 6**.

[17] Pucci 2010, fig. 8.

[18] This fabric difference does not seem to be related to a chronological factor, nor there is a connection between fabric and specific rim shapes.

[19] Venturi 2010, figs. 7.9 and 9.1.

[20] This percentage it is not negligible as it is at other sites such as Tell Afis, cf. Venturi 2007, p. 261. However, it should be pointed out that the selection of the sherds in the field may have strongly influenced these ratios making the percentage of painted pottery always greater than it was in reality.

from Alalakh IV-III both in terms of the shapes, as well as in the decorations and seems to continue a tradition of painted pottery from the Late Bronze Age I. Among the imports, a monochrome single handled bowl (**Fig. 3.2**) belongs to the Late Cypriot III horizon[21] (a similar bowl was also found in Alalakh IV)[22] and three small body sherds are in the painted Nuzi/Atchana tradition.

A very significant change in the spatial use of the area occurs at the following level II_11; a series of pebble floors, mud brick silos, and graves occupy the area, so that it seems possible that a break in the architectural sequence occurred and the spatial organization of this area at least was radically changed (**Fig. 1.2**). By contrast, the assemblage belonging to this level II_11 shows strong elements of continuity with the former level; simple ware sherds represent the majority of the assemblage and the same shapes (conical platters with incurving, square or triangular rim **Figs. 2.5**, **2.8**), as well as globular cooking pots with doubled folded rims (identical to **Fig. 2.15**) are the most common ones. Fabric and surface treatment of both the simple ware and of the cooking pots do not vary from the previous level. Among the 19 painted rim sherds, the closed vessels common in the earlier assemblages with oblique lines disappear and fragments of open vessels with horizontal bands are the only painted sherds available in the assemblage. Among the few imported sherds (all body sherds except for one), it is possible to identify those from Cyprus (three fragments of White Slip II and five of Red Lustrous Spindle Bottles), and one single but large piece of an Atchana Ware beaker (A27550).[23]

Level II_10 directly on top of II_11 seems to continue without interruption in the use of this area as an open pebbled space with grain silos (**Fig. 1.2**). This time, the excavated area being larger, it is possible to connect this open area to two structures separated by a street or alley. From an architectural point of view nothing changes in the use of the area or in the building techniques.

The very rich pottery assemblage generally assigned to this level should, at this point, be divided into the following two groups: the sherds found on and inside the floors of this level and those found in the "filling layer" between these structures and the following level II_09. The first group basically consists of an assemblage similar to the previous ones; a vast majority of simple ware open platters (**Figs. 2.7**, **2.9**, **2.11**, **2.12**), shell tempered cooking pots with doubled folded external rims (**Figs. 2.17** and **2.18**), while a few painted potsherds different from the ones found in the earlier levels, now appear (**Fig. 4.13**). The second assemblage, i.e. the one found in the fill layer (marked in the plates as II_10_fill), shows more relevant changes; examples of painted monochrome pottery are not only more numerous, but two main new shapes suddenly

21 Åström 1972, XV, V, 4.
22 Woolley 1955, p. 356 (ATP/38/27).
23 Published in McEwan 1937.

appear, deep bowls with outcurving rims (or bell-shaped bowls) start to become a common shape (cf. **Fig. 4.6-10**), as well as (although only in minor numbers), shallow carinated bowls with flared painted rims (**Fig. 4.4**). The painted patterns range from geometric elements (plain bands, wavy lines, plain or cross-hatched triangles) to figural elements (birds and fishes). Painted decoration, which appears mainly on open vessels and the tradition of geometrically decorated shoulders (**Fig. 2.16**), seems to be completely abandoned together with the sharp angular shapes (i.e. angular shoulders or angular bases). The variety of decorative patterns, their arrangement on the vessel surfaces, and the shapes in the assemblage, which characterize the fill layer during the passage from phase M to N, seem to be related to a LH IIIC horizon. Although the imported fragment of a bell-shaped bowl with antithetic spirals (**Fig. 4.6**) is similar to the pieces with antithetic spirals from Tarsus,[24] which have been generally dated to the LH IIIC Early,[25] early this pattern developed over a long period of time (LH IIIB to LH IIIC Late)[26] and may not be a good marker for specific dating. Moreover, the spirals from Chatal seem to differ slightly from the usual ones, that is, the starting point of the stem is not aligned with the spiral itself, as it is usual in antithetic spirals without stems. In the same way, cross hatched triangles on a frieze (**Fig. 4.14**) and simple horizontal bands (**Figs. 4.7** and **4.8**) are extremely common in the LH horizon and are not chronologically indicative. By contrast the plain painted bowls with reserved line under the internal rim (**Fig. 4.9**) are considered as typical starting from the LH IIIC middle period.[27] In addition wavy line patterns on a large framed field (**Fig. 3.1**, **Fig. 3.3** and **Fig. 4.10**), originating from the granary style of LH IIIC middle period, suggest a middle date for the LH IIIC period for this fill layer.[28]

Several patterns such as fish (**Fig. 4.3** and **4.13**), birds (**Fig. 4.13**), together with stylized caprids (**Fig. 4.12**) are the most common decorative figural patterns and are typical in the Late Helladic III repertoire; in particular, the figural decoration in a horizontal frieze seems to be common in the LH IIIC period, however, no exact match could be identified especially for geometrized figures such as those in **Fig. 4.12**, which are probably a local interpretation of LH patterns. On the other hand, the quadruped with tree in **Fig. 4.5** seems to refer to a local tradition of "palm tree and ibex."[29] The shapes also fit into the Late Helladic tradition, ranging from very common

[24] Goldman 1937, fig. 41; Mountjoy 2005, p. 109, fig. 9–10.

[25] Cf. Mountjoy 2005, p. 84.

[26] Dothan and Zuckerman 2004, p. 37; Mountjoy 1986, FS 50; Venturi 2007, p. 298.

[27] Mountjoy 1986, p. 156; Mountjoy 2007, p. 224 dates it to the LH IIIC middle advanced, French 2007, p. 181 assigns this pattern to the period starting from the LH IIIC middle advanced. These dates refer to the Greek mainland, while it seems that on Crete this pattern already started during the LH IIIC early cf. Mountjoy 1999, pp. 512–513.

[28] cf. Lehmann 2008, p. 493, pp. 517–518 Fig. 4. The wavy line pattern in Afis phase IV slightly differs from the examples from Chatal, cf. Venturi 2007, pp. 278–279, fig. 69.3, 69.6.

[29] Venturi 2007, p. 287.

deep bowls (Furumark Shape 285)[30] and kraters with flat rims (probably FS282), to more seldom monochrome deep bowls and carinated cups with high handles (FS240).

Among the imports, besides a few (five body pieces probably belonging to the same bowl), body fragments of White Slip II milk bowls, and of Atchana painted beakers (three body sherds), the two deep bowls described above (one with antithetic spirals, **Fig. 4.6**, and the one with reserved lines **Fig. 4.9**), show a fabric completely different from the local painted examples (fine, with no temper and pink), and are thus considered imported. This change in the painted pottery tradition, the arrival of new shapes and the evident connections to a "Helladic" tradition of this fill layer mark the passage from phase M to N.

In Area V the sequence from phase M to phase N can again be easily identified according to the assemblages. However, the small extent of the trench precludes a clear understanding of the sequence and the number of excavated levels per phase is different from Area II, so that it is not possible to establish a one-to-one connection between the two areas. In Area V the earliest excavated context is the architectural level, V_06 (**Fig. 1.1**). Several walls with stone foundations belong to this level without a clear building plan; by contrast, their orientation may suggest that they belong to slightly different building phases, so that it is likely that level V_06 comprises more than one occupational period. Grave b-S-61 was dug during level V_06 and partially destroyed some of the walls mentioned above. The grave goods included a Red Lustrous spindle bottle and a Base Ring II jug, both imported from Cyprus .[31]

The assemblage from this level again includes several classes, among which the main one is simple ware. Also in this area, conical platters with incurving or thickened internal rims (**Fig. 2.10**) are the main shapes which occur, while combed decoration is frequently employed on closed vessels. Cooking pots with shell temper and triangular external rims can be considered the common shape in this class, although quartz grit is very common and used at the same time as shell temper. Again the few painted monochrome sherds belong to closed vessels with oblique lines painted on the shoulders or deep bowls with horizontal bands, and again both belong to the same painted local tradition well known from Alalakh VII-IV.

The following level V_05 includes only a single stone wall with some floor patches. The locus was identified on the base of its elevation above sea level rather than on the actual presence of horizontal interfaces such as floors. However, there are a few changes in the pottery assemblage; again simple ware conical platters (**Fig. 2.4**), triangular shaped cooking pots, and one White slip II rim sherd. It should be noted here that among the usual closed vessels with painted monochrome decoration, a few sherds

[30] Furumark 1941 classification of shapes is employed (abbreviated FS) here, because, although it is in some aspects outdated, it is still commonly used. Cf. Mountjoy 1986.

[31] The grave was published in McEwan 1937, fig. 1.

display different motifs such as one figural example (**Fig. 4.5**), suggesting a progressive change, which will become evident in the following level.[32]

The assemblage changes at the following level V_04, where only painted monochrome decorated sherds were collected belonging to deep bowls with everted rims or to kraters with flat rims. This is a phenomenon similar to the one observed in Area II with the sole, but relevant difference in this case, being that the total number of collected sherds is extremely small to be representative of each class. The structural remains do not indicate any relevant change; a single wall with the same orientation and the same building technique as the one from the previous period occupies the excavated area.

Chronological Limits of Phase M

The absolute chronological dates of the phase M period are based on the imported objects and pottery. If we take into consideration both areas and all levels of period M, it is evident that fragments of Nuzi/Atchana ware are frequent, although in very small and not-diagnostic pieces (except for the archaeologically complete beaker mentioned above). These imports may establish a parallel with levels IV-II at Alalakh, i.e. with a date starting from the mid-15th century BC onwards, however, their low number and poor state of preservation may indicate that either this type of "luxury" tableware, despite its proximity to Alalakh, was not imported to the site of Chatal or that it was no longer a fashionable item.[33] The majority of the imports were from Cyprus; Red Lustrous Spindle Bottles and White Slip II milk bowls fragments are common in the phase M repertoires. The distribution of WSII seems to be related mainly to the 13th century BC,[34] while Red Lustrous Spindle Bottles have a long period of production and distribution (from the mid-17th century to the end of the 13th century BC),[35] although at Alalakh the highest number of imports was found at level III together with LHIIIA2 pottery,[36] i.e. from the 14thcentury BC. Late Helladic imports are extremely few but they definitely belong to a Late Helladic IIIC horizon; in particular,

[32] However, the existence of "collared" cooking pots with quartz grit similar to Afis VIII, of a single but large fragment of a fine small bowl (Swift 1958, fig. 12) similar to Alalakh V-VII palace ware, and the larger number of combed pale brown bi-conical craters (which are also frequent in Afis VIII, cf. Venturi in this book), may indicate that the excavations in this area also reached older (LBI?) levels.

[33] Nuzi painted Ware was found at the "end of level IV, common in level III, most abundant in level II," Woolley 1955, p. 347. Atchana Ware is more abundant in Level II (Woolley 1955, p. 350). The beaker from Chatal (A27550) belongs to the "Atchana Ware" group.

[34] At Tell Abu al Kharaz the WSII was found in Phase 7 and dated to 1380–1290, cf. Fischer 1999, at Tell Kazel the WS II was found in Area IV lev. 5 upper floor and dated to the Late Cypriot IIb–c, cf. Badre 2006; at Deir el-Balah the White slip II was found on floor IX and dated to the 19th dynasty, i.e. to the 13th century, cf. Killebrew et al. 2006. However the time period of the distribution of this class of pottery occupies the 14th to the end of the 13th centuries, cf. Eriksson 2007.

[35] Manning et al. 1998, p. 335; Eriksson 1993, p. 119.

[36] For this new dating of the imports see Yener (this volume).

the painted bowls with reserved lines as well as the wavy line style on the bowls appear to be related to a LH IIIC middle tradition, which is commonly dated to the mid-12th century. Thus, according to these elements it is possible to suggest for the excavated levels of phase M a date to the 14th and 13th centuries BC, and the mid-12th century for the end of this phase.[37]

Moreover, the standardized repertoire of simple ware conical platters with incurving rims may suggest two very different origins. On the one hand it is similar to the Late Bronze Age platters from Tarsus and Kinet Höyük, which are frequently identified with a chronological indicator for the LB II period. However, due to the fact that these vessels were not imported from Anatolia but were locally produced and consequently are subject to regional variations, it is only possible to interpret them as indicating standardization, but it is not possible to use them as a chronological element. On the other hand, these conical platters with angular internal rim and elevated ring base may also refer to a local tradition of pottery production visible also in Alalakh[38] and therefore should be considered as the continuation of a local tradition.

Phase N: Architecture and Pottery

Architectural levels belonging to phase N were excavated in all sectors on the mound, suggesting that at least during this phase the whole mound was inhabited. In Area II, not only was the orientation of the walls maintained and not only were some of the walls built on top of the older ones, but also the structures appear to be similar in shape and spatial organization to the previous ones (**Fig. 5**). This area was then gradually built up with the large open areas reduced by construction of more houses, reflecting a denser urban population. The sequence of structural levels in Area II belonging to phase N (four structural levels from II_09 to II_05) is characterized by a change in the general orientation of the structures during period II_08/II_07 and by a denser population of this area. The function of the area and the type of dwelling structures seem to have remained the same, although the large open pebbled areas with silos gradually disappeared and the system of streets and consequently of the neighbouring structures was rearranged. By contrast in Area V, it is only possible to establish a general continuity in the orientation of the structures built one on top of the other and the existence of a mound wall with square towers at least at Level V_02 (the excavated area was large enough), where several open pebbled spaces adjoined it.

The pottery assemblage of phase N is characterized by a large majority of painted monochrome pottery, which imitates the shapes and decorative patterns of the Late

[37] Both the continuity of some shapes and the continuity of the architectural levels in Area II exclude the existence of a gap in the settlement occupation.

[38] Woolley 1955, pottery types 5 and 6a found mainly in levels V and IV.

Helladic IIIC middle, late, and sub-Mycenaean periods as well as local developments. As far as the ratio is concerned, it is important to point out that assemblages were selected in the field and probably all the painted monochrome decorated diagnostic sherds were collected and brought to Chicago , but not all the simple ware or cooking ware sherds. Therefore, it is likely that the painted to unpainted ratio is somewhat overrepresented in all levels. However, even though this error recurs in every analysed context, it alone does not explain the striking proportion of painted pottery in phase N assemblages, which in level II_08 reaches 94 % of the whole repertoire.[39]

A pale brown, fine or medium fine clay with polychrome grit and very frequent organic inclusions characterizes the fabric of the painted decorated pottery. The surface is frequently left untreated; a simple wash or self-slip is seldomly used, while a proper slip is almost absent. By contrast the few imported pieces are characterized by fine ware, also pale brown or pinkish fabric, by rare organic inclusions, and a fine slip, usually paler than the ware itself.

The bell-shaped bowl (FS244), hemispherical bowls, carinated cups (FS240), strainer jugs (FS155), which are all well-known Helladic IIIC shapes, are extremely common in the assemblage of phase N. The bell-shaped bowls maintain their globular shape, while the bowls with flaring rim from the earlier level (**Fig. 4.4**) become shorter (**Fig. 6.4**). They are very similar to carinated bowls of the Late Helladic tradition (**Fig. 6.3**) and probably are a more elaborated version of simple bi-conical bowls (**Fig. 6.6**). Painted decoration is also employed on earlier shapes, such as the well-known conical platters, which in part keep their incurving rim shapes (**Fig. 6.7**) but for the most part, show simplified square rims (**Fig. 6.5**). Large hemispherical bowls with everted rims (**Fig. 6.8**) seem to completely replace the more ancient shape with angular internal rims. Necked jars with simple rims (**Fig. 6.14**), as well as feeding bottles (**Fig. 3.5**), and strainer jugs (**Fig. 6.11**) are common shapes in the painted monochrome class.

The painted patterns are mainly geometrical, tend to be more and more simplified during phase N, and they are very often organized in rows (**Fig. 6.14**). Wavy lines are now more narrow-framed (**Fig. 6.3**; **6.5**), while a "palmette" hanging from the rim of the bowls (**Fig. 6.1**) or on closed vessels (**Fig. 6.10**) becomes an extremely common pattern as do loops hanging at the base of handles (**Fig. 6.15**). The "palmette" can be probably interpreted as derivative from Late Helladic patterns such as the tassel (FM72), which seems to become more elaborated during the sub-Mycenaean period,[40] while the hanging loops at the base of the handle, are common motifs in the Aegean

[39] All percentages are calculated on rim sherds.

[40] A very similar piece was found at Tell Tayinat, cf. Harrison 2010, fig. 4.7.

and at Tell Afis.[41] The figural patterns (usually on a closed vessel) are rare finds percentage wise, but keep the same motifs as in the earlier assemblages (**Fig. 6.11**). By contrast, the deep bowl (**Fig. 6.9**) is a rare shape and is probably linked to a different earlier and local tradition. The plain painted bowls with reserved decoration are common (**Figs. 6.2**, **6.13** and **3.6**) both in red and black.

The simple ware class does not completely disappear, however, large-scale production of conical platters decreases significantly, incurving rims progressively disappear, and the painted wares appear to be the common tableware now; although the same standardization of dimensions and shapes is not as in the earlier phase. By contrast cooking pots keep their old shapes; globular vessels with external thickened rim, short collar, and shell temper (**Fig. 6.12**).

Chronological Limits of Phase N

Considering that the beginning of phase N can be identified with the sudden but massive appearance of local imitations of LH IIIC middle phase ceramics, this local production appears in a simple fill level between two similar structural phases with no traces of destruction or sudden break. Also, this "new local trend" continues uninterrupted and therefore it seems evident that not only the transition from phase M to N was smooth, but also that this "new" local painted tradition settled and flourished at the site developed during phase N. From a chronological point of view it is possible to set this transition during the second half of the 12th century BC.

Moreover, although the number of local imitations of LH IIIC late is extremely high during phase N, and seem to represent an important local production, Mycenaean imports are extremely rare (**Fig. 6.3**); the majority consisting of body fragments. At the more recent levels still dating to phase N, the imports are also not numerous and originate mainly from Cyprus with several examples of White Painted Wheel made cups and bowls. A large fragment of an imported Protogeometric amphora and two fragments of Euboean bowls with hanging semicircles in the more recent levels of this phase set the end of this phase to a relatively late period. These imports together with two fragments of Black on Red juglets seem to mark the end of phase N during the second half of the 9th century BC.

Conclusion: the Anatolian and Mycenaean influences

The large distribution and the overwhelming number of conical platters in the assemblages of phase M support the idea of a standardized multifunctional vessel; the shape and size could allow comparisons with the so called "drab ware" from Tarsus,

[41] Mountjoy 1986, fig. 261; Venturi 2007, fig. 85.

Kinet Höyük and Kilise Tepe. This term "drab ware" has been employed to identify pottery bearing surface scraping, poor quality fabric, pottery marks on the surface and it is mostly related to an Anatolian sphere of influence.[42] Consequently, according to these definitions, the lack of scraping, or of a particular gritty fabric, or of wheel or rope traces on the bottom, and of potmarks prevent conclusive identification of the sherds from Chatal with "Drab Ware." These standardized shapes may be related generally to the Anatolian region because they allow similarities with the Hattusha repertoire and because they slightly differ from earlier assemblages at Alalakh VII-IV.[43] However, several similarities of this repertoire to regional local assemblages may also suggest a well rooted local tradition rather than a relation with a general Anatolian pottery tradition.

In an attempt to identify distinctive pottery features which may be considered Anatolian as opposed to Syrian ones, and thus following Glatz, who identifies five "typical Anatolian shapes," it is only possible to point out two elements.[44] The miniature bowl is extremely similar to the piece from Chatal (**Fig. 2.3**) and "stepped" platters can be only identified in those shapes with squared and slightly angular rim (**Fig. 2.5**), but their relatively simple shape may be not distinctive. Besides these two shapes, the other platters with hooked internal rim, folded internal, or simply thickened internal rims found at Chatal are very standardized and common; their shape is identical both to Anatolian and Syrian pieces.[45]

Moreover, it is impossible to establish a direct connection between the Hittite conquest of the area and the massive use of apparently Anatolian pottery shapes. In 2001 Gates proposed an identification of this mass-produced limited standardized repertoire with the Tudhaliya conquest of Cilicia although in a recent article, these shapes seem to already be present at level 15 at Kinet, i.e. at a level which predates the Hittite conquest of the area.[46] In Tarsus these shapes suddenly appear "instead of the sharply profiled carinated bowls of LBI," so that they are directly connected with a Late Bronze II horizon.[47] At Kilise Tepe platters with inverted rims were found in the

[42] To my knowledge there is no clear or uniform description of this pottery class. However, on the one hand Goldman (1938, p. 36; 1937), who was the first to use this term for a specific Late Hittite Pottery class in Tarsus, does not mention scraping rather only a "brown to red ware" colour, chaff temper and varied grits (Goldman 1956, p. 203), while both Summers (1993, pl. 104) and Gates (1996, p. 294; 1997, p. 274; 2001) mention scraping and potmarks in connection with this pottery. Schoop 2006 has emphasized that "more than half of the drab ware pottery is still undistinguishable from older assemblages in terms of quality," so that this deterioration of the technical standard in the Hittite pottery concerns less than half of the whole production.

[43] The shapes 5 and 6a at Atchana are in part similar and were found in level Alalakh V and IV (Woolley 1955, p. 322 and pl. 109), the stepped or hooked incurving rims seems to be typical for the Anatolian region cf. Müller-Karpe 1988; Parzinger 1992, pl. 15, 16, 22, and not common in Syria.

[44] Glatz 2009, Fig. 2.

[45] Cf. Fischer 1963, pl. 83 and 100; Parzinger 1992, pl. 15, 22; Venturi 2010, fig. 6 and 8.

[46] Gates 2001; Gates 2006, p. 293.

[47] Goldman 1956, p. 203.

Late Bronze Age repertoire, although it should be noted here, that very similar shapes were also found in the EBA assemblage from the same site.[48]

At Chatal Höyük it is only possible to state that the simple ware class in phase M represents almost two-thirds of the whole repertoire. Among these, more than half of the shapes can be interpreted as related to Anatolian or of local traditions, but these shapes are, in any case, locally produced, that is, related to local fabric variations. Moreover, it is not possible to affirm on the basis of the Chatal assemblage, whether these shapes were also common in earlier levels (as is apparently the case at Kinet), or that they characterize only a later part of the LBA (as in Tell Afis and in Tarsus), because the earlier levels (underneath II_12) were not excavated. Thus, not only the idea of a strong Anatolian influence linkage and the political Hittite presence remains a hypothesis, but also the connection between the Hittite occupation of the area, which is certain, and an Anatolian influence on the material culture requires further research.[49] Only eight biconvex seals, some of which bear traces of hieroglyphs were found and are in general extremely similar to those found at Kilise Tepe.[50] A single bronze bull figurine found at Chatal Höyük may also in part support this Anatolian link.[51] On the other hand, the red burnished pottery sherds, which were collected in Phase M levels, cannot be definitely identified with red burnished Hittite pottery having no definitive similarities between either the shape or the surface treatment. Only one single red burnished spouted bowl, found in one of the trenches dug on the mound, can be interpreted as a typical "Hittite" red burnished production.[52]

From an architectural and stratigraphic point of view, it is possible to point out a change in the spatial organization of at least the southeastern part of the settlement, which took place during phase M. Here a massive structure was replaced by rural dwelling units with large open areas, where grain was kept and the dead were buried. Neither the massive structure nor the following buildings can be related to an Anatolian or non–Anatolian tradition, but this sequence may suggest only that rural elements could have experienced an insecure political situation during phase M and have moved to the town.[53] Before and after this change in the settlement, the material culture did not immediately change nor apparently did any foreign elements arrive, while the possible Anatolian tradition mentioned above remained predominant.[54]

48 Postgate and Thomas 2007, cf. LBA platter 616, fig. 388 with EBA platter 310, fig. 372.

49 For this problem cf. Venturi (this volume).

50 Postgate and Thomas 2007, nos. 1471, 1472, 1473 and 1475.

51 Neither the eight seals nor the figurine were found in phase M contexts, rather in later ones or on the surface.

52 This bowl (A26873) has long open spout, vertical stranded handle and high foot.

53 The only slope excavated down to this phase was located in Area II, where external erosion prevented the preservation of the mound walls for all levels. For this reason, it is not possible to state the existence of a mound wall during phase M.

54 Mitannian influence or presence is even less visible; a few Nuzi/Atchana imported wares (all body sherds except for one) and several Mitannian cylinder seals, which were found both in these levels

During the end of phase M and the beginning of phase N, no breaks are visible in the structural sequence, settlement levels gradually become denser, parallel with the sudden change in the pottery production; local painted pottery imitating the LH IIIC middle tradition starts to become the most commonly produced class. Besides determining the area of origin for the Late Helladic pottery imported to Chatal Höyük,[55] the main unresolved problem is an explanation of how it was possible that such a massive and sudden imitation of foreign pottery took place when the number of imported vessels of the same type was so low. It seems likely that only the arrival of external foreign elements can explain the massive local production of this kind of pottery. This theory dates back to beginning of the 20th century and has been partially reconsidered in recent times, not only in order to explain archaeological sets of data similar to the one at Chatal Höyük, but also as a consequence of recent discoveries of written documents.[56] Therefore, it seems possible that this pottery imitation was not connected to a general "influence" but to the local presence of "external peoples," who moved to the Amuq area. Furthermore, if this hypothesis is correct, then the structural evidence at Chatal Höyük suggests that the arrival of external people was not directly related to any break in the settlement but was subsequent to a change in urban density, i.e. "foreign," possibly eastern Mediterranean people arriving in a period of urban shrinkage and population decrease. This new population settled down, mixing with the local traditions, and started a new local tradition of painted, decorated pottery which continued during the whole of phases N and O, i.e. until the 6th century BC.

In conclusion, although the political implications suggested by the Chatal Höyük materials remain hypothetical, the material clearly shows the manifold cultural elements, which during different periods affected a secondary and provincial town in a region, and not only experienced different political powers, but was also at the border between different cultures.

LIST OF WORK CITED

ÅSTRÖM, P.
1972 *The Late Cypriot Bronze Age Architecture and Pottery,* The Swedish Cyprus Expedition: IV part 1C. Lund: The Swedish Cyprus Expedition.

BADRE, L.
2006 "Tell Kazel-Simyra: A Contribution to a Relative Chronological History in the Eastern Mediterranean during the Late Bronze Age," *Bulletin of the American Schools of Oriental Research* 343: 45–75.

belonging to phase M and in the later ones. Probably the structural levels belonging to the Mitannian period at Chatal are still to be excavated.

[55] For this problem see Venturi 2007, pp. 406–407, who suggest a Aegean origin.

[56] Venturi 2010; Niemeier 2001; Liverani 1987; Hawkins 2009; also Janeway 2008.

BRAIDWOOD, R. J.
1937 *Mounds in the Plain of Antioch an Archaeological Survey,* OIP 48. Chicago: Chicago University Press.
BRAIDWOOD, R. J., and BRAIDWOOD, L. S.
1960 *Excavations in the Plain of Antioch I,* OIP 61. Chicago: Chicago University Press.
ERIKSSON, K.
1993 *Red Lustrous Wheel-made Ware,* SIMA 103. Jonsered: Paul Åströms Förlag.
2007 *The Creative Independence of Late Bronze Age Cyprus: An Account of the Archaeological Importance of White Slip Ware,* Denkschriften der Gesamtakademie 38. Wien: Österreichische Akademie der Wissenschaften.
FISCHER, F.
1963 *Die Hethitische Keramik von Bogazköy,* WVDOG 75. Berlin: Mann.
FISHER, P. M.
1999 "Chocolate-on-White Ware: Typology, Chronology and Provenance. The Evidence from Tell Abu al-Kharaz, Jordan Valley ," *Bulletin of the American Schools of Oriental Research* 313: 1–29.
FRENCH, E.
2007 "Late Helladic III C Middle at Mycenae ," *LH III C Chronology and Synchronisms,* Veröff. der Mykenischen Kommission Band 28, edited by S. Deger-Jalkotzy and M. Zavadil, pp. 175–188. Wien: Österreichische Akademie der Wissenschaften.
FURUMARK, A.
1941 *Mycenaean Pottery I: Analysis and Classification.* Stockholm: Kungliga Vitterhets Historie och Antikvitets Akademien.
GATES, M. H.
1996 "Archaeology in Turkey," *American Journal of Archaeology* 100: 277–335.
1997 "Archaeology in Turkey," *American Journal of Archaeology* 101: 241–305.
2001 "Potmarks at Kinet Höyük and the Hittite Ceramic Industry," *La Cilicie: espaces et pouvoirs locaux (2e millénaire av. J.C. 4e siècle ap. J.C.). Actes de la table ronde Internationale d'Istanbul,* Varia Anatolica 13, edited by E. Jean, A. M. Dinçol, S. Durugönül, pp. 137–158. Istanbul and Paris: Institut français d'études anatoliennes.
2006 "Dating the Hittite Levels at Kinet Höyük: a Revised Chronology," *Structuring and Dating in Hittite Archaeology,* BYZAS 4, edited by D. P. Mielke, J. Schoop, U. D. Seeher, pp. 293–309. Istanbul: Ege Yayınları.
GEVIRTZ, S.
1967 "A Spindle Whorl with Phoenician Inscription," *Journal of Near Eastern Studies* 26: 13–16.
GILBOA, A. and SHARON, I.
2003 "An archaeological Contribution to the Early Iron Age Chronological Debate: Alternative Chronologies for Phoenicia and their Effects on the Levant, Cyprus and Greece," *Bulletin of the American Schools of Oriental Research* 332: 7–80.
GLATZ, C.
2009 "Empire as Network: Spheres of material interaction in Late Bronze Age Anatolia," *Journal of Anthropological Archaeology* 28: 127–141.
GOLDMAN, H. ed.
1956 *Excavations at Gözlü Kule, Tarsus. Vol. II: From the Neolithic through the Bronze Age.* Princeton: Princeton University Press.

GOLDMAN, H.
1937 "Excavations at Gözlü Kule, Tarsus, 1936," *American Journal of Archaeology* 41: 262–286.
1938 "Excavations at Gözlü Kule, Tarsus , 1937," *American Journal of Archaeology* 42: 30–54.
HAINES, R. C.
1971 *Excavations in the Plain of Antioch II: the Structural Remains of the Later Phases,* OIP 95. Chicago: Chicago University Press.
HARRISON, T. P.
2010 "The Late Bronze/Early Iron Age Transition in the North Orontes Valley," *Societies in Transition. Papers presented on the occasion of the 20th Anniversary of the new Excavations in Tell Afis*, Studi e Testi Orientali 9, edited by F. Venturi, pp. 83–102. Bologna: Clueb.
HAWKINS, J. D.
2009 "New Light in a Dark Age," *Near Eastern Archaeology* 72: 164–173.
HENDRIX R. E., PHILIP R. D., BJØRNAR J. S.
1997 *Ancient Pottery of Transjordan*, Berrien Springs: Institute of Archaeology/Horn Archaeological Museum.
JANEWAY, B.
2008 "The Nature and Extent of Aegean Contact at Tell Tayinat and Vicinity in the Early Iron Age: evidence of the Sea Peoples?," *Scripta Mediterranea* 27–28: 123–146.
KILLEBREW, A. E., GOLDBERG, P. and ROSEN, A. M.
2006 "Deir el-Balah: A Geological, Archaeological and Historical Reassessment of an Egyptianizing 13th and 12th Century BCE Center," *Bulletin of the American Schools of Oriental Research* 343: 97–19.
KROGMAN, W. M.
1949 "Ancient cranial types at Chatal Höyük and Tell al Judaidah," *Belleten* XIII: 407–477.
LEHMANN, G.
2008 "Decorated Pottery Styles in the Northern Levant during the Early Iron Age and their Relationship with Cyprus and the Aegean," *Ugarit Forschungen* 39: 487–550.
LEVENSON, J. D.
1973 "The Spindle Whorl Inscription from Chatal Höyük: a Forgery," *Bulletin of the American Schools of Oriental Research* 209: 37–40.
LIVERANI, M.
1987 "The Collapse of the Near Eastern Regional System at the End of the Bronze Age: the Case of Syria," *Centre and Periphery in the Ancient World,* edited by M. Rowlands, M. Larsen, K. Kristiansen, pp. 66–73. Cambridge: Cambridge University Press.
MANNING, S. W., MONKS, S. J., STEEL, L., RIBEIRO, E. and WEINSTEIN, J. M.
1998 "Late Cypriot Tombs at Maroni Tsaroukkas, Cyprus," *The Annual of the British School at Athens* 93: 297–351.
MCEWAN, C. W.
1937 "The Syrian expedition of the oriental institute of the University of Chicago," *American Journal of Archaeology* 41: 8–13.
MEYER, J.-W.
2008 *Die eisenzeitlichen Stempelsiegel aus dem 'Amuq-Gebiet: Ein Beitrag zur Ikonographie altorientalischer Siegelbilder,* OBO 28. Freiburg: Academic Press Fribourg.

MOUNTJOY, P. A.
1986 *Mycenaean Decorated Pottery: a Guide to Identification,* Studies in Mediterranean Archaeology 73, Goteborg: Paul Åströms Förlag.
1999 "Late Minoan IIIC/Late Helladic IIIC: Chronology and Terminology,"*Melemata. Studies in Aegean Archaeology presented to Malcom H. Wiener as He enters His 65. Year,* Aegeum 20, edited by P. Betancourt, V. Karageorghis, R. Laffineur and W.-D. Niemeier, pp. 511–516. Liège: Université de Liège
2005 "The Mycenaean Pottery from the 1934–1939 Excavations at Tarsus," *Field Season 2001-2003 of the Tarsus-Gözlükule Interdisciplinary Research Project,* edited by A. Öyzar, pp. 83–134. Istanbul: Ege Yayınları.
2007 "A Definition of LH III C Middle," *LH III C Chronology and Synchronisms,* Veröff. der Mykenischen Kommission Band 28, edited by S. Deger-Jalkotzy and M. Zavadil, pp. 221–242. Wien: Österreichische Akademie der Wissenschaften.
MÜLLER-KARPE, A.
1988 *Hethitische Töpferei der Oberstadt von Hattusha,* Marburger Studien zur Vor- und Frühgeschichte 10. Marburg: Lahn.
NIEMEIER, W.-D.
2001 "Archaic Greeks in the Orient: Textual and Archaeological Evidence," *Bulletin of the American Schools of Oriental Research* 322: 11–32.
PARZINGER, H.
1992 *Die Oberstadt von Hattuša. Hethitische Keramik aus dem zentralen Tempelviertel,* Boğazköy-Hattuša. Ergebnisse der Ausgrabung 15. Berlin: Gebr. Mann.
POSTGATE, N. and THOMAS, D. eds.
2007 *Excavations at Kilise Tepe, 1994-98,* BIAA Monograph 30. Oxford: Oxbow Books.
PUCCI, M.
2010 "The Chatal Höyük Publication Project: a work in progress," *Proceedings of the 6th International Congress on the Archaeology of the Ancient Near East, vol. 2,* edited by P. Matthiae et al., pp. 567–580. Wiesbaden: Harassowitz.
SCHOOP, U.-D.
2006 "Dating the Hittites with Statistics: Ten Pottery Assemblages from Bogazköy-Hattusa," *Structuring and Dating in Hittite Archaeology,* BYZAS 4, edited by D. P. Mielke, U.-D. Schoop, J. Seeher, pp. 215–240. Istanbul: Ege Yayınları.
SUMMERS, G.
1993 *Tille Hoyuk 4: The Late Bronze Age and the Iron Age Transitions,* British Institute of Archaeology at Ankara Monographs 15. Ankara: David Brown Book Co.
SWIFT, G.
1958 "The Pottery of the Amuq Phases K to O, and its Historical Relationships." Unpublished dissertation, University of Chicago.
VENTURI, F.
2007 *La Siria nell'età delle trasformazioni,* Studi e Testi orientali 8. Bologna: Clueb.
2010 "Cultural Breakdown or Evolution? The impact of Change in 12th Century BC Tell Afis," *Societies in Transition, papers presented on the occasion of the 20th Anniversary of the new Excavations in Tell Afis,* Studi e Testi Orientali 9, edited by F. Venturi, pp. 1–27. Bologna: Clueb.
WOOLLEY, L.
1955 *Alalakh. An Account on the excavations at Tell Atchana in the Hatay, 1937–1949,* Reports of the Research Committee of the Society of Antiquaries of London 18. Oxford: Oxford University Press.

YENER, A. ed.
2005 *The Amuq Valley Regional Projects, Volume 1: Surveys in the Plain of Antioch and Orontes Delta, Turkey, 1995-2002,* OIP 131. Chicago: The University of Chicago Press.

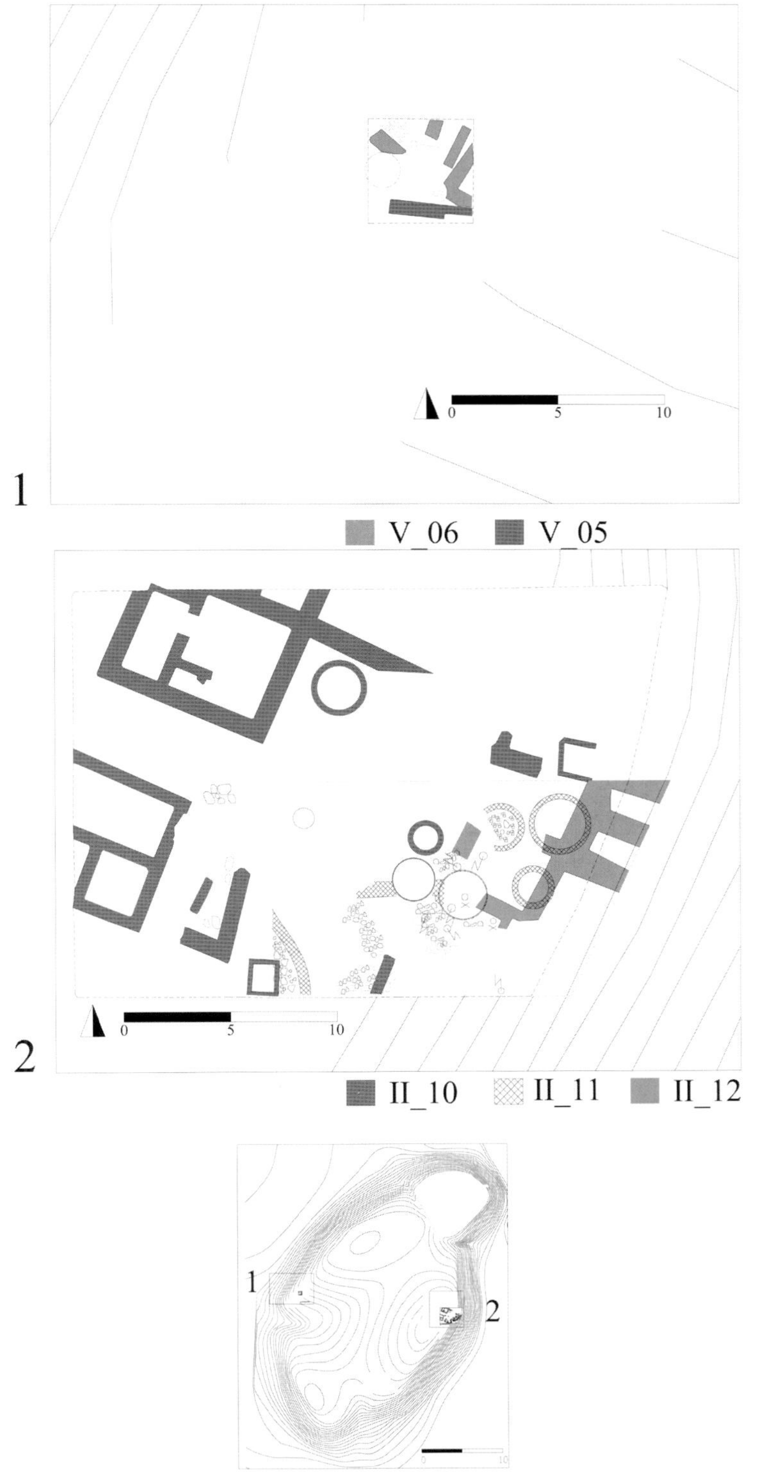

Fig. 1 Phase M. Structural Remains from Area V (1.1) and II (1.2). Adapted from Haines 1971: pl. 29 and 37.

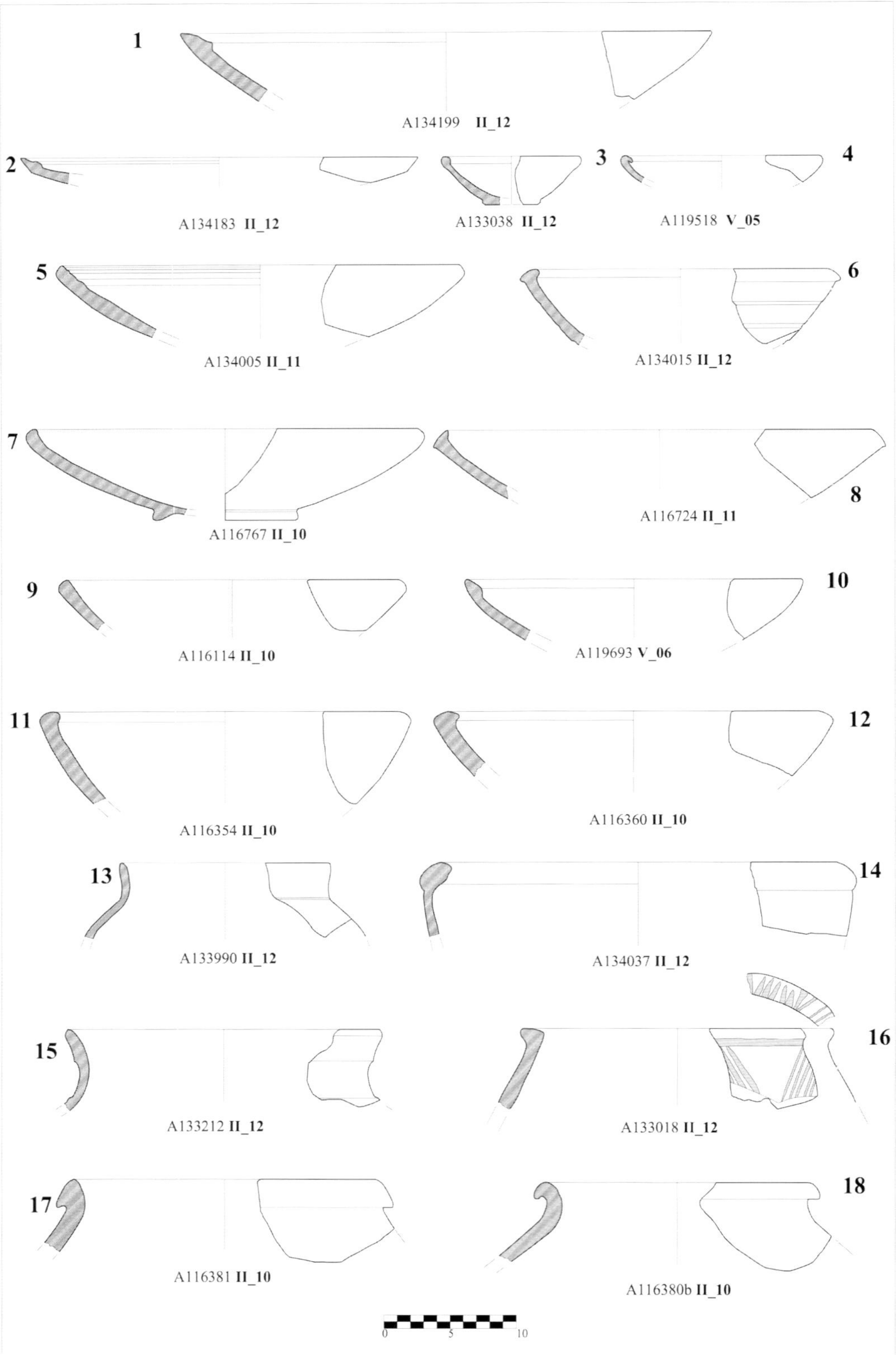

Fig. 2 Phase M, pottery assemblage. The locus is indicated in bold under each sherd. Grey hatch = red paint. Scale 1:5.

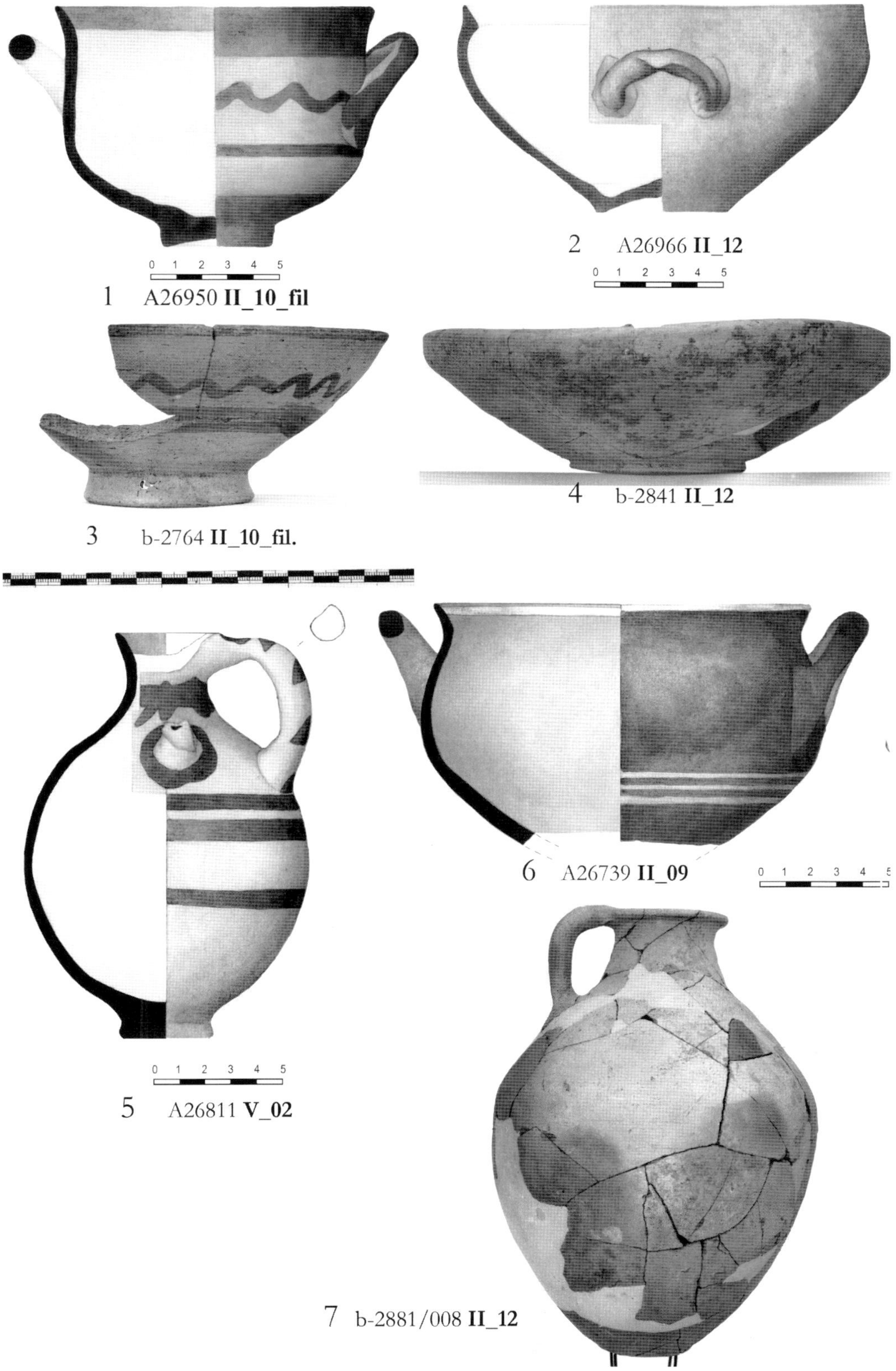

Fig. 3 Drawings and photo of complete vessels.
Drawings A26950, A26966 and A26811 (T. d'Este) in scale 1:5;
pictures b-2764, b-2841 and b-2881 are from original negatives of the excavations.

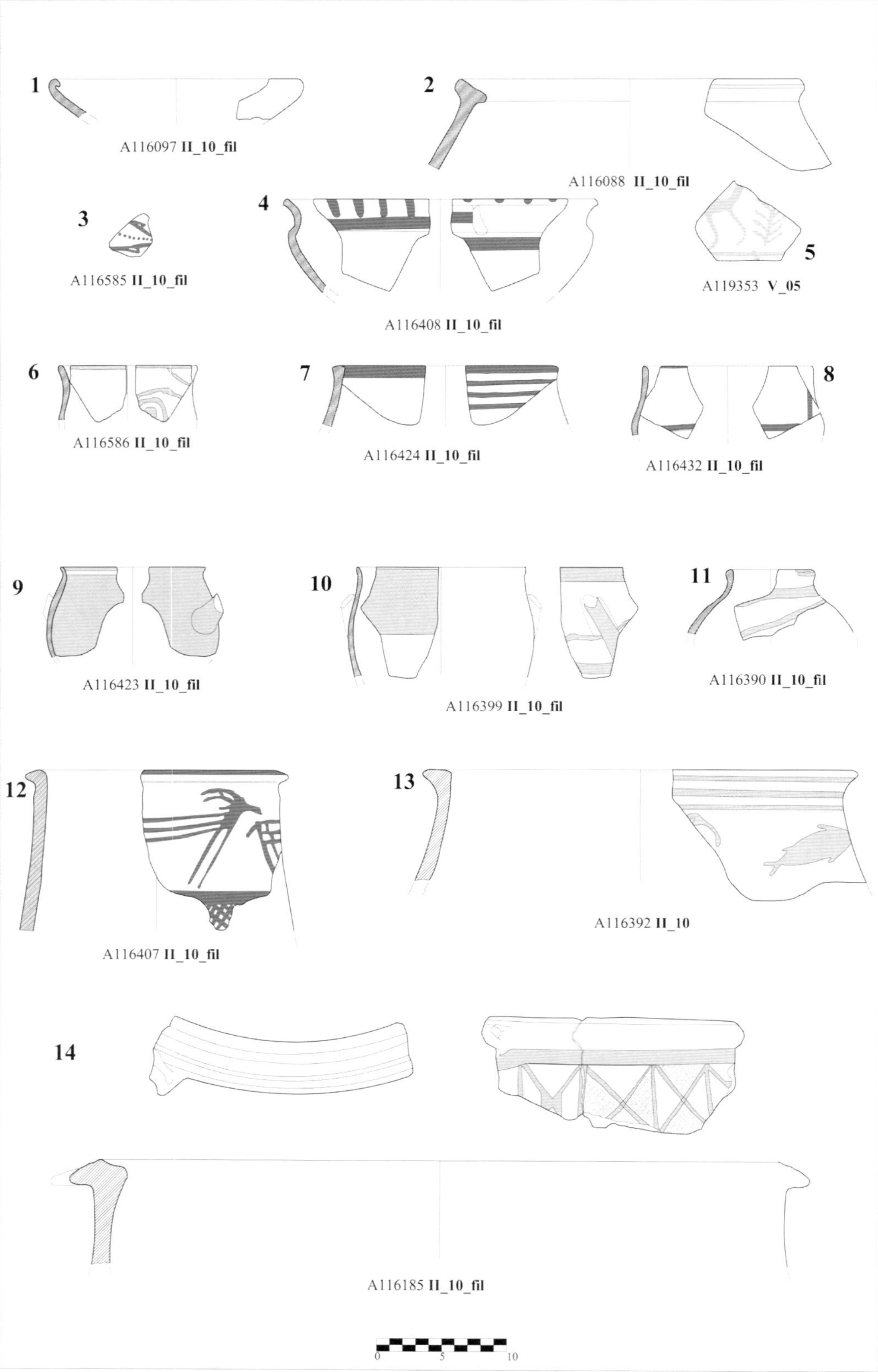

Fig. 4 Phase M/N, pottery assemblage. The locus is indicated in bold under each sherd. Black hatch = black paint, grey hatch = red paint. Scale 1:5.

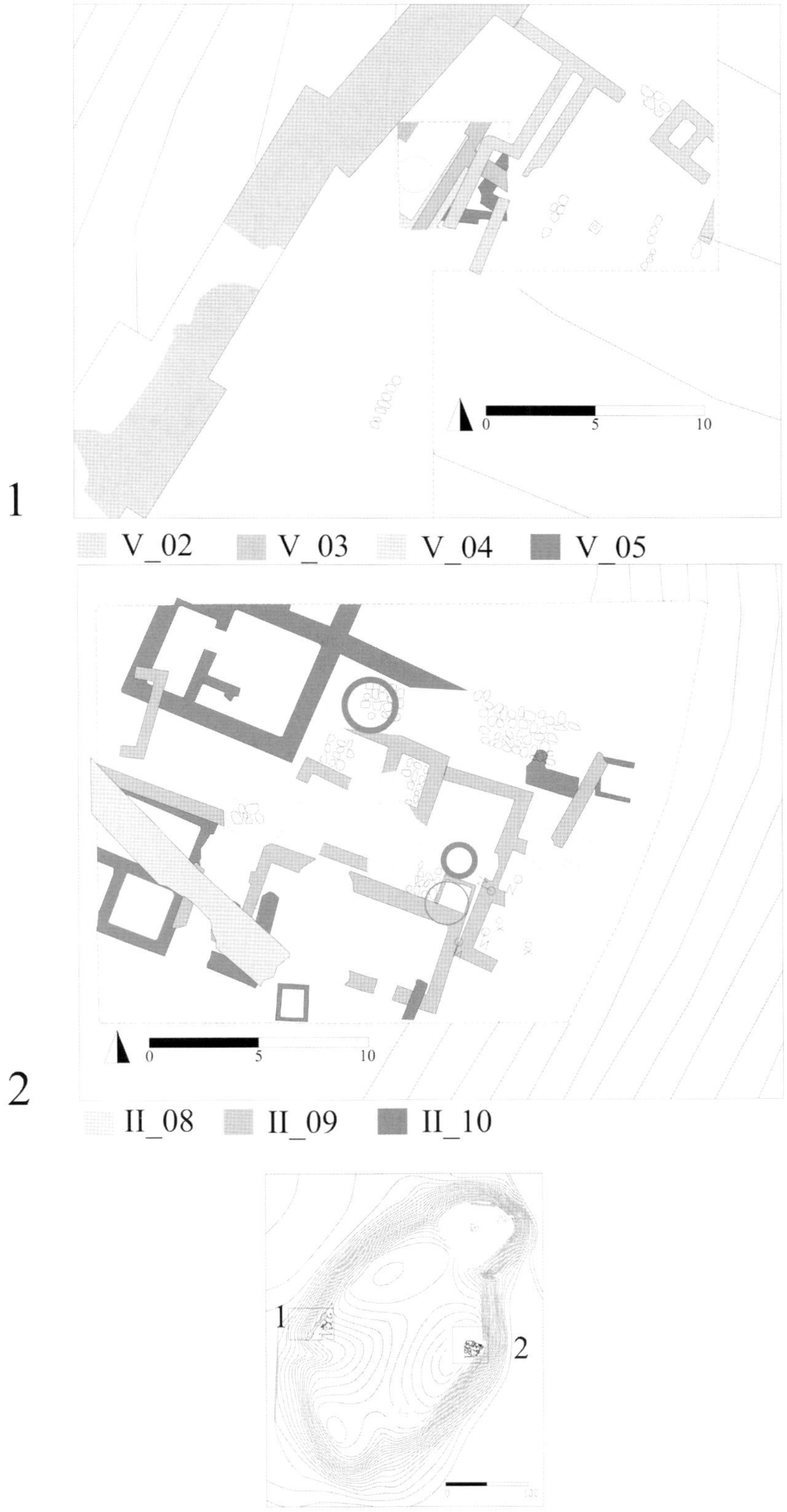

Fig. 5 Phase N. Structural Remains from Area V (top) and II (bottom). Adapted from Haines 1971: pl. 29 and 37.

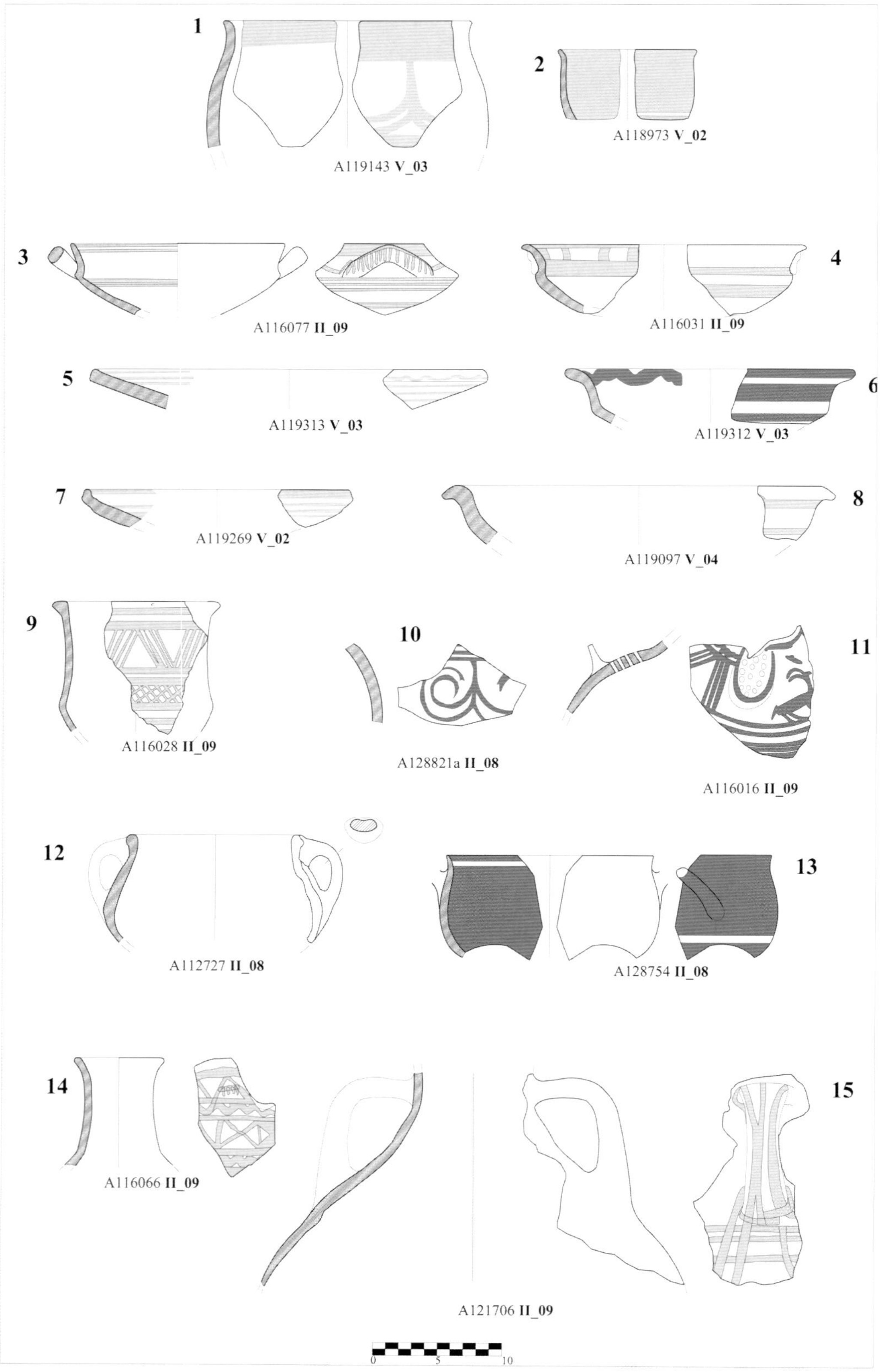

Fig. 6 Phase N, pottery assemblage. The locus is indicated in bold under each sherd. Black hatch = black paint, grey hatch = red paint. Scale 1:5.

CHAPTER 5

THE CRISIS OF QATNA AT THE BEGINNING OF THE LATE BRONZE AGE II AND THE IRON AGE II SETTLEMENT REVIVAL. A REGIONAL TRAJECTORY TOWARDS THE COLLAPSE OF THE LATE BRONZE AGE PALACE SYSTEM IN THE NORTHERN LEVANT

Daniele MORANDI BONACOSSI
Director, Archaeological Mission
of the University of Udine to Mishrifeh/Qatna
Dipartimento di Storia e Tutela dei Beni Culturali
Università degli Studi di Udine
Vicolo Florio 2/B
33100 Udine - Italy
E-mail: daniele.morandi@uniud.it

ABSTRACT

The paper explores the urban layout and organization of the city of Qatna during the LBA, focusing on the Royal Palace and the system of subsidiary palaces surrounding it (Lower City Palace and Southern Palace) and the domestic architecture in the upper and lower towns excavated up to now. The crisis that affected the site at the beginning of the LBA II and the continuation of life at the settlement until the end of the LBA are also investigated. The archaeological evidence indicates that the following Early Iron Age marks a break in the occupational continuity at the site, which appears to be settled again only from the end of the Iron Age I and the beginning of the Iron Age II onwards within a radically changed political, socio-economic and cultural context. *

* Acknowledgements. I am deeply indebted to Aslıhan Yener (Koç University, Istanbul) for inviting me to the inspiring conference on Late Bronze-Iron Age relations between Syria and Anatolia and for supplying new information concerning the chronology and stratigraphy of the late phases of Alalakh based upon recent results from her project. I would like to acknowledge the help and support of Graham Philip (University of Durham) and Karin Bartl (DAI, Damascus), who discussed the results of their own surveys in the Homs and Middle Orontes Regions with me. I also benefitted greatly from the discussions on the palaeography of the newly excavated texts from the Lower City Palace that I had with Jesper Eidem (The Netherlands Institute for the Near East, Leiden) and on Middle and Late Bronze Age Egyptian scarabs imported into Syria that I had with Vanessa Boschloos (Royal Museums of Art and History, Brussels) and Alexander Ahrens (DAI, Damascus). Finally, I am grateful to The Oriental Institute Museum (University of Chicago) and the Director of The Oriental Institute, Prof. Gil J. Stein, for having given me photographs of the colossal head from Tell Ta'yinat together with permission to publish them in this article.

The perspective on the occupation, crisis, and revitalization of the site is broadened by an analysis of the changes in the settlement system between the second and first millennia BC in the area directly surrounding Mishrifeh/Qatna, as well as in the wider region of the Middle Orontes Valley.

Introduction

Archaeological and historical research during recent decades has shown that the structural crisis and collapse of Late Bronze Age centralized state bureaucracies in the Northern Levant was the result of the complex interplay of various political, economic, social, environmental, and ethnic factors and has emphasized the role played by dynamics inherent in the system, rather than calling on external disruptive factors.[1]

In academic debate, the disintegration of palace economies as the consequence of the systemic collapse, or rather failure, of the palace system itself has often been explored as a basically sudden, synchronous, and uniform development, which occurred in a short time lapse, the early 12th century BC, and affected the entire Levantine and Anatolian world. It is clear that the roots of the crisis, however, were remote and deeply seated in the historical and cultural context of the preceding centuries and their regional peculiarities.[2] This paper aims to bring into focus more sharply the regionally and chronologically heterogeneous and diversified character of the breakdown process of Late Bronze centralized administrations in the Northern Levant. An examination of the settlement history of Mishrifeh/Qatna and the Middle Orontes Valley (central-western, inner Syria) during the Late Bronze and Iron Ages (**Fig. 1**) and comparison with those documented in other regions of the Northern Levant makes clear the way in which the system's collapse was the collective consequence of markedly different trajectories with regionally diversified genesis, pace, and outcome. The use of a generalized and synchronous framework for the analysis of the crisis and collapse of the Late Bronze palace system is misleading and risks overshadowing the regional particularities and the complexity of this multifaceted process.

Qatna during the Late Bronze Age

After the pioneering explorations conducted in the 1920s by Count Robert du Mesnil du Buisson,[3] the new excavation project conducted since 1999 by the Syrian, German-Syrian, and Italian-Syrian Missions at Mishrifeh/Qatna has radically

[1] Marfoe 1979; Liverani 1987 and 2001; Neumann and Parpola 1987; essays in Ward and Sharp Joukowsky 1992; Oren 2000; Venturi 2007 and 2010; Kaniewski *et al.* 2010; Gates 2010; Harrison 2010.

[2] See also McClellan 1992, p. 170; Venturi 2007, pp. 381–383; de Martino 2009, pp. 21–22.

[3] Du Mesnil du Buisson 1926, 1927, 1930 and 1935.

changed our understanding of the urban organization of the ancient city of Qatna during the Late Bronze and Iron Ages.[4] Firstly, the archaeological evidence concerning Qatna's urban layout and its development between the mid second and the early first millennia BC will be reviewed in the light of recent archaeological excavations; while in the second part of the paper, the change of settlement patterns in the Mishrifeh region and the Middle Orontes Valley from the Late Bronze to the Iron Age will be considered.

In the long urban history of Mishrifeh, which started with the first mid-sized Early Bronze IV urban centre,[5] the end of the Middle Bronze and the early Late Bronze Age constitutes a crucial phase in the city's urban development and in the shaping of its image as a royal capital. Over a span of a few centuries, a centralized programme of public and institutional building was accomplished involving both the upper and lower cities. The core of this endeavour was the construction of an imposing new Royal Palace next to the northern scarp of the acropolis terrace dominating the northern lower city at the end of the Middle Bronze II, which remained in use until its final destruction in a fierce conflagration around 1340 BC (**Figs. 2–3**).[6] This huge building of about 142 × 90 m (1.3 ha) exhibits in its plan a combination of elements characteristic of the western Syrian tradition,[7] together with typically Syro-Mesopotamian features. The latter are evident in the layout of the exceptionally monumental ceremonial and reception suite consisting of a large colonnaded audience chamber (Hall C) with access to the throne room (Hall B) and a second, even more imposing ceremonial chamber (Hall A), probably dedicated to the royal ancestor cult,[8] from which an underground corridor led to the royal burial chambers.[9] The typological similarities between the plan of the reception unit of the Royal Palace of Qatna and Courtyard 106 and Rooms 64 and 65 of the so-called palace of Zimri-Lim at Mari are clear.[10]

The palace was not only vast, but also lavishly furnished. Several rooms around the reception suite were decorated with wall paintings featuring Aegean-like motifs, such as those found in the Late Minoan IA Aegean sites and the Levantine palaces of Alalakh VII, Tell Kabri, and Tell el-Dab'a.[11] The presence in diverse wings of the Royal Palace of wall paintings that were very close to Aegean examples in technique,

[4] Morandi Bonacossi 2007a; Pfälzner 2007 and 2009a; Al-Maqdissi and Morandi Bonacossi 2009a and 2009b; Morandi Bonacossi 2009a and 2009b.

[5] Morandi Bonacossi 2007a, 2008a, 2008b and 2009c.

[6] On the palace and its chronology, see Novák 2004, Morandi Bonacossi 2007b; Pfälzner 2007 and 2009a.

[7] Absence of large courtyards, widespread use of basalt orthostats, wood and columns, hypostyle halls, galleries, presence of a royal hypogeum.

[8] Pfälzner 2005 and 2007, p. 50.

[9] Al-Maqdissi *et al.* 2003; Pfälzner 2007, pp. 55–69 and 2009b.

[10] Parrot 1958.

[11] Pfälzner (in collaboration with Constance von Rüden) 2008; von Rüden 2009.

style and iconography[12] indicates that the Qatna court, along with those of the other Syro-Palestinian regional states, participated in the far-flung network of long-distance trade and inter-palace prestige relations that connected the mid-second millennium eastern Mediterranean and the Levant as far as the Nile Delta.[13] Broad evidence of this is also provided by the Egyptian and Egyptianizing imagery abundantly present in seals and sealings, ivories, precious metalwork, and stone vessels from the palace and the royal hypogeum.[14]

The area occupied by the representative Royal Palace unit (4500 sq m) constituted a third of that of the entire building, thus leaving only a relatively limited space for other functions such as administrative, residential and storage units. This may have been one of the reasons which determined the elaboration of a system of two subsidiary palaces surrounding the north and south of the Royal Palace during the Late Bronze I, which was the actual pivot of the city's political and economic power.

Less well known, but of particular interest, is the 'Lower City Palace' (**Figs. 4–5**),[15] a vast and well-structured building, not yet fully excavated, known at present to contain more than 60 rooms and cover over 2200 sq m.[16] This large building with at least three main phases of use (K 14-K 12) shows the typical hallmarks of second-millennium palace architecture with an entrance unit (Room I, Courtyard J and Room S), which was partly decorated (Room S) with Aegean-like wall paintings similar to those found in the Royal Palace. These rooms lead to a reception suite with the same thick concrete floors found in the Royal Palace, consisting of a large hall (F) and a throne room (D) with a column base in the centre of the entrance (**Fig. 6**). The reception unit was flanked to the north and south by service wings with a cellar for beverages (H), a bathroom (M), kitchens (C and Q), and storage rooms where numerous earthenware cooking vessels were found (AA and U). To the north of the reception suite a vast Courtyard (V) was located in the eastern part of which were three large ovens. These were probably used to cook large quantities of food, which might have been consumed during communal meals in the nearby monumental hall F and could be reached through Rooms U, AA, and throne room D. The courtyard was bounded

[12] Large numbers of wall painting fragments were found not only in Room N in the northern wing of the palace, but also in the debris of the eastern wing of the building, suggesting that rooms decorated with Aegean-like wall paintings existed in an upper storey of the palace situated above the ground floor storage rooms.

[13] Caubet 1998; Feldman 2006 and 2007; Fischer 2007.

[14] Dohmann-Pfälzner 2009; Turri 2009; Pfälzner 2009c; Roßberger 2009; Ahrens 2009.

[15] Luciani 2006a, pp. 404–406; Morandi Bonacossi 2009a and Morandi Bonacossi in press.

[16] According to the preliminary results of a geoelectric prospection conducted in 2010, however, the building seems to cover an area approximately double that excavated so far (the geophysical survey was conducted in cooperation with the *Istituto Nazionale di Oceanografia e di Geofisica Sperimentale* of Trieste as part of the project "ARCHAEOIMAGE. Archaeological excavations and geophysical survey work at Mishrifeh/Qatna," funded by the Friuli Venezia Giulia Regional Administration; grant no. 454/ LAVFOR/2009).

to the N by a large storage room (AB), where two parallel rows of circular depressions for storage vessels were found. In the heart of the palace, therefore, a large group of spatially and functionally connected rooms was devoted to ceremonial functions, possibly including communal feasting and service functions such as food and drink storage, cooking, warehousing earthenware vessels, and bathrooms.

All the rooms of the southern wing of the reception suite (E, G, H, L-N) were beautifully decorated with red-painted lime plasters. In the entrance and reception units several doorways were ornamented with basalt orthostats and the walls were built with the half-timber construction technique also found in the Alalakh IV palace[17] and probably also widely employed in Qatna's Royal Palace.[18]

The last phase of use of the building (K 12) contained valuable late Middle Cypriot and especially Late Cypriot ceramics imported from the eastern Mediterranean[19] and Late Helladic IIIA2 Mycenaean pottery from the Argolis.[20] Over a thousand pieces of durable animal material inlays, mainly elephant ivory, but also antler and bone[21] belonging to Phase K 12 were found scattered in several rooms of the palace (R, Y, BJ). At least part of these were originally antler wall decorations, which fell onto the building's floors during the collapse of the mud-brick walls. On the floors and in the fill of the Phase 12 and 13 rooms, copper/bronze objects such as toggle pins, needles, tools were found, as well as weapons such as arrows and spearheads and a chariot wheel-hub cover. Other finds were a piece of gold sheet, together with many vitreous beads, administrative documents such as numerous cuneiform tablets connected with food deliveries for the workforce, military and animals (R, T, AE, Y and BA),[22] seals and clay sealings (A, G, K, T, AE), and an *in situ* steatite scarab with its gold mount from the floor of Room AC in the northern part of the building, which bears an inscription with the royal title and epithets of Amenhotep III (*c.* 1390–1352 BC).[23]

This is not the place for a detailed discussion of the architecture, stratigraphy, and chronology of this interesting and important building.[24] For the purpose of this article, it suffices to say that whereas the Royal Palace was destroyed around the mid-14th century BC in a devastating blaze, the Lower City Palace (Phase K 12) was abandoned in the same period and probably under the same general circumstances, but

[17] Woolley 1955, pp. 126, 224–226, fig. 71 and pl. XXVIIb.

[18] In the few parts of the palace, where standing mud-brick walls are preserved, such as some of the eastern palace wall, the use of wooden beams to strengthen the brickwork has been recorded in the archaeological excavation conducted by the Italian team.

[19] Few sherds of Red-on-Black, White Painted V-VI, White Painted IV-VI Cross Line Style and White Slip I and a larger amount of White Slip II and Base Ring I ceramic fragments cf Luciani 2008.

[20] As was demonstrated by NAA analyses conducted on several Mycenaean sherds at the University of Bonn by H. Mommsen and R. Jung.

[21] Luciani 2006a and Luciani 2006b; Morandi Bonacossi 2008c; Turri 2009 and Turri in press.

[22] Eidem 2003, 2007 and 2009.

[23] The scarab was identified by Vanessa Boschloos (Royal Museums of Art and History, Brussels).

[24] For a more detailed presentation of the Lower City Palace, see Morandi Bonacossi in press.

without suffering a similarly traumatic event. As for the preceding Phase 13 of the Lower City Palace, it would seem reasonable to propose a date in the early 14th century, before the LH IIIA2 phase Mycenaean ceramics start to appear in the region (*c.* 1375 BC).[25] Such dating is suggested by the local ceramic materials, the absence of Late Helladic IIIA2 period Mycenaean pottery, numerous fragments of which, on the other hand, have been recovered from the following phase, and the discovery of a scarab of Amenhotep III, which should be considered to be most probably contemporary with its context. Still uncertain is the chronology of the earliest phase of use of the Lower City Palace (K 14); more excavation and further study of the, as-yet limited, related pottery assemblages are needed. For the time being, however, a preliminary dating of the first phase of use of the palace to the 15th century BC based on the pottery, clay sealings, and the palaeography of a fragmentary cuneiform tablet recovered from Room AE[26] seems reasonable.

However, what is relevant for the present article is that with the construction of the Lower City Palace, which probably took place over a century after the erection of the massive Royal Palace, we are confronted with the appearance in Qatna's urban and functional layout of a large and important building erected in the northern lower city at the foot of the upper town close to the Royal Palace and directly facing the northern city gate. The palace has already furnished ample evidence that reception, administrative, economic, residential, and possibly even production activities were centred there. Although the identity of the owner whether the person or institution of the Lower City Palace is as-yet unknown, the building's extension, the well-structured organization of its representative suite according to the characteristic canons of second millennium BC Syrian palace architecture, and its lavish decoration[27] are all elements that suggest that the Lower City Palace had a special and important function within the city's organization and that it was the seat of a prominent authority and figure, possibly a major member of Qatna's royal family. This is confirmed by the richness of the materials recovered from its last phase of use[28] such as the presence in it of administrative paraphernalia[29] and "Aegyptiaca," especially the Amenhotep III scarab, possibly a diplomatic gift of the Pharaoh to the building's owner, notwithstanding the cleaning out of the building that must have taken place before its abandonment.

In Levantine Late Bronze urban centres, the presence of a royal household fed the need for prestigious objects[30] and Qatna's location on important commercial routes explains the presence of high status imported goods. Therefore, it is not surprising to

[25] Mountjoy 1993.
[26] Jesper Eidem, personal communication.
[27] Basalt orthostats, columns, Aegean-style figured wall paintings, painted plaster, and antler wall decorations.
[28] Fine imported pottery, ivory, antler, bone inlays, and metal objects.
[29] Seals and sealings and cuneiform tablets with administrative content.
[30] Feldman 2006; Heinz 2009.

find sumptuous ornaments such as antler wall decorations, an Egyptian royal scarab, and other rich materials in the Lower City Palace, which might have been a building that, besides its other functions,[31] was also used to store foreign gifts or was a diplomatic reception area.[32] The possibility that some imported goods and diplomatic gifts were stored in the Lower City Palace[33] after they had been received in the Royal Palace cannot be excluded.

In about the same period, immediately to the south of the Royal Palace, the 'Southern Palace' was constructed; it was a smaller building with about twenty rooms and the same concrete floors and half-timber construction technique seen in the Royal and Lower City Palaces.[34] To the south of the building, a further room possibly pertaining to it was found which contained the basalt bases of four columns.[35] From this building the small basalt statuette of a sitting bareheaded man, probably representing an ancestor figurine, was recovered.[36] Unfortunately, the Southern Palace's fragmentary state of preservation, the heavy Iron Age II overburden, and the substantial lack of archaeological materials from this building, which had been carefully emptied and cleaned before its abandonment in around the mid-14th century BC, preclude a more accurate dating of its construction or the functional interpretation of the surviving rooms. However, judging from its layout, the size of some of its rooms, the quality of the installations,[37] lime plasters and concrete floors, and the presence of the small basalt ancestor statue, it would appear plausible that this structure had an official administrative and residential function.

The destruction of the Royal Palace around 1340 BC during the reign of King Idanda, against the general background of the Syrian military campaigns of the Hittite king Shuppiluliuma I (the "six-year-campaign") as indicated by the cuneiform sources, constituted a major, dramatic break in the history of the city.[38] Roughly at the same time the Royal Palace was destroyed, the whole system of Late Bronze palaces at

[31] For instance, its location and proximity to the northern city gate might suggest that the building was also used to control the in- and outflow of goods and persons through this gate.

[32] For example, in Tell Kazel the walls and floors of some rooms of a large 13th century public building (Building II) on the acropolis were decorated with shells. These rooms have been interpreted as a unit of the building used to receive or accommodate diplomatic guests, who needed to be impressed by the richness of the local court cf Capet 2003, figs. 13, 25; Badre 2006, p. 80 and fig. 11. The same kind of shell floor covering is also known from another Levantine palace context, namely that of the Strata VIII and VIIB palace at Megiddo dating to the 15th–13th centuries BC cf Loud 1948, figs. 50, 52.

[33] Possibly in Room AC, where the Amenhotep III scarab was found together with numerous vitreous-material beads and also a piece of gold sheeting. The presence in this room of precious and high-status objects might suggest that this was the "treasury" of the palace.

[34] Al-Maqdissi 2003a, pp. 1500–1505 and Al-Maqdissi 2003b, pp. 235–239.

[35] Al-Maqdissi 2003a, p. 1502.

[36] Al-Maqdissi 2007.

[37] Such as the doorway thresholds and the toilet contained in a room.

[38] On the possible historical and political background of the palace blaze, see the two different scenarios depicted by Novák-Pfälzner 2003, pp. 133–135 (destruction of the Royal Palace of Qatna by Shuppiluliuma's army) and Richter 2002, pp. 614–616 and Richter 2003, pp. 168–171 and 178–182,

Qatna fell into disuse. Both of the subsidiary palaces, the Lower City Palace, and the Southern Palace were abandoned during the mid-14th century BC presumably as a consequence of the Royal Palace's destruction and the accompanying disruption, although the exact contemporaneity of these events cannot of course be established with certainty from the available archaeological evidence.

Until recently, the destiny of the city after its seizure and the destruction of the Royal Palace was known only from a limited number of cuneiform texts. From the letters of Akizzi[39] we learn that Qatna continued to be settled during the reign of Idanda's successor and that it was looted and destroyed by Shuppiluliuma as mentioned in the Shattiwaza treaty.[40] However, until the recent archaeological excavations at Mishrifeh, no direct physical evidence of the site's occupation dating to immediately after the destruction of the Royal Palace (that is, to the second part of the LBA II) had been uncovered. The last few years' excavation activity, however, has brought to light the first known constructions of a 'post-palace' period at Qatna dating to the late 14th and 13th centuries BC.

In this period the abandoned Southern Palace was replaced by a pottery workshop,[41] whilst above the Lower City Palace, two large adjacent courtyards or enclosures were built bounded by walls extending beyond the excavation limits (Phase K 11).[42] The function of these structures cannot be established, even though the discontinuity with the architecture of the underlying palace is unmistakable. Furthermore, Late Bronze Age II residential buildings have been identified in two regions of the site, on the acropolis as well as in the lower town and date to a period following the destruction of the Royal Palace. Houses were excavated by the Syrian team in Area Q next to the *Coupole de Loth* and by the Italian team in Area T1, immediately to the east of the Royal Palace.[43]

In particular, the dwelling excavated by the Italian Mission was built directly on the levelled destruction debris formed by the fallen walls of the east wing of the Royal Palace. The pottery inventories from this dwelling's phases of use allow us to date it to the final Late Bronze II[44] and show similarities with the ceramic assemblages retrieved from the houses of the *Coupole de Loth*.[45] This meagre evidence is certainly not even enough to permit a sketchy outline of the occupation of Qatna at the close of the Late Bronze Age, which has to remain one of the aims of future excavation at

who identifies the enemy of Idanda as "one of the smaller or medium-sized Syrian states that opposed the Hittite coalition (e.g., Amurru)" cf Richter 2005, pp. 125.

[39] Knudtzon 1907–1915, pp. 52–56; Moran 1992.

[40] Laroche 1966, p. 51 and Beckman 1999, p. 43, No. 6 §4.

[41] Al-Maqdissi 2002, pp. 196–198.

[42] Luciani 2002, pp. 152–158.

[43] Al-Maqdissi 2008, p. 12, figs. 15–16; Morandi Bonacossi *et al.* 2009, pp. 93–105.

[44] Morandi Bonacossi *et al.* 2009, pp. 96, 101.

[45] Shadi Chabo, personal communication.

the site. However, the rather poor quality of the architectural technique and the building materials used in the construction of the Area Q and T1 houses and the Area K enclosure/courtyard walls, together with the fact that despite the excavation of numerous areas to date in Qatna's upper and lower towns, no other evidence of final Late Bronze Age II occupation has come to light until now, would seem to suggest a picture of scant and impoverished occupation of the site. Settlement continued in the second half of the 14th and 13th centuries BC during a major crisis period for the city, which had by now been reduced in size and lost its importance and regional role.

For approximately three centuries after the end of the 13th century, no archaeological information regarding Qatna is available. The last possible mention of Qatna's name is in an early 12th century text from Emar, which refers to the destruction of a land of KUR*qa-ad/t/ṭ-na* by a "governor of the land of Sukhi."[46] Adamthwaite recently identified this toponym as Mishrifeh,[47] although in the present writer's opinion the possibility of reference to the site of Qattunam/Qattun/Qatni on the Lower Khabur cannot be excluded.

MISHRIFEH DURING THE LATE IRON I -EARLY IRON II AND ITS CONNECTIONS WITH THE 'AMUQ REGION

The archaeological work conducted at Mishrifeh up to now has not yielded evidence that the site was continually occupied during the Iron Age I. The oldest Iron Age levels recorded at the present date to the late 10th–early 9th century BC, *i.e.* to the Iron IC-Iron II transition.[48] This would suggest the existence of a rather long occupational gap in Mishrifeh's settlement history corresponding to almost the entire span of Iron I. It is, therefore, not surprising that the toponym Qatna does not occur again in the following Iron Age II and III Luwian, Aramaic, and cuneiform sources related to the region and that the name of the site is currently unknown in this period.[49]

After the three centuries of the Iron Age I during which the site remained unsettled in the late Iron I (Iron IC) and especially during Iron II, Mishrifeh was reoccupied under totally different structural conditions and in a radically changed historical, socio-political, and economic regional scenario now dominated by the newly emerged

[46] Arnaud 1985-1987 (Emar VI), p. 263, l. 24.

[47] Adamthwaite 2001, pp. 275–278; cf Répertoire géographique des textes cunéiformes 12/2, p. 226.

[48] Morandi Bonacossi 2007a, pp. 83–84 and Morandi Bonacossi 2009b, p. 120. The Iron Age periodisation used in this paper is that proposed by Mazzoni 2000.

[49] The possibility that the place name *qt* ⌜*n*⌝ mentioned twice on the mid-8th century BC inscribed slabs found by the Danish expedition at Hama corresponds to Qatna has recently been denied by Lipiński 2000, pp. 272–274, due to the association of the place name with the toponym *Rg*, which probably corresponds to the ar-Ruğ Depression east of the Middle Orontes. For this reason Lipiński prefers to interpret the toponym *qt* ⌜*n*⌝ as the old name for Qastun, an important tell in the northern Ghab Depression to the southeast of Tell Qarqur.

Luwian-Aramaean polities. Recent epigraphic and archaeological research has revealed that the ʿAmuq and Aleppo plains and possibly also the Middle Orontes Valley as far as the Hama region were part of the "Land of Palistin/Walistin," which in the 11th/10th century BC was ruled by an individual named Taita, "hero and king of the Land of Palistin," and the capital of which has to be sought at the site of Tell Taʿyinat in the northern Orontes Valley.[50] The following 9th century BC was marked by the first serious disruption in the new political landscape of the Early Iron Age polities, provoked by the earliest Assyrian penetration in Northern Syria and the Middle Orontes Valley under Shalmaneser III, who defeated a Syrian coalition in Qarqar in 853 BC.[51]

The position of the late Iron Age I site of Mishrifeh within this new political landscape cannot be ascertained on the basis of the archaeological and textual evidence available currently. The nature and size of this first Late Iron I and early Iron II settlement has not yet clearly emerged from the archaeological research that has been conducted.[52] Occupation evidence has been found in only two excavation areas so far, located in the northern lower town and in the central part of Mishrifeh's upper town.[53] This suggests that the site, which grew out of the Iron I phase of crisis and desertion, was a rather small settlement distinguished by relatively large buildings combining residential and productive functions erected in the area above the Lower City Palace (Area K). One of these, the so-called 'Jeweller's House', furnished evidence of household activities, including food production and storage, metal craftwork, and possibly also of a domestic shrine (**Fig.** 7).

Due to the limited evidence available, the political and administrative affiliation of this settlement cannot be established with certainty. However, the proximity of Mishrifeh to the site of Hamath, whose large royal complex on the summit of the acropolis is known from the late Iron I Phase E2 (*c.* 925–800 BC),[54] suggests that it might have belonged to the sphere of influence of the city of Hamath, which during Taita's reign was perhaps part of the 'Land of Palistin,' as indicated by the presence in the region of inscriptions with the name of Taita (Luwian stelae from Meharde and Sheizar).[55]

[50] For the inscriptions mentioning Taita and the Land of Palistin and their archaeological contexts, see Hawkins 2000 and 2009 and this volume; Harrison 2009 and 2010 and Kohlmeyer 2009. Lately Sass 2010 has proposed lowering the dating of Taita's reign to the late 10th century BC, thus making it approximately contemporary with the reoccupation of Mishrifeh during the late Iron IC.

[51] Dion 1997 and 2006; Grayson 2001; Lipiński 2000 and Sader 1987.

[52] Morandi Bonacossi 2009b, p. 120.

[53] Here (Operation H) only an occupation horizon was detected characterized by pits dug into the razed Royal Palace walls.

[54] Fugmann 1958, pp. 275–277.

[55] Hawkins 2009, pp. 169–170. However, the dedication inscription of Taita from Meharde and the funerary stela of his wife from Sheizar cannot necessarily be seen as a proof of Taita's political control of the Middle Orontes Valley.

This possible connection of the Hama and perhaps even of the Mishrifeh regions to Taita's kingdom, the heart of which was centred in the North Orontes Valley, could be echoed in a set of three basalt human heads of different sizes found at Mishrifeh. These sculptures share iconographic features and stylistic similarities with the head of the unfortunately very fragmentary colossal statue of an enthroned king from Tell Ta'yinat, originally stated to have been found in the citadel Gateway VII,[56] but probably erected in the courtyard of Building XIV (**Fig. 8**).[57] The fragmentary inscription from the statue's throne (Tell Ta'yinat 1), which is now on display at The Oriental Institute Museum of Chicago, mentions the country Wadasatini and the name of Halparuntiya, perhaps the author of the inscription and the king represented by the statue, who could be the Qalparunda, king of Unqi, named by Shalmaneser III in 857 and 853 BC.[58] According to Hawkins, a mid-9th century date for the inscription and the statue, which was probably mutilated by the Assyrians when the area was conquered by Tiglath-pileser III in 738 BC, would appear consistent with the palaeography of the hieroglyphs and the style of the colossal statue's head. This dating receives further support from the context in which the fragmentary enthroned king statue was found, assigned by the excavator to the First Building Period of Tell Ta'yinat.[59]

The three basalt heads found at Mishrifeh must also date to approximately the same period. Two of them unfortunately do not have precise archaeological provenance and their chronological assignment can rest only on art historical considerations. One is now exhibited in the Aleppo National Museum and is slightly larger than natural size (**Fig. 9**).[60] This well preserved basalt head was uncovered in 1894 in the area of the northern wing of the Royal Palace,[61] where Iron Age levels are found; it is a male head with gaunt modelling of the face and elegantly carved spiral-like curls arranged in a cap-shaped headdress. The curls and headdress show the same form and vigorous execution of those of the fragmentary colossal basalt head from Tell Ta'yinat and the rendering of the ears is also very similar, so that an early Iron Age II date for this sculpture can be safely proposed. The same curly hair also appears on a possibly contemporary, carved basalt orthostat depicting two charioteers driving over an enemy, which was found by Perdrizet and Fossey in 1896, allegedly near Tell Ta'yinat.[62]

The second head was found at Mishrifeh after the end of du Mesnil du Buisson's excavations in 1929, although no information is known about its exact provenance

56 Haines 1971, pp. 41–66.
57 Harrison 2009, p. 179.
58 Hawkins 2009, pp. 166–167.
59 Haines 1971, p. 64.
60 Clermont-Ganneau 1898, p. 26 and Ploix de Rotrou 1932, p. 6, no. 10 and fig. 8.
61 The supposed find-spot of the basalt head is recorded in du Mesnil du Buisson 1926, pp. 312–313, figs. 26 and 30.
62 Braidwood 1937, p. 33, fig. 7 and Harrison 2009, p. 178.

within the site. The head, which is now in the Hama Museum, is less well preserved and of less artistic merit than the one from Aleppo. However, it shows the same execution of the curls, ears and mouth, and the same slender structure of the face with prominent cheekbones although it is not in a cap-shaped headdress.

Finally in 2002, the Italian Mission working in Area K found a small basalt head measuring 16 × 12 × 12 cm in a pit belonging to a late Iron I context preceding the above-mentioned 'Jeweller's House' (**Fig. 10**).[63] The workmanship is very schematic and rough, although not devoid of power and expressive force. This sculpture also features curly hair, which is, however, only coarsely outlined on the top of the head.

All these male basalt heads dating from between the Iron IC and Iron IIA show common traits in style, composition, and iconographic features, which are also significantly found in the monumental basalt head of the enthroned figure from Tell Ta'yinat. These similarities do not, of course, allow any general, or even less, a political conclusion to be drawn concerning the possible extension of the Land of Palistin as far down as the Mishrifeh area, but they constitute an important link worthy of note and may connect the two regions and their artistic milieus. Whether this link might have some significance in terms of cultural, or possibly even broader ties between Ta'yinat and the Middle Orontes Valley during the Early Iron Age — as suggested by the stela from Meharde and the funerary monument of Taita's wife from Sheizar — remains an open question. Only the discovery of new archaeological evidence would allow us to explore this issue further. In any case, it seems important to add this little piece of documentary evidence to the debate.

Mishrifeh during the Late Iron II

The Iron Age II at Mishrifeh saw the revival of occupation at the site, coinciding with the termination of the drought event that affected the Mediterranean belt of Syria from the late 13th/early 12th centuries to the 9th century BC.[64] Evidence of rather intensive settlement with private dwellings, official and productive buildings, as well as large intensive storage areas dated in particular to the 8th century BC (Iron IIB) by pottery assemblages and radiocarbon determinations, has been uncovered in almost all excavation areas explored so far. This indicates that the 'Aramaean' settlement of Mishrifeh encompassed a rather large portion of the site (**Fig.** 7). Since I have already discussed the Iron II occupation of Mishrifeh elsewhere,[65] in this paper I will limit myself to emphasizing how the layout, organization, size, and function of the new Iron II settlement differed greatly from those of the smaller late 10th–early 9th century

[63] This sculpture has already been briefly discussed in Morandi Bonacossi 2009b, pp. 130–131, fig. 13.
[64] Kaniewski *et al.* 2010.
[65] Morandi Bonacossi 2009b, pp. 120–126.

site. The presence of official architecture at Mishrifeh, large productive and intensive storage areas, and dwelling quarters, as well as its vast size and location at the centre of a local settlement pattern composed of rural "satellite" villages show that during the Iron II Mishrifeh was a local urban centre in the region situated immediately to the south of Hamath, which until 720 BC and the conquest by the Assyrian army under Sargon II was the capital of a major Luwian-Aramaean kingdom. The available archaeological evidence suggests that Mishrifeh may have been part of this Iron Age polity, perhaps as an important wool and textile producer, as would be suggested by the numerous specialized buildings and installations for textile manufacture and dyeing found at the site.

Settlement trends in the Qatna region and the Middle Orontes valley during the Late Bronze and Iron Ages

Archaeological research conducted by the Italian Mission at Mishrifeh and in the surrounding region includes a regional survey of the site environs along the Mishrifeh wadi system. Studies of the survey results and comparison with those of similar ongoing projects in adjacent areas yield a picture of the evolution of settlement distribution in the Mishrifeh and Middle Orontes regions during the Late Bronze and Iron Ages (**Fig. 11**).

Whilst the Iron Age II corresponds to the period of the greatest and most widespread development in the occupation of the region surrounding Mishrifeh, where 20 dispersed rural settlements were inhabited (**Fig. 12**), no surface evidence of an Iron I occupation could be detected in the survey pottery assemblages. This does not necessarily accurately reflect the actual settlement situation, due to the difficulty of identifying Iron I ceramic diagnostics especially in surface collections, but suggests in any case, a drastic decline in the occupation of the Mishrifeh environs after the end of the Late Bronze Age II. The Iron I break in the settlement continuity at Mishrifeh is, therefore, mirrored by a parallel trend in the occupation history of its hinterland.

The fact that most of the surveyed Late Bronze sites date from the Late Bronze I–early Late Bronze II period is highly suggestive (**Fig. 13**). It seems, therefore, that the fall of Qatna with the destruction of its royal palace in the mid-14th century BC marked the beginning of a long crisis period not only for the city, which continued to be settled although in an impoverished condition until the end of the Late Bronze, but also for its hinterland. This came to an end only with the vigorous Iron Age II settlement revival.

Interestingly enough, such a trend has also been recorded in the adjacent Middle Orontes Valley to the south of Rastan.[66] The Homs Survey, conducted by G. Philip

[66] Philip and Bradbury 2010, fig. 1.

and his team in the basalt landscape to the northwest of Homs on the Orontes left bank (Northern Study Area), has evidenced a clear decline in settlement in the later part of the Late Bronze Age (14th–13th centuries BC).

It is quite remarkable that the Late Bronze Age II settlement decline appears to be more pronounced in the Northern Study Area (*i.e.* the region immediately adjacent to the western limit of our Qatna survey area), than towards the south around Tell Nebi Mend/Qadesh, where much greater continuity has been be recorded.[67] Furthermore, unlike Qatna, where the Late Bronze II after the destruction of the Royal Palace is already a period of crisis and decline, the 14th and 13th centuries BC at Qadesh (Phases C-A) seem to be a time of revival after a phase of decay corresponding to the Late Bronze I (Phases F-D).[68] This occupation evidence suggests that the divergent settlement trajectories of the Qatna environs and the Northern Study Area on one hand, and the Qadesh region on the other, reflect the differing fortunes of these two important polities towards the end of the Late Bronze Age.

In the Homs Survey too, there is very little that is recognizable as Early Iron Age[69] and no material of this period has been found so far at Nebi Mend itself. Iron II material, on the other hand, is widespread, especially across the marl landscape of the survey area (South Study Area).[70]A similar development has also been recorded in the Middle Orontes Survey conducted immediately to the north by K. Bartl and M. Al-Maqdissi.[71] The settlement distribution tends to remain basically stable from the Late Bronze (26 sites) to the Iron Age (29 sites) with two main settlement concentrations in the great Orontes Bend to the northeast of Rastan and to the north of Hama.[72] The Iron Age I has not, to date, been identified in the surface material from the sites in this stretch of the Orontes Valley, even though recent excavation at Tell al-Nasriyah, located about 15 km to the NNW of Hama on the eastern Orontes bank have shown the existence as at Hama itself of a cremation necropolis covering the time range from the late Late Bronze II/Iron I to the early Iron II, thus indicating continuity in the settlement development of the site from the Late Bronze to the beginning of the Iron Age II.[73]

67 Philip forthcoming.
68 Bourke 1993.
69 Philip 2007, pp. 240–241.
70 Philip 2007, p. 241; Whincop 2007.
71 Bartl and Al-Maqdissi 2007, p. 248, fig. 4.
72 Bartl and Al-Maqdissi forthcoming. Unfortunately information about settlement pattern development in the survey region during the Late Bronze Age is not available.
73 Tenu and Rottier 2010, p. 26; Faivre 2010, pp. 38–39.

Conclusions

Analysis of the archaeological evidence obtained from surveys in the Mishrifeh environs and the adjacent stretch of the Middle Orontes Valley yields a convincing picture of how the collapse of an important polity like Qatna in the mid-14th century BC at the time of Shuppiluliuma's campaigns in Syria triggered instability in the region and the dramatic depopulation of an area probably reaching as far as the basalt landscape to the west of the Orontes Valley. On the other hand, the continuity of occupation at the nearby site of Qadesh and the flourishing of its polity during the Late Bronze II are mirrored by the parallel stability of settlement evidenced by archaeological field survey in the surrounding territory.

The 'early crisis' already present during the Late Bronze II of single important polities or regional urban centres in the Northern Levant before the systemic collapse of centralized state bureaucracies in the early 12th century BC, would certainly have been an important factor in the early structural destabilization of the entire Late Bronze Age palace system and especially of its political, social, economic, and demographic fabric. Archaeological research in Syria and southeastern Turkey has documented developments, which parallel those seen at Qatna in other important urban centres; during the late 14th or 13th century BC, these suffered substantial destruction and/or were radically reduced in extension and significance entering thereafter into a period of strong decline. Hama and Tell Munbaqa, for instance, are good examples of the early decline of significant Late Bronze Age II urban sites in Syria.[74] Similarly, the results of the new excavation project at Tell Atchana have shown that the final destruction of Late Bronze Age Alalakh occurred already around 1300 BC and not in the early 12th century BC as believed by Woolley. [75]

[74] The settlement of Phase G3 at Hama, dating to the Late Bronze IB-IIA shows a prosperous urban development including the construction of drains, a possible palace with an extended storage sector in Square I 10 (Fugmann 1958, p. 119, figs. 142–143) and a second building with a porticoed passageway perhaps belonging to some sort of mansion in Square O 12, which were both destroyed by fire at the time of the Syrian military campaigns of Shuppiluliuma I. Whereas the settlements of the following Phases G2 and especially G1of the Late Bronze IIA have a more domestic character marked by the construction of small houses and seem to have been already strongly reduced in extension cf Fugmann 1958, p. 124, fig. 152; for the dating of the G3-1 ceramic assemblages, cf Mazzoni 2002, pp. 131–132. For a recent revision of the Period G stratigraphy according to which Phase G1 should be assigned to the following Early Iron Age Phase F2, cf Riis and Buhl 1990, p. 18. In any case, the first destruction of the Hama G3 urban site and the following reduction of the settlement's size seem to be contemporary with the destruction of the Royal Palace and the beginning of the crisis of Qatna during the Early Late Bronze II and might be linked to Shuppiluliuma's campaigns.

The Late Bronze Age settlement of Tell Munbaqa consisted of an upper and a lower town fortified by a massive city wall with gates cf Machule 1988, p. 37. The lower town was divided into two distinct quarters: the area of the *Innenstadt* and *Ibrahim Garten*, which was occupied during the entire Late Bronze Age cf Machule 1987, pp. 101–102 and Machule 1990, p. 21, and the so-called *Außenstadt*, which shows only a Late Bronze I occupation cf De Feyter 1989, p. 254. During the Late Bronze II, therefore, the size of the city was greatly reduced.

[75] Aslıhan Yener, personal communication, and Yener, this volume.

Such an early and progressive, albeit localized, political, economic, and demographic weakening of the regional scenario of the Northern Levant could have been a major long term cause of deterioration in the overall system, seriously damaging and undermining it and hence foreshadowing the subsequent final collapse making it more severe and definitive.

In conclusion, the early crisis of the Qatna Late Bronze Age "regional system" during the mid-14th and 13th centuries and its chronological, and probably also causative correlation with the parallel destruction and crisis of Hama G3-G2 and the similar case of Alalakh well illustrate an essential point that should be taken into account when dealing with the systemic collapse of Late Bronze palace economies. This phenomenon did not consist of the sudden, monolithic, and simultaneous collapse of a system homogeneously and contemporaneously present in the Eastern Mediterranean, the Levant and Anatolia, but as the two different political and settlement trajectories of Qatna and Qadesh and their regions show it was a process which occurred at a pace that could be strongly differentiated locally and regionally.

It is a fact, however, that only a fortunate integration of high resolution archaeological evidence from excavations and regional surveys, on one hand, with detailed data from written sources, on the other, permits such a diversified approach. This favourable combination is indeed unfortunately rather uncommon.

References

Adamthwaite, M. R.
2001 *Late Hittite Emar. The Chronology, Synchronisms, and Socio-Political Aspects of a Late Bronze Age Fortress Town*, Leuven-Paris-Sterling: Peeters.

Ahrens, A.
2009 "Alabastren und Amphoren. Die Steingefäße," *Schätze des Alten Syrien. Die Entdeckung des Königreichs Qatna*, edited by Landesmuseum Württemberg in Zusammenarbeit mit M. Al-Maqdissi, D. Morandi Bonacossi and P. Pfälzner, pp. 236–239. Stuttgart: Theiss Verlag.

Al-Maqdissi, M.
2002 "Ergebnisse der sechsten Kampagne der syrischen Ausgrabungen in Mišrife-Qatna im Jahr 2000," *Mitteilungen der Deutschen Orient-Gesellschaft* 134: 193–206.
2003a "Recherches archéologiques syriennes à Mishirfeh-Qatna au nord-est de Homs (Émèse)," *Comptes Rendus des Séances de l'Académie des Inscriptions et Belles-Lettres*, pp. 1487–1515.
2003b "Ergebnisse der siebten und achten syrischen Grabungskampagne 2001 und 2002 in Mishrife-Qatna," *Mitteilungen der Deutschen Orient-Gesellschaft* 135: 219–245.
2007 "Notes d'Archéologie Levantine. VI bis. À propos d'une statuette en basalte trouvée à Mishirfeh-Qatna," *Al-Rafidan* 28: 75–82.
2008 "Réflexions sur Qatna et sa région," *Studia Orontica* III: 3–41.

Al-Maqdissi, M., Dohmann-Pfälzner, H., Pfälzner, P. and Suleiman, A.
2003 "Das königliche Hypogäum von Qatna," *Mitteilungen der Deutschen Orient-Gesellschaft* 135: 189–218.

AL-MAQDISSI, M. and MORANDI BONACOSSI, D.
2009a "Stadtmauer und Akropolis. Das Stadtbild im 2. Jahrtausend v. Chr.," *Schätze des Alten Syrien. Die Entdeckung des Königreichs Qatna*, edited by Landesmuseum Württemberg in Zusammenarbeit mit M. Al-Maqdissi, D. Morandi Bonacossi and P. Pfälzner, pp. 130–133. Stuttgart: Theiss Verlag.
2009b "Die Geschichte geht weiter. Mishrifeh in der Eisenzeit," *Schätze des Alten Syrien. Die Entdeckung des Königreichs Qatna*, edited by Landesmuseum Württemberg in Zusammenarbeit mit M. Al-Maqdissi, D. Morandi Bonacossi and P. Pfälzner, pp. 278–285. Stuttgart: Theiss Verlag.

ARNAUD, D.,
1985–1987 *Recherches au pays d'Aštata: Emar VI: Les textes sumériens et accadiens*, Paris: Editions Recherches sur les Civilisations.

BADRE, L.
2006 "Tell Kazel-Simyra: A Contribution to a Relative Chronological History in the Eastern Mediterranean during the Late Bronze Age," *Bulletin of the American Schools of Oriental Research* 343: 65–95.

BARTL, K. and AL-MAQDISSI, M.
2007 "Ancient Settlements in the Middle Orontes Region between ar-Rastan and Qal'at Shayzar. First Results of Archaeological Surface Investigations 2003-2004," *Urban and Natural Landscapes of an Ancient Syrian Capital. Settlement and Environment at Tell Mishrifeh/Qatna and in Central-Western Syria. Proceedings of the International Conference held in Udine, 9-11 December 2004*, Studi Archeologici su Qatna 1, edited by D. Morandi Bonacossi, pp. 243–252. Udine: Forum Editrice.
forthc. *Archaeological Prospecting on the Middle Orontes. Survey Work between ar-Rastan and Qalat Shayzar.*

BECKMAN, G.
1999 *Hittite Diplomatic Texts*, Atlanta: Scholars Press.

BOURKE, S.
1993 "The Transition from the Middle to the Late Bronze Age in Syria: The Evidence from Tell Nebi Mend," *Levant* 25: 155–196.

BRAIDWOOD, R.
1937 *Mounds in the Plain of Antioch: An Archaeological Survey*, Oriental Institute Publications 48, Chicago: The University of Chicago Press.

CAPET, E.
2003 "Tell Kazel (Syrie), Rapport préliminaire sur les 9e-17e campagnes de fouilles (1993–2001) du Musée de l'Université Américaine de Beyrouth. Chantier II," *Berytus* 47: 63–121.

CAUBET, A.
1998 "The International Style: a point of view from the Levant and Syria," *Aegaeum* 18: 105–114.

CLERMONT-GANNEAU, C.
1898 "Tète de statue archaïque de Mouchrifè," *Recueil d'Archéologie Orientale* II: 26–27.

LAROCHE, L.
1966 *Catalogue des textes Hittites* (CTH), Paris: Klincksieck.

DE FEYTER, T. C.
1989 "The Aussenstadt Settlement of Munbaqa, Syria," *To the Euphrates and Beyond. Archaeological Studies in Honour of Maurits N. van Loon*, edited

by O. Haex, H. Curvers and P. Akkermans, pp. 237–256. Rotterdam-Brookfield: A.A. Balkema.

DE MARTINO, S.
2009 "Anatolia after the Collapse of the Hittite Empire," *From the Aegean to the Adriatic: Social Organisations, Modes of Exchange and Interaction in Postpalatial Times (12th-11th BC)*, edited by E. Borgna and P. Càssola Guida, pp. 21–28. Roma: Edizioni Quasar.

DION, P.
1997 *Les Araméens à l'âge du Fer. Histoire politique et structures sociales*, Paris: Librairie Lecoffre.
2006 "Tell 'Acharneh in the Kingdom of Hamath," in *Tell 'Acharneh 1998–2004. Rapports préliminaires sur les campagnes de fouilles et saison d'études*, edited by M. Fortin, pp. 43–48. Turnhout: Brepols.

DOHMANN-PFÄLZNER, H.
2009 "Meisterwerke der Bildkunst in Miniaturformat," *Schätze des Alten Syrien. Die Entdeckung des Königreichs Qatna*, edited by Landesmuseum Württemberg in Zusammenarbeit mit M. Al-Maqdissi, D. Morandi Bonacossi and P. Pfälzner, pp. 182–185. Stuttgart: Theiss Verlag.

DU MESNIL DU BUISSON, R.
1926 "Les ruines d'el-Mishrifé au Nord-Est de Homs (Émèse)," *Syria* 7: 289–325.
1927 "L'ancienne Qatna ou les ruines d'el-Mishrifé au N.-E. de Homs (Émèse). Deuxième campagne de fouilles 1927," *Syria* 8: 227–301.
1930 "Compte rendu de la quatrième campagne de fouilles a Mishrifé-Qatna," *Syria* 11: 146–163.
1935 *Le site archéologique de Mishrifé-Qatna*, Paris: de Boccard.

KNUDTZON, J. A.
1907–1915 *Die El-Amarna-Tafeln* (EA), Leipzig: J.C. Hinrichs.

EIDEM, J.
2003 "The Cuneiform Tablets," *Akkadica* 124: 164–167.
2007 "Notes on the Topography of Late Bronze Age Qatna. New Evidence from the 'Lower City Palace' Tablets," *Urban and Natural Landscapes of an Ancient Syrian Capital. Settlement and Environment at Tell Mishrifeh/Qatna and in Central-Western Syria. Proceedings of the International Conference held in Udine, 9-11 December 2004*, Studi Archeologici su Qatna 1, edited by D. Morandi Bonacossi, pp. 297–304. Udine: Forum Editrice.
2009 "Von Stadttoren und Bier," *Schätze des Alten Syrien. Die Entdeckung des Königreichs Qatna*, edited by Landesmuseum Württemberg in Zusammenarbeit mit M. Al-Maqdissi, D. Morandi Bonacossi and P. Pfälzner, pp. 114–115. Stuttgart: Theiss Verlag.

FAIVRE, X.
2010 Les jarres cinéraires de Tell al-Nasriyah, Syrie (Mission syro-française de l'Oronte), *Studia Orontica* VII-VIII: 33–59.

FELDMAN, M. H.
2006 "Frescoes, Exotica, and the Reinvention of the Northern Levantine Kingdoms during the Second Millennium B.C.E.," *Representations of Political Power: Case Histories from Times of Change and Dissolving Order in the Ancient Near East*, edited by M. Heinz and M. H. Feldman, pp. 39–65. Winona Lake: Eisenbrauns.

2007 *Diplomacy by Design. Luxury Arts and an "International Style" in the Ancient Near East, 1400–1200 BCE*, Chicago.

FISCHER E.
2007 "Der so genannte Internationale Stil der Späten Bronzezeit," *Ugarit-Forschungen* 39: 803–886.

FUGMANN, E.
1958 *Hama. Fouilles et recherches de la Fondation Carlsberg 1931–1938, II. L'architecture des périodes pré-hellénistiques*, Copenhague: Fondation Carlsberg.

GATES, M.-H.
2010 "Potters and Consumers in Cilicia and the Amuq during the "Age of Transformations" (13th–10th Centuries BC)," *Societies in Transition. Evolutionary Processes in the Northern Levant between Late Bronze Age II and Early Iron Age*, edited by F. Venturi, pp. 65–81. Bologna: Clueb.

GRAYSON, A. K.
2001 "Assyria and the Orontes Valley," *Bulletin of the Canadian Society for Mesopotamian Studies* 36: 135–144.

HAINES, R. C.
1971 *Excavations in the Plain of Antioch II*, Oriental Institute Publications 95, Chicago: The University of Chicago Press.

HARRISON, T. P.
2009 "Neo-Hittites in the "Land of Palistin." Renewed Excavations at Tell Ta'yinat on the Plain of Antioch," *Near Eastern Archaeology* 72/4: 174–189.
2010 "The Late Bronze/Early Iron Age Transition in the North Orontes Valley," *Societies in Transition. Evolutionary Processes in the Northern Levant between Late Bronze Age II and Early Iron Age*, edited by F. Venturi, pp. 83–102. Bologna: Clueb.

HAWKINS, J. D.
2000 *Corpus of Hieroglyphic Luwian Inscriptions*. I, *Inscriptions of the Iron Age*. Berlin: De Gruyter.
2009 "Cilicia, the Amuq, and Aleppo. New Light in a Dark Age," *Near Eastern Archaeology* 72/4: 164–173.

HEINZ, M.
2009 "Imports - Consumer Goods, Gifts or Private Property? The Story behind the Material Evidence for External Relations in Late Bronze Age *Kumidi* (Kamid el-Loz)," *Interconnections in the Eastern Mediterranean. Lebanon in the Bronze and Iron Ages. Proceedings of the International Symposium, Beirut 2008*, BAAL Hors-Série VI, pp. 311–322. Beirut.

KANIEWSKI, D., PAULISSEN, E., VAN CAMPO, E., WEISS, H., OTTO, T., BRETSCHNEIDER, J. and VAN LERBERGHE, K.
2010 "Late Second-Early First Millennium BC Abrupt Climatic Changes in Coastal Syria and Their Possible Significance for the History of the Eastern Mediterranean," *Quaternary Research* 74: 207–215.

KOHLMEYER, K.
2009 "The Temple of the Storm God in Aleppo during the Late Bronze and Early Iron Ages," *Near Eastern Archaeology* 72/4: 190–202.

LIPIŃSKI, E.
2000 *The Aramaeans: Their Ancient History, Culture, Religion*, Leuven-Paris-Sterling: Peeters.

LIVERANI, M.
1987 "The Collapse of the Near Eastern Regional System at the End of the Bronze Age: The Case of Syria," *Centre and Periphery in the Ancient World*, edited by

M. Rowlands, M. Larsen and K. Kristiansen, pp. 66–73. Cambridge: Cambridge University Press.
2001 *International Relations in the Ancient Near East, 1600-1100 B.C.*, New York: Palgrave.

LOUD, G.
1948 *Megiddo II, Seasons of 1935–39*, Chicago: University of Chicago Press.

LUCIANI, M.
2002 "Operation K," *Excavating Qatna I. Preliminary report on the 1999 and 2000 campaigns of the joint Syrian–Italian–German archaeological research project at Tell Mishrifeh*, Excavating Qatna 1, edited by M. Al-Maqdissi, M. Luciani, D. Morandi Bonacossi, M. Novák and P. Pfälzner, pp. 145–168. Damascus: Salhani Publishing.
2006a "Palatial Workshops at Qatna?," *Bagdader Mitteilungen* 37: 403–429.
2006b "Ivory at Qatna," in *Timelines. Studies in Honour of Manfred Bietak, Vol. III*, Orientalia Lovaniensia Analecta 149, edited by E. Czerny, I. Hein, H. Hunger, D. Melman, and A. Schwab, pp. 17–37. Leuven-Paris-Sterling: Peeters.
2008 "The Late MB to Early LBA in Qatna with Special Emphasis on Decorated and Imported Pottery," *The Bronze Age in the Lebanon*, edited by M. Bietak and E. Czerny, pp. 115–126. Vienna: Verlag der Osterreichischen Akademie der Wissenschaften.

MACHULE, D., BENTER, M., BOESSNECK, J., DE FEYTER, T. C., KARSTENS, K., KLAPPROTH, H.-H., KOELLING, S., KUNZE, J., TEZEREN, Ö., VON DEN DRIESCH, A. and WERNER, P.
1987 "Ausgrabungen in Tall Munbaqa 1985," *Mitteilungen der Deutschen Orient-Gesellschaft* 119: 73–134.

MACHULE, D., BENTER, M., CZICHON, R. M., KARSTENS, K., KLAPPROTH, H.-H., MAYER, W., PAPE, W. and PETER, W.
1988 "Ausgrabungen in Tall Munbaqa 1986," *Mitteilungen der Deutschen Orient-Gesellschaft* 120: 11–50.

MACHULE, D., BENTER, M., CZICHON, R. M., GERLACH, I. and WERNER, P.
1990 "Ausgrabungen in Tall Munbaqa 1988," *Mitteilungen der Deutschen Orient-Gesellschaft* 124: 11–40.

MARFOE, L.
1979 "The Integrative Transformation: Patterns of Socio-Political Organisation in Southern Syria," *Bulletin of the American Schools of Oriental Research* 234: 1–42.

MAZZONI, S.
2000 "Syria and the Periodization of the Iron Age: A Cross-Cultural Perspective," *Essays on Syria in the Iron Age*, edited by G. Bunnens, pp. 31–60. Louvain-Paris-Sterling: Peeters.
2002 "The Late Bronze Age Pottery Production in Northwestern Central Syria," *Céramique de l'âge du Bronze en Syrie, I. La Syrie du sud et la vallée de l'Oronte*, edited by M. Al-Maqdissi, V. Matoïan and C. Nicolle, pp. 129–142. Beyrouth.

MCCLELLAN, T. L.
1992 "Twelfth Century B.C. Syria: Comments on H. Sader's Paper," *The Crisis Years: The 12th Century B.C. from beyond the Danube to the Tigris*, edited by W. Ward and M. Sharp Joukowsky, pp. 164–173. Dubuque: Kendall/Hunt Publishing.

MORAN, W. L.
1992 *The Amarna Letters*, Baltimore: The Johns Hopkins University Press.

MORANDI BONACOSSI, D.
2007a "Qatna and its Hinterland during the Bronze and Iron Ages. A Preliminary Reconstruction of Urbanism and Settlement in the Mishrifeh Region," *Urban and Natural Landscapes of an Ancient Syrian Capital. Settlement and Environment at Tell Mishrifeh/Qatna and in Central-Western Syria. Proceedings of the International Conference held in Udine, 9-11 December* 2004, Studi Archeologici su Qatna 1, edited by D. Morandi Bonacossi pp. 65–90. Udine: Forum Editrice.
2007b "The Chronology of the Royal Palace of Qatna Revisited. A Reply to a Paper by Mirko Novák, *Egypt and the Levant* 14, 2004," *Egypt and the Levant* 17: 221–240.
2008a "The EB/MB Transition at Tell Mishrifeh: Stratigraphy, Ceramics and Absolute Chronology. A Preliminary Review," *The Bronze Age in the Lebanon. Studies on the Archaeology and Chronology of Lebanon, Syria, and Egypt. Contributions to the Chronology of the Eastern Mediterranean*, edited by M. Bietak and E. Czerny, pp. 127–152. Vienna: Austrian Academy of Sciences Press.
2008b "Excavations on the Acropolis of Mishrifeh, Operation J. A New Early Bronze Age III – Iron Age III Sequence for Central Inner Syria. Part 1: Stratigraphy, Chronology and Architecture," *Akkadica* 129/1: 55–127.
2008c "Face Plaque," *Beyond Babylon. Art, Trade, and Diplomacy in the Second Millennium B.C.*, edited by J. Aruz, K. Benzel and J. M. Evans, p. 234. New York.
2009a "Der Unterstadtpalast," *Schätze des Alten Syrien. Die Entdeckung des Königreichs Qatna*, edited by Landesmuseum Württemberg in Zusammenarbeit mit M. Al-Maqdissi, D. Morandi Bonacossi and P. Pfälzner, pp. 156–159. Stuttgart: Theiss Verlag.
2009b "Continuity and Change in the Town Planning and Material Culture of Iron Age II and III Mishrifeh, Central Syria," *Syria* 86: 119–132.
2009c "Tell Mishrifeh and its Region during the EBA IV and the EBA-MBA Transition. A First Assessment," *The Levant in Transition*, Palestine Exploration Fund Annual Series IX, edited by P. J. Parr, pp. 56–68. London and Leeds: Maney Publishing.
in press "The Lower City Palace at Qatna," *Qatna and the Networks of Bronze Age Globalism*, edited by P. Pfälzner.
MORANDI BONACOSSI, D. DA ROS, M., GARNA, G., IAMONI, M. and MERLINO, M.
2009 "The 'Eastern Palace' and the residential architecture of Area T at Mishrifeh/Qatna. Preliminary Report on the 2006–2008 Excavation Campaigns of the Italian Component of the Syro-Italian Archaeological Project," *Mesopotamia* 44: 61–112.
MOUNTJOY, P. A.
1993 *Mycenaean Pottery. An Introduction*, Oxford: the Oxford University School of Archaeology.
NEUMANN, J. and PARPOLA, S.
1987 "Climatic Change and the 11th-10th Century Eclipse of Assyria and Babylonia," *Journal of Near Eastern Studies* 46: 161–182.
NOVÁK, M.
2004 "The Chronology of the Royal Palace of Qatna," *Egypt and the Levant* 14: 299–317.
NOVÁK, M. and PFÄLZNER, P.
2003 "Ausgrabungen im bronzezeitlichen Palast von Tall Mišrife / Qatna 2002. Vorbericht der deutschen Komponente des internationalen Kooperationsprojektes," *Mitteilungen der Deutschen Orient-Gesellschaft* 135: 131–145.

OREN, E. D.
2000 *The Sea Peoples and their World: A Reassessment*, Philadelphia: University Museum.

PARROT, A.
1958 *Le palais: architecture*, Bibliothèque archéologique et historique 68, Paris: Paul Geuthner.

PFÄLZNER, P.
2005 "Syrien: Qatna. Ahnenkult im 2. Jahrtausend v. Chr.," *Welt und Umwelt der Bibel* 2/2005: 56–59.
2007 "Archaeological Investigations in the Royal Palace of Qatna," *Urban and Natural Landscapes of an Ancient Syrian Capital. Settlement and Environment at Tell Mishrifeh/Qatna and in Central-Western Syria. Proceedings of the International Conference held in Udine, 9-11 December 2004*, Studi Archeologici su Qatna 1, edited by D. Morandi Bonacossi, pp. 29–63. Udine: Forum Editrice.
2008 (in collaboration with C. von Rüden) "Between the Aegean and Syria: The Wall Paintings from the Royal Palace of Qatna," *Fundstellen. Gesammelte Schriften zur Archäologie und Geschichte Altvorderasiens ad honorem Hartmut Kühne*, edited by D. Bonatz, R. M. Czichon and F. J. Kreppner, pp. 95–118. Wiesbaden: Harrassowitz.
2009a "Macht und Reichtum in der Königsresidenz," *Schätze des Alten Syrien. Die Entdeckung des Königreichs Qatna*, edited by Landesmuseum Württemberg in Zusammenarbeit mit M. Al-Maqdissi, D. Morandi Bonacossi and P. Pfälzner, pp. 164–171. Stuttgart: Theiss Verlag.
2009b "Residenz der toten Herrscher. Die Königsgruft," *Schätze des Alten Syrien. Die Entdeckung des Königreichs Qatna*, edited by Landesmuseum Württemberg in Zusammenarbeit mit M. Al-Maqdissi, D. Morandi Bonacossi and P. Pfälzner, pp. 200–203. Stuttgart: Theiss Verlag.
2009c "Zwischen Tradition und Innovation. Die Goldschmiede von Qatna," *Schätze des Alten Syrien. Die Entdeckung des Königreichs Qatna*, edited by Landesmuseum Württemberg in Zusammenarbeit mit M. Al-Maqdissi, D. Morandi Bonacossi and P. Pfälzner, pp. 220–227. Stuttgart: Theiss Verlag.

PHILIP, G.
2007 "Natural and Cultural Aspects of the Development of the Marl Landscape East of Lake Qatina during the Bronze and Iron Ages," *Urban and Natural Landscapes of an Ancient Syrian Capital. Settlement and Environment at Tell Mishrifeh/Qatna and in Central-Western Syria. Proceedings of the International Conference held in Udine, 9-11 December 2004*, Studi Archeologici su Qatna 1, edited by D. Morandi Bonacossi, pp. 233–242. Udine: Forum Editrice.
forthc. "Expansion, Contraction and Continuity: Long-term Settlement Change in Western Syria. A View from the Orontes Valley."

PHILIP, G. and BRADBURY, J.
2010 "Pre-Classical Activity in the Basalt Landscape of the Homs Region, Syria: Implications for the Development of 'Sub-Optimal' Zones in the Levant during the Chalcolithic-Early Bronze Age," *Levant* 42/2: 136–169.

PLOIX DE ROTROU, G.
1932 *Le Musée national d'Alep. Catalogue sommaire.*

BELMONTE MARÍN, J. A.
2001 *Répertoire Géographique des Textes Cunéiformes 12.2. Die Orts- und Gewässernamen der Texte aus Syrien im 2. Jt. v. Chr.*, (RGCT). Wiesbaden: Harrassowitz.

RICHTER, TH.
2002 "Der "Einjährige Feldzug" Shuppiluliumas I. von Khatti in Syrien nach Textfunden des Jahres 2002 in Mishrife/Qatna," *Ugarit-Forschungen* 34: 603–618.
2003 "Das 'Archiv des Idanda," *Mitteilungen der Deutschen Orient-Gesellschaft* 135: 167–188.
2005 "Qatna in the late Bronze Age: Preliminary Remarks," *Studies on the Civilization and Culture of Nuzi and the Hurrians* 15: 109–126.
RIIS, P. J. and BUHL, M. L.
1990 *Hama. Les objets de la période dite syro-hittite (âge du fer)*, Copenhague: Fondation Carlsberg.
ROSSBERGER, E.
2009 "Schmuck für Könige und Götter. Funde aus der Königsgruft," *Schätze des Alten Syrien. Die Entdeckung des Königreichs Qatna*, edited by Landesmuseum Württemberg in Zusammenarbeit mit M. Al-Maqdissi, D. Morandi Bonacossi and P. Pfälzner, pp. 228–233. Stuttgart: Theiss Verlag.
RÜDEN, VON C.
2009 "Ein Hauch von westlichem Luxus. Die Wandmalerei," *Schätze des Alten Syrien. Die Entdeckung des Königreichs Qatna*, edited by Landesmuseum Württemberg in Zusammenarbeit mit M. Al-Maqdissi, D. Morandi Bonacossi and P. Pfälzner, pp. 176–181. Stuttgart: Theiss Verlag.
SADER, H.
1987 *Les états araméens de Syrie depuis leur fondation jusqu'à leur transformation en provinces assyriennes*, Wiesbaden: Franz Steiner Verlag.
SASS, B.
2010 "Taita, King of Palistin: ca. 950–900 B.C.E.?" *Near Eastern Archaeology online.*
TENU, A. and ROTTIER, S.
2010 "Le cimetière à crémation de Nasriyah, Syrie (Mission syro-française de l'Oronte)", *Studia Orontica* VII-VIII: 21–32.
TURRI, L.
2009 "Elfenbein. Prestigeobjekte der Elite," *Schätze des Alten Syrien. Die Entdeckung des Königreichs Qatna*, edited by Landesmuseum Württemberg in Zusammenarbeit mit M. Al-Maqdissi, D. Morandi Bonacossi and P. Pfälzner, pp. 188–191. Stuttgart: Theiss Verlag.
in press "Ivory, Bone and Antler in Late Bronze and Iron Age Qatna," *Qatna and the Networks of Bronze Age Globalism*, edited by P. Pfälzner.
VENTURI, F.
2007 *La Siria nell'età delle trasformazioni (XIII-X sec. a.C.). Nuovi contributi dallo scavo di Tell Afis*, Bologna: Clueb.
WARD, W. and SHARP JOUKOWSKY, M., eds.
1992 *The Crisis Years: The 12th Century B.C. from beyond the Danube to the Tigris*, Dubuque: Kendall/Hunt Publishing.
WHINCOP, M. R.
2007 "The Iron Age II at Tell Nebi Mend: Towards an Explanation of Ceramic Regions," *Levant* 39: 185–212.
WOOLLEY, C. L.
1955 *Alalakh. An Account of the Excavations at Tell Atchana in the Hatay, 1937–1949*, Oxford: Oxford University Press.

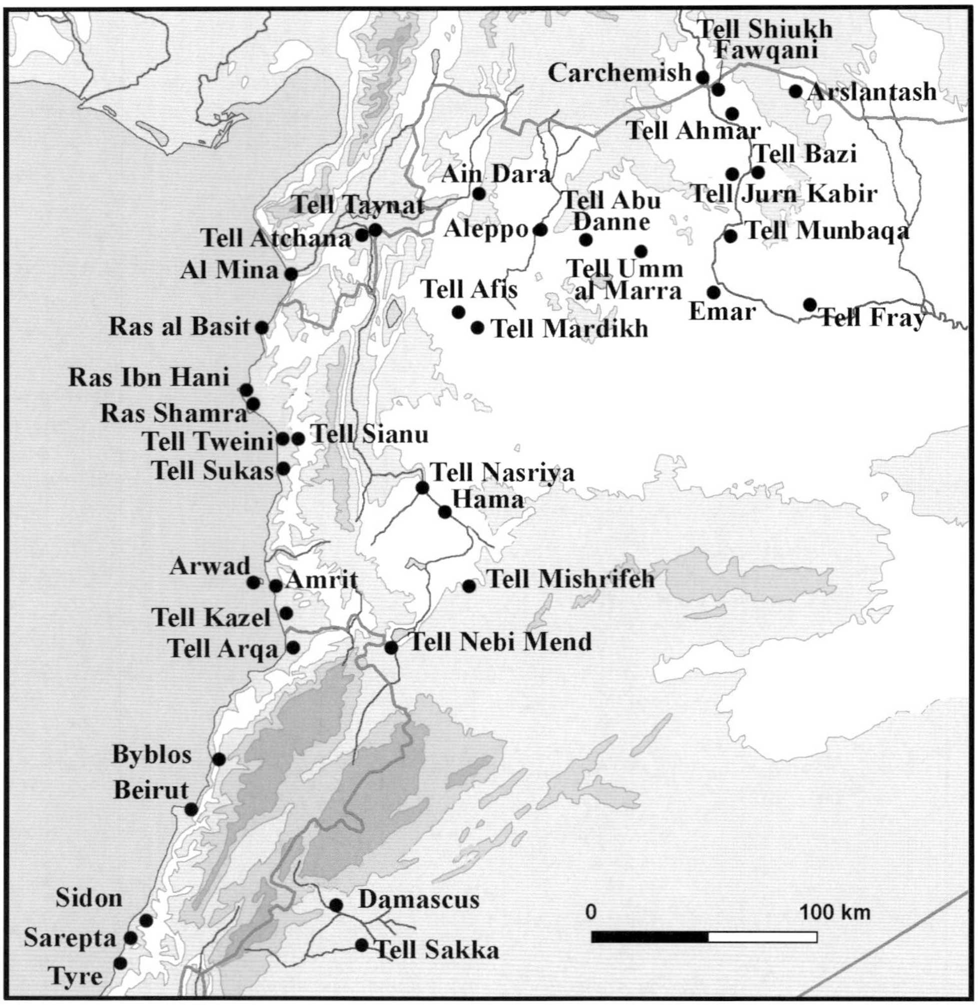

Fig. 1 Map of the Northern Levant with main Late Bronze and Iron Age sites (drawing: L. Turri).

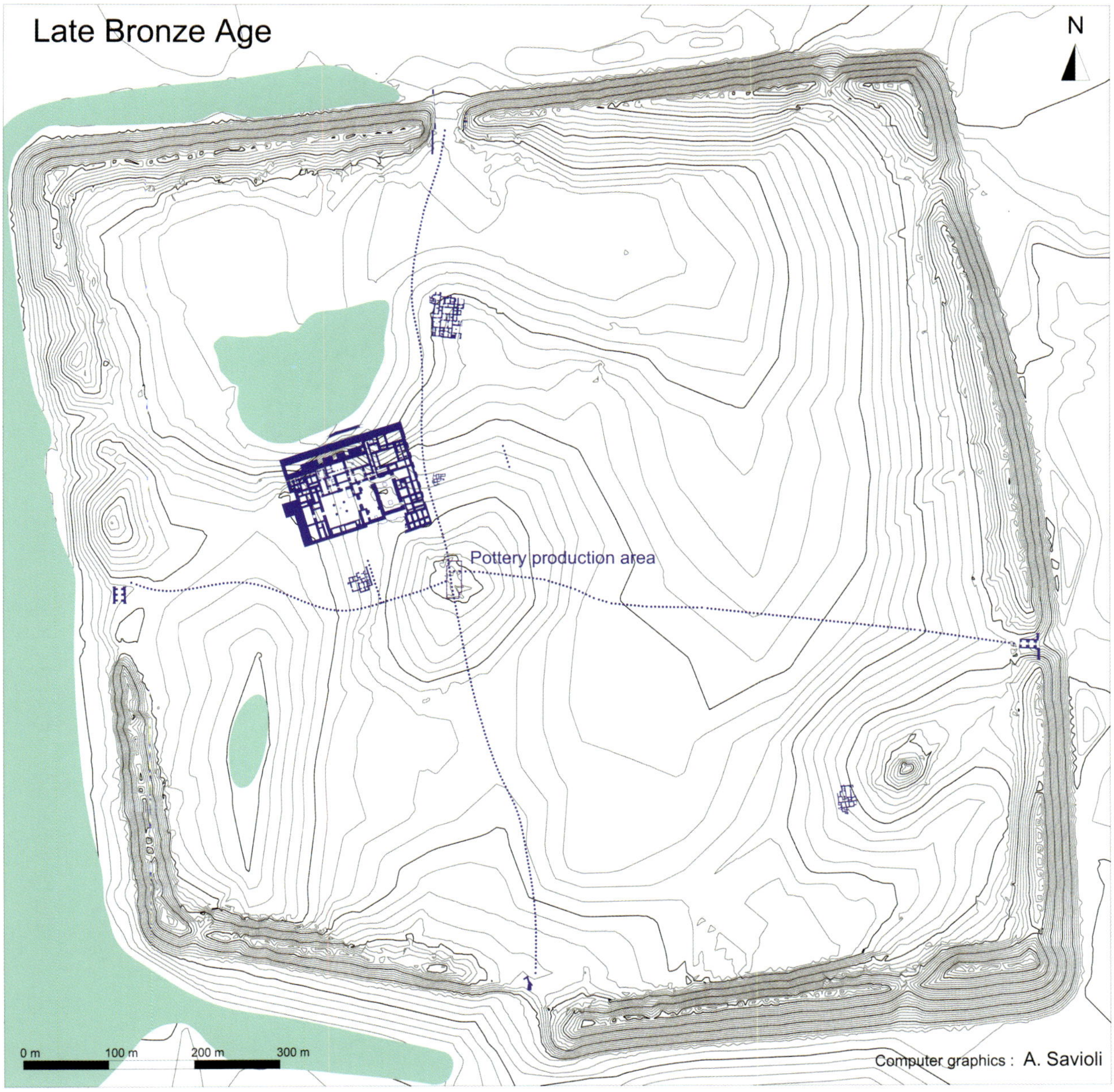

Fig. 2 Topographic map of Mishrifeh with main excavated Late Bronze Age buildings (drawing: A. Savioli).

Fig. 3 Schematic plan of the Royal Palace.

Fig. 4 Schematic plan of the Lower City Palace (drawing: A. Savioli).

Fig. 5 View of the Lower City Palace from the north (photograph: J. Ballester Serrano).

Fig. 6 View of the reception suite of the Lower City Palace from the SSW (photograph: J. Ballester Serrano).

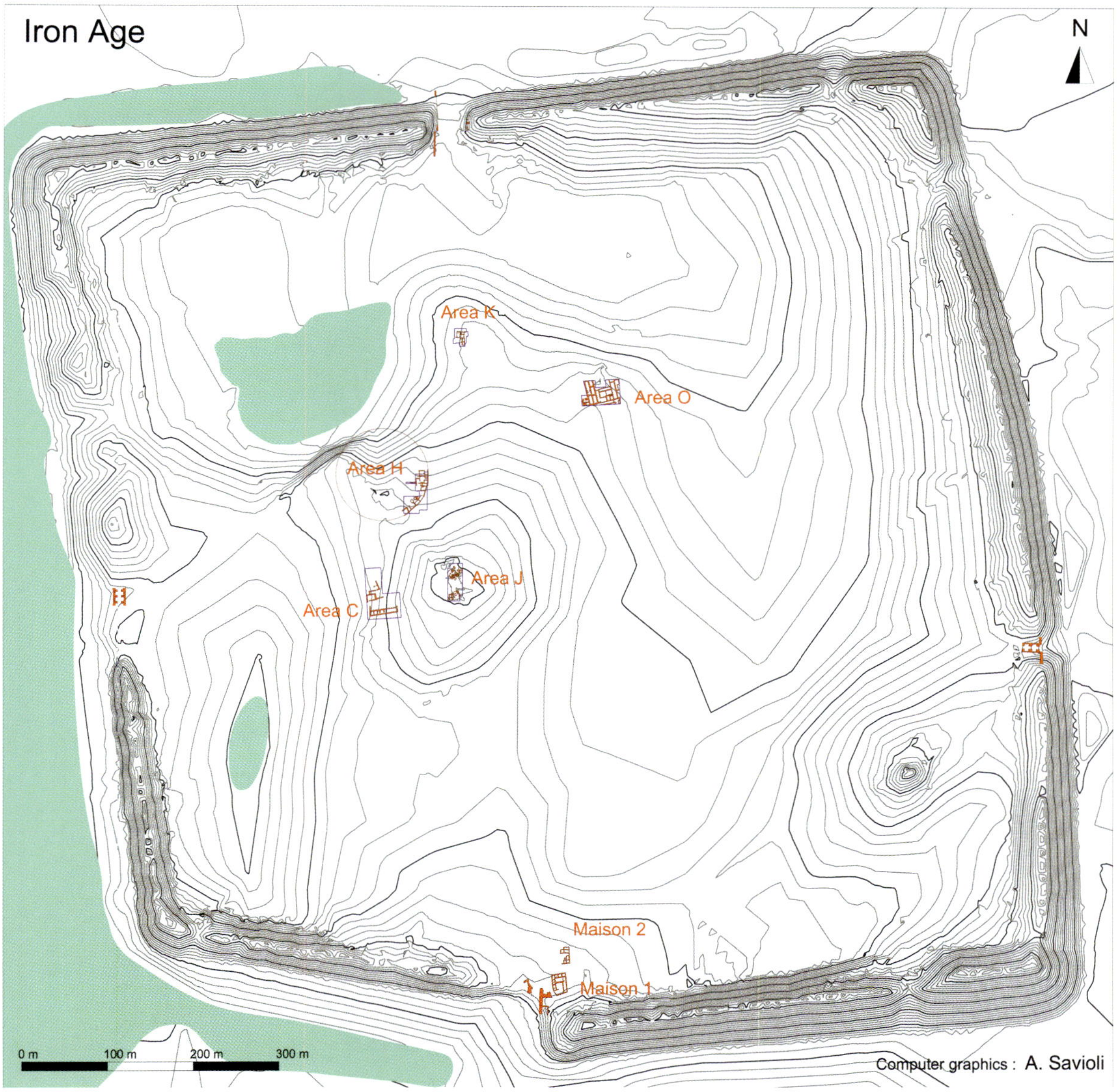

Fig. 7 Topographic map of Mishrifeh with main excavated Iron Age buildings (drawing: A. Savioli).

Fig. 8 Head of the Ta'yinat enthroned figure (photograph courtesy of The Oriental Institute Museum, University of Chicago).

Fig. 9 The basalt head in the Aleppo National Museum (from Ploix de Rotrou 1932, fig. 8).

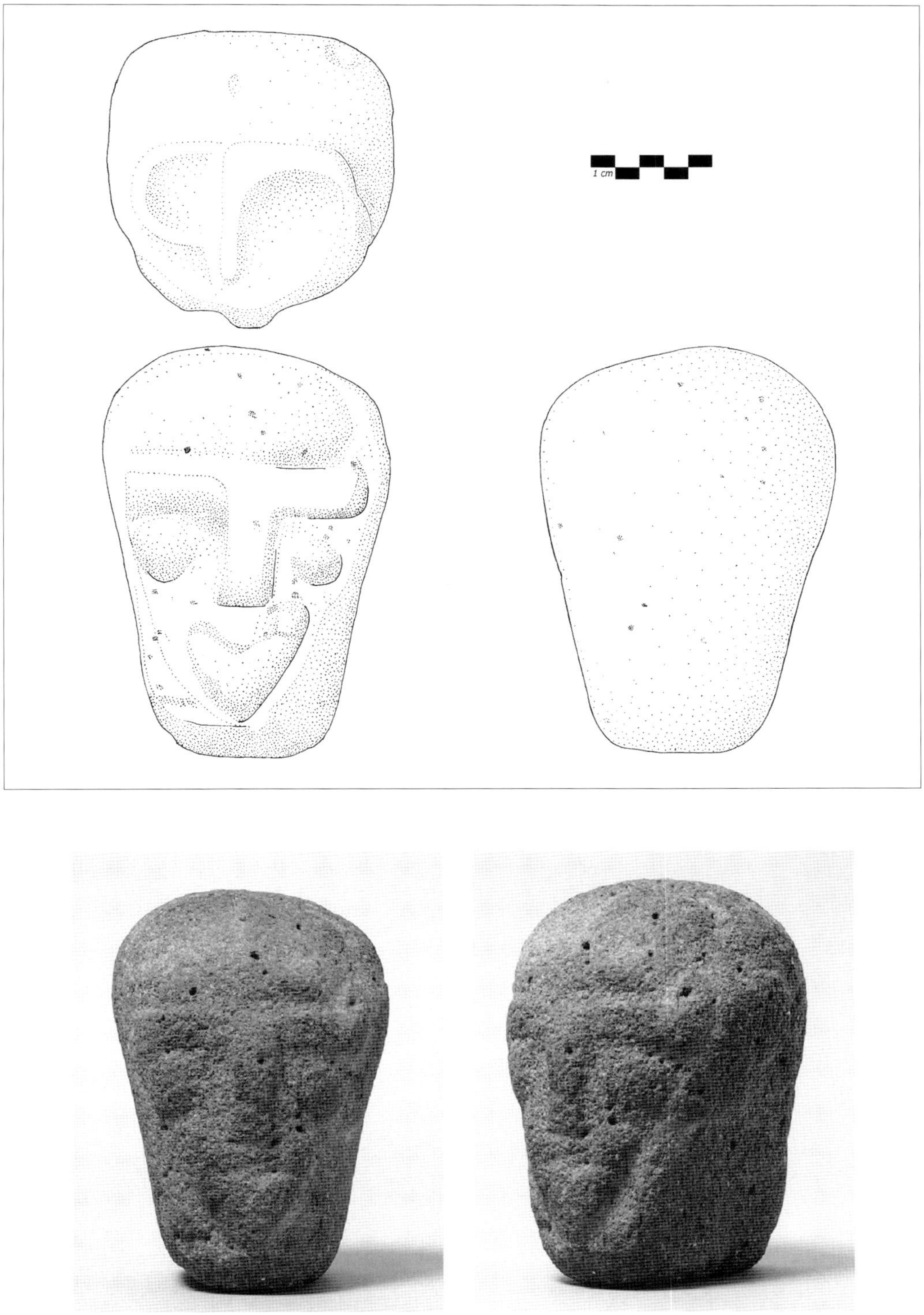

Fig. 10 The Area K basalt head
(photographs: M. Cusin, drawings: P. Vedovetto).

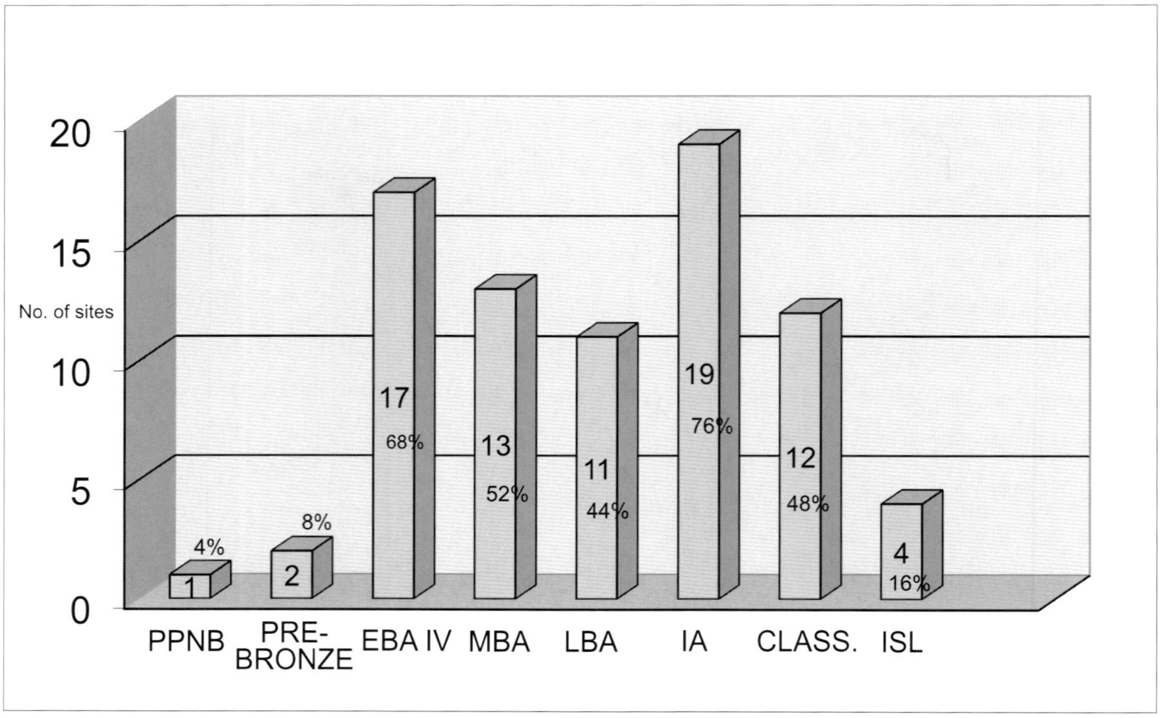

Fig. 11 The distribution of settlements in the Mishrifeh region by period.

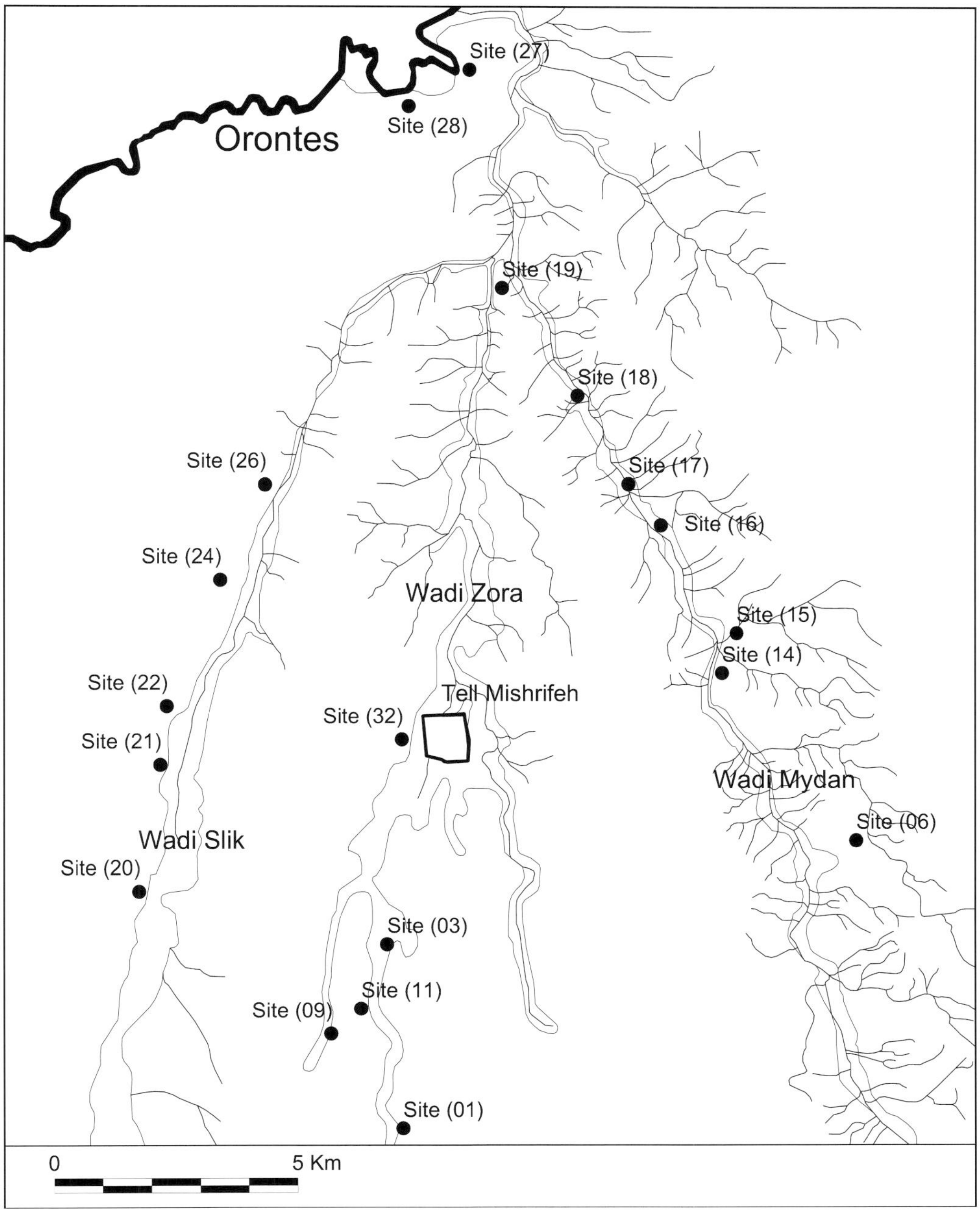

Fig. 12 Distribution map of Iron Age II/III sites around Mishrifeh (drawing: A. Savioli).

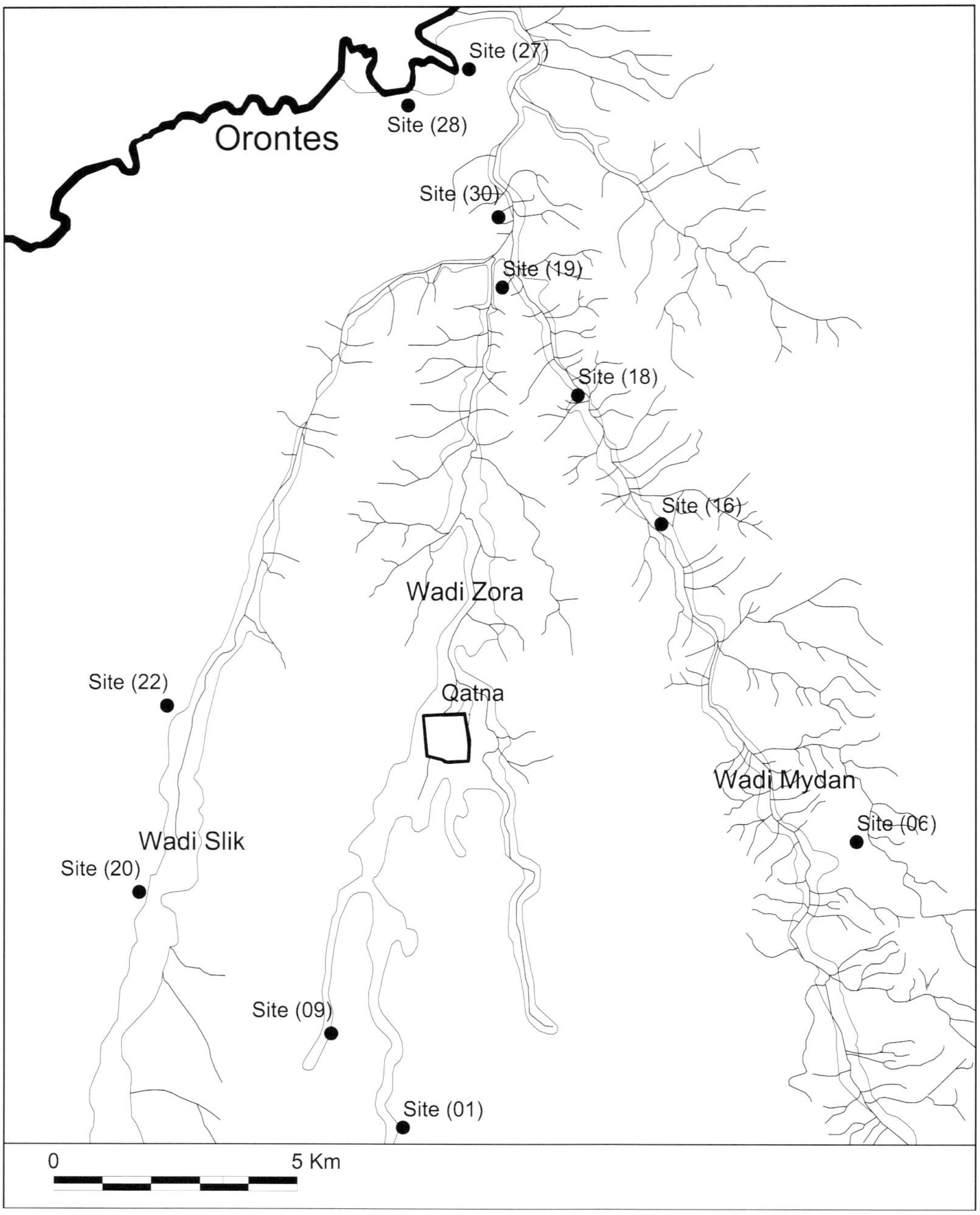

Fig. 13 Distribution map of Late Bronze Age sites around Mishrifeh (drawing: A. Savioli).

CHAPTER 6

SHEDDING NEW LIGHT ON THE ELUSIVE LATE BRONZE AND EARLY IRON AGES AT TELL 'ACHARNEH (SYRIA)

Michel FORTIN
Université Laval, Québec, Canada
E-mail: michel.fortin@hst.ulaval.ca

and

Lisa COOPER
University of British Columbia, Vancouver, Canada
E-mail: licooper@interchange.ubc.ca

ABSTRACT

Following a widely accepted interpretation of some second millennium literary documents, Tell 'Acharneh may represent the remains of the ancient city of Tunip. Several texts refer in particular to the existence of this important city, located in the Orontes valley, during the Late Bronze Age. Until now, however, no remains of this period had been revealed on this prominent archaeological site dug by a Canadian team, led by the two authors, since 1998. But, during the 2009 campaign and particularly the 2010 season, we came upon substantial remains of this period and the ones that followed: Early Iron Age I and II.

Tell 'Acharneh, a substantial site in the middle Orontes valley (Syria), is one of the most conspicuous considering the following features:[1]

— its size: 1.2 km N-S by 500/600 m E-W, for a total surface of 72 hectares;
— many of its components are still visible on the ground: a wide and circular pisé city wall/rampart, a main citadel and a secondary one with a "postulated" city gate in between, leading to a lower town encircled by the rampart;
— its strategic setting in a right-angle bend of the course of the river Orontes, which itself served as a natural moat;

[1] For a more detailed description of the site, see: Fortin 2006b.

— its strategic location in the middle of a low plain forming an extension to the southern end of the middle Orontes valley: this situation had already been shown by Courtois during his pioneering survey in 1970[2] and then confirmed by us in 2004 and 2006.[3] The site is visible from everywhere in the depressed plain ("*cuvette*") at the southern end of the Middle Orontes valley.

The historical context

Before the beginning of our excavations at Tell 'Acharneh in 1998, we were well aware that this site must have corresponded to a major Aramaean city on the basis of information provided by a cuneiform inscription chiselled onto a piece of basalt which had been found just beside the main tell. This stela had been discovered by chance in 1924, when the bridge over the Orontes River, which was still being frequently used by local traffic, had been rebuilt.[4] It was purposely left there by the Assyrian king Sargon II (or one of his high ranking officers who commanded his army and carried out his instructions while he was in his capital)[5] only a short time after the conclusion of the 720 BC campaign against Hamath. From the text of this official proclamation, it seems likely that the Assyrian troops conquered the city that stood at the location of modern Tell 'Acharneh — but whose ancient name is not mentioned — in the process of controlling the region which at that time was inhabited by Aramaean communities. We therefore surmise that 'Acharneh probably corresponded to one of the major Aramaean cities during this period of time, and that because of its strategic location directly on the banks of the Orontes River, it must have been part of the core of the Aramaean Hamath kingdom.[6]

In spite of this information, however, it remains to be determined when exactly 'Acharneh became an Aramaean city. It must have been somehow Aramaicized by the time of Shalmaneser III's military expedition against Hamath in 853 BC, as it sided with the coalition of Aramaean cities defeated at Qarqar. Interestingly, an elevation view of its defensive city wall with gateways, towers, and battlements dated from some decades earlier may be featured on one of the sixteen famous embossed metallic gate bands belonging to a temple that was constructed by Shalmaneser III at the site of Balawat. It is often argued that the artists of the bronze bands "would have had some knowledge, probably eye witness knowledge, of the buildings" they depicted[7] although this opinion is questioned by some scholars.[8] Band number IX, which refers to the

[2] Courtois 1972, p. 79, 1973, pp. 55, 59, 62–65.
[3] Fortin 2007a, 2007b.
[4] Thureau-Dangin 1933; Frame 2006.
[5] Na'aman 2007, pp. 168–169.
[6] Dion 1997, pp. 160–161.
[7] Tucker 1994, p. 116.
[8] Jacoby 1991.

well-known capture of Qarqar by Shalmaneser III in 853 BC, shows, in addition to *Warwar*, two other Aramaean cities that were attacked, *Pargā/Bargā* and *Adā/Adennu*. These are described as "belonging to Urhilēnu, the Hamatite" according to the epigraphs on the band.[9] Since they are represented by a river, it is logical to think that they correspond to major Aramaean towns of the Hamath kingdom, which were established on the banks of the Orontes River.[10] This would seem particularly so since geography was an "organizing principle" strictly followed by artists from the time of Shalmaneser III[11] and moreover, "both registers in each band [of the Balawat bronze bands] showed incidents from one campaign."[12] Thus, if the visual narrative is trustworthy (the sequential organization of the bands on the door panels is still disputed by some scholars)[13]ʿAcharneh is a good candidate for one of the depicted cities. In our reconstruction of the sequence of events, then, ʿAcharneh would have experienced a first attack by the Assyrian troops of Shalmaneser III in 853 BC. This attack was followed by a program of reconstruction before the city was taken one last time in 720 BC by Sargon II and his troops because of its resistance to the Assyrian invasion, as inferred by the ʿAcharneh inscription mentioned above. The reconstruction and reoccupation of ʿAcharneh following the destruction of 853 BC might bear the mark of Assyrian influence since the Hamath kingdom, which would have included the city of ʿAcharneh, accepted an Assyrian overlordship in 842 BC. This period of Assyrian hegemony lasted until the end of the 9th century, at which time the Aramaean king Zakkur seized power over Hamath.[14]

Before the Aramaean king Zakkur came into power, the kingdom of Hamath "had a mixed population."[15] This included Semitic tribes of Aramaeans who had settled here and there in the region[16] as early as around 1100 BC, since Tiglath-pileser I had to contend with them in the course of a military expedition into North Syria.[17] The name "Aramaeans" first appeared in inscriptions related to this campaign. The region also included Luwian populations, the presence of whom have been confirmed so far by twenty-one Hieroglyphic Luwian inscriptions discovered in the modern town of Hama or in its vicinity.[18] The city of Hamath itself was under the leadership of a Hittite dynasty. Thus, although its citadel, excavated by the Danish team in levels F

9 Grayson 1996, pp. 74–76, A.O.102.
10 Sader 1987, p. 225 n. 98.
11 Marcus 1987.
12 Reade 1979, p. 70.
13 For instance: Hertel 2004; Schachner 2007; Curtis and Tallis 2008, pp. 11–15.
14 Hawkins 1982, p. 435; Dion 2006, p. 46
15 Dion 2006, p. 45.
16 Dion 2006, p. 44.
17 Bunnens 2009, p. 68.
18 Hawkins 2000, pp. 398–415.

and E and dated to the 10th and early 9th centuries BC has been labelled "Aramaean," it should probably be more appropriately defined as "Hittite."[19]

Hieroglyphic Luwian inscriptions were found in three localities very close to Tell 'Acharneh; Qalat al-Mudiq, Meharde and Sheizar. Since these sites are easily visible from the summit of the main tell at 'Acharneh, it would be reasonable to think that some Luwian elements settled down at Acharneh in the Early Iron Age as well. Noteworthy is the fact that the stelae from Meharde and Sheizar[20] refer to king Taita of the land of *Padasatini* or *Wadasatini* (a toponym now read *Palistin*), the very same individual mentioned on the reliefs from the Temple of the Strom God at Aleppo.[21] Hawkins[22] and Harrison[23] have suggested recently that this king was the head of a kingdom located in the Amuq Plain, with its capital at Tell Ta'yinat. Between the 11th and 10th centuries BC, it extended to the environs of Hama. During this period, therefore, it is likely that Tell 'Acharneh would have been somehow associated with, or even incorporated into, the "Land of Palistin," a Neo-Hittite Early Iron Age "rump" state centered at Tell Ta'yinat.

Hawkins[24] even sees a possible connection between the toponym "*Palistin*" and the Philistines, one of the "Sea Peoples" who appear at the end of the Bronze Age as seaborne raiders on the Levantine coast: "we may perhaps envisage an intrusive group of Sea Peoples settlers in the north Levant and their territory being designated by a form of *Palistin*." In this regard, it is relevant to mention two inscriptions from Medinet Habu, written in the years 5 and 8 of the reign of Ramses III (c.1180 BC), the pharaoh who defeated the Sea Peoples at land and at sea. These texts refer to the conquest of the Amurru kingdom by the Sea Peoples and the submission of its population.[25] Tell 'Acharneh, which was known as Tunip at that time,[26] had just been integrated into this kingdom!

An external wall of Medinet Habu shows a relief representation of Tunip as it would have looked during this period; a three-story high fortress surrounded on three of its sides by a moat. The fact that the city is shown attacked by soldiers of Ramses III[27] implies that Tunip was no longer an ally of the Egyptians at the end of the Late Bronze Age. This situation contrasts with the beginning of the Late Bronze Age, when Tunip was on such good terms with Egypt that it was "personified" on a pylon erected

[19] Hawkins 2000, p. 402.
[20] Hawkins 1979, 1995, p. 97.
[21] Hawkins 2000, pp. 415–419, 2009, p. 169.
[22] Hawkins 2009, pp. 169–172.
[23] Harrison 2009a, p. 181, 2009b.
[24] Hawkins 2009, p. 171.
[25] Klengel 1992, pp. 182–184.
[26] Klengel 1995.
[27] Pritchard 1969, pl. 344.

by Amenophis I (1525–1504 BC) at Karnak[28] and that the king of Tunip was sending letters written on clay tablets to his "brother," the Pharaoh Akhenaton (1351–1334 BC) at his capital Amarna.[29] Those letters even allude to a "colonisation" of Tunip by Egyptians and to a remodelling of the city into an Egyptian town. Tunip seems to have been then under the tutelage of Egypt[30] as its citizens clearly asked in a letter for its protection against the Hittites.[31]

This period of friendship came to an end after the battle of Qadesh (1275 BC). Ramses II led an attack against the city of Tunip because this city had endeavoured to maintain a good relationship with the Hittites, the foe against whom Egyptians had fought at Qadesh, 80 km to the south of Tell ʿAcharneh. The pharaoh had been right about Tunip's divided loyalties; the name of Tunip appears in Hittite texts,[32] namely in an itinerary, which describes it as a station used by the troops of Suppiluliuma I (1344–1322 BC) during their campaigns into Syria. One could easily cross the Orontes River there, as it is shallow and there is a ford. Many scholars agree that during the time after the Amarna period, the Hittites were able to take control of the northern region of Inner Syria, including the Ghab Valley, where Tell ʿAcharneh is located.[33]

Judging from the numerous written and iconographic documents briefly referred to here, if the identification of Tell ʿAcharneh with Tunip is correct,[34] one should expect a major Late Bronze Age level of occupation at Tell ʿAcharneh. It should contain within it the remains of the material culture of the various people — Hittites and Egyptians — who tried to secure its alliance during this time, not to mention traces of the attacks led on the city by these groups and the phases of reconstruction that followed.

Archeological evidence: campaigns 1998–2004

Archaeological evidence gathered by our team during field campaigns at Tell ʿAcharneh between 1998 and 2004[35] confirmed the existence of occupation during the second phase of the Iron Age (900–720 BC; IA II). On the other hand, only a small amount of material for the Late Bronze Age and the early Iron Age (IA I) has been as-yet obtained,[36] and it was clearly insufficient to demonstrate any kind of

[28] Redford 1979.
[29] Goren *et al.* 2002, 2003, 2004, pp. 116–121.
[30] Klengel 1992, pp. 97, 104–105.
[31] Freu 1992, p. 66, 2009, p. 21.
[32] Klengel 1992, pp. 113, 163.
[33] Still other scholars argue, however, that the Hittites' role in Syria has been overestimated. See Gromova 2007, p. 307.
[34] Klengel 1995; Goren *et al.* 2002, 2003, 2004, p. 121.
[35] Fortin and Cooper 2006; Fortin ed. 2006.
[36] Cooper 2006, pp. 148–149.

continuity between these periods. This situation contrasts with other contemporary sites in the region such as Tell Afis, where a clear continuity in the occupation from LBA to IA I is well documented.[37] Moreover, at several sites in the Amuq valley further to the north, the transitional LB/IA period — long perceived as an interruptive period following the passage of the Sea Peoples in the Levant — is now established as of a period of continuity marked by the creation of rump Neo-Hittite states at the beginning of the Iron Age.[38]

In 'Acharneh's TE trench, we came upon a large cobbled floor surrounded by walls. Sherds dating to the Iron Age II period (900–720) were found embedded in the floor between the cobble stones.[39] This installation is comparable to a cobble-floored building at Tell Afis from which Iron Age II sherds were similarly uncovered.[40] We were also able to observe a defensive glacis made of distinctive layers of earth containing EBA-MBA pottery and figurines, which was adjacent to and had been thrown up against the cobbled space.[41] Although constructed some time during the Iron Age, this defensive structure was clearly constructed of earth mined from other parts of the settlement where extensive Bronze Age occupation had occurred many centuries before.

A similar multi-layered defensive glacis was encountered in the area of the postulated northern gate of the city, where there is a large opening in the massive earthen rampart that encircles the site.[42] We are inclined to think that this glacis was constructed as a precaution against the Assyrian troops of Shalmaneser III, whose campaigns against a coalition of Aramaean cities in the west culminated in the battle at Qarqar in 853. Alternatively, it may have been built in the aftermath of such a defeat — so vividly commemorated on the Balawat Gates' bronze bands — and in anticipation of further attacks. Whatever the precise motivation and date of these defensive constructions, they appear to have been in use when Sargon II took the city in 720 and erected the well-known stela, and reflect well the city's part in the coalition of Aramaean cities that he defeated.

'Acharneh's circuit rampart, which upon first inspection seemed typical of a Levantine MBA fortification,[43] appears also to date to the Iron Age since it appears to be associated with traces of a major building of Iron Age II date found in the CVB area of the Lower Town.[44] In all, Tell 'Acharneh's occupation seems comparable to a similar situation at Qatna nearby, where urban life flourished during the Iron Age II, and

[37] Mazzoni 1998b; Venturi 2000, 2007.
[38] Harrison 2007, 2009a, 2009b; Hawkins 2009.
[39] Fortin 2006d, pp. 114–116, 2006e, pp. 125–128.
[40] Cecchini 2000; Soldi 2009, p. 103.
[41] Fortin 2006d, pp. 117–118, 2006e, p. 125.
[42] Fortin 2006e, pp. 125–133.
[43] Burke 2008.
[44] Cooper and Fortin 2004; Fortin 2006c, p. 92, 2006e, pp. 136–138.

the Aramaean settlement encompassed practically the entire site.[45] But the question remains as to exactly when the Iron Age city was built at Tell ʿAcharneh. Can its founding be traced back to the Iron Age I? And what happened to the Late Bronze Age city of Tunip?

Campaign 2009: test trench

In order to find some answers to those questions, we returned to the field in 2009 and opened a small test trench measuring 5 × 2,5 m at the top of a wadi formed by rain run-off on the southern flank of the main tell; *Wadi Operation* (*WO*) 1. It is precisely the transitional LB/IA period we tried to elucidate through this operation at Tell ʿAcharneh.

During this brief campaign (three weeks), we uncovered a 5 m deep stratigraphic sequence consisting of three clearly distinct levels (**Fig. 1**).

Level 1

The first level is characterized by a cobbled surface, clearly visible in section, with a fill above it, the thickness of which varies from 0.5 to 2 meters. Cobbles were cemented together with a white clayish material and the whole surface was originally covered with a fibre mat, the print of which could be easily observed in the white clay between the cobbles. This cobbled floor belonged to a major building we could trace into the section to the east of the trench.

The cobbled surface had several fragments of pottery purposefully inserted among the cobbles. Ceramics relevant for the dating of this floor were also collected in the fill directly above it. These sherds belong to red slipped and burnished bowls (**Fig. 2:1**), the forms of which compare well to shapes found in Iron Age II contexts in sector CVB in the lower town of Tell ʿAcharneh,[46] and large ovoid pithoi with thickened rims and heavy, solid-footed bases (**Fig. 2:4–10**), which are particularly numerous and offer the same range of fabric types and production technologies as those observed on Iron II specimens found in other sectors of the site.[47] There were also sherds from deep bowls or kraters with expanded rims (**Fig. 2:3**)[48] and globular, hole mouth cooking pots with thickened, internally rounded rims (**Fig. 2:2**).[49]

A few painted sherds (**Fig. 2:11–12**), some featuring bands of red paint similar to those already found elsewhere on the main mound at Acharneh, as well as a bodysherd

[45] Morandi Bonacossi 2009, p. 120.
[46] Cooper 2006, fig. 1:6–11.
[47] Cooper 2006, figs. 4:12–17, 10–11, 16–17; Boileau 2006, pp. 197–199.
[48] Cooper 2006, figs. 2:6–13; 3:1–9.
[49] Cooper 2006, fig. 9:3–9.

featuring bichrome decoration whose best parallels date back to the early part of the Iron Age, were found in the fill above the cobbled floor. We have already speculated that the principal mound at 'Acharneh, unlike the Lower Town, was inhabited in the earlier Iron I period.[50] These painted wares in sounding WO, which are probably residuals from an earlier occupation, also seem representative of that Iron I period.

The cobbled surface probably represents a construction that took place sometime in the Iron II period (900–720 BC), and approximately contemporary with the similar cobbled space found in TE1a–b–c on the main mound, some 40 meters to the north-east of WO1, although a few meters higher.[51]

Level 2

This Iron Age II cobbled floor lies right above a 1,20 m thick layer of reddish, bricky debris material coming from the destruction of wide walls that most probably belonged to a major building. To make the area even at the time of the area's reoccupation, the occupants filled the depressions between the bricky debris with brown earth. This is our second level. The occupation period of the building made of red bricks, disaggregated by a major fire, is obviously earlier than the Iron II cobbled surface above, but by how many years?

Sherd fabrics and forms retrieved from this second level are different from those of Iron Age II sherds from the layer above. They include several small cups with flaring rims, which are the hallmark of the Middle Bronze Age (**Fig. 3**:1–3). Also present are bowls featuring internal swollen rims (**Fig. 3**:4–5), similar to those found at Qatna, Ebla, and along the Euphrates River, where they are believed to date to the final MBII and into the LBI.[52] A few bowls with bevelled rims were recovered (**Fig. 3**:6), comparable to those found at Arqa Phase L, where they are dated to the Late Bronze Age; at Qatna, where they have been fit specifically within the Late Bronze II horizon at that site; and at Tell Afis in LBIIB.[53] Another bowl with an out-turned rim (**Fig. 3**:7) has parallels to examples coming from Late Bronze Age strata at Tell Afis, and which seem to continue into the Iron I period.[54] Rims of deep cups, which are corrugated or grooved below the rim (**Fig. 3**:9), are elsewhere regarded as dating to the end of the MBII and into the LBI period.[55]

Among the pots, kraters and storage receptacles (**Fig. 4**), one continues to see forms that are typical of the Middle Bronze Age horizon of the Northern Levant (**Fig. 4**:1–4),

[50] Cooper 2006, pp. 148–149, 155.
[51] Fortin 2006b, pp. 114–116, 2006e, pp. 125–133.
[52] Morandi Bonacossi *et. al.* 2009, p. 81, fig. 15:1–2.
[53] Thalmann 2006, pl. 117: 13; Morandi Bonacossi *et al.* 2009, p. 101, fig. 32:4–6; Venturi 1998, fig. 5:13; 2007, fig. 48:9 (phase Vb).
[54] Venturi 1998, fig. 5:5; 2007, fig. 48:13–14; Mazzoni 1998, fig. 17:3.
[55] Morandi Bonacossi *et al.* 2009, p. 81, fig. 15:10.

although vessels with later dates are also attested. Particularly striking is the appearance of two-handled cooking pots with flanged rims (**Fig. 4:7**), which do not appear at Tell Afis until the very start of the Iron Age (Iron I) and which continue into the early Iron II period.[56] Similar cooking pots have now also been documented in Iron I levels at Tell Tayinat.[57] This second level is also characterized by the appearance of large pithos jars. One of these has an internally swollen rim (**Fig. 4:8**), which finds a good parallel at Tell Afis from the LBIIB,[58] but the other pithos rims (**Fig. 4:9–10**) compare well with those which first appear in Iron I levels at Afis and which continue to propagate into the Iron II. Such pithoi are certainly well known from Iron II levels at Tell Acharneh.[59]

This second level made of red bricky debris and associated brown fill, found as a thick deposit right under the cobbled surface, contains a mix of ceramic material that includes not only an abundance of Middle Bronze Age forms, but also sherds dating to the Late Bronze and the early part of the Iron Age. Although this rubble contains within it debris from constructions that date back to the Middle Bronze Age, the final deposition of these layers must be attributed to no earlier than the Iron I period (1200/1150–900 BC).

Level 3

The building made of red-brick walls just mentioned had been erected on top of a purposely created fill — our third level — made up of earth and fragments of mudbrick walls from the occupational level below. The fill was retained by a 3 m high dry stone thin wall. At first sight, we inferred that elements of this fill, such as the wall remains, were originally erected during the period immediately prior to the second level, i.e. the Late Bronze Age. To be sure, none of the ceramics from this level 3 can be dated to the Iron Age. But, it turned out that none of the pottery can be assigned a date from the Late Bronze Age either! Indeed, almost all of the pottery from the contexts in level 3 dates to the Early and Middle Bronze Ages (**Fig. 5**). The Early Bronze Age specimens, which include, for example, fragments of painted caliciform cups, bowls with vertical ribbed rims, and vertical or slightly out-turned rim pots (**Fig. 5:1–5**), compare well with sherds found elsewhere at Hama, Ebla, Mishrifeh-Qatna, Al-Rawda and elsewhere at ʿAcharneh itself.[60] All of the pieces belong within the EBIV horizon. The Middle Bronze Age forms, which include inturned-rim bowls,

[56] Venturi 1998, fig. 8; 2007: fig. 62:4, 7–10; Mazzoni 1998, fig. 18:15–16.

[57] Harrison 2010, fig. 7:4.

[58] Venturi 1998, fig. 10:7.

[59] Venturi 2007, fig. 63; Cooper 2006, figs 10–11, 16–17.

[60] Fugmann 1958, fig. 93:3H352, 3H353; fig. 98:3G98, 3G773; fig. 103:3C89; Matthiae 1980, fig. 21; Morandi Bonacossi et al. 2003, fig. 5:9; Boudier 2007, pl. I: 8–14; Cooper 2006, fig. 18:1–5.

pots and cooking vessels with everted rims (**Fig. 5:6–15**), and decoration in the form of comb incising, are very comparable to MBIIA and B assemblages occurring elsewhere at Tell 'Acharneh, and many other sites in Western Syria.[61]

On the basis of this finding, therefore, we cannot do otherwise than to assign a Middle Bronze date to the brick and stone constructions, and associated fill of Level 3. It is noteworthy that of the numerous sherds collected and classified from these earlier lots within WO, almost none of the material can be dated any later than the Middle Bronze Age.

At the end of our 2009 campaign, we had to admit that the well-known LBA town of Tunip was still very much elusive at Tell 'Acharneh. Tell Afis, a site close and comparable to Tell 'Acharneh, offers a similar situation: the "Aramaean town of IA II seems to lie directly upon the ruins of the MB town, without any architectural evidence for LB or IAI periods."[62] Nevertheless, at Afis, this situation prevails only on the northern side of the tell. On the acropolis, the Late Bronze and Iron Age I periods are largely attested.[63]

Campaign 2010: the LBA level at last

With some issues still remaining to be resolved, in the spring of 2010, we extended our *WO* 1 trench further north into the tell, in a 10 × 10 square, with the objective of exposing a larger area for each of the three levels described above. As these very recent results are still being analyzed and will be presented later on in a more detailed manner in a proper preliminary report, we will comment here only on the evidence gathered in relation to the transitional LB/IA period.

An IA II cobbled floor II

The first level of occupation could clearly be identified as a floor made of stone cobbles with potsherds inserted in between. This is the same cobbled floor encountered in 2009, exposed over a wider area. The floor is limited on the east and north by two long walls made of boulders set at right angles (**Fig. 6**). Sherds from this floor, similar to those found in 2009, continue to confirm its Iron Age II date (900–720 BC). The function of this room still eludes us, though.

[61] Cooper 2006, figs 23–26; Morandi Bonacossi et al. 2003, figs 6–7; Fugmann 1958, fig. 109:3B721; fig. 110:3H982, 3B912.

[62] Soldi 2009, p. 100; Mazzoni 2000, pp. 8–9; Venturi 2007, p. 126.

[63] Soldi 2009, p. 100.

An IA I (?) fill and soil erosion layers

Our 2010 operation confirmed that this IA II structure, characterized by a cobbled floor, had cut and been set into layers of earlier debris which were found at a higher altitude in the areas around it. In all probability, these layers should be attributed to the Iron Age I period (1100–900 BC) although the ceramic material is not sufficient to confirm this date, at least for the moment. A larger portion of these layers will be excavated next season.

LBA storage rooms

Right underneath the IA II cobbled floor, brick walls, burned to a flamboyant red colour, were found *in situ*. The red bricky debris unearthed in Level 2 in 2009 represents destroyed sections of these walls. The walls had been burned by a violent fire, so much that several parts of them crumbled as we tried to uncover them; fortunately they are clearly visible in section. We have been able to confirm that these red-fired brick walls delineate a series of three rooms obviously designed for storage purposes since big jars, one meter in height, were found *in situ* within the rooms:

— a first room produced 13 large jars, complete but in several fragments, aligned in three rows (**Fig.** 7);
— a second room, to the north of the first one, revealed the tops of two jars still in the ground, found at the very end of the campaign;
— a third room, to the west of the first one, yielded seven large jars, complete but crushed into many pieces (**Fig. 8**).

The original dimensions of these storerooms are impossible to establish since they have not yet been fully excavated. The same goes for the floors, which have not been reached yet: in the first storeroom, once we had removed the jars, more rim jars appeared below, leading us to conclude that another level of jars awaits us underneath!

The large storage jars (**Fig. 10**) can be compared to similar examples from the last phase of occupation of the Royal Palace at Qatna[64] which is dated between 1500 BC to the destruction of the palace in the middle of the 14th century BC. Similar jars have also been found in Hama G, dated to the Late Bronze Age.[65] Finally, most recently, in field T to the east of the Royal Palace of Qatna, large storage jars, complete but crushed, have been found in storerooms in a very similar arrangement as those in the Tell ʿAcharneh storerooms[66] and they are dated to the LBA I (1550–1350 BC). Since

[64] Sievertsen 2007, fig. 7; Pfälzner 2007, fig. 20.
[65] Fugmann 1958, fig. 143: S. No. R.1.
[66] Gallet and Maqdissi 2010, pp. 31–32, fig. 2b.

the Qatna storerooms are part of a palace, could it not be that the three (so far) storerooms found at Tell 'Acharneh are also part of a series of storerooms forming a section of a palace?

At the southern limit of trench *WO1* was found a very thick wall, 2.35 m wide, made of mudbricks laid on a pebble foundation (**Fig. 9**). Due to its location on the very edge of the main tell, we are inclined to interpret it as a city wall. LBA ceramic material found in an occupational layer leaning against the base of this wall suggests that the wall too should date to the Late Bronze Age. It appears that at some point, a second wall foundation was added to its external face so as to form some sort of a bastion projecting out some 1.60 m. Such a form matches the representation of Tunip's fortifications as depicted on the external face of one of the walls of the Egyptian temple of Medinet Habu.[67]

Conclusion

Although it may sound slightly premature to announce it before the full completion of the data analysis just recently collected in the field, we believe we have finally found the LBA level of Tell 'Acharneh, at least on the main tell.[68]

This level comprises a building of considerable importance judging by its enormous capacity for storage as we have discovered thus far. Nevertheless, the events taking place after the destruction of this Late Bronze Age structure, and their relationship to the ensuing Iron Age phases still remain elusive at Tell 'Acharneh. We know that Tell 'Acharneh experienced some Iron I occupation before its more substantial, urban expansion in the Iron II period, but the nature of this occupation, the identity of the settlement's occupants, and their precise relationship to the city's preceding Late Bronze Age, are tantalizing issues that still require further resolution.

References

Boileau, M.-C.
2006 "The Pottery from Tell 'Acharneh, Part II: Technological Considerations," in *Tell 'Acharneh 1998–2004*, Subartu 18, edited by M. Fortin, pp. 191–213. Turnhout: Brepols.

Boudier, T.
2007 "La poterie d'al-Rawda (Syrie intérieure) dans son context regional à la fin du Bronze ancien," in *Céramique de l'âge du Bronze en Syrie. II: L'Euphrate et la region de Jézireh*, edited by M. al-Maqdissi, V. Matoïan and C. Nicolle, pp. 23–41. Beyrouth: IFPO.

[67] Pritchard 1969, pl. 344.

[68] It would not been completely obliterated by an extensive Aramaean IA II reconstruction as Fortin suggested earlier: 2006a.

BUNNENS, G.
2009 "Assyrian Empire Building and Aramization of Culture as seen from Tell Ahmar/Til Barsib," *Syria* 86: 67–82.
BURKE, A. A.
2008 *"Walled up to Heaven". The Evolution of Middle Bronze Age Fortification Strategies in the Levant.* Winona Lake: Eisenbrauns.
CECCHINI, S. M.
2000 "Un bâtiment mystérieux sur l'acropole de Tell Afis", in *Proceedings of the First ICAANE. Roma, May 18th-23rd 1998*, edited by P. Matthiae *et al.*, pp. 199–212. Roma.
COOPER, L.
2006 "The Pottery from Tell ʿAcharneh, Part 1: Typological Considerations and Dating According to Excavated Areas in the Upper and Lower Towns, 1998–2002," in *Tell ʿAcharneh 1998–2004,* Subartu 18, edited by M. Fortin, pp. 140–190. Turnhout: Brepols.
COOPER, L. and FORTIN, M.
2004 "Tell ʿAcharneh in the Middle Orontes Valley and the Assyrian Presence in Syria", in *From the Upper Sea to the Lower Sea: Studies on the History of Assyria and Babylonia in Honour of A. Kirk Grayson*, edited by G. Frame, pp. 17–56. Istanbul: Nederlands Instituut voor het Nabije Oosten.
COURTOIS, J. C.
1972 "Les *Tells* du Ghab. La moyenne vallée de l'Oronte à l'âge du Bronze, " in *Actes du colloque Apamée de Syrie. Bilan des recherches archéologiques 1969–1971*, edited by J. and J.-Ch. Balty, pp. 79–84. Bruxelles.
1973 "Prospection archéologique dans la moyenne vallée de l'Oronte (El Ghab et Er Roudj - Syrie du nord-ouest)," *Syria* 50: 53–99.
CURTIS, J. E. and TALLIS, N., ed.
2008 *The Balawat Gates of Ashurnasirpal II.* London: The British Museum Press.
DION, P.-E.
1997 *Araméens à l'âge du Fer: histoire, politique et structures sociales.* Paris: Gabalda.
FORTIN, M.
2006a "À la recherche de l'ancienne Tunip à Tell ʿAcharneh, dans la vallée de l'Oronte (Syrie)," in *Les espaces syro-mésopotamiens. Dimensions de l'expérience humaine au Proche-Orient ancien. Volume d'hommage offert à Jean-Claude Margueron*, Subartu 17, edited by P. Butterlin *et al.*, pp. 212–221. Turnhout: Brepols.
2006b "Tell ʿAcharneh: localisation, description et recherches antérieures", in *Tell ʿAcharneh 1998–2004,* Subartu 18, edited by M. Fortin, pp. 3–23. Turnhout: Brepols.
2006c "Tell ʿAcharneh: rapport préliminaire sur la campagne préparatoire de 1998," in *Tell ʿAcharneh 1998-2004* (Subartu 18), edited by M. Fortin, pp. 82–105. Turnhout: Brepols.
2006d "Tell ʿAcharneh: rapport préliminaire sur la campagne de fouilles de 2001," in *Tell ʿAcharneh 1998–2004,* Subartu 18, edited by M. Fortin, pp. 106–119. Turnhout: Brepols.
2006e "Tell ʿAcharneh: rapport préliminaire sur la campagne de fouilles de 2002," in *Tell ʿAcharneh 1998–2004,* Subartu 18, edited by M. Fortin, pp. 120–139. Turnhout: Brepols.
2007a "La vallée du Ghab: Nouvelle prospection archéologique," in *Urban and Natural Landscapes of an Ancient Syrian Capital. Settlement and Environment at Tell Mishrifeh/Qatna and in Central-Western Syria. Proceedings of the International*

Conference held in Udine, 9–11 December 2004, Studi Archeologici su Qatna 1, edited by D. Morandi Bonacossi, pp. 253–268. Udine: Forum Editrice.

2007b "Reprise de la prospection de la moyenne vallée de l'Oronte (Syrie) par une mission syro-canadienne: 2004–2006," *Journal of the Canadian Society for Mesopotamian Studies* 2, pp. 19–41.

FORTIN, M., ed.

2006 *Tell 'Acharneh 1998–2004. Rapports préliminaires sur les campagnes de fouilles et saisons d'études. Preliminary Reports on Excavation Campaigns and Study Season*, Subartu 18, Turnhout: Brepols.

FORTIN, M. and COOPER, L.

2006 "La mission canadienne à Tell 'Acharneh (Syrie): à la recherche de l'ancienne Tunip," *Mouseion. Journal of the Classical Association of Canada/Revue de la Société des études classiques* 6: 163–201.

FRAME, G.

2006 "The Tell 'Acharneh Stela of Sargon II of Assyria," in *Tell 'Acharneh 1998–2004,* Subartu 18, edited by M. Fortin, pp. 49–68. Turnhout: Brepols.

FREU, J.

1992 "Les guerres syriennes de Suppiluliuma et la fin de l'ère amarnienne," *Hethitica* 11: 39–101.

2009 "Qatna et les Hittites," *Studia Orontica* 6: 9–23.

FUGMANN, E.

1958 *Hama: fouilles et recherches, 1931–1938, v. 2, pt. 1: L'architecture des périodes pré-Hellénistique.* Copenhague: Nationalmuseet.

GALLET, Y. and AL-MAQDISSI, M.

2010 "Archéomagnétisme à Mishirfeh/Qatna: nouvelles données sur l'évolution de l'intensité du champ magnétique terrestre au Moyen-Orient durant les derniers millénaires", *Akkadica* 131: 29–46.

GOREN, Y. *et al.*

2002 "Petrographic Investigations of the Amarna Tablets," *Near Eastern Archaeology* 65/3: 196–205.

2003 "The Expansion of the Kingdom of Amurru According to the Petrographic Investigation of the Amarna Tablets," *Bulletin of the American Schools of Oriental Research* 329: 1–11.

2004 *Inscribed in Clay. Provenance Study of the Amarna Tablets and other Ancien Near Eastern Texts.* Tel Aviv: Emery and Claire Yass publications in archaeology.

GRAYSON, A. K.

1996 *Assyrian Rulers of the Early First Millennium BC, II (858–745BC). Royal Inscriptions of Mesopotamia, Assyrian Periods.* Toronto: University of Toronto Press.

GROMOVA, D.

2007 "Hittite Role in Political History of Syria in the Amarna Age Reconsidered," *Ugarit-Forschungen* 39: 277–310.

HARRISON, T. P.

2007 "Neo-Hittites in the North Orontes Valley: Recent Investigations at Tell Ta'yinat," *Journal of the Canadian Society for Mesopotamian Studies* 2: 59–68.

2009a "Lifting the Veil on a "Dark Age": Ta'yinat and the North Orontes Valley during the Early Iron Age," in *Exploring the Longue Durée. Essays in Honor of Lawrence E. Stager,* edited by J. D. Schloen, pp. 171–184. Winona Lake: Eisenbrauns.

2009b "Neo-Hittite in the "Land of Palistin": Renewed Investigations at Tell Ta'yinat on the Plain of Antioch," *Near Eastern Archaeology* 72/4: 174–189.

2010 "The Late Bronze/Early Iron Age Transition in the North Orontes Valley," in *Societies in Transition. Evolutionary Processes in the Northern Levant between Late Bronze Age II and Early Iron Age,* edited by F. Venturi, pp. 83–102. Bologna: CLUEB.

HAWKINS, J. D.

1979 "The Hieroglyphic Luwian Stelae of Meharde-Sheizar," in *Florilegium Anatolicum. Mélanges offerts à Emmanuel Laroche,* pp. 145–156. Paris: De Boccard.

1982 "The Neo-Hittite States in Syria and Anatolia," in *The Cambridge Ancient History,* Vol. III, pt. 1. *The Prehistory of the Balkans; the Middle East and the Aegean World, tenth to eighth centuries B.C.,* edited by J. Boardman *et al.,* pp. 372–441. Cambridge: Cambridge University Press.

1995 "The Political Geography of North Syria and South-East Anatolia in the Neo-Assyrian Period," in *Neo-Assyrian Geography,* edited by M. Liverani, pp. 87–101. Roma: Università di Roma "La Sapienza".

2000 *Corpus of Hieroglyphic Luwian Inscriptions. Vol. I: Inscriptions of the Iron Age.* Berlin-New York: Walter de Gruyter.

2009 "Cilicia, The Amuq, and Aleppo. New Light in a Dark Age," *Near Eastern Archaeology* 72/4: 164–173.

HERTEL, T.

2004 "The Balawat Gate Narratives of Shalmaneser III," in *Assyria and Beyond. Studies Presented to Mogens Trolle Larsen,* edited by J. G. Dercksen, pp. 299–315. Leiden: Nederlands Instituut voor het Nabije Oosten.

JACOBY, R.

1991 "The Representation and Identification of Cities on Assyrian Reliefs," *Israel Exploration Journal* 41: 112–131.

KLENGEL, H.

1992 *Syria 3000 to 300 BC A Handbook of Political History.* Berlin: Akademie Verlag.

1995 "Tunip und Andere Probleme der historischen Geographie Mittelsyriens," in *Immigration and Emigration within the Ancient Near East. Festschrift E. Lipinski,* edited by K. Van Lerberghe and A. Schoors, pp. 125–134. Louvain: Uitgeverij Peeters en Departement Oriëntalistiek.

MARCUS, M. I.

1987 "Geography as an Organizing Principle in the Imperial Art of Shalmaneser III," *Iraq* 49: 77–90.

MATTHIAE, P.

1980 *Ebla. An Empire Rediscovered.* Garden City, New York: Doubleday & Company.

MAZZONI, S.

1998a *The Italian Excavations of Tell Afis (Syria): from Chiefdom to an Aramaean State.* Pisa: Edizioni ETS.

1998b "The Late Iron I and Early Iron II Levels," in *Tell Afis (Siria). Scavi sull'acropoli 1988–1992. The 1988–1992 Excavations on the Acropolis,* edited by S. M. Cecchini and S. Mazzoni, pp. 163–171. Pisa: Edizioni ETS.

2000 "Syria and the Periodization of the Iron Age. A Cross-cultural Perspective," in *Essays on Syria in the Iron Age,* Ancient Near Eastern Studies Supplement 7, edited by G. Bunnens, pp. 31–59. Louvain: Peeters.

MORANDI BONACOSSI, D.

2009 "Continuity and Change in the Town Planning and Material Culture of Iron Age II and III Mishrifeh, Central Syria," *Syria* 86: 119–132.

MORANDI BONACOSSI, D. *et al.*
2003 "The Mishrifeh/Qatna 1999–2002. A Preliminary Report of the Italian Component of the Joint Syrian-Italian-German Project. Part 2," *Akkadica* 124: 144–204.
2009 "The "Eastern Palace" and the Residential Architecture of Area T at Mishrifeh/Qatna. Preliminary Report on the 2006–2008 Excavation Campaigns of the Italian Cimponent of the Syro-Italian Archaeological Project," *Mesopotamia* 44: 61–112.
NA'AMAN, N.
2007 "Sargon II's Second *Palû* according to the Khorsabad Annals," *Tel Aviv* 34: 165–170.
PFÄLZNER, P.
2007 "Archaeological Investigtions in the Royal Palace of Qatna", in *Urban and Natural Landscapes of an Ancient Syrian Capital: Settlement and Environment at Tell Mishrifeh/Qatna and in CentralWestern Syria*, edited by D. Morandi Bonacossi, pp. 29–64. Udine: Forum.
PRITCHARD, J. B.
1969 *The Ancient Near East in Pictures Related to the Old Testament.* Princeton: Princeton University Press.
READE, J.
1979 "Narrative Composition in Assyrian Sculpture," *Baghdader Mitteilungen* 10: 52–110.
REDFORD, D. B.
1979 "A Gate Inscription from Karnak and Egyptian Involvement in Western Asia during the Early 18th Dynasty," *Journal of the American Oriental Society* 99/2: 270–287.
SADER, H. S.
1987 *Les états araméens de Syrie depuis leur fondation jusqu'à leur transformation en provinces assyriennes.* Beirut.
SCHACHNER, A.
2007 *Bilder eines Weltreichs. Kunst- und kulturgeschichtliche Untersuchungen zu den Verzierungen eines Tores aus Balawat (Imgur-Enlil) aus der Zeit von Salmanassar III, König von Assyrien,* Subartu 20. Turnhout: Brepols.
SIEVERSTEN, U.
2007 "New Research on Middle Bronze Age Chronology of Western Syria", in *The Synchronisation of Civlisations in the Eastern Mediterranean in the Second Millennium B.C. II,* edited by M. Bietak and E. Czerny, pp. 423–430. Vienna: Verlag der Österreichischen Akademie der Wissenschaften.
SOLDI, S.
2009 "Aramaeans and Assyrians in North-Western Syria: Material Evidence from Tell Afis," *Syria* 86: 97–118.
THALMANN, J.-P.
2006 *Tell Arqa — I. Les niveaux de l'âge du Bronze.* Beyrouth: Institut français du Proche-Orient.
THUREAU-DANGIN, F.
1933 "La stèle d'Asharné," *Revue d'assyriologie et d'archéologie orientale* 30: 53–56.
TUCKER, D. J.
1994 "Representations of Imgur-Enlil on the Balawat Gates," *Iraq* 56: 107–116.

VENTURI, F.
1998 "The Late Bronze Age II and Early Iron I Levels," in *Tell Afis (Siria). Scavi sull'acropoli 1988–1992. The 1988–1992 Excavations on the Acropolis*, edited by S. M. Cecchini and S. Mazzoni, pp. 123–162. Pisa: Edizioni ETS.
2000 "Le premier Age du Fer à Tell Afis et en Syrie septentrionale," in *Essays on Syria in the Iron Age*, Ancient Near Eastern Studies Supplement 7, edited by G. Bunnens, pp. 505–536. Louvain: Peeters.
2007 *La Siria nell'età delle trasformazioni (XIII-X sec. A.C.). Nuovi contributi dallo scavo di Tell Afis,* Studi e Testi Orientali 8, Serie Archeologica 1. Bologna: CLUEB.

Fig. 1 Stratigraphy of the *Wadi Operation* (2009) showing three distinct levels.

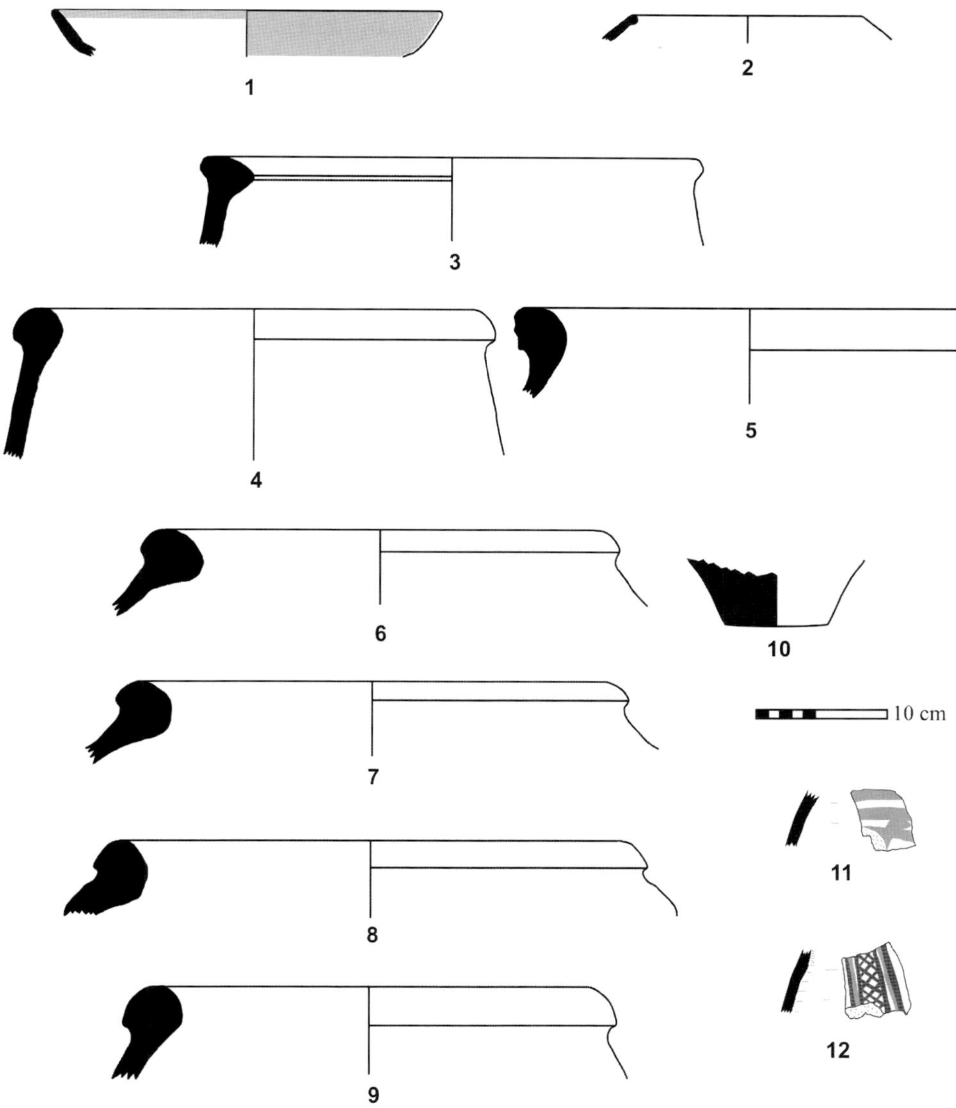

Fig. 2 WO Level 1 – Cobbled Floor and Fill Directly Above.

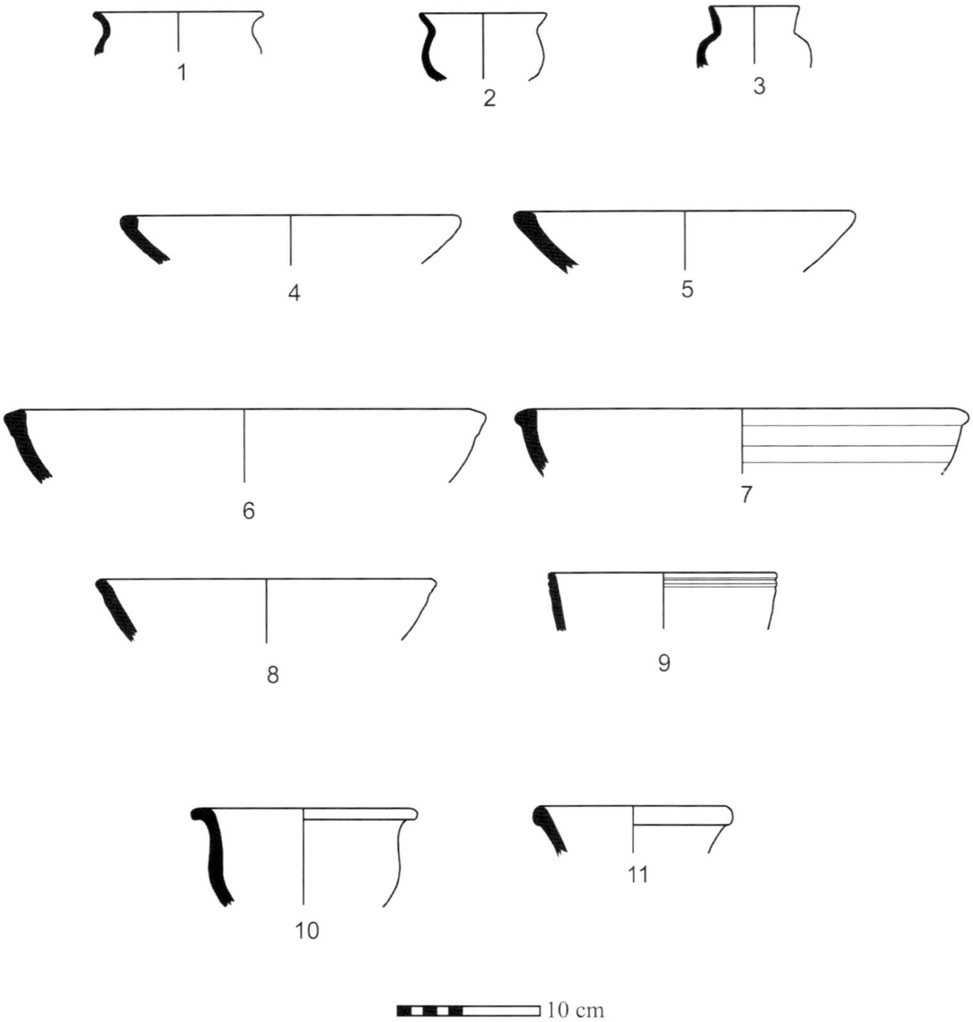

Fig. 3 WO Level 2 – Red Bricky Debris and Brown Fill.

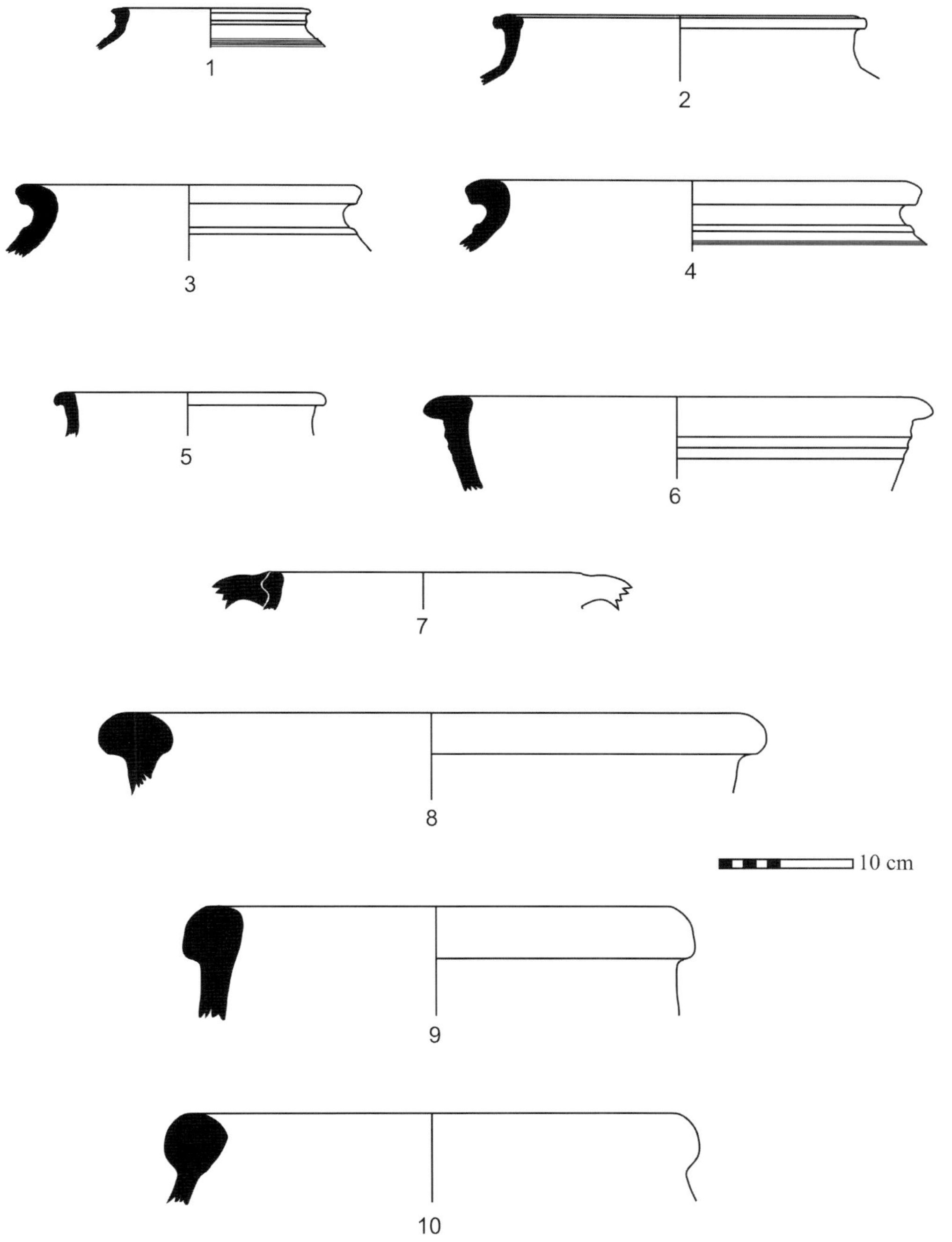

Fig. 4 WO Level 2 – Red Bricky Debris and Brown Fill.

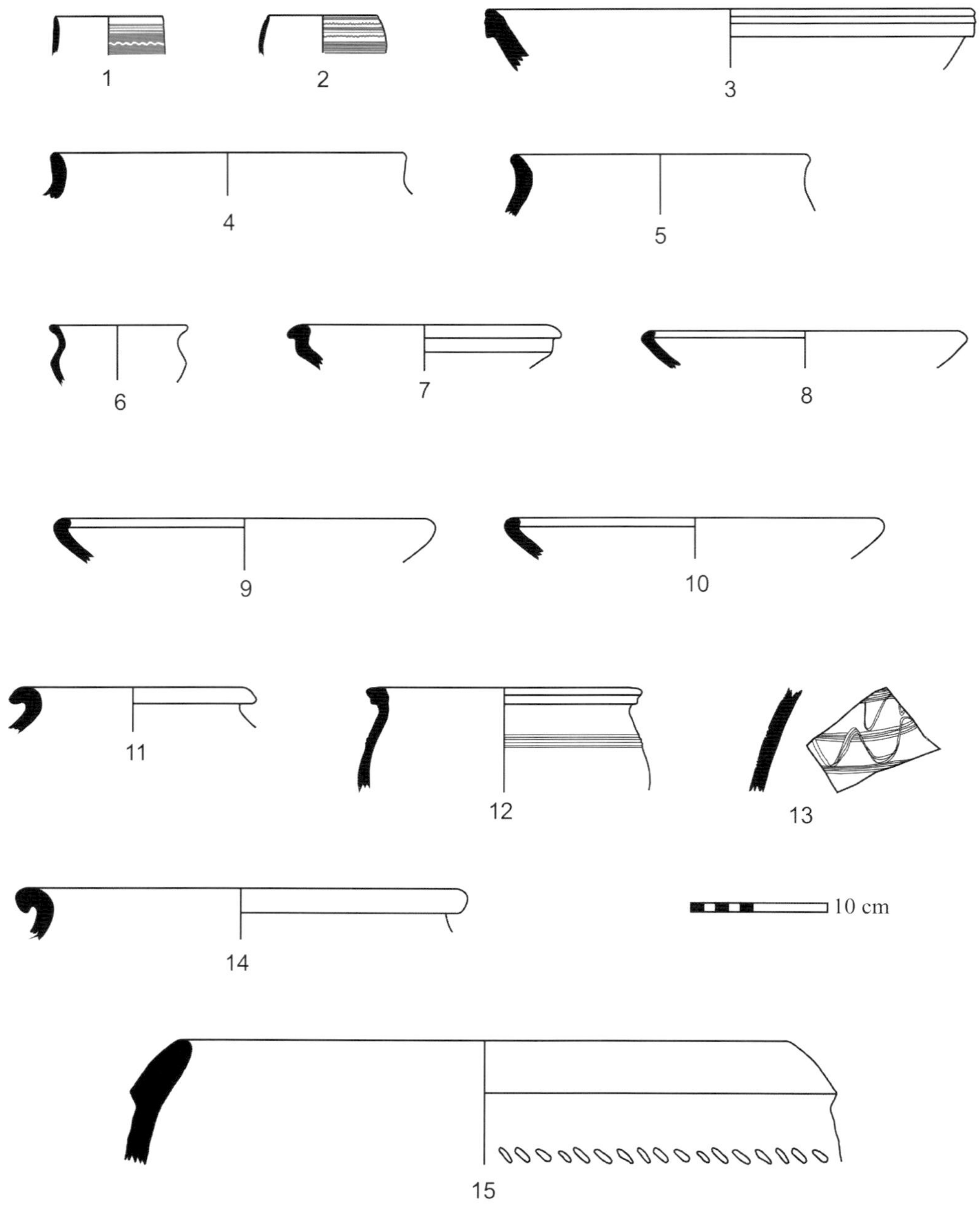

Fig. 5 WO Level 3.

Fig. 6 Early Iron Age II cobbled floor limited to the north and the east by stone walls.

Fig. 7 Late Bronze Age storage room with 13 complete jars still *in situ*.

Fig. 8 Late Bronze Age storage room with seven crushed jars.

Fig. 9 Stone foundations of the mud-brick Late Bronze Age city wall?

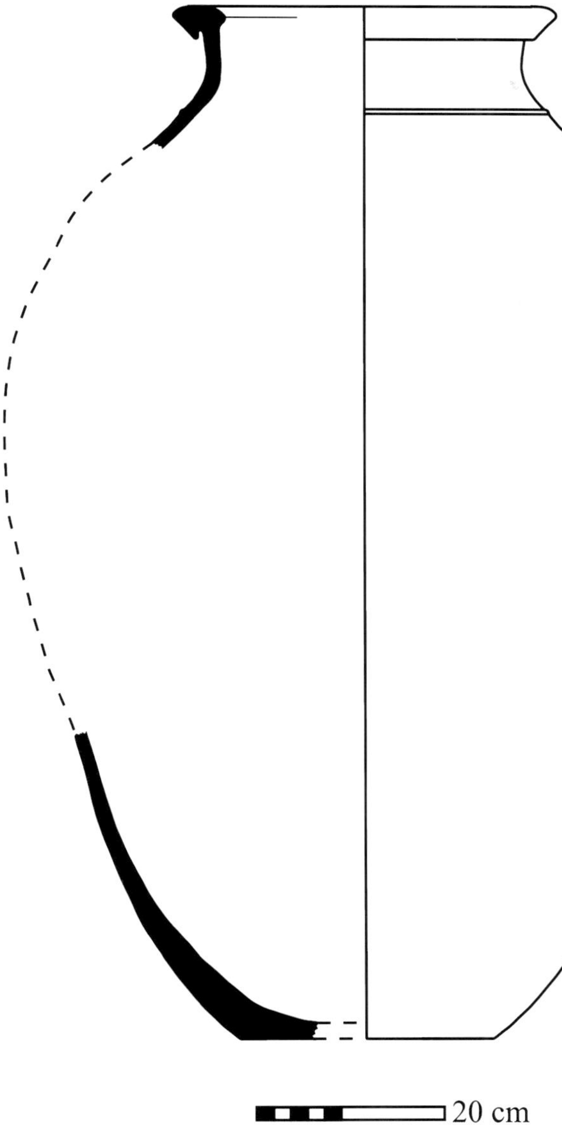

Fig. 10 An Excavated Jar from one of the LBA Storage Rooms in WO.

CHAPTER 7

SABUNIYE: A LATE BRONZE-IRON AGE PORT SETTLEMENT ON THE NORTHEASTERN MEDITERRANEAN COAST

Hatice PAMIR
Mustafa Kemal University Faculty of Sciences –Letters,
Tayfur Sökmen Campus
31040 Antakya/Hatay, Turkey
E-mail: haticepamir@gmail.com

ABSTRACT

Sabuniye is located on a natural hill in the Orontes Delta and on the north bank of the Orontes River, about 6 km inland from the Mediterranean coast. The geographical position of Sabuniye and the presence of imported wares at the site suggest that it was an important LBA to IA trade post/port in the northeastern Mediterranean before the port site at Al-Mina was in use. This presentation aims to discuss the continuity of the site and the trade relations of Sabuniye, which was the trade post/port of the Amuq Plain sites such as Alalakh at Tell Atchana mound and Kunulua at Tell Tayinat mound during the Late Bronze through the Iron Age.

INTRODUCTION

Sabuniye lies on the southern prominent point of a natural hill and the northern bank of the Orontes River. Approximate site area measurements are 120 (NW-SE) × 80 (NE-SW) m for a total of ca.1 ha in size, including the hilltop and the south slope area;[1] although an earlier publication mentions ca. 1.2 ha in size, now it is considered to be slightly smaller (**Fig. 1**). It is located around 55 m above sea level and 30 m above the present floodplain, which extends to the north,west and South of the site.. The western and northern edges of the natural rocky outcrop, on which the mound lies are very steep and appear to have been artificially cut while the southern slopes rise more gently with terraces. The site may extend further to the south, but on the northern part of the hilltop, the sandstone bedrock is already visible on the ground. Thus, the main occupation of the mound is limited to the southern part of the natural hill. This may be due to heavy cultivation activities and there is a possibility that

[1] Pamir 2005, p. 71

the original occupation spread to encompass the entire hilltop area. The site is now heavily damaged by cultivation activities and large cuts are visible on the mound in the southwest and southeast. The southeast slope was transformed into a terraced field and some field systems can be observed on the hilltop.The summit is about 30 m above floodplain, and from it the site has strategic views of the delta, the Mediterranean, and the river.

The Delta region is located in the Hatay Province, southeast Turkey at the mouth of the Orontes River (**Fig. 2**). The Orontes River flows from Lebanon, through Syria and the Amuq Plain; after passing through highland topography, it reaches the Orontes Delta, making a flood plain flow basin measuring about 6 km before emptying its water into the Mediterranean Sea.

Recent paleogeographic research on the Orontes Delta showed that geomorphological changes occurred due to environmental conditions in historical processes. The coastline of the Delta was raised by tectonic movements 1. 2 m in the southern part of the Delta and 1.7 m in the northern of the Delta 2500–2800 years ago; a second such uplift movement occurred 1400 years ago and added another 0.7–0.8 m.[2] Öner's research in 2002 and 2003[3] revealed very important results for the settlement history of the trade ports of Sabuniye as well as Iron Age II-III Al-Mina in the delta. According to the results, the coastline was located in between Al-Mina and Sabuniye after the Middle Holocene (BP 7000–5000) and the delta seems to be a bay in that period. The sedimentation continually filled the bay densely through a 5000 year process and the delta acquired its present shape. In addition, alluvial sediments of the Orontes River carried by small streams, as well as erosion and sand dune movements by the action of wind or waves effected and changed the geomorphological condition of the delta. The results revealed that Sabuniye was not on the coast and but environmentally it was closer to the coastline, that is, to the Orontes river mouth than it is in the present. When settlement began on Sabuniye the delta plain level was -10 m lower than the present level. An even more important result is that since the coastline was located between Al-Mina and Sabuniye, Al-Mina was under sea level during the Late Bronze and Early Iron Age.[4]

The topographical features of the northern Levantine region are characterized by steep mountain ranges running parallel to the coastline, which give very few means of access to the inland regions and the Orontes Delta is one of the few port areas there. Thus, the Orontes Delta is the gateway from the Amuq Plain to the Mediterranean

[2] Pirazzoli et al 1991, pp. 290–310.

[3] Öner 2008, pp. 1–25. The paleogeographich research was part of the ODAP and AVRP (Amuq Valley Regional Projects) research. Coring sondages were carried out on the delta around the mound of Sabuniye, along the Orontes River course in the delta, and on the present coastline.

[4] Öner 2008, pp. 10–12, fig. 13, 14, 15. According to coring results when Al-Mina was settled in the 8th century BC it was situated on the coast thus on the flood plain and river sediments which covered previous flood plain sediments.

Sea. Furthermore, these two areas have to be considered as interacting historical units. The Amuq Valley is strategically situated between the Upper Tigris and Euphrates river systems of eastern Turkey/Northern Syria, Iraq, and the Mediterranean Sea. As emphasized before by many scholars, the Amuq Valley is at the crossroads of overland routes[5] and the following four principal cultural zones are connected by the natural corridors of the river valleys in this interaction zone: Anatolian, eastern Mediterranean (Aegean-Cypriot), Levantine, Palestinian (Egyptian and Canaanite), and northern Syro-Mesopotamian (Hurrian/Mitanni and Assyrian Babylonian).[6]

The best known archaeological expedition in the delta region was led by C. Leonard Woolley in the late 1930s. Two sites, Sabuniye and Al-Mina, were discovered by Woolley in 1936. He excavated Al-Mina between 1936 and 1937 and Al-Mina was introduced as the major Greek colony in the Levant.[7] A total of three soundings were executed at Sabuniye during his excavation at Al-Mina in 1936. It was only mentioned in a few passages in the Al-Mina excavation report.[8] Woolley argued that Sabuniye was settled during the Bronze Age as a residential area of the Greek merchants who traded at Al-Mina. He also suggested that the Late Bronze Age of Al-Mina was swept away when the river course of the Orontes changed. However, the results of the Sabuniye soundings were never published in detail and even the location of the site was gradually forgotten by the academic community.

The new research program at Sabuniye was named the Orontes Delta Archaeological Project (hereafter ODAP), which conducted a series of surface surveys at the site between 1999 and 2005.[9] After a six-year survey program, the Sabuniye excavation started in 2008 and continued in 2009 (**Fig. 3**).

Material culture

The collections of the Sabuniye excavations and surveys have yielded significant amounts of artefacts of non-local production. In addition to these, a small number of examples from the 1936-1937 sounding are housed at the Hatay Archaeological Museum, the British Museum, the Ashmolean Museum, the Classical Museum of Cambridge University, and the Institute of Archaeology in London. Only the Late Bronze and Iron Age I-III materials in the collections are presented in this article.[10]

[5] Braidwood 1937, p. 10; see also Alkım 1969, p. 280.
[6] Yener 2005, p. 2.
[7] Woolley 1937, pp. 1–15; Woolley 1938, pp. 133–170.
[8] Woolley 1937, pp. 11–12; Woolley 1938, pp. 8–9.
[9] Yener, Harrison and Pamir 2002, pp. 289–302; Pamir and Nishiyama 2002, pp. 294–314; Pamir 2005, pp. 67–98; Pamir 2006, pp. 535–544.
[10] The ODAP is currently researching the previously excavated materials in museum collections. This work is ongoing and was supported by the American Research Institute in Turkey (ARIT).

The Sabuniye collections in the Hatay Archaeological Museum included three scarab seals in white stone dated to the LB/Iron I periods.[11] Two important artefacts from the Sabuniye 2008 excavations include a scarab dating to Thutmosis III with his royal sign on it. The other is a cylinder seal. The first example is a limestone scarab beetle with wings spread out and on the seal base is a cartouche with the name of Thutmosis III (*Mn-hpr-r*) (**Fig** 4).[12] Thutmosis III (ruled from 1479 to 1425 BC) campaigned to north Syria seventeen times and conquered many towns. His seventh military campaign was against the port cities of the northern Levant. All the surplus grain, which was produced in Syria, was stored in the harbors that he recently conquered and was used for the support of the military and civilian Egyptian presence ruling Syria.[13] The scarab seems to imply that there is evidence of his traders or his activity in Sabuniye during his military campaigns.

The second example is a complete LB II (15th century BC) cylinder seal from the survey (**Fig.** 5). It is cut in the Mitannian style depicting a worshipper facing a tree of life with two horned animals, necks crossed behind; similar specimens were found at Tell Atchana/Alalakh.[14] The Sabuniye cylinder seal is of black stone from the surface collection of the 2008 excavation campaign (**Fig.** 6). It is carved with extremely fine lines and has figures with cartoonish arms, legs, and drillings. It is very similar in stylistic composition to the so-called binary group in North Syria, similar to Ras Shamra/ Ugarit examples dated to the Late Bronze II.[15] It might belong to a unique group, which should be included with the Egyptian influenced north Syrian stamp seal group.[16] Another cylinder seal from Sabuniye is a dark green stone in the Hatay Museum collections was previously published by Collon.[17] It depicts a figure that stands facing right carrying a bow over his right shoulder and raises his hand up; he wears a horned headdress and shoes with upturned toes in the Hittite style. He approaches a figure, which raises his right hand and is seated on a high backed, gate legged chair; few details of this figure remain, but he wears a pointed head dress which may be horned, and he seems to be robed. Grouped in front of two figures are a star, two drill holes, two crosses, a triangle and a sign; grouped behind the figures are

[11] Hatay Archaeological Museum Inventory No: 6875, 6863, 6923. All of the recorded Sabuniye finds from the Al-Mina collection have not been published so far.

[12] The preliminary stylistic analysis was made by Dr. Hasan Peker, Istanbul University, Faculty of Letters, Department of Ancient Cultures and Languages. Also see Jaeger 1982.

[13] Redford 2003, p. 218.

[14] See for example, Collon 1982, pp. 39–40, 54.

[15] Hammade 1994, p. 113, no. 455.

[16] The preliminary stylistic analysis was made by Prof. Dr. Süleyman Özkan, Ege University, Department of Ancient History.

[17] Hatay Archaeological Museum Inv. No.: 10302. Published by Collon 1982, pp. 124–125, cat. no 114.

a lituus, sign, a drill hole, an oval shape, and a bird. [18] The seal was dated to the 13th century BC and confirmed by parallels from Emar, Carchemish and Ugarit, when Hittite political influence was strong in northern Syria.[19]

The ceramics

The Sabuniye assemblage yielded fragmentary vessels of Cypriot origin and number more than 60 pieces, indicating close connections with the island. The imported Cypriot wares are represented by Middle Cypriot III/Late Cypriot I Red on Black, and Red on Red samples, Late Cypriot II Base Ring II, White Slip II, Late Cypriot White Shaved wares and the local production of Late Cypriot IIIC wares.[20] The majority of the series is represented by the Late Bronze Cypriot II-III milk bowls at Sabuniye (**Figs 7a, 7b**).[21] Cypriot White Slip II ware mainly consists of "milk bowl" shapes, which can often be found in the major LB sites in the coastal areas of the northern Levant.[22]

Mycenaean pottery in the Sabuniye assemblage is represented by three types; LH IIIA2, LH IIIC (**Figs 8–9**) [23] and Early Iron Age transitional period sherds (**Fig. 10**). [24] These were collected during the surveys in1999–2007 and the 2008 excavation. Almost all pieces of LH IIIC are surface finds and non stratified, therefore, it is very difficult to date the pieces stylistically to individual LH IIIC phases.[25] The LH IIIC and Late Bronze/Early Iron Age sherds in the Sabuniye collection are the local adaptations of Mycenaean models.[26] They were either imported, or were a local imitation of an Aegean ceramic industry, or made by resettled Aegean potters who sought to continue production of a long standing ceramic tradition, perhaps with local influence.[27] The LH IIIC pottery in the Levant is considered to be a local

[18] Collon 1982, p. 124.
[19] Collon 1982, p. 125.
[20] Pamir 2002, p. 307, fig. 11, p. 309 fig. 13: 4–9; 2005, p. 82, fig. 3.7/1–4, 7–8.
[21] Pamir 2002, p. 307 fig. 11 nos. 4–6; 2005, pp. 72, 82, fig. 3.7:1–4.
[22] Yon 2001, pp. 117–126.
[23] The preliminary analysis of the imported pottery during the 2002 survey collection was made by R.B. Koehl. The study of the imported pottery of Middle Cypriote/Late Cypriot I, Late Bronze III and Late Cypriot II and III has not been completed yet. Some of the samples were published in Pamir 2002: p. 306 fig. 10.1, fig. 13 1–3, p. 310; see also Pamir 2005, pp. 82–83, fig. 3.7: 5–6, 88–89, fig. 3.11: 2.
[24] Some of the samples from Sabuniye survey were published in Pamir 2005, pp. 82–83, fig. 3.7: 9–12, fig. 3.11: 1.
[25] The same situation has been discussed for the LH IIIC wares of Tarsus excavations, see Mountjoy 2005, pp. 84–85.
[26] Pamir 2005, p. 82, fig. 3.7: 9–12.
[27] These have as yet not been analyzed. Gagne 2008, p.106 debates the presence of LH III A-C pottery and gives the results that "Neutron Activation Analysis suggested that the most of the Mycenaean III A-B pottery found in Cyprus, especially Enkomi, was manufactured at Tiryns where along with Boeotian Thebes and Perati,..." however "Mycenaean IIIC:1 pottery in Cyprus was locally made or was imported from different parts of Greece perhaps Crete or from the Levant. "

production[28] at the beginning of the 12th century BC after the destructions by the so-called "Sea Peoples." Only nine coastal sites in Syria and Palestine have yielded LH IIIC vases or fragments; in several cases most certainly of local manufacture.[29] The new evidence of Mycenaean LH IIIC middle phase 1 from the Alalakh excavations[30] and slightly later from the Tayinat excavations[31] together with its existence in Sabuniye suggests the regional and trade relations with the Amuq Valley of LH IIIC pottery at Sabuniye.

The Sabuniye Iron Age II assemblage has yielded imported Cypriot Geometric wares, Red Slip burnished wares, a fragment of Black Figured Attic vase depicting a mythological scene,[32] and Iron Age II Cypriot White Painted and Bichrome wares dating to the 7th to 6th centuries (**Fig. 11**). Another group of imports come from different Aegean production centers. Two pieces in the Sabuniye collection are painted in the Wild Goat style produced in a western Anatolian pottery center, possibly Miletus (**Fig. 12**). There are parallel examples from Candarlı that are dated to the end of 7th and the beginning of 6th centuries BC.[33] A fragmentary krater with Attic Red Figured style painted ware was found during the 2009 excavation. A mythological *Kentauromakhia* scene is depicted in which *Herakles* is fighting with a *kentauros* (centaur) and Athena on one side and running female figures and a *Herme* altar on the other side of the krater (**Fig. 13**). Stylistic analysis demonstrates that the vase is to be dated to early 5th century BC and was produced by Attic Red Figure potters and painters.[34]

One noteworthy find in this area of the trench was a basalt plate (**Fig. 14**). One third of the plate was broken, but it is one of the typical forms of basalt vessels dated to the 8th century BC. It has two handles on the outer rim, which were curved out from the body of the vessel. It has a ring base and the interior is well polished. Similar specimens are reported from sites in the northern Levant, such as Hama,[35] Zincirli,[36] Carchemish,[37] and Tell Halaf.[38]

[28] Dothan and Zukerman 2004, pp. 1–54. Analyses of the Mycenaean IIIC: 1b pottery from Ekron and Ashdod indicate that it was locally produced; Asaro et al 1971, pp. 169–75, Cline 1994, p. 62, typologically it closely resembles assemblages of Mycenaean IIIC:1b found on Cyprus and the Helladic mainland.

[29] Vanschoonwinkel 2006, p. 49, fig. 3. Eight coastal sites were listed in the article.

[30] Yener (this volume).

[31] Janeway 2008, pp. 129–136; Harrison (this volume).

[32] Pamir 2005, p. 84, fig. 3.8, p. 88 fig. 3.11, p. 90, fig. 3.12, p. 92, fig. 3.14.

[33] Özkan 1999, Catalogue no. 74.

[34] Boardman 1988, pp. 111–113, figs. 163, 195–198.

[35] Riis 1990, p. 70, no. 72.

[36] von Luschan and Andrae 1943, p. 21, nos, n–q.

[37] Woolley 1939–40, pp. 31, 36, 37, pl. 16c2.

[38] Hrouda 1962, pp. 67, 70, pl. 51.

Discussion

The Sabuniye collection contains sufficient non-local material showing its regional and interregional relations. As yet, the earliest non-local materials from Sabuniye are Late Bronze Cypriot, Mycenaean wares, and Egyptian scarabs. All Late Bronze imported wares and scarab from Sabuniye show that the relations of the site were a part of the northern Levantine trade network during the Late Bronze Age II and III dating to the 15th century through 12th centuries BC. Its situation on the Orontes River gorge at the beginning of a natural and safe pass between the Amuq plain and the Mediterranean coast, established Sabuniye as a port settlement both for trade and travel from the coast into the rich centers of the Amuq plain.

Fifty-five sites were recorded by ODAP surveys in 1999, 2002–2005 of which five sites were pre-classical sites in the delta.[39] The two Bronze Age sites, Sabuniye and Virşa Tepe, are located on the hilltop overlooking the delta. The pottery assemblages of Virşa Tepe are mainly of local production, however, the Sabuniye pottery assemblage has yielded LB/IA imported products from Egypt, Greece mainland, Aegean, Cyprus, and Levant. A pre classical site on the lower Orontes valley is Kaletepesi situated as a stopover/station between Sabuniye and the Amuq Plain, and is located on a natural low hill on the northern bank of the river valley near Aknehir (**Fig. 15**).

Imported Aegean ceramics and their local imitations were found at Amuq mounds such as Tell Atchana/ Alalakh and 21 other sites dating to the Late Bronze Age. These sites are distributed all over the plain with a concentration in the southern part of the valley. Aegean imports reached the plain during the first phase of the Late Bronze Age (Amuq M), which is represented by the finds on five sites. Cypriot White Slip II was found at Yassıyurt (AS 6),[40] Topraklı-Baytarlı (AS 40), and imported Mycenaean pottery was uncovered at Atchana, Chatal Höyük and Tell Judaidah, which are situated along the east-west route; Yassıyurt is in the north (**Fig. 15**).[41] In the Late Bronze Age, this East-West trade activity in the Mediterranean was controlled from the inland by the trade/administrative center, Alalakh (Tell Atchana). The trade route is divided in two directions after reaching Atchana, one towards the Belen Pass, which went over the Amanus Mountain range and the other safer, closer route was connected to the Mediterranean coast as the sea trade network. This route passes through the Amuq plain, follows the Orontes River valley, and reaches the Delta at the Mediterranean coast (**Fig. 16**). Situated strategically at the beginning of the Delta, Sabuniye was on the northern bank of the river course.

39 Pamir 2005, pp. 67–98.
40 AS initials connotate the Amuq Survey recording system.
41 Verstraete and Wilkinson 2000, p. 188, fig. 12a.

Aegean imports between the Aegean and the eastern Mediterranean start in the latter half of the 14th century.[42] The importation of Late Bronze Age Aegean related products to the Amuq which are commonly Mycenaean III A2 styles, occurs during Amuq M at Atchana[43] and this phase ended around the 13th century BC.[44] Swift describes the second phase of the imported material as Amuq N, which is the transitional phase marked by local imitations of Aegean pottery, LH III C1 dated to the mid 12th century BC.[45] This type of pottery, which was found on 19 sites including Tell Judaidah, Chatal Höyük, Alalakh/Atchana, and Tell Tayinat, had a wider distribution than the earlier Aegean imports, indicating perhaps that it circulated among a wider range of social groups or communities.[46] The renewed excavations in 2004 at Tell Tayinat in the Amuq plain have yielded several LH IIIC 1 wares such as a *skyphos*, or bell-shaped example with one or two horizontal handles[47] with similar counterparts in the Sabuniye collections. The similar patterns typical of the LH IIIC transitional wares have also been observed in Cilicia (Tarsus)[48] and Cyprus, where they have been related to changes in economic organization.[49] Local imitations of LH IIIC painted wares and early Iron Age painted wares of North Syria as well as Cypriot wares from the Sabuniye collection show that despite the declining Mycenaean trade on the Levantine coast, Sabuniye was still active and was one of the few sites along the north Levantine coast which contained LBA and Iron Age I occupation. Very fresh data from Alalakh Level 0 with LH IIIC1 middle phase 1 ceramics[50] shows that despite the devastating destruction of the "Sea Peoples" the interrelation of the Eastern Mediterranean, the trade network between Sabuniye and Alalakh still continued. The quantity and the proportion of the imported material in the whole Sabuniye collection indicates that the bulk of the Late Bronze Age and the Iron Age imports are from the Aegean and Cyprus.

The Sabuniye collection contains Iron Age II and III imported sherds; among them, Cypro-Geometric ware is the largest group of Aegean imports. However, contrary to Sabuniye, Al-Mina, located on the northern bank of the Orontes river course and much closer to the coast, has yielded an imported wares series dating to the Iron Age II and III. The series starts with Euboean Geometric and continues with almost

[42] Koehl 2010, p. 82; Swift 1958, pp. 63–64 regarded Aegean imports as starting during Amuq M, and continuing to the end of the period to about 1400 BC; The Amuq N phase cannot be dated earlier than the 12th century BC.

[43] Koehl 2010, p. 82.

[44] Atchana Level I is now dated to the late 14th C with an abandonment in the 13th C. No LH IIIB occurs at Alalakh. see Yener this volume.

[45] Swift 1958, pp. 63–64.

[46] Swift 1958, pp. 63–64; Verstraete and Wilkinson 2000, p. 188.

[47] Janeway 2008, p. 129.

[48] Swift 1958, p. 120; Mountjoy 2005, pp. 87–132.

[49] Verstraete and Wilkinson 2000, pp. 188–189.

[50] New evidence from Atchana LH IIIC early phase 1 see Yener in this volume.

all samples of Athens and Corinthian, Ionian, Aegean black and red figured series. This series also has Cypriot, Levantine and Egyptian productions. The quantity and proportion of the imported IA II–III material in Sabuniye collection is less than the Al-Mina collections.

The imported Greek, Protogeometric (Attic), Geometric and Sub Geometric pottery as well as Cypro- Geometric wares were found at or near the surface over most of the three sites in the Amuq; Tell Tayinat, Chatal Höyük and Tell Judaidah.[51] In addition, several hundred sherds of many Greek wares and a small number of whole vases came from Amuq O (950–550 BC) levels from Tayinat and Chatal Höyük and fewer from Judaidah.[52] With few exceptions, the sherds came from open vessels, preponderantly small *skyphoi*, cups and bowls, although a fair number of krater fragments were also unearthed.[53] The amount of Greek geometric pottery from the Amuq mounds is greater than the sporadic pieces found at Syria and Levant sites with the exception of Al-Mina. Furthermore, the quantity and variety of the Greek geometric pottery from the Amuq is indeed impressive and the amount from Tell Tayinat alone is second only to Al-Mina.[54] In general, it should be stressed that the range and types of Greek pottery from the Amuq are very similar to those of Al-Mina levels X-V. The Geometric II period marks the beginning of relations between the Aegean/Greek centers and Near East trade centers. The majority of the imported wares are small cups, Euboean *skyphoi* with pendant semi circles, and kraters. The series starts with Euboean Geometric wares and continues with almost all examples of Athens and Corinthian, Ionian, and Aegean Black and Red Figured wares, plus Cypriot, Levantine, and Egyptian imports. As Kantor and Swift pointed out, it may safely be assumed that the Amuq supplies came in by way of Al-Mina, and that it was the harbour, presumably the main one, of the Kingdom of Hattina, which was one of the sites important at that time, and probably was the capital, Tell Tayinat (**Fig. 16**). [55]

A recently published Assyrian account of Tiglath Pilesar's conquests in 738 BC lists conquered places on the north Syrian coastline and gives the name "*Ah-ta- [a]* " the trading post by the edge of the sea, the place of the kingship's " store" (a storehouse) on the river plain/delta between Kel Dağ (Jebel Aqra, Mt. Cassius) and the Amanus mountain.[56] *Ah-ta-[a]* is thought to be described as a trading post on the coast.[57] As Lane Fox suggested either Ah-ta-a is itself this 'trading post by the edge of the sea',

[51] Swift 1958, pp. 124–125, 151–155.
[52] Swift 1958, p. 153.
[53] Saltz 1978, p. 81.
[54] Saltz 1978, p. 80.
[55] Kantor 1962, p. 93; Swift 1958, p. 153.
[56] Lane Fox 2009, p. 106 footnote 10: He referred to Tadmor 1994 Stele IIB Lines on p. 105 (Tadmor, H., 1994. Inscriptions of Tiglath-Pileser III, King of Assyria). Boardman 2002, p. 328 had doubts with this theory.
[57] Zadok 1996, pp. 11–13.

surely Al-Mina on the seashore, or Ah-ta-a is one place, possibly Sabuniye, and the trading post is Al-Mina, while the "place of the kingship's 'store" is the same or yet another site".[58] The words *Potamoi Karon* were used to mention the mouth of the Orontes River and its environs. The non-Greek word *Karon* may have derived from *karu (n)*: the name *Potamoi Karon* would then mean 'River(s) of the Trading post', referring to the mouth of the Orontes on which Al-Mina stood: the uncertain 'royal storehouse' in Tiglath Pilesar' s list may well be the same place.[59] Two epigraphical documents as well as the imported materials testify to the rich port settlement in the delta during the Iron Age.

Conclusions

It is clear that a trade route from the Amuq plain was connected to the Delta area and to the Late Bronze Age site of Sabuniye. In the Late Bronze Age this Mediterranean East-West trade activity was controlled from the inland by the trade/administrative center, Alalakh (Tell Atchana) and from the coast by the trade post, Sabuniye. Woolley proposed that Al-Mina was the port of Alalakh, though there is no material of the Late Bronze and Early Iron Age at the site.[60] But, recent research and excavations at Sabuniye disproved his thesis and proved that it was the Late Bronze Age port of Alalakh. Three cylinder seals from the Sabuniye collections, a Mitannian cylinder 15th Atchana style, a seal dated to the 13th century BC during the time Hittites ruled at Atchana, and another seal from the 15th century BC commonly used in North Syria, suggest trade relationships between the two sites and traders' existence at Sabuniye. Egyptian imports and imitations show the impact of Egyptian activities at Sabuniye and the Delta during the Late Bronze Age through the Iron Age. After Alalakh was deserted at the end of the Bronze Age and after a brief occupation in the early Iron Age, Tell Tayinat was inhabited. Soon after, it became the political, economical, and cultural center of the plain. During the early Iron Age transitional phase, Sabuniye was still settled and was actively the port of the Delta and Amuq sites. Its trade was mainly controlled by the important site, Tell Tayinat in the Amuq.

The Sabuniye pottery collection proved that it had been inhabited during all the periods represented by ten levels of the harbor site, Al-Mina, as well as LB and IA1 before Al-Mina. It is certain that this was the place where the merchants lived and who did business with eastern Mediterranean sea trade from the LB through the Persian period. Woolley's excavations at Al-Mina revealed mainly warehouses, and there were no free standing houses, which fairly pointed out Al-Mina's port function.

[58] Lane Fox 2009, p. 106.
[59] Lane Fox 2009, p. 109.
[60] Woolley 1959, p. 153.

Various theories about Al-Mina have been generated without taking into account the existence of Sabuniye and environmental changes in the Delta. One theory by Kearsley was that Al-Mina was settled first by Greek colonists, or alternatively, it was exploited as a Greek mercenary settlement in the pay of Assyria,[61] or there might have been only seasonal occupation by Greeks,[62] or founded by Phoenicians whose merchants traded there alongside Greeks and Cypriots.[63] New results of recent paleogeographical research carried out on the Delta proved that the environmental changes effected the settlement history in the Delta between Sabuniye and Al-Mina. When Sabuniye was settled, the location of Al-Mina was under sea level, and Sabuniye was the location for harbour facilities since it was closer to the coastline and provided safety anchorage on the river course. The four hundred years gap between Al-Mina and Alalakh could be explained by the ecological effects on the morphology of the Delta. Sabuniye was settled first and functioned as port or trade post in the Delta until changing ecological and possibly political conditions which would have affected the Sabuniye settlement. It seems that it lost its strategic position as a port which shifted to Al-Mina in the mid 8th century BC. almost four hundred years later than the destruction of Alalakh. Even if Al-Mina was established as a new port and the port activities shifted to Al-Mina, there is no reason that the settlers of Sabuniye left their residences. This time traders stayed at Sabuniye as the residential location and they did business at Al-Mina at the port. A majority of imported materials of Iron Age II-III at Al-Mina were never compared to a place in the eastern Mediterranean. During Iron Age II-III periods Sabuniye's imported materials are fairly less than at Al-Mina. Although the excavation on Sabuniye has just started, at least the Iron Age III levels of Sabuniye gives a domestic aspect of the site with its finds. An imported basalt stone plate dating to the 8th century BC, a wild goat style *oinoche* dating to the 7th century BC, and Attica Red Figured krater dating to the beginning of 5th century BC found on the floor of a house at Sabuniye suggests the different tastes of the peoples who lived at Sabuniye rather than port trade activity.

In sum, the trade route between the inland and the eastern Mediterranean cities and beyond was carried out with the coordination of the coastal city as a trade post and the inland city as a trade centre. This connectivity mutually affected the development and settlement patterns of both areas and sites. The interrelationship between the coastal city as port and the inland centre can be observed through the relations of Alalakh in the Amuq Plain and Sabuniye on the Delta during the Late Bronze Age and Iron Age I and Tayinat and Sabuniye during Iron Age I. Al-Mina takes over as the trade post of the delta during the Iron Age II-III, and sea trade was controlled by

[61] Kearsley 1999, pp. 109–134.
[62] Boardman 2002, p. 327.
[63] See Pamir 2002, p. 294 and footnote 3.

Al-Mina and Tayinat in the Amuq plain, and Sabuniye has played the role of the residential place for the traders. Interestingly, a similar binary collaboration during the subsequent Hellenistic and Roman Periods can be observed between Antioch in the Amuq plain and Seleuceia Pieria in the Delta.

Bibliography

ALKIM, B. A.

1969 "The Amanus Region in Turkey: New Light on the Historical Geography and Archaeology," *Archaeology* 22: 280–289.

ASARO, F. and PERLMAN, I.

1973 "Provenience Studies of Mycenaean Pottery Employing Neutron Activation Analysis," *Acts of the International Archaeological Symposium "Mycenaeans in the Eastern Mediterranean," Nicosia 27th March 2nd April 1972*, pp. 213–224. Nicosia: Department of Antiquities of Cyprus.

BOARDMAN, J.

1988 *Athenaian Red Figure Vases: The Archaic Period.* London: Thames and Hudson.

2002 "Al-Mina: The Study of a Site," *Ancient West and East* Vol.1: No. 2. Leiden-Boston: Brill.

BRAIDWOOD, R. J.

1937 *Mounds in the Plain of Antioch, an Archaeological Survey*, Oriental Institute Publications 18. Chicago: The University of Chicago.

COLLON, D.

1982 *The Alalakh Cylinder Seals: A new catalogue of the Actual Seals Excavated by Leonard Woolley at Tell Atchana, and from Neighbouring Sites on the Syrian-Turkish Border.* British Archaeological Reports, International Series 132. Oxford: British Archaeological Reports.

CLINE, E.

1994 *Sailing the Wine Dark Sea: International Trade and Late Bronze Age Aegean,* BAR International Series 591. Oxford: British Archaeological Reports.

DOTHAN, T. and ZUKERMAN, A.

2004 "A Preliminary study of the Mycenaean IIIC:1 Pottery Assemblages from Tel Mikne-Ekron and Ashdod," *Bulletin of American Schools of Oriental Research* 333: 1–54.

GAGNE, L.

2008 "The problem of Regional Variation of Mycenaean IIIC:1 Pottery: The View from Cyprus," in *Cyprus, The Sea Peoples and The Eastern Mediterranean: Regional Perspectives of Continuity and Change: Scripta Mediterranea* Vol. XXVII – XXVIII, edited by A. Percival and T. P. Harrison, pp. 105–112. Toronto: Canadian Institute for Mediterranean Studies.

HAMMADE, H.

1994 *Cylinder Seals from the Collections of the Aleppo Museum, Syrian Arab Republic. 2. Seals of known province.* Oxford: British Archaeological Reports.

HROUDA, B.

1962 "Die Kleinfunde aus Historischer Zeit," in *Tell Halaf*, Bd. IV., edited by M. F. von Oppenheim. Berlin: Orient Forschung Institute.

JAEGER, B.

1982 *Essai de classification et datation des scarabées Menkhéperr.* Fribourg: Editions Universitaires.

JANEWAY, B.
2008 "The Nature and Extent of Aegean Contact at Tell Ta'yinat and Vicinity in the Early Iron Age: Evidence of the Sea Peoples?" *Scripta Mediterranea* Vol. XXVII-XXVIII, edited by A. Percival and T. P. Harrison, pp. 123–146. Toronto: Canadian Institute for Mediterranean Studies.

KOEHL, R. B.
2010 "Mycenaean Pottery," in *The Atchana, Ancient Alalakh Volume 1: The 2003–2004 Excavation Seasons*, edited by K. A. Yener, pp. 81–84. İstanbul: Ege Yayınları.

KANTOR, H. J.
1962 "A Bronze Plaque with Relief Decoration from Tell Tainat," *Journal of Near Eastern Studies* 21: 93–117.

LANE FOX, R.
2009 *Travelling Heroes, Greeks and Their Myths in the Epic Age of Homer*, 2nd edition. London: Penguin Books.

MOUNTJOY, P. A.
2005 "The Mycenaean Pottery from the 1934–1939 Excavations at Tarsus," *Field Seasons 2001–2003 of the Tarsus-Gözlükule Interdisciplinary Research Project*, edited by A. Özyar, pp. 83–134. İstanbul: Ege Yayınları.

ÖNER, E.
2008 "Asi Delta Ovasında Alüvyal Jeomorfoloji ve Paleocoğrafya Araştırmaları (Antakya/Hatay)," *Ege Coğrafya Dergisi* 17/1–2, pp. 1–25. İzmir: Ege Üniversitesi Coğrafya Bölümü.

ÖZKAN T.
1999 *İzmir Arkeoloji Müzesi Seramik Kataloğu.* Ankara: T.C. Kültür ve Turizm Bakanlığı Anıtlar ve Müzeler Genel Müdürlüğü.

PAMIR, H.
2005 "The Orontes Delta Survey," in *The Amuq Valley Regional Projects, Vol. 1: Surveys in the Plain of Antioch and Orontes Delta, Turkey 1995–2002,* Oriental Institute Publications 131, edited by K. A. Yener, pp. 67–98. Chicago: University of Chicago Press.
2006 "Al-Mina and Sabuniye in the Orontes Delta: The Sites," in *Greek Colonization: An Account of Greek Colonies and Other Settlements Overseas* Vol. 1, edited by G. R. Tsetskhladze, pp. 535–544. Leiden-Boston: Brill.

PAMIR, H., and NISHIYAMA, S.
2002 "The Orontes Delta Survey: Archaeological Investigations of Ancient Trade Stations/Settlements," in *Ancient West & East* 1/2: 294–314.

PIRAZZOLI, P. A., LABOREL, J., SALIÈGE, F., EROL, O., KAYAN, I., and PERSON, A.
1991 "Holocene Raised shorelines on the Hatay Coasts (Turkey): Palaeoecological and Tectonic Implications," *Marine Geology* 96: 296–310.

REDFORD, D. B.
2003 *The Wars in Syria and Palestine of Thutmose III.* Leiden-Boston: Brill.

RIIS, P. J., BUHL, M.-L.
1990 *Hama. Fouilles et recherches de la Fondation Carlsberg 1931-1938, II 2: Les objets de la période dite Syro-Hittite (âge du fer).* Kopenhagen: National Museets Skrifter.

SALTZ, D. L.
1978 "Greek Geometric Pottery in the East, the Chronological Implications." Unpublished Ph.D diss. Harvard University.

SWIFT, G. E.
1958 "The Pottery of the Amuq Phases K to O and its Historical Relationships," Unpublished Ph.D dissertation, University of Chicago.

VANSCHOONWINKEL, J.
2006 "Mycenaean Expansion," *Greek Colonisation: An Account of Greek Colonies and other Settlements Overseas* Vol. 1, edited by G. R. Tsetskhladze, pp. 41–114. Leiden-Boston: Brill.
VERSTRAETE, J., and WILKINSON, T.
2000 "The Amuq Regional Archeological Survey," in 'The Amuq Valley Regional Project 1995–1998,' K. A. Yener, C. Edens, T. P. Harrison, J. Verstraete, and T. Wilkinson, pp. 179–192, *American Journal of Archaeology* 104: 163–220.
VON LUSCHAN, F., ANDRAE, W.
1943 *Ausgrabungen in Sendschirli V: Die Kleinfunde von Sendschirli.* Mittheilungen aus den Orientalischen Sammlungen / Königliche Museen zu Berlin; Heft 15. Berlin: De Gruyter.
WOOLLEY, C. L.
1937 "Excavations near Antioch in 1936," *The Antiquaries Journal* 17: 1–15.
1938 "Excavations at Al-Mina, Sueidia," *Journal of Hellenic Studies* 58:1–2, pp. 1–30, pp. 133–170.
1959 *A Forgotten Kingdom, Being a record of the results obtained from the excavations of two mounds Atchana and Al-Mina in the Turkish Hatay*, 2nd Edition. London: Max Parrishe and Co Ltd.
YENER, K. A.
2005 "The Amuq Valley Regional Projects," *The Amuq Valley Regional Projects, Vol.1: Surveys in the Plain of Antioch and Orontes Delta, Turkey 1995–2002* Oriental Institute Publications 131, edited by K. A. Yener, pp. 1–16. Chicago: University of Chicago.
2010 *The Atchana, Ancient Alalakh Volume 1: The 2003–2004 Excavations Seasons*, İstanbul: Koç University.
YENER, K. A., EDENS, C., HARRISON, T. P., VERSTRAETE, J., and WILKINSON, T.
2000 "The Amuq Valley Regional Project 1995 – 1998," *American Journal of Archaeology 104/2:* 163–220.
YENER, K. A., HARRISON, T., PAMIR, H.
2002 "University of Chicago, Oriental Institute, 2000 Yılı Hatay Aççana, Tayinat Höyükleri ve Samandağı Yüzey Araştırmaları," *19.Araştırma Sonuçları Toplantısı* Vol. 2, pp. 289–302. Ankara: T. C. Kültür Bakanlığı, Anıtlar ve Müzeler Genel Müdürlüğü,
YON, M.
2001 "White Slip ware in northern the Levant," *The White Slip Ware of Late Bronze Age Cyprus Proceedings of an International Conference organized by the Anastasios G. Leventis Foundation, Nicosia in Honour of Malcolm Wiener, Nicosia, 29th-30th October 1998,* edited by V. Karageorghis, pp. 117–126. Wien: Verlag der Osterreichischen Akademie der Wissenschaften.
ZADOK, R.
1996 "Geographical and Onomastic Remarks," *NABU (Nouvelles assyriologiques bréves et utilitaires)* I: 11–13.

Fig. 1 Sabuniye, view from the west (Sabuniye Archive).

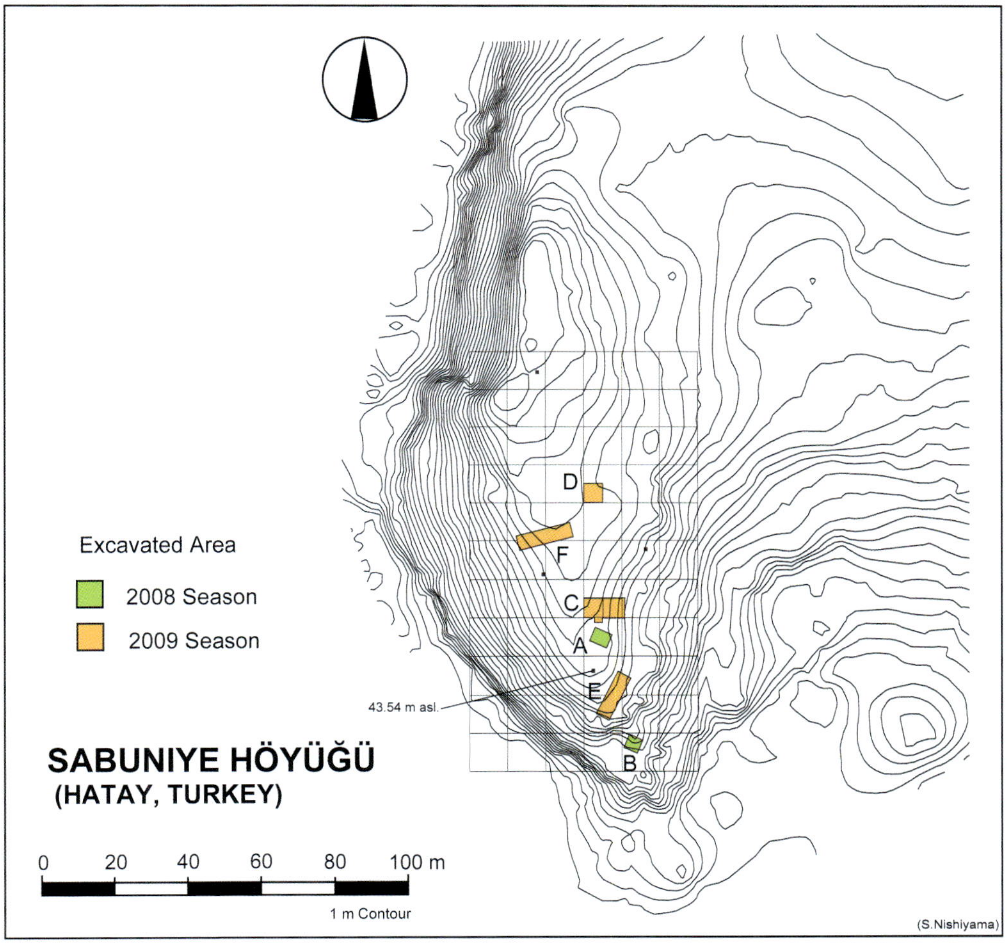

Fig. 3 Sabuniye site map
(drawn by S. Nishiyama, H. Inan after H. Tsumura and Y. Hayakawa).

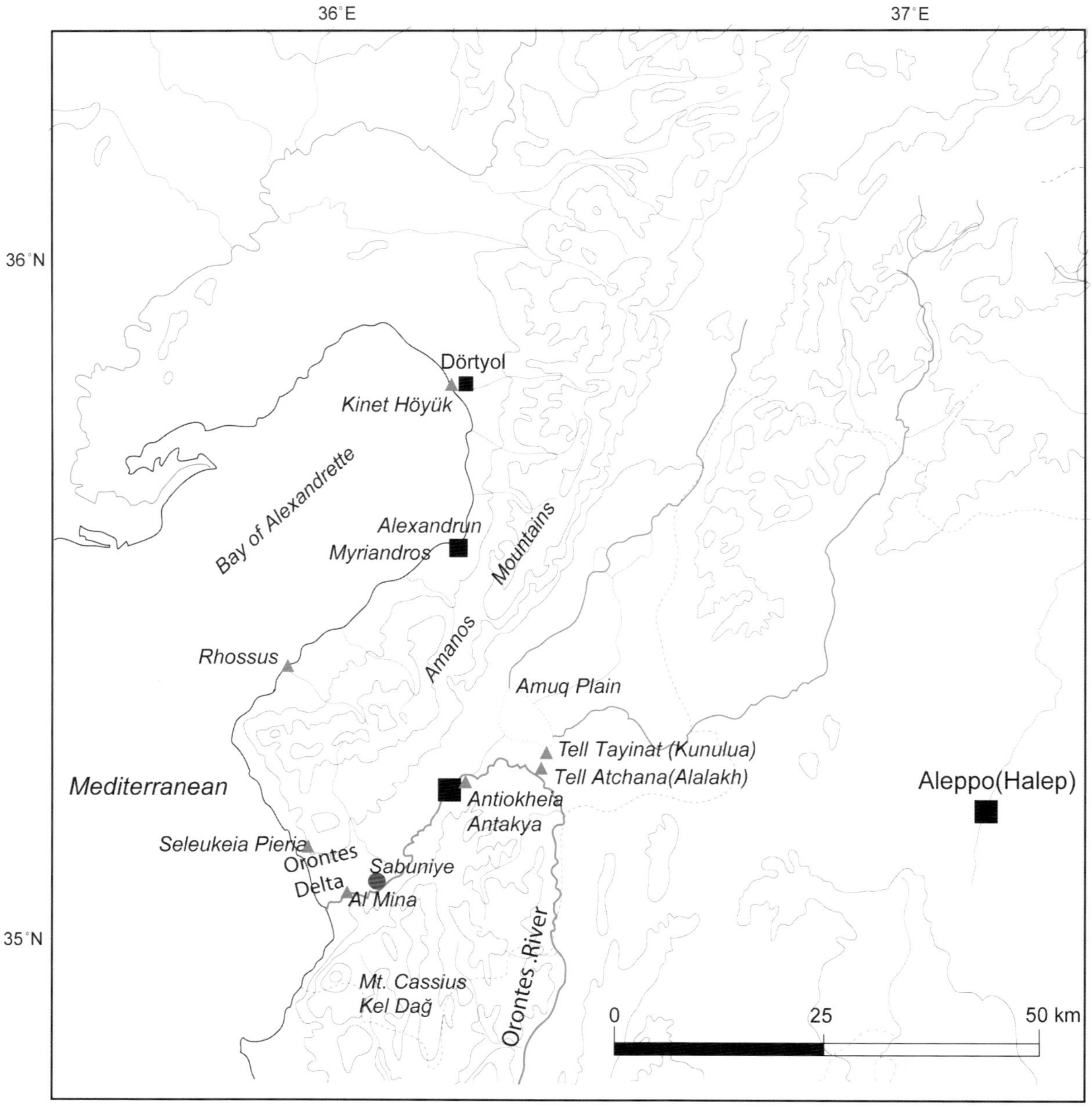

Fig. 2 Northwestern Levant and Sabuniye (ODAP Archive).

Fig. 4 Egyptian Scarab (Sabuniye Archive).

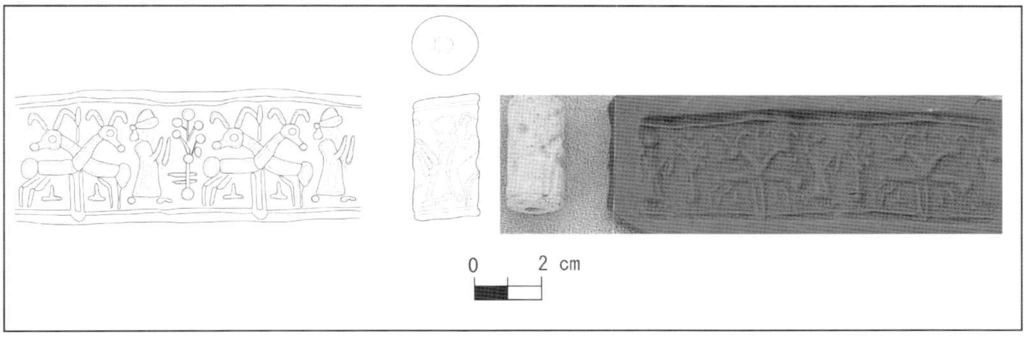

Fig. 5 Late Bronze Age Mitannian style cylinder seal (ODAP Archive).

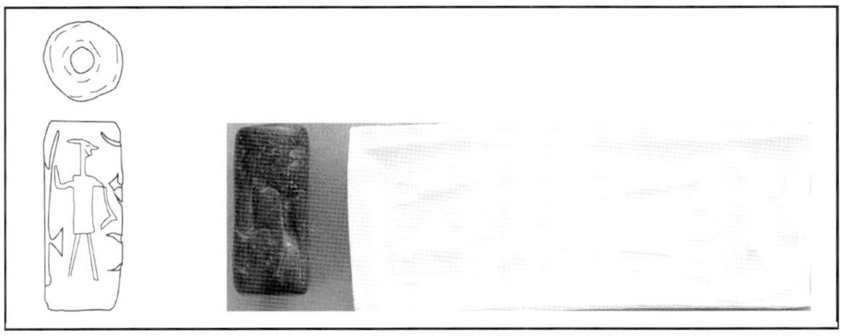

Fig. 6 Late Bronze Age cylinder seal (Sabuniye Archive).

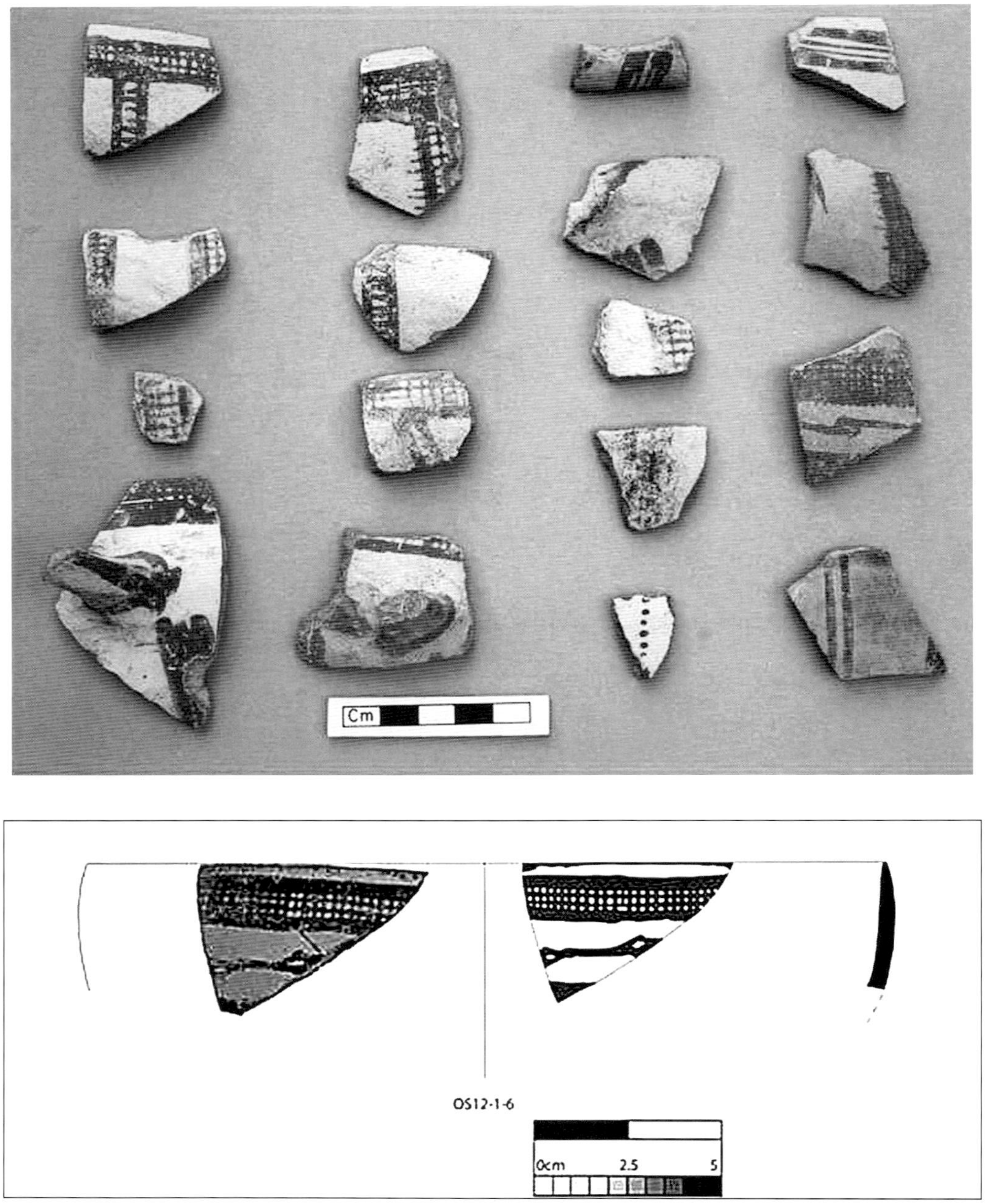

Fig. 7 Fragments of Late Cypriote White Slip II milk bowls (ODAP Archive).

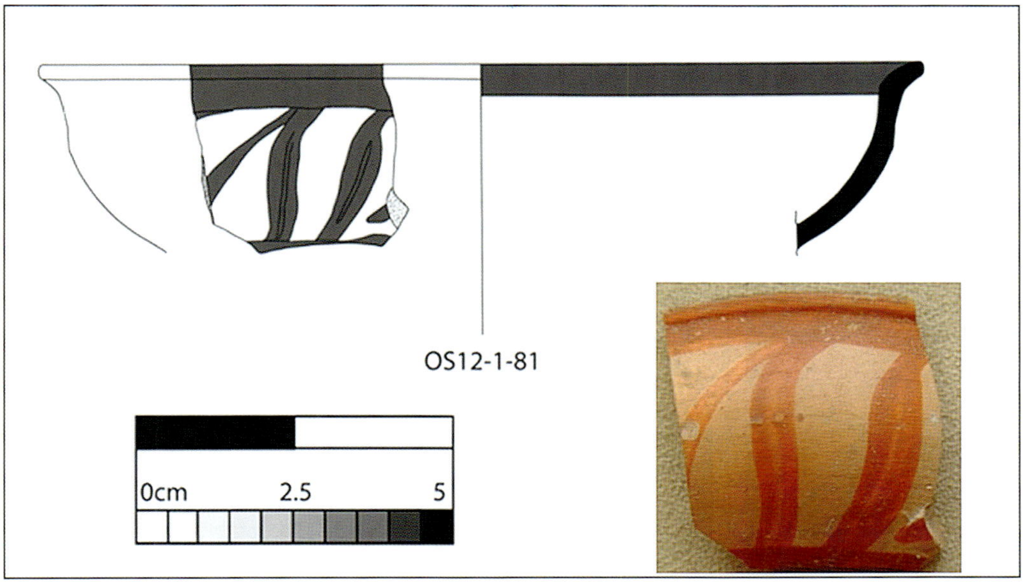

Fig. 8 Fragments of Mycenaean imports a, b, c, d, f, g: LH III A2. (Sabuniye Archive).

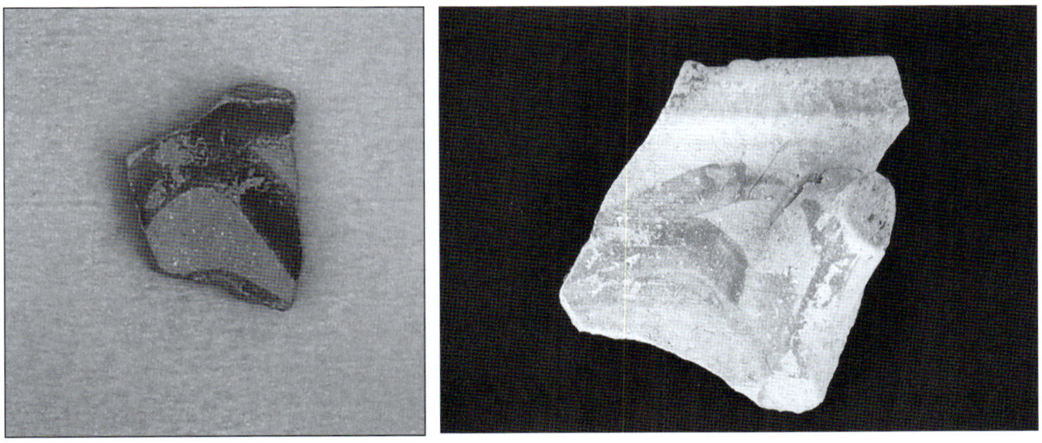

Fig. 9 Fragments of LH IIIC bowls, red paint wavy line decoration, (Sabuniye Archive).

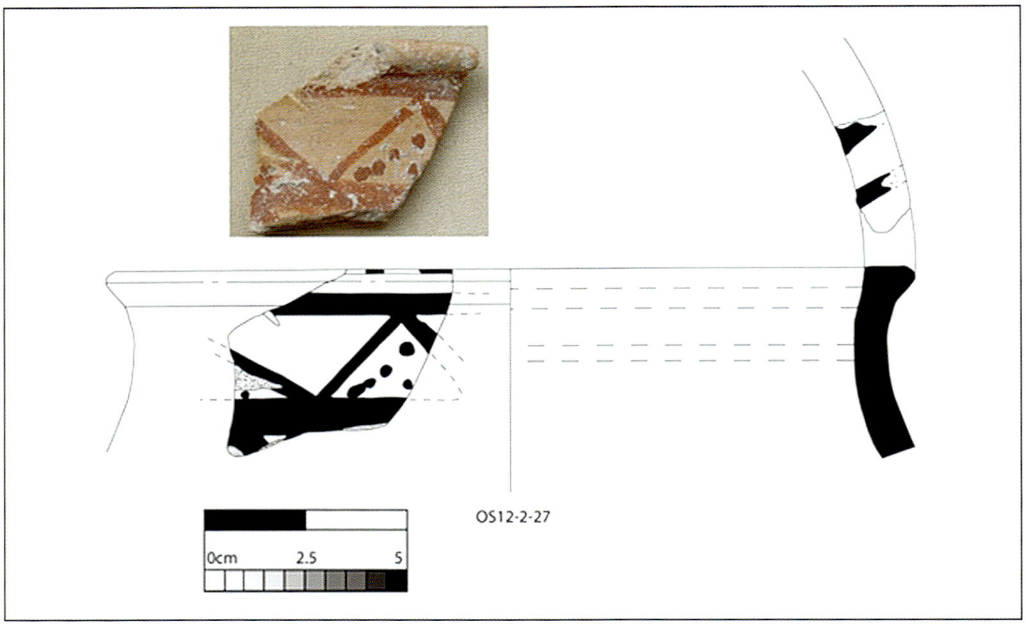

Fig. 10 Fragment with line decoration between two horizontal bands, red paint, Iron Age I (Sabuniye Archive).

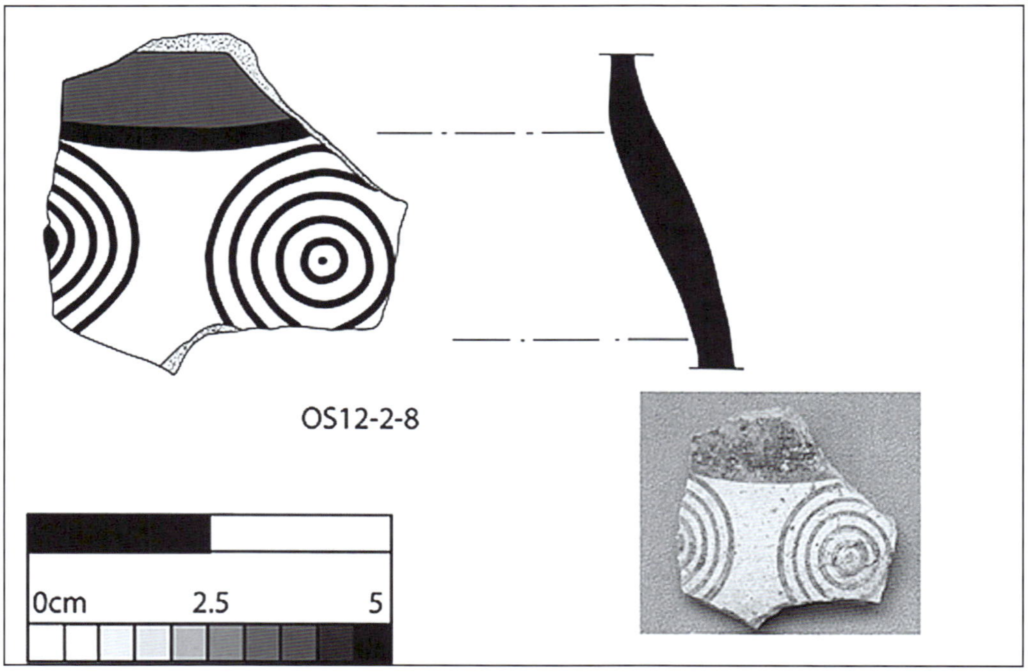

Fig. 11 Fragment of Cypriote bichrome juglet (Sabuniye Archive).

Fig. 12 Fragment of Oinochoe with wild goat style decoration (Sabuniye Archive).

Fig. 13 Fragments of Attican red figured krater (Sabuniye Archive).

Fig. 14 Bazalt Stone plate (Sabuniye Archive).

Fig. 15 Site distrubution of the late bronze and early iron age imported wares (drawn by Pamir, after S. Batiuk).

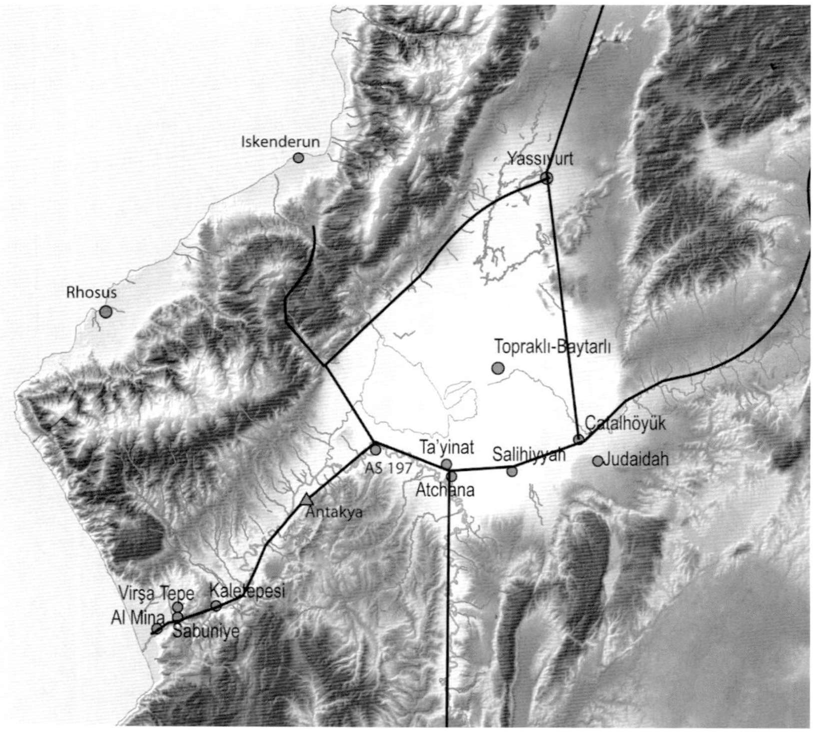

Fig. 16 Trade route in the Amuq and the Orontes Delta (drawn by Pamir, after S. Batiuk).

CHAPTER 8

A RE-EVALUATION OF THE LATE BRONZE TO EARLY IRON AGE TRANSITIONAL PERIOD: STRATIGRAPHIC SEQUENCE AND PLAIN WARE OF TARSUS-GÖZLÜKULE

Serdar YALÇIN
Columbia University
Department of Art History and Archaeology
826 Schermerhorn Hall
1190 Amsterdam Avenue
New York, NY 10027, USA
E-mail: sy2226@columbia.edu

ABSTRACT

Tarsus-Gözlükule is one of the prehistoric sites on the Cilician plain providing a continuous stratigraphy of the transition from the Late Bronze to Early Iron Age. In this study the site's stratigraphic sequence and the change in its plain ware assemblage have been investigated. The re-evaluation of the stratigraphy revealed that there are at least seven successive architectural layers from the destruction of the Hittite settlement until the end of the Early Iron Age. The analysis of these layers demonstrates a decline in the economic conditions of the site following the destruction of the Hittite town.

A re-analysis of the plain wares of Tarsus-Gözlükule has added new forms, which derived from the Hittite Monochrome Ware, to the ceramic corpus of the site. Present study also substantiates the view of G. M. A. A. Hanfmann arguing the continuation of the Hittite monochrome tradition in the Early Iron Age plain wares of Gözlükule. This continuity is particularly visible in jar and bowl forms. These results, combined with the emergence of foreign elements such as painted pottery in ceramics and an apsidal structure in architecture, show that the Late Bronze to Early Iron Age transition brought about both continuity and change at Tarsus-Gözlükule. *

* This paper is a short version of an MA thesis supervised by Prof. Aslı Özyar and submitted to the Institute of Social Sciences at Boğaziçi University, Istanbul in 2005. The full catalogue with further comments will be published in the second volume of the Tarsus-Gözlükule Field Reports series. This research was made possible by the Boğaziçi University Tarsus-Gözlükule Interdisciplinary Research Project, funded by academic research projects (BAP) no. 02R101, 00R104. I would like to thank Prof. Aslı Özyar, Assist. Prof. Elif Ünlü and Prof. Zainab Bahrani for editing this paper and for their valuable comments and suggestions.

The transition from the Late Bronze to Early Iron Age was a period of social and economic turmoil in the eastern Mediterranean. During this period, the great powers of the Late Bronze Age either collapsed, as in the case of the Hittite kingdom, or entered into a period of political instability and administrative fragmentation, as in the case of Egypt. Numerous sites across the region, such as Mycenae, Hattuša, Emar and Ugarit, suffered from serious destructions, and some did not last into the Iron Age. On the other hand, a more gradual transition rather than a complete break can be observed especially in Assyria and the Neo-Hittite kingdoms in Southern Anatolia and Northern Syria. Cultural and political aspects of the Late Bronze Age did not perish altogether, but seem to have lasted in these regions.

The goal of this paper is to understand how this period of economic and political transformation is reflected in the archaeological record of Tarsus-Gözlükule in Cilicia, which was an important Hittite administrative center during the Late Bronze Age. The excavations carried out by a team from Bryn Mawr College headed by Hetty Goldman showed a continuous stratigraphic sequence at Tarsus during the Transitional Period.[1] Especially the painted pottery coming from this sequence is representative of the emergence of new elements at the site after the destruction of the Hittite town. In this context, a re-analysis of the architectural remains and plain ware pottery from the same layers helps us to see a more complete picture of the transformation that the Late Bronze Age community of Tarsus experienced during the Transitional Period. What are the architectural differences between the Late Bronze Age and Early Iron Age towns of Gözlükule? Did the Hittite ceramic tradition last into the Iron Age, or did it also show signs of drastic change as in the case of the emergence of painted pottery?

The following analysis presents new data to answer these questions as well as some new insights concerning the Hittite ceramic repertoire in the Late Bronze Age layers of Tarsus. I argue that the Hittite ceramic corpus of the settlement has a broader shape spectrum than previously assumed. Additionally, confirming the ideas of Hetty Goldman and George M. A. A. Hanfmann in the excavation reports, the Iron Age plain wares of Gözlükule, to a large extent, represent a continuation of the Late Bronze monochrome forms. A severe decline in architecture is attested, which hints at a break with the preceding Hittite tradition. These results, combined with the emergence of foreign elements such as the painted pottery in ceramics and an apsidal structure in architecture, show that the Late Bronze to Early Iron Age transition brought about both continuity and change at Tarsus-Gözlükule.

[1] Goldman 1956, 1963.

A SURVEY OF THE CHANGE IN THE PLAIN WARE TRADITION ACROSS THE HITTITE GEOGRAPHY FROM THE LATE BRONZE TO EARLY IRON AGE

Originated from the fine ceramics of the Old Assyrian colony period and Old Hittite Kingdom in Central Anatolia, the Hittite Monochrome Ware or the so-called 'drab' ware is one of the most distinctive elements of the Hittite material culture during the Late Bronze Age.[2] It became the dominant ceramic group across the Hittite lands with its standardized coarse fabric and shapes from the 15th to the beginning of the 12th centuries BC.[3] This special ware includes a variety of vessel types produced mainly for storage and daily use.[4] They are all wheel-made, not slipped and have no decoration, but in some occasions potters' marks were used as a sign of professional potters' industry.[5] The most characteristic shapes of the monochrome ware are bowls and plates, cooking pots, jars with everted ledge rims and large pitchers with rounded or pointed bases. All are standardized in terms of their shapes, fabric and firing but slight variations occur, particularly in rim shapes.[6]

Large quantities of the Hittite Monochrome Ware were uncovered in a wide geography extending from Mersin-Yumuktepe in Cilicia, to Dündartepe in the Pontic region, from Beycesultan in the inland Aegean to the Keban region in the east (**Fig. 1**).[7] Its standardization and broad distribution across the Hittite lands and its disappearance in many locations right after the collapse of the Hittite kingdom demonstrate the role of the central Hittite administration in imposing the use of this ware on local populations. As Gates suggested, the use of this uniform pottery assemblage across such a wide geography might indicate Hittite political and economic control over the provinces.[8]

Following the collapse of the Hittite administration, regional differences re-emerge in ceramics across its former territories (**Fig. 2**). After the destruction of the Late Bronze Age towns, Monochrome Ware disappeared in many sites such as Gordion, Norşuntepe and Korucutepe.[9] At Hattuša, it survived, but was replaced by new types of pottery after a short period of time.[10] At Kinet the fabrics and shapes of the pottery assemblage show only a superficial resemblance to the preceding Late Bronze II corpus in the sub-Hittite phase of the settlement.[11] It seems that the standards set for

[2] Müller-Karpe 2000, p. 257; see also Schoop 2003, p. 168.
[3] Müller-Karpe 2000, p. 257.
[4] Parzinger and Sanz 1992, p. 15.
[5] Gates 2001, 140.
[6] Müller-Karpe 1988; see also Parzinger and Sanz 1992, pp. 15–33.
[7] Müller-Karpe 2000, p. 257.
[8] Gates 2001, p. 138.
[9] Henrickson 1994, pp. 107–124; Köroğlu 2003, p. 232.
[10] Seeher 1999, p. 331; Genz 2000, p. 36.
[11] Gates 2006, p. 304.

homogenous mass-production declined during this period. With the onset of the Early Iron Age, Hittite pottery totally disappeared at this site as well.

One of the most striking characteristics of the post-Hittite period in Anatolia is the re-appearance of hand-made pottery in many sites such as Hattuša, Gordion, Norşuntepe and Korucutepe after more than a millennium of use of the wheel.[12] Shortly after the destruction of the Hittite towns, hand-made pottery emerged in Gordion, Norşuntepe and Korucutepe as the single present ceramic type. In Hattuša it replaced the last vestiges of the wheel-made Monochrome Ware in the middle and last phases of the Early Iron Age.

Another change is the emergence of painted pottery in many sites. In coastal Southern Anatolia, LH IIIC pottery appears suddenly in the ceramic corpus along with the Late Bronze–Early Iron Age Transitional Painted Pottery at Tarsus, Kilisetepe and Kinet.[13] It was later replaced by Cypro-Cilician painted pottery at the turn of the 1st millennium BC. In Central Anatolia, too, painted decoration re-emerged on hand-made pottery as in Hattuša, or on wheel-made ceramics as in Kaman.[14] In the same period finishing techniques such as polishing and slipping became popular again particularly in Central Anatolia and the upper Euphrates region. Almost all ceramics found in the Early Iron Age levels of Boğazköy were polished to some extent.[15] Likewise, the pottery assemblage at Korucutepe was generally finished with a slip during the same period.[16]

All these developments indicate the disintegration of the standardized ceramic production in the Hittite kingdom and changes in pottery production techniques in many places. However, as Genz suggested, what is termed as change in certain locations such as Central and Eastern Anatolia actually might be the resurgence of local traditions which were suppressed by the Hittite influence in the Late Bronze Age.[17] On the other hand, the appearance of LH IIIC in Southern Anatolian sites may be indicative of the arrival of newcomers from the west to this region.[18]

Hittite plain ware, as mentioned above, vanished rapidly in some sites, whereas it showed resilience in others such as Kaman-Kalehöyük, Lidar, Oylum and Tell Afis, although it was no longer the only ceramic group.[19] In these sites, ceramics derived from Hittite forms seem to have lasted until the 11th century BC. In the ceramic

[12] Genz 2004, p. 24; also see Henrickson 1994, p. 107; Winn 1980, p. 156; Köroğlu 2003, p. 233.

[13] Goldman 1956, pp. 205–209; see also French 1975; Mountjoy 2005; Postgate 1998, p. 134; Postgate and Thomas 2007, pp. 121–152; Symington 2001, p. 172; Gates 2006, p. 304. For a definition of the Late Bronze to Iron Age transitional ware, see Ünlü 2005.

[14] Genz 2000, 2004; see also Matsumura 2000, p. 126.

[15] Genz 2004, p. 24.

[16] Winn 1980, p. 156.

[17] Genz 2004, pp. 37–45.

[18] The appearance of LH IIIC pottery at Tarsus is examined in detail by Goldman (1956), Slane (1987), and Mountjoy (2005); see also Mommsen *et al* (2011).

[19] Omura, 1997, 1998, 2000; see also Müller 1999; Özgen and Helwing 2003; Venturi 2000.

assemblage of Tarsus the plain ware shapes persisted even into the early 1st millennium BC.[20] The continuation of the Monochrome Ware in these sites might be related to several issues. First of all, the physical proximity of the sites such as Tell Afis in the Orontes Valley, and Lidar and Oylum in the middle Euphrates region to the neo-Hittite centers such as Carchemish and Melid/Malatya must have played a role in this continuity. As we know, various aspects of the Hittite *koine* such as hieroglyphic Luwian script and aspects of iconography persisted in the Neo-Hittite states during the Iron Age. In this respect, it is not surprising that Hittite pottery survived as well near these centers.

Another reason for the survival of Hittite pottery might simply be the continuation of ceramic workshops. The craft of pottery production is known to be a conservative one, in which potters are not willing to change their generations-old ways of producing ceramics. In this context, the potters in some Hittite sites did not necessarily stop using techniques and forms, which they had been using for centuries, after the demise of Hittite political authority around 1200 BC. On the other hand, they clearly absorbed new ideas. This would explain why in the Early Iron Age we see pottery forms derived from Hittite monochrome typology, but with painted decoration, for instance, at Tarsus and Porsuk.[21] Such an imaginative approach seems not to have been possible in the strictly standardized ceramic production process of the Late Bronze Age.

The Late Bronze to Early Iron Age Transition at Tarsus-Gözlükule

What kind of change or continuity do we have at Tarsus during the Transitional Period? Which aspects of the Late Bronze Age material culture survived; which perished? What were the new elements and where were their origins? An analysis of the plain wares of Gözlükule along with a review of its architectural remains will help us to answer these questions.

Gözlükule is one of the mounds in Anatolia providing an uninterrupted sequence of the Transitional Period. Architectural layers of this phase were initially published in the Bronze and Iron Age volumes of the Goldman excavations and analyzed as Late Bronze IIb and Early Iron Age phases.[22] In the present study, Late Bronze IIa, IIb (LB IIa and IIb) and Early Iron Age phases of Gözlükule are considered as a continuous sequence, and discussed along with relevant architectural and ceramic remains to detect continuities and changes at the site. The Bryn Mawr College excavations were carried out in two areas of the mound called Section A and Section B. All of the

[20] See the following discussion.

[21] Goldman 1963, fig. 115. 70; see also Dupré 1983, pl. 55, no: 76–80.

[22] Goldman 1956, 1963. Also in 1980s Dorothy Slane re-evaluated the Late Bronze Age levels of the site in her dissertation (1987).

information used in the following discussion, however, is obtained from Section B since a continuous sequence of the Transitional Period is present only in this area (**Fig. 3**). The Goldman publication of architectural remains, the stratigraphic development of pottery proposed by Hanfmann and the field diaries of the former Gözlükule excavations form the basis of the analysis given below.

From the destruction of the Hittite town (LB IIa) to the end of the Early Iron Age, there are at least seven successive architectural layers dating to the Transitional Period at Tarsus-Gözlükule (**Fig. 4**). LB IIa is the phase of the Hittite New Kingdom occupation, during which monumental religious and administrative buildings were attested both in Section A and Section B. In Section A, remains of a freestanding monumental temple building covered the entire excavated area. In Section B, the architectural layout is defined by large-scale, at least two-storied buildings separated by a broad street extending in north-south direction.[23] Both the scale of these buildings and associated finds such as bullae bearing administrative and royal names indicate that this was the administrative district of the Hittite settlement. The ceramic assemblage of this phase is entirely composed of the Hittite Monochrome Wares.[24]

All layers postdating the LB IIa town at Gözlükule contained scanty architectural remains. In this respect, Gözlükule, following the destruction of the Hittite town, turned into a "squatter's settlement", as Goldman labeled it.[25] The successive settlements lacked in size and quality of the building techniques compared to those of the preceding Hittite period. This deterioration in the architectural realm must be a reflection of economic decline and the demise of the Hittite political authority at ancient Tarsa. The only exceptional architectural feature of this era is an apsidal building, which appeared at the site at the beginning of the Early Iron Age (**Fig. 5**). This structure stands out from its surrounding with its freestanding location and distinctive stone foundations, but compared to the structures of the LB IIa phase, it is still poor in terms of its size and construction quality.

Apsidal structures, which had no precursors at Tarsus preceding the Early Iron Age, are generally encountered in the Aegean and western Anatolian context. They appear earliest in the Late Chalcolithic period on either side of the Aegean and continue to be used sporadically in this region until the archaic Greek period.[26] In this context, the construction of an apsidal building at Tarsus might be ascribed to a surmised group of new settlers with western affinities in Cilicia. The emergence of LH IIIC ceramics at the site during the LB IIb phase along with the Transitional Painted

[23] Goldman 1956, pp. 50–58.

[24] Goldman 1956, pp. 203–205.

[25] Goldman 1956, p. 58.

[26] Numerous apsidal houses found across the Aegean and Western Anatolian sites are discussed in Warner (1979), Mazarakis-Ainian (1989), Pappa and Besios (1999), Bakır *et al.* (2001, p. 26) and Drerup (1969, pp. 26–29).

Pottery supports such a view (**Fig.** 4).[27] As shown by the recent study of Mommsen *at al* these special Aegean ceramics were either locally produced at the site or imported from Cyprus and eastern Aegean.[28] This situation shows not only the arrival of a population from the Aegean in Cilicia, but also the region's new position within the changing trade patterns in the Eastern Mediterranean after the end of the Late Bronze Age system.

It is difficult to understand the function of the apsidal structure at Tarsus. Its size, freestanding location and distinctive foundations differentiate this building from all other excavated structural remains of the Transitional Period at the site. Additionally, some later Aegean examples of apsidal and oval houses from Lesbos might have been used for cultic purposes.[29] In this respect, the structure at Gözlükule might have had a special function. However, its badly disturbed floor levels did not provide any material to confirm such a use.[30]

Finally, what kind of a development do we observe in the plain wares of Gözlükule from the Hittite period to the end of the Early Iron Age? In the excavation reports, Goldman made no distinction between the monochrome wares of the LB IIa period and the post-destruction LB IIb levels, stating that no real change or development in either fabric or shape can be discerned between the two phases.[31] The characteristic shapes such as bowls and plates with thickened rims or jars with everted ledge rims continue in abundance. The difference between the wares of these two periods is the presence of more brown and buff colored wares among the LB IIb specimens as opposed to the more reddish wares in the LB IIa period. Goldman's observation is confirmed in the present re-analysis as well. LB IIb and Early Iron Age plain ware fragments seem to have predominantly buff, brown and gray surface colors.[32] This difference between the Hittite and Transitional Period wares implies a significant change in the control of firing process in pottery production. In the absence of state control, Tarsian potters seem to have lacked the technology, which gave the Hittite Monochrome Wares their distinctive reddish color.

The re-analysis of the Transitional Period plain wares of Gözlükule was able to add new shapes to the published repertoire of Goldman and Slane.[33] A small jar with flaring rim datable to either LB IIa or in IIb levels has its parallel at the Hittite layers of

[27] Goldman 1956; Mountjoy 2005; for the emrgence of the Transitional Painted Pottery at Tarsus, see also Ünlü 2005.

[28] Mommsen *et al.* 2011, pp. 912–913.

[29] Drerup 1969, p. 26–29; Spencer 1995, p. 297.

[30] Goldman 1963, p. 3.

[31] Goldman 1956, pp. 203–205; see also Mountjoy 2005.

[32] Yalçın 2005, pp. 101–120.

[33] Re-evaluation of the entire Gözlükule ceramic assemblage was initiated by the Boğaziçi University Tarsus- Gözlükule Interdisciplinary Research Project. First results of this process on painted pottery were published in Özyar (2005).

Boğazköy and Porsuk (**Fig. 6 k**).[34] Additionally, various bowl forms found at Gözlükule can be compared to the Hittite material from Boğazköy. Two shallow bowls with slightly thickened and slanted rims from LB IIb period again have their parallels from the Hittite New Kingdom and Transitional Period levels of Boğazköy, and the transitional levels of Tell Afis (**Fig. 6 a–b**).[35] Bowls with s-formed profiles known from the Boğazköy corpus are represented at Tarsus both in the LB IIb and Early Iron Age corpus (**Fig. 6 c–d**).[36]

Two bowls with thickened, flat-top rims are particularly significant, because they are not only paralleled with the Hittite New Kingdom period material from Boğazköy, but also variations of these shapes became quite popular in the Iron Age phases of Tarsus (**Fig. 6 e–f**).[37] In the space available this shall suffice to illustrate long-lasting influence of the Late Bronze Age ceramic tradition at the site.[38]

In addition to these examples, which are closely related to monochrome forms, some new plain ware shapes emerged in the LB IIb period of Gözlükule as well. A deep bowl with a thickened flat-top rim slanted inward and a jar with a flat-top rim rounded on the exterior have no similarity with Hittite monochrome typology and local predecessors at Gözlükule (**Fig. 6 i–j**). The bowl is different from the Hittite plain ware tradition in terms of its shape, dark brown surface color and very coarse fabric. The closest parallels for the jar are from Tell Jurn Kabir and Tell Sheikh Hassan in northern Syria dating to the 9th to 5th centuries BC.[39] The Tarsus fragment dates to the LB IIb period and is thus considerably earlier.

With the transition to the Early Iron Age, one does observe change and continuity simultaneously in the ceramic tradition of Gözlükule. During this period, the latest remnants of Late Bronze Age ceramics such as LH IIIC and Transitional Painted Pottery were replaced by Cypro-Cilician painted pottery characterized by concentric-circled decoration (**Fig. 4**).[40]

On the other hand, when we look at the plain ware repertoire of Gözlükule, we see that Hittite monochrome forms continued particularly to influence jar and bowl types of the Early Iron Age. For instance, jars with everted ledge rims are among the most

[34] Though this jar definitely comes from the Late Bronze Age strata of the site, its exact stratigraphic location is not fully clear. For its parallels in Boğazköy and Porsuk, see Parzinger and Sanz 1992, tafel 47.20; Dupré 1983, No: 152.

[35] Parzinger and Sanz 1992, abb. 19. 5.1 and 5.2; see also Venturi 2000, fig. 6, no: 8 and fig. 8, no: 2.

[36] Parzinger and Sanz 1992, p. 26.

[37] Parzinger and Sanz 1992, tafel 36, no: 5 and abb. 19. I. 3. 2; see also Goldman 1963, fig. 117. 194 and fig. 126. 717.

[38] The full catalogue of this research project along with further comments will be published in the second volume of the Tarsus-Gözlükule Field Reports series.

[39] Eidem and Ackermann 1999, fig. 8, no: 12 and 14; see also Schneider 1999, abb. 14, Typ. 25. 13–17.

[40] Goldman 1963, p. 20.

frequent Hittite monochrome shapes in many sites such as Boğazköy.[41] At Gözlükule, examples of these forms are present not only at the Late Bronze Age levels, but also in the later phases of the Early Iron Age implying a remarkable continuity of the Monochrome Ware tradition perhaps into the 10th century BC (**Fig. 6 l–n**).[42] Similar forms were also found in the transitional layers of Lidar and Tell Afis.[43]

New elements appeared in the plain ware repertoire of Gözlükule in the Early Iron Age as well. Two bowls with triangular rim profiles pointed at the top appeared at the site along with the Cilician painted pottery during the second phase of the Early Iron Age, which corresponds to the disappearance of the last vestiges of LH IIIC and Transitional Painted Pottery (**Fig. 6 g–h**). The latter has a slight carination on its body; the surface of the former is very well polished. Similar forms continued to be used at the site in later phases of the Iron Age.[44] The closest parallels to the Gözlükule bowls in terms of size and shape come from the 9th to 7th century layers of Tell Jurn Kabir.[45] These examples demonstrate that in addition to continuity some new elements emerged in the plain wares of Tarsus-Gözlükule during the Iron Age.

Conclusions

The collapse of the Hittite kingdom at the beginning of the 12th century BC resulted in the resurgence of regional differences in ceramics across its former territories. In the Early Iron Age, distinct local ceramic traditions were in use in the area extending from Gordion in northwest Anatolia to Korucutepe in the upper Euphrates valley. Under the Hittite authority this vast territory was entirely dominated by the Monochrome Ware. New features of the Transitional Period in ceramics are the re-emergence of hand-made technique and painted pottery. While hand-made traditions were in use mainly in central and eastern Anatolian sites, painted pottery was produced in a wider geography including Cilicia, central and eastern Anatolia. In addition to these abrupt changes, the monochrome tradition of the Late Bronze Age survived in some regions such as the middle Euphrates valley or parts of Cilicia. This continuity might be a result of either ongoing Hittite political authority in form of the new Neo-Hittite states and/or due to the survival of the Late Bronze Age pottery workshops and their practices into the Early Iron Age.

Within this larger picture, Tarsus shows aspects of both continuity and change in its Transitional Period material culture. The Early Iron Age plain wares of the site

41 Parzinger and Sanz 1992, Abb. 14, A.2.2., A.2.3.

42 For examples of these forms from the Late Bronze levels of Gözlükule, see Goldman 1956, fig. 389–390.

43 Müller 1999, Abb. 3, CA 01; see also Venturi 2000, fig. 6.13–16, and fig. 8.6.

44 Goldman 1963, fig. 120. 268.

45 Eidem and Ackermann 1999, fig. 8, Group C, no. 6.

display strong affinities with the preceding Hittite tradition as well as new elements. The continuity is substantiated with the ongoing popularity of some jar and bowl shapes almost unchanged until the end of the Early Iron Age. Some plain ware bowl forms, on the other hand, appear new within the Gözlükule corpus and compare well to north Syrian types. The emergence of LH IIIC, the appearance of local Transitional Painted Pottery and the construction of an apsidal structure are further material evidence for changing circumstances at Tarsus-Gözlükule. Some of these elements seem to have an Aegean and western Anatolian origin. Thus, the Early Iron Age inhabitants of Tarsus might have combined aspects of their Late Bronze Age Hittite heritage with the new elements brought into Cilicia by a new group of settlers from the west. The plain ware forms, which were related to the Iron Age repertoire in North Syria, on the other hand, indicate that the old connection between Cilicia and North Syria also persevered during the Transitional Period and later parts of the Iron Age.

BIBLIOGRAPHY

BAKIR, G., ERSOY, Y., FAZLIOĞLU, Ü., ÖZBAY, F., ÖZEN, B. and ZEREN, M.
1999 "1998 Klazomenai Kazısı," *Kazı Sonuçları Toplantısı 21, Vol. 2*: 47–56.

DRERUP, H.
1969 *Griechische Baukunst in Geometrischer Zeit, Archaeologia Homerica, Kapitel O, Band. II.* Göttingen: Vandenhoeck u. Ruprecht

DUPRÉ, S.
1983 *Porsuk I. La Ceramique de l'Age du Fer.* Paris: Editions Recherche sur les Civilisations.

EIDEM, J., and ACKERMANN, R.
1999 "The Iron Age Ceramics from Tell Jurn Kabir," in *Iron Age Pottery in Northern Mesopotamia, Northern Syria and South-Eastern Anatolia*, edited by A. Hausleiter and A. Reiche, pp. 309–324. Münster: Ugarit-Verlag.

FRENCH, D.
1975 "A Reassessment of the Mycenaean Pottery at Tarsus," *Anatolian Studies 25*: 53–75.

GATES, M.-H.
2001 "Potmarks at Kinet Höyük and the Hittite Ceramik Industry," in *La Cilicie: Espaces et Pouvoirs Locaux: Actes de la Table Ronde Internationale d'Istanbul, 2-9 Novembre 1999*, edited by E. Jean, A. M. Dinçol and S. Durugönül, pp. 137–157. Istanbul: Institut Français d'Études Anatoliennes.
2006 "Dating the Hittite Levels at Kinet Höyük: A Revised Chronology," in *Strukturierung und Datierung in der Hethitischen Archäologie: Voraussetzungen – Probleme – Neue Ansätze*, edited by D. P. Mielke, U.-D. Schoop and J. Seeher, pp. 293–310. Istanbul: Ege Yayınları.

GENZ, H.
2004 *Büyükkaya. I. Die Keramik der Eisenzeit.* Mainz: Verlag Philipp von Zabern.

GOLDMAN, H.
1956 *Excavations at Gözlükule, Tarsus, Vol. II, From the Neolithic through the Bronze Age.* Princeton: Princeton University Press.

1963 *Excavations at Gözlükule, Tarsus, Vol. III., The Iron Age*. Princeton: Princeton University Press.

HENRICKSON, R. C.

1994 "Continuity and Discontinuity in the Ceramic Tradition of Gordion during the Iron Age", in *Anatolian Iron Ages 3*, edited by D. H. French and A. Çilingiroğlu, pp. 95–129. Ankara: British Institute of Archaeology at Ankara.

KÖROĞLU, K.

2003 "The Transition from the Bronze Age to Iron Age in Eastern Anatolia," in *Identifying Changes: The Transition from Bronze Age to Iron Ages in Anatolia and its Neighboring Regions*, edited by B. Fischer, H. Genz, E. Jean and K. Köroğlu, pp. 231–243. Istanbul: Türk Eskiçağ Bilimleri Enstitüsü.

MATSUMURA, K.

2000 "On the manufacturing techniques of Iron Age ceramics of Kaman-Kalehöyük," *Kaman-Kalehöyük 9*: 119–135.

MOMMSEN, H., MOUNTJOY, P. and ÖZYAR, A.

2011 "Provenance Determination of Mycenean IIIC Vessels from the 1934–1939 Excavations at Tarsus- Gözlükule by Neutron Activation Analysis," *Archaeometry, 53*: 900–915.

MOUNTJOY, P. A.

2005 "The Mycenaean Pottery from the 1934–1939 Excavations at Tarsus," in *Field Seasons 2001–2003 of the Tarsus-Gözlükule Interdisciplinary Research Project*, edited by A. Özyar, pp. 83–134. Istanbul: Ege Yayınları.

MÜLLER, U.

1999 "Die eisenzeitliche Keramik des Lidar Höyük," in *Iron Age Pottery in Northern Mesopotamia, Northern Syria and South-Eastern Anatolia*, edited by A. Hausleiter and A. Reiche, pp. 403–434. Münster: Ugarit Verlag.

MÜLLER-KARPE, A.

1988 *Hethitische Töpferei der Oberstadt von Hattuša*. Marburg: Hitzeroth.

1999 "Untersuchungen in Kuşaklı 1998," *Mitteilungen des Deutschen Orient-Gesellschaft* 131: 57–90.

2000 "Die Keramik des Mittleren und Jüngeren hethitischen Reiches: Die entwicklung der anatolischen Keramik – ihre formen und Funktionen", in *Die Hethiter und Ihr Reich*, edited by J. Frings, pp. 256–264. Stuttgart: Theiss.

OMURA, S.

1997 "1995 Yılı Kaman-Kalehöyük Kazıları," *18. Kazı Sonuçları Toplantısı I*: 212–201.

1998 "1996 Yılı Kaman-Kalehöyük Kazıları," *19. Kazı Sonuçları Toplantısı I*: 311–322.

2000 "1998 Yılı Kaman-Kalehöyük Kazıları," *21. Kazı Sonuçları Toplantısı I*: 217–228.

ÖZGEN, E. and HELWING, B.

2003 "On the Shifting Border between Mesopotamia and the West: Seven Seasons of Joint Turkish-German Excavations at Oylum Höyük," *Anatolica XXIX*: 61–85.

ÖZYAR, A., ed.

2005 *Field Seasons of 2001-2003 of the Tarsus-Gözlükule Interdisciplinary Research Project*. Istanbul: Ege Yayınları.

PAPPA, M. and BESIOS, M.

1999 "The Makriyalos Project: Rescue Excavations at the Neolithic Site of Makriyalos, Pieria, Northern Greece," in *Neolithic Society in Greece*, edited by P. Halstead, pp. 108–120. Sheffield: Sheffield Academic Press.

PARZINGER, H. and SANZ, R.

1992 *Die Oberstadt von Hattuša: Hethitische Keramik aus dem zentralen Tempelviertel*. Mainz: Gebr. Mann Verlag.

POSTGATE, J. N.
1998 "Between the Plateau and the Sea: Kilisetepe 1994–1997," in *Ancient Anatolia: 'Fifty Years' Work by the British Istitute of Archaeology at Ankara*, edited by R. Matthews, pp. 127–141. London: British Institute of Archaeology at Ankara.
POSTGATE, N. and THOMAS D., eds.
2007 *Excavations at Kilise Tepe 1994–98: From Bronze Age to Byzantine in Western Cilicia.* London: British Institute of Archaeology at Ankara.
SCHNEIDER, E.
1999 "Die eisenzeitliche Keramik von Tell Sheikh Hassan," in *Iron Age Pottery in Northern Mesopotamia, Northern Syria and South-Eastern Anatolia*, edited by A. Hausleiter and A. Reiche, pp. 325–346. Münster: Ugarit Verlag.
SCHOOP, U.-D.
2003 "Pottery Traditions of the Later Hittite Empire: Problems of Definitions," in *Identifying Changes: The Transition from Bronze Age Iron Ages in Anatolia and its Neighboring Regions*, edited by B. Fischer, H. Genz, E. Jean and K. Köroğlu, pp. 167–177. Istanbul: Ege Yayınları.
SEEHER, J.
1999 "Die Ausgrabungen in Bogazköy-Hattuša 1998," *Archäologischer Anzeiger*: 317–341.
SLANE, D. A.
1987 "Middle and Late Bronze Age architecture and Pottery in Gözlükule, Tarsus: A New Analysis." Unpublished Ph.D diss. Bryn Mawr College.
SPENCER, E.
1995 "Early Lesbos between East and West: A 'Gray Area' of Aegean Archaeology," *The Annual of the British School of Athens* 90: 269–306.
SYMINGTON, D.
2001 "Hittites at Kilise Tepe," in *La Cilicie: Espaces et Pouvoirs Locaux: Actes de la Table Ronde Internationale d'Istanbul, 2-9 Novembre 1999*, edited by E. Jean, A. M. Dinçol and S. Durugönül, pp. 168–184. Istanbul: Institut Français d'Études Anatoliennes.
ÜNLÜ, E.
2005 "Locally Produced and Painted Late Bronze to Iron Age Transitional Period Pottery of Tarsus-Gözlükule," in *Field Seasons 2001–2003 of the Tarsus – Gözlükule Interdisciplinary Research Project*, edited by A. Özyar, pp. 145–168. Istanbul: Ege Yayınları.
VENTURI, F.
2000 "Le premiere age du Fer a Tell Afis en Syrie Septentrionale," in *Essays on Syria in the Iron Age*, Ancient Near Eastern Studies Supplement 7, edited by G. Bunnens, pp. 505–536. Leuven: Peeters.
WARNER, J.
1979 "The Megaron and Apsidal House in Early Bronze Age Western Anatolia: New Evidence from Karataş," *American Journal of Archaeology* 83: 133–147.
WINN, M. M.
1980 "The Early Iron Age pottery," in *Korucutepe 3*, edited by M. N. van Loon, pp. 155–175. Amsterdam: North-Holland Pub. Co.
YALÇIN, S.
2005 "A Re-evaluation of the Late Bronze to Early Iron Age Transitional Period: Stratigraphic Sequence and Plain Ware of Tarsus-Gözlükule." Unpublished M.A. Thesis. Boğaziçi University.

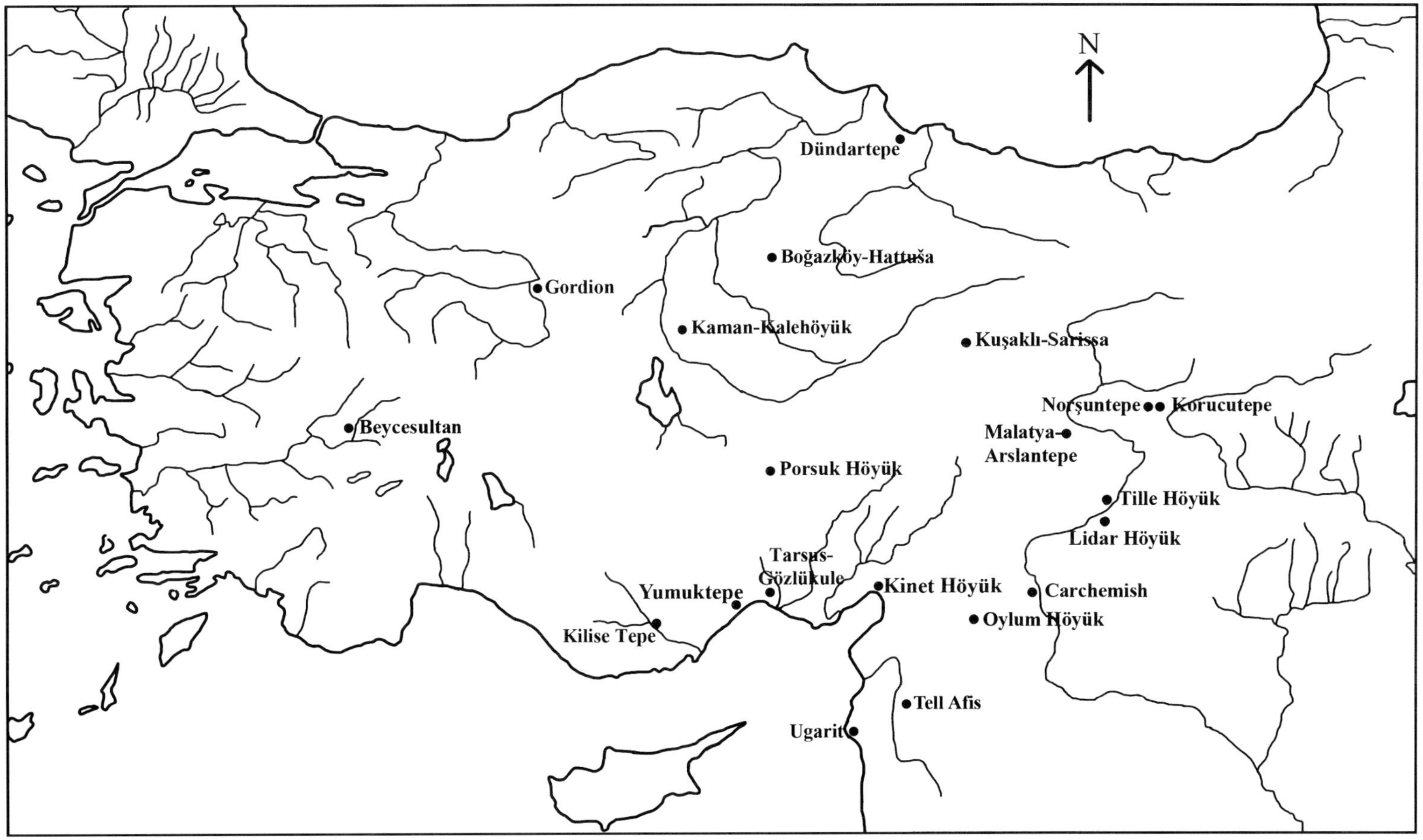

Fig. 1 Anatolia and Northern Syria: Sites producing the Hittite Monochrome Ware in their Late Bronze Age levels.

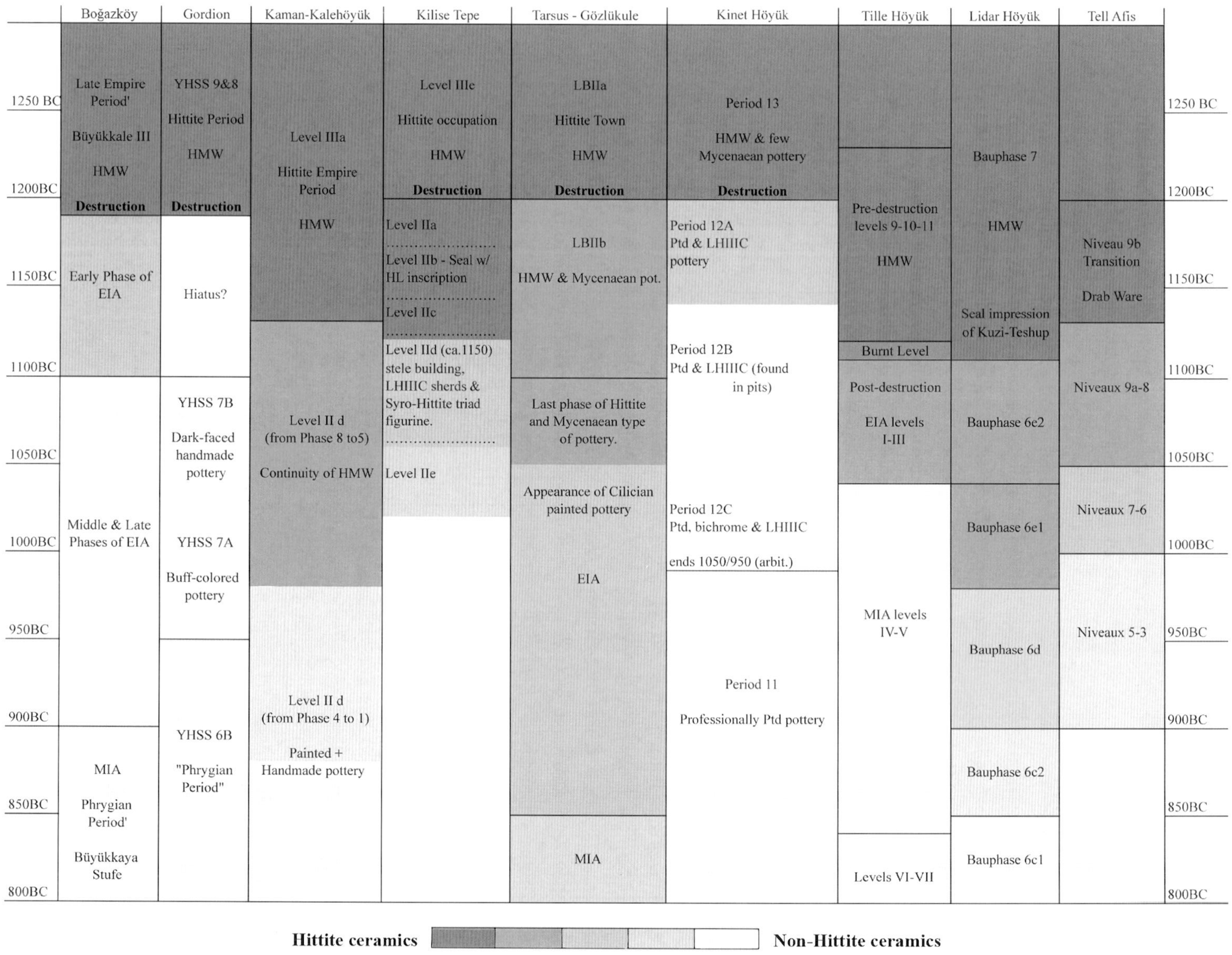

Fig. 2 Continuity of the Late Bronze monochrome tradition in terms of its typology and proportion within the ceramic assemblages of the Early Iron Age settlements across the former Hittite lands.

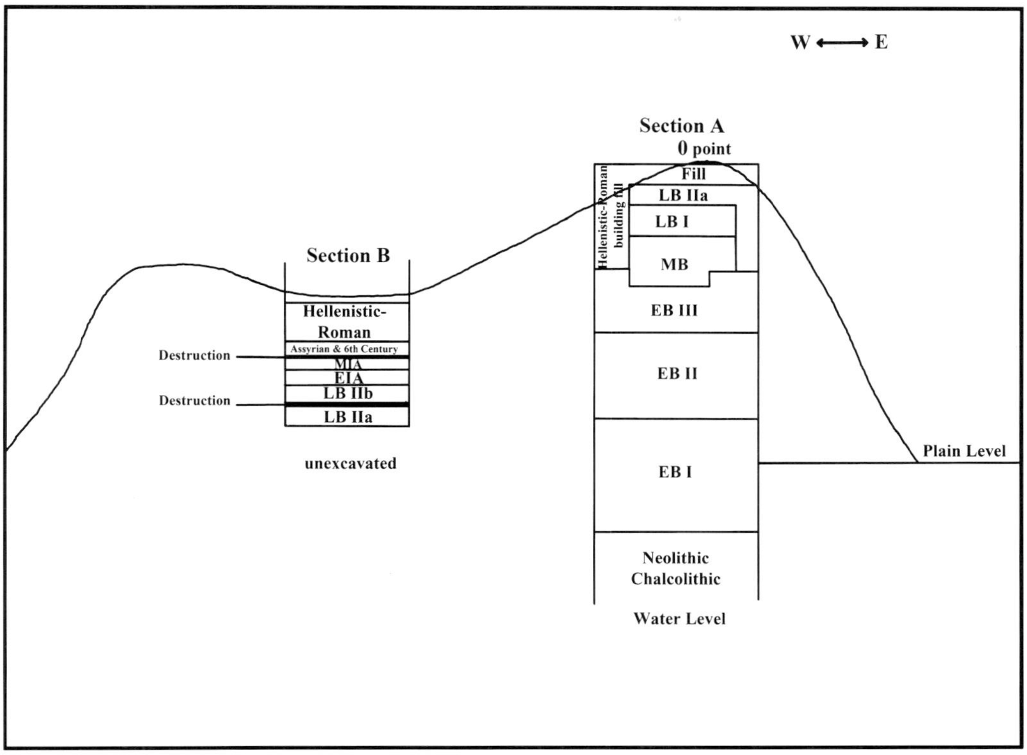

Fig. 3 Stratigraphy of the mound of Gözlükule as revealed by the Goldman excavations in Section A and B.

Level	Subphase	Elevation	Architectural Remains	Undecor. Pottery	Decor. Pottery
EIA	IV	15.00 - 15.44m	Jw at 15.44-15.30m, Jo at 15.30m, U at 15.25m, 'P' at 15.00m(?)	PW	CPP
	III	15.15 - 15.50m	Jw at 15.50m, U at 15.45m, W at 15.47 m, T at 15.47m, 'P' at 15.15m.	PW	CPP
	II	15.80m	Jw at 15.80m	PW	CPP
	I	15.47 - 16.40m	U at 15.70m, W at 15.70-15.60m & Phantom level at 'P'	HMW - PW	TPP - LHIIIC
LBII b	Late	15.79 - 16.43m	Room below U, & 'P' at 15.79	HMW	TPP - LHIIIC
	Middle	15.50 - 16.47m	Town built in either side of a street in N-S direction. Units L, R & Q.	HMW	TPP - LHIIIC
	Early	15.93 - 18.25m	DD & 'P' at 15.93m	HMW	
LBII a		16.50 - 19.14m	Hittite Temple (Section A), East, West & South Houses (Section B)	HMW	

HMW: Hittite Monochrome Ware PW: Plain Ware TPP: Transisitonal Painted Pottery CPP: Cilician Painted Pottery

Fig. 4 Summary of the architectural levels and associated ceramic types of Tarsus- Gözlükule during the Transitional Period.

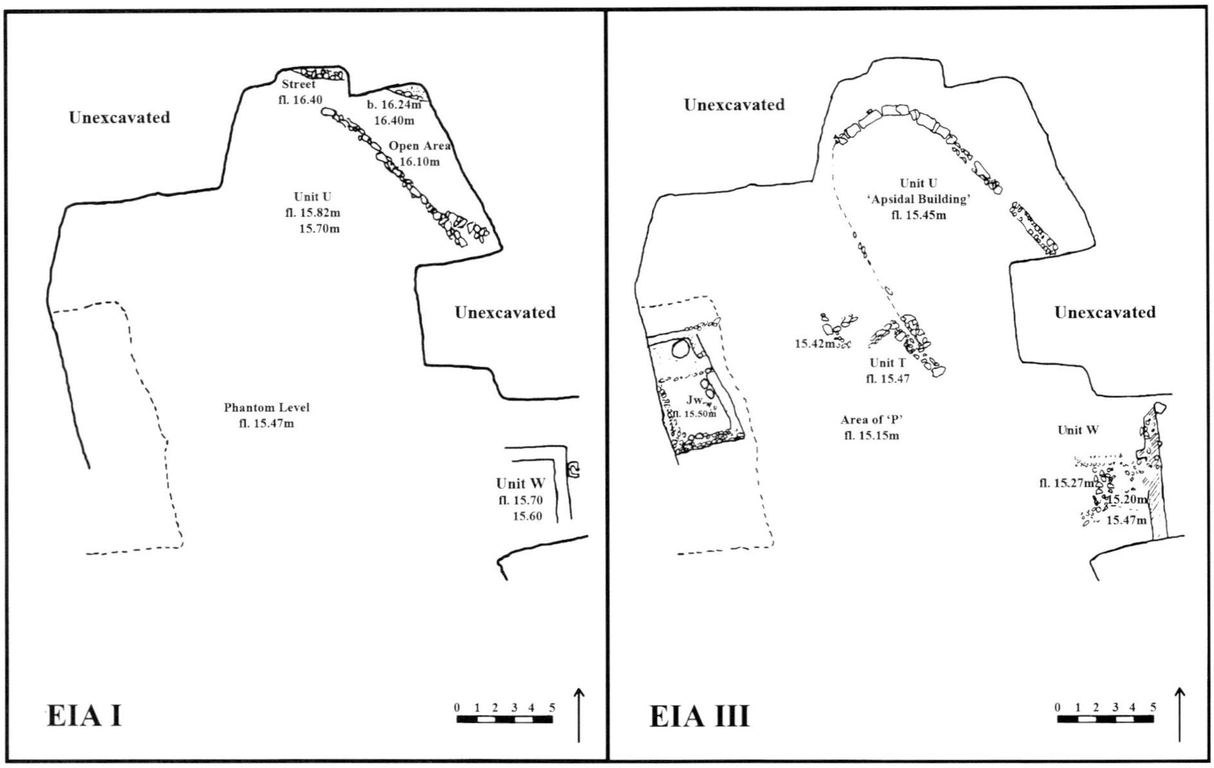

Fig. 5 The apsidal structure in its different architectural phases during the Early Iron Age at Tarsus-Gözlükule (after Goldman 1963).

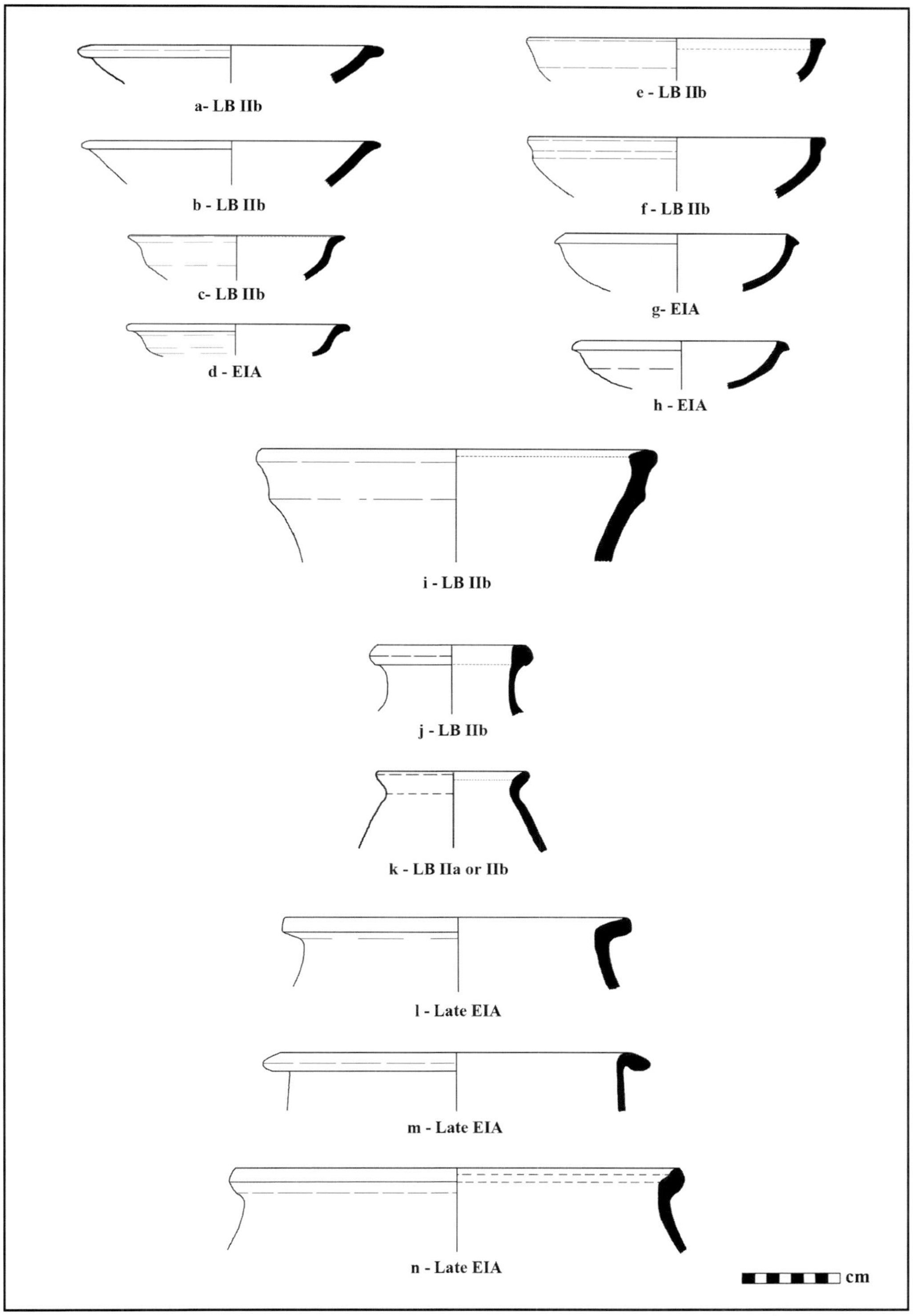

Fig. 6 A selection of bowl and jar forms from the LB IIa, IIb and Early Iron Age layers of Tarsus-Gözlükule.

CHAPTER 9

EXPLORING SIRKELI HÖYÜK IN THE LATE BRONZE AGE AND ITS INTERREGIONAL CONNECTIONS

Ekin KOZAL
Department of Archaeology
Faculty of Sciences and Letters
Çanakkale Onsekiz Mart University, Turkey
E-mail: ekozal08@gmail.com

ABSTRACT

Sirkeli Höyük, as one of the largest sites in Smooth Cilicia, was excavated between 1992-96 and in 1997 by B. Hrouda and H. Ehringhaus respectively. Preliminary reports mention the presence of periods from the Chalcolithic to the Roman Periods. Renewed excavations under the direction of M. Novak since 2006 focus mainly on the settlement history, chronology, and cultural relations. In this perspective, this article deals with the interregional relations of Sirkeli Höyük in the Late Bronze Age. A small selection of pottery and artifacts are chosen here to exemplify the presence of Late Bronze Age and its interregional relations. *

INTRODUCTION

Late Bronze Age levels were discovered in the excavations of Mersin-Yumuktepe,[1] Mersin-Soli,[2] Tarsus-Gözlükule,[3] Tatarlı Höyük,[4] Kinet Höyük[5] in Smooth Cilicia. The findings from these excavations and from other sites in the neighboring regions, such as central Anatolia and the Amuq Plain are representative of the corpus of the Late Bronze Age material in this region. A common regional character is evident in Smooth Cilicia in this period. Substantial Late Bronze Age levels are present in all excavated sites, which are characterized by a sound central Anatolian influence on the

* I would like to thank K.A. Yener for organising the symposium and its publication; M. Novák for providing the opportunity to work with the documentation of old excavations; Cornelia Wolf for illustrations; T.E. Şerifoğlu for his comments on the article.

[1] Garstang 1953; Sevin and Köroğlu 2004; Jean 2006; Manuelli 2009.

[2] Yağcı 2001; 2003a–b; 2007.

[3] Goldman 1956, pp. 183–229; Kozal 2005; Mountjoy 2005.

[4] Girginer 2008.

[5] Gates 2001, 2004, 2006, 2008, 2009.

pottery production[6] and a certain number of imports from Cyprus, the Levant, and Mesopotamia.[7] Sirkeli Höyük is located on the bank of Ceyhan River between Tarsus-Gözlükule and Kinet Höyük on the route between Anatolia and the Levant as well as Mesopotamia. In addition, a relief of Muwatalli II was carved out on the rocky outcrops of the site.[8] As a background to this evidence, there have been some questions about whether the site has a Late Bronze Age settlement. It has been put forward by A. Ünal that the relief of Muwatalli II might have been carved to define a geographical marker in the landscape and that a Late Bronze Age settlement is not present at Sirkeli Höyük but on the nearby mound across the river on the outskirts of Yılan Kalesi.[9] Sirkeli Höyük was occupied since the Chalcolithic Period[10] and substantial remains as well as dense material culture are preserved from the Middle Bronze[11] and Middle Iron Ages.[12] If there was a hiatus between these periods, its reasons were never touched upon by A. Ünal and B. Hrouda. Re-analysis of the documents of the old excavations and the findings from the renewed excavations demonstrate the presence of Late Bronze Age in Sirkeli Höyük.

After J. Garstang's one season of work in 1936–37, a compact preliminary report had been published that did not yield enough material to answer this question.[13] M.V. Seton-Williams surveyed the site in 1951 and published some Late Bronze Age wares.[14] However, survey finds were not strong enough to deal with this question. Thereafter, B. Hrouda conducted five seasons of excavations in 1992–96,[15] which were followed by one excavation season under the directorship of H. Ehringhaus in 1997.[16] The presence of the Late Bronze Age especially in the stone building above and behind the reliefs was discussed among these two scholars without a detailed examination of the pottery. In this respect the issue is being reconsidered by the new Turkish-German joint team.[17] The problematic issue of whether there are Late Bronze Age levels will be dealt with here based on the publications and the documentation of the older excavations as well as the evidence from the recent excavations.

The first archaeological publication about Sirkeli was done by J. Garstang, who described five trenches that were opened by his team (Trench A-E). J. Garstang also

[6] Gates 2001; Symington 2001; Jean 2006.
[7] Kozal 2006.
[8] Güterbock in Garstang 1937; Ehringhaus 2005, pp. 95–99.
[9] Ünal 2002, pp. 146–147.
[10] Hrouda 1997a, pp. 98; Kroll in Hrouda 1997a, pp. 105–107; Ahrens et al. 2010, pp. 55–56.
[11] Hrouda 1997a, pp. 98–100; Ahrens et al. 2010, pp. 56–57.
[12] Hrouda 1997, pp. 121–126; Ahrens et al. 2010, pp. 62–64.
[13] Garstang 1938.
[14] Seton-Williams 1954.
[15] Hrouda 1997a, 1997c.
[16] Ehringhaus 1999a, 1999b.
[17] Ahrens et al. 2008, 2009, 2010; Novak and Kozal 2010.

mentioned Late Bronze Age finds from Trench C and E. The material from Trench C cannot be validated as he published only the material illustrations from Trench E.[18] Among the small number of illustrated vessels from Trench E, a red banded globular bottle with double handle on the shoulder is noteworthy. It has a cylindrical narrow neck, an everted rim and a vertical handle with a vertical groove that cuts the handle slightly.[19] In general, this form has plain and painted variations. In Anatolia, the most numerous group of this form is found at Kültepe, where a clear chronological distinction between the plain and painted ones is obvious. The plain bottles were discovered in level II, whereas painted ones are from level Ib. Three painted examples at Kültepe were encountered, two of which were decorated with red and brown concentric circles. In contrast to the others, the third example has irregularly painted circles. All the painted ones were found in graves.[20] Comparable examples from Lidar Höyük are not painted, but some are decorated with slightly incised concentric circles. They are assigned to Lidar level 5 and 5/4, which were dated to MB III by G. Kaschau.[21] Another painted example made of blue faience is found in a child's grave belonging to level 4, dated to the beginning of MB IIIA. The painting consists of horizontal and vertical bands on the shoulder.[22] Other parallels from Cilicia were unearthed at Tarsus-Gözlükule and the Kinet Höyük excavations. The Tarsus example, which is painted with concentric circles, was found in a LB I context.[23] The Kinet Höyük bottle is being dated to MB II by M.-H. Gates.[24] As pointed out by K. Emre, this type of bottle shows strong affiliations with the pottery from North Syria and North Mesopotamia.[25] According to Einwag, who studied the distribution of this ware, the type is also common in Tuttul/Tell Bi'a and Mari.[26] The bottle from Sirkeli was dated to the lowest level of Trench E that was assigned to the Hittite Imperial period by J. Garstang. However, we cannot rely on J. Garstang's chronology for this site. Thus, this bottle from Sirkeli would need to be dated according to typological parallels which point to the connections of Sirkeli with northern Syria and Mesopotamia already in the MB II or potentially in the LB. So far the Tarsus bottle is the only example from a LB I context in Anatolia. However, B. Einwag mentions LB examples from some sites the Upper Euphrates.[27] Two examples were found in Egypt at Tell

[18] Garstang 1938, pp. 22–23, Pl. XV–XVII.

[19] Garstang 1938, Pl. XV:4.

[20] Emre 1994, pp. 93, 96, figs. 1–10, 19–20, Pl. XII; Emre 1963, p. 95, Pl. XXVII:2.

[21] Kaschau 1999, pp. 225, 234, 242, 246, 249, 263, 268, Pls. 99:13, 150:1, 206:4, 236:2, 242:1, 257:3, 353:2–3, graves 103:1–2 and 199:1

[22] Kaschau 1999, pp. 176, 266, Pl. IX, grave 126:6, Pl. G:4.

[23] Goldman 1956, pp. 193–194, Pl. 308:1024

[24] Paper "Kinet Höyük Çalışmaları, 2009" presented by M.-H. Gates at the 32. *Uluslararası Kazı, Araştırma, Arkeometri Sempozyumu, 24-28 Mayıs 2010*, İstanbul.

[25] Emre 1994.

[26] Einwag 2007, pp. 202–205.

[27] Einwag 2007, p. 205.

el-Daba from phase D/3, which were identified as imports by K. Kopetzky.[28] The origin of this type was discussed by M.-H. Gates[29] and B. Einwag[30] as it is widely distributed from Anatolia to Egypt, pointing to the Levant or the Upper Euphrates as its source.

M. V. Seton-Williams mentioned Sirkeli in the list of sites, which has red and brown burnished wares and "local base ring," which is defined as "metallic and hard" by her.[31] Since these wares were not illustrated and poorly described, it is not possible to make any comparisons and further examination. Reexamination of the pottery may, however, contribute to this issue.

A monumental building made of gigantic stones was excavated during the directorship of B. Hrouda and H. Ehringhaus, which is architecturally bound to the back of the outcrop with the relief. While H. Ehringhaus interpreted it as a "Stonehouse [Hegur]" of the Hittite king,[32] B. Hrouda pointed to a small number of finds from the Late Bronze Age.[33] In the current excavations since 2006, another building was discovered with substantial high walls. Although the pottery from the destruction fill of the building dates to the Middle Iron Age, the pottery assemblage from the fill on its plastered floor contained only Late Bronze Age Plain Wares. These are already published elsewhere.[34] This deposit points to the last use of the floor in the Late Bronze Age. The building was then reused in the Middle Iron Age; the plastered floor remained below the later Iron Age floor level and the walls were reinforced with new wall additions. Therefore, the Late Bronze Age contexts were disturbed by these rebuilding activities. However, a few dispersed Late Bronze Age sherds were found among each Middle Iron Age deposit. Early Iron Age pottery is very small in number throughout the site, probably indicating a reduction in the size of the settlement. The same stratigraphical relationship might be the case for the monumental building but a date cannot be proposed without a re-examination of the deposits.

B. Hrouda's excavations yielded a stamp seal of central Anatolian origin,[35] a Syrian terracotta figurine,[36] and crescent-shaped objects,[37] which already show the connections of Sirkeli Höyük in the Middle Bronze Age. Excavations by H. Ehringhaus yielded another five crescent shaped clay objects. All have two holes on both their ends and two have round marks. Three were discovered in operation 17.1-south.

[28] Kopetzky 2008, pp. 219, 235–236, fig. 23:1–2.
[29] Gates 1998, p. 71, fig. 2.
[30] Einwag 2007, pp. 204–205.
[31] Seton-Williams 1954, fig. 4.
[32] Ehringhaus in Hrouda 1997, p. 115.
[33] Hrouda 1997, p. 118.
[34] Ahrens et al. 2008, pp. 300–301, fig. 5; Ahrens et al. 2010, pp. 59–60, fig. 6.
[35] For parallels see Kozal in Ahrens et al. 2010, p. 57, fn. 24 and also Boehmer and Güterbock 1987, pp. 26–27, Pl. V–VI.
[36] For parallels see Kozal in Ahrens et al. 2010, p. 57, fn. 25.
[37] Ehringhaus 1999a, pp. 131–132, fig. 33.

Another one came from operation 16.1 at the foot of a pisé wall (M20) in the Late Bronze Age building. The fifth was found in operation 18.1-west on the floor of a room with the smelting furnace. H. Ehringhaus mentions parallels from Konya-Karahöyük level I-V (310 pieces)[38] and Kilise Tepe MB level (five pieces).[39] Although these objects are mainly found in levels dating to the Middle Bronze Age, H. Ehringhaus notes that they appear to be in use at the beginning of Late Bronze Age at Sirkeli.[40] Here, it should be noted that other examples of these objects are also found in Anatolia at Tarsus-Gözlükule LB I (26 pieces),[41] Mersin-Yumuktepe level X (2 pieces),[42] Beycesultan levels II-IV/MB-SB (41 pieces),[43] Demircihöyük EB I (8 pieces),[44] Alacahöyük Old Hittite-Hittite Imperial Period (17 pieces),[45] and Alişar level II and Hittite Imperial Period (23 pieces).[46] According to these observations, the crescent-shaped objects can thus be dated to the periods from the Early to the Late Bronze Ages. However, they are more common in the Middle Bronze Age. The examples from Sirkeli should be dated according to their context, which is Late Bronze I. Different uses of these objects were proposed; for example, as loom weights or tokens. H. Ehringhaus mentions the studies of J. Weingarten and G. Vogelsang-Eastwood, who view these administrative devices as part of a regulated administrative system.[47]

A White Painted Pendant Line Style juglet fragment was newly identified among the documentation of the older excavations pointing to relations with Cyprus (**Fig. 1.1**). This find represents the earliest Cypriot find from the 2nd millennium in Cilicia. Other examples are known from Kültepe Ib[48] and Alalakh[49] in Anatolia. Sirkeli sherd was discovered in 1996 in Trench 16.2 in or under the stone plastered ground. A fragment of Red-on-Black was encountered on the stone plastered ground (**Fig. 1.2**). These wares are associated with MB II Amuq-Cilician and Plain Wares. These levels were generally dated towards the end of Middle Bronze II. Additionally, four other Red-on-Black/Red fragments were found in the same level in the neighboring Trench 18.1 with the same associated wares (**Figs. 1.3–6**). A single example was present in Trench 14 as well (**Fig. 1.7**). In Trench 16.1 among the Middle Iron Age fill deposit a residual White Slip II bowl rim was found in locus 5 (**Fig. 2.8**).

[38] Alp 1994, pp. 69–72, Pl. 144–245.
[39] Baker in Baker et al. 1995, pp. 186–187, Pl. XXVa–b.
[40] Ehringhaus 1999a, pp. 131–132, fig. 33.
[41] Goldman 1956, pp. 319, 324, fig. 441, 11.
[42] Garstang 1953, p. 217, fig. 137.
[43] Mellaart and Murray 1995, p. 118, fig. O.19–23, Pl. XIVa–b.
[44] Obladen-Kauder in Baykal-Seeher 1996, pp. 238, 241, Pl. 1.
[45] Koşay and Akok 1973, pp. 28–30, Pl. 48–49.
[46] Schmidt 1932, p. 149, fig. 189; von der Osten 1937, pp. 273, 275, fig. 300.
[47] Ehringhaus 1999a, p. 132; Weingarten 1990; Vogelsang-Eastwood 1990.
[48] Åström 1989.
[49] Author's studies on the material.

In the loci of the same Trench 10–11, residual four plain ware thick plates were found among the Middle Iron Age assemblage. Three of them are undecorated plates with thickened rim (**Figs. 2.9–12**). Counterparts are known from Kinet Höyük[50] and Tarsus-Gözlükule LB II.[51] One has a red banded circular decoration inside and a pot mark on the exterior, which is not completely preserved (**Fig. 2.12**). Plates with red banded circular paint are known from Alalakh IV.[52] Plates with potmarks are represented in Kinet Höyük[53] and Alalakh,[54] besides other central Anatolian sites. Another sherd with a potmark (**Fig. 2.13**) is similar to those from Kinet Höyük.[55] Recent excavations also yielded Late Bronze Age plain wares with light brown fabric with a variety of inclusions with different densities. The surface is smoothed. Most common forms are plates, deep bowls and jugs. Plates have thickened, rounded and slightly inturned rims, whereas deep bowls have everted rims.[56]

Another imported ware is the black impressed ware of a not as-yet defined origin. Two examples were found in Sirkeli Höyük, one from Hrouda's[57] and the other from the recent excavations.[58] The ware has a dark gray to black slip and its surface is decorated with white filled incised parallel lines, zigzags and points. Parallels were discovered in Kilise Tepe in LB II,[59] in Tarsus in LB I-II[60] and at the Alalakh excavations from Woolley's Level V contexts.[61]

Late Bronze Age small finds from the recent excavations comprise an anthropomorphic terracotta figurine (Sİ07A-294), two miniature bronze ingots (Sİ07A-14 and 115),[62] and a bronze scale pan (Sİ07A-9).[63] The terracotta figurine is represented by the part of the foot with a typical Hittite shoe with the upturned tip. Another typical feature of the Hittite figurines is the extension at the heel for attaching the figure to another place or object. These kinds of representations are known from reliefs (e.g. Boğazköy-Yazılıkaya) and other Hittite bronze figurines such as the one from Dövlek.[64] This part is apparently broken in the Sirkeli example.

[50] Gates 2006, pp. 305–306, fig. 8–9.
[51] Goldman 1956, pp. 203–205, 209–210, fig. 316–17, 384; Slane 1987, pp. 387–390, 443, 445–446, Pl.122–123, 150–151.
[52] Woolley 1955, p. 318, Pl. 88e; Mullins 2010, fig. 3.3–1.
[53] Gates 2001.
[54] Woolley 1955, p. 352, Pl. 108.
[55] Gates 2001, fig. 6.
[56] Ahrens et al. 2008, pp. 300–301, fig. 5; Ahrens et al. 2010, pp. 59–60, fig. 6.
[57] Hrouda 2000, pp. 73–74, Pl. 23:2.
[58] Ahrens et al. 2008, p. 90, fig. 21.
[59] Symington 2001, p. 170, fig. 8.
[60] Goldman 1956, pp. 204, 218, Cat. No. 1232–1234.
[61] Woolley 1955, p. 342, Pl. 100–101; Mullins 2010, pp. 60–61.
[62] For parallels see Kozal in Ahrens et al. 2010, p. 60.
[63] Ibid.
[64] Emre 2002, p. 230, fig. 11.

CONCLUSIONS

Although the Late Bronze Age assemblages were found in limited areas under or in the thick Middle Iron Age leveling and destruction fill, these few finds indicate that there was a Late Bronze Age settlement at Sirkeli Höyük and that it was involved in interregional relations. The new excavations in Area A in the northwest terrace of the mound show the complications of dating these remains. The deposit on the floor of the building indicates its last occupation or the destruction phase. Excavation in the step trench on the northwestern slope under the level of the building included disturbed assemblages with a small number of diagnostic pottery due to the erosion. Black impressed ware was found in the level dating to prior to the construction of the northwestern building, putting forward the possibility that this might date to Late Bronze I. The destruction of the walls and the way their stones were rolled down point out that the building was constructed on the edge of the terrace. Its topographical position and comparisons with other sites brought up the question whether the building could belong to a fortification. Even though examination of these assemblages provides information on the history of the building and the topography of the site on that slope, these assumptions surely need to be verified with larger scale excavations.

The connections with Cyprus and Syria began in the Middle Bronze II. The presence of single examples of White Slip II, Base ring II, and Red Lustrous Wheel-made wares shows that the connections continued in the Late Bronze Age. However, another aspect of the relations, namely the involvement of the site in copper trade should also be examined by sourcing the metal finds.

The presence of central Anatolian affiliated pottery and finds at different sites in Cilicia raised questions about the extent of Hittite influence in this region. Late Bronze Age assemblages of Sirkeli Höyük are not large enough to contribute to this issue. However, these wares in association with the other finds mentioned above demonstrate that Sirkeli Höyük was most probably a typical Middle and Late Bronze Age Cilician site, easily comparable to other Cilician sites in Tarsus, Mersin, Adana and Dörtyol. Its location on the crossroads from central Anatolia to the Levant and Mesopotamia indicates that it was one of the significant sites in Cilicia in the Late Bronze Age.

BIBLIOGRAPHY

AHRENS, A., KOZAL, E., KÜMMEL, C., LAUBE, I., and NOVÁK, M.

2008 "Sirkeli Höyük – Kulturkontakte in Kilikien: Vorbericht über die Kampagnen 2006 und 2007 der türkisch-deutschen Mission," *Istanbuler Mitteilungen* 58: 67–107.

2009 "Sirkeli Höyük in Kilikien – Festung oder Kultstadt?" *Antike Welt* 3/2009: 42–46.

AHRENS, A., KOZAL, E, and NOVÁK, M.
2010 "Sirkeli Höyük in Smooth Cilicia. A General Overview from the 4th to the 1st Millennium BC," in: *Proceedings of the 6th International Congress on the Archeology of the Ancient Near East, May, 5th-10th, "Sapienza" –Università di Roma*, Vol. 2, edited by P. Matthiae, F. Pinnock, L. Nigro, N. Marchetti, pp. 55–74. Wiesbaden: Harrassowitz Verlag.

ALP, S.
1994 *Konya Civarında Karahöyük Kazılarında Bulunan Silindir ve Damga Mühürleri (Zylinder- und Stempelsiegel aus Karahöyük bei Konya)*. Ankara: Türk Tarih Kurumu Yayınları.

ÅSTRÖM, P.
1989 "Early Connections Between Anatolia and Cyprus," in *Anatolia and the Ancient Near East. Studies in Honor of Tahsin Özgüç*, edited by K. Emre, B. Hrouda, M. Mellink, N. Özgüç, pp. 15–17. Ankara: Türk Tarihi Kurumu Yayınları.

BAKER, H. D., COLLON, D., HAWKINS, J. D., POLLARD, T., POSTGATE, J. N., SYMINGTON, D., and THOMAS, D.
1995 "Kilise Tepe 1994," *Anatolian Studies* 45: 139–189.

BAYKAL-SEEHER, A. and OBLADEN-KAUDER, J.
1996 *Demircihöyük. Die Ergebnisse der Ausgrabungen 1975–78. Die Kleinfunde.* Mainz am Rhein: Philipp von Zabern.

BOEHMER R. M. and GÜTERBOCK, H. G.
1987 *Glyptik aus dem Stadtgebiet von Bogazköy.* Berlin: Gebrüder Mann Verlag.

EHRINGHAUS, H.
1999a "Vorläufiger Bericht über die Ausgrabung auf dem Sirkeli Höyük, Provinz Adana/Türkei im Jahre 1997," *Istanbuler Mitteilungen* 49: 83–140.
1999b "Grabungen am Sirkeli Höyük 1997" XX. *Kazı Sonuçları Toplantısı*, pp. 383–397. Ankara: Ministry of Culture and Tourism.
2005 *Die Felsreliefs der hethitischen Großreichszeit.* Mainz: Philipp von Zabern.

EINWAG, B.
2007 "Early Second Millennium Pottery of the Euphrates Region," *Proceedings of International Colloquium. From Relative Chronology to Absolute Chronology: The Second Millennium BC in Syria-Palestine. Rome 29th November-1st December 2001*, edited by P. Matthiae, F. Pinnock, L. Nigro, L. Peyronel, pp. 195–208. Rome: Bardi Editore.

EMRE, K.
1963 "The Pottery of the Assyrian Colony Period According to the Building Levels of the Kanis Karum," *Anatolia* 7: 87–99.
1994 "A Type of Syrian Pottery from Kültepe/Kanis," in *Beiträge zur Altorientalischen Archäologie und Altertmskunde. Festschrift für Barthel Hrouda zum 65. Geburstag*, edited by P. Calmeyer, K. Hecker, L. Jakob-Rost, C. B. F. Walker, pp. 91–96. Wiesbaden: Harrassowitz Verlag.
2002 "Felsreliefs, Stelen, Othostaten. Großplastik als Monumentale Form Staatlicher und Religiöser Repräsentation," in *Die Hethiter und Ihr Reich*, edited by Kunst- und Ausstellungshalle der Bundersrepublik Deutschland in Bonn, pp. 218–233. Bonn: Konrad Theiss Verlag.

GARSTANG, J.
1937 "Explorations in Cilicia. The Neilson Expedition: Preliminary Report," *Liverpool Annals of Archaeology and Anthropology* 24: 52–68.
1938 "Explorations in Cilicia. The Neilson Expedition: Preliminary Report II," *Liverpool Annals of Archaeology and Anthropology* 25: 12–23.

1953 *Prehistoric Mersin: Yümük Tepe in Southern Turkey*. Oxford: Clarendon Press.

GATES, M.-H.

1998 "Dialogues Between Ancient Near Eastern Texts and the Archaeological Record: Test Cases from Bronze Age Syria," *Bulletin of the American Schools of Research* 270: 63–91.

2001 "Potmarks at Kinet Höyük and the Hittite Ceramic Industry," in *Kilikia: Mekanlar ve Yerel Güçler (M.Ö. 2. binyıl – M.S. 4. yüzyıl), Uluslararası Yuvarlak Masa Toplantısı Bildirileri İstanbul, 2-5 Kasım 1999*, edited by É. Jean, A.M. Dinçol, S. Durugönül, pp. 137–157. Paris: De Boccard.

2004 "2002 Season at Kinet Höyük (Yeşil-Dörtyol, Hatay)," 25. *Kazı Sonuçları Toplantısı*, Vol. 1, pp. 405–416. Ankara: Ministry of Culture and Tourism.

2006 "Dating the Hittite Levels at Kinet Höyük: A Revised Chronology," in *Structuring and Dating in Hittite Archaeology*, edited by D. P. Mielke, U. D. Schoop, J. Seeher, pp. 293–309. İstanbul: Ege Yayınları.

2008 "2006 Season at Kinet Höyük (Yeşil-Dörtyol, Hatay)," 29. *Kazı Sonuçları Toplantısı*, Vol. 2, pp. 281–191. Ankara: Ministry of Culture and Tourism.

2009 "2007 Season at Kinet Höyük (Yeşil-Dörtyol, Hatay)," 30. *Kazı Sonuçları Toplantısı*, Vol. 2, pp. 351–368. Ankara: Ministry of Culture and Tourism.

GIRGINER, K. S.

2008 "Ceyhan/Tatarlı Höyük Kazı Çalışmaları 2007," *Haberler* 26: 15–17.

GOLDMAN, H.

1956 *Excavation at Gözlü Kule, Tarsus*. Vol. 2. *From the Neolithic through the Bronze Age*. Princeton: Princeton University Press.

HROUDA, B.

1997a "Vorläufiger Bericht über die Ausgrabungsergebnisse auf dem Sirkeli Höyük/Südtürkei von 1992–1996," *Istanbuler Mitteilungen* 47: 91–150.

1997b "'Damnatio memoriae?'Neue Beobachtungen am Relief Nr. 2 bei Sirkeli/Türkei," *Antike Welt* 28/6: 471–474.

1997c "Vorläufiger Bericht über die Ausgrabungsergebnisse auf dem Sirkeli Höyük / Südtürkei von 1992–1995," XVIII. *Kazı Sonuçları Toplantısı*, pp. 291–311. Ankara: Ministry of Culture and Tourism.

2000 "Sirkeli I: Zu Beziehungen mit Syrien und dem östlichen Mittelmeer," in *Periplus: Festschrift für Hans-Günter Buchholz zu Seinem Achtzigsten Geburstag am 24. Dezember 1999*, Studies in Mediterranean Archaeology Vol. CXXVII, edited by P. Åström, D. Sürenhagen, pp. 73–76. Jonsered: Paul Åströms Förlag.

JEAN, É.

2006 "The Hittites at Mersin-Yumuktepe: Old Problems and New Directions," in *Structuring and Dating in Hittite Archaeology*, edited by D. P. Mielke, U. D. Schoop, J. Seeher, pp. 311–339. İstanbul: Ege Yayınları.

KASCHAU, G.

1999 *Lidar Höyük. Die Keramik der Mittleren Bronzezeit*, Archaeologica Euphratica 3. Mainz am Rhein: Philipp von Zabern.

KOPETZKY, K.

2008 "The MB IIB-Corpus of the Hyksos Period at Tell El-Daba," *The Bronze Age in the Lebanon. Studies on the Archaeology of Lebanon, Syria and Egypt*, edited by M. Bietak, E. Czerny, pp. 195–242. Vienna: Verlag der Österreichischen Akademie der Wissenschaften.

KOŞAY, H. Z. and AKOK, M.

1973 *Alacahöyük Excavations. Preliminary Report on Research and Discoveries*. Ankara: Türk Tarih Kurumu Yayınları.

KOZAL, E.
2005 "Unpublished Middle and Late Cypriot Pottery from Tarsus-Gözlükule," in *Field Seasons 2001–2003 of the Tarsus-Gözlükule, Interdisciplinary Research Project,* edited by A. Özyar, pp. 135–144. İstanbul: Ege Yayınları.
2006 *Anatolien im 2. Jt. v.u.Z. und die Hinterlassenschaften materieller Kultur aus dem Ostmittelmeerraum, insbesondere Zyperns.* http://tobias-lib.ub.uni-tuebingen.de/volltexte/2006/2481/ (27 December, 2008).

MANUELLI, F.
2009 "Local Imitations and Foreign Imported Goods. Some Problems and New Questions on Red Lustrous Wheel-made Ware in the light of the new excavations of the Southern Step Trench at Yumuktepe/Mersin," *Altorientalische Forschungen* 36/2: 251–267.

MELLAART, J. and MURRAY, A.
1995 *Beycesultan.* Vol. III, Part II, *The Late Bronze Age and Phrygian Pottery, Middle and Late Bronze Age Small Objects.* Oxford: The British Institute of Archaeology at Ankara.

MOUNTJOY, P. A.
2005 "The Mycenaean Pottery from the 1934–38 Excavations at Tarsus," in *Field Seasons 2001–2003 of the Tarsus-Gözlükule, Interdisciplinary Research Project,* edited by A. Özyar, pp. 78–112. İstanbul: Ege Yayınları.

MULLINS, R. A.
2010 "A Comparative Analysis of the Alalakh 2003–2004 Season Pottery with Woolley's Levels," in *Tell Atchana, Ancient Alalakh.* Vol 1. *The 2003–2004 Excavations Seasons* edited by K. A. Yener, pp. 51–66. İstanbul: Koç University Press.

NOVAK, M. and KOZAL, E.
2010 "Sirkeli Höyük'te 2008 Yılı Çalışmaları," 31. *Kazı Sonuçları Toplantısı,* Vol.3, pp. 477–490. Ankara: Ministry of Culture and Tourism.

VON DER OSTEN, H. H.
1937 *The Alishar Hüyük Seasons of 1930-32 Part II,* Oriental Institute Publications XXIX. Chicago: The University of Chicago Oriental Institute Publications.

ÖZGÜÇ, N.
1968 *Seals and Seal Impressions of Level Ib from Karum Kanish.* Ankara: Türk Tarih Kurumu Yayınları.

SCHMIDT, E. F.
1932 *The Alishar Hüyük Seasons of 1928 and 1929,* Oriental Institute Publications XIX. Chicago: The University of Chicago Oriental Institute Publications.

SEVIN, V. and KÖROĞLU, K.
2004 "Late Bronze Age at Yumuktepe: New Evidence from Step-Trench South 2004," in *Mersin-Yumuktepe A Reappraisal,* edited by I. Caneva, V. Sevin, pp. 73–83. Lecce: Congedo Ediotre.

SETON-WILLIAMS, M. V.
1954 "Cilician Survey,"*Anatolian Studies* 4: 121–174.

SLANE, D.
1987 "Middle and Late Bronze Age Architecture and Pottery in Gözlü Kule, Tarsus: A New Analysis." (Unpublished dissertation) Ann Arbor: University Microfilms International.

SYMINGTON, D.
2001 "Hittites at Kilise Tepe," in *Kilikia: Mekanlar ve Yerel Güçler (M.Ö. 2. binyıl – M.S. 4. yüzyıl), Uluslararası Yuvarlak Masa Toplantısı Bildirileri İstanbul, 2-5 Kasım 1999,* edited by É. Jean, A. M. Dinçol, S. Durugönül, pp. 167–184. Paris: De Boccard.

ÜNAL, A.
2002 *Hititler Devrinde Anadolu*, Vol.1, İstanbul: Arkeoloji ve Sanat Yayınları.
VOGELSANG-EASTWOOD, G.
1990 "Crescent Loomweights?" in *Oriens Antiquus* 29: 97–113.
WEINGARTEN, J.
1990 "The Sealing Structure at Karahöyük and Some Administrative Links with Phaistos in Crete," *Oriens Antiquus* 29: 63–95.
WOOLLEY, L.
1955 *Alalakh: An Account of the Excavations at Tell Atchana in the Hatay, 1937–1949*. Oxford: The Society of Antiquaries.
YAĞCI, R.
2001 "The Importance of Soli in the Archaeology of Cilicia in the 2nd Millennium B.C.," in *Kilikia: Mekanlar ve Yerel Güçler (M.Ö. 2. binyıl – M.S. 4. yüzyıl), Uluslararası Yuvarlak Masa Toplantısı Bildirileri İstanbul, 2-5 Kasım 1999*, edited by É. Jean, A. M. Dinçol, S. Durugönül, pp. 159–165. Paris: De Boccard.
2003a "The Stratigraphy of Cyprus WS II and Mycenaean Cups in Soli Höyük Excavations,"in *Identifying Changes: The Transition from Bronze to Iron Ages in Anatolia and its Neighbouring Regions. Proceedings of the International Workshop* (Istanbul, November 8-9, 2002), edited by B. Fischer, H. Genz, É. Jean, K. Köroğlu, pp. 93–106. İstanbul: Ege Yayınları.
2003b "Beyaz Astarlı (White Slip) II Kapları ve I.Ö. II. Binde Kıbrıs Soli İlişkileri," *Adalya* 6: 1–19.
2007 "Soli/Pompeiopolis 2005 Yılı Kazıları," 28. *Kazı Sonuçları Toplantısı*, Vol. 2, pp. 175–184. Ankara: Ministry of Culture and Tourism.

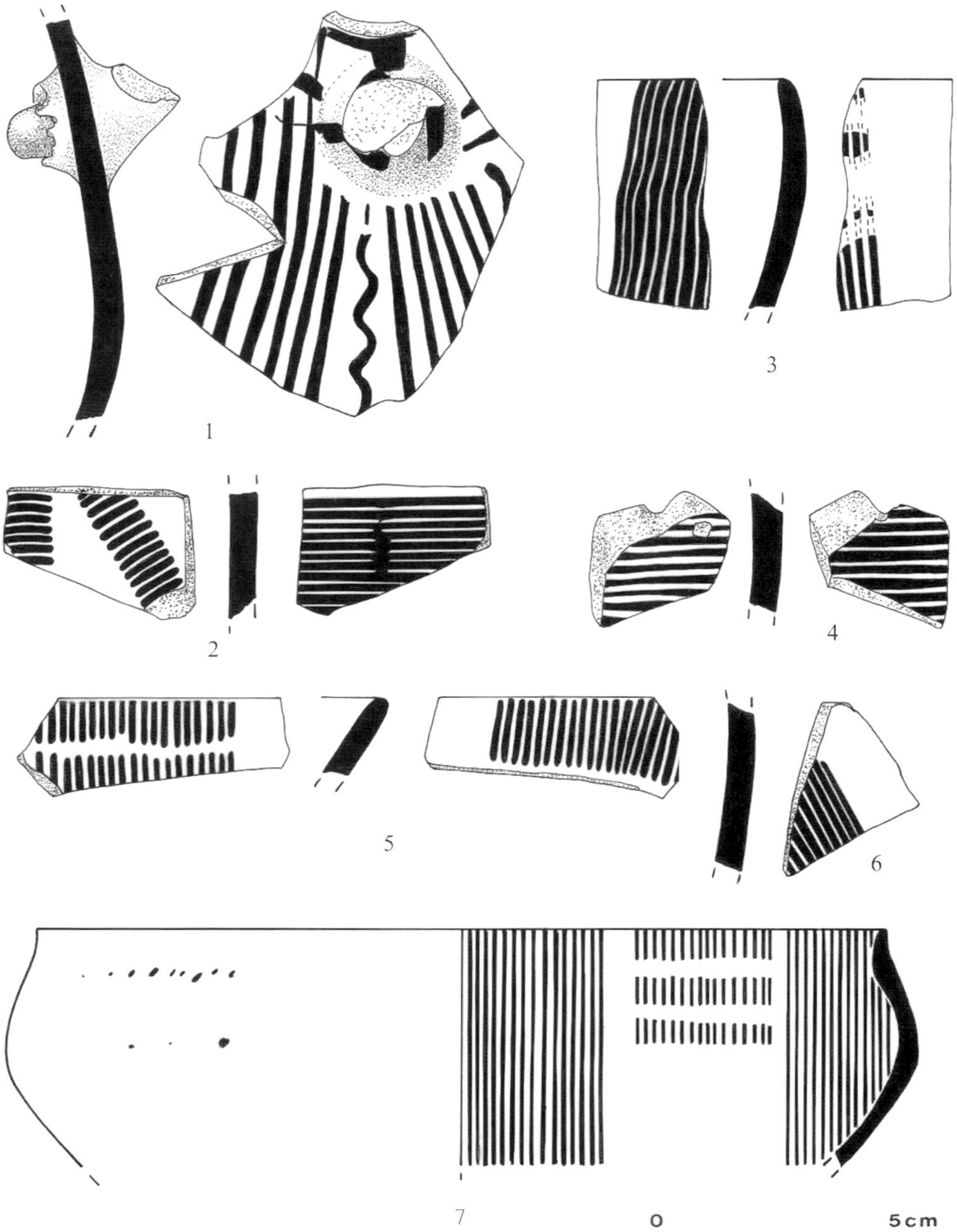

Fig. 1 MB II-MB III/LB I Cypriot imports.

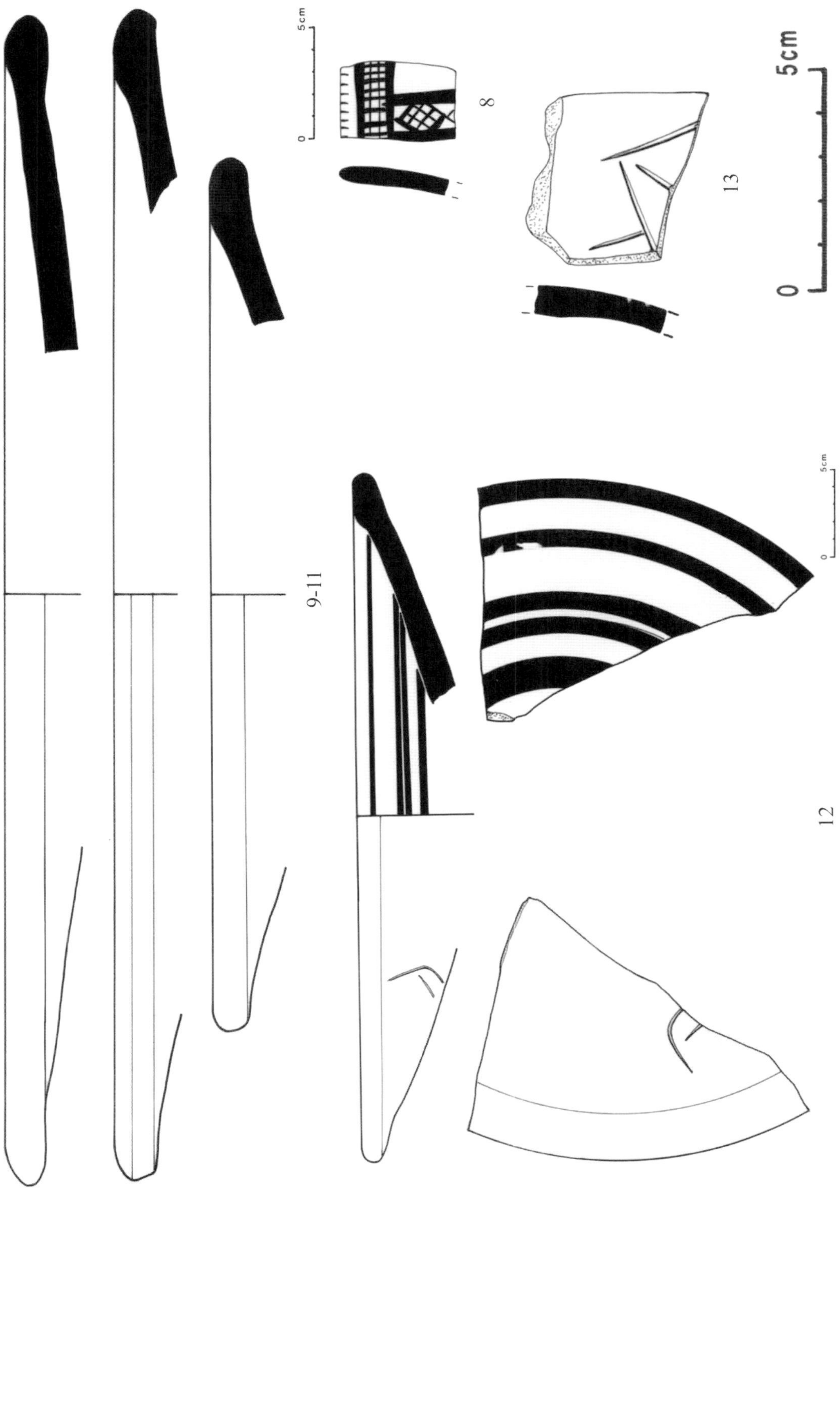

Fig. 2 LB plates (9-13) and a LB II Cypriot White Slip bowl fragment (8).

CHAPTER 10

THE TRANSITION FROM THE LATE BRONZE AGE TO THE EARLY IRON AGE AT TELL AFIS, SYRIA (PHASES VII–III)

Fabrizio VENTURI

ABSTRACT

The Levant was involved in profound changes between the end of the 13th century BC and the beginning of the 12th century BC; the fall of the Hittite Empire in north western Syria and the withdrawal of Egyptian domination from Canaan created a sudden power vacuum and gave rise to important changes in the material culture. The disintegration of the city state system, the arrival of new populations such as the "Sea Peoples," the settlement of Aramaic tribes (in the case of Syria), continuity and discontinuity in the reorganization of societies; these are all topics linked to this much-debated period. The analysis of such phenomena, made possible by abundant documentation from Cyprus and the cities of the Philistine Pentapolis, has been given new evidence from the northern Levant, thanks to increasing information from Cilicia, the Amuq, and new excavations on the Syrian coast. To this documentation we can add the evidence from the site of Tell Afis, situated on the north western Syrian plateau. The long stratigraphical sequence that was uncovered has allowed us to define an extensive picture of the material culture and architecture of the site on the eve of the changes which swept through the Levant at the end of the Late Bronze Age. Furthermore, it enabled us to analyse the processes through which the site subsequently developed a new urban and cultural model in the so-called "Dark Age."

INTRODUCTION

The transition from the Late Bronze Age to the Iron Age in the Levant is marked by the collapse of the Egyptian and Hittite empires, which dominated the political scene during the 14th–13th centuries BC, and by the fall of city state administrative and political systems, which led to a period of crisis called the "dark age." A long tradition of studies and debates focussing on this period has been devoted to regions such as Cyprus and the southern Levant and it has been demonstrated that these centuries were not as dark as previously believed, but rather an arc of time characterized by a wide-reaching dynamic of cultural interactions stimulated by the crisis of the dominant powers.

In recent decades increasing research and the important archaeological and textual discoveries coming from both the Turkish and Syrian sides shed new light on our knowledge of the period and enable us to deal with this complicated issue from a Northern Levant perspective as well. Tell Afis is one of the sites, which, thanks to its uninterrupted stratigraphical sequence covering a span from the 13th to the 10th century BC, allows an analysis of the cultural and urban development of a town on the eve of the important transformations which took place at the end of Late Bronze Age and the beginning of Early Iron Age in the Levant.

The site is situated in Syria in the district of Idlib, on the border of a fertile plateau, called Jazr in the medieval period, 40 km from the Bab el Hawa pass and 60 km SW of Aleppo.[1] The Late Bronze Age/Early Iron Age sequence has been investigated in area N[2] and E4, respectively on the eastern and western slopes of the acropolis (**Fig. 1**). The results of area E4 will be presented here, summing up the findings of 23 years of archaeological activity, already published in preceding articles, preliminary reports and books[3], and adding new unpublished information coming from the latest two campaigns.

Late Bronze Age II

Architecture

Three phases (VII–VI and Vb) can be ascribed to this period. In phase VII, the area was occupied by residence F (**Fig. 2**), partly exposed in its western limits on a surface of 450 sq. m. The building shows a coherent plan divided into distinct sectors. The doors in the rooms were systematically set in the opposite corners, creating a bent-axis circulation. The southern sector is composed of rooms F4-5-6-11. As the floors of these *loci* have not yielded any material *in situ*, it is difficult to suggest any kind of function. The F6 floor presents numerous re-pavings and burnt traces, so we can therefore suggest some industrial activities. Even if badly damaged by later pits, Room F11 is clearly a pillared room (7.5 x 5 m) divided into two parts on its longitudinal axis by a row of wooden supports. The three bases preserved were made of a single flat

[1] In the Seventies, together with Ebla/Tell Mardikh and Tell Tuqan, the site was part of a wide excavation project directed by Prof. P. Matthiae. Since 1986, the site has been under the direction of Prof. S. Mazzoni.

[2] Affanni 2005.

[3] The excavation in area E4 started in 1988 and since 1992 has been conducted under my direction. Since 2004 the work has been accomplished with the co-direction of Barbara Chiti, who is also responsible for the CAD rendering of the plans of phases VII-IV-III. The most recent preliminary reports on the area are in Chiti 2005; Pedrazzi 2002, 2005; Venturi 2002, 2005. A comprehensive presentation of the excavation results is in Venturi 2007. About the LB II/EIA sequence in area E4, see also Venturi 2008b, 2010.

roughly cut stone (75 × 50 × 40 cm) sunken into the floor. The northern sector was the most important area of the building and has its main space in room F8 (8 × 4.5 m), equipped with a low bench set against its southern wall. From this locus it was possible to reach the kitchen F3 through the narrow vestibule F7, and the small secondary rooms F1-2 to the west. Kitchen F3 was equipped with a *tannur*, and a horseshoe-shaped hearth. Some vessels and grinding stones lay near its eastern wall. Rooms 1-2 display high-quality architecture with heavily plastered floors and walls. These two *loci* lack materials *in situ*, but in the south eastern corner of room F2, a cuneiform tablet in the Hittite language was found in 2008. A third door in room F8 opens towards the north into F12, the excavation of which was accomplished during the 2009 campaign. Unfortunately the western part of this narrow space (5 × 2.5 m) has been almost completely lost owing to a rectangular pit from phase Vb. In any case, the eastern part was well-preserved and contained a big storage jar, a shallow plate, a burnished one-handled lentoid asymmetrical pilgrim flask, and four cuneiform tablets; three in local crude reddish clay and one made of fine greenish clay of the same type as the one found in F2. This tablet, like the F2 one, was written in the Hittite language. The excavation of room F13 in 2010 revealed four more badly damaged tablets, one of these again, written in Hittite. The scattered arrangement of these texts suggests that they belong to a more numerous *corpus* located elsewhere in the building and testify to its public function.[4]

Residence F was intentionally abandoned, its walls razed and the rooms filled. With phase VI, the area was occupied by an open-air industrial complex. The only dwelling, consisting of a single rectangular room, was arranged just above room F12 of building F, but the majority of the area was occupied by sunken firing installations (**Figs. 3-4**) and pits. The lack of any waste material residues makes it difficult to identify the functions of these productive equipment. Structure 9002 (**Fig.** 4) was an oval pit (4 × 2.30 × 2.30) lined with mud bricks. The vitrification of the inner coating and the burnt wooden elements found in the filling suggest that it was a combustion chamber. Despite evidence of intensive use, this occupation must have occurred for only a short period; we presume that these installations could have been functional for the building of the residences of the following important urban period represented by phase Vb.

This phase is now exposed over about 800 sq. m and testifies to a complete rebuilding of the area with changes in the urban plan (**Fig.** 5). The surface previously occupied by building F was divided into two distinct blocks by a paved street C, along which smaller residences abutted. Even if smaller in size, these residences do not show

[4] The other six tablets made of local clay found in rooms F12-13 were basically administrative texts written in Akkadian. The whole *corpus* of texts from building F has been published in Archi-Venturi 2012, p. 47.

any loss in building technique. In particular, residence A is delimited by 2 m thick walls and is characterized by the use of large squared stones for door frames and staircases. The plan consisted of a wide central room A1 accessible from a bent-axis vestibule A6 and a group of secondary rooms surrounding the main central space. Room A1 was divided into two parts by a wooden structure and was probably the reception room. The secondary rooms, A2-A7, had a storage function and they contained all the pottery *in situ*. The southern building B, despite its northern 3-metre-thick wall, has a more domestic aspect. The main space is represented by the broad room B1 divided into two parts by a row of six stone pillar bases. The dimensions (8.50 × 6.50 m) of the room are slightly bigger than those of F11 in phase VII, but the clearest difference is represented by the pillars, which are now made of ashlar rectangular blocks (65 × 40 cm), 100-120 cm high, laid directly on the floor. They divided the space into two distinct sections of different sizes; the larger western part was plastered, while on the contrary, the eastern part was stone-paved.[5] Even if a door on street C was set towards the NE, B1 was accessible only through rooms B2–B6. It was certainly the real focus of the house; as a matter of fact, the majority of the material was arranged in its western part, where many activities took place (storage, food transformation and cooking). Room B5, equipped with three *tannurs*, was probably a kitchen.

The Pottery[6]

The three analyzed phases show a homogeneous pottery assemblage without remarkable changes from one period to another, from which we can highlight some well-identifiable features. The pottery industry shows a strong standardisation of forms and pottery types. In phase Vb, the mass-produced local plain ware makes up 84% of the total selected diagnostic sherds. Imported pottery is completely lacking and the presence of painted pottery is negligible. The most ubiquitous fabric in common ware shows a prevalent reddish-yellow surface colour (Munsell soil charts 7.5YR6/6 or 5YR6/8). Cross-sections have an inner very pale brown (10YR7/4) colour and greyish core. The clay is composed of a high percentage of black and white mineral inclusions, and surface-finishing, such as burnishing or slip are very rare.

Distinctive for the period is the high proportion of shallow bowls with rounded or small, flat base. The high standardisation of the production led to a great simplification of rim-types, which are simple, bevelled or outwardly thickened (**Figs 7.1–11**). The same type of clay was also used for kraters which frequently display rectangular or triangular flaring rim (**Figs. 7.12–14, 16**), but the thick flat rims with inner projection are also well attested (**Fig. 7.15**). When preserved, the body of the kraters shows

[5] For a discussion on pillar buildings in the Levant, see Venturi 2008a.
[6] All the pottery presented in this article is drawn by Sergio Martelli.

a gently curved profile and a ring base (**Figs. 7.12–13**). Other distinctive forms are the one-handled fusiform jar (**Figs. 8.1–3**) and a krater-jar, 60–80 cm tall, with a straight-sided profile, small flat base, and a low carination (**Figs. 8.4–5**). Also typical of the three Late Bronze Age phases is the use of pot marks on the big storage jars (**Fig. 9**).

Even if the pottery production of Tell Afis appears to be completely local, it shares some trends with the Anatolian *milieu* of the 14th–13th centuries BC. The high percentage of common poorly finished pottery, the incidence of shallow bowls in the total amount of the corpus, and the lack of fine or imported wares also characterized the so-called drab ware production during the last part of the Hittite period in many central Anatolian and Cilician sites. Our site lacks some of the typical Hittite diagnostic open shapes, such as the plate with stepped rim or the bowl with thickened inward rim, but the most prevalent bevelled or thickened outward rim (**Figs. 7.4–8**) are also common in Hattusha,[7] Tille Höyük,[8] and Gordion.[9] Moreover, among the forms which are an expression of local tradition, some shapes resemble Anatolian types. The examples of one-handled fusiform jars with narrow neck and pointed base collected in phase Vb (**Figs. 8.1–3**)[10] have good parallels from Hattusha,[11] Tarsus ,[12] Tille Höyük,[13] and Gordion.[14] The form is attested also in Alalakh level II and Emar,[15] that is, in Mukish and Ashtata, which were under Hittite control during the 13th century BC. H. Genz suggests a possible Hittite origin for these two samples.[16] The southernmost examples come from Late Bronze Age levels in Tell Kazel.[17]

Complete or almost complete krater-jars with a low carination in phase Vb come from rooms A7 (**Fig. 8.4**) and B1 (**Fig. 8.5**), but rim sherds related to this form (**Figs. 8.6–10**), flaring rectangular or outwardly-thickened with inner projection are widespread on floors and destruction layers of this phase, testifying to common use during this period. Good parallels come from the 13th/early-12th century BC contexts in Tell Fray, Malatya III, and Tell Kazel.[18] This type of jar became typical in the

[7] Müller-Karpe 1988, figs. 33–34; Parzinger and Sanz 1992, fig. 19 (types 5.1–2), figs. 26.17, 58.2, 6, 10–13.

[8] Summers 1993, pp. 47–48, fig. 43.4–7.

[9] Voigt and Henrickson 2000, p. 344, figs. 17.9.4–6, 10–13.

[10] Fig. 8.1 was found in the open area just north of residence A (Pedrazzi 2007, type 7–2–3, fig. 3.45.a). Fig. 8.2 was collected in pit 9502, cut into the open space just west of the SW outer wall of building B. Fig. 8.3 comes from area N1, the step trench excavated on the eastern slope of the acropolis. It belongs to phase VIIb which corresponds stratigraphically to phase Vb of area E4.

[11] Müller-Karpe 1988, p. 31, type K2, fig. 3.2; Parzinger and Sanz 1992, figs. 10.18, 13.5.

[12] Goldman 1956, fig. 322.1192.

[13] Summers 1993, fig. 54.2.

[14] Voigt and Henrickson 2000, fig. 17.11.

[15] Woolley 1955, pl. CXI, type 39; Caubet 1982, p. 73, fig. 31.

[16] Genz 2006, p. 502.

[17] Pedrazzi 2007, pp. 95–96, fig. 3.45b. See Pedrazzi 2010, pp. 55–56 for a different opinion on the origin of the Syrian one-handle fusiform jars.

[18] Pfälzner 1995, fig. 183a; Pecorella 1975, p. 100, fig. 10.3; Capet 2003, p. 113, fig. 48a.

Hittite imperial period and the same shapes and rims are known in Alişar Hüyük,[19] Kuşakli,[20] and Hattusha.[21]

The big storage jars from the three Late Bronze Age II phases at Tell Afis were frequently incised with marks. These signs were made before firing and were generally placed on the shoulder of the vessel, apart from the jar in fig. 9.1. The range of mark-types used at Tell Afis has counterparts in several Anatolian sites.[22] The crossed shield (**Fig. 9.1**) seems to be a rough version of Kinet Höyük type nos. 34.[23] It is also well-known in central Anatolia during the Hittite imperial period. In Alaca Höyük as in Kinet Höyük, it is used on bowls,[24] while in Kuşakli[25] it appears on vessels morphologically similar to the krater-jars of Tell Afis.[26] The triangle, divided in two parts by a vertical line (**Fig. 9.2**), has its best comparison in Hattusha, Alaca Höyük, and Tarsus .[27] It is the only sign in Tell Afis associated with a krater-jar vessel and in this case, the relationship between vessel form and sign is particularly useful in defining a possible link between the Tell Afis production and that of Anatolia. The trident-shaped mark (**Figs. 9.3, 5–6**) was incised in Hattusha on jars or below vertical handles.[28] It is also well-known in Cilicia; it appears in Kinet Höyük phase 15 but is more common in phase 14.[29] In Tarsus[30] we find both the sharp (**Figs. 9.3, 6**) and the rounded version (**Fig. 9.5**).

A bronze lugged axe (**Fig. 6**) discovered beneath the floor of the pillared room B1, buried there before the construction of the building, could have an Anatolian origin. The shape is common in north central Anatolia,[31] but no comparable examples have been found in Syria.[32]

The most important evidence related to Anatolian links between the Idlib region and the Hittite homeland is obviously represented by the three cuneiform tablets in the Hittite language found in building F. Following the translation by A. Archi, two letters were sent by a "lord of the country" to the local governor, who in the second

[19] Fischer 1963, figs. 11.14, 12.7.

[20] Müller-Karpe 2001, p. 329, figs. 12.2–3.

[21] Müller-Karpe 1988, fig. 15 (T1r), 16–17 (T2k); Parzinger and Sanz 1992, figs. 3.6–9, 19.17, 24.21–23, 28.1.

[22] For fig. 9.5, see also Pedrazzi 2005, p. 59, fig. 45.8.

[23] Gates 2001, fig. 6.

[24] Koşay 1951, figs. 1–20.

[25] Müller-Karpe 1998, p. 114, fig. 15.8, p. 159, fig. 39; 2001, p. 332, fig. 12.2–3.

[26] Some scholars suggest that this mark could have a relationship with the Hittite hieroglyph "king" Müller-Karpe 2001, p. 332.

[27] Seidl 1972, p. 76, fig. 23, B36; Koşay 1944: p. 54, pl. XXXIX; Goldman 1956, fig. 318.1136.

[28] Seidl 1972, p. 76, fig. 23, B30–33.

[29] Types 21–23, 14th–13th centuries BC see Gates 2001, fig. 6, nos. 21–23.

[30] Goldman 1956, p. 204, figs. 318.1132, 319.1150.

[31] Erkanal 1977, type I, figs. 1.11, 2.13–14, type III, fig. 2.23.

[32] A similar axe was found in the destruction level of Hama phase E. Even if it comes from an Iron II context, a Late Bronze Age Anatolian provenience is suggested cf. Riis and Buhl 1990, p. 114, fig. 53, nos. 319.

letter bears a Semitic name, Ashmakh-ya (TA.09.E.203). But most important is the text of the first letter (TA.08.E.1) in which the sender informs the official in charge of Afis that he has had to delay his departure because the queen, after reaching him, fell ill. He thinks, however, that he will reach Izziya in three days from the moment in which his letter is sent. From Hittite sources, we know that the town of Izziya must be located in Cilicia[33] and is related to vows carried out by a queen, probably Puduhepa. A. Archi also argues that the queen mentioned in the Afis texts could be the wife of Hattushili III and therefore, the Tell Afis tablet dates to the reign of this king. The sender, following Archi's hypothesis, could have been residing in Alalakh, the most important governor's seat, which was situated halfway between Tell Afis and Cilicia.[34]

Even if these texts confirm the political links between Tell Afis, Kizzuwatna, Mukish, and the great king of Hatti in the mid-13th century BC, it is more difficult to establish a direct connection between this political scenario and the production choices of the Tell Afis potters during phases VII–VI and Vb. With the aim of verifying the antecedents to this production at the site, during the 2009 campaign we opened a trench below room F4. We then identified our phase VIII. Statigraphically, it lies between the top of the Middle Bronze Age fortification and the construction of building F. It is divided into three sub-phases for a total thickness of less than one metre. The structures are basically of a domestic nature: a horse-shoe-shaped hearth and stone banquettes set on uneven, low-quality floors. The study of the materials is still at a preliminary stage, but we can already underline some important points. The phase VIII pottery horizon appears to be completely different from the following phases, starting with shapes (**Fig. 10**); bowls have mainly rounded or pointed, inwardly thickened rims; kraters have rectangular, often grooved rims; jars have grooved or pinched rims; decoration is mainly impressed, incised or combed, and above all, the clay has a completely different aspect. Common wares show higher firing and have a pinkish to light red core and external pale yellow surface. Finer classes have homogenous pale yellow colour. In other words, these forms and fabrics are more familiar to the local Middle Bronze Age[35] or to 16th–15th BC Inner Syrian contexts, such as the middle Euphrates sites Tell Hadidi,[36] Tell Munbaqa,[37] or El Qitar.[38] We can suggest

[33] M. Forlanini has proposed an identification with Issos, the place of Alexander's battle, the modern Kinet Höyük Forlanini 1988, p. 147.

[34] Archi-Venturi 2012, p. 45–46.

[35] For the bowls with inward thickened rim (fig. 10.1–7), see Mazzoni 1998, figs. 21.2, 3, 11–12 (Tell Afis); Fiorentino 2006, fig. 34 (Tell Tuqan). For the closed bowl of fig. 10.10, see Matthiae 1989, fig. 51.1 (Tell Mardikh/Ebla).

[36] Dornemann 1981, cfr. TA fig. 10.16 with figs 4.12–13, 5.6; TA fig. 10.17 with fig. 6.8; TA fig. 10.8 with figs 14.18, 21.

[37] De Feyter 1989, cfr. TA fig. 10.5, 7 with figs. 6.15–16.

[38] McClellan 1985, cf. TA fig. 10.15 with fig. 4.P; TA fig. 10.9 with fig. 4.N, TA fig. 10.12 with fig. 5.D, 6.D; Mc Clellan 1986: Tell Afis figs. 10.1–7 with fig. 7.

two different hypotheses; a chronological gap between phases VIII and VII or a strong continuity of Late Bronze I tradition in the site until phase VII. In both cases, the massive production of pottery with external reddish yellow surface and its typical forms must be considered a phenomenon limited to phases VII–VI–Vb and basically attributable to the 13th century BC.

The Early Iron Age

The Architecture

The Late Bronze Age sequence ended with the destruction of the Vb buildings, an event which could be ascribed to the general picture of instability, which affected the Levant at the beginning of the 12th century BC. Although the area underwent complete reconstruction, phase IV preserved some patterns of the previous urban organisation (**Fig. 11**), such as the same street C, lined by two new houses. However, the architecture shows a completely different appearance. The high-quality Late Bronze Age residences are now replaced by domestic units equipped with benches, ovens, and other domestic furniture. A change in storage methods is testified by the use of circular sunken silos employed in considerable numbers, inside the domestic units, and in communal wide-open areas, used not only for storage purposes, but also as dumps (**Fig. 13**).

Phase III documents a further step in the urban development of the area, which regained a coherent urban layout (**Fig. 12**). The two houses were razed and then completely rebuilt. The ancient street C was still in use, but the construction of the southern unit made it a narrow passage,1.5 m wide. Towards the north and south, the wide yards were overlapped by new domestic units divided by parallel streets with SW-NE orientation. The disappearance of the communal yards and the close arrangement of the urban space led to the abandonment of the silos as storage facilities.

The Pottery

The events which brought about the dramatic end of phase Vb did not lead to a complete change in the material culture of the site. As in architecture, we do not see a total break in the local tradition. In particular, in cooking and storage ware there is a clear continuity in shapes, which evolved from previous forms. The Early Iron Age carinated cooking pot with thick rim and rounded base (**Fig. 14.2**) and the big storage jars (**Fig. 14.4**) are clearly inspired by Late Bronze Age models (**Figs. 14.1, 3**). However, at the same time we have some significant changes. The one-handle fusiform jars and the krater-jars completely disappear and, even if the big *pithoi* derive from their Late Bronze Age predecessors, the practice of marking them with distinctive signs went out of use.

Undoubtedly the most striking difference between the Late Bronze Age and Early Iron Age cultural horizons is represented by the appearance of the new Aegean-inspired Mycenaean IIIC:1 and local monochrome painted pottery. Mycenaean IIIC: 1 is a fine ware with a pink (5YR7/3) or very pale brown (10YR7/4) colour. The vessels are smoothed and sometimes slipped (5Y8/3 pale yellow), but never burnished, giving the surface and the painting a matt aspect.

The most common shape is represented by the deep bell-shaped bowl, decorated during phase IV with few geometric motifs. The single or double wavy line (**Fig. 15.4–7**), the monochrome black decoration with reserved bands (**Figs. 15.1–2**) and the tricurved arch[39] are stylistically linked to the White Painted Wheelmade III/ Proto White Painted ware in Cyprus,[40] and to the Aegean LH IIIC middle-late,[41] dating phase IV to a period between the end of the 12th and the first half of the 11th century BC. However, the style of the decoration, together with the shape of deep bowls characterized by an accentuated s-profile and everted rim, find their best counterpart in the Amuq production, as we know from the Swift-phase N[42] and the recent excavations in field I in Tell Tayinat.[43] Rarer, but belonging perfectly to this period is the shallow angular bowl with strap handles, decorated with horizontal bands (**Fig. 15.3**).[44] During phase III, the presence of deep bowls diminishes and the decorations become simpler, executed with horizontal bands.

Mycenaean IIIC: 1 ware is clearly distinguishable from the local painted ware. The clay of the latter is coarser and includes chaff, a temper little-used previously. Nevertheless, the rough aspect of the clay is compensated by an accurate surface treatment, due to the introduction of stroke-burnishing. Painting is always monochrome red. Black painting or bichrome (**Fig. 16.1**) appear only at the end of phase III. The most common motifs used in Tell Afis are the horizontal wavy line (**Fig. 16.14**), the zig-zag (**Fig. 16.6**), and the hatched triangles, antithetic (**Figs. 16.5, 11**) or arranged in rows (**Figs. 16.8, 12**). Rims of bowls and kraters are frequently decorated with dots or lines (**Figs. 16.3, 9–10, 16**). The commonest decoration for vertical handles consists of vertical lines which divide into antithetical tails, single or double (**Figs. 16.7, 16**). The Tell Afis motifs fall within the typological range of the Hama and Amuq N repertoire.[45] The decoration of handles with antithetical tails is

[39] Pedrazzi 2002, fig. 24.2.

[40] Karageorghis and Demas 1985, pl. CCXII.5030, 5483; Mountjoy 2005b, p. 173, figs. 19.14–15; 174, fig. 20.18, p. 175, fig. 21.28.

[41] Mountjoy 1999, figs. 58.440–441, 238.601, 473.13.

[42] Swift 1958, figs. 19–21.

[43] Janeway 2008, fig. 4.1; Harrison 2010, figs. 4.7, 9.

[44] In Cyprus and Greece , this form became popular in the LCIIIA-B/LHIIIC early-middle (Mountjoy 1999, fig. 97.213; Mountjoy 2005b, fig. 9.39). In the Northern Levant, it is attested in Mycenaean IIIC: 1 contexts in Tarsus (Mountjoy 2005a, fig. 15) and Ras Ibn Hani (Bounni *et al.* 1979, p. 249, fig. 25).

[45] Riis 1948, figs. 130A.3, 10, 11, 17, 48, 50, 81; Swift 1958, figs. 23–24; Harrison 2010, fig. 5.4.

also attested in Tarsus[46] and was particularly appreciated in the Dodecanese Islands during the 12th–11th centuries BC.[47] In particular, the band encircling the lower part of the handle of fig. 16.7 has exact parallels in Rhodes in LHIIIC middle.[48]

The affirmation of Mycenaean IIIC:1 and the local painted pottery concerns mainly table ware and even if their incidence in the total amount of sherds is not striking (they represent respectively 4% and 11% of the whole *corpus*), the introduction of new forms, such as the Mycenaean IIIC:1 deep bell shaped bowls, the shallow bowls with ring base (**Figs. 16.3, 9–10**)[49] and the amphoroid kraters (**Figs. 16.6, 14, 16**), caused a decrease in the massive production of common tableware shapes; the incidence of shallow bowls with rounded base and hemispherical bowls diminishes drastically from 30% to 10%, whereas the incidence of other classes such as storage or cooking ware remains basically unaltered.

Conclusions

A general overview of the area E4 sequence shows the cultural continuity of the site from a diachronical perspective. The close overlapping of architectural phases and the persistence of local features in the urban layout and material culture are clear evidence of the strong roots of the local social and cultural framework. Nevertheless, the destruction which occurred at the end of phase Vb divides the sequence into two different periods represented by phases VII–VI–Vb for Late Bronze Age II and IV–III for Early Iron Age with their own specific features; two distinct snapshots of a society in evolution through the historical events affecting the region in this troubled period.

During 13th century BC, Tell Afis was a well-developed urban centre characterized by sophisticated architecture. The low-quality fabric of the pottery, the marked standardization of forms and the cuneiform texts show the existence of a complex economy and a centralised administrative system. Judging by the contexts of the two texts in Hittite found in building F, the local governor of Tell Afis was under the direct control of a Hittite authority: the "lord of the country" who resided in Alalakh.[50] Therefore the textual evidence seems to indicate that neither Karkemish nor Aleppo were the controlling powers in the region as might be suggested for a mid-13th century BC political scenario.[51] Rather they seem to outline a diplomatic axis towards Kizzuwatna and Mukish. Control of the Tell Afis region certainly had strategic implications. The

[46] Goldman 1956, fig. 391.
[47] Mountjoy 1998, p. 54, fig. 10; Mountjoy 1999, fig. 463.15.
[48] Mountjoy 1999, fig. 437.263.
[49] The diffusion of this type of ring-based shallow bowls, decorated with horizontal bands and with simple rim decorated with dot or lines is also testified in the Amuq (Swift 1958, fig. 18) and Hama (Riis 1948, figs. 101, 130.86, 87, 89, 101).
[50] Archi-Venturi 2012, p. 47.
[51] Klengel 2001, p. 265.

Jazr was one of the transit points towards the inner Syrian provinces and was, like the Amuq, a fertile plan important for the supply of cereals. Therefore Hittite interest in stable control of the region is perfectly understandable.

More difficult is defining a correlation between the Hittite political role in the region and those elements in the Tell Afis material culture, which seem to be linked to the Anatolian plateau. We know that after the Shuppiluliuma I and Murshili II campaigns, the Hittites controlled the North Syrian provinces. However, the textual evidence shows that the central power appeared disinterested in an effective annexation of the conquered territories; apart from Aleppo and Karkemish, it limited its control over them, installing what G. M. Beckman called "a thin layer of imperial bureaucracy."[52] The correlation between Hittite expansion and the diffusion of their material culture inside the empire's borders is an issue still subject to debate, and for provincial sites is complicated by the difficulty in understanding how and at which level the local traditions of the periphery interacted with the central power strategies. The paucity of Anatolian elements in the material culture of sites such as Ugarit and Emar confirms that Hittites did not feel it necessary to impose their cultural model on the conquered Syrian provinces.[53] However, a quite different situation occurred in areas closer to the Hittite homeland, such as Kizzuwatna or Mukish, directly controlled by the Great King through governors.[54] C. Glatz suggests that in the territories from Cilicia to the Euphrates, Hittite central power established an intermediate form of external control which led to local processes of adoption of imperial cultural elements.[55]

Despite its southern position, Tell Afis was probably affected by a similar political status, and the hypothesis that some elements in material culture could have been influenced by this relationship can not be completely rejected. Moreover, it must be underlined that the presence of these elements at Tell Afis is restricted to phases VII–VI–Vb; they appeared for the first time in building F and in connection with its textual evidence, and disappeared after the destruction of the Vb residences at the end of Late Bronze Age.[56]

At the beginning of the Early Iron Age, phase IV shows a fully-developed architectural tradition, even if only with a rural dimension; the intensive use of silos indicates the persistence of a solid agro-pastoral economy which had evidently felt little effect of the problems which led to the end of the phase Vb residences. However, the

[52] Beckman 1992, p. 49.

[53] Genz 2006, p. 505.

[54] Concerning the diffusion of drab ware in the peripheral sites, see Goldman 1956, pp. 204–205 (Tarsus); Gates 2006 (Kinet Höyük); Symington 2001 (Kilise Tepe); Summers 1993, pp. 47–48 (Tille Höyük) and Henrickson 1995 (Gordion).

[55] Glatz 2009, pp. 140–141.

[56] Tell Afis has also presented two biconvex seals from Iron Age I–II contexts in areas G and N, which could however be related to the same Late Bronze Age II political context see Archi 1998, pp. 367–368; Cecchini 2002, p. 50, fig. 33.1.

appearance at the beginning of the Iron Age of Aegeanized pottery also places Tell Afis in the complex discussion about the Sea Peoples, their origins and the role they played in the fall of the Late Bronze Age system. The idea that the collapse in the Northern Levant happened for internal reasons and that we must suggest substantial continuity for the southern provinces, formerly under Hittite control, is now widely accepted. The style of the reliefs in the Ain Dara and Aleppo temples,[57] and the mention of King Kuzi Teshub in the Lidar Höyük *bullae* confirm this hypothesis.[58] On the other hand, the strong appearance in the Northern Levant of locally-produced Aegeanized pottery at the beginning of the 12th century BC does not fit well into this reconstruction and must be further understood. If this phenomenon appears fuzzier on Cyprus and on the Syro-Lebanese coast, where a stronger link with the Mediterranean commercial network kept alive the taste for Mycenaean products until the end of 13th century BC, a clear break is particularly evident at Tell Afis, and in Cilician sites such as Tarsus[59] and Kinet Höyük,[60] where the Aegeanized Mycenaean IIIC: 1 and the local derivative class overlapped the monochrome drab ware production. Although during XII-XI centuries BC, Tell Afis preserved the older Late Bronze Age II trend in cooking and storage activities, the radical change in forms and decoration of table ware reflects modifications to the local daily habits in terms of consumption of food and libation. This must consequently be interpreted as a relevant change in the local social framework.[61]

Leaving aside the complex issue regarding the origins of these new elements in the material culture, what seems clear once again following the Tell Afis evidence is the close link between NW Syria, Cilicia, and the Amuq. The exchange of information between these regions must have been facilitated by the same channels existing at the time of Hittite control of the southern provinces. However, particularly interesting in this sense is the figure of Taita, the king responsible for the inscriptions found in the storm-god temple in Aleppo.[62] If the Taita mentioned in the inscriptions found near

[57] Mazzoni 1997, pp. 298–301; Kohlmeyer 2008, pp. 122–124.

[58] Kuzi Teshub was the successor of Talmi Teshub, the king of Karkemish, a contemporary of the last Hittite king Shuppiluliuma II. Therefore his kingdom should be placed in the mid-12th century BC (Hawkins 1988).

[59] Between phases LBIIa and LBIIb see Goldman 1956, pp. 203–207.

[60] Gates 2010, pp. 66–70.

[61] It must however be emphasised that the Tell Afis excavations have not revealed the wide spectrum of discontinuity in material culture found, for example, in the "Philistine" sites. Apart from pottery, few other elements in the Tell Afis Early Iron Age phases can be convincingly considered clear evidence of the presence of new people in the site. In phases IV-III, the typical EIA cylindrical loomweights were commonly used. These simple objects made of crude clay appear in the Levant at the very beginning of EIA and testify to the adoption of new weaving techniques (Cecchini 2000), often related to the incoming Sea People (see for example Stager 1995: p. 346, pl. 6). The three bronze violin-bow fibulae found in phase IV also appear in the Eastern Mediterranean at the beginning of EIA, frequently associated with the Sea People's movements (Venturi 2005, p. 75, fig. 54.7; Venturi 2008b, p. 370, fig. 7.9).

[62] Gonnella *et al.* 2005.

Hama[63] can be identified with the same Taita in Aleppo, it should suggest the existence in the 11th–10th centuries BC of a powerful kingdom extending from the Amuq to Hama, with a possible capital in Kunulua/Tell Tayinat. If we accept such a possibility, then we must also accept that the affirmation of this political entity and the spread of Aegeanized elements in the Northern Levant chronologically and geographically overlapped.[64]

All those issues rest on a preliminary interpretation and await further developments in the research; nevertheless, beyond the difficulty of establishing historical processes, the evidence coming from Tell Afis shows how the different regions in the north-eastern corner of the Mediterranean between the 13th and 10th centuries BC were strictly related by common or similar trends in material culture, foreshadowing close relationships and exchanges of cultural information – complex dynamics which can best be analysed and understood through a trans-regional approach, to be developed, as the title of this symposium properly suggests, "across the border."

Bibliography

AFFANNI, G.

2005 "Area N1: le fortificazioni del Ferro I," in Tell Afis (Siria) 2002–2004, edited by S. Mazzoni, *Egitto e Vicino Oriente* XXVII: 85–89.

ARCHI, A.

1998 "A Biconvex Seal from Tell Afis," in *Scavi sull'acropoli 1988-1992. The 1988–1992 Excavations on the Acropolis*, edited by S. M. Cecchini, S. Mazzoni, pp. 367–69. Pisa: edizioni ETS.

ARCHI, A. and VENTURI, F.

2012 "Hittites at Tell Afis. I. New Evidence of Cultural Links between Syria and Anatolia through Analysis of Late Bronze Age II Tell Afis Material Culture II. The Cuneiform Tablets," *Orientalia* 81: 1–55.

BECKMAN, G. M.

1992 "Hittite Administration in Syria in the Light of the Texts from Khattusha, Ugarit and Emar," *Bibliotheca Mesopotamica* 25: 41–49.

BOUNNI, A., LAGARCE, J., LAGARCE, E., SALIBY, N. and BADRE, L.

1979 "Rapport préliminaire sur la deuxième campagne de fouilles (1977) à Ibn Hani (Syrie)," *Syria* 56: 217–291.

CAPET, E.

2003 "Tell Kazel (Syrie), Rapport préliminaire sur les 9–17 campagnes de fouilles (1993–2001) du Musée de l'Université Américaine de Beyrouth, chantier II," *Berytus* 47: 63–118.

[63] Taita is cited in the two funerary *stelae* found in Meharde and Sheizar see Jasink 1995, pp. 103–105; Hawkins 2000, pp. 365–367.

[64] A possible correlation between the figure of Taita and the cultural processes in the Northern Levant at the beginning of the Early Iron Age is further emphasised by the recent new reading by Professor D. Hawkins of the toponym *Padasatini* in the inscription Aleppo 6 related to this king, with *Palistin* see Hawkins 2009, pp. 169–172.

CAUBET, A.

1982 "La céramique, in *Meskéné-Emar. Dix ans de travaux 1972–1982,*" edited by D. Beyer, pp. 71–86. Paris: Recherche sur les civilisations.

CECCHINI, S. M.

2000 "The Textile Industry in Northern Syria during the Iron Age According to the Evidence of the Tell Afis Excavations," in *Essays on Syria in the Iron Age*, Ancient Near Eastern Studies, suppl. 7, edited by G. Bunnens, pp. 211–234. Louvain Paris, Sterling, Virginia.

2002 "Area N: presentazione e cronologia," in Tell Afis (Siria) 2000–2001, edited by S. Mazzoni, *Egitto e Vicino Oriente* XXV: 47–53.

CHITI, B.

2005 "Area E4b nord: Bronzo Tardo II-Ferro I," in Tell Afis (Siria) 2002–2004, edited by S. Mazzoni, *Egitto e Vicino Oriente* XXVII: 62–69.

DE FEYTER, T.

1989 "The Aussenstadt Settlement of Munbaqa, Syria," in *To the Euphrates and Beyond: Archaeological Studies in Honour of M.N. van Loon*, edited by O. M. C. Haex, H. H. Curvers, P. M. M. G. Akkermans, pp. 237–256. Rotterdam; Brookfield: A. A. Balkema.

DORNEMANN, R. H.

1981 "The Late Bronze Age Pottery Tradition at Tell Hadidi, Syria ," *Bulletin of the American School of Oriental Research* 241: 29–48.

ERKANAL, H.

1977 *Die Äxte und Beile des 2. Jahrtausends in Zentralanatolien,* Prähistorische Bronzefunde 9, Band 8. Munich: C.H. Beck.

FIORENTINO, R.

2006 "Le campagne 1978, 1981 e 1986. La ceramica," in *Tell Tuqan. Ricerche archeologiche nella regione del Maath (Siria)*, edited by F. Baffi, pp. 51–111. Lecce: Congedo Editore.

FISCHER, F.

1963 *Die hethitische Keramik von Bogazkoy.* Berlin: Gebr. Mann.

FORLANINI, M.

1988 "La regione del Tauro nei testi hittiti," *Vicino Oriente* 7: 129–169.

GATES, M. H.

2001 "Potmarks at Kinet Höyük and the Hittite Ceramic Industry," in *La Cilicie: espaces et pouvoir locaux (2e millenaire av. J.C. 4e siècle ap. J.C.). Actes de la table ronde Internationale d'Istanbul 2-5 novembre 1999*, edited by É. Jean, A. M. Dinçol, S. Durugönül, pp. 137–158. Institut Français d' Études Anatoliennes G. Dumézil. Istanbul-Paris: De Boccard.

2006 "Dating the Hittite Levels at Kinet Höyük: a Revised Chronology," in *Structuring and Dating in Hittite Archaeology*, BYZAS 4 edited by D. P. Mielke, U. D. Schoop, J. Seeher, pp. 293-309. Istanbul.

2010 "Potters and Consumers in Cilicia and the Amuq During the "Age of Transformations" (13th–10th Centuries BC)," in *Societies in Transition. Evolutionary Processes in the Northern Levant between Late Bronze Age II and Early Iron Age*, Studi e testi orientali 9, Serie Archeologica 2, edited by F. Venturi, pp. 65–81. Bologna: CLUEB.

GENZ, H.

2006 "Hetitische Präsenz im Spätbronzezeitlichen Syrien: Die archäeologische Evidenz," *Baghdader Mitteilungen* 37: 499–509.

GLATZ, C.
2009 "Empire as network: Spheres of material interaction in Late Bronze Age Anatolia," *Journal of Anthropological Archaeology* 28: 127–141.

GOLDMAN, H.
1956 *Excavations at Gözlu Kule, Tarsus* . Vol. 2. *The Neolithic through the Bronze Age.* Princeton: Princeton University Press.

GONNELLA, J., KHAYYATA, W. and KOHLMEYER, K.
2005 *Die Zitadelle von Aleppo und der Tempel des Wettergottes.* Münster: Rhema.

HARRISON, T. P.
2010 "The Late Bronze/Early Iron Age Transition in the North Orontes Valley," in *Societies in Transition. Evolutionary Processes in the Northern Levant between Late Bronze Age II and Early Iron Age, papers presented on the occasion of the 20th anniversary of the new excavation in Tell Afis, Bologna, 15th november 2007*, Studi e testi orientali 9, Serie Archeologica 2, edited by F. Venturi, pp. 83–102. Bologna: CLUEB.

HAWKINS, J. D.
1988 "Kuzi Teshub and the "Great Kings" of Karkemish," *Anatolian Studies* 38: 99–108.
2000 *Corpus of Hieroglyphic Luwian Inscriptions.* Berlin: Walter de Gruyter.
2009 "Cilicia, the Amuq and Aleppo: New Light in a Dark Age," *Near Eastern Archaeology* 72: 164–173.

HENRICKSON, R. C.
1995 "Hittite Pottery and Potters: the View from Late Bronze Age Gordion," *Biblical Archaeologist* 58(2): 82–90.

JANEWAY, B.
2008 "The Nature and Extent of Aegean Contact at Tell Ta'yinat and Vicinity in the Early Iron Age: Evidence of the Sea Peoples?" *Scripta Mediterranea* 27–28: 123–146.

JASINK, A. M.
1995 *Gli stati neo-ittiti. Analisi delle fonti scritte e sintesi storica*, Studia Mediterranea 10. Pavia: G. Iuculano.

KARAGEORGHIS, V. and DEMAS, M.
1985 *Excavations at Kition V. The Pre-Phoenician Levels*, Department of Antiquities Cyprus. Nicosia: Zavallis Press.

KLENGEL H.
2001 "Einige Bemerkungen zur hethitischen Herraschaftsordnung in Syrien," in *Akten des IV Internationalen Kongresses für Hethitologie. Würzburg, 4-8 Oktober 1999*, Studien zu den Boğazköy Texten 45, edited by G. Wilhelm, pp. 255–271. Wiesbaden: Harrassowitz Verlag.

KOHLMEYER, K.
2008 "Zur Datierung der skulpturen von 'Ain Dara," in *Fundstellen. Gesammelte Schriften zur Archäologie und Geschichte Altvorderasiens ad honorem Hartmut Kühne*, edited by D. Bonatz, R. M. Czichon, F. J. Kreppner, pp. 119–130. Wiesbaden: Harrassowitz Verlag.

KOŞAY, H.
1944 *Ausgrabungen von Alaca Höyük, ein Vorbericht über die im Auftrage der Türkischen Geschichtskommission im Sommer 1936 durchgeführten Forschungen und Entdeckungen.* TTKY Vol. 2a. Ankara: Türk Tarih Kurumu basımevi.
1951 *Alaca Höyük Kazisi 1937–39. Ilk Rapor/Les Fouilles d'Alaca Höyük. Rapport Préliminaire 1937–39.* TTKY Vol. 5. Ankara: Türk Tarih Kurumu basımevi.

MATTHIAE, P.
1989 *Un impero ritrovato. Dai Primi scavi alle ultime scoperte.* Torino: Giulio Einaudi Editore.
MAZZONI, S.
1997 "L'arte siro-hittita nel suo contesto archeologico," *Contributi e Materiali di Archeologia Orientale* VII: 287–327.
1998 "Area E1. Late Chalcolitic, Early, Middle and Late Bronze I Ages. Materials and Chronology," in *Scavi sull'acropoli 1988-1992. The 1988-1992 Excavations on the Acropolis*, edited by S. M. Cecchini, S. Mazzoni, pp. 9–100. Pisa: Edizioni ETS.
MCCLELLAN, T. L.
1985 "The Second Season of the Australian Excavations at el-Qitar, 1983–84," *Abr Nahrain* 23: 315–324.
1986 "El-Qitar: Third Season of Excavation 1984–85," *Abr Nahrain* 24: 83–106.
MOUNTJOY, P. A.
1998 "The East Aegean-West Anatolian Interface in the Late Bronze Age: Mycenaeans and the Kingdom of Ahhiyawa ," *Anatolian Studies* 48: 33–68.
1999 *Regional Mycenaean Decorated Pottery.* Rahden: Verlag Marie Leidorf.
2005a "The Mycenaean Pottery from the 1934–1939 Excavations at Tarsus ," in *Field Seasons 2001–2003 of the Tarsus–Gözlükule. Interdisciplinary Research Project*, edited by A. Özyar, pp. 83–134. Istanbul: Ege Yayınları.
2005b "The End of the Bronze Age at Enkomi Cyprus: the problem of Level IIIB," *British School of Athens* 100: 125–214.
MÜLLER- KARPE, A.
1988 *Hethitische Töpferei der Oberstadt von Khattusha. Ein Beitrag zur Kenntnis Spätgroßreichszeitlicher Keramik und Töpferbetriebe unter Zugrundelegung der Grabungsergebnisse von 1978–82 in Boğazköy.* Marburg/Lahn: Hitzeroth.
1998 "Untersuchungen in Kuşakli 1997," *Mitteilungen der Deutschen Orient-Gesellschaft zu Berlin* 130: 93–174.
2001 "Untersuchungen in Kuşakli 2000," *Mitteilungen der Deutschen Orient-Gesellschaft zu Berlin* 133: 225–249.
PARZINGER, H. and SANZ, R.
1992 *Die Oberstadt von Khattusha. Hethitische Keramik aus dem Zentralen Tempelviertel.* Berlin: Gebr. Mann Verlag.
PECORELLA, P. E.
1975 *Rapporto preliminare delle campagne 63–68. Il livello imperiale eteo e quelli neo etei*, Orientis Antiqui Collectio XII. Roma: Centro per le antichità e la storia dell'arte del Vicino Oriente.
PEDRAZZI, T.
2002 "Area E: l'occupazione del Bronzo Tardo II-Ferro I. Il settore nord," in Tell Afis – Siria 2002–2004, edited by S. Mazzoni, *Egitto e Vicino Oriente* XXV: 33–38.
2005 "Lo scavo dell'area E4a: Bronzo Tardo II-Ferro I," in Tell Afis – Siria 2002–2004, edited by S. Mazzoni, *Egitto e Vicino Oriente* XXVIII: 56–60.
2007 *Le giare da conservazione e trasporto del Levante. Uno studio archeologico dell'economia fra Bronzo Tardo II e Ferro I (1400–900 a.C. ca.).* Pisa: Edizioni ETS.
2010 "Globalisation Versus Regionalism: LBII/Iron I Transition in Coastal Syria from the Storage Jars Point of View," in *Societies in Transition. Evolutionary Processes in the Northern Levant between Late Bronze Age II and Early Iron Age,*

papers presented on the occasion of the 20th anniversary of the new excavation in Tell Afis, Bologna, 15th november 2007, Studi e testi orientali 9, Serie Archeologica 2, edited by F. Venturi, pp. 53–64. Bologna: CLUEB.

PFÄLZNER, P.
1995 *Mittanische und Mittelassyrische Keramik. Eine Chronologische, Funktionale und Produktionsökonomische Analyse* (Berichte der Ausgrabung Tall Sehikh Hamad, Dur-katlimmu). Berlin: Reimer.

RIIS, P. J.
1948 *Les cimetières à crémation. Hama. Fouilles et Recherches de la Fondation Carlsberg 1931–1938.* II, 3 (=NS I). Copenhague: 1. Kommission hos Gyldendalske Boghandel, Nordisk Forlag.

RIIS, P. J. and BUHL M. L.
1990 *Hama. Les objets de la période dite syro-hittite (âge du fer).* Copenhague: Nationalmuseet.

SEIDL, U.
1972 *Gefässmarken von Boğazköy*, Wissenschaftliche Veröffentlichungen der Deutschen Orient-Gesellschaft 88. Berlin: Gebrüder Mann.

STAGER, L. E.
1995 "The Impact of the Sea People in Canaan (1185–1050 BCE)," in *The Archaeology of Society in the Holy Land*, edited by T. E. Levy, pp. 333-348. London.

SUMMERS, G. D.
1993 *Tille Höyük 4. The Late Bronze Age and the Iron Age Transition.* London: British Institute of Archaeology at Ankara.

SWIFT, G. F. Jr.
1958 "The Pottery of the 'Amuq Phase K to O and Its Historical Relations" (unpublished Ph.D. Dissertation). Chicago: University of Chicago.

SYMINGTON, D.
2001 "Hittites at Kilise Tepe," in *La Cilicie: espaces et pouvoir locaux (2e millenaire av. J.C. 4e siècle ap. J.C.). Actes de la table ronde Internationale d'Istanbul 2-5 novembre 1999*, edited by É. Jean, A. M. Dinçol, S. Durugönül, pp. 167–184. Institut Français d' Études Anatoliennes G. Dumézil. Istanbul-Paris: De Boccard.

VENTURI, F.
2002 "Area E: l'occupazione del Bronzo Tardo II-Ferro I. Il settore Sud," in Tell Afis (Siria) 2000–2001, edited by S. Mazzoni, *Egitto e Vicino Oriente* XXV: 29–32.

2005 Tell Afis. L'Area E4b sud: Bronzo Tardo II-Ferro I, in Tell Afis (Siria) 2002–2004, edited by S. Mazzoni, *Egitto e Vicino Oriente*, XXVIII: 69–76.

2007 *L'età delle trasformazioni in Siria (XIII-X sec. a.C.). Nuovi contributi dallo scavo di Tell Afis*, Studi e testi orientali 8, Serie Archeologica 1. Bologna: CLUEB.

2008a "Eléments de continuité dans l'architecture domestique du Levant à travers l'âge obscur; le cas des maisons aux piliers," in *Proceedings of the 4th International Congress of the Archaeology of the Ancient Near East, 29th march – 3rd april* 2004, edited by H. Kühne, R. M. Czichon, R. Janoscha Kreppner, pp. 587–600. Wiesbaden: Harrassowitz Verlag.

2008b "The Sea People in the Levant: a North-Syrian Perspective," in *Proceedings of the 5th International Congress of the Archaeology of the Ancient Near East,* edited by J. M. Cordoba, M. Molist, M. C. Perez, I. Rubio, S. Martinez, pp. 365–382. Vol. III. Madrid: Publications Service of the Universidad Autonoma of Madrid.

2010 "Cultural Breakdown or Evolution? The Impact of Changes in 12th B.C. Tell Afis," in *Societies in Transition. Evolutionary Processes in the Northern Levant between Late Bronze Age II and Early Iron Age, papers presented on the occasion of the 20th anniversary of the new excavation in Tell Afis, Bologna, 15th november 2007*, Studi e testi orientali 9, Serie Archeologica 2, edited by F. Venturi, pp. 1–27. Bologna: CLUEB.

VOIGT, M. M. and HENRICKSON, R. C.

2000 "The Early Iron Age at Gordion: The Evidence from the Yassihöyük Stratigraphic Sequence," in *The Sea People and Their World: a Reassessment*, edited by E. Oren, pp. 327–360. Philadelphia: The University Museum; University of Pennsylvania .

WOOLLEY, C. L.

1955 *Alalakh. An Account of the Excavations at Tell Atchana in the Hatay, 1937–49.* Oxford: The Society of Antiquaries.

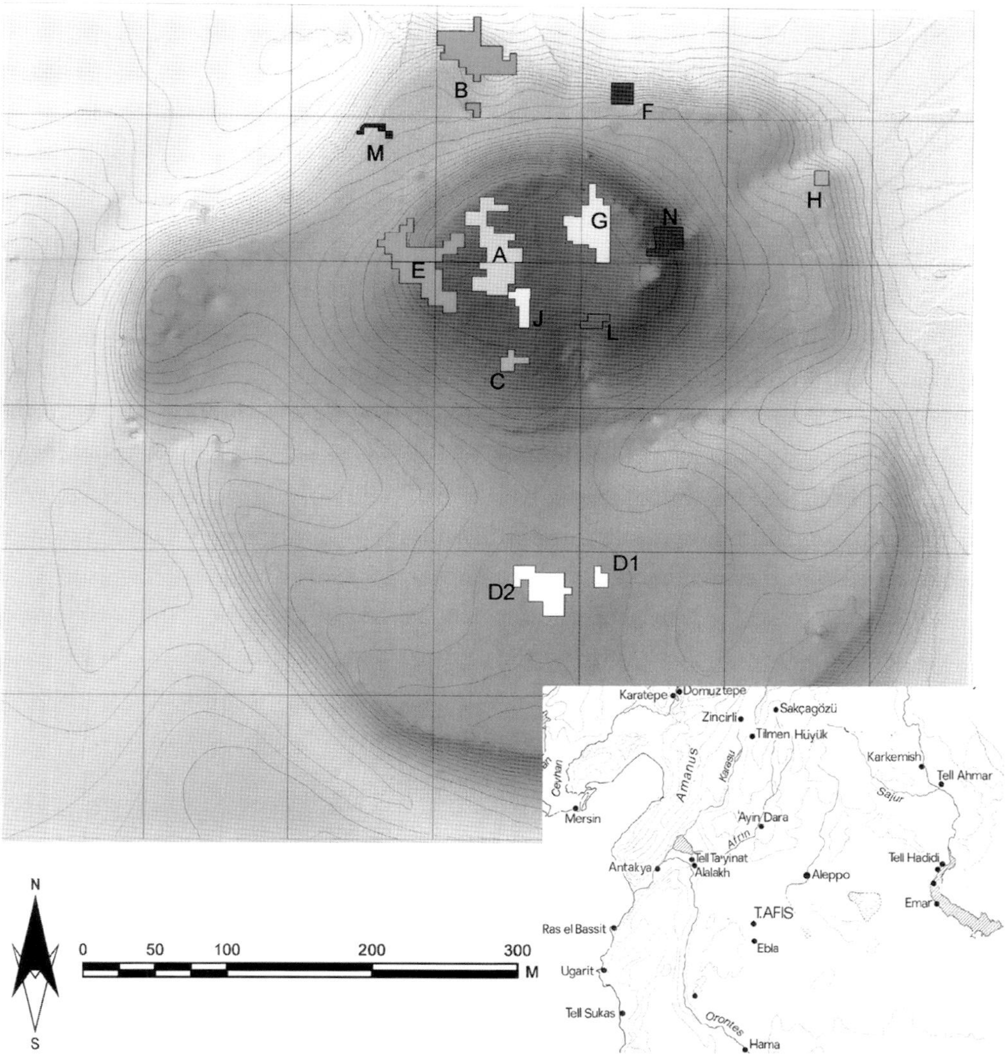

Fig. 1 Tell Afis and the excavated areas.

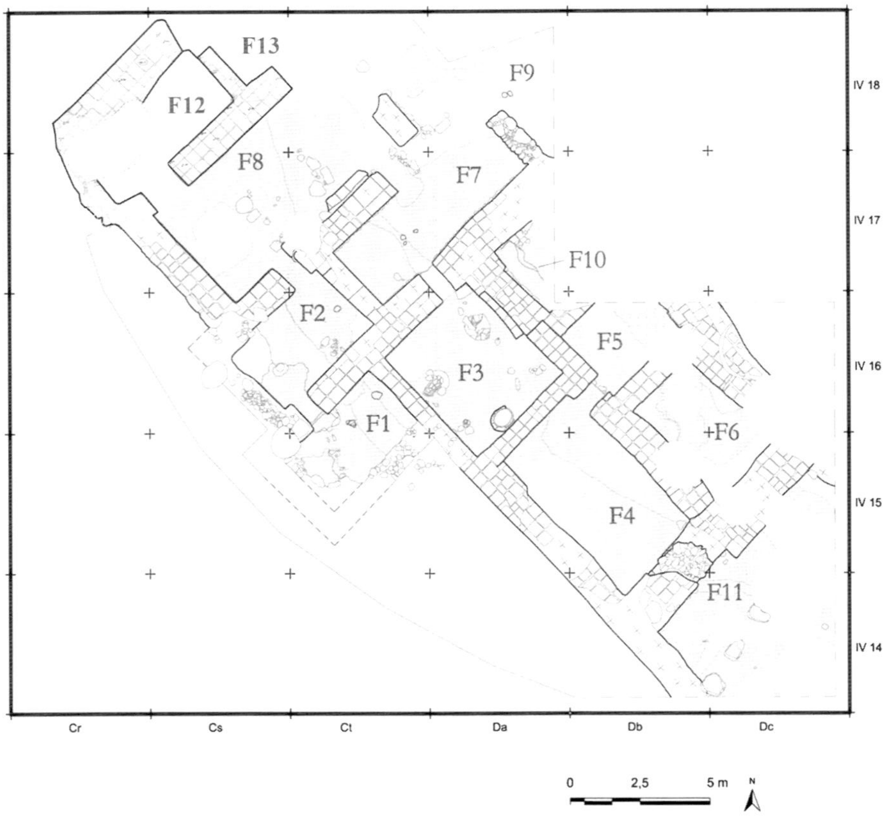

Fig. 2 Building F (phase VII).

Fig. 3 Kiln 7977 (phase VI).

Fig. 4 Structure 9002 (phase VI).

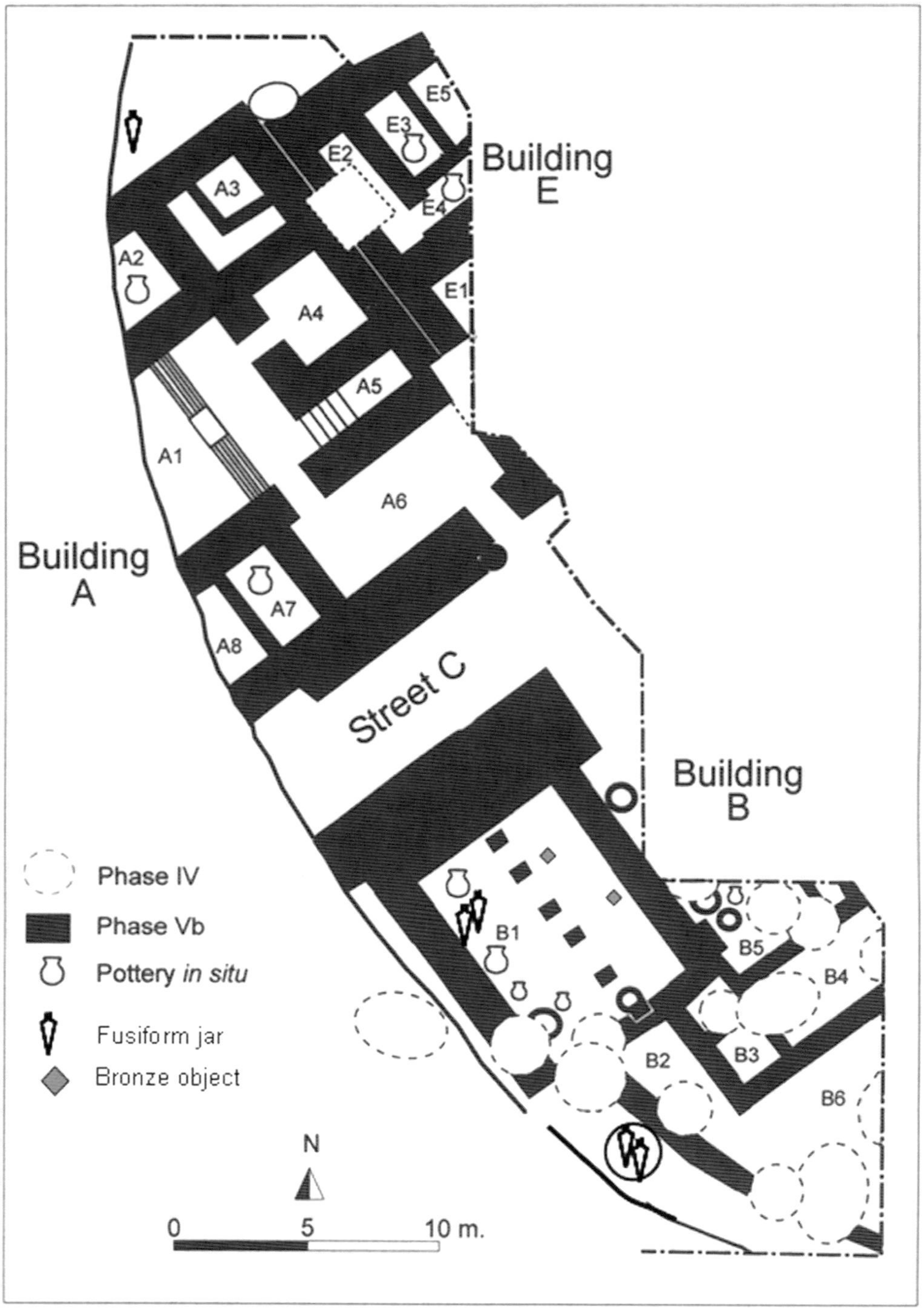

Fig. 5 The buildings of phase Vb.

Fig. 6 The bronze lugged axe TA.07.E.530/A (phase VI).

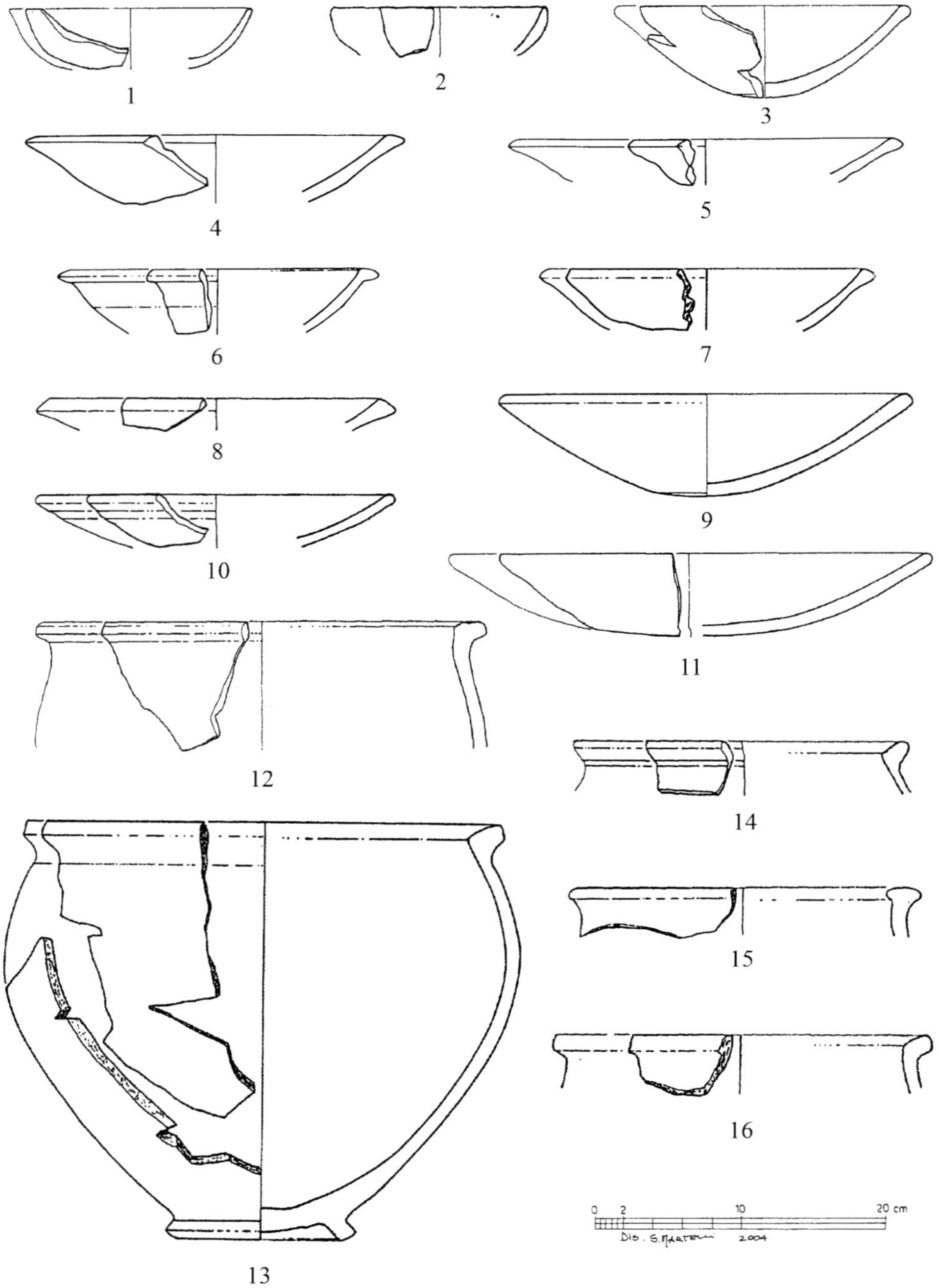

Fig. 7 Shallow bowls (nos. 1-11) and kraters (nos. 12-16).

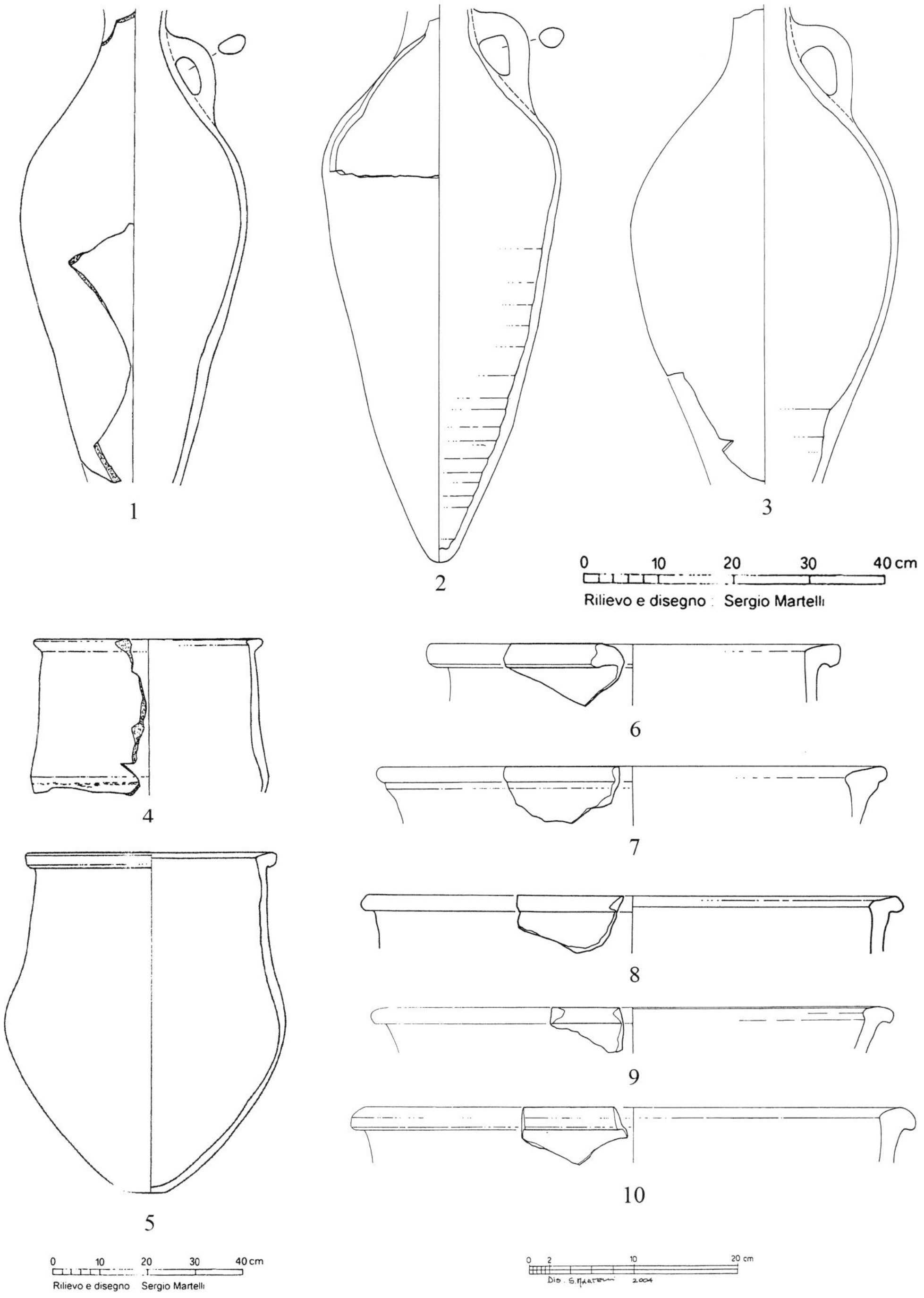

Fig. 8 Fusiform jars (nos. 1-3) and krater-jars (nos. 4-10).

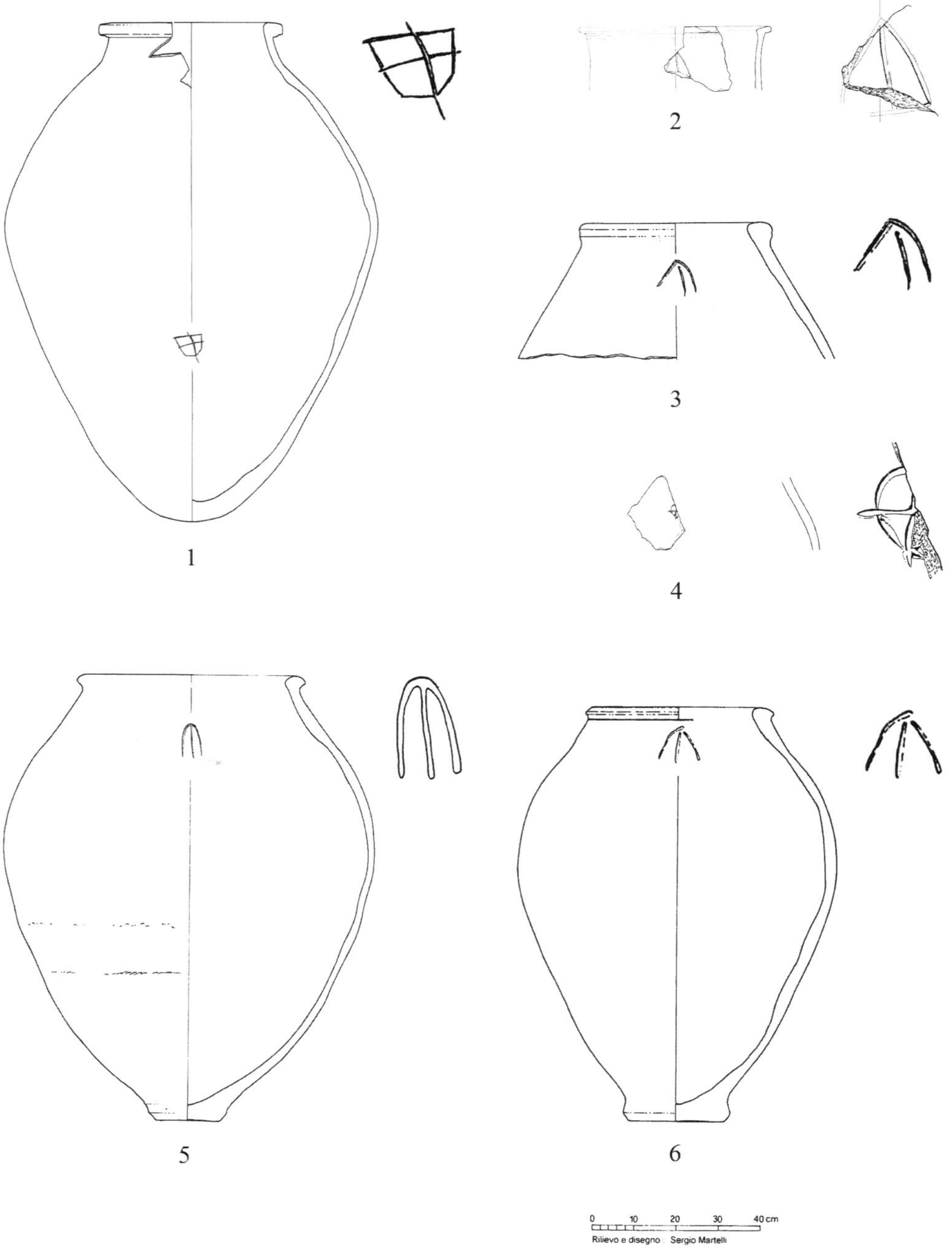

Fig. 9 Potmarks on storage jars: phase VII (nos. 1), VI (nos. 2-3), Vb (nos. 4-6).

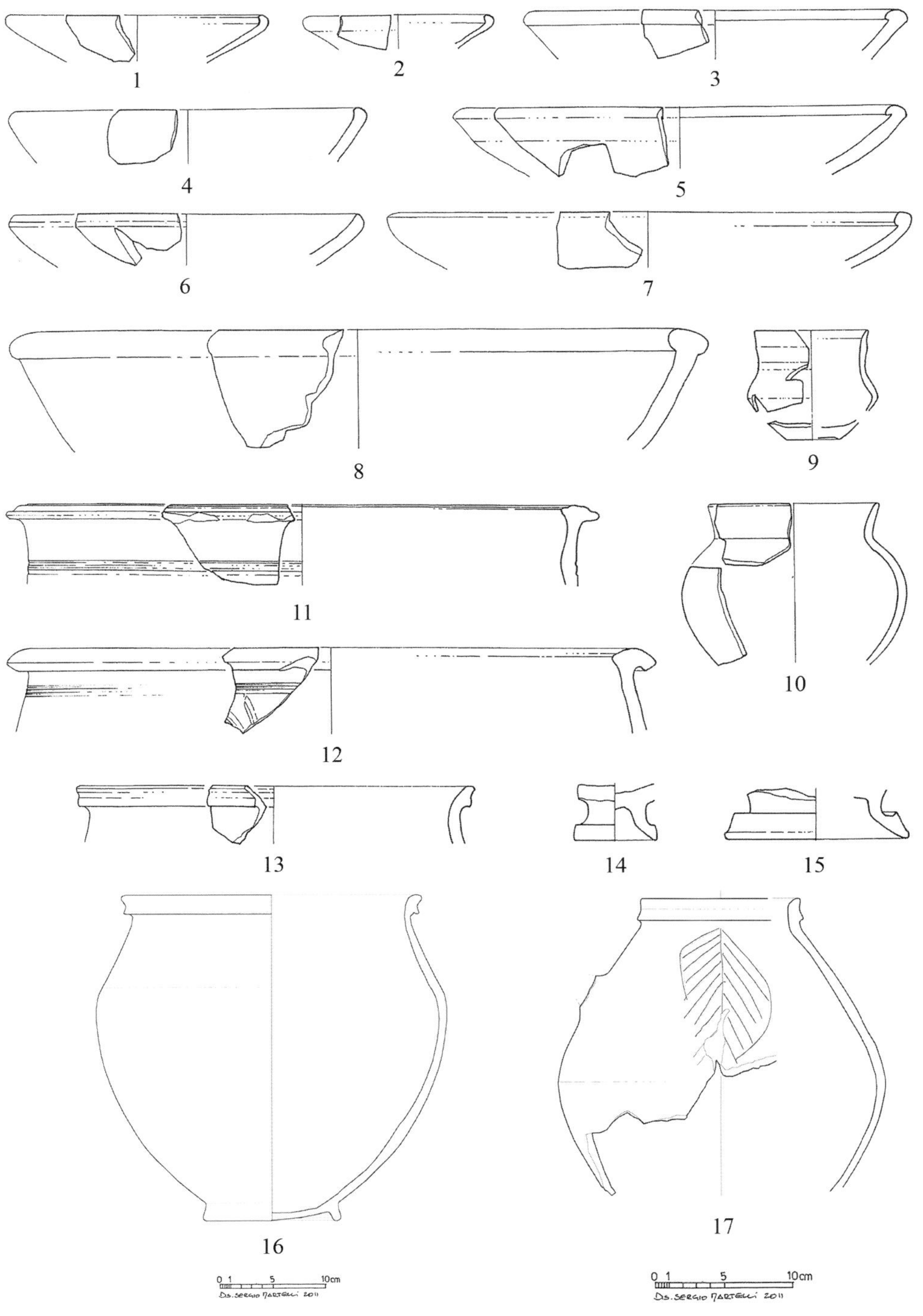

Fig. 10 The pottery of phase VIII.

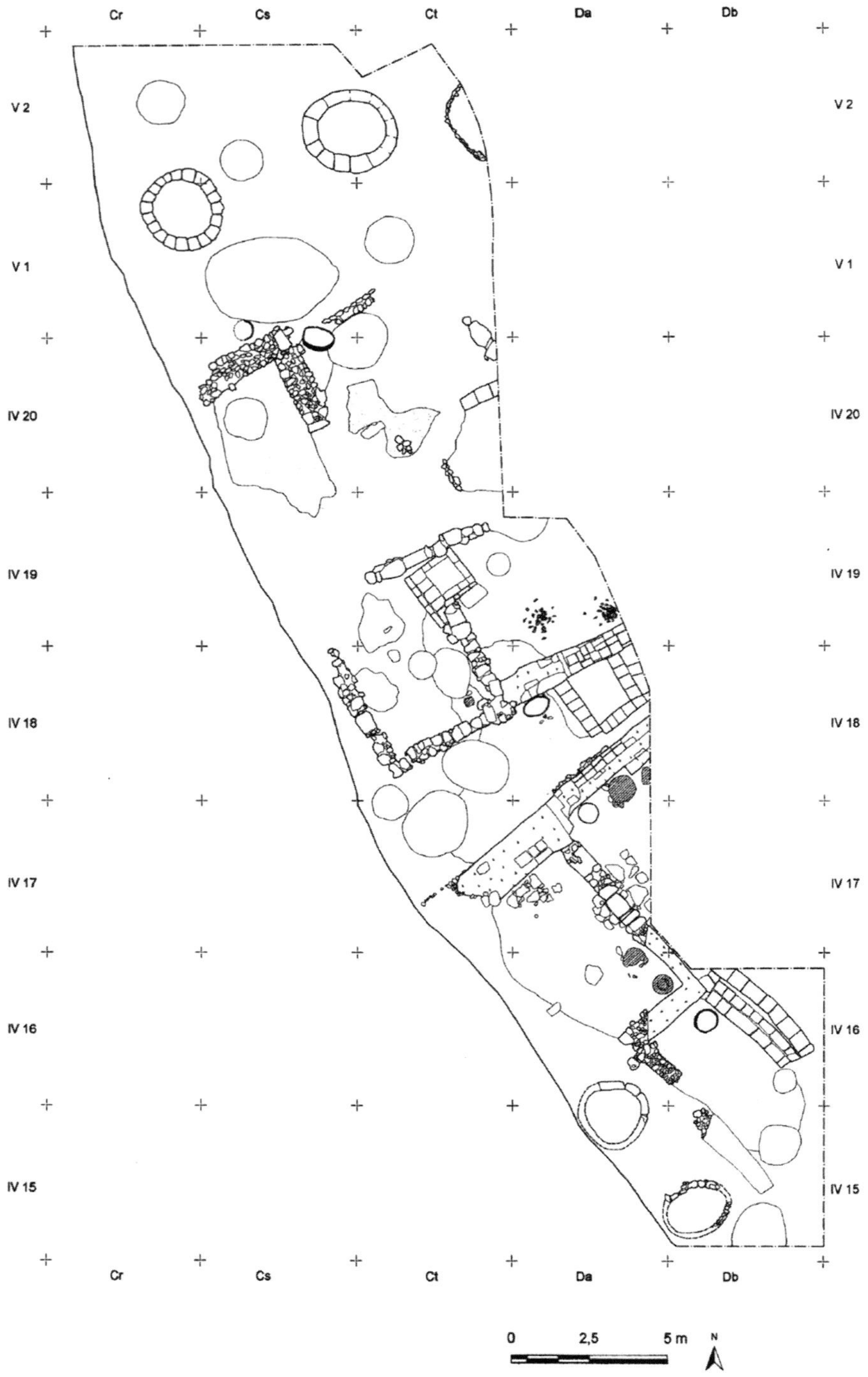

Fig. 11 Phase IV.

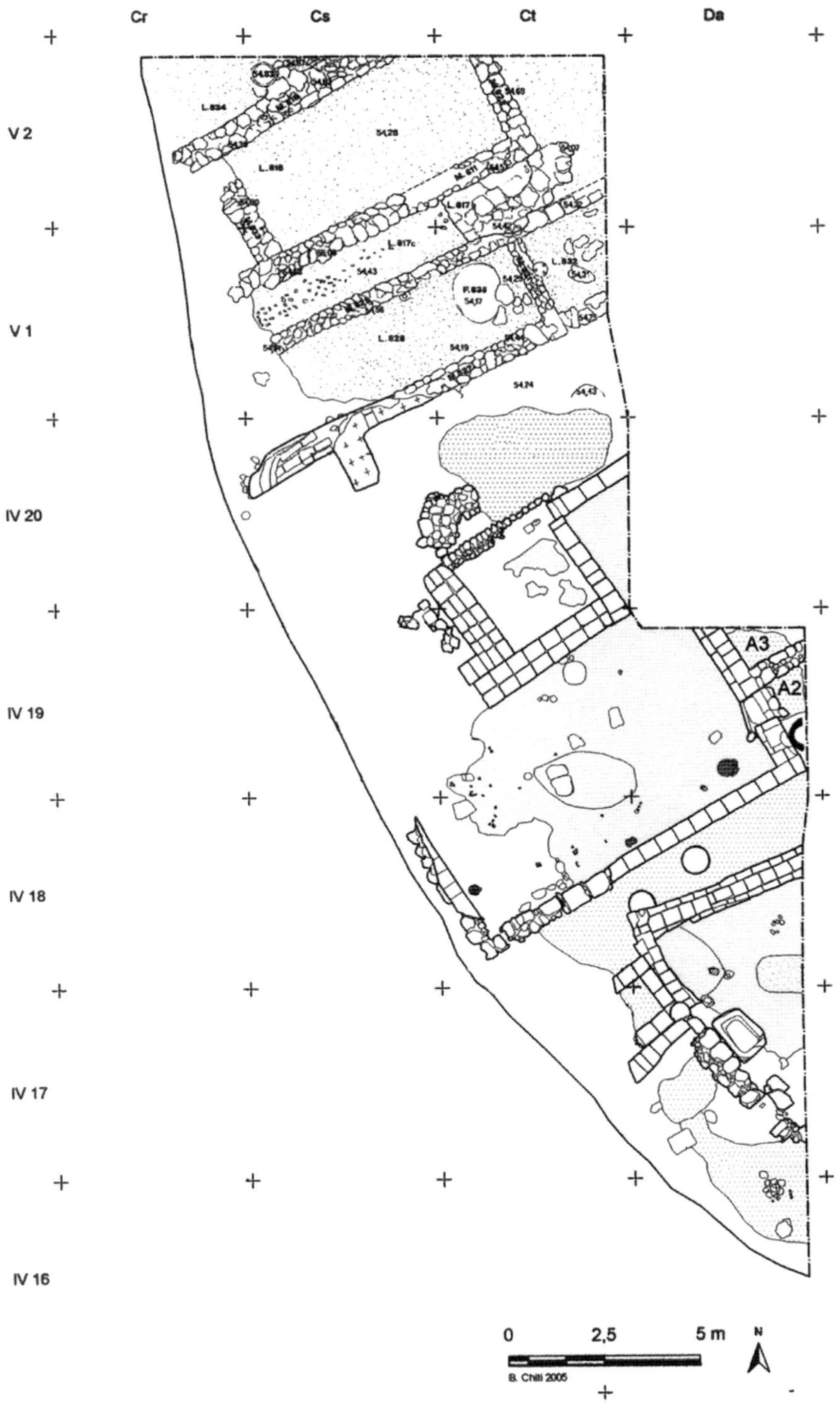

Fig. 12 Phase III.

Fig. 13 Silos and pits in phase IV.

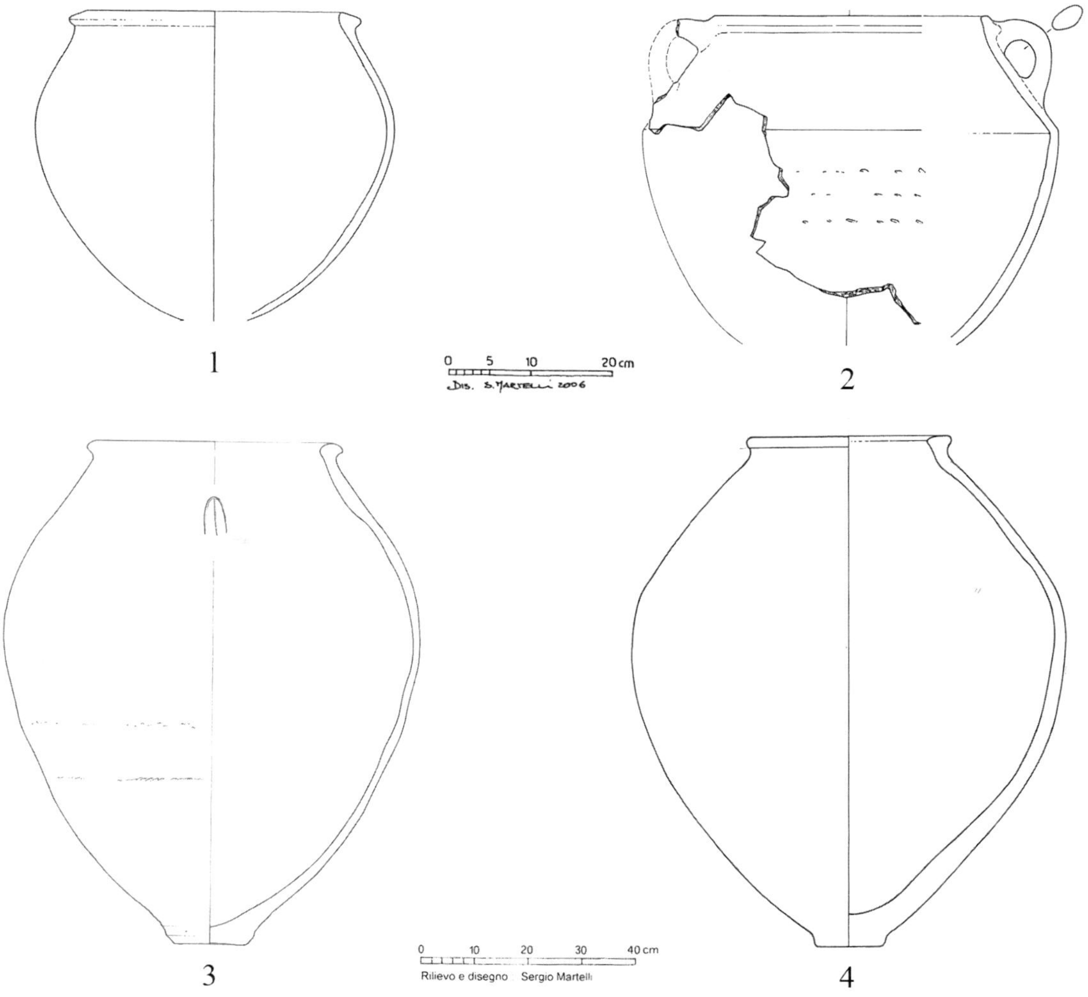

Fig. 14 Continuity in storage and cooking ware shapes between Late Bronze Age II (nos. 1, 3) and Early Iron Age (nos. 2, 4).

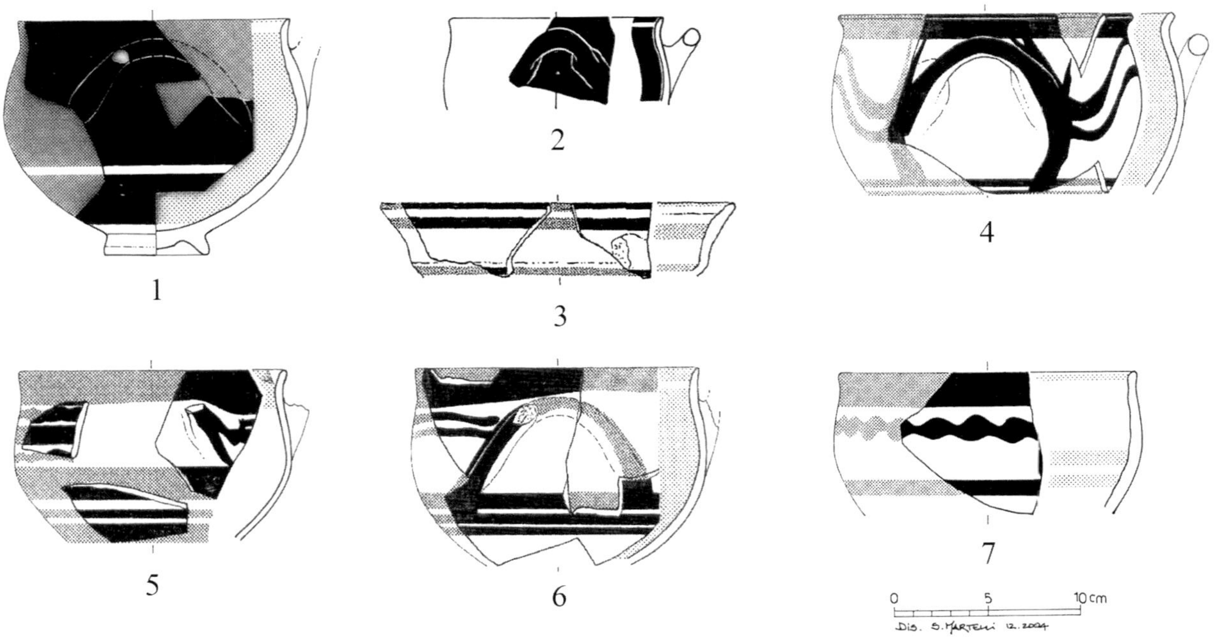

Fig. 15 The Mycenaean IIIC:1 deep bell-shaped bowls (phase IV).

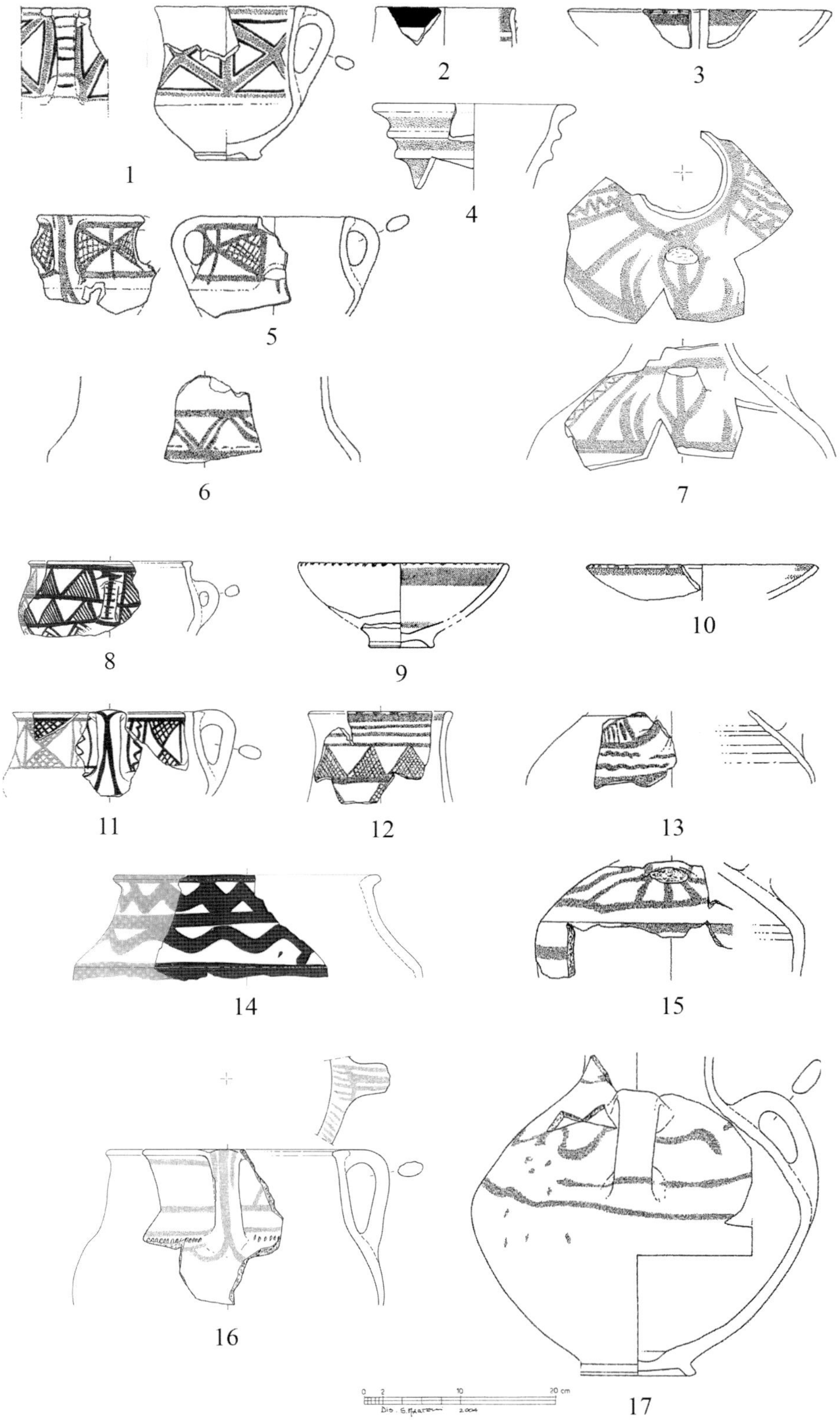

Fig. 16 The local painted monochrome pottery: phase III (nos. 1-7), phase IV (nos. 8-17).

Section B

EXCAVATIONS IN EASTERN TURKEY AND EASTERN SYRIA

CHAPTER 11

ACROSS ASSYRIA'S NORTHERN FRONTIER: TELL FEKHERIYE AT THE END OF THE LATE BRONZE AGE

Peter V. BARTL

and

Dominik BONATZ
Freie Universität Berlin
Institute of Ancient Near Eastern Archaeology
Hüttenweg 7
14195 Berlin, Germany
E-mail: bonatz@zedat.fu-berlin.de, pvb@zedat.fu-berlin.de

ABSTRACT

Since 2006, renewed excavations at Tell Fekheriye in the Khabur headwater region have yielded important remains from the Mittani and Middle Assyrian periods. The architectural sequence at the western slope of the Tell shows a gradual change from monumental to administrative household architecture as well as the use of the same area as a burial ground at the end of the Middle Assyrian period. Many seal impressions on clay sealings and cuneiform tablets from different occupation phases attest to activities of the Assyrian central administration at this place. From the perspective of this site the establishment of regular large-scale networks cutting across Assyria's political boundaries and an extensive Middle Assyrian state characterized by a more uniform material culture and ideological basis than seen previously can be investigated. The archaeological materials and textual sources recently discovered at Tell Fekheriye will therefore be discussed against the backdrop of geopolitical developments and interregional relations in the late second millennium BCE. *

* The Tell Fekheriye project of the Institute of Ancient Near Eastern Archaeology at the Freie Universität Berlin and the Directorate of Antiquities and Museums of the Syrian Arab Republic is conducted in cooperation with Dr. ʿAbd al-Masih Bagdo, Director of the Department of Antiquities and Museums in Hasseke. It is under the kind sponsorship of the Director of Antiquities and Museums in Syria, Dr. Basam Jamous, and the Director of Excavation, Dr. Michelle al-Maqdissi. Since 2006 the fieldwork is carried out in collaboration with the Slovakian Archaeological and Historical Institute (SAHI) which also gives financial support to the project. Since 2009, it is generously sponsored by the German Research Foundation (DFG).

INTRODUCTION

At the end of the 14th century BC, the Assyrian state began to expand towards the Syrian Jezirah and the Anatolian piedmont. The conquest of territories which had previously formed the core of the Mittani state resulted in a rapid change of the political and cultural landscape, the materialisation of which is tangible at every excavated site with Middle Assyrian occupation levels.[1] However, as quickly as the Assyrian territorial state became established in this area it started to disperse. Even throughout its flourishing period during the 13th century BC, regional developments and signs of self-governance stood in contrast to the idea of a centralised state that was cherished for so long. After this century, the decentralisation of Assyria's western provinces seems to be a matter of fact. But this event does not mark a distinct break in the history of this region, as political structures, ethnic shifts and cultural developments emerged from pre-existing traditions. With this in mind, the chronological distinction between the Late Bronze Age and Iron Age almost seems useless, as it does nothing besides strengthen the biased view of our archaeological record.

Therefore, when referring to the end of the Late Bronze Age at Tell Fekheriye, the authors do not intend to fix the conclusion of this period in absolute terms. Instead, they consider it a crucial phase in the settlement history of the site, during which both continuities and discontinuities are the proper measurement values of transition. This transition started with the Assyrian advent during the early 13th century BC, but was not yet complete as their political power diminished only about 100 years later. Assyrian traits, at least in cultural terms, certainly persisted at the site, primarily visible in the burial complex addressed in the later part of this article.

With the evidence at hand it is still not possible to bridge the gap between the late Late Bronze Age settlement and Iron Age occupation during the Neo Assyrian period at Tell Fekheriye. However, based upon the architectural sequence as well as material and textual finds, it is possible to provide a detailed account of the transforming significance of the site that reveals itself both from a diachronic and synchronic perspective. For example, the importance of Sikāni as place of worship for the Aramaean storm-god, mentioned in the bilingual inscription on the Tell Fekheriye statue (see below), apparently derives from a late 3rd millennium BC cult tradition.[2] From this

The authors wish to thank the organizers of the conference at the Koç University, "Across the Borders", for including this contribution in the very extensive discussion about the Late Bronze–Iron Age relations between Syria and Anatolia, which also provided many stimuli for our future research at Tell Fekheriye.

[1] The archaeological data and sources for this westward Middle Assyrian expansion are compiled in Tenu 2009a.

[2] The Ur III period text TIM 6,15,17 identifies Sikāni with the goddess of the Khabur (*dḪaburitum Siganki*) making it most plausible that the Sikāni of the late 3rd millennium BC has to be located at the same place as the Iron Age Sikāni, i.e. at Tell Fekheriye (Müller-Kessler and Müller 1995, pp. 240–241).

religious center, a political center emerged during the middle of the 2nd millennium BC, a time when Tell Fekheriye might be identified with the Mittani residence Waššukanni. So far, the subsequent Middle Assyrian occupation is the period archaeologically attested to best. Here we do not only have the chance to study changes in the structures of political governance, but also to view the relevance of the site in relation to the widespread phenomenon of a long-lasting transition beginning at the end of the Late Bronze Age.

GEOGRAPHY AND GEOPOLITICAL BACKGROUND

Tell Fekheriye is situated on the fringe of the modern town Ras al-'Ain, which lies in the center of the karst spring area forming the actual head of the Khabur River in north-eastern Syria (**Fig. 1**). The specific environmental situation is reflected in the toponym Ras al-ʿAin, meaning "head of the spring," which derives from the Roman-Byzantine Rhesaina and the Akkadian *rēš ina* already mentioned in the annals of the Assyrian king Adad-narari II (911–891 BC).[3] Today, the Syrian-Turkish border just runs 1 km north of the site where it separates Ras al-'Ain from the Turkish town of Ceylanpınar. About 45 km to the south of Tell Fekheriye, the Jebel 'Abd al-'Aziz rises to form the natural barrier to the arid zones of the Syrian steppes. The fertile upper Mesopotamian plain stretches to the north bordered by the Tur 'Abdīn about 50 km to the northeast. Access to the Anatolian highlands is granted via the plain of Harran and the Şanlıurfa region about 80 km northwest of Tell Fekheriye.

Due to this geographic setting, conditions for human life at the head of the Khabur are favorable in several respects. They allow settlement in a fertile landscape with a rich natural supply of water and quick access to the natural resources of the Anatolian mountains. Therefore, it is not surprising that early in antiquity a dense settlement system developed in this area with Tell Fekheriye and the nearby Tell Halaf as its most prominent sites. It is an important task for archaeologists to observe how this settlement system was transferred and shaped by the different ancient polities who were in control.

At the beginning of the 2nd millennium BC the historical situation in north eastern Syria can be described as one of emergent imperialism. This process, however, had several initial steps and was slowed down by the lack of control over people and territories. For example, a recently published itinerary from Mari dating to the time of Samsî-Addu reveals several toponyms along the western Khabur, which were relevant for what is apparently proclaimed in this text as a safe journey through contested territories.[4] The last station mentioned in the itinerary is Zalluhân, the centre of the

[3] Grayson 1991, p. 153, A.0.99.2.101–102.
[4] Charpin 2009 and 2010.

synonymous kingdom, to be located at the mouth of Wadi Jirjib, ca. 15 km south of Tell Fekheriye. The text was written by one of the tribal chiefs, Yarîm-Addu, who was loyal to the Yahdun-Lîm dynasty in Mari. It reflects the activities of a faithful ally within the realm of Samsî-Addu's Upper Mesopotamian kingdom but also tells us about the difficulties in maintaining access to the western periphery.[5]

It was only when the Mittani kings established their state in the middle of the 2nd millennium BC, that the Khabur triangle region became the centre of a large political system.[6] It is during this time that the name Waššukanni appears for the first time as a capital city's name in the contemporary Hittite sources.[7] The political situation changed again with the Assyrian annexation of the region at the beginning of the 13th century BC. It then became the rich agrarian hinterland of the Middle Assyrian territorial state and a political frontier to the Anatolian highlands. Despite the fact that the Assyrians also penetrated northward of the Tur 'Abdīn mountains and into the upper Tigris region,[8] the southern foothills remained as the actual border line of the empire. A system of districts (*paḫutu*) including cities (*ālu*), fortified agrarian domains (*dunnu*), and fortresses (*birtu*) developed along this line which often followed the urban plan of the Mittani period.[9] Political governance, however, was no longer based in local milieus but endured a strong Assyrian impact on the existing rural Hurrian and semi nomadic Sutaean populations.

For the purpose of this article, it will be argued that Tell Fekheriye played a central role for the establishment of the Middle Assyrian hegemony in this area and that the material evidence from the same site can be used to study the development and extent of Assyrian culture in the west until the end of the 2nd millennium BC.

Middle Assyrian presence at Tell Fekheriye: The textual and iconographic evidence

The series of Assyrian conquests in the Khabur triangle started with Adad-narari I (1295–1264 BC), who claimed to have destroyed the cities of Mittani from Taidu to Irridu including the city of Waššukanni.[10] Tell Fekheriye might have been one of the places threatened by the Assyrian king but since it is not yet certain that the site can be identified with Waššukanni, speculation on such a conquest must be confirmed by archaeological evidence. In the course of the renewed Syrian-German excavations at Tell Fekheriye parts of a monumental building from the Mittani period have been

5 Charpin 2009, p. 64, 2010, p. 37.
6 Kühne 1999.
7 See Crasso 2009, pp. 222–224.
8 Radner 2004, pp. 72–73.
9 Cancik-Kirschbaum 2000, Wiggermann 2000.
10 Grayson 1987, p. 131, A.0.76.1.8–11; p. 136, A.0.76.3.26–37.

exposed in Area C at the western slope of the mound (see below). This architecture, together with the associated finds, which include a large number of Mittani style seal impressions, attest to the existence of a Mittani settlement with some sort of administrative function prior to the arrival of the Assyrians. The mud-brick ruins in this small sector of the site show no traces of violent destruction. Instead the rooms of the emptied building seem to have been deliberately filled and the walls leveled in order to create a platform for a new building.

This process can be connected to the Middle Assyrian occupation of the site.

The earliest absolute dates for the Middle Assyrian presence are given by the clay tablets, which were discovered in a deposit between the aforementioned monumental building and the lowest floor of the subsequent Middle Assyrian building (House I). During the excavations in 2009 and 2010 a total of 51 tablets and tablet fragments were recovered from this deposit (loc. C–1035/C-1199) (**Fig. 2**). They had been discarded in this area shortly before the construction of the new building started. As for the stratigraphic context of the architectural features in this trench, the texts document an intermediate phase which has as yet not been excavated.

A very preliminary translation of the texts by Eva Cancik-Kirschbaum confirms that they belonged to the administration of the local palace. Where this palace and the original archive are to be located demands further investigations. The eponyms mentioned on some of the texts, most notable Mušabšiu-sibitti, date the whole corpus to the first third of the reign of Šalmaneser I, i.e. around 1250 BC.[11] The larger tablets measuring up to 28 cm in length and up to 24 cm in width list the distribution of a high amount of grain to families and cohorts of male workers. Both groups are employed as labourers by the palace and are under the supervision of its officials. Among the smaller tablets are legal documents and letters. Three of them were found within their unopened and sealed clay envelopes. The letters are comparable to the 'letter orders' found at Tell Khuera (the Assyrian Ḫarbe).[12] One letter (TF 6375) contains orders for military troops and mentions the palace of Waššukanni in this context. Another letter deals with the transport of horses and donkeys to Taidu (TF 4772). Other toponyms, which have been gathered from these texts are Kurda, Alu-ša-Sîn-rabi, Assur, and Ninua. They prove that Tell Fekheriye was part of the regional and supra-regional Middle Assyrian communication system but are not yet sufficient evidence for the identification of the site itself.

The texts also give no explicit answer as to when exactly the Assyrians took control over the site, but they confirm that a fully developed state administration already existed there in the early reign of Šalmaneser I. Some of the Assyrian personal names

[11] For Mušabšiu-sibitti see Saporetti 1979, p. 83 (with references) and also Freydank 1991, pp. 191, 194. The same eponym is mentioned on one of the texts found in same area by the American team in 1940 (Güterbock in McEwan et al. 1958, pp. 86, 90, text no. 10:13).

[12] Jakob 2009, pp. 8–9.

mentioned in the texts reflect a local patronym as they use the river "Khabur" as topical element for example. This observation points to people who have lived in the region for more than one generation, therefore, bringing us back to the time of Adad-narari I.

The function of an early Assyrian outpost at the head of the Khabur was twofold. First, it became the designated administrative center for a large agricultural hinterland. The distribution of high amounts of grain, mentioned in the ration lists, obviously served to stabilize the activities of a peasant community who exploited the cultivable land along the Khabur. The agrarian expansion was spearheaded by the dunnu-system, the fortified agricultural production centers, which may have been modelled from the dimtu-system established in the Mittani period.[13] The high productivity of such a dunnu is well documented in the Middle Assyrian archive from Tell Sabi Abyad on the northern Balikh, which dates to the later reign of Tukulti-Ninurta I (1233–1198 BC).[14] In order to organize and to protect an efficient system of land tenure it was important to have a strong base of economic and political control. Therefore, the second importance of Tell Fekheriye would have been in the coordination of the regional communication and its links to the Assyrian capital Assur. It can be assumed that Tell Fekheriye consequently served as the starting point for military operations and colonization projects directed towards the Balikh valley in the west and the Anatolian mountains in the north.

Most of these aspects are reflected in the correspondence between the 'vizier' (*sukallu*) Sîn-mudammeq in Aššukanni and his superior in Dūr Katlimmu, the 'grand vizier' (*sukallu rabi'u*) and 'King of the land of Hanigalbat' (*šar māt Ḫanigalbat*), Aššur-iddin. The texts from Tell Sheikh Hamad, which include nine letters sent by Sîn-mudammeq to Aššur-iddin, were written within a period of ca. 50 years between the reigns of Šalmaneser I and Tukulti-Ninurta I.[15] Thus, they are probably slightly later than the aforementioned texts from Tell Fekheriye. Considering the strong possibility that Tell Fekheriye can be identified with Waššukanni/Aššukanni, they are of great importance for the history of this site. Even without such an identification, these texts remain important in sketching a clear picture of the challenges in managing a strategic key site at the northern periphery of the Assyrian empire.

Sîn-mudammeq vividly describes his efforts in fighting against enemies who came from the mountains down to the plains causing damage to several of the towns under his supervision. He also mentions chasing after refugees and trying to protect the caravan routes as far as Carchemish on the Euphrates. The difficulties of managing a productive agriculture and struggling with locust plagues and famine are frequently

[13] Koliński 2001.
[14] Wiggermann 2000.
[15] Cancik-Kirschbaum 1996, p. 9.

reported. All these problems are reinforced by the notorious lack of an adequate labour force and military troops.[16] Additional information to this situation is given by the texts from Ḫarbe/Tell Khuera.[17] These include several letter orders sent by Sîn-mudammeq to his subordinate, the *bēl pāḫete* ('district governor') in Ḫarbe.[18]

The written sources from Dūr Katlimmu and Ḫarbe testify that Sîn-mudammeq was coordinating the military and civil affairs in a region which stretched from Saḫlala/Tell Sakhlan on the upper Balikh river ca. 125 km west of Tell Fekheriye to the area of Hasseke ca. 80 km to the southeast of the site.[19] Near Hasseke, for example, Sîn-mudammeq was engaged in the water management of the Khabur channel, which ran down to Dūr Katlimmu.[20] One of his main concerns was the control of the piedmont zone south of the Tur 'Abdīn, which in particular is the area of the Kašiyāri Mountains mentioned in Assyrian texts as far as the region of Niḫriya in the northwest.[21] Furthermore, we know that Sîn-mudammeq had his residence in Aššukanni but we are not yet sure about the identification of this town with Tell Fekheriye. Nevertheless, if we take this site as a theoretical point of reference for Sîn-mudammeq's activities, a clear picture of its geo-strategic importance emerges. Tell Fekheriye lies at the center of all these activities and it is hence more than probable that it served as an important logistic base for the Assyrian dominion in the upper Mesopotamian piedmont.

Assumptions about the political status of Tell Fekheriye can be substantiated by the administrative finds from the area of House I and House II, which were erected after the dismantlement of the previous monumental building and built over the depositions containing the bulk of tablets dated to the reign of Šalmaneser I. In 1940, the American excavation under the direction of C. McEwan had already found several Middle Assyrian tablets in a sector of House I. Three of these texts mention the name Aššur-iddin and it has been convincingly argued to identify him with the same person who later became the *sukallu rabi'u* of the western empire.[22] The strong possibility that Aššur-iddin was among the main authorities in the administration of the Middle Assyrian Tell Fekheriye is furthermore stressed by the glyptic evidence from House I. The reconstruction of a nearly complete seal design from about 50 fragmentary

[16] Cancik-Kirschbaum 1996: pp. 94–139, text nos. 2–8.

[17] Jakob 2009.

[18] Tell Khuera lies ca. 74 km west of Tell Fekheriye and Ras al-'Ain. For a detailed discussion of Sîn-mudammeq's correspondence with the district governor and *ḫaziānu* ('mayor') in Ḫarbe and its relevance for the identification of Aššukanni with Tell Fekheriye see Jakob 2009, pp. 4–6, pp. 8–9 and Bonatz forthcoming.

[19] For the important communication route between Saḫlala/Tell Sakhlan, Ḫarbe/Tell Khuera and Aššukanni/Tell Fekheriye (?) see Jakob 2009, p. 8, pp. 45–46.

[20] Cancik-Kirschbaum 1996, pp. 129–139, text no. 8.

[21] For the localization of Niḫriya in the Urfa region see below.

[22] Texts nos. 3, 4 and 9; see Güterbock in McEwan et al. 1958, p. 87; Cancik-Kirschbaum 1996, p. 23.

impressions on clay lumps found in the northern part of this house, and one impression from House II, both show a contest between a winged human-headed lion and a winged bull with a small reclining winged calf on the base between the two opponents (**Fig. 3**). The triangular composition and the plastic modelling of the figures are typical for the Middle Assyrian mature style. Impressions of the same seal had already been found during the American excavations in the context of House I[23] and on a document from Tell Sheikh Hamad (DeZ 2529), which deals with the administrative affairs of Aššur-iddin and Sîn-mudammeq in Waššukanni. This document makes it quite plausible to identify the owner of the seal with Aššur-iddin.[24] The seal of Sîn-mudammeq depicting an ostrich hunt, which has been firmly identified on several documents and clay envelops from Tell Khuera,[25] also appears at Tell Fekheriye on a broken clay envelope (TF 7255) and a fragment of a bulla with cord-marks on its back (TF 6293).

The evidence is clear enough to assume there was a period of time when both high ranking officials were actively involved in the administration in Tell Fekheriye. Concerning the length of that period, two or three different temporal scenarios can be developed. The first is the phase when Aššur-iddin might have started his career as *sukallu* in the Khabur triangle region during the late reign of Šalmaneser I. Later, when he moved to the lower Khabur, Sîn-mudammeq apparently became his successor in this region. However, two texts, one from Tell Sheikh Hamad (DeZ 2529), the other from Tell Khuera (TCH 92.G.218) attest that Aššur-iddin returned to the northern districts to carry out administrative duties in Aššukanni and Ḫarbe as well.[26] This would have been a phase of intensive collaboration between Aššur-iddin and Sîn-mudammeq, in which Tell Fekheriye obviously played a significant role. Around the middle of the reign of Tukulti-Ninurta I, the career of Aššur-iddin ended and thereafter Šulmānu-mušabši, and later Ilī-padda, took up the position of the *sukallu rabi'u*.[27] During that time Sîn-mudammeq remained active in his office and it is therefore safe to assume that his sealed documents found at Tell Fekheriye belong to the phase when he quite independently acted as the coordinator of the Assyrian districts in the north western part of the empire.[28] A further two text documents

[23] Kantor in McEwan et al. 1958, p. 73, pl. 71, design XI.

[24] Cancik-Kirschbaum 1996, pp. 22–23. The text is still not edited but discussed in this volume. The drawing of the impressions of this seal on DeZ 2529 kindly shown to us by Hartmut Kühne confirms the correspondence with the impressions of the same seal found in Tell Fekheriye (Bonatz et al. 2008, pp. 111–112, n. 31).

[25] Janisch-Jakob 2009, p. 185, seal motif 3.

[26] For the historical information gained from these texts see Cancik-Kirschbaum 1996, p. 23 and Jakob 2009, p. 52.

[27] Cancik-Kirschbaum 1996, p. 21.

[28] This is why he probably also gets in a conflict with the sukallu rabiu Ilī-padâ who had his private farmstead (dunnu) at Tell Sabi Abyad at the upper Balikh (Wiggermann 2006; see also Jakob 2009, p. 6).

specifically confirm the concentration of administrative activities at this phase. One is the fragment of a letter (TF 3168) from House I, dated by the eponym Eru-appla-iddina, to the end of the reign of Tukulti Ninurta I. The letter is addressed to a person who was the son of a certain Sami and who is designated as someone from Aššukanni.[29] The other text (TF 4772) found in the filling of a burial pit in House II mentions the eponym Sarniqu, who is also among the last eponyms of Tukulti-Ninurta's reign.[30] This document deals with a person from Niḫriya who had been in charge of organising the transport of cattle to Assur. Niḫriya is the place where Tukulti-Ninurta had fought a victorious battle against the Hittite king Tutḫaliya at the beginning of his reign.[31] Under Assyrian control thereafter, the probable location of Niḫriya at Kazane Höyük in the Şanlıurfa region[32] would show how Tell Fekheriye continued to interact in the long-distance transport and communication routes between Assyria's capital and the Anatolian borderland.

In conclusion, we can reconstruct a continuous historical development of the Middle Assyrian Tell Fekheriye on the base of textual and iconographic evidence from at least the early reign of Šalmaneser I until the end of the reign of Tukulti-Ninurta I. The names of the two high ranking Assyrian officials discussed in this context stand above other officials whose activities are attested to by the texts and nearly 200 clay sealings on jars and door pegs with different seal impressions found in the area of Houses I and House II. These official documents prove that both houses fulfilled important functions as administrative places mainly in the later part of Tukulti-Ninurta's reign. Some of the material including the pottery may well date beyond this period but no absolute date later than the reign of Tukulti-Ninurta is yet given. Therefore, speculations about an abrupt end in the use of the administrative quarter at Tell Fekheriye coinciding with the death of the Assyrian king are possible.[33]

The end of Tukulti-Ninurta's reign is indeed considered as the starting point of political fragmentation and the loss of central administration in the western Assyrian empire.[34] This process, however, is not necessarily to be equaled with the decline of Assyrian presence in the upper Mesopotamian area. Being Assyrian in political or cultural terms includes two aspects, which have to be separated in this context. The pre-existence of Assyrian traits in the material culture becomes especially important when

[29] For the translation of this text and the date of the eponym see G. Chambon in Bonatz et al. 2008, pp. 130–131.

[30] For this eponym see Saporetti 1979, p. 121, with references and Freydank 2005, p. 52.

[31] Singer 1985.

[32] As suggested by Charpin and Ziegler 2003, p. 23, p. 46, n. 157. Current excavations at Kazane Höyük are under the direction of Patricia Wattenmaker in association with Şanlıurfa Museum.

[33] Bonatz forthcoming.

[34] See esp. A. Tenu 2009a, pp. 255–263 and B. Brown (forthcoming) who both collected the textual and archaeological data which lead to an understanding of the changing structures of Middle Assyrian presence in the western Jezirah in the 12th and 11th centuries BC.

the investigation of the transition from the Late Bronze Age to the Iron Age, that is, the changes from the Middle Assyrian to the Aramaean period soon begins. This task, as preliminary as it is, leads us back to the archaeological record and to a reassessment of the stratigraphy at Tell Fekheriye, which will be discussed in the second part of this article.

Late Bronze Age – Iron Age transition at Tell Fekheriye from a stratigraphical point of view: continuity or discontinuity?

A brief outline of the stratigraphy has already been given, yet for an in depth understanding of the transition from the Middle Assyrian period to the succeeding period it is essential to reinvestigate those occupational levels in more detail, as far as they are present at Tell Fekheriye. In this case not only the ideologically and religiously charged location of the site at the source of the Khabur, but also its vicinity and thus interaction with the nearby Tell Halaf has to be taken into consideration. In the following, an attempt will be made to present the archaeological evidence of the Middle Assyrian occupation in the area of House I and House II, their abandonment and the successive utilisation of the area on the western slope of the main mound at Tell Fekheriye under special consideration of the Bronze Age – Iron Age transition and possible cultural or ethnic affiliations respectively.

Middle Assyrian architecture has been found in several areas of the site during different archaeological expeditions (**Fig.** 4). On the terrace along the western slope of the main mound, the first excavations under the direction of Calvin McEwan revealed the remains of a 13th century building in Sounding VI[35] which was a starting point for linking the old results with new investigations. Thus in 2001, work in that area was resumed by a Syrian-German mission under Alexander Pruß and Abd al-Masih Bagdo,[36] but was discontinued after one year due to financial restraints. When the new excavation project commenced in 2006 it was possible to investigate the stratigraphic sequence in several so far untouched areas of the site as well as to add to and complete the stratigraphic sequences already provided by previous soundings.

With regard to the important study of the character of the settlement it was proven that an extensive Middle Assyrian settlement existed at Tell Fekheriye. Architectural features from this period were excavated not only in Area C and Step Trench D, where a connection to the excavations of the American team and A. Pruß's trench were found, but also in Area B in the east of the main mound. In all areas excavated so far the youngest Middle Assyrian levels are located at an average height of approximately 354.50m above sea level. If we consider the location of the areas, the minimal

[35] McEwan et al. 1958, pp. 4–6, 42–46.
[36] Pruß and Bagdo 2002.

extent of the Late Bronze Age settlement can be estimated to be at least ca. 10 to 12 ha.

Since the remains of the Middle Assyrian occupation on the western terrace start to appear directly underneath the modern surface, it is possible to investigate these layers on a large scale and to precisely describe the layout of the architecture, its stratigraphic relationships, and its functional character. The architecture is embedded between the abovementioned Middle Assyrian debris with cuneiform tablets and sealings and accumulation of the early the Iron Age. Yet none of the latter activities have drastically destroyed the Middle Assyrian architecture, which is thus well preserved and whose remains were excavated along the terrace over a length of about 110 m between Area C in the north and Area D in the south. The western facade of these buildings can be traced along the whole terrace and be subdivided into at least two architectural units in Area C (House I and House II) and another one unit in Area D (so far unlabelled), with several building phases and phases of occupation each (**Fig. 5**).

The architecture of the Middle Assyrian House I is very distinct and was described before[37] as being grouped around a central courtyard, having two floor levels with associated finds and being terraced due to the slope of the ancient mound from east to west. So far only the western part of this building has been exposed during the expedition of the Oriental Institute in 1940 and consisted of a long L-shaped corridor (7), a unit of three rooms abutting it (4, 5, 6), a large reception room to the south (1), a central courtyard (2), as well as a second courtyard to the east (3). Observations on building techniques and stratigraphic relations allow a division in several room units and suggest a progression of buildings that started with the huge reception room as part of the oldest building phase of the building, whereas the part to the north of it must have been built separately and added to the existing architecture as it is clearly visible by a join in the western facade. This room unit, consisting of a single room, was abutted in the north by the aforementioned western room unit with Rooms 4 to 7, which has approximately the same size. Despite the fact that the floors of the rooms were heavily destroyed by two earlier excavations, 70 years of exposure to the elements and, last but not least, because the American excavators ignored or missed the floor levels and thus continued excavating under the foundation level of the walls,[38] further research has presented a more detailed picture of the internal stratification and functionality of the building unit. Room 6 at the northern end gives detailed information on the construction of a bathroom and drainage installation with a drainage pit at the northern end of the western room unit. It is located outside the narrow part of the northern wall of Room 6 opposite the toilet and allows wastewater to be drained into a sewer paved with fragments of backed bricks, which passes under the

[37] McEwan et al. 1958, pp. 4–6; Pruß and Bagdo 2002.
[38] McEwan et al. 1958, pp. 4–6, n. 2; Pruß and Bagdo 2002, p. 322, n. 23.

mud-bricks of the wall. The upper part of the soakage pit was slightly conical, tapering towards the top and covered by several large capstones and shards (**Fig. 6**). Similar installations are known from many other sites such as Tell Barri,[39] Tell Asmar, Tell Beydar, Tell Hariri, Tell Bi'a, Yorgan Tepe, Tell al-Uhaymir, and Tell Telloh and have mostly been identified with bathrooms and toilets. Also other interpretations are plausible, yet little convincing, for instance the use of the installation for craft activities.[40]

Also noteworthy is a sewer east of the room unit that runs parallel to Rooms 5 and 6 and connects the central courtyard Room 2 with an unexcavated area north of Room 6. It is made of two rows of stones bordering the drainage canal that is about 30cm in depth and 15 cm in width. The top is covered by a layer of larger capstones and sherds of large storage vessels.

The area between the western room unit with the sewer canal and Room 8 in the east is characterised by several small single-rowed mud-brick walls and ovens (tannurs). They form part of a production area that is bordered by a diagonally running wall to the north of House I and comprises two standard sized tannurs and one slightly bigger oven. From the stratigraphic point of view it is clear that the area had already been used for economic purposes and kitchen activities before the construction of House I, as parts of this layer were covered by the courtyard and Room 8. Yet the diagonal wall to which the installations are connected does not seem to have lost its function in later periods as is witnessed by it being the northern perimeter for House I.[41]

To the east, the situation looks different. A single room (Room 8) about 4 m × 4 m in size with two door openings, was built northeast of the central courtyard (Room 2) and allows passage from this courtyard to the area to the east and thus the proposed second courtyard on a slightly higher terrace (Room 3). In this general area a concentration of several clay tablets was already found in 1940 and our investigations revealed nine more fragments of letters and administrative documents in the rubble on the pebble floor of the courtyard in front of and in Room 8, which can largely be dated to the reign of Tukulti-Ninurta I (1233–1198 BC).[42] Moreover, numerous seal impressions have been found on clay sealings for jars and other storage facilities and

[39] In the palace of Adad-nirari I cf. Pecorella and Benoit 2008b, pp. 70–75, fig. 74.a–b.

[40] As suggested in Margueron 2008.

[41] This can be proposed with relative certainty, even if the stratigraphic connection to the western room unit is hidden under the baulk and its eastern end and thus connection to Room 8 has been destroyed by later graves and wells. Because the floor levels in this area are heavily disturbed by younger levels and previous excavations, it cannot be said with absolute certainty, whether the production area was also part of an early phase of House I as suggested in Bonatz et al. 2008, pp. 112–113, fig. 13, for several installations further to the south, as long as the huge amount of data has not been processed and analysed in detail.

[42] One of which is already published by Gregory Chambon in Bonatz et al. 2008, Appendix I, pp. 130–131.

clay lumps associated with administrative and sealing activities. With the new finds it becomes clear that Room 8 has to be connected with administrative activities, possibly accounting and also the preparation of clay for sealings.[43] Three consecutive door socket stones next to an opening in the eastern wall as well as a repair in the wall and a succession of tramples indicate three phases of use of the room. Yet this room's connection to the rest of the building is thus far only given via a small wall to its south that connects it with the reception room and at the same time separates both pebbled courtyards.

Both cuneiform tablets and sealings thus offer a good opportunity to equate the exact find spots, floor levels, and construction phases of House I described in the older expeditions with our results. It becomes clear that despite different assessments and difficulties with the allocation in the past, the small archive of fragmented letters and administrative documents, whose bulk can be dated to the reign of Tukulti-Ninurta I must belong to the phase of utilisation of House I.

Another room unit is situated east of the reception-room. As this unit has not been excavated completely it is hard to give any satisfactory interpretation. A rectangular room (Room 9) has been excavated, which abuts the eastern end of Room 1 and has two doorways opening to the south and the north, respectively, making that room a transit room to access the second courtyard (Room 3) from the south.

The first evidence for a second Middle Assyrian building along the terrace was found in 2001 by the Syrian-German expedition in the south-western corner of House I.[44] Work was resumed in 2006 and continues until today, confirming the existence of further buildings with the same alignment of the western facade as House I. The architecture of the building designated House II as excavated so far, can be subdivided into at least three main phases of occupation and rebuilding. It has to be noted that the general layout is quite similar to that of House I. One room unit is situated to the west; this was the one that was first excavated. A reception room is located south of this unit, a production area to the north and probably an open courtyard were found in the center. The eastern part of this building is, however, as it is with House I, still covered under the main mound.

The western room unit is the best explored part of the building so far and the one that has the closest resemblance to House I. In the architecture's original building phase a corridor (Room 3) and three adjacent rooms (Rooms 1, 2 and 4) can be observed. The latter is a stone paved bathroom with a toilet in its northern wall that is connected to a cesspit in Room 1 by a ceramic sewage pipe. Aside from the sewage pit that is similarly constructed to the one in House I, a polygonal oven suggests a production or kitchen area.

[43] As described before on pages 10–11.
[44] Pruß and Bagdo 2002, pp. 320–325.

At large, due to these major similarities between both Middle Assyrian House I and House II, and the fact that they form part of a uniformly constructed complex of buildings contributing to the homogeneous character of the area, one could almost speak of a Middle Assyrian housing estate row.

For all Middle Assyrian buildings excavated so far, official and administrative activities are attested for their main phase of occupation and probably for some of their later phases of utilisation as well. Not only in House I but also in House II some Middle Assyrian clay sealings with seal impressions have been excavated. One of them is a remarkably well preserved impression of the seal of Aššur-iddin, lots of which were found in and around Room 8 of House I (**Fig. 3**). A clay tablet (TF 4772) with reference to a limu-date at the end of the reign of Tukulti-Ninurta I has been excavated in a secondary context, but probably originates from House II.[45] Thus an absolute and approximate relative date is given within the reign of Tukulti-Ninurta I that is supported by the pottery assemblage, which corresponds to Middle Assyrian standard forms of the Middle-Jezireh IIA and B periods.

Already during the occupational phase of House I and House II, yet not later than after their abandonment, several double jar burials have been dug (**Fig.** 7). This is supported by the fact that the graves are orientated along the walls and in the corners of rooms, suggesting that the building was still occupied or at least that the walls were still standing above ground and were clearly visible when the graves were dug. Five of them, which were largely ignored or missed by the American expedition, are located under the floor level of House I[46] with another two under the floors of House II. One burial was found by Moortgat in the so called Türbe-trench in 1955.[47] It is a not entirely exceptional phenomenon for this period that graves, especially those of children, are placed in a jar or a double jar burial under the floor of a dwelling.

Their burial customs are quite uniform consisting of two big vessels, in which the body of the deceased was placed in a flexed position. In order to hold these vessels in position they have often been fixed with one or several mud-bricks that were placed between the edge of the pit and the jars. The grave goods can have a large variety. Smaller jars, carinated bowls or nipple base goblets were often found outside of the burial vessels,[48] sometimes also placed next to the burial jars or in a niche in the grave pit. In some cases a ritual offering in form of bones of the extremities, shoulder blades and skull of a small ruminant animal (sheep or goat) are preserved in the fill of the grave (**Fig. 8**).

[45] Compare in this article on page 273 and Bonatz forthcoming.

[46] Except for burial I in House I, Room 4 which has been excavated but not published in detail (H. Kantor in McEwan et al. 1958, p. 45, pl. 20b,c).

[47] Moortgat 1957, p. 22, Fig. 8.

[48] Bonatz et al. 2008, fig. 12.

Inside the two burial-jars, and associated with the body of the deceased, mostly beads of different shapes and materials, golden earrings and bronze bracelets, a variety of finds has been identified.

Comparable double jar burials have been found at Tell Hariri,[49] Tell Knēdiğ,[50] Tell Taban,[51] Tell Mohammed 'Arab,[52] Tell Mohammed Diyab,[53] Assur[54] and Tell Barri.[55] The exact date of these graves can momentarily be established via stratigraphic observations and pottery comparisons, which place them at the end of the Middle Assyrian period during the use and after the abandonment of House I, a date conforming to the dates of similar burials at other sites. This date is also supported by a radiocarbon sample taken and processed by the Poznań Radiocarbon Laboratory (sample TF1148), that offers a timeframe for one of the graves (C–32) between 1120 and 920 cal BC (2 sigma) (**Fig. 9**).

The succeeding levels and layers can be described as being quite homogeneous yet partly destroyed by earlier expeditions, or cut by later pits, wall foundations and antique industrial installations. However, from the scarce evidence we have, it can be concluded that an approximately 80 to 100 cm thick Late Bronze Age – early Iron Age level with numerous tannurs and other workshop installations covers the remains of the Middle Assyrian buildings on a large scale and separates them from the younger levels of the Roman Period.

Thus it seems that before and after the occupation of House I, this area was not built up properly but rather an open space with a scattered occupation and has been used for food preparation, other economic purposes as well as a burial ground as will be shown below.

During the excavation in 1940 and 2001 several graves were investigated, which were different from the aforementioned double jar burials and hard to date by any conventional means. Both Helene Kantor[56] and Alexander Pruß[57] noticed that some of the grave goods could be dated to the early Iron Age or the Late Assyrian period. Since the initiation of the new Syrian-German mission at Tell Fekheriye in 2006 another 30 graves of that kind have been exposed.[58] (**Fig. 10**)

The vast majority consists of grave pits at the base of which a rectangular mudbrick enclosure is erected, in which the deceased is placed in a stretched position on

[49] Jean-Marie 1999.
[50] Martin 2005, pp. 55–62.
[51] Numoto in Numoto et al. 2008, pp. 4–6.
[52] As reported in Sauvage 2005, p. 48, fig. 1.
[53] Sauvage 2005, pp. 49–50.
[54] Haller et al. 1954.
[55] Pecorella 2003, pp. 48–53, p. 70; Pecorella and Benoit 2008a, pp. 57–63, pp. 127–141.
[56] Kantor 1958, p. 46, p. 51.
[57] Pruß and Bagdo 2002, p. 321.
[58] One grave from Area A has already been published in Bonatz et al. 2008, pp. 99–100, fig. 3.

his back. These burials usually have a roof made of mud-bricks standing on edge forming a triangular pediment.[59] These brick graves[60] are oriented in a north-south or an east-west direction respectively, and cut the walls and fill of the Middle Assyrian buildings without any regard for the older architecture. Thus they must have been dug when the buildings on the western slope of the ancient mound had already lost their function, were abandoned, and their walls were no longer standing visibly above ground. However, it is rarely possible to establish the exact floor level from where they were dug into the ground due to later disturbances and pits, making it almost impossible to assign them to any of the levels by stratigraphic means. Moreover, the situation on the western slope of the high mound is responsible for a difference in the graves' base-level of about two meters from east to west. Thus for an exact dating, several characteristics have to be combined.

One of the main characteristics is a set of pottery usually deposited at the bottom of the grave pit next to or on top of the grave architecture near the head of the deceased. The set consists of a large jar originally filled with a liquid and often decorated with an incision, a nipple base goblet at the bottom of the jar and a small bowl to cover the mouth. Initially, dating these graves was slightly difficult as the shapes of the different pottery vessels have a very long time span of use, lasting from the beginning Late-Assyrian period well into the Roman-Parthian era.[61] This is attested in the Roman-Parthian graveyard at Tell Sheik Hamad (Magdala) where a continuous use or even reuse of vessel forms known from the Late Assyrian period can be observed.[62] The architecture of the graves presents a similar dilemma, as the type with the distinct gable construction is mainly used in this period, as can be seen in numerous sites such as Uruk, Babylon, Nimrud, Assur, Nippur, Yorgan Tepe, Tell Knēdiğ, Tell ed-Der and Seleucia,[63] but can be found in other periods of Northern Mesopotamia, like the Middle and Late Assyrian period at Tell Mohammad 'Arab,[64] Tell Barri,[65] Tell Sabi Abyad, Tell Khuera or Tell Mohammed Diyab[66] as well.

Yet despite the long life span of the vessel shapes there is growing evidence for a date in the period of the Late Bronze Age – Iron Age transition. An increasing number of

[59] Typologically these graves can be further subdivided. A small group, thus far represented by only three examples, has a slightly different brick covering. Here two rows of vertically standing mud-bricks cover the architecture, leaning against a small wall at the top end of the grave. Yet another sub-group shows a covering made of one or two rows of lying mud-bricks.

[60] Sometimes called mud-brick cist graves, brick graves, mud-brick lined graves, graves with mud-brick architecture and 'Lehmziegelkistengrab' in German, or 'Tombe construite' in French respectively.

[61] See Novák in Novák et al. 2000, pp. 15–16, fig. 9, 11–12; This has already been discussed in Bonatz et al. 2008, pp. 100, 110 n. 26.

[62] Römer-Strehl in Novák et al. 2000: pp. 130–131, fig. 445, 461–462.

[63] Bonatz et al. 2008, p. 100 n. 16.

[64] E.g.: Grave 50V:55 cf Roaf 1984, p. 146 (Period a), p. 148 (Period e).

[65] Pecorella 2003, pp. 43–57.

[66] Sauvage 2005.

nipple base goblets of typical Middle and Late Assyrian type have been found, moreover a white frit bowl with black drops on the rim, that has parallels in Middle Assyrian burials in Üçtepe (level 9),[67] Tell Barri (strato 33C)[68] and Mohammed 'Arab (phase e),[69] stresses this fact as well.[70]

In addition, the deceased have few grave goods. Mainly bronze pins were found to secure the shroud and bronze foot-rings, except in several burials where bronze or iron bracelets, a few beads of semi-precious stone, a golden earring and infrequently some small pottery bowls deposited near the chest of the individual or in its hands were discovered.

Several characteristics stand out that can clearly be associated with burial customs and rituals being performed during inhumation. One of them is a small carinated bowl with smoke residue placed on top of the grave architecture or in a niche in the wall of the cist. It is possible that they were used to illuminate the grave during the inhumation ceremony.[71] The fill of the grave shaft also often contains the extremities of small ruminant animals (sheep or goat) as it is in the case of the aforementioned double jar burials. Exact stratigraphic observations result in questions concerning the visibility of the burials after their deposition. In some cases it might be possible that the mouth of the vessel with its cover and the aforementioned animal were above ground at least for a certain period of time. This is witnessed by the skeletal remains of the aforementioned animals jutting out over the edge of the pit in two cases. These burial customs, especially the food offerings, are almost identical in material and deposition,[72] and the type of pottery contained within the graves show some remarkable overlapping. Despite varying grave types and different customs, which might point to different social, cultural or even ethnic backgrounds, despite stratigraphic discrepancies, and despite the fact that the exact date of abandonment of the younger graveyard is still a matter of debate, even if it can be postulated that the set of pottery accompanying the deceased overlaps with even younger periods until the Roman-Parthian period, a certain continuity and strong local tradition can be observed.

In 2010 additional radiocarbon analyses of the three inhumations have been conducted, which confirm a date sometime between 1290 and 830 BC[73] and form a good basis for the further study of these graves (**Fig. 9**).

[67] An inhumation of a woman and a baby as published in Sevin 1989, fig. 12:2.

[68] Pecorella and Benoit 2008a, pp. 127–142, fig. 131a; Pecorella and Benoit 2008b, p. 98, fig. 95b.

[69] Roaf 1984, p. 148, fig. 6.02, grave 49U:29.

[70] A similar example has also been found in Tell Fekheriye itself – yet out of context – by Anton Moortgat in 1955 (Moortgat 1957, p. 22, fig. 10).

[71] Similar interpretations have been given for other Iron Age graves by Kulemann-Ossen and Martin (2008, p. 242, p. 245).

[72] This burial custom can be observed at cremations as well, as witnessed by Tombe 1498 at Tell Mohammed Diyab (Sauvage 2005, pp. 49–50).

[73] The samples were processed at the Poznań Radiocarbon Laboratory and the results were calibrated using OxCal 4.1 (2010) with a probability rate of 95,4% (2 sigma).

Accordingly, the majority of the graves[74] can approximately be dated to the end of the Middle Assyrian or early Late Assyrian period and thus to the Late Bronze Age – Iron Age transition. During that period the area of the Middle Assyrian houses was used as a graveyard for a possible Assyrian or Assyrianised (?) population.[75] After the abandonment of the area as a living quarter, debris accumulated and only scarce building activities can be observed. The area seems to have been used as a graveyard over a considerable time.

Besides these graves only a few remains of Neo-Assyrian architectural features were found, with the exception of the so called 'bit hilani' building excavated by the American expedition in 1940 at the northern slope of the mound. Parts of this building were reached in a deep sounding in Area A. In the other excavation areas, however, only fragmentary and secondary evidence was produced despite the layers indicated in the section drawings by Anton Moortgat.[76] It is therefore conceivable that as a result of the interaction between Tell Fekheriye and the neighbouring Tell Halaf, the focus of the settlement shifted to Guzana in the first millennium, which is reflected in the archaeological evidence. Yet Tell Fekheriye remains a religiously and ideologically charged site at the source of the Khabur River and an important center for the cult of the weather god of the Khabur and his wife Šala being worshiped in the city of Sikāni. This is according to the statue of Adad-it'i (Hadad Yis'i), a bilingual inscription in Assyrian cuneiform and Aramaean alphabetic script, which records that the statue had stood in the temple of the weather god of Guzana in the town Sikāni, which some scholars suggest to be derived from Aššukanni.[77]

Thus, strictly from a stratigraphic point of view, a structural transition from the Late Bronze Age to the Iron Age can be observed after substantial Mittani occupation and building activities, which is followed by two well represented and, due to the finding of cuneiform tablets, now better understood Middle Assyrian levels. One can probably be assigned to the reign of Shalmaneser I (1263–1234); however, it yields no substantial architecture yet. The second level comprises a row of houses showing several utilisation phases, which can approximately be dated to the reign of Shalmaneser I

[74] In addition to those graves, two further types have been identified. Stratigraphically closely connected to these graves are five jar burials of infants. They consist of a large mostly ovoid vessel with an infant placed inside. In one case the mouth of the jar is covered with a mud-brick and has a design incised on it before firing that shows a tree.

Inhumations seem to be part of the necropolis as well and show different characteristics. Two examples contain the bones of an individual placed in a flexed or contracted position respectively. Another inhumation shows a rather peculiar burial custom, with the body of the individual being placed in a small pit in a sitting position with contracted legs.

[75] Cultural or ethnic affiliations are hard to establish as long as clear picture of the composition of the population is incoherent. This will be one of the aims of the project for the future. Yet it is possible to gain a first insight from the onomastic sources of the clay tablets (Bonatz forthcoming).

[76] Moortgat 1957, fig. 7.

[77] A more detailed discussion of this subject and references to older literature will be published in Bonatz forthcoming.

(1263–1234BC) and Tukulti-Ninurta I (1233–1198BC). During or after the occupation of this building, a graveyard was established within the walls of the building. This is comparable to many Middle Assyrian buildings, where mostly young children were buried under the floors of the houses. After the abandonment of the area as a living quarter, debris accumulated and only scarce building activities can be observed. The area seems to have been used as a working and cooking area and as a graveyard over a considerable period of time.

The graves themselves show interesting features as well. Both the double jar burials and the stratigraphically slightly younger graves with mud-brick architecture show overlapping burial customs including food offerings in the fill of the pit that are almost identical in material and deposition. Even if the exact date of abandonment of the younger graves is still a matter of debate it can be postulated that the set of pottery accompanying the deceased overlaps with even younger periods until the Roman-Parthian period. This can be seen as a strong local tradition. Thus, despite the fact that the graves are of different kinds, which might point to a different cultural background or social status of the population, a certain continuity of local traditions is observable.

Maybe these tendencies can be seen within the context of a declining settlement size and a possible shift of settlement activities to the neighbouring Tell Halaf in the early tenth century BC. An Aramaean kingdom was established at Tell Halaf after the early Iron Age (ca. 1200–1000 BC) settlement which had evidence of grooved or groovy pottery (Rillenkeramik), possibly associated with an Anatolian population.[78] How these changes in cultural identity affected the settlement at Tell Fekheriye will have to be investigated in a broader approach when more adequate data is available. However, from the data at our disposal now, a picture of substantial change arises which occurred at the end of the Middle Assyrian empire, when during the reign of several weak kings new ethnic groups emerge and settle there.[79] At least parts of the settlement seem to have been abandoned, as can be observed at Giricano in the Upper Tigris valley for instance, where, after ca. 1069/68 BC, the settlement was left due to Assyrian-Aramaean conflicts and another group of settlers used the site.[80] Changes like this are, however, not reflected in the burial customs at Tell Fekheriye, as is typical for other Iron Age graveyards, for example in Tell Shioukh Faouqâni and other sites where cremations occur.[81]

Since only fragmentary evidence for changing circumstances has yet been found at Tell Fekheriye, and due to the close proximity of the neighbouring Tell Halaf, which became a centre of Aramaean settlement in the region, it can be assumed that local

78 Novák 2009, pp. 93–94.
79 Kantor 1958, pp. 22, 25, notices a lack of pottery.
80 Radner 2004, pp. 115–116.
81 Tenu 2009b, pp. 83–96. See also: Sauvage 2005.

traits and especially a long Assyrian tradition existed. Although non-Aramaean ethnic elements remained present in this area, they were exposed to changing influences. Thus the character of the area exposed so far changes drastically from a densely settled Middle Assyrian administrative quarter to a scattered occupation and use of the area as a ground for graves in the early Iron Age.

The potential to address and, at some point in time give more satisfactory answers to these questions, is enormous, and future excavations will help to better understand the processes of Late Bronze Age – Iron Age transition in Northern Mesopotamia.

Bibliography

Bonatz, D.

forthcoming "Tell Fekheriye in the Late Bronze Age. Archaeological Investigations into the Structures of Political Governance in the Upper Mesopotamian Piedmont," in *The Archaeology of Political Space. The Upper Mesopotamian Piedmont in the Second Millennium BC*, Topoi. Berlin Studies of the Ancient World, edited by D. Bonatz. Berlin: Walter de Gruyter.

Bonatz, D., Bartl, P. V., Gilibert, A. and Jauss, C.

2008 "Bericht über die erste und zweite Grabungskampagne in Tell Feḫerīye 2006 und 2007," *Mitteilungen der Deutschen Orientgesellschaft* 140: 89–135.

Brown, B.

forthcoming "Settlement Patterns of the Middle Assyrian State: Notes Toward an Investigation of State Apparatuses," in *The Archaeology of Political Space. The Upper Mesopotamian Piedmont in the Second Millennium BC*, Topoi. Berlin Studies of the Ancient World, edited by D. Bonatz. Berlin: Walter de Gruyter.

Cancik-Kirschbaum, E. Ch.

1996 *Die mittelassyrischen Briefe aus Tall Šēḫ Ḥamad*, Berichte der Ausgrabung Tall ŠēḪ Ḥamad / Dūr-Katlimmu 4, Berlin: Dietrich Reimer.

2000 "Organisation und Verwaltung von Grenzgebieten in Mittelassyrischer Zeit," in *Landscapes. Territories, Frontiers and Horizons in the Ancient Near East, Papers presented to the XLIV Rencontre Assyriologique Internationale, Venezia, 7-11 July 1997*, Part II. *Geography and Cultural Landscapes*, edited by L. Milano et al., pp. 5–8. Padova: Sargon srl.

Charpin, D.

2009 "Un itinéraire paléo-babylonien de long du Habur," in *Entre les fleuves – I. Untersuchungen zur historischen Geographie Obermesopotamiens im 2. Jahrtausend v. Chr.,* Berliner Beiträge zum Vorderen Orient 20, edited by E. Cancik-Kirschbaum and N. Ziegler, pp. 59–74. Gladbeck: PeWe-Verlag.

2010 "An Old Babylonian Itinerary along the Ḫābūr," in *Studia Chaburensia* 1, edited by H. Kühne, pp. 33–48. Wiesbaden: Harrassowitz.

Charpin, D. and Ziegler, N.

2003 *Florilegium Marianum V. Mari et le proche-orient à l'époque amorrite, essai d'histoire politique*, Mémoires de N.A.B.U. 6, Paris: SEPOA.

CRASSO, D.
2009 "The Region of the Upper Euphrates: The Hittite Perspective," in *Entre les fleuves – I. Untersuchungen zur historischen Geographie Obermesopotamiens im 2. Jahrtausend v. Chr.,* Berliner Beiträge zum Vorderen Orient 20, edited by E. Cancik-Kirschbaum and N. Ziegler, pp. 211–231. Gladbeck: PeWe-Verlag.

FREYDANK, H.
1991 *Beiträge zur mittelassyrischen Chronologie und Geschichte,* Schriften zur Geschichte und Kultur des Alten Orients 21, Berlin: Akademie Verlag.
2005 "Zu den Eponymenfolgen des 13. Jahrhunderts v. Chr. in Dūr-Katlimmu," *Altorientalische Forschungen* 32/1: 45–56.

GRAYSON, A. K.
1987 *Assyrian Rulers of the Third and Second Millennium BC (to 1115 BC),* The Royal Inscriptions of Mesopotamia. Assyrian Periods Volume 1. Toronto: University of Toronto Press.
1991 *Assyrian Rulers of the Early First Millennium BC I (1114–859 BC),* The Royal Inscriptions of Mesopotamia. Assyrian Periods Volume 2. Toronto: University of Toronto Press.

HALLER, A.
1954 *Die Gräber und Grüfte von Assur,* 65. Wissenschaftliche Veröffentlichung der Deutschen Orient-Gesellschaft. Berlin: Gebr. Mann Verlag

JANISCH-JAKOB, D. I.
2009 "Die Siegelabrollungen auf den mittelassyrischen Tafeln aus Tell Chuēra," in *Die mittelassyrischen Texte aus Tell Chuēra in Nordost-Syrien*, Vorderasiatische Forschungen der Max Freiherr von Oppenheim-Stiftung, Bd. 2. Ausgrabungen in Tell Chuēra in Nordost-Syrien, edited by S. Jakob, pp. 185–189. Wiesbaden: Harrassowitz.

JAKOB, S.
2009 *Die mittelassyrischen Texte aus Tell Chuēra in Nordost-Syrien*, Vorderasiatische Forschungen der Max Freiherr von Oppenheim-Stiftung, Bd. 2. Ausgrabungen in Tell Chuēra in Nordost-Syrien. Wiesbaden: Harrassowitz.

JEAN-MARIE, M.-L.
1999 *Tombes et Nécropoles de Mari*, Bibliothèque archéologique et historique, volume CLIII. Mission archéologique de Mari, volume V. Beyrouth: IFAPO.

MARTIN, L.
2005 "Eisenzeitliche Gräber," in *Tall Knēdiğ*, 113. Wissenschaftliche Veröffentlichung der Deutschen Orient-Gesellschaft, edited by E. Klengel-Brandt, S. Kulemann-Ossen, L. Martin, pp. 52–62. Saarwellingen: Saarländische Druckerei & Verlag.

KOLIŃSKI, R.
2001 *Mesopotamian dimatu of the Second Millennium BC,* BAR International Series 1004. Oxford: Archaeopress.

KANTOR, H.
1958 "Miscellaneous Small Objects and Burials," in *Soundings at Tell Fakhariyah*, Oriental Institute Publications 79, edited by C. McEwan et al., Chicago: University of Chicago Press.

KÜHNE, C.
1999 "Imperial Mittani: An Attempt at Historical Reconstruction," in *Nuzi at Seventy-Five,* Studies on the Civilization and Culture of Nuzi and the Hurrians, Vol. 10, edited by D. I. Owen and G. Wilhelm, pp. 203–222. Bethesda: CDL Press.

KULEMANN-OSSEN, S. and MARTIN, L.
2008 "Gefässsets, Schmuck und Waffen: Zum Umgang mit den Toten am Tell Knēdiğ im 3. und 1. Jahrtausend v. Chr.," in *Fundstellen. Gesammelte Schriften zur Archäologie und Geschichte Altvorderasiens ad honorem Hartmut Kühne,* edited by D. Bonatz, R. M. Czichon and F. J. Kreppner, pp. 233–250. Wiesbaden: Harrassowitz.

MARGUERON, J.
2008 "Notes d'archéologie et d'achitecture Orientales 15 – Installations hygiéniques ou artisanales?" *Syria* 85: 175–222.

MCEWAN, C., BRAIDWOOD, L. S., FRANKFORT, H., GÜTERBOCK, H. G., HAINES, R. C., KANTOR, H- J. and KRAELING, C. H.
1958 *Soundings at Tell Fakhariyah.* Oriental Institute Publications 79. Chicago: University of Chicago Press.

MOORTGAT, A.
1957 "Archäologische Forschungen der Max Freiherr von Oppenheim-Stiftung im nördlichen Mesopotamien 1955," *Abhandlungen der Arbeitsgemeinschaft für Forschung des Landes Nordrhein-Westphalen* 62: 5–24.

MÜLLER-KESSLER, C. and KESSLER, K.-H.
1995 "Zum Kult des Wettergottes von Guzana," in *Eski Yakon Doğu Kültürleri Üzerine İncelemeler. In Memoriam İ. Metin Akyurt,* edited by A. Erkanal et al., pp. 239–244. Istanbul.

NOVÁK, M.
2009 "Zur Geschichte der aramäisch-assyrischen Stadt Gūzāna," in *Vorbericht über die erste und zweite syrisch-deutsche Grabungskampagne auf dem Tell Halaf,* Vorderasiatische Forschungen der Max Freiherr von Oppenheim-Stiftung, Bd. 3. Ausgrabungen auf dem Tell Halaf in Nordost-Syrien, edited by A. el-M. Baghdo, L. Martin, M. Novák and W. Orthmann pp. 93–98. Wiesbaden: Harrassowitz.

NOVÁK, M., OETTEL, A., WITZEL, C.
2000 *Der parthisch-römische Friedhof von Tall Šēḫ Ḫamad / Magdala,* Berichte der Ausgrabung Tall Šēḫ Ḫamad / Dūr-Katlimmu 5. Berlin: Dietrich Reimer.

NUMOTO, H.
2008 *Excavations at Tell Taban, Hassake, Syria.* Hiroshima: Letterpress.

PECORELLA, P. E.
2003 *Tell Barri/Kahat. La Campagna del 2000.* Florence: Firenze University Press.

PECORELLA, P. E. and BENOIT, R. P.
2008a *Tell Barri/Kahat. La Campagna del 2003.* Florence: Firenze University Press.
2008b *Tell Barri/Kahat. La Campagna del 2004,* Florence: Firenze University Press.

PRUSS, A. and BAGDO A.-M.
2002 "Tell Fecheriye. Bericht über die erste Kampagne der deutsch-syrischen Ausgrabungen 2001," *Mitteilungen der Deutschen Orientgesellschaft* 134: 311–329.

RADNER, K.
2004 *Das mittelassyrische Tontafelarchiv von Giricano/Dunnu-ša-Uzibi. Ausgrabungen in Giricano I,* Subartu 14. Turnhout: Brepols.

ROAF, M.
1984 "Excavations at Tell Mohammed 'Arab in the Eski Mosul Dam Salvage Project," *Iraq* 46.2: 141–156.

SAPORETTI, C.
1979 *Gli eponimi medio-assiri,* Bibliotheca Mesopotamica 9. Malibu: Undena Publications.

SAUVAGE, M.
2005 "Incinération et inhumation à l'époque médio-assyrienne (XIIIe-XIIe s. av. J.-C.): le cas de Tell Mohammed Diyab (Syrie du Nord-Est)," *KTÈMA* 30: 47–54.

SEVIN, V.
1989 *Excavations at Üçtepe Kazıları*. İstanbul: Arkeoloji ve Sanat Yayınları.

SINGER, I.
1985 "The Battle of Niḫriya and the End of the Hittite Empire," *Zeitschrift für Assyriologie und Vorderasiatische Archäologie* 75: 100–123.

TENU, A.
2009a *L'expansion médio-assyrienne. Approche archéologique*, BAR International Series 1906. Oxford: Archaeopress.
2009b "Assyrians and Arameans in the Euphrates Valley viewed from the cemetery of Tell Shiukh Fawqâni," in *Assyrian and Aramean Interaction (Actes de la Table Ronde tenue au 6ICAANE, Rome, 5-11 mai 2008)*, edited by A. Tenu and C. Kepinski, *Syria* 86: 83–96.

WIGGERMANN, F. A. M.
2000 "Agriculture in the Northern Balikh Valley. The Case of Middle Assyrian Tell Sabi Abyad," in *Rainfall and Agriculture in Northern Mesopotamia,* MOS Studies 3, edited by R. M. Jas, pp. 171–231. Istanbul and Leiden: Nederlands Historisch-Archeologisch Inst.
2006 "The Seal of Ilī-padâ, Grand Vizier of the Middle Assyrian Empire," in *The Iconography of Cylinder Seals,* Warburg Institute Colloquia 9, edited by P. Taylor, pp. 90–99. London: Warburg Inst.

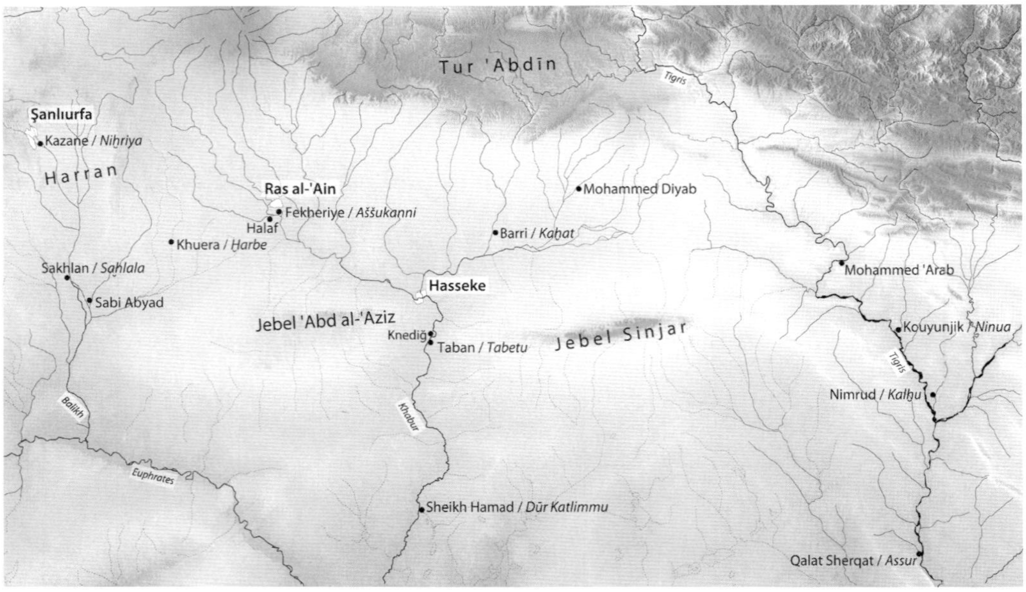

Fig. 1 Map showing location of sites mentioned in the text (black dots) and of modern towns (white areas).

Fig. 2 Cuneiform tablets in situ in deposit C–1035 and C–1191.

Fig. 3 Reconstruction of the seal of a high Assyrian official, probably Aššur-iddin.

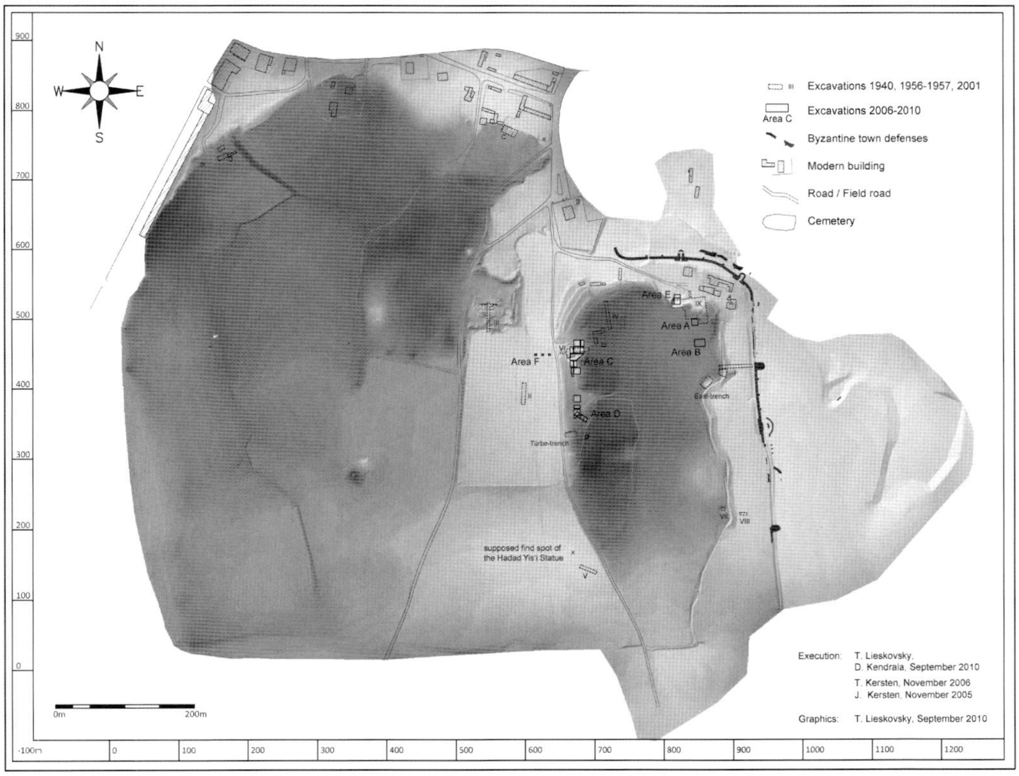

Fig. 4 Plan of the site.

Fig. 5 Plan of the Middle Assyrian buildings on the western terrace of the mound.

Fig. 6 Aerial photograph of House II and detail of bathroom of House II.

Fig. 7 Double jar burial C–1036 before and after opening the jars.

Fig. 8 Mud-brick cist graves C–1307 (foreground) and C–1325 (upper right).

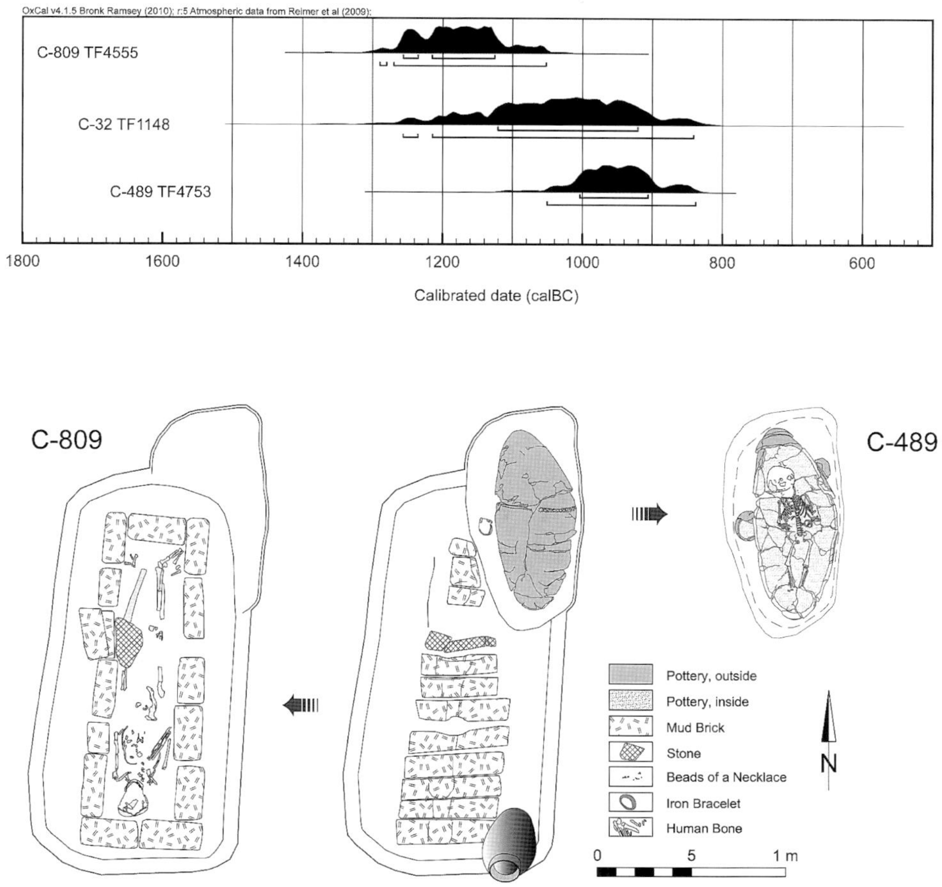

Fig. 9 Radiocarbon dates of three selected graves.

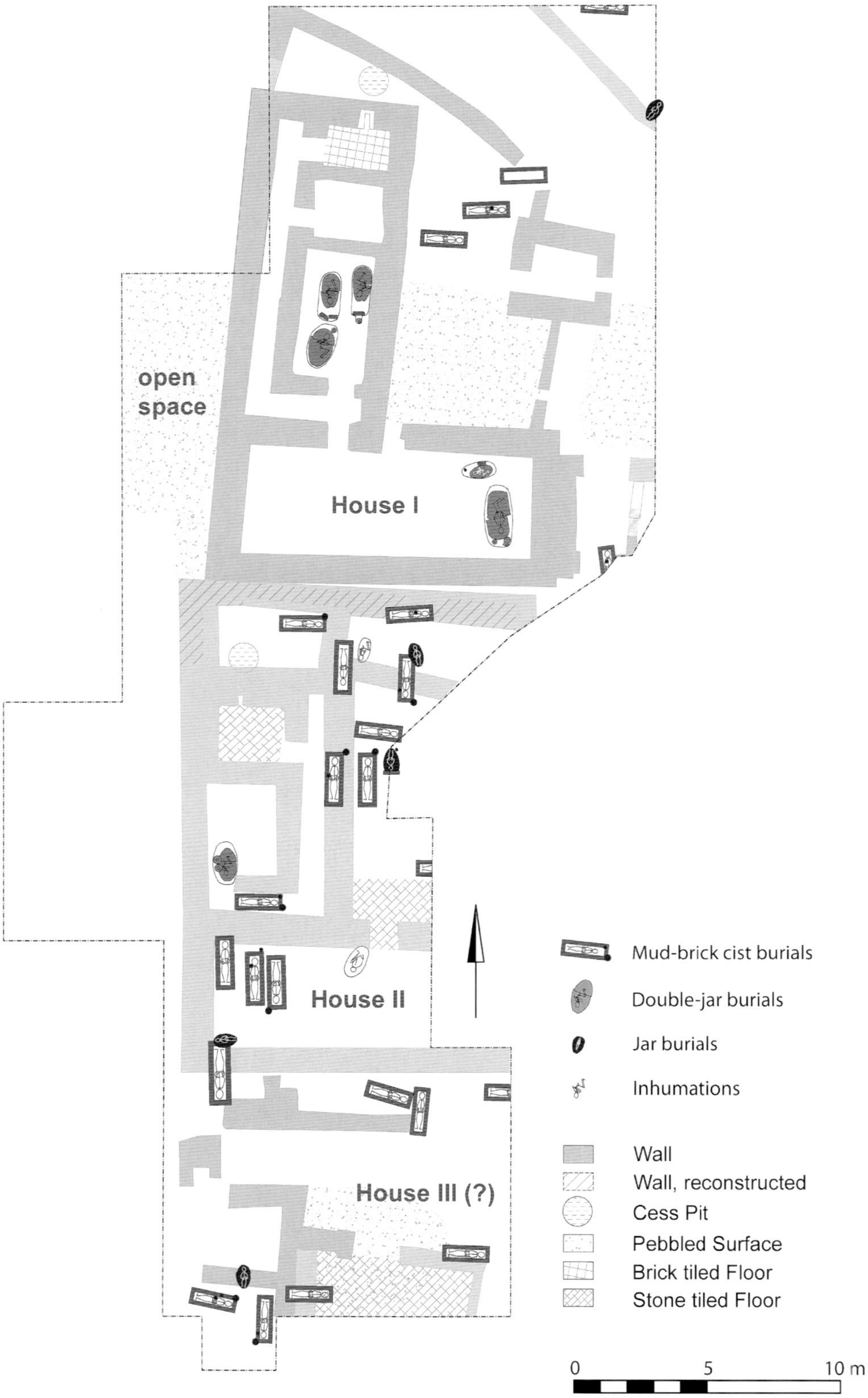

Fig. 10 Plan of the necropolis on the western terrace of the main mound.

CHAPTER 12

BETWEEN THE MUŠKU AND THE ARAMAEANS THE EARLY HISTORY OF GUZANA/TELL HALAF

Mirko NOVÁK
Universität Bern
Institut für Archäologische Wissenschaften
Abteilung für Vorderasiatische Archäologie
Länggassstrasse 10
CH-3012 Bern
Switzerland
E-mail: novak@iaw.unibe.ch

ABSTRACT

One of the main goals of the renewed Syro-German excavations in Tell Halaf is the reconstruction of its history during the Iron Age. According to the ceramics discovered in the earliest Iron Age levels, the predecessor settlement of the Aramaean town of Gozan/ Guzana was founded by immigrants from Eastern Anatolia. Probably they were settled outside the gates of the Middle Assyrian provincial town of Aššukanni, modern Tell Fekheriye, by the Assyrian government in the early 11th century. After the occupation by Aramaean tribes and its reconquering by the Assyrians the town underwent major reconstructions and changes in its layout.[1] *Thus, several breaks can be traced in the material culture of the site, each time followed by distinguished acculturations.*

INTRODUCTION

In 2006 a Syro-German mission started new excavations at Tell Halaf in northeastern Syria, precisely 77 years after the end of the large-sized explorations of Max von Oppenheim at this site. It revealed both a prehistoric settlement with a characteristic type of painted pottery and the capital of an Aramaean principality with a previously unknown monumental art dating to the early Iron Age. The new project is conducted by the General Directorate of Antiquities and Museums in Damascus and the Museum

[1] The project is co-directed by Abdel Mesih Baghdo (Damascus/Hassake), Lutz Martin (Berlin) and the present author. The prehistoric levels are investigated by Jörg Becker (Halle). I thank the General Directorate of Antiquities and Museums and all the authorities of the Syrian Arab Republic for their helpful support and all colleagues involved in the project for their ambitious work, which made this overview possible. Alexander Ahrens requires thank for improving the manuscript. I am indebted to Aslıhan Yener for offering the opportunity to participate at the present volume.

of Ancient Near Eastern Art in Berlin in collaboration with the Universities of Munich, Tübingen and Halle-Wittenberg.

Besides other aims, the new research has gained further information on the chronology of the Iron Age settlement and revealed new and unexpected insights into the early history of the ancient city of Guzana.Surprisingly, there is now evidence for the settlement being founded by immigrants from southeastern Anatolia, prior to the well-known state formation of the Aramaeans during the 10th century BC.

The Site

Tell Halaf is situated in Northern Mesopotamia at one of the sources of the Khabur-River, the major tributary of the Euphrates. One of the main trade routes connecting Assyria with the Northern Levant and the Mediterranean passed through the region, known in Neo-Assyrian times as the *harran šarri*, i.e. the "King's Road" (**Fig. 1**, the route starting in Ḥalab and running through Ḫarrān, Gūzāna and Naṣibīna to Ninuwa). It is flanked by the Tur Abdin mountain range to the north and the Jebel Abdel-Aziz to the south, both running in an east-west direction. The area comprises good conditions for agriculture since it is located within the stable rain-fed zone and is additionally supplied with water by a large number of natural sources. Nowadays, Tell Halaf lies immediately south of the Syrian-Turkish border near the modern twin towns of Ra's al-Ain (Syria) and Ceylanpınar (Turkey).

Just 2.5 km to the east lies Tell Fekheriye, ancient Waššukanni/Sikani, with which Tell Halaf formed a twin site. The regional urban centre always changed between these two sites; Pre-Pottery Neolithic levels are attested at Tell Fekheriye, Pottery Neolithic and Chalcolithic occupation at Tell Halaf. The Bronze Age is present at Tell Fekheriye again and the Iron Age, including the Hellenistic period, appears at Tell Halaf. The last shift back to Tell Fekheriye, which became the core of modern Ra's al-Ain, took place during the Parthian period.

The archaeological site of Tell Halaf consists of a high mound, the location of the Iron Age citadel (**Figs 2 and 3**), and an extended lower town, enclosing the citadel to the west, south, and east. Altogether, the Iron Age settlement covers an area of approximately 75 ha. Within the fortified citadel, a number of buildings were excavated by Max von Oppenheim during his campaigns in 1911–13 and in 1929.[2] The most prominent were the so-called *Hilani* or "Western Palace" in the western area with the adjacent "Scorpion's Gate", and the "Northeastern Palace". While the former was extensively decorated by monumental caryatid statues and carved relief slabs and is dated by inscriptions of the Aramaean ruler Kapara (Fig. 4), the latter lacked direct

[2] The results were published by Schmidt 1943, Langenegger *et al.* 1950; Moortgart 1955; Hrouda 1962; Cholidis and Martin 2010. A reappraisal of the former excavations is given by Orthmann 2002.

indications for a chronological date. Therefore, it was labelled as the dwelling palace of Kapara by the first excavators. Other important buildings discovered by Oppenheim on the mound were two massive mudbrick tombs north of the *Hilani* and a number of burials close to the southern citadel gate, of which two contained female statues for an ancestor cult. In the lower town, the "Cultic Room," presumably another tomb with statues for an ancestor cult, an Assyrian temple, a couple of dwelling houses and large parts of the defensive wall were excavated.

Apart from these, Oppenheim and his team discovered large quantities of painted pottery dating to the prehistoric occupation of the site. Thus, Tell Halaf gave its name to a period of the late Pottery Neolithic in Northern Mesopotamia.

The Renewed Excavations

The goals of the joint Syro-German mission are the following: investigation of the nature and chronology of the prehistoric settlement, the chronology of the Iron Age town, the spatial organisation and functional structure of ancient Guzana, the acculturation processes of the Aramaeans at the time of their domination, and after the incorporation of the polity into the Assyrian empire, the "cultural orientation" of the Hellenistic settlement and the organisation of subsistence throughout the occupation history.

A number of excavation areas have been opened since 2006:[3] Sector A explored the area of the *Hilani* and the southern part of the citadel, Sector B was dedicated to the investigation of the prehistoric levels and Sector C stretched all over the eastern part of the citadel, including the "Northeastern Palace". In the lower town the operations concentrated on the "Cultic Room" (Sector D), the "City Temple" (Sector E), the fortification wall (Sector F) and the residences south of the river Khabur in the eastern part of the lower town (Sector G).

The First Settlers: "Chaff Tempered Ware People" and "Groovy Pottery People"

Tell Halaf contains a considerably extended prehistoric settlement, which was inhabited during the entire Pottery Neolithic (i.e. "Hassuna" and "Halaf") and the Chalcolithic (i.e. "Late Ubaid" and "Uruk") periods. Well constructed building remains, e.g. a large house excavated in 2009 (**Fig.** 5), attest to the importance of the site during these periods. Most of these houses consisted of a circular room and an adjacent rectangular room. Due to the results of the recent excavations, it seems that

[3] On the recent excavations *cf.* Baghdo et al. 2009; Martin and Novák 2010.

the prehistoric site consisted of a series of smaller mounds neighbouring each other with deep depressions in between.

Neither the old nor the renewed excavations have brought to light any indications for a Bronze Age settlement at Tell Halaf, except for very few sherds. Obviously, the site was abandoned for nearby Tell Fekheriye, which at that time formed the urban centre of the area and can well be identified as the Mittani capital Waššukanni and the Middle-Assyrian provincial town Aššukanni

Middle Assyrian domination over the Khabur triangle partly collapsed after the last campaigns of Tiglath-Pileser I in the late 11th century BC, whereas it continued uninterrupted into Neo-Assyrian times in the areas around Hassake and the lower Khabur, as indicated by the results of the excavations at Kahat (Tell Barri), Tabete (Tell Taban), Šadikanni (Tell Ajaja) and Dūr-Katlimmu (Tell ŠeikhHamad).

This "period of change" is represented by the replacement of the administrative buildings at Tell Sabi Abyad, Tell Chuera (and presumably also at Tell Fekheriye) by cemeteries. At Tell Halaf, a sequence of simple domestic architectural units on the northern slope of the mound and the so-called *"Terrassenschüttung"* to the east and north of the *Hilani* represent the earliest occupation after a hiatus of almost 1000 years.

The *"Terrassenschüttung,"* a massive filling consisting of hard and sterile mud, was accumulated inside the depressions between the former prehistoric mounds to create an even surface for the new buildings. The pottery found in it and within some small house units discovered at the northern slope of the citadel mound was a wheel made, crude, and chaff tempered ware with simple forms consisting of thick sides and profiles, mainly bowls and pots (**Fig. 6**). Besides that, a few sherds of the hand-made "Groovy Pottery", known from sites along the Upper Euphrates[4], were discovered (**Fig.** 7). K. Bartl[5] has drawn attention to the fact that Oppenheim's excavations had already revealed examples of this pottery, which was attributed to the prehistoric levels by mistake. Only few parallels of these wares were discovered in the Khabur region so far. This could be explained by the fact that most of the other sites like Tell Barri, Tell Taban, Tell Ajaja and Tell ŠeikhHamad were never lost to Assyrian control (and culture respectively). Some sherds of the "Groovy Pottery" found at Kahat (Barri Phase 2)[6] can be dated to the period immediately after the reign of Aššur-bēl-kala (1073–56 BC).

The historical background of the appearance of the "Groovy Pottery" is unclear. However, it seems most unlikely that this pottery can be seen as trade good or even as container of organic transportation good. It is obviousely a ceramic made for cooking,

[4] *Cf.* Müller 1999.
[5] Bartl 1989.
[6] d'Agostino 2009.

eating and drinking. Since it is far from being a luxury ware, it is most probably really the indication for people, who brought their ceramic from other regions to Upper Mesopotamia during their migration. One possibility is a connection with groups coming from the Upper Euphrates region, which are mentioned by Tiglath-Pileser I as *Mušku* and *Kašku*, former subjects of the, at that time collapsed Hittite Empire (**Fig. 8**).[7] It is not unlikely that they were re-settled close to the still existing city of Aššukanni after their defeat. Thus, the new village was founded on a ruined prehistoric mound and became the core of the future site of Guzana.

From Assimilation to Refoundation: The Emergence of the Aramaeans

Along with the growth of the village, an assimilation of Assyrian culture took place. The area in the northwest of the mound, now flattened by the artificial filling of the depressions between the peaks, became a burial ground. Several mudbrick cist graves were built, not unlike the late Middle Assyrian tombs known from Tell Fekheriye, dated to the 11th or early 10th century BC. Four similar graves were excavated in 2007–2009, all situated north and northeast of the later *Hilani*-Palace. The best preserved of these contained the skeleton of a 15 year old girl and a considerable number of grave goods, like textiles, a necklace with a large number of beads, a scarab and several iron rings (**Fig. 9**). The pottery vessels, which were deposited close to the head of the deceased, are reminiscent of the pottery from the late Middle Assyrian layers and tombs from Tell Fekheriye. Nevertheless, they are thick and chaff-tempered, still in the tradition of the local ware. Max von Oppenheim had discovered two monumental mud brick tombs right to the north-east of the *Hilani* with an uncertain stratigraphic relation to Kapara's building.[8] One of them was not plundered and found intact; it contained elite grave goods, e.g. several appliqués made of gold and a number of ivory carvings. It now seems probable that both tombs belonged to the same cemetery, just like the cist graves recently discovered, and thus predate Kapara.

The architecture of the tombs and cist graves, as well as the objects, clearly show that the assimilation of Middle Assyrian culture by the local population had already reached a high degree at that time. Furthermore, the luxury grave goods, consisting of precious materials like gold, iron, and ivory, indicate the existence of a new local elite, now competing with the inhabitants of Aššukanni.

Already during the 11th century BC Aramaean tribes emerged in the areas of Upper Mesopotamia and beyond. Tiglath-Pileser I had to defend the Assyrian empire against

[7] Tiglath-Pileser I mentions in his inscriptions that 20.000 people from Mušku had attacked the province of Katmuhu. 4000 Kašku and Urumu, both former subjects to the Hittite king occupied the cities of Shupria. The Mušku came from Alšu, an area along the Upper Euphrates, from which the "Groovy Pottery" probably derived. Cf. Baghdo *et al.* 2009, p. 93.

[8] *Cf.* Orthmann 2002, pp. 47–50.

these raiding tribes, mostly on the banks of the Euphrates and in the Syrian steppe. His son Aššur-bēl-kala had to face the aggressors even along the Upper Khabur. In the early 10th century, Aramaic tribes founded a number of principalities on the grounds of the former Middle Assyrian Empire (**Fig. 10**). The most prominent were those of the Temanides in Nasibina, Gidara and to the west of the Kaššiyari mountains (i.e. the Tur Abdin mountain range), as well as Bit-Zammani along the Upper Tigris and Palê/Bit-Bakhiani at the sources of the Khabur.[9]

The earliest rulers known from Palê are Hadianu and his son Kapara.[10] Since the former is only known from the written sources of the latter, it can be doubted if he ever ruled in a residential city; perhaps he was still just the chief of a nomadic tribe. Kapara claimed in his inscriptions that he had "done what his father and grandfather never did," probably the act of building a palace in an urban capital. His principality is named Palê in his inscription, the later designation of the principality, Bit-Bakhiani, does not appear yet. Obviously, Bakhiani was a successor of Kapara, who was not a direct precendant and the founder of a new dynasty. The capital of his kingdom was named Gozan/Guzana, the ancient name of Tell Halaf.

After a period of weakness and reconsolidation, Assyria re-started its expansion to the west in the early 9th century. Adad-nerari II collected the tribute of the Aramaic kingdoms of the Khabur and Balikh. Later, he seized Nasibina and Gidara and re-founded Huzirina near Harran. When he appeared at Guzana, its ruler Abisalamu was wise enough to pay tribute and subordinate himself to Assyria. Nevertheless, he did not open his capital city for the Assyrians, but met the Assyrian king in Sikani, former Aššukanni, a city with an Assyrian history.

In the two generations to follow, Bit-Bakhiani remained loyal to Assyria until the replacement of the local dynasts by Assyrian governors.

The Aramaic City of Guzana

It was probably Kapara who chose Tell Halaf as the capital of his Aramaic kingdom. No inscriptions of any of his predecessors, e.g. his father Hadianu mentioned above, were discovered so far.

The layout of the town was changed dramatically. The former burial ground in the northwest of the mound was abandoned, in some cases the architecture of the mud brick cists tombs was heavily damaged by the new structures. The area became the building ground for a representative palace in the western Syrian "*Hilani* style," decorated with huge caryatide statues of the main deities at its entrance and a large number of relief slabs along the south and north façades. Connected to the palace, the so-

[9] *Cf.* Sader 1987; Lipinski 2000.
[10] *Cf.* Dornauer in Cholidis and Martin 2010.

called "Scorpion's Gate" gave access to the inner part of the citadel. It also contained rich and monumental decorations.

The whole mound was transformed into a fortified citadel, accessible only from the south via a gate. An inner part of the citadel was separated from an outer one by another defensive wall. The "Scorpion's Gate" was part of this inner wall. Presumably the fortified Lower Town was also founded in this period.

Since the former cemetery was abandoned for the *Hilani* palace, a new burial ground had to be established. The area immediately south of the citadel's fortification and east of the outer citadel gate was chosen as the burial place of the elites. Oppenheim discovered a number of chapel-like buildings, each consisting of one or two rooms. Two of them contained monumental statues, depicting women sitting and holding cups in their right hands (**Fig. 11**). This specific kind of statue was dedicated and linked to the ancestor cult and already had a long tradition in Syria at that time, similar to Middle Bronze Age statues from Qatna and Ebla clearly indicate. Below one of the statues, an urn was discovered containing the cremated bones of the deceased and some luxury grave goods. It is of high interest that the burial customs had apparently drastically changed with the foundation of the Aramaen city; inhumation, exclusively practiced in the early cemetery, was now replaced by cremations. The reason behind this change is still unknown, but it might be seen in the light of Neo-Hittite influence.

From Vassals to Governors: The Accession of Guzana

Early in the 9th century, Guzana became a vassal to the Assyrians and remained that for at least two generations. Bit-Bakhiani is only rarely mentioned by Assurnasirpal II and Shalmanessar III. The site contributed troops to the Assyrian army and paid its tribute regularly. At Tell Fekheriye, a statue of a certain Hadda-yiš'i[11] was discovered. He is shown as a worshipper in front of the local Storm God of Sikani.[12] In his bilingual inscription he claims himself to be "governor" (Assyrian version) or "king" (Aramaic version) of Guzana. Although his name argues for an Aramaic origin, his father's name Šamaš-nuri is clearly Akkadian/Assyrian. Thus, it is uncertain if Hadda-yiš'i was a descendant of the local Aramaic dynasty, integrating himself into the governmental system of the Assyrian Empire, or an Assyrian official, who took the position of a local king for the sake of being better accepted by the local population. This would be similar to the function of the Middle Assyrian governor of Upper Mesopotamia as "King of Hanigalbat." An identification of his father with the Assyrian eponym of the year 866 would be in favour with the latter solution. If so, Guzana was already

[11] Abu Assaf *et al.* 1982.

[12] On the Storm God of Sikani and Guzana *cf.* Kessler and Müller-Kessler 1995.

completely incorporated into the Assyrian provincial system during the reign of Shalmanesser III, the period to which the statue should thus date.

Guzana became one of the most important provincial towns of the Assyrian Empire. Its governor had the right to be limmu eponym in the 16th or 17th year of each Assyrian king. Probably Šamaš-nuri was first eponym, who owed this honour to his position as governor of Guzana. The activities of his successor Mannu-ki-Assur, eponym of the year 793, are well attested by his archive, discovered by Max von Oppenheim in the southern part of his palace.

Only two events disturbed the peaceful history of Guzana as provincial town and seat of a regional governor. In 808 BC, Adad-nerari III undertook a campaign against the city. Due to the lack of any further information, the reason for that military act remains completely obscure. In 761–758 Guzana participated, together with Arrapha and Kalhu, in a revolt against the eunuch Šamši-ilu, the true ruler of the empire at that time.[13] The city was besieged for two years and then finally captured. After that, it remained the seat of a governor until the fall of the Assyrian Empire in 609 BC. Even afterwards the town was of some importance until it was abandoned in the Parthian period.

A Provincial Town: Guzana in the Assyrian Period

The architectural layout of the city of Guzana was once again completely changed during the Assyrian period. Although the fortification walls of the Lower Town and the citadel and some major buildings like the *Hilani*-Palace were kept in use, the inner structure of the citadel was again modified. Huge and high mudbrick terraces were built in the south and east of the citadel, both incorporating and overbuilding the fortification wall and stretching out of the former limit of the citadel into the area of the Lower Town.

The southern mud brick terrace became the substructure of the residences of the elite, which were well preserved and contained rich inventories. The cemetery of the Kapara period was thoroughly covered by this terrace, without destroying the ancestor statues.

The eastern part of the citadel was chosen to be the area of the governor's palace, erected on top of a massive mud brick terrace (**Fig. 12**). The building, which was founded in the 9th century, saw one major reconstruction with significant changes in its formal and functional layout. Since the archive of Mannu-ki-Assur was discovered within the debris of this first phase, the reconstruction must have occurred after 793 BC, presumably caused by severe damages during the capture of Guzana in 758 BC. The second phase of the palace was succeeded by a third phase with nearly

[13] Baghdo *et al.* 2009, p. 96.

the same layout. Due to the date of the inventories discovered on these floors, the occupation of the palace lasted at least until the Late Babylonian period.

The Lower Town of Guzana was densely inhabited during the Neo-Assyrian period. Apart from a temple built on an artificial platform, ordinary houses and elite residences were also excavated. The discovery of the statue of a certain Kammaki, presumably a member of one of the Aramaic elite families of Guzana, living in the 8th century BC is also of interest (**Fig. 13**).[14] The style of the statue is clearly in the tradition of the other ancestor statues known from the cemetery at the citadel gate and from the so-called "Cultic Room" close to the southern border of the city. This highlights the still vivid Aramaic traditions at Guzana, also exemplified by the emergence of the Aramaic script and language even in the official administration of the town.

Conclusions

As this short overview aimed to demonstrate, a re-evaluation of the results of Max von Oppenheim's excavations in the light of the new research may give new insights into the early history of Iron Age Tell Halaf, the ancient city of Guzana. As opposed to the presumptions based exclusively on early research, the town does not appear to be established by Aramaeans *ex nihilo*. It seems that a small settlement was founded by immigrants coming from the north, from areas in the southeast of the collapsed Hittite empire. The Aramaeans, who gained control over the region during the 10th century, moved the administrative center from Tell Fekheriye in favor of their new residential city Guzana. How and why this happened are still open questions, hopefully to be answered in the future by further excavations.

Bibliography

ABU ASSAF, A., BORDREUIL, P. and MILLARD, A. R.
1982 *La statue de Tell Fekheriyé et son inscription bilingue assyro-araméene*, Paris (= Etudes Assyriologiques 7).

D'AGOSTINO, A.
2009 "The Assyrian-Aramaean Interaction in the Upper Khabur: The Archaeological Evidence from Tell Barri Iron Age Layers," *Syria* 86: 17–41.

BAGHDO, A. M., MARTIN, L., NOVÁK, M. and ORTHMANN, W. eds.
2009 *Tell Halaf: Vorberichte über die erste und zweite syrisch-deutsche Grabungskampagne*, Wiesbaden (*Vorderasiatische Forschungen der Max Freiherr von Oppenheim-Stiftung* 3,1).

BARTL, K.
1989 "Zur Datierung der altmonochromen Ware vom Tell Halaf," in *To the Euphrates and Beyond. Archaeological Studies in Honour of Maurits N. van Loon*, edited

[14] Röllig 2003.

by O. M. C. Haex, H. H. Curvers and P. M. M. G. Akkermans, 257–274. Rotterdam.

CHOLIDIS, N. and MARTIN, L. eds.
2010 *Tell Halaf V. Im Krieg zerstörte Denkmäler und ihre Restaurierung*, Berlin/New York.

HROUDA, B.
1962 *Tell Halaf IV.Die Kleinfunde aus historischer Zeit*, Berlin.

KESSLER, K. and MÜLLER-KESSLER, CHR.
1995 "Zum Kult des Wettergottes von Guzana," in *Eski Yakin Doğu Kültürleri Üzerine İncelemeler*, edited by A. Erkanal et al., pp. 239–244. Istanbul.

LANGENEGGER, F., MÜLLER, K. and NAUMANN, R.
1950 *Tell Halaf II. Die Bauwerke*, Berlin.

LIPINSKI, E.
2000 *The Aramaeans*, Orientalia Loveniensia Analecta 100. Leuven.

MARTIN, L. and NOVÁK, M.
2010 "Aramäer und Assyrer auf dem Tell Halaf," *Archäologie in Deutschland* 6/2010: 6–11.

MOORTGAT, A.
1955 *Tell Halaf III. Die Bildwerke*, Berlin.

MÜLLER, U.
1999 "Die eisenzeitliche Keramik des Lidar Höyük," in *Iron Age Pottery in Northern Mesopotamia, Northern Syria and South-Eastern Anatolia*, edited by A. Hausleiter and A. Reiche, pp. 403–434 (*Altertumskunde des Vorderen Orients* 10). Münster.

ORTHMANN, W.
2002 *Die aramäisch-assyrische Stadt Guzana*, Saarbrücken.

RÖLLIG, W.
2003 "Das Sitzbild des Kammaki vom Tell Halaf," in *Altertumswissenschaften im Dialog. Festschrift für Wolfram Nagel*, Alter Orient und Altes Testament 306, edited by R. Dittmann, Chr. Eder and B. Jacobs, pp. 421–432. Münster.

SADER, H.
1987 *Les États Araméens de Syrie*, Beiruter Texte und Studien 36. Wiesbaden and Beirut.

SCHMIDT, H.
1943 *Tell Halaf I. Die Prähistorischen Funde*, Berlin.

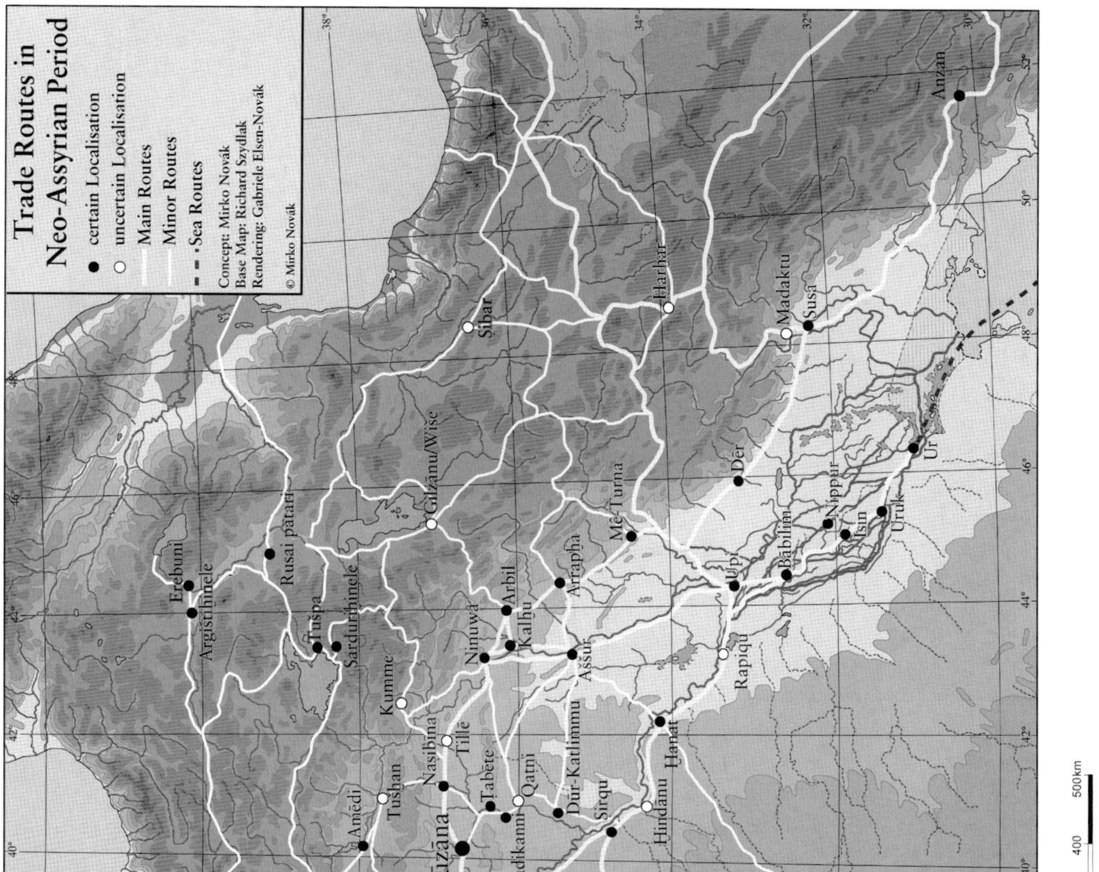

Fig. 1 Map showing the Road System in Ancient Near East during the Iron Age.

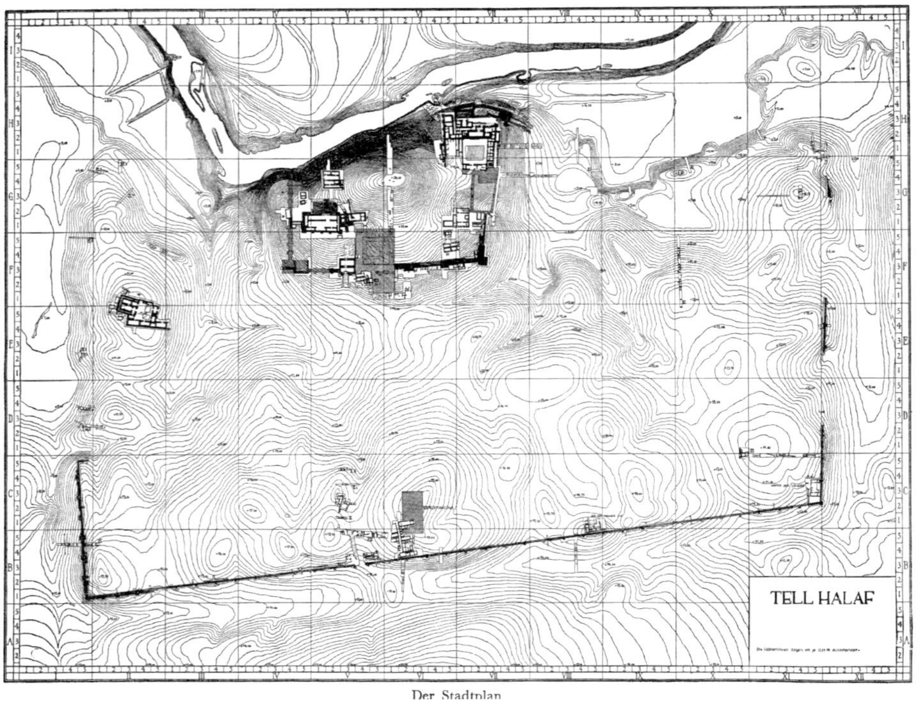

Fig. 2 Plan of the City of Guzana.

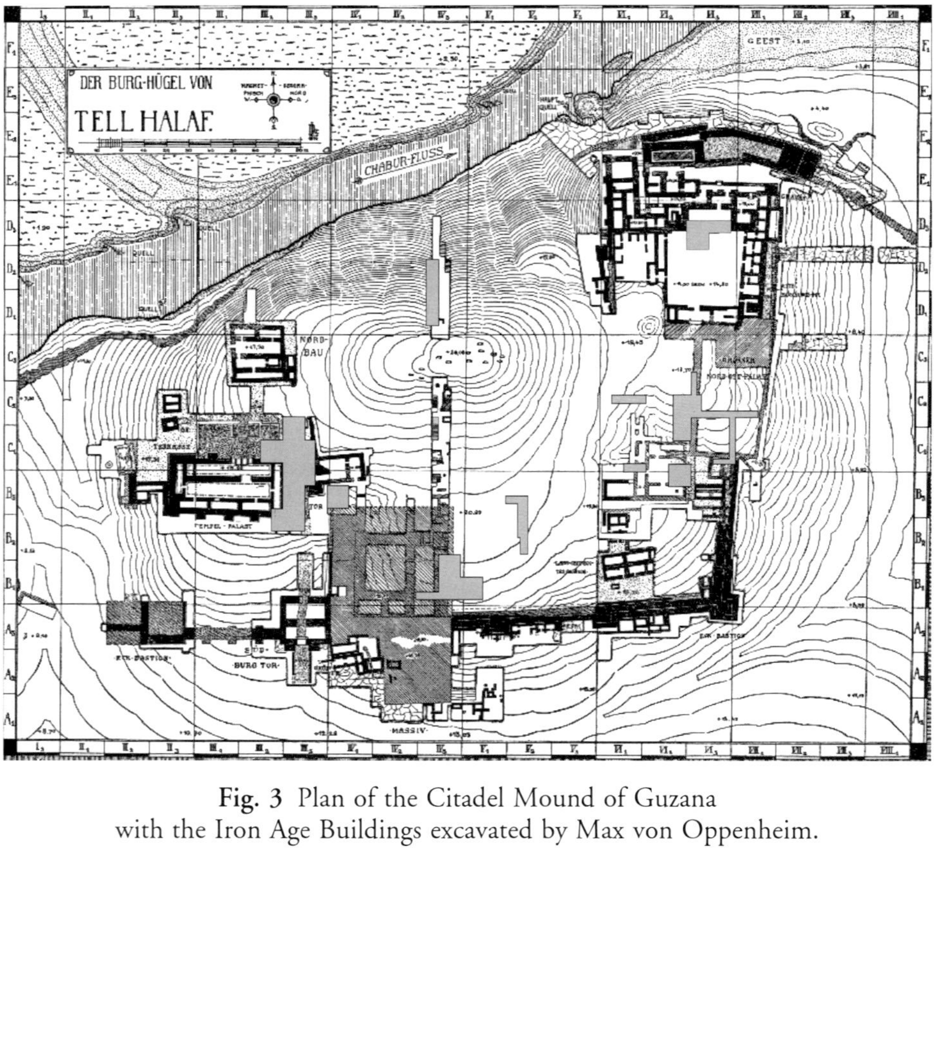

Fig. 3 Plan of the Citadel Mound of Guzana
with the Iron Age Buildings excavated by Max von Oppenheim.

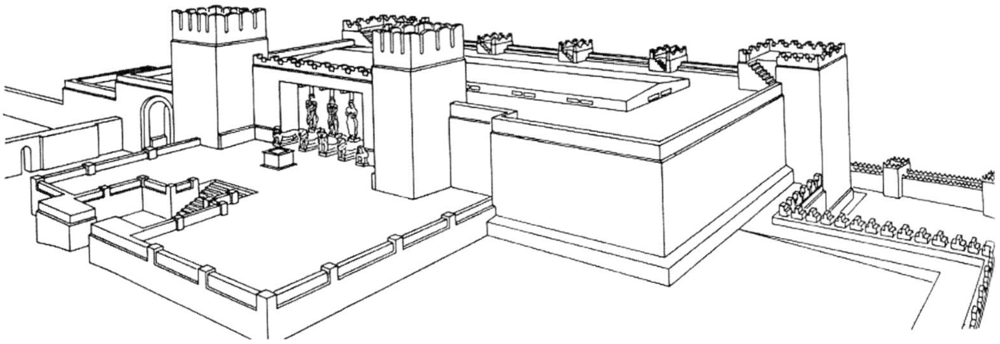

Fig. 4 Reconstruction of the *Hilani*-Palace.

Fig. 5 Building from the Halaf-Period excavated in 2009 (Photo by G. Mirsch).

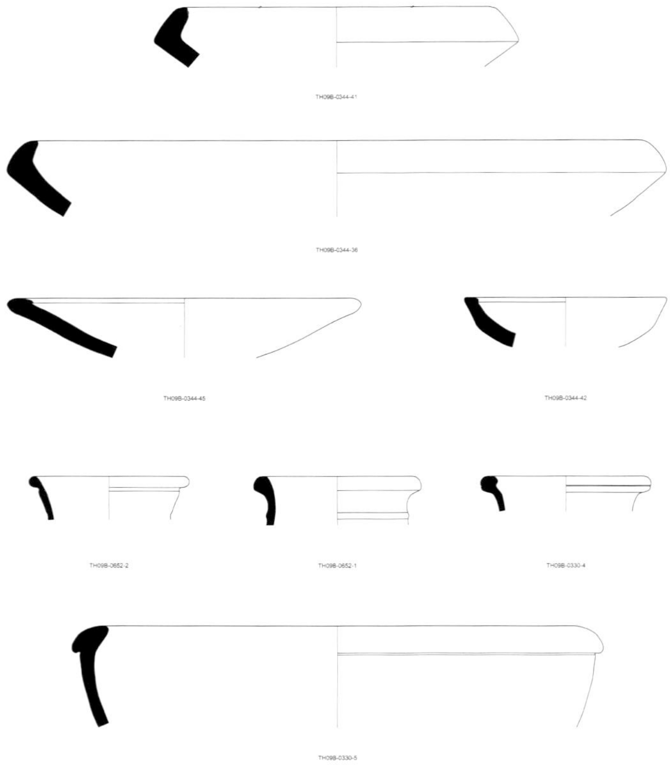

Fig. 6 Early Iron Age "Chaff-tempered Ware" from the new Excavations (drawing by Ch. Radovanov and G. Elsen-Novák).

Fig. 7 Sherd of the "Groovy Pottery" discovered below the Governor's Palace (Photo by L. Simons).

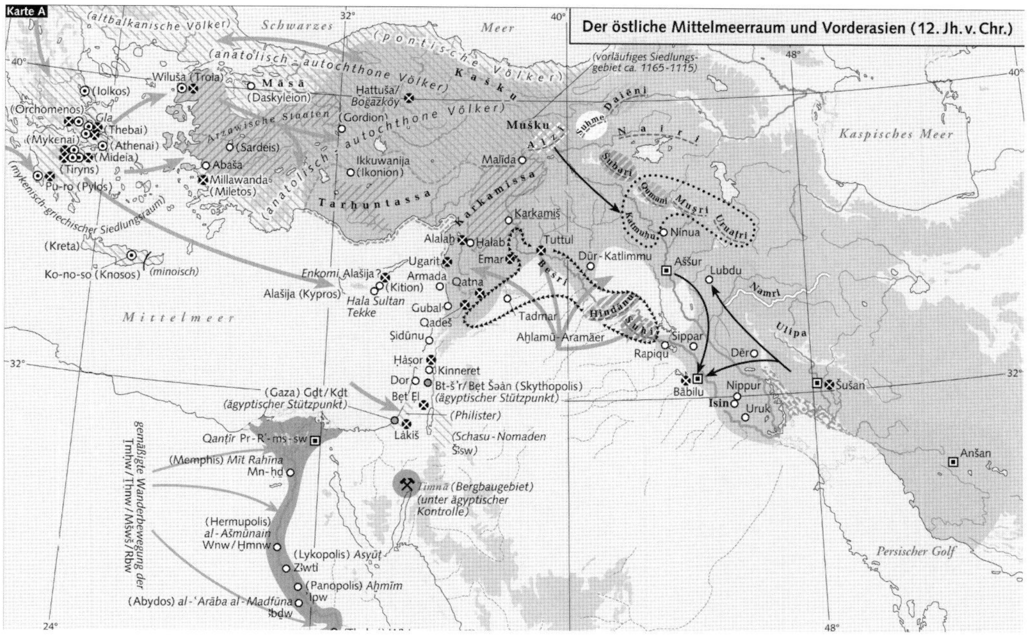

Fig. 8 Map showing the political Situation during the 12th/11th century BC (rendering by R. Szydlak for *Der Neue Pauly*, *Historischer Atlas der Antiken Welt*).

Fig. 9 Mud Brick Cist Grave discovered in 2008 (Photo by L. Simons).

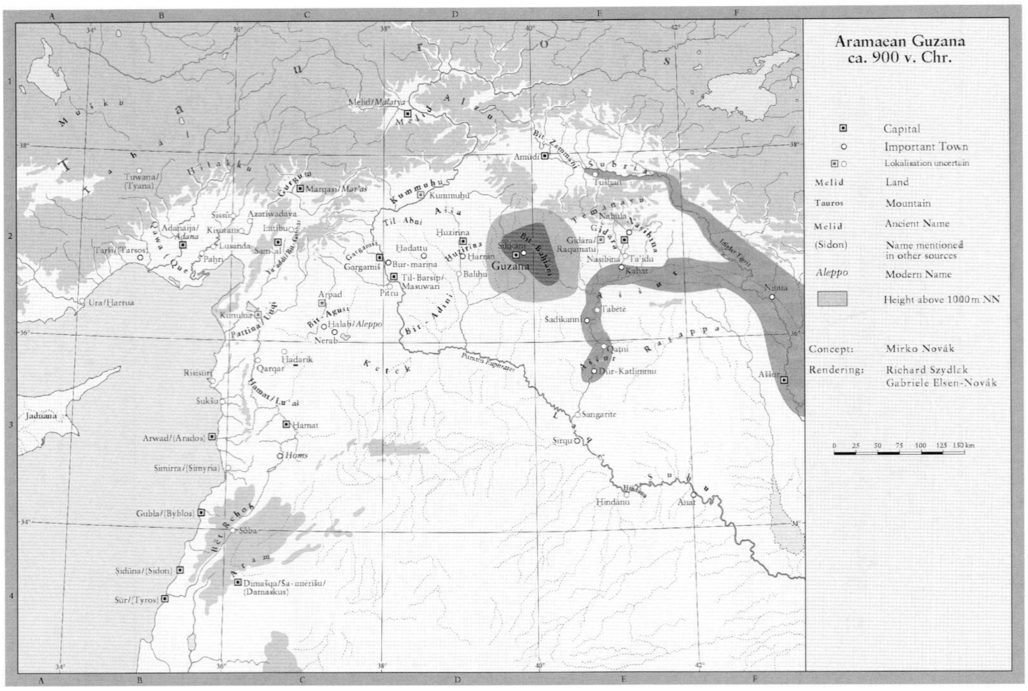

Fig. 10 Map showing the Extension of the Aramaean Principality of Palê/Bīt-Bakhiani.

Fig. 11 Ancestor's Cult Statue of an Elite Woman discovered above a Cremation Burial east of the Citadel Gate.

Fig. 12 Overview on the new Excavations of the Southern Part of the Assyrian Governor's Palace (Photo by D. Vogl).

Fig. 13 Statue of Kammaki, son of the scribe Ilu-le'i (taken from Röllig 2003, p. 432).

CHAPTER 13

SOME IMPLICATIONS OF REVISED C14 AND DENDROCHRONOLOGICAL DATING FOR THE "LATE BRONZE LEVELS" AT TİLLE HÖYÜK ON THE EUPHRATES

Geoffrey D. SUMMERS
Adjunct Associate Professor
Koç University Research Center
for Anatolian Civilizations
Istanbul
Turkey
E-mail: summersgd@gmail.com

ABSTRACT

Very recent re-examination of the burnt timbers from the monumental gate at Tille Höyük on the Euphrates River has implications for both Tille Höyük itself and the wider region during the transition from the Late Bronze Age to the Iron Age. AMS dating and a consequent reassessment of the dendrochronology has lowered the dates for the construction of the first phase of the gate, and thus of the pottery associated with it. This lower dating of the gate also impacts on the date of post-destruction levels at Tille and by extension on the Early Iron Age chronology at other excavated sites in South-Eastern Turkey. This paper addresses some of the implications of the lower dating.[*]

Between 1979 and 1990 the British Institute of Archaeology at Ankara under the direction of David French conducted rescue excavations at Tille Höyük, a medium sized settlement mound on the west bank of the Euphrates River in the province of Adıyaman. The site is now submerged by the waters of the Atatürk Dam (**Figs. 1 and 2**). When I joined the team in 1984 the excavation of well preserved structures of the latest Iron Age level was at an advanced stage.[1] At this time earlier strata could be glimpsed in the sides and bottoms of pits that had been dug down from medieval and Hellenistic levels and which had been emptied in the course of controlled stratigraphic

* Güzin Eren, Cheedem Ozkan and Françoise Summers assisted with illustration. I thank Nicholas Postgate and Marie-Henriette Gates for helpful discussion and Noël Siver for assiduous reading of the text, as well as Aslıhan Yener and an anonymous referee for suggesting improvements. Errors and opinions are entirely my own.

[1] Blaylock 2009, Level X.

excavation. The lowest of these strata to be thus exposed, towards the western edge of the mound, included parts of what was clearly a monumental structure built of large mudbricks. This entire level seemed to have been destroyed by fire. Sherds extracted from the burnt debris clearly resembled what had already become known as Late Imperial Hittite "drab ware" that was generally thought to mark the end of the Late Bronze Age in the Keban region, particularly at the site of Norşuntepe.[2]

The final excavation report on this Burnt Level and earlier strata, published as *Tille Höyük 4: The Late Bronze Age and the Iron Age Transition,* contained an appendix by Peter Kuniholm, Shana Tarter and Carol Griggs that offered dendrochronological dates for the two phases of a substantial gateway which had surely formed a part of defences on the western side of the mound. These dates were based on such carbonised wood as it had been possible to recover from the Burnt Level, the majority of samples coming from the gateway (**Fig. 3**). At least some of the timber elements found in the passage appeared to have been planks rather than beams. The burnt wood was not well preserved and difficult to lift, while analysis of the samples at Cornell was made yet more difficult by the mistaken use of plaster of paris to bind together charcoal that delaminated as it was exposed. The initial publication presented two dates, one for each of the two phases of the Gateway. Confidence in the legitimacy of these dates was inspired by the completely independent identifications of two building phases, one stratigraphic made by the present author, the other dendrochronological made by the Cornell team.[3] The date suggested for the construction of the first phase in *Tille Höyük IV* was 1209 +/-37 BCE while the modification was put at 1140 +/-37 BCE. In 1995 the entire dendrochronological sequence for Anatolia constructed by Peter Kuniholm and his team at Cornell was moved down, with the result that the felling date for timbers used in the modifications to the gateway was lowered to one side or other of 1101 BCE. In yet another reassessment this date was then raised to 1123 +4/-7 BCE. Stuart Blaylock perspicaciously regarded these dates as provisional.[4] In 2009 Carol Griggs and Sturt Manning at the Malcolm and Carolyn Wiener Laboratory for Aegean and Near Eastern Dendrochronology at Cornell University published in *Radiocarbon* the results of their careful re-examination of the Tille Höyük charcoals.[5] These new results provided two, or perhaps three dates, for the cutting of the oak timbers incorporated into the Tille Höyük gateway. The first and last of these dates can fairly safely be taken to coincide with the two building phases of the gateway that, as just noted, were independently identified through both excavation and by the Cornell team's original dendrochronological study. According to this most recent study, construction of the first phase should

[2] Korbel 1985 and 1987, Müller 2005, pp. 108–112.
[3] Kuniholm *et al.* in Summers 1993, p. 180.
[4] Blaylock 2009
[5] Griggs and Manning 2009.

now be placed at about 1150 BCE while modifications to the standing gate structure are now calculated to have been made approximately 60 years later, that is, around 1090 BCE (**Table 1**). The length of time that elapsed between the felling of the trees and destruction of the Gateway by fire is uncertain. While there is no good reason to question the archaeological indications, as they were understood at the time of the excavation, that the fire consumed the entire settlement and was not restricted to the gateway, no evidence was recovered that permits us to decide whether the fire was a result of hostile action or of some unfortunate accident. On the other hand, the date of about 1090 BCE for the modifications to the gateway are not incompatible with the theory that the destruction was related with the campaigns of the Assyrian King Tiglath-Pileser I (1114–1076) into the Middle Euphrates region.[6] In any event the burnt defences do not seem to have been replaced but, rather, to have slowly crumbled.[7] The length of the hiatus following the conflagration is difficult to assess, as indeed is the amount of time that should be allotted to the poor structures and pits that were identified as falling between the Burnt Level and Blaylock's Early Iron Age Level I.[8]

	TİLLE GATE PHASE 1	TİLLE GATE PHASE 2
Old Dates	*c.* 1210 +/-37 BCE	*c.* 1140 +/-37 BCE
Revised Dates	*c.* 1193 +4/-7 BCE	*c.* 1123 +4/-7 BCE
NEW DATES	***c.* 1150 BCE**	***c.* 1090 BCE**

Table 1: Cornell felling dates for the Tille Höyük Gate.
The fire is now to be dated to some unknown time after *ca.* 1090 BCE.

The complexities of archaeometric dating methods are such that archaeologists have little choice but to cautiously accept these new dates from Cornell in the expectation that the level of scientific rigour now applied is so stringent that they are, in all probability, correct. On the other hand, that there is no glaring archaeological evidence to arouse suspicion about these newly revised dates for Tille Höyük might be thought to provide some measure of comfort. The positive approach adopted here entails an attempt to unravel some of the ramifications of the new chronology for our understanding of the end of the Late Bronze Age and the beginning of the Iron Age in this portion of the Euphrates basin and beyond. The longstanding view that the Hittite capital, Hattuša, and other cities that lay within the bend of the Kızılırmak: Oymaağaç, Hittite Nerik; Ortaköy, Hittite Šapinuwa; Kuşaklı (Sivas), Hittite Sarissa; and Kuşaklı/Uşaklı (Yozgat), Hittite Zippalanda, to take only the most obvious,[9]

[6] Summers 1993, p. 11; Venturi 2007, p. 44 and Blaylock 2009, p. 22.
[7] Blaylock 2009, pp. 62–78.
[8] Blaylock 1999, pp. 62–63.
[9] For a recent appraisal of Hittite geography see Forlanini 2008.

were destroyed by sackings and burnings which marked the collapse of complex urban civilisation, and that a similar and presumably related event can be indisputably recognised at Ugarit, still seem to hold true even if there might be some need of fine tuning. However, it has long been recognized that this simple picture of twelfth century collapse is not applicable across the entire Eastern Mediterranean and the Ancient Near East.[10] By the same token, it is as well to remember that "Late Bronze Age" and "Iron Age" are terms that we archaeologists have invented and which we use as convenient labels in our attempts to impose order, and preferably simplicity, on the realities of historical and archaeological complexities which we study. Thus, while the date of the destruction by fire of the gateway at Tille Höyük is now recognised as falling significantly later than the long accepted 1200–1180 date for the collapse of the Hittite core, Stuart Blaylock might not be incorrect in retaining the idea this dramatic event can usefully be taken to mark the end of the Late Bronze Age at Tille Höyük.[11] Further, dividing the Late Bronze Age from the Iron Age at the Tille Höyük Burnt Level is not inconsistent with the situation reported in the upper Tigris area, notably at Ziyaret Tepe and Giricano, but also seen more generally. Along the upper Tigris River as well as across the Jazirah the Late Bronze Age is marked by the end of the Middle Assyrian Period rather than by events on the northern fringes of the Anatolian Plateau.[12] But neither the archaeological nor the historical trajectories of Hatti and Middle Assyria were the same. My own preference is to use "Transitional" for the two phases of the Tille Höyük gateway and to begin the Early Iron Age with Blaylock's "Deposits pre-dating Level I".[13] While the extent of any hiatus between the Burnt Level at Tille Höyük and the Deposits pre-dating Level I occupation of the earliest Iron Age might be unclear, the orientations of these first Iron Age structures are clearly different to those of the Burnt Level. There are, however, no obvious indications of a lengthy period of abandonment.[14] Stubs of the Burnt Level walls were still extant when the earliest archaeologically coherent structural level, Iron Age Level I, was built with ruinous mudbrick walling occasionally incorporated into the new scheme. Assessment of the extent to which the ceramics display continuity from the Burnt Level into the Early Iron Age must await publication of *Tille Höyük 3.2.*[15]

[10] For instance, Ward and Joukowsky, editors, 1992.

[11] Blaylock 2009, p. xx. However, on pp. 62–63 Blaylock describes Early Iron Age "Deposits predating Level I" which include a structural phase followed by pits that "suggests the passage of a significant passage of time".

[12] Roaf and Schachner 2005,

[13] Blaylock 2009, pp. 62–63; Transitional is preferable to "Sub-Hittite" which carries both cultural and historical connotations.

[14] Blaylock 2009, pp. 62–67 with inset to Figure 5.11 on page 67.

[15] Blaylock, *Tille Höyük* 3.2, in preparation.

"Late Bronze Age Levels" at Tille Höyük

In the light of the new, lower, date for the cutting of the trees used in the construction of the first phase of the Tille Höyük gate, it is perhaps helpful to revisit the Late Bronze Age levels in their entirety.

In *Tille Höyük 4* the pre-Burnt Level strata excavated in the deep sounding on the northwestern corner of the mound were divided into eleven levels, numbered 1 to 11 from the lowest upwards.[16] It is worth re-emphasising that the area of Early Iron Age remains exposed by excavation was very restricted. In addition, there were many intercutting pits of the kind that make close stratigraphic control difficult at the best of times, and even more so given the ever greater haste with which it was necessary to conduct these rescue excavations as completion of the Atatürk Dam approached ever nearer. In *Tille Höyük IV* it was suggested that not only the Burnt Level but all of the excavated strata that preceded it should be dated to the Late Bronze Age. Included in this assessment was the suggestion that there were close parallels between the houses in Tille Level 3 (**Fig.** 4) and Late Bronze Age houses at Emar on the Syrian stretch of the Euphrates River.

Support for this dating came in the form a single Mycenaean sherd (**Fig.** 5) and bifacial seal of well-known Hittite type (**Fig.** 6), neither of which was recovered from a really secure context. Distinctive pottery, a hand-made combed ware and cooking pots with triangular lugs bearing two or three simple impressions (**Fig.** 7), had no known parallels at the time of their discovery, with the result that these ceramics were thought to have been locally produced during the earlier part of the Late Bronze Age. Absent from the assemblages were "Hittite" red slipped ceramics and other hallmarks of Hittite material culture, such as red lustrous ware, libation arms or spindle bottles. However, subsequent publication of excavations at Lidar Höyük and Kurban Höyük demonstrate beyond doubt that this material and the levels in which they were found (Levels 1–8 in the Deep Sounding) should be attributed to the Middle Bronze Age.[17] That the Mycenaean sherd and the biconvex seal were intrusive into Middle Bronze Age levels seems an inevitable conclusion. This reassessment would not be over worrisome were it not for the fact that these two finds now represent the only clear evidence that might point to occupation at Tille Höyük during the Imperial Hittite period. Furthermore, there is no material at all that looks as though it could be related to the Hittite Old Kingdom. While it is true that only a restricted portion of the mound was examined beneath the Burnt Level, 11 years of excavation failed to produce any stray material belonging to the Imperial Hittite period. With regard to the biconvex seal, I see no reason why it

[16] Summers 1993, pp. 17–30.
[17] Algaze 1990; Kaschau 1999.

cannot belong to the same period as the monumental gateway. The fragment of stirrup jar, Elizabeth French kindly informs me, should be ascribed to LH IIIA2/B1 the manufacture of which can be dated to a few years either side of 1300 BC. The date and circumstances of the deposition of this single exotic sherd, however, is open to question.[18]

It may thus be concluded that there was no occupation at Tille Höyük during the time of the Hittite Empire, or at least none of significance. Furthermore, it is difficult to identify any evidence for Imperial Hittite occupation within the entire region of the Atatürk Dam. No Hittite Empire period levels have been reported at the excavated sites of Lidar Hoyük, Gritille, Kurban Höyük or Titrish Höyük. Nor, to the best of my knowledge, was there an Imperial Hittite period occupation at the huge mound of Samsat. Additionally, no site with traces of later second millennium occupation was recognised in the course of the Adıyaman Survey which achieved reasonably complete coverage of the area within Adıyaman province now flooded by the Atatürk Dam.[19] Given the historical importance of Carchemish, downstream from the sites just mentioned, in the later decades of the Hittite Empire this perceived absence of Hittite material in the lower reaches of the Euphrates River north of the Syrian border is somewhat surprising. Perhaps, however, we should rethink Carchemish itself and our, or at least my, assumption that the Imperial Hittite levels of substance lie just below those of the Iron Age that are so well known. Maybe the footprint of the Hittite Empire on the archaeological landscape of Southeastern Turkey and northern Syria is rather slighter than many of us had assumed?

Revised Plans of the First Phase of the Monumental Gate at Tille Höyük

The reconstructed plan of the earliest phase of the Tille Höyük Gateway presented in *Tille Höyük IV* (reproduced here as **Fig. 8** at top) was based on the (wrong) assumption that it had been built in the last decades of Hittite Empire Period, i.e. some short while before *c.* 1180 BCE. Thus the standard Hittite plan of a two chambered gate piercing a casemate wall was suggested. In the recent, more modest, reconstruction, this gateway has been reduced to a single rectangular chamber. An outwork or small buttress provided added protection on the northern side, beyond an internal tower with a rectangular depot containing pithoi that was entered from above (**Fig. 9** at top).[20]

[18] As perspicaciously noted by Collon 1993, p. 173, No.6.

[19] For Samsat see now Özgüç 2009, for the Adıyaman Survey see Blaylock, French and Summers, 1990 and Blaylock 1998b. Lidar Höyük is further discussed below.

[20] This reassessment of the Tille Höyük is presented in greater detail, with the same drawings, in Summers 2010.

The Modified and Burnt Gate

Principle alterations in the second phase of the gateway are now thought to comprise a narrowing of the inner entrance by extension of the flanking buttresses and the addition of substantial stone footings in front of the southern side (**Fig. 9** at bottom).

Some Implications

It is clearly necessary to now completely revise earlier interpretations of this evidence pertaining to the dating of the two phases of the gateway at Tille Höyük. No longer can the remains of the Burnt Level be seen as the embodiment of control over a river crossing from the Hittite Empire through into the Hittite revival of what Timothy Harrison has characterised as a Hittite "rump state" having its capital at Carchemish. Rather, it would now seem, the reoccupation of the mound at Tille (following a long Late Bronze Age hiatus) and the concomitant construction of substantial, but by no means "imperial", defences might be better thought to reflect the rise of the new state on the North Syrian Euphrates together with a new political and strategic concern directed towards control of the river and its limited crossing points in a territory that stretched as far upstream as Melid (Arslantepe, Malatya) on the edge of highlands to the north.[21]

Discussion

Several issues are raised by the new chronology and the reappraisal presented above. Firstly, late Hittite Empire potting traditions can be shown to have continued, albeit in a somewhat degenerate fashion, after the demise of the Hittite core in the Central Highlands of Anatolia. As set out fully in *Tille IV*, Hittite-derived drab ware was in use during the first phase of the gateway at Tille Höyük, now put at around 1150 BCE.[22] Much of this pottery continues to be wheel-made while the exteriors are often scraped, both characteristics of Late Bronze Age potting techniques. On the other hand, rigid standardisation disappears following the demise of a strong overarching state. Certain forms, notably broad-rimmed plates and bowls with internal rims, are absent (**Fig. 10**). By the time of the burning at Tille Höyük, which destroyed the second phase of the gateway, production of plates had ceased whilst other forms had degenerated yet further. As outlined above, the construction of the second phase should perhaps be put about 1090, an unknown number of years

[21] Frangipane and Liverani, this volume.

[22] There was some discussion about the utility of the term "drab ware" at the symposium. Arguably this term is useful even though the occurrence of this rather miserable class of pottery can now be shown to have continued (without potmarks) after the collapse of the Imperial Hittite core.

before the destruction. Potmarks are entirely absent. It is significant that during this long decline of pottery manufactured in a Hittite style there is no evidence whatsoever for painted decoration.

If it is indeed correct that in this portion of the Euphrates Basin and neighbouring regions immediately to the west and east there was little permanent settled occupation during the second half of the Second Millennium BCE it becomes incumbent to seek explanation. In formal discussion during this symposium it was asked if the paucity of evidence for occupation in the Late Bronze Age was a matter of recognition in a zone where taxonomic indicators of Hittite material culture, as known on the Anatolian Plateau, are rare. However, it was just such an assumption that influenced the lower, incorrect, dating of Middle Bronze Age occupation at Tille Höyük in the early 1990s. Another possibility sometimes mooted is a period of adverse climatic conditions such as may have made the region unsuitable for the kind of large-scale rain-fed agriculture on which urban centres depend. But caution is required before the invocation of such climatic or environmental explanations, which trend towards determinism. After all, it was in the time of the Hittite Empire that the Great Kings contested control of North Syria with Egypt. But rainfall in North Syria would always have been lower than along the Turkish stretch of the Euphrates.[23] Perhaps one helpful approach might be to step back from the concept of the Euphrates River as a border or boundary. While the river certainly formed the eastern limit of the Roman Empire for much of its existence, it did not form a cultural boundary in Chalcolithic or Early Bronze Age times when it seems rather to have been a route. It is perhaps also relevant to remind ourselves that in the 20th century CE, before construction of the dam, there were no major settlements on either bank of the Euphrates between the Anatolian Plateau and the Syrian border, not least because of the paucity of drinking water.

To return to Tille Höyük, a long stratified sequence of Early Iron Age phases and sub-phases followed the destruction of the Gateway.[24] Sometime into this sequence there appears the very distinctive and much discussed grooved ware, called ribbed ware at Tille Höyük. Large sherds of a limited range of vessels were excavated, although no pieces were found *in situ* and no complete pots were recovered.[25] Nevertheless, this material was undoubtedly restricted to one horizon within which it formed only one component of the entire ceramic repertoire. At first this stratified sequence appeared to be at variance with evidence from Norşun Tepe and other sites in the Keban region as well as with Lidar Höyük in the southeastern area of the Atatürk Dam, and also

[23] See Blaylock 2009, 1 for comparison of recent preciptation in Adıyaman and Syria and for the broader setting of Tille Höyük in general.

[24] Blaylock 1998a, 1999 and forthcoming.

[25] By *in situ* it is meant that grooved ware was not found in direct association with floors or surfaces on which it had been used. However, the majority of large sherds were recovered from a restricted horizon with the result that their stratigraphic position within the Tille Höyük sequence is firm.

with sites such as Ziyaret Tepe and Giricano in the region of the proposed Ilusu Dam on the Upper Tigris River.[26] The new dates for Tille Höyük reinforce Stuart Blaylock's tentative conclusion that grooved ware would best be placed in the ninth century BCE.[27] The similarities between the limited repertoire of spouted cooking pots from Tille and similar vessels from both the Keban and the Ilusu Dam regions do not permit much chronological leeway even if the duration at Tille Höyük is somewhat shorter than at certain other sites. Nowhere in the southeast of Turkey does this grooved ware appear to be dominant in pottery assemblages, thus it might seem somewhat unwise to equate this distinctive pottery with a mass movement of people. Whether grooved ware, which is very widely distributed, marks a limited infiltration of newcomers, perhaps intermingling with settled folk, was a specialised product manufactured by specialists for a specific purposes or, more probably, requires some other more sophisticated explanation, it is not possible to decide. Equally hard to decide on present evidence is the precise cultural and chronological relationship between this grooved ware found along the Euphrates and Tigris Rivers and similar grooved pottery from Eastern Turkey, particularly the Van region, where a continuation of the tradition, now wheel-made, through the eighth century seems an inescapable fact.[28] Where this style, or more correctly these styles, of grooved pottery may have originated remains for the moment as mysterious as the identification of its makers.

To summarise, Tille Höyük now appears not to have been occupied in the Late Bronze Age. An assumption that the position of Tille, on the right bank of the Euphrates River at a location where it was presumably possible to ford the river in summer, provided it with minor strategic importance towards the end of the Late Bronze Age turns out to have little or no foundation. Settlement in earlier periods, and maybe also in later ones, is perhaps to be explained by the presence of sweet water rather than fordability of the river. New, lower, dendro-AMS 14C-wiggle-matched dating from the Cornell laboratory suggests that the earliest phase of the gateway belongs to a time shortly after the collapse of the Hittite core on the Anatolian Plateau. With regard to ceramics, the drab ware pottery associated with the first phase of the gateway bears none of the potmarks that seem to indicate production within the borders of a strong state.[29] Early Iron Age painted wares are absent in these earliest Iron Age levels, not making their first appearance until sometime in the tenth century following the period that elapsed between the second phase of the gateway and the devastating fire. Grooved ware, as long thought, does not make its appearance at Tille Höyük much if at all before the ninth century.

[26] Müller 1999 and 2003; Schachner 2003.
[27] Blaylock 1999.
[28] See particularly the overview by Konyar 2005, and most recently Erdem 2009.
[29] E.g. Gates 2001 and 2006; Postgate 2007 and 2010.

Finally, dendrochronology combined with AMS 14C dating techniques increasingly offers precision in dating not otherwise obtainable in the absence of historical sources.

BIBLIOGRAPHY

ALGAZE, G.

1990 *Town and Country in Southeastern Anatolia.* Vol. II: *the Stratigraphic Sequence at Kurban Höyük*, OIP 110. Chicago: Oriental Institute.

BLAYLOCK, S.

1998a "Rescue Excavations by the BIAA at Tille Höyük, on the Euphrates, 1997–1990," in *Ancient Anatolia*, edited by R. Matthews, pp. 177–194. London: British Institute of Archaeology at Ankara.

1998b "Adıyaman Survey 1985–1991," in *Ancient Anatolia*, edited by R. Matthews, pp. 101–110. London: British Institute of Archaeology at Ankara.

1999 "Iron Age Pottery from Tille Höyük, South-Eastern Turkey," in *Iron Age Pottery in Northern Mesopotamia, Northern Syria and South-Eastern Anatolia*, edited by A. Hausleiter and A. Reiche, pp. 263–286. Munster: Altertumskunde des Vorderen Orients 10, Ugarit Verlag.

2009 *Tille Höyük 3.1: The Iron Age: Introduction, Stratification and Architecture.* London: British Institute at Ankara.

Forthcoming *Tille Höyük 3.2: The Iron Age: Pottery, Finds and Conclusions.* London: British Institute at Ankara.

BLAYLOCK, S., FRENCH, D. H. and SUMMERS, G. D.

1990 "The Adıyaman Survey, an Interim Report," *Anatolian Studies* 40: 81–135.

COLLON, D.

1993 "The Seals from Tille Höyük of the Late Bronze Age and Earlier," in *Tille Höyük 4: The Late Bronze Age and the Iron Age Transition*, by G. D. Summers, pp. 171–177. London: British Institute of Archaeology at Ankara.

ERDEM, A.

2009 "Van Gölü Havzası'nda Bulunan Demir Çağ Yivli Çanak Çömleğinin Urartu Kalelerindeki Varlığı," in *Studies in Honour of Altan Çilingiroğlu: a Life Dedicated to Urartu on the Shores of the Upper Sea,* edited by H. Sağlamtimur, E. Abay, Z. Derin, A. Ü. Erdem, A. Batmaz, F. Dedeoğlu, M. Erdalkıran, M. B. Baştürk and E. Konakçı, pp. 299–307. Istanbul: Arkeoloji ve Sanat.

FORLANINI, M.

2008 "The Central Provinces of Hatti: an Updating," in *New Perspectives on the Historical Geography and Topography of Anatolia in the II and I Millenium B.C.,* Collana di studi sulle civiltà dell'Oriente antico 16, edited by K. Strobel, pp. 145–188. Firenze: Eothen.

GATES, M.-H.

2001 "Potmarks at Kinet Höyük and the Hittite Ceramic Industry," in *La Cilicie: espaces et pouvoirs locaux (IIe millénaire av. J.-C. - IVe siècle ap. J.-C.),* Varia Anatolica 13, edited by É. Jean, A. M. Dinçol and S. Durugönül, pp. 137–157. Istanbul.

2006 "Dating the Hittite Levels at Kinet Höyük: a Revised Chronology," in *Strukturierung und Datierung in der hethitischen Archäologie. Voraussetzungen - Probleme - Neue Ansätze. Structuring and Dating in Hittite Archaeology. Requirements - Problems - New Approaches. Internationaler Workshop, Istanbul, 26-27. November 2004*, BYZAS 4, edited by D. P. Mielke, U.-D. Schoop and J. Seeher, pp. 293–309. Istanbul. Veröffentlichungen des Deutschen Archäologischen Instituts.

GRIGGS, C. B. and MANNING, S. W.
2009 "A Reappraisal of the Dendrochronology and Dating of Tille Höyük (1993)," *Radiocarbon* 51: 711–720.

KASCHAU, G.
1999 *Lidar Höyük: Die Keramik der Mittleren Bronzezeit*, Mainz and Rhein: von Zabern.

KONYAR, E.
2005 "Grooved Pottery of the Lake Van Basin: A Stratigraphical and Chronological Assessment," *Colloquium Anatolicum* 4: 105–127.

KORBEL, G.
1985 *Die spätbronzezeitliche Keramik von Norşuntepe*, Hannover: Institut für Bauen und Planen in Entwicklungslädern.
1987 *Materialheft spätbronzezeitliche Keramik Tarsus (Grabung Hetty Goldman)*, Hannover: Institut für Bauen und Planen in Entwicklungslädern.

KUNIHOLM, P. I., TARTER, S. L. and GRIGGS, C. B.
1993 "Dendrochronological Report," in *Tille Höyük 4: The Late Bronze Age and the Iron Age Transition*, by G. D. Summers, pp. 179–190. London: British Institute of Archaeology at Ankara.

MÜLLER, U.
1999 "Die eisenzeitliche Stratigraphie von Lidar Höyük," *Anatolian Studies* 49: 123–132.
2003 "A Change to Continuity: Bronze Age Traditions in Early Iron Age," in *Identifying Changes: The Transition from Bronze to Iron Ages in Anatolia and its Neighbouring Regions, Proceedings of the International Workshop Istanbul, November 8-9, 2002*, edited by B. Fischer, H. Genz, É. Jean and K. Köroğlu, pp. 137–149. Istanbul: Türk Eskiçağ Bilimleri Enstitüsü.
2005 "Norşuntepe and Lidar Höyük: Two Examples for Cultural Change in Early Iron Age," in *Proceedings of the 5th Anatolian Iron Ages Colloquium held at Van in 2001*, edited by A. Çilingiroğlu and G. Darbyshire, pp. 107–114. London: British Institute of Archaeology at Ankara.

ÖZGÜÇ, N.
2009 *Samsat: Sümeysat, Samosata, Kumaha, Hahha, Hahhum: Bir Başkent ve Kalenin Uzun Yaşamının 6000 Yıllık Döneminden Kesitler*, Ankara: Türk Tarih Kurumu.

POSTGATE, J. N.
2007 "The ceramics of centralisation and dissolution: a case-study from Rough Cilicia," *Anatolian Studies* 57: 141–150.
2010 "The Debris of Government: Reconstructing the Middle Assyrian State Apparatus from Tablets and Potsherds," *Iraq* 72: 19–37.

ROAF, M. and SCHACHNER, A.
2005 "The Bronze Age to Iron Age Transition in the Upper Tigris Region: New Information from Ziyaret Tepe and Giricano," in *Proceedings of the 5th Anatolian Iron Ages Colloquium held at Van in 2001*, edited by A. Çilingiroğlu and

G. Darbyshire, pp. 115–123. London: British Institute of Archaeology at Ankara.

SCHACHNER, A.
2003 "From the Bronze to the Iron Age: Identifying Changes in the Upper Tigris Region, the Case of Giricano," in *Identifying Changes: The Transition from Bronze to Iron Ages in Anatolia and its Neighbouring Regions, Proceedings of the International Workshop Istanbul, November 8-9, 2002*, edited by B. Fischer, H. Genz, É. Jean and K. Köroğlu, pp. 151–163. Istanbul: Türk Eskiçağ Bilimleri Enstitüsü.

SUMMERS, G. D.
2010 "Revisiting the End of the Late Bronze Age and the Transition to the Early Iron Age at Tille Höyük," *Iraq* 72: 193–200.

SUMMERS G. D. with contributions by D. COLLON, P. KUNIHOLM, S. TARTER and C. GRIGGS
1993 *Tille Höyük 4: The Late Bronze Age and the Iron Age Transition*. London: British Institute of Archaeology at Ankara.

VENTURI, F.
2007 *La Siri nell'età delle transformazioni (XIII-X sec. a.C.). Nuovi contributi dallo scavo di Tell Afis*. Bolognai: CLUEB.

WARD, W. A. and JOUKOWSKY, M. S. eds.
1992 *The Crisis Years: the 12th Century B.C.* Dubuque: Kendall Hunt.

Fig. 1 The last days of Tille Höyük (photo. Tuğurl Çakar, BIAA Archive 9031).

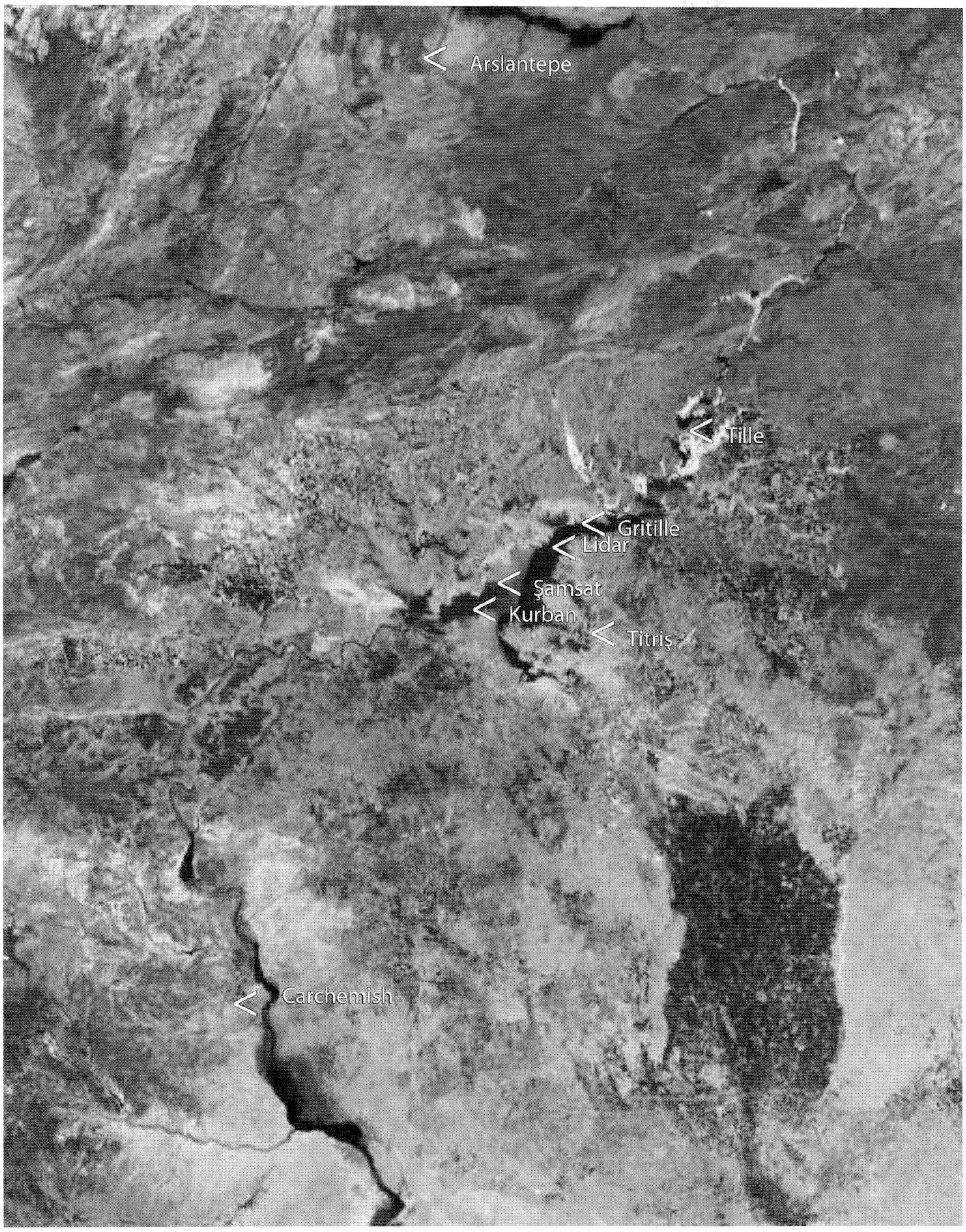

Fig. 2 The Euphrates River between Arslantepe, Malatya, and Carchemish together with the approximate location of Tille Höyük and other sites within the Atatürk Dam Region mentioned in the text.

Fig. 3 Part of the gateway at Tille Höyük showing the burnt timbers in the passage which were used for dendrochronology (adapted from Summers 1993, figure 22).

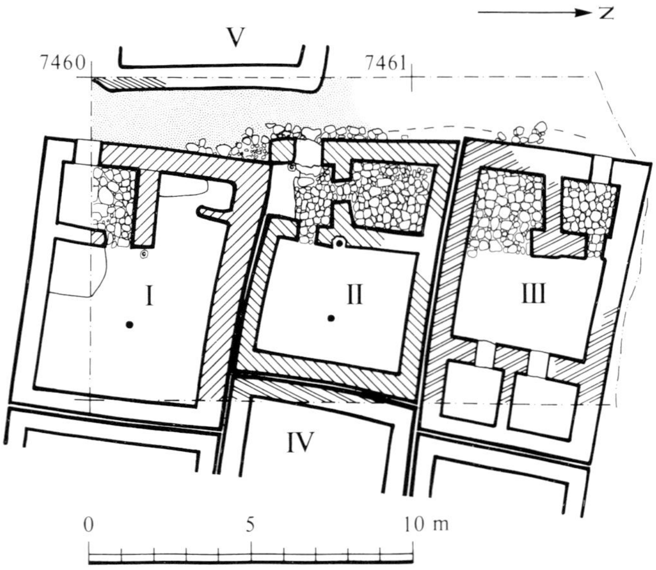

Fig. 4 Middle Bronze Age houses fronting onto a narrow street (adapted from Summers 1993, figure 19b).

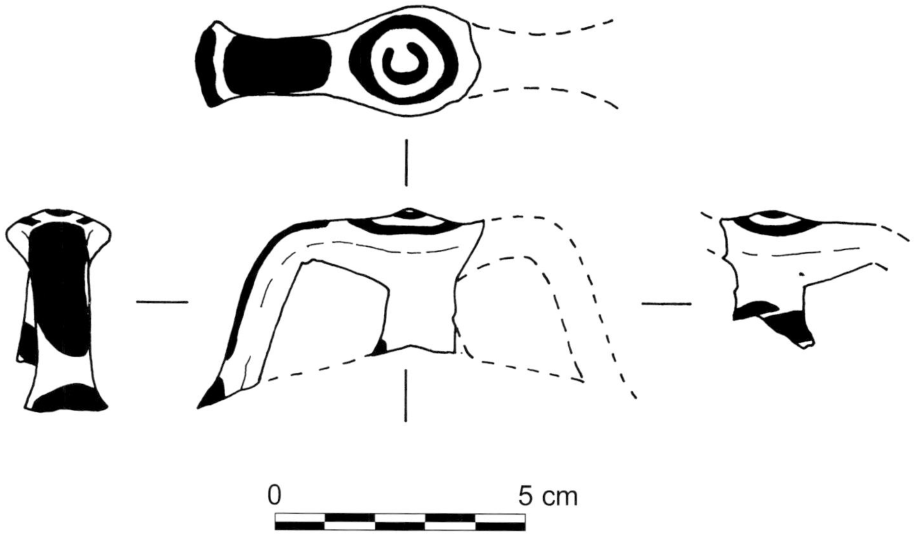

Fig. 5 Fragment of a Mycenaean LH IIIA2/B1 stirrup jar, maximum height 4 cm. (adapted from Summers 1993, figure 35.1).

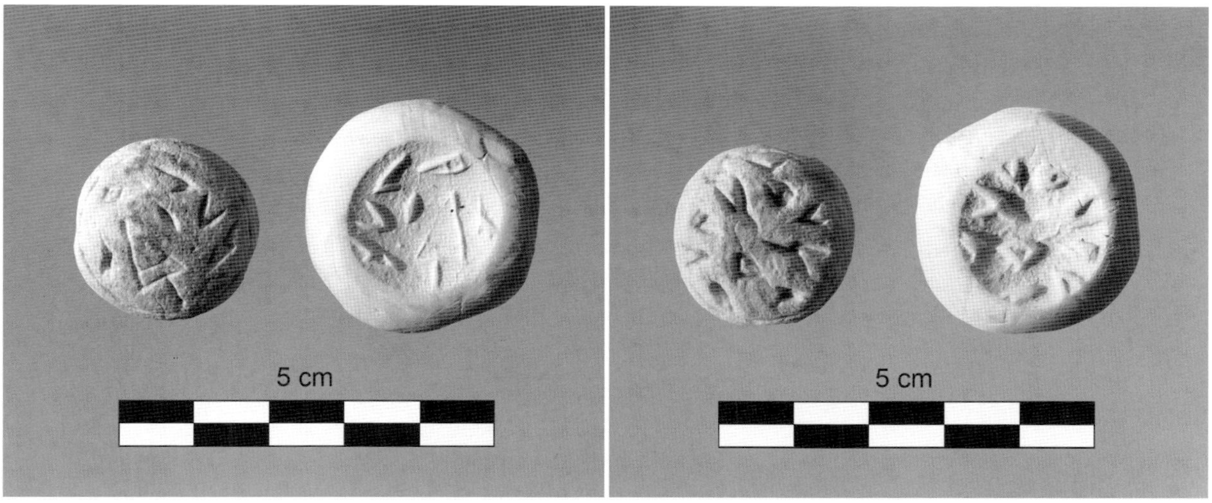

Fig. 6 Biconvex seal, *ca.* actual size
(photos Tuğurl Çakar, BIAA Archive 8817 & 8820).

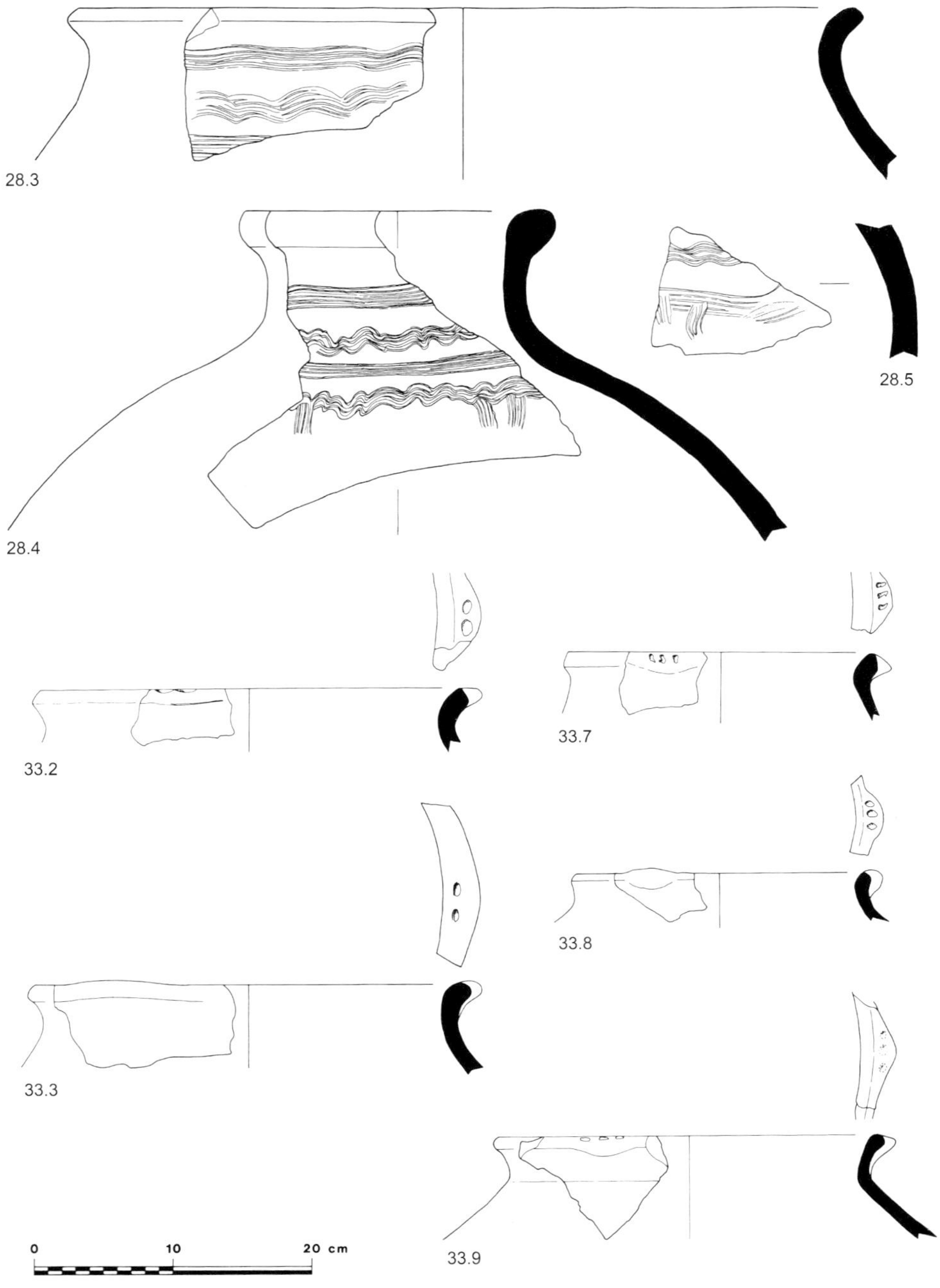

Fig. 7 Middle Bronze Age hand-made combed ware, above, and cooking pots with impressed triangular lugs, below (adapted from Summers 1993, figure 28 nos 3-5 and figure 33 nos 2–3 and 7–9).

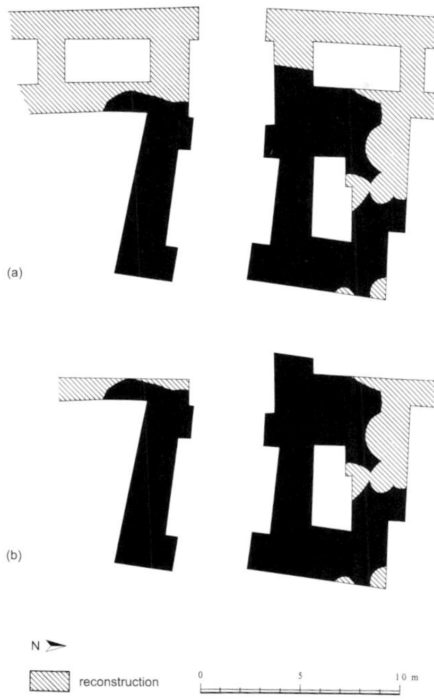

Fig. 8 The two phases of the Tille Höyük gate as reconstructed in the original excavation report (Summers 1993, figure 26).

Fig. 9 The two phases of the Tille Höyük gate with the more modest reconstructions suggested in Summers 2010, figure 2. The gate itself is reduced to a single chamber while the casemate wall disappears.

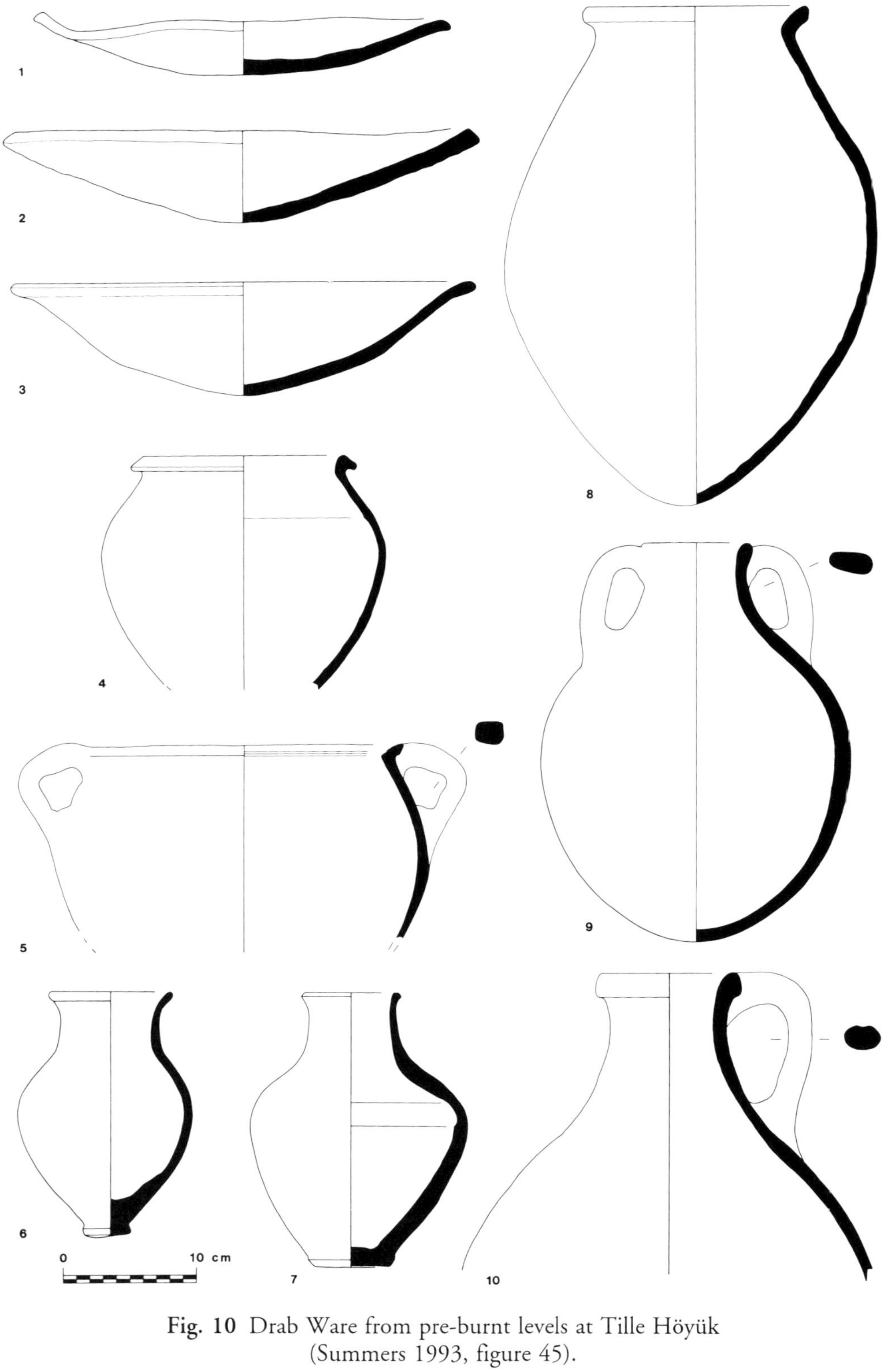

Fig. 10 Drab Ware from pre-burnt levels at Tille Höyük (Summers 1993, figure 45).

CHAPTER 14

THE LATE BRONZE AGE TO EARLY IRON AGE TRANSITION: A PERSPECTIVE FROM THE UPPER TIGRIS RIVER

Timothy MATNEY
Professor of Archaeologhy
Affiliation: University of Akron
Address:
Department of Anthropology and Classical Studies
University of Akron
241 Olin Hall
Akron, OH 44325-1910, USA
E-mail: matney@uakron.edu

ABSTRACT

This chapter explores the transition from the Late Bronze to Early Iron Ages in the upper Tigris River valley of southeastern Turkey. Recent archaeological surveys and excavations in advance of the planned Ilısu hydroelectric dam near the modern Syrian border have greatly improved our understanding of the ancient occupational history of the region, yet certain time periods are still poorly documented. The upper Tigris River valley was conquered by the armies of both the Middle and Late Assyrian kings and formed an important border province within their empires. A brief period of imperial weakness lasting from c. 1069–882 BC during the Early Iron Age led to an Assyrian abandonment of the region. Archaeologists have long assumed that indigenous Anatolian populations, termed here "Upper Tigridians," moved into the region to fill a power vacuum left by the Assyrian retreat. The pattern that has emerged after fifteen years of salvage archaeology, however, suggests that while the Upper Tigridians utilized the former Assyrian lands along the river during the Early Iron Age, they did not establish permanent settlements. Rather, Upper Tigridian mobile agropastoralists utilized the river valley resources, while their permanent settlements were located away from the river in areas which provided greater defensive opportunities.

INTRODUCTION

One of the clear themes that emerged at the *Across the Border* symposium was the highly variable regional responses to social, political, ecological, and environmental shifts seen across the ancient Near East at the end of the Late Bronze Age. Unlike many of the other regions of Anatolia and Syria that were discussed at the symposium, the terminology and general framework for the transition from the Late Bronze Age to the Early Iron Age within the upper Tigris River valley, when taken in isolation, is reasonably unproblematic. In most respects, the chronology of the Assyrian cuneiform texts correlates well with archaeological evidence excavated to date along the upper Tigris River. Schachner and others had previously outlined this chronology at the "Identifying Changes" workshop in Istanbul in 2002.[1] The basic framework — a period of "indigenous" control of the region during the Early Iron Age sandwiched between two centralized imperial Assyrian occupations during the Late Bronze (Middle Assyrian) and Middle Iron (Late Assyrian) Ages — still seems to fit the data coming from a number of excavations within the Ilısu Dam archaeological salvage area where we have seen intensive archaeological activity over the past decade and a half.

In brief, the Late Bronze Age in the upper Tigris River valley is associated with the presence of Middle Assyrian imperial interests, centered on the urban sites of Üçtepe, probably the provincial capital of Ta'idu, and Ziyaret Tepe, Middle Assyrian Tushhum [**Fig. 1**]. A number of smaller associated settlements with Middle Assyrian ceramics are also documented along the river, such as Kavuşan Tepe, Hakemi Use, Salat Tepe, and Grê Dimsê.[2] The end of Middle Assyrian occupation in the upper Tigris River valley can be dated through the discovery of a cache of Middle Assyrian cuneiform tablets at Giricano Tepe. These texts identify Giricano as Dunnu-ša-Uzibi, a fortified agricultural center a few kilometers northwest of the urban administrative center of Ziyaret Tepe/Tušhum, and are dated on internal evidence to 1069 or 1068 BC.[3] Roaf and Schachner argue that shortly after this date, the Middle Assyrian kings lost control of the region.[4] Similarly, the beginning of the subsequent Late Assyrian occupation is marked most forcefully by the well-known inscription of king Ashurnasirpal II on a stele found in the Ninurta Temple at Kalhu/Nimrud in which the king describes his rebuilding of the city of Tušhan/Ziyaret Tepe, including the reconstruction of the fortifications, the building of a palace, the erection of a monument, and the re-peopling of the upper Tigris River valley by the Assyrians who had left due to hunger and famine.[5] The stele inscription dates to 882 BC and can be taken to portray the re-establishment of Assyrian control in the upper Tigris River valley. Ashurnasirpal II and his successors extended imperial control throughout the region through a chain of fortified centers along the Tigris River: Tušhan/Ziyaret Tepe, Tidu/Üçtepe, and Sinabu/ Pornak.[6] We have treated the settlement system of the Late Assyrian period

[1] Schachner 2003; Fischer et al. 2003.
[2] For a summary see Tenu 2009.
[3] Roaf and Schachner 2005; Radner 2004.
[4] Roaf and Schachner 2005 p. 119.
[5] Grayson 1991; Roaf in Matney et al. 2002, pp. 49–51.
[6] Kessler 1980.

elsewhere.[7] There is widespread agreement on these general points of chronology and historical geography.

Rather than looking at these intensively-studied Middle and Late Assyrian imperial systems, however, the focus of this chapter is the relatively poorly-understood Early Iron Age occupation in the upper Tigris River valley during the intervening period of political weakness in the Assyrian heartland, c. 1069–882 BC. While the major Assyrian administrative center of Tušhum/Ziyaret Tepe and the smaller agricultural stations such as Dunnu-ša-Uzibi/Giricano were abandoned by the Assyrians, the area was clearly not unutilized. The beginning of the Early Iron Age was marked by radical changes in the regional material culture in the upper Tigris River valley arguing for major differences in who was utilizing the area, and the way the resources were used in the absence of the Assyrian imperial bureaucracy. For the sake of discussion, the Early Iron Age non-Assyrian inhabitants of the region will be referred to as "Upper Tigridians," used here as a purely geographical and temporal label free of ethnic, political, or linguistic affiliations, although these issues are discussed below briefly, as are the material differences seen at the Early Iron Age Upper Tigridian sites. It is vital to note that the changes from the Late Bronze to Early Iron Ages outlined here for the upper Tigris River valley are not seen uniformly across the Assyrian imperial periphery and must, therefore, not be extended uncritically to other areas. For example, Kühne has shown that the lower Khabur River region in Syria maintained an Assyrian connection throughout the Late Bronze Age to Iron Age transition despite the growing presence of other groups such as Aramaeans and that the lower Khabur River served as a buffer zone between the Assyrian heartland and the Aramaeans to the north and west.[8]

In this chapter, the upper Tigris River valley is further subdivided into two discrete areas. The broader region comprises a long stretch of the Tigris River from the region north of Diyarbakir to near the Syrian border. The region comprises a low river valley with an elevation less than 550 m, surrounding uplands and foothills ranging in elevation up to 1000 m, and the mountainous zones of the Taurus Mountains and the Tur Abdin [**Fig. 1**]. The first of these zones, the lowlands, is now well explored due to work within the Ilısu Dam salvage area. The second zone, the uplands and foothills, have been surveyed but few sites are excavated. For purposes of this chapter, the lowland area — following roughly the 550 m isohyet stretching between the modern city of Bismil and the confluence of the river with its major tributary the Batman Su — is treated as a separate region termed here for convenience the "Bismil-Batman Corridor" [**Fig. 2**]. This geographical separation is a vital distinction in the arguments that follow. As discussed below, there are significant reasons for singling out the

[7] Matney 2010.
[8] Kühne 2009; 2010.

Bismil-Batman Corridor for consideration. The lowland valley to the west of modern Bismil, including the excavated settlement of Üçtepe, lies within the kingdom of Bit Zamani, and appears to follow a different occupational history than the Bismil-Batman Corridor. Furthermore, the geography and especially the accessibility of sites within the uplands and foothills above the 550 m isohyet, such as Kazıktepe (possibly Early Iron Age Damdammusa), similarly create a different occupational pattern. Finally, the lowland valley to the east of the Batman Su confluence does not contain much agricultural land and the river itself is confined to a deep, narrow bed of limited utility for transport or irrigation, although Early Iron Age sites such as Hirbemerdon Tepe show that this marginal region is of importance to the Upper Tigridians. In other words, the Early Iron Age utilization of the Bismil-Batman Corridor can be narrowly defined and contrasted to patterns of occupation in the immediately surrounding areas based on a combination of geographical, environmental, ecological, and political factors. Throughout this chapter, then, the inclusive term "upper Tigris River valley" will refer to the broader area seen in Figure 1, while the more specific term "Bismil-Batman Corridor" will refer specificially to the area at or below roughly 550m in elevation between modern Bismil and the Batman Su seen in Figure 2.

The Nature of 'Upper Tigridian' Society

One issue that speaks directly to the theme of the *Across the Border* conference is the nature of this "indigenous" or Upper Tigridian occupation during the Early Iron Age. Is it more appropriate to characterize the social, political, and material shifts seen archaeologically as a deliberate reaction to Assyrian domination, as Szuchman has recently suggested, or perhaps to view them more generally as part of a broader Aramaesation process as suggested by Postgate?[9] To what degree can we reconstruct on present evidence the social, political, and economic systems in place during the Early Iron Age? In addressing these issues, we are forced to question some basic assumptions that have become entrenched within our research and which are the result, in part, of our biased source materials. The functioning of the Assyrian empire in its peripheries — an important topic — has received a great deal of attention.[10] Most of this discussion on imperial organization in the frontier provinces is Assyro-centric, an understandable bias since the cuneiform sources provide considerable detail on many aspects of imperial practice. Unfortunately, however, this has meant that the Upper Tigridian populations tend to be given a passive role to the machinations and interests of the imperial Assyrians. The Assyrians arrive in the valley, so others retreat. The Assyrians retreat during a period of imperial weakness, so others come in to fill in the power

[9] Szuchman 2009; Postgate 1992.
[10] For example, Parker 2001.

vacuum left behind. In this chapter, the opposite perspective is explored; we visualize the Late Bronze to Early Iron Age transition not from an imperial viewpoint, but rather from the perspective of the Upper Tigridians at the point in time when Middle Assyrian domination wanes and the Late Bronze Age closes.

An interesting issue, but one which cannot be settled here, is the ethnic identity of the Upper Tigridians. Szuchman has cogently discussed the political evolution of the Aramaean kingdom of Bit Zamani which appears to encompass much of the upper Tigris River region with its capital at Amedi, modern Diyarbakır, during the Early Iron Age.[11] Szuchman notes, however, that the section of the upper Tigris River under consideration here — the Bismil-Batman Corridor — fell outside of the direct control of Bit Zamani, which lay generally to the west and north.[12] While it seems highly likely that the region we are considering was home to a significant Aramaean population in the Early Iron Age, we might expect to find a mosaic of different settlement types and activities to be practiced by a number of different ethnic groups. "Tribal social structures are fluid, and accordingly allow for flexibility in adapting to internal or external changes and threats. This flexibility can be expressed in shifting political allegiances, geographic boundaries, and social identities."[13] The sedentarization process which transformed Aramaean nomadic pastoralist communities into a collection of small chiefdoms and kingdoms spread across northern Mesopotamia was probably inaugurated in the Late Bronze Age during a time a political stability under the Middle Assyrian kings and was fully in place by the early 9th century BC,[14] but that process, extending across the entire Early Iron Age, cannot be reconstructed exclusive of other actors in the upper Tigris River valley.

Admittedly, it is tempting to suggest that the Upper Tigridians were simply an Aramaean tribal group based on the visibility of the Aramaeans in the cuneiform record. Shortly before the abandonment of the region by the Middle Assyrians, the annals of Tiglath-pileser I described an Assyrian military campaign against the Ahlamû/Aramaeans in 1111 BC in northern Mesopotamia.[15] Likewise, immediately before the reassertion of Assyrian control in the early 9th century BC, Ashurnasirpal II's father, Tukulti-Ninurta II, described a political structure in which Bit Zamani was dominant in the region when the kingdom was ruled by a non-Assyrian named Amme-ba'li.[16] In other words, chronologically on either side of the Early Iron Age, the Assyrian textual record describes the presence of Aramaean tribes and kingdoms in the vicinity. Despite this evidence, we will retain the more neutral term "Upper

[11] Szuchman 2009.
[12] Szuchman 2009, Fig. 1.
[13] Szuchman 2009, pp. 60–61.
[14] Szuchman 2008.
[15] Grayson 1991, p. 23.
[16] Kuhrt 1995, p. 482; Szuchman 2009, p. 56; D'Agostino, forthcoming.

Tigridian;" there is a danger in viewing the Ahlamû/Aramaeans as a single cultural entity and without stronger evidence it would be premature to declare the entire upper Tigris River valley as an Aramaean kingdom during the Early Iron Age.

Material Evidence for Upper Tigridian Occupation

It is useful to review of the material evidence that marks the Upper Tigridian populations in the Early Iron Age. As numerous scholars have noted, the most immediately recognizable material marker of the Early Iron Age is a type of ceramic called variously, Grooved or Groovy Pottery. In the upper Tigris River region this pottery is mostly handmade, often in the form of simple slightly closed bowls, sometimes with handles or spouts, bearing a very characteristic horizontal incised grooving below the rim on the exterior. Along the river and in the surrounding upland areas, it is found on small sites, or concentrated in restricted areas of larger multi-period settlements.

Past studies have used Groovy Pottery as both a chronological marker and as an ethnic marker; both of these formulations have serious methodological flaws. Chronologically, Groovy Pottery is clearly associated with the Early Iron Age. The interesting chronological question is really when the use of this type of pottery starts and ends. It is now clear that the use of Groovy Pottery in the upper Tigris River region does not end with the reassertion of Late Assyrian imperial control in the early 9th century BC. At Ziyaret Tepe, for example, in Operation L on the High Mound, indigenous Early Iron Age ceramics are found on the same floors as Late Assyrian forms, showing that these earlier ceramic types persisted well into the Middle Iron Age.[17] Likewise, the development and continuation of the Groovy Pottery ceramic tradition into the 7th century BC has been documented in eastern Anatolia,[18] so it is hardly controversial to conclude that Groovy Pottery dates to both the Early and Middle Iron Ages. Less clear is whether or not Groovy Pottery is a good indicator of a clear chronological break between the Late Bronze Age and Early Iron Age. To date, there are no unambiguous examples of Groovy Pottery being found in primary Late Bronze Age archaeological contexts in the upper Tigris River valley, suggesting that this ware was perhaps a new arrival in the Early Iron Age. With the caveat that the Late Bronze Age levels at the upper Tigris River valley sites are still not fully documented, present evidence appears to support this contention.

We must be careful not to try and equate the use of Groovy Pottery with specific ethnic identities. Previous attempts to link Groovy Pottery to historically-attested ethnic groups have been rejected. For example, Sevin's idea that this pottery could be

[17] Matney *et al.* 2009, p. 54.
[18] Köroğlu 2003.

linked to the Mushku has now been largely discounted.[19] Roaf and others have argued convincingly that this material culture cannot be unambiguously linked to any particular group, indeed preferring to note that it overlaps geographically with the Assyrian toponym of the Nairi Lands.[20] Likewise, there appears to be no strict correspondence between the distribution of this ceramic horizon and the much broader process of Aramaesation which occurred linguistically across the Near East in the late second millennium BC. In short, we have no means to prove that this particular ceramic horizon ever correlated neatly with the boundaries of any singular cultural group. The ubiquity and long period of use for Groovy Pottery is probably not tied to its technical qualities, such as simplicity of form, ease of production, or durability, but rather to its function and the general conservative nature of the potting tradition. It is better to describe the distribution of this pottery, as well as other features and archaeological data, as indicative of a broad social strategy that probably encompassed many peoples of different origins, languages, and ethnicities.

One of the most striking characteristics of the Early Iron Age occupations in the Bismil-Batman Corridor is the paucity of mudbrick structures found at sites with Groovy Pottery and other Early Iron Age material culture indicators. What few pieces of architecture that we do find in the Bismil-Batman Corridor comprise thin stone wall foundations, a practice at variance with both Middle and Late Assyrian buildings which are more substantial and built, in general, of mudbrick. In fact, there is not a single complete Early Iron Age room from the Bismil-Batman Corridor sites despite nearly fifteen years of archaeological activity in the area.

At **Ziyaret Tepe**, the bulk of the evidence for Early Iron Age utilisation of the site comes from a very large storage pit, later used as a trash dump excavated in the Operation E step-trench.[21] Although only exposed in a very small, shallow cut, a few small walls possibly of Early Iron Age date were found on the eastern edge of the high mound.[22] These remains are only tentatively dateable and, in any case, are quite ephemeral. Pits with Early Iron Age Groovy Pottery are found elsewhere in the upper Tigris River valley, for example, at **Kavuşan Tepe**.[23] Of particular interest was the discovery by Ökse at **Salat Tepe** of an Early Iron Age pits, some 5m in diameter, with horseshoe-shaped hearths on the floor, that she interpreted as possibly indicative of temporary semi-subterranean dwellings, possibly the remnants of winter pastures of nomadic tribes. Some of the pits were small and might have been granary storage or processing pits.[24] Finally, pits and disturbed remains, including "some piles of

[19] Sevin 1991; see also Blaylock 2009, p. 25.
[20] Roaf and Schachner 2005, p. 120.
[21] Matney et al. 2002, p. 65; McDonald in Matney and Rainville 2005, pp. 23–26.
[22] Matney et al. 2003, pp. 186–187.
[23] Kozbe and Köroğlu 2004.
[24] Ökse and Görmüş 2006, p. 190.

stones which originally may have belonged to buildings" along with Groovy Pottery were present in the uppermost layers of **Giricano**.[25] The only site along the river west of the confluence with the Batman Su which has much Early Iron Age architecture is **Kenan Tepe**, where scattered remains of both stone and mudbrick walls have been interpreted as a "small village or hamlet that contained a few relatively large domestic structures interspersed with outdoor work areas."[26] However, the published plans from Kenan Tepe comprise a few isolated wall segments and no coherent rooms or buildings have emerged from the excavations.[27] From the published data it is not yet clear whether Kenan Tepe represents a year-round village occupation, or a more ephemeral use of the site.

In short, what we have yet to find in the Bismil-Batman Corridor is a well-preserved Early Iron Age village with clear evidence for significant permanent occupation. It is possible that this pattern is simply the result of the vagaries of archaeological sampling, or that the Early Iron Age remains were removed by subsequent activities and taphonomic processes. A more parsimonious explanation, however, and the one discussed below, is that the Bismil-Batman Corridor was only utilized by nomadic pastoralists during the Early Iron Age and that there were no permanent villages occupied by the Upper Tigridians.

This is not to say that Upper Tigridians did not use the Bismil-Batman Corridor area. Their ceramics and other remains are found at the sites noted above and, importantly, we have excavated evidence for their settlements in adjacent regions. For example, immediately east of the area under consideration, in an area which was of marginal interest to the Assyrians and with limited agricultural potential, Laneri has documented clear evidence for permanent habitation at Early Iron Age Hirbemerdon Tepe.[28] In Phase IVA at Hirbemerdon Tepe, Laneri found scattered remains of stone architecture in the northern sector of the High Mound (Area A and Step Trench AC) and an important room with mortars, pestles, ovens, assumed to be used for bread production.[29] Unfortunately, most of the immediate highland areas adjacent to the river are not accessible for modern excavation as they lie outside of the Ilısu Dam salvage area and excavation permits for these sites are, at present, not available. On present evidence, there appears to be two components to Upper Tigridian society; (1) a group of mobile pastoral nomads who utilized the Bismil-Batman Corridor between 1069 and 882 BC but who chose not to settle there permanently; and (2) a contemporary settled population in the upland or adjacent

[25] Roaf and Schachner 2005, p. 117.
[26] Parker 2003, p. 533.
[27] Parker 2003, Fig. 8.
[28] Laneri et al. 2009; also cited in D'Agostino forthcoming b.
[29] Üçtepe has an Early Iron Age occupational strata (Level 8) which fits this pattern, but the site lies within the area of Bit Zamani and is, therefore, not considered further here. See Köroğlu 1998; Szuchman 2009, Fig. 1.

environmentally marginal areas of the broader upper Tigris River valley living in villages and hamlets.

Examining the data collected by surface surveys conducted both along the river and in the immediate upland areas, especially along the main Tigris River tributaries where we have good survey evidence, the Early Iron Age does not appear to have an urban component. Sites are small and, to the extent that we can characterize them given the paucity of excavated settlements, they are primarily agricultural in nature. Using Algaze's survey material, Parker noted 19 sites in the upper Tigris River valley had Groovy Pottery, and hence Early Iron Age occupation.[30] Nine of these sites were less than one hectare in size; the largest was over three hectares according to Parker, although it seems likely that this is an overestimation of size. It is interesting to note that Parker suggests a two-tier settlement pattern for the Early Iron Age sites overall with ten villages (larger than 1 ha) and nine hamlets (smaller than 1 ha), [31] a pattern predicted by Alizadeh's model of mobile agropastoralists, discussed below and applicable to the Bismil-Batman Corridor.[32]

Based purely on settlement sizes, then, the entire sedentary Early Iron Age population of the upper Tigris River valley and its immediate uplands was very small. If we assume that all of these small sites were occupied simultaneously and to their full extent, and if we accept a rough figure of 100 persons per hectare of site, then the entire settled population of the upper Tigris River valley and uplands is something on the order of 3000 persons spanning a period of 180 years. This population is spread out over an area of some 400 km^2, as surveyed by Algaze and his team in the late 1980s.[33] This level of population density — very roughly 7.5 persons per square kilometer — is more characteristic of semi-nomadic groups than of settled agriculturalists. Finally, based on our admittedly small dataset, there appears to be no evidence of large-scale specialized production or workshops. This may be, as noted above, simply a function of sampling bias. However, it is important to note that spatially there is morphological variation in Groovy Pottery and it appears not to have been centrally-produced. Parker reported the presence of kilns in the Early Iron Age levels at Kenan Tepe, possibly for small-scale metal working or pottery production, but these remain outliers to the general pattern.[34]

To summarize, there are five elements of the Upper Tigridian use of the Bismil-Batman Corridor during the Early Iron Age that must be considered further; (1) its geographical proximity to the uplands and high Taurus Mountains; (2) its non-urban

[30] Parker 2003.

[31] Parker 2003, pp. 539–530. This pattern can be expanded to cover both the Upper Tigris and Batman river valleys where "sites dating to the Early Iron Age may fall into two site size categories," Parker 2001, p. 175.

[32] Alizadeh 2010.

[33] Algaze et al. 1991.

[34] Parker et al. 2004, p. 591.

settlement pattern with a two-tier site hierarchy in the uplands surrounding the river valley; (3) its lack of architectural remains along the river valley itself; (4) the presence of large grain storage silos at sites along the Bismil-Batman Corridor; and (5) the wide distribution of handmade ceramic wares.

A Model of Upper Tigridian Society

The model proposed in this chapter is that there are two components of Upper Tigridian society, a nomadic and a settled component. The former component utilizes the existing mounds along the Bismil-Batman Corridor for both agricultural and pastoral activities, while the latter component is settled in small towns and villages in the uplands and foothills away from the Tigris River. It seems likely that both components share some attributes, such as the Groovy Pottery ceramic style. There is nothing to suggest that they distinguished themselves culturally or ethnically, although our data are too sparse to say this with any certainty.

One modern parallel for Upper Tigridian society worth considering here is that of recent pastoral nomadic populations of Iran. As is well established, among these groups ethnographers found chiefdoms with leaders possessing formal settled residences, and where both settled and nomadic components of the same population exist side-by-side. Alizadeh has recently discussed these modern groups as analogues to ancient populations responsible for the rise of the Elamite state in southwestern Iran.[35] He examined the relationship between groups in the Zagros Mountains and the lowlands of Elam concluding that the highland mobile pastoralists, whom he calls "mobile agropastoralists,"[36] were able to dominate the lowland areas of Elam and create a diversified economy leading to the emergence of the Elamite state. Thus, mobile pastoralism and settled farming are seen as two sides of the same system.[37] Interestingly, he notes that these mobile agropastoralists had a two-tier settlement hierarchy with permanent towns and villages, significant crop storage, trade, and yet they did not possess a politically centralized state. Possible parallels with the Upper Tigridians in the Early Iron Age described above are clear.

Significantly, there is a similarity in terms of geographical diversity between the two regions, although Alizadeh is discussing a social and political evolution on a much larger scale than what is proposed here for the upper Tigris River valley. The Upper Tigridian populations of the Early Iron Age enjoyed a close proximity to the Taurus

[35] Alizadeh 2010.

[36] Szuchman terms such groups "tribal societies with mobile components" (Szuchman 2008, p. 401) and also cites a similar concept introduced by Salzman 1972, who discusses "multi-resource nomads" such as the Yarahmadzai and Gamshadzai who rather than migrating to lowlands for winter pasture, live off stored supplies, protecting their flocks inside their tents.

[37] Alizadeh 2010, p. 354.

Mountains which would have provided them with access to the easily defendable, resource-rich foothills and high mountains. A similar geographic situation in the Zagros uplands and foothills favored the development of the Elamite state in Iran, as posited by Alizadeh.

The implication is that, in terms of the Upper Tigris region in the Early Iron Age, larger centers, away from the Tigris River itself, would serve as bases for the sedentary component of these populations. Certainly by the end of the Early Iron Age, Ashurnasirpal II in the annals of his second campaign describes the area south of the river valley as being occupied by both small permanent villages such as Mariru, from which the Assyrian army carried off livestock, as well as larger settlements, such as Damdammusa and the town of Tela where some 3000 men were gathered to defend the town. It is conceivable that sites like Tela represent chiefly residences, to which scattered populations were drawn in times of crisis. However, the few small sites found along the Tigris River, with scatters of Groovy Pottery, storage pits, but lacking real architecture, served a different function altogether.

Parallels for the integration of nomadic and settled elements of the same cultural group are widespread. For example, the annals of Tiglath-pileser I reporting on his military campaign against the Ahlamû-Aramaeans, noted that in addition to devastating their nomadic forces, he also "conquered six of their cities at the foot of Mount Bišri."[38] While not within the geographical region covered in this paper, this reference adds to the general understanding that nomadic and settled segments of the same populations were well known. Postgate reviewed sources from the Middle Assyrian texts for nomadic elements, showing that they are well attested from the early second millennium BC onwards.[39] Ristvet has reached similar conclusions looking at the landscape of the Khabur River region during the Middle Bronze Age.[40] The texts from Mari and Tell Leilan, for example, describe northern Mesopotamian kingdoms as collections of people initially, both sedentary and nomadic, and as places secondarily. She notes the discontinuous nature of territorial states and the importance of tribal identities to settled places, suggesting that in some instances small villages should be correlated with herding groups and nomadic lineages. In other words, small settlements "represent glorified pastoralist camps that were only seasonally occupied."[41]

Applying Alizadeh's concept of mobile agropastoralists to the situation of Upper Tigridians utilizing the river valley, one might expect to find a lack of permanent architecture, the presence of storage pits, and a widespread distribution of Groovy Pottery, all noted above. The upper Tigris River valley was, until recently in modern historic times, a transitional zone where groups migrating from the Syrian Jazirah

[38] Grayson 1991, p. 23.
[39] Postgate 1976.
[40] Ristvet 2008.
[41] Ristvet 2008, p. 594.

south of the Tur Abdin would bring their flocks in the spring, camping for a period of time before moving on to the high Taurus mountains for the summer, returning in the fall before reaching their winter pastures in the lower elevations of the Jazirah.[42] The Bismil-Batman Corridor is located roughly halfway between the edges of the Syrian steppe and the high mountains and its well-watered floodplain would have provided ample food for large flocks. The high mounds, like Ziyaret Tepe, Salat Tepe, Grê Dimsê, and Kenan Tepe serve as natural promontories and would have been an ideal spot from which to keep watch over domestic herds, providing a moderate protection from bandits and wild animals. This is not to say that the Upper Tigridian populations followed the same nomadic routes as later pastoralists, but rather that a segment of their population employed a similar general semi-nomadic strategy.

The lack of permanent structures of any substantial size is thus explained by the short stays in the valley as the small populations move with their herds. The handmade pottery Groovy Pottery, rather than the wheel-made wares of the Late Bronze and Middle Iron Ages, demonstrates the convenience of this technology for a mobile population. Certainly there is a wide distribution of Groovy Pottery; Elazığ, Malatya, the Van Basin, northwestern Iran, Transcaucasia.[43] The large storage pits seen at Ziyaret Tepe and Salat Tepe are also understandable using modern parallels. During both the planting and harvesting seasons, nomadic pastoralists would have sown seeds, perhaps by hand in unplowed fields along the rich river floodplain in the spring, returning in the late summer or early fall to reap their harvest. Rather than transporting large quantities of grain, the storage pits were utilized to create a stockpile of grain for later use. Stores consumed in the spring could have been replenished in the fall when the flocks were brought out of the high mountains, so a ready supply of grain for humans and animals would have been available in underground storage silos.

In this model, the sites of the Bismil-Batman Corridor are not villages at all in the sense of places of permanent residences, but are really just temporary stations where grain processing took place, with storage over winter for consumption during the spring. Some sites might have thus been occupied temporarily on a seasonal basis, perhaps for as long as a few months, while others — perhaps Kenan Tepe is the best candidate — might have had very small permanent occupations. The location of the temporary sites was chosen primarily for protection, sight lines, and for access to good grazing land and water. Such a model again has parallels elsewhere. Lyonnet, for example, in discussing the role of pastoral nomads in Early Bronze Age Syria suggests that villages in the region were "mainly used as storage places with numerous silos,

[42] Matney et al. 2007, pp. 28–29, with references.
[43] Köroğlu 2003, p. 239.

and only a few of them offered houses not necessarily used all the year around," [44] and even large settlements might have only housed a very small permanent population.

Clearly, a careful consideration of geographical context is critical to the application of this model. The model of mobile agropastoralism with settled towns suggested by Alizadeh for the Zagros Mountains region and extended here to the Upper Tigridians contrasts with the situation in those geographical regions at a greater physical distance from the Taurus-Zagros chain. For example, recent scholarship by D'Agostino outlining the historical development of the Ahlumû/Aramaeans as enemies of the Assyrian state during the Late Bronze and Early Iron Ages looks in particular at the region of Tell Barri and the upper Khabur region.[45] Here the influence of Early Iron Age mobile agropastoralists appears less significant. D'Agostino believes that the tribal structure of the pastoralists in this region involves significant mobility and economic flexibility, but does not include the settlement traditions outlined by Alizadeh for the Zagros Mountain area. The difference here is primarily geography and environment; the lowland pastoralists lack access the necessary mountain and upland resources for the model to apply.

The Theme of the Conference

Returning to the conference theme, if this model of Upper Tigridian society in the Early Iron Age is upheld by new evidence, then the collapse of the Middle Assyrian *dunnu* system and the abandonment of the northern Assyrian frontier in the mid-11th century BC did not create a power vacuum into which rushed the emergent Aramaean kingdoms. Rather, the picture portrayed here is of a long, narrow stretch of land in which there was little permanent habitation during the 180 or so years of the Early Iron Age. Mobile agropastoralists, representing only one social element of local chiefdoms or kingdoms centered elsewhere, like Damdammusa and Amedi, seem to have utilized existing mounds as temporary halting places. The disappearance of the Middle Assyrians, from the perspective of the Upper Tigridians, was an economic opportunity to access the rich river valley more readily than during times of Assyrian strength. There was no push by emergent polities to create new towns and cities in the Bismil-Batman Corridor at the end of the Late Bronze Age. The obvious question that arises, then, is why the Upper Tigridians did not choose to settle in such a rich agricultural area.

One plausible explanation for the lack of permanent Early Iron villages is that the Bismil-Batman Corridor was simply too dangerous to settle. Despite the abandonment of the major urban center of Tušhum/Ziyaret Tepe and supporting sites such

[44] Lyonnet 2009, p. 180.
[45] D'Agostino 2009.

as Dunnu-ša-Uzibi/Giricano, the threat of a possible return of the Assyrian army was always present, and eventually realized in the early 9th century BC. Perhaps the Bismil-Batman Corridor was a contested zone between emerging Aramaean polities themselves and was, therefore, difficult or impossible to colonize; unfortunately, we have no written sources to inform us of Aramaean internal politics. In any case, it seems clear that mobile agropastoralists came to the abandoned places along the river with their flocks, planted, harvested, and stored crops in silos dug into the mounds, but did not invest time in extensive permanent building projects. Rather than emulating the Middle Assyrian pattern of land usage, the Upper Tigridian polities of the Early Iron Age engaged a radically different perspective which saw the river and its valley as a place to use and move through, rather than as a place to colonize. Near Eastern archaeologists (this one included) have long been blinkered by our assumption that, as Szuchman succinctly summarizes, "the archaeology of nomadism... is limited to identifying the ancient 'campsite' or 'tentsite'."[46] We expected to find settled Early Iron Age villages along the river and failed to imagine other possibilities. In this case, envisioning a more fluid, dynamic social fabric allows us to expose the weaknesses in our methodology and to present a more nuanced explanation of the past.

References cited

ALGAZE, G. et al.
1991 "The Tigris-Euphrates Archaeological Reconnaissance Project: A Preliminary Report of the 1989–1990 Seasons," *Anatolica* 17: 175–240.

ALIZADEH, A.
2010 "The Rise of the Highland Elamite State in Southwestern Iran: 'Enclosed' or Enclosing Nomadism?," *Current Anthropology* 51(3): 353–383.

BARNARD, H. and WENDRICH, W., editors
2008 *The Archaeology of Mobility: Old World and New World Nomadism*, Cotsen Advanced Seminars 4. Los Angeles: Cotsen Institute of Archaeology, UCLA.

BLAYLOCK, S.
2009 *Tille Höyük 3.1. The Iron Age: Introduction, Stratification and Architecture*, The British Institute at Ankara Monograph 41. London: The British Institute of Archaeology at Ankara.

D'AGOSTINO, A.
forthcoming "The Upper Khabur and Upper Tigris valleys between the end of the Late Bronze Age and the beginning of the Iron Age: an assessment of the archaeological evidence (settlement patterns and pottery assemblages)," in *Empires after Empire. Anatolia, Syrian and Assyria after Suppiluliuma II (ca. 1200–800/700 B.C.), Proceedings of the Interdisciplinary Workshop held at Klagenfurt, December 4-6th 2008*, Eothen 17, edited by K. Strobel. Firenze: LoGisma Editore.

46 Szuchman 2008, p. 405.

2009 "The Assyrian–Aramaean Interaction in the Upper Khabur: The Archaeological Evidence from Tell Barri Iron Age Layers," *Syria* 86: 17–41.

FISCHER, B., GENZ, H., JEAN, É., and KÖROĞLU, K., editors

2003 *Identifying Changes: The Transition from Bronze to Iron Ages in Anatolia and its Neighbouring Regions.* Istanbul: Türk Eskiçağ Bilimleri Enstitüsü.

GRAYSON, A. K.

1991 *Assyrian Rulers of the Early First Millennium BC I (1114–859 BC)*, Royal Inscriptions of Mesopotamia, Assyrian Periods 2. Toronto: University of Toronto Press.

KESSLER, K.

1980 *Untersuchungen zur historischen Topographie Nordmesopotamiens nach keilschriftlichen Quellen des 1. Jahrtausends v. Chr.* Wiesbaden: Dr. Ludwig Reichert Verlag.

KÖROĞLU, K.

2003 "The Transition from Bronze Age to Iron Age in Eastern Anatolia," in *Identifying Changes: The Transition from Bronze to Iron Ages in Anatolia and its Neighboring Regions*, edited by B. Fischer, H. Genz, É. Jean, and K. Köroğlu, pp. 231–244. İstanbul: Türk Eskiçağ Bilimleri Enstitüsü.

1998 *Üçtepe I. Yeni Kazı ve Yüzey Bulguları Işığında Diyarbakır/Üçtepe ve Çevresinin Yeni Assur Dönemi Tarihi Coğrafyası.* Ankara: Türk Tarih Kurumu Basımevi.

KOZBE, G. and KÖROĞLU, K.

2004 "Kavuşan Höyük 2002 Yılı Kazısı," *Kazı Sonuçları Toplantısı* 25: 279–288.

KÜHNE, H.

2009 "Interaction of Aramaeans and Assyrians on the Lower Khabur," *Syria* 86: 43–54.

2010 "The Rural Hinterland of Dūr-Katlimmu," in *Dūr-Katlimmu 2008 and Beyond*, Studia Chaburensia 1, edited by H. Kühne, pp. 115–128. Wiesbaden: Harrassowitz Verlag.

KUHRT, A.

1995 *The Ancient Near East, c. 3000–330 BC.* (Routledge History of the Ancient World). London: Routledge.

LANERI, N., SCHWARTZ, M., VALENTINI, S., D'AGOSTINO and NANNUCCI, S.

2009 "The Hirbemerdon Tepe Archaeological Project: The First Four Seasons of Archaeological Work at a Site in the Upper Tigris River Valley, SE Turkey," *Ancient Near Eastern Studies* 46: 212–276.

LYONNET, B.

2009 "Who Lived in the Third-millennium "Round Cities" of Northern Syria?," in *Nomads, Tribes, and the State in the Ancient Near East: Cross-disciplinary Perspectives*, Oriental Institute Seminars 5, edited by J. Szuchman, pp. 179–200. Chicago: The Oriental Institute of the University of Chicago.

MATNEY, T.

2010 "Material Culture and Identity: Assyrians, Aramaeans, and the Indigenous Peoples of Iron Age Southeastern Turkey," in *Agency and Identity in the Ancient Near East: New Paths Forward*, edited by S. Steadman and J. Ross, pp. 129–147. London: Equinox Publishing Ltd.

MATNEY, T., GREENFIELD, T., HARTENBERGER, B., KESKIN, A., KÖROĞLU, K., MACGINNIS, J., MONROE, W., RAINVILLE, L., SHEPPERSON, M., VORDERSTRASSE, T. and WICKE, D.

2009 "Excavations at Ziyaret Tepe, 2007–2008," *Anatolica* 35: 37–84.

MATNEY, T., RAINVILLE, L., KÖROĞLU, K., KESKIN, A., VORDERSTRASSE, T., FINDIK, N.Ö., and DONKIN, A.

2007 "Report on Excavations at Ziyaret Tepe, 2006 Season," *Anatolica* 33: 23–74.

MATNEY, T. and L. RAINVILLE, editors
2005 "Archaeological Investigations at Ziyaret Tepe 2003–2004," *Anatolica* 31: 19–68.
MATNEY, T., ROAF, M., MACGINNIS, J. and MCDONALD, H.
2002 "Archaeological Excavations at Ziyaret Tepe, 2000 and 2001," *Anatolica* 28: 47–89.
ÖKSE, A. T. and GÖRMÜŞ, A.
2006 "Excavations at Salat Tepe in the Upper Tigris RegionL Stratigraphical Sequence and Preliminary Results of the 2005–2006 Seasons," *Akkadica* 127: 167–197.
PARKER, B. J.
2003 "Archaeological Manifestations of Empire: Assyria's Imprint on Southeastern Anatolia," *American Journal of Archaeology* 103: 525–557.
2001 *The Mechanics of Empire: The Northern Frontier of Assyria as a Case Study in Imperial Dynamics*. Helsinki: The Neo-Assyrian Text Corpus Project.
PARKER, B., CREEKMORE, A. and SWARTZ DODD, L.
2004 "The Upper Tigris Archaeological Research Project (UTARP): A Preliminary Synthesis of the Cultural History of Kenan Tepe," in *Salvage Project of the Archaeological Heritage of the Ilısu and Carchemish Dam Reservoirs: Activities in 2001*, edited by N. Tuna, J. Greenhalgh, and J. Valibeyoğlu, pp. 581–629. Ankara: Centre for Research and Assessment of the Historic Environment.
POSTGATE, J. N.
1992 "The Land of Assur and the yoke of Assur," *World Archaeology* 23(3): 247–263.
1976 "Nomads and Sedentaries in the Middle Assyrian Sources," in *Nomads and Sedentary Peoples*, edited by J. S. Castillo, pp. 47–56. Mexico City: El Colegio de Mexico.
RADNER, K.
2004 *Das Mittelassyrische Tontafelarchiv von Giricano/Dunnu-ša-Uzibi*, Subartu 14; Excavations at Giricano 1. Turnhout: Brepols.
RISTVET, L.
2008 "Legal and archaeological territories of the second millennium BC in northern Mesopotamia," *Antiquity* 82: 585–599.
ROAF, M. and SCHACHNER, A.
2005 "The Bronze Age to Iron Age transition in the upper Tigris region: new information from Ziyaret Tepe and Giricano," in *Anatolian Iron Ages 5: Proceedings of the Fifth Anatolian Iron Ages Colloquium held at Van, 6–10 August 2001*, edited by A. Çilingiroğlu and G. Darbyshire, British Institute at Ankara Monograph 31, pp. 115–123. London: British Institute at Ankara.
SALZMAN, P. C.
1972 "Multi-resource Nomadism in Iranian Baluchistan," in *Perspectives on Nomadism*, edited by W. Irons and N. Dyson-Hudson, pp. 60–68. Leiden: Brill.
SCHACHNER, A.
2003 "From the Bronze Age to the Iron Age: Identifying Changes in the Upper Tigris Region. The Case of Giricano," in *Identifying Changes: The Transition from Bronze to Iron Ages in Anatolia and its Neighbouring Regions*, edited by B. Fischer, H. Genz, É. Jean, and K. Köroğlu, pp. 151–163. Istanbul: Türk Eskiçağ Bilimleri Enstitüsü.
SEVIN, V.
1991 "The Early Iron Age in the Elazığ Region and the Problem of the Mushkians," *Anatolian Studies* 41: 87–97.

SZUCHMAN, J., editor
2009b *Nomads, Tribes, and the State in the Ancient Near East: Cross-disciplinary Perspectives*, Oriental Institute Seminars 5. Chicago: The Oriental Institute of the University of Chicago.

SZUCHMAN, J.
2009a "Bit Zamani and Assyria," *Syria* 86: 53–64.
2008 "Mobility and Sedentarization in Late Bronze Age Syria," in *The Archaeology of Mobility: Old World and New World Nomadism*, Cotsen Advanced Seminars 4, edited by H. Barnard and W. Wendrich, pp. 397–412. Los Angeles: Cotsen Institute of Archaeology, UCLA.

TENU, A.
2009 *L'expansion médio-assyrienne: Approche archéologique*. BAR International Series 1906. Oxford: John and Erica Hedges, Ltd.

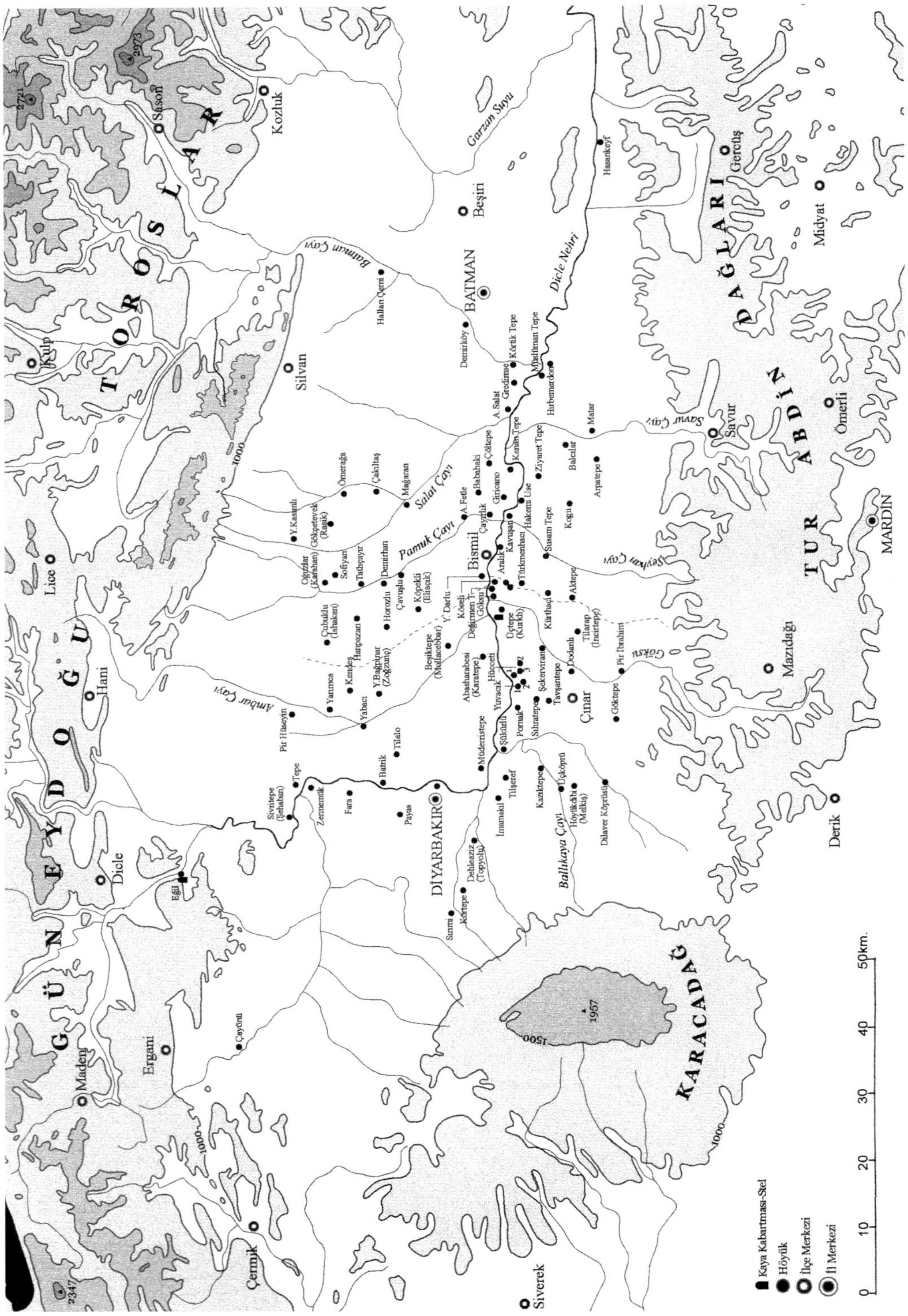

Fig 1 Map of the upper Tigris River valley showing principal ancient sites.
This map is reproduced with the kind permission of Prof. Dr. Kemalettin Köroğlu.

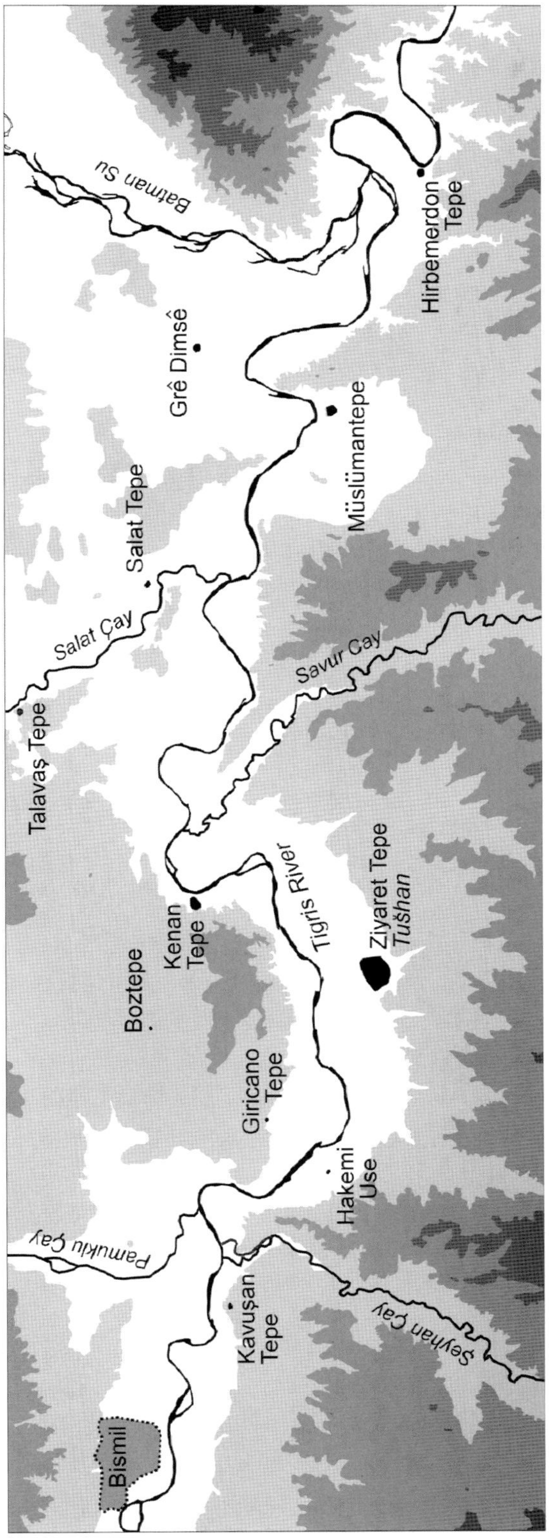

Fig. 2 Map of the "Bismil-Batman Corridor" region of the upper Tigris River valley showing principal ancient sites.

CHAPTER 15

NEO-HITTITE MELID: CONTINUITY OR DISCONTINUITY?

Marcella FRANGIPANE
Sapienza Università di Roma, Italy
E-mail: marcella.frangipane@uniroma1.it

and

Mario LIVERANI
Sapienza Università di Roma, Italy
E-mail: mliver@mclink.it

Introduction

(M. Frangipane)

The excavations of the Late Bronze and Iron Age levels, as everybody knows, were suspended at Arslantepe for many decades, mainly due to the unearthing of major remains of the fourth and third millennia BCE in the SW area of the mound. The Chalcolithic and Early Bronze levels, which yielded new crucial knowledge about the history of the region in those periods and the developments of "early urban" and "early state" societies[1] had demanded extensive investigations and attracted the bulk of our energies and efforts for several years.

To a certain extent, it is precisely the constant increase in our knowledge of the proto-history of Arslantepe and our growing perception of the sharp and repeated breaks in continuity that have characterised the peculiar development of the site for millennia that has driven us to revisit once again, with a new methodology and on different bases, the question of the revival in the fortunes of the site in the Late Bronze Age. Furthermore, we will focus new attention on the causes and features of the new supposed 'crisis' it underwent at the end of the 2nd millennium BCE, and its consequences affecting the subsequent evolution towards different forms of power and political organisation in the Iron Age. Thus, in 2007–2008, we resumed the activities in the NE area of the mound, immediately to the west of the large old trench where the famous Lion Gate had been apparently located.

[1] Palmieri 1973, 1997; Frangipane, Palmieri 1983; Frangipane *et al.* 2001; Frangipane, ed. 2004, 2007.

In the first two years of excavations in this new sector opened in the NE area of the mound, an interesting sequence of levels relating to the period immediately after the end of the Late Bronze Age (the 'imperial' phase) and covering the first centuries of the Iron Age (the first phase of the Neo-Hittite development) have been brought to light. This sequence illustrates a series of changes that took place in architecture and material culture during the first development of the Iron Age, documenting what seems to be an actual and unexpected interruption in the architectural, and possibly political, continuity in the history of Melid, as it is shown by Mario Liverani in this paper and by Federico Manuelli.[2] Despite its preliminary character, therefore, the information that has emerged from the renewal of the investigation in the Neo-Hittite levels at Arslantepe is in my opinion, already worthy of being introduced into the general debate on the themes proposed by this conference.

The characteristics that seem to emerge from the hypothesised arrangement and transformation of the settlement in these periods appear, in general terms, to be comparable with similar features and trends observable in the period of the first political centralisation at the end of the 4th millennium. In both cases, the centre of Arslantepe was monumental and small in size and was a kind of citadel, certainly fortified in the period of the Hittite and Neo-Hittite state; in both cases the sequences were characterised by very sharp breaks and discontinuity, which are distinctive traits in the history of this site.

I may suggest that such site arrangements, as well as its developmental breaks and discontinuity were probably due first of all to the internal structure of Arslantepe society and the political systems it produced over time. Even though these systems, of course, changed sometimes radically in their institutional and organisational forms, they may have indeed retained certain basic distinctive structural features on which traditional relations, power and population were founded. Another important reason for these breaks would certainly have been the site's location on a geographical, political and cultural border between the Taurus/Anti-Taurus mountains and the Euphrates Valley environment, between the mining zones of the North Eastern mountainous region and those of the Circumpontic areas; in summary, between the Syro-Mesopotamian, Central Anatolian, and Transcaucasian cultural worlds. This location plotted the curve full of breaks, declines, and revivals in Arslantepe's development, as well as enabling it to open up to different worlds and make it receptive to alternatively different prevailing cultural influences.

But what are these distinguishing structural features of Arslantepe societies and the way they related with the world around them; features which must have shaped the forms of power and their frequent "collapses", perhaps until the second and first millennia BCE? First of all, I believe that what characterised life on the site during its

[2] Manuelli in the present volume.

most prosperous periods was the fact that it never underwent a proper urbanisation process, and particularly during phases in which the site was the capital, this resulted in a clash between a structured and strong central power and a small settlement, mostly occupied by public structures. For example, this first occurred with the development of the period VI A palatial centre in the final Late Chalcolithic period (LC 5), when the monumental public area occupied most of the SW slope of the mound, while the settlement itself actually seems to have shrunk in size from what it had been in the previous period VII (LC 3–4). It probably occurred once again during the Hittite empire expansion in the Late Bronze II period, certainly becoming the salient feature of the Neo-Hittite kingdom of Melid when Arslantepe seems to have been a fortified citadel, which was evidently much smaller than other contemporary centres to the south. We have found evidence to show that in the Late Bronze I (the Old Kingdom phase) the whole mound was occupied as far as the SW slopes (**Fig. 1**), where we have found dwellings full of *in situ* materials.[3] The LB I fortification unearthed in the NE area, which consisted of an imposing earthen wall with a rectangular gate made of a double chamber of a clearly Central Anatolian type,[4] seems to have continued around the whole settlement according to the evidence found on this wall along the western flank of the mound. Its traces indeed leads one to hypothesize that it may have surrounded the entire mound including the southern sector of the settlement. Conversely, no traces of occupation in the Empire phase (Late Bronze II) or the Neo-Hittite phase (Iron Age) have been found in the SW part of the hill. During this time, a new powerful regional centre developed again, which most probably already had been under the influence of the Hittite empire. Certainly in the following period of the small neo-Hittite kingdom of Melid, there is evidence to show that the site shrank in size and was restricted to a smaller and fortified area.

We do not know yet whether there was a lower town; but as it can be plausibly assumed, even if there had been a lower settled area, from the evidence gathered in the course of our survey at Arslantepe in 2003–2006,[5] we may safely suggest that — exactly as had occurred in the fourth millennium — instead of a real town as such, there may have been a concentration of small villages, houses, and hamlets around the political centre and its public areas.

The second distinctive feature of Arslantepe is the constantly recurring visits and interference of nomadic and seminomadic pastoralist groups in the life of the town. Their presence appears most evidently in the form of seasonal settlements during periods of political crisis and are indirectly and continuously attested throughout the whole history of the site.

[3] Palmieri 1983, pp. 101, 385.
[4] Palmieri 1978.
[5] Di Nocera 2008, 2009.

The 2008 and 2009 excavation campaigns have also confirmed this as a very prominent and characteristic feature during the Iron Age, marking a phase of abandonment of the site (approximately in the 10th century BCE), which seems to have been seasonally occupied by groups of *squatters* after the destruction by fire of the post-imperial citadel. The existence of a monumental area in a post-imperial phase has been documeneted by a huge town wall built on the ruins of the "Imperial Gate" (excavated by P.E. Pecorella)[6] with a possible gate structure of its own preceding the later arrangement of the town entrance at the time of the Lion Gate. These new achievements of the recent excavations will be thoroughly and with greater detail presented below by M. Liverani.

The Late-Bronze to Iron Age Transition at Arslantepe: Preliminary Results

(M. Liverani)

History and Main Targets of the Arslantepe Excavation

The Neo-Hittite remains at Arslantepe, especially the sculptured slabs and statues still visible on the top of the mound or kept in the village nearby,[7] provided the starting stimulus for the archaeological investigation of the site. During the thirties of the past century, Louis Delaporte excavated the "Lions' Gate", which is now in the Ankara Museum of Anatolian Civilizations.[8] The proposed date of the sculptured reliefs, based on their style, was quite high —the end of the second millennium.[9] But the gate was still in use half a millennium later, when the city was destroyed by Sargon II in 712 BCE, therefore its stratigraphic position (in the last Neo-Hittite level)[10] was not in agreement with so high a date. The search started for an earlier gate, from which the reliefs could have been removed to be reused in the Lions' Gate. During the late forties, Claude Schaeffer and his architect, W. Forrer, dug an enormous trench under the Lions' Gate and they did find the remains of a gate, a "triple gate", with sculptured lions; but their preliminary reports were rather contradictory as to their stratigraphic position and dating of the remains.[11] In any case, Schaeffer did not publish nor leave any map, stratigraphy, or any other kind of record. Ten years later, when the

[6] Pecorella 1975.
[7] See e.g. the Gertrude Bell photos in the web-site http://www.gerty.ncl.ac.uk.
[8] Delaporte 1940.
[9] Delaporte 1940, pp. 31 and 57; Akurgal 1946, 1949, pp. 139–141; Orthman 1971, pp. 91–100, 463–464.
[10] Delaporte 1939.
[11] Schaeffer 1948, pp. 342–343 speaks of a gate identical to (although smaller than) the Lion's Gate, 1.15 m. above it, therefore an older gate; W. Forrer *apud* Schaeffer 1951, first suggests a date in the 12th–11th century, but then says that the gate "fait partie du dernier palais dont Delaporte a dégagé quelques éléments"; see also Weidner 1952–53.

Italian mission started working on the site,[12] the dig in the area was enlarged and deepened down to the Hittite Imperial gate published by Pecorella,[13] located in the very same position as the later Lions' Gate;[14] but it was too ancient and too well preserved to be identified with the one from which the reliefs could have been removed.

After an intermission of 40 years, the excavation of the northern area was resumed in 2008, in order to clarify both the stratigraphy and the topography of the area. In terms of topography, the Lions' Gate opened on a wide plaza paved in stone slabs and bordered by important buildings along its sides. Delaporte excavated one of them to the west of the plaza, but his tragic death in a Nazi concentration camp prevented him from publishing it.[15] In terms of stratigraphy, the renewed excavation of the buildings (still extant) associated with the gate and the plaza (no longer extant) can provide the correct answer. A further point in our program was to get down to the underlying levels in order to fill the gap between the Imperial Hittite level of the 13th century BCE and the Neo-Hittite and Assyrian levels of the 8th century BCE.

A specific clue to both aims was provided by the presence of a big wall (M159) in mud bricks on a stone foundation, a city wall ca. four meters wide, and as many in preserved height, built above the Imperial Gate level and underlying the Lions Gate and associated buildings.[16] The wall, which was entirely burnt by a huge fire, was most probably provided with a gate as well: perhaps the gate found by Schaeffer; and in any case the long expected city gate of the 11th century from which the reliefs could have been removed.

In a few words, we can say that our 2008 campaign reached the first planned results; by exposing an important pillared hall (**Fig. 2**) structurally and stratigraphically connected to the Lions' Gate and by getting the pottery inventory, which provided for the first time the date of the gate and which will be discussed by Federico Manuelli in his own paper. The 2009 campaign targeted the second point by starting to descend under the pillared hall. The 2010 campaign reached the level of the city wall (M159) and the top of an important building in greenish mud bricks (A1279). We need another campaign to reach the floor of this building and its stratigraphic connection with the Imperial Gate, a connection already visible (and quite clear) in the profile on the western wall of the big Schaeffer trench (**Fig. 3**).[17] But we already have some clues to describe the history of Melid in the transition from the Late Bronze Age to the Early Iron Age and then to the Middle Iron Age in a way that is markedly different from the one generally accepted until now. But before entering into historical interpretations, we have to describe our excavation in more detail.

[12] Puglisi and Meriggi 1964.

[13] Pecorella 1975.

[14] See the superposed maps in Pecorella 2004, p. 168.

[15] Delaporte 1940, pl. XI.

[16] The wall should have been exposed by Schaeffer, since it was already at sight at the beginning of the Italian activities, see Puglisi and Meriggi 1964, pp. 18–19 and fig. 5.

[17] The section published by Pecorella 1975, pl. I is inaccurate in various decisive points.

The Pillared Hall of the Middle Iron Age

The building that Delaporte excavated and left unpublished (A1139+) has been cleaned, mapped, and removed (**Fig. 4**)[18] after 70 years of abandonment. Both the plan of the building, which is similar to other buildings in the Assyrian periphery,[19] and its stratigraphic position (Neo-Assyrian Level One in Delaporte's terms) confirm that we are dealing with a Neo-Assyrian building, presumably built soon after the conquest of the site by Sargon. The base of this building was built upon and abutted against a mud brick platform (M157) similar to the Assyrian ones found by Delaporte in the central area of the mound, and was most probably part of a large terraced building on the northern slope of the mound.[20]

Once the building A1139+ and the mud brick platform M157 had been cleaned, mapped, and removed, the pillared hall (**Fig. 5**) appeared, which was a room 18 × 12 m (walls excluded) oriented EW (A1142).[21] The foundations of the N and W walls were partly dug into the ground. Their inner faces were visible, but the outer face of the walls abutted a pre-existing cut. The S wall was partly visible beyond a deep modern trench dating to Schaeffer's activities. The E side opened onto the paved plaza inside the Lion's Gate, which was still in use after the Assyrian conquest; but this part was badly preserved because of later (i.e. Assyrian) overlay. The hall is characterized by two rows of four pillars each, of which only the bases were preserved, whereas three of them had been completely cut away by the modern trench. Furthermore, a uniform paving was entirely built of medium sized river pebbles. The pillars were regularly spaced and big enough to sustain an upper floor. Size, pillars, homogeneous paving, and the absence of any feature such as benches, bins, pits, and fireplaces, point to a ceremonial use such as a wide hall for receptions, obviously connected with the city gate.[22]

From the cut in the Schaeffer trench, it was clear that 20-30 cm under the cobble paving, there was another paving in smaller river pebbles clearly corresponding to an earlier and original phase of the same building. We, therefore, removed the entire upper paving and we exposed the lower paving (A1168) with the perimeter walls remaining the same.[23] The lower paving was less well preserved but we can see that the hall had originally been paved in large stone slabs in the perimeters and in small river pebbles in the central area (**Fig. 6**). Instead of the two rows of huge pillars, there were three rows of thin columns, whose round bases were partly preserved and partly removed leaving a round empty space. A reasonable reconstruction is a hall with

[18] Liverani 2010, pp. 650–654; Delaporte 1940, pl. I.
[19] See lastly Manuelli 2009.
[20] Delaporte 1939, pl. 8–9.
[21] Liverani 2010, pp. 657–660.
[22] Liverani 2011.
[23] Liverani 2010, pp. 661–665.

a central space open to the sky, surrounded by a roofed portico along the walls; but a completely covered area sustaining a terrace rather than a second floor remains a possibility as well.

The date of the two phases of the hall have been established thanks to the pottery fragments in the sealed fill between the two pavings and are discussed in the paper by Federico Manuelli.[24] In rough terms, we can say that the hall was originally built around 825 BCE, restored around 750 BCE, and finally destroyed around 710 BCE.

From the architectural point of view, the presence of the pillars or columns and the pebble paving require some comments which are intended to suggest different functions and uses for the first structural arrangement vs. the second. Pillared and columned halls are alien for obvious reasons to the mud brick architecture of the Mesopotamian lowlands. However, they are quite frequent in a variety of forms in the highlands from Central Anatolia, through Eastern Anatolia and Iranian Azerbaijan, to the Central Zagros. These include square halls with multiple rows of columns, rectangular halls with two or just one row of columns, columned porticos, big storerooms in public buildings, and small storerooms in private houses which appear by the Late Bronze period, but are prevalent especially during Early-Middle Iron Age. This entire set of sub-types will find its culmination and coordination in the large palaces of the Achaemenid empire. We cannot discuss the development of the architectural type[25] here, which would require an entire monograph, the Levant providing rich additional evidence, mostly at the domestic level;[26] but it is clear that our hall in Neo-Hittite Melid provides a previously missing link; a link in space between the Phrygian and the Urartian sites and also, in part, a link in time between the 13th century Hittite Büyükkale and the 9th–8th century halls. As for the paving with river pebbles, it is quite typical of Neo-Hittite architecture. Obviously, paving in pebbles and also in stone slabs is more functional and more frequent in external areas such as courtyards and lanes, but is also attested in covered rooms.[27]

The original arrangement of our hall appears to be more convenient for a functional use presumably connected with the city gate, that is, for hosting the guard corps, checking incoming persons, and merchandise. The paving would be coherent with an occasional admittance of horses, while the formal, "full time" stables of the type known from Bastam to Megiddo, belong to a more specialized sub-type.[28] However, the second arrangement with an homogeneous paving and no additional features, is more convenient for a "ceremonial" use such as for audiences or banquets. Such a use has

[24] See also Manuelli 2010; s.d. 1.

[25] Extensive treatment in Liverani 2011; see already Margueron 2001; Miglus 2004; also Forbes 1983, pp. 49–59 (Urartian area only).

[26] On pillared houses in the Levant see the recent syntheses by Braemer 1992 and by Herzog 1997.

[27] Liverani 2010, pp. 659–660.

[28] Liverani 2012; on stables see Holladay 1986; Cantrell – Finkelstein 2006.

a long history in the highland areas of the Near East starting at least from Building D at Boğazköy (14–13th centuries), through the columned halls at Hasanlu (11th–10th centuries), to the Phrygian *megarons* at Gordion and Kerkenes, the various halls in the Urartian sites (8th–7th centuries), such as Bastam, Altintepe, Arinberd, Kef Kalesi, and many others. They also exist in the Median sites of the same date at Godin Tepe and Nush-i Jan, finally culminating in the *apadana* of the Achaemenid palaces (6th–5th centuries).[29] We have, however, to consider the size; the Achaemenid halls of Susa and Persepolis are ten times bigger than their Urartian and Median models, and 25 times bigger than the Melid hall (**Fig.** 7). Of course the Persian architects derived the type of the *apadana* from the Median halls, which were closer to them in time, space, and in cultural connections. But the Middle Iron Age halls had their forerunners neither in Urartu nor in Media, where no monumental architecture is attested in the Late Bronze Age, but in Imperial Hittite Anatolia, so that the role of Melid and presumably also of other Neo-Hittite sites becomes relevant for the transmission of the type.

The Sequence of the Early Iron Age

The transmission of the type remains, however, a problem at Arslantepe itself — a problem that we are trying to solve by exploring the remains belonging to the Early Iron Age by digging under the pillared hall down to the "Imperial Gate." The possibility of getting a continuous sequence from the Hittite Imperial level through the level of the burnt city wall to the level of the Lions' Gate (and our pillared hall) would provide important historical results. I can anticipate here that our results seem to provide an image of the history of Melid that is quite different from the previously accepted one. I hardly need to reiterate that the commonly accepted historical reconstruction is characterized by long and enduring continuity. First of all, the early kings of Melid are the immediate descendants of Kuzi-Teshub, who was king of Carchemish in the early 12th century.[30] Moreover, there are so many kings of Melid, especially during the 12th – 11th centuries, that the hypothesis of two parallel dynasties has been advanced. Finally, several kings are known in the Middle Iron Age also, whose names are generally different in Assyrian and in local inscriptions.[31]

Consequently, we removed a good half of the columned hall, leaving the best preserved western part, and we went down on an area of 180 square meters. In the 2009 campaign, we recovered the poorly preserved remains of a building (A1210+) under the columned hall with the very same orientation of the hall and ultimately of the Lions' Gate. This was an orthogonal orientation, which was almost exactly NS. Espe-

[29] See chart and literature in Liverani 2011.

[30] Hawkins 1988; 1994; 2002a–b.

[31] Standard reconstructions of the history of Melid are provided by Hawkins 1993; 1998; 2000, pp. 283–288. See also Archi 2004 and Liverani 2004.

cially important is the fact that the terrace wall, later used to delimit the pillared hall towards the Lions' Gate and the paved courtyard, was already in existence in an earlier, rougher version (M170+188) in connection with this "early orthogonal building" (A1210+). But the major surprise was to find out that both after and especially before the "early orthogonal building", the sequence was characterized by very poor remains of squatters' occupations, which were small and large plastered pits (**Fig. 8a**), postholes, small bins (**Fig. 8b**), alignments of bricks, and fireplaces. The entire squatters' occupation was located above the burnt city wall as well as adjacent to it and above the decay of its mud bricks, sloping down from the top of the wall towards the SE, that is, inside the citadel. Clearly the burnt city wall remained in sight as a huge ruin in the process of decay for a long time, with rain and snow washing away the mud bricks. The area hosted the poor structures of a community that cannot be imagined as urbanized. Federico Manuelli shows in his paper how the ceramic horizon of this phase is quite different (totally local) from the one when the gate and the hall were in function and relevant outer connections are documented.

Admittedly, the excavated area is small and it is legitimate to doubt that it could legitimately represent the entire site. Yet our excavated area is located in a strategic position next to the northern city gate, probably the only city gate, and could not host squatters if the citadel was occupied by public buildings. Note that in Neo-Hittite times, the Arslantepe mound seems to have been entirely occupied by the citadel public buildings, while the common population may have lived outside the walls in a lower town — which apparently left no trace due to the intensive agricultural exploitation — and/or in small villages and hamlets in the surroundings. But during the Early Iron Age, when the citadel was occupied by squatters, where were the kings and, where is the continuity?

The second major surprise came during the 2010 campaign, which was that the main crisis of the city was not due to or contemporary with the collapse of the Hittite empire, but was postponed by some 150 years. The "Imperial Gate" and the related city wall underwent a total destruction by a huge fire, resulting in a deep layer of collapsed bricks all over the area of the gate. But immediately or shortly afterwards, another city wall was built anew, together with important buildings inside the city gate (A1279). This arrangement was short-lived, ending in abandonment (no trace of fire), but was followed by the building of still another city wall (M159) connected with a city gate, most probably the one that Schaeffer found. This gate may have functioned for a century to be finally destroyed by a second fire, which also left a layer of burnt collapsed bricks. In order to better visualize the sequence of events and the stratigraphy of layers, a summary chart is provided of the entire sequence as we can reconstruct it now (**Fig. 9**). At this point, two topics have to be better clarified. The first is the nature of the main structures of the post-imperial but pre-squatting period, the second is chronology.

The main structures identified so far belonging to our level 10 are the following: a few remains of the stone foundation of the city wall embedded below the stone foundation of M159, the "Green Building" (**Fig. 10**) (A1279), which was an impressive building measuring some 11 × 16 m, partly cut away by Schaeffer, partly excavated by Pecorella,[32] and partly now excavated by ourselves. In addition, an external floor connected the two, which is visible in section but not yet reached by our excavation. The "Green Building" bears no trace of fire, its floor (where reached by Pecorella) was empty and the building was most probably abandoned.

The main structures belonging to our level 8 are the following: the city wall (M159), which had been built above the remains of the wall of level 10, and its floor inside the citadel (A1278). Slightly later, a wall (A1278 M1), perpendicular to M159 was probably added with the purpose of hosting a city gate. For sure, the gate was totally cut away by the Schaeffer dig, but we found two sculptured slabs on the floor of A1278, close to M1, which were quite similar (in one case, identical) to other slabs discovered at Arslantepe (one in the Malatya Museum, two in the Ankara Museum), and most probably came from the Schaeffer Gate.[33] At first impression, we may have the stratigraphic proof that the Lions' Gate decoration originally belonged to an earlier gate, as was always suspected on stylistic grounds;[34] but the relation between the decoration of the 11th century gate and that of the Lions' Gate requires further study. As to the decoration of this earlier gate, it is even possible that the fire put an end to a work in progress; our two slabs were in a perfect state of preservation and were found lying on the floor in the open space at the intersection of M1 with M159, as if not yet placed into their final position.

As for chronology, pending both the study of the pottery and radiocarbon dates, which are both still in progress, the indications provided in the chart are obviously preliminary. We take for granted that the Imperial Gate was destroyed by a huge fire at the beginning of the 12th century, and 1180 is an approximate date. We also have various bits of evidence for a date of the destruction of M159 / A1278 around 1070 BCE, suggesting the author of the destruction could have been Ashur-bel-kala in 1073–72.[35] In between 1180 and 1070, the date of the shift from our phase 8 to our

[32] Pecorella 1975, pl. XLIV–XLV and fig. G–I.

[33] The sculptured slabs will be shortly published by Federico Manuelli.

[34] See fn. 3 above.

[35] Full discussion in Liverani, s.d. [After the present paper had been completed, we received information from Dr Pinar Ertepinar, METU Ankara, that the paleo-magnetic date just obtained for the destruction of the burnt fortification wall M159 is to be lowered to 970 BCE; in this case our "Post-Imperial Period" should be extended, and our "Squatting Period" reduced, accordingly. But for the moment, pending our C14 dates of the entire sequence, we keep the chronology as announced at the "Across the Border" conference. The paleomagnetic dating on samples from Arslantepe are in progress in the Fort Hoofddijk Paleomagnetic laboratory of Utrecht University and Geomagnetism Laboratory of University of Liverpool].

phase 10 at ca. 1120 is clearly artificial and approximate. Of course, during the 2010 campaign we collected several carbon samples from layer 9, which is the destruction layer resulting from the burnt collapse of bricks from M159, and whose analysis will confirm or change our tentative chronology.

Historical Considerations

The early kings of Melid, who were the descendants of Kuzi-Teshub, and are mostly attested from steles at the northern border of the Melid territory, would have to be dated to the period between ca.1180–1070 BCE. These are also the dates for "Sulumeli" (the traditional reading of his name), whose reliefs decorated the Post-Imperial Gate (A1278 M1). In this period Melid underwent several troubles: The period starts and ends in two huge fires, one destroying the Imperial Gate, and the other destroying M159 and the Post-Imperial Gate; in addition the intermediate building(s) were abandoned. Yet building activities, which include city walls and gates, their iconic decoration, plus important edifices, testify to the flourishing and importance of the city, no doubt a palatine city, the capital of a kingdom. The city wall was standing when Tiglath-pileser I received the submission of Allumara in the first quarter of the eleventh century. But at the end of this period, around 1070, a destructive event suddenly stopped building activities. The city wall, city gate, and the entire citadel were not reconstructed, and remained in a state of partial abandonment for a few centuries. The poor remains of a prolonged squatters' occupation seem to rule out the possibility that the citadel was the seat of a royal palace. If the kings of Melid still existed, they would have been living somewhere else. Some building activity started again only around 900 BCE and only by 830 BCE did the site attain high levels of monumental structures, the obvious proxies for a strong political order, i.e. the Melid known from Urartian and Assyrian texts to have been a strategic kingdom and a flourishing cultural centre.

Such a process of decay and recovery, which is new when compared to the traditional reconstruction of Melid history in terms of continuity is, however, quite normal in a wider perspective. It corresponds to the well known trajectory from the collapse of Late Bronze Age polities through the "Dark Age" of the Early Iron Age[36] to recovery in the Middle Iron Age, to the final collapse following the Assyrian conquest. We could say that the archaeological excavation at Arslantepe is substituting a real Melid to the hypothetical Melid reconstructed before.

But, while in some regions, such as Central Anatolia through the Syrian coast to the Southern Levant, the crisis started immediately after the collapse of Late Bronze

[36] Recent literature includes Herr 1997; Joffe 2002; Grabbe (ed.) 2008; on the Syro-Anatolian area see Venturi 2007.

centres, possibly as a direct effect of the destructions produced by foreign invaders, in the area of the Upper Euphrates, from Carchemish to Melid, there was a prolongation of city life and political order that lasted a century. In particular, the city wall and gate of the 11th century at Tille Höyük seems to be quite a good parallel to the post-imperial revival of Melid;[37] and also Tell Bazi could have undergone a similar process.[38] But this phenomenon is not limited to the Upper Euphrates basin. On the one hand we have to give due attention to the recently discovered kingdom of Taita, the Philistine[39] and the sculptured decoration belonging to his polity,[40] while on the other hand, the 12th century was a period of strong political and military activity in Assyria under Tiglath-pileser I, in Babylonia under Nebuchadnezzar I, and in Elam from Shutruk-Nakhunte to Shilkhak-in-Shushinak. The main collapse, especially east of the Euphrates, seems to be connected with the spread of Aramaean tribes around 1070–1050 BCE.[41]

As to the Middle Iron Age, the story of our pillared hall seems to fit quite well into the development of the historical situation. The utilitarian room (A 1168), dated on ceramic grounds to the period ca. 830–750 BCE, corresponds in quite exact terms to the phase of Urartian influence on Melid, as documented by the statements in their own inscriptions of Menua, Argishti I, and Sarduri I, and parallels the "feudal" crisis of Assyria. The ceremonial hall (A 1142), dated to the period ca. 750–710 BCE, corresponds to the phase of Assyrian prominence following the victory of Tiglath-pileser III at Kishtan in 743. Finally, building (A 1139+) is dated ca. 710–680, both on stratigraphic grounds and on the presumption that it corresponds to the phase of Assyrian provincial presence at Melid after Sargon's conquest in 712. We are confident that future campaigns will provide additional evidence, but already now we can establish a reasonable correlation between stratigraphy and historical sources in the troubled period between the end of the Late Bronze age (with its 12th-11th century prolongation) and the great recovery of urbanism, monumental architecture, and celebratory art that characterized the Middle Iron Age.

[37] See Summers 1990, 1993, pp. 9–15, 30–39, 55–56; 2010; and his paper in the present volume. Also, Blaylock 1999.

[38] Lastly Otto 2006, pp. 18–21; on chronology see also Venturi 2007, pp. 35–36, 417–426.

[39] Harrison 2009a–b; Hawkins 2009; and their papers in the present volume. See also Sass 2010a–b.

[40] In addition to the decoration of the Aleppo citadel temple, also the 'Ain Dara reliefs belong to the same chronological horizon (see Stone and Zimanski 1999; Mazzoni 1997), together with the slabs discovered at Aslantepe in 2010.

[41] On the current views of the problems of the imperial heritage and of the Neo-Hittite/Aramaean interactions see Novak 2002. On the rise of the Aramaeans see Sader 1992 and comments by McClellan 1992; Venturi 2007, pp. 420–426.

BIBLIOGRAPHY

AKURGAL, E.
1946 *Remarques stylistiques sur les reliefs de Malatya.* Istanbul: Pulhan Matbaası.
1949 *Späthethitische Bildkunst.* Ankara: Archaeologisches Institut der Universitaet Ankara.

ARCHI, A.
2004 "Malitiya-Meliddu: Arslantepe nelle fonti scritte", in *Alle Origini del Potere. Arslantepe, la collina dei leoni*, edited by M. Frangipane, pp. 173–174. Milano: Mondadori/Electa.

BLAYLOCK, S.
1999 "Iron Age Pottery from Tille Höyük, South East Turkey," in *Iron Age Pottery in Northern Mesopotamia, Northern Syria and South Eastern Anatolia*, edited by A. Hausleiter and A. Reiche, pp. 263–286. Munster: Ugarit-Verlag.

BRAEMER, F.
1982 *L'architecture domestique du Levant à l'âge du Fer.* Paris: Editions Recherche sur les civilisations.

CANTRELL, D. O. and FINKELSTEIN, I.
2006 "A Kingdom for a Horse. The Megiddo Stables and Eighth Century Israel," in *Megiddo, IV. The 1988–2002 Seasons*, edited by I. Finkelstein, D. Ussishkin and B. Halpern, pp. 643–665. Tel Aviv: Institute of Archaeology, Tel Aviv University.

DELAPORTE, L.
1939 "La troisième campagne de fouilles à Malatya," *Revue Hittite et Asianique* 5: 43–56.
1940 *Malatya.* Vol. 1. *La porte des lions.* Paris: De Boccard.

FORBES, TH. B.
1983 *Urartian Architecture*, BAR International 170. Oxford: BAR.

FRANGIPANE, M.
1997 "A 4th millennium temple/palace complex at Arslantepe-Malatya. North-south relations and the formation of early state societies in the northern regions of Greater Mesopotamia," *Paléorient* 23/1: 45–73.

FRANGIPANE, M. (ed.)
2004 *Alle Origini del Potere. Arslantepe, la Collina dei Leoni.* Milano: Mondadori/ Electa.
2007 *Arslantepe* Cretulae. *An Early Centralised Administrative System Before Writing*, Arslantepe vol. V. Roma: Dip. di Scienze dell'Antichità, Università La Sapienza.

FRANGIPANE, M. and PALMIERI, A. eds.
1983 "Perspectives on Protourbanization in Eastern Anatolia: Arslantepe (Malatya). An Interim Report on 1975–1983 campaigns,"*Origini* XII/2: 287–574.

FRANGIPANE M., DI NOCERA, G.M., HAUPTMANN, A., MORBIDELLI, P., PALMIERI, A.M., SADORI, L., SCHULTZ, M., and SCHMIDT-SCHULTZ, T.
2001 "New Symbols of a New Power in a "Royal" Tomb from 3000 BC Arslantepe, Malatya (Turkey)," *Paléorient* 27/2: 105–139.

GRABBE, L. L., ed.
2008 *Israel in Transition. From Late Bronze II to Iron IIa (c. 1250–850 B.C.E.).* Vol. 1, *The Archaeology*, Journal for the Study of the Old Testament, Supplement 491. New York – London: Clark International.

HARRISON, T. P.
2009a "Neo–Hittites in the "Land of Palistin," *Near Eastern Archaeology* 72: 174–189.

2009b "Lifting the Veil on a 'Dark Age': Ta'yinat and the North Orontes Valley during the Early Iron Age," in *Exploring the Longue Durée. Essays in Honor of L. E. Stager*, edited by J. D. Schloen, pp. 171–184. Winona Lake IN: Eisenbrauns.
2013 "Tayinat in the Early Iron Age", this volume, pp. 61–87.

HAWKINS, J. D.
1988 "Kuzi-Tešub and the 'Great Kings' of Karkamiš," *Anatolian Studies* 38: 99–108.
1993 "Melid. A. Historisch," in *Reallexikon der Assyriologie* 8, pp. 35–41. Berlin: De Gruyter.
1994 "The End of the Bronze Age in Anatolia: New Light from Recent Discoveries," in *Anatolian Iron Ages 3*, edited by A. Çilinigiroğlu and D. H. French, pp. 91–94. Ankara: British Institute of Archaeology.
1998 "Hittites and Assyrians at Melid (Malatya)," in *XXXIV International Assyriology Congress, Istanbul*, edited by H. Erkanal, V. Donbaz and A. Uğuroğlu, pp. 63–78. Ankara: Türk Tarih Kurumu.
2000 *Corpus of Hieroglyphic Luwian Inscriptions*, Vol. I–II. Berlin – New York: Walter de Gruyter.
2002a "Anatolia: The End of the Hittite Empire and After," in *Die nahöstlichen Kulturen und Griechenland an der Wende vom 2. zum 1. Jahrtausend v. Chr.*, edited by E. Braun-Holzinger and H. Matthäus, pp. 144–151. Möhnesee: Bibliopolis.
2002b "Die Erben des Großreiches, I–II", in *Die Hethiter und ihr Reich*, pp. 56–59 and 264–273. Bonn: Wissenschftliche Buchgesellschaft.
2009 "Cilicia, the Amuq, and Aleppo. New Light in a Dark Age," *Near Eastern Archaeology* 72: 164–173.
2013 "The Luwian Inscriptions from the Temple of the Storm-God of Aleppo", this volume, pp. 493–500.

HERR, L. G.
1997 "The Iron Age II Period: Emerging Nations," *Biblical Archaeologist* 60: 114–183.

HERZOG, Z.
1997 *Archaeology of the City. Urban Planning in Ancient Israel and Its Social Implications*. Tel Aviv: Institute of Archaeology, Tel Aviv University.

HOLLADAY, J. S.
1986 "The Stables of Ancient Israel," in *The Archaeology of Jordan and Other Studies Presented to S. H. Horn*, edited by L. T. Geraty and L. G. Herr, pp. 103–165. Berrien Springs MI: Andrews University Press.

JOFFE, A. H.
2002 "The Rise of Secondary States in the Iron Age Levant," *Journal of the Economic and Social History of the Orient* 45: 425–467.

KOHLMEYER, K.
2008 "Zur Datierung der Skulpturen von 'Ain Dārā," in *Fundstellen. Gesammelte Schriften zur Archäologie und Geschichte Altvorderasien ad honorem Hartmut Kühne*, edited by D. Bonatz, R. M. Czichon and F. J. Kreppner, pp. 119–130. Wiesbaden: Harrassowitz.

LIVERANI, M.
2004 "Gli Ittiti sulle rive dell'Eufrate," in *Alle Origini del Potere. Arslantepe, la collina dei leoni*, edited by M. Frangipane, pp. 161–165. Milano: Mondadori/Electa.
2010 "Il salone a pilastri della Melid neo-hittita," *Scienze dell'Antichità* 15: 649–675.

2011 "The Pillared Hall of Neo-Hittite Melid: a New Link in the Development of an Architectural Type," in *Studi in onore di A. Invernizzi*, edited by C. Lippolis and S. de Martino, pp. 91–111. Firenze.

2012 "From Melid through Bastam to Megiddo: Stables and Horses in Iron Age II," in *Studies Presented to F. M. Fales*, edited by G. B. Lanfranchi, pp. 443–458. Wiesbaden.

in press "Melid in the Early and Middle Bronze Age: Archaeology and History," forthcoming in *The Ancient Near East in the 12th–11th Centuries BCE: Archaeology and History*, edited by G. Galil.

MANUELLI, F.

2009 "Assyria and the Provinces. Survival of Local Features and Imposition of New Patterns in the Peripheral Regions of the Empire," *Mesopotamia* 44: 113–127.

2010 "Some Remarks on the Late Bronze Age Pottery Assemblages from Arslantepe," in *Proceedings of the 6th ICAANE (Roma 2009)*, Vol. III, edited by P. Matthiae, F. Pinnock, L. Nigro and N. Marchetti, pp. 399–409. Wiesbaden: Harrassowitz.

2011 "Pottery as an Indicator of Changing Interregional Relations in the Upper Euphrates Valley," this volume, pp. 373–391.

in press 1 "Iron Age Ceramic Movements and Usages at Arslantepe," forthcoming in *Mesopotamia.*

in press 2 "Malatya-Melid between the Late Bronze and the Iron Age: Preliminary Observations on the Pottery Assemblages" (Klagenfurt conference: *Empires after the Empire. Anatolia, Syria and Assyria after Šuppiluliuma II (ca. 1200–800/700 B.C.)*, 4.–6. 12. 2008), forthcoming as *Eothen 17*, Florence: LoGisma Editore.

MARGUERON, J.-C.

2001 "Salles à piliers dans l'architecture mésopotamienne, anatolienne et iranienne (fin 2e et début 1er millénaires)," in *Migration und Kulturtransfer*, edited by R. Eichmann and H. Parzinger, pp. 451–471. Berlin: R. Habelt

MAZZONI, S.

1997 "L'arte siro-hittita nel suo contesto archeologico," *Contributi e Materiali di Archeologia Orientale* 7: 287–327.

MCCLELLAN, TH. L.

1992 "12th Century B.C. Syria," in *The Crisis Years: The 12th Century B.C.*, edited by E. W. Eard and M. Sharp Joukowsky, pp. 164–173. Dubuque Iowa: Kendal / Hall Publishing Company.

MIGLUS, P. A.

2004 "Die Säule in Assyrien," in *Assyria and beyond. Studies Presented to M. T. Larsen*, edited by J. G. Dercksen, pp. 421–428. Leiden: Nederlands Instituut voor het Nabije Oosten.

NOVÁK, M.

2002 "Akkulturation von Aramäern un Luwiern und der Austausch von ikonographischen Konzepten in der späthethitischen Kunst," in *Brüchenland Anatolien?*, edited by H. Blum, B. Faist, and P. Pfälzner, pp.147–171. Tübingen: Attempto Verlag.

ORTHMANN, W.

1971 *Untersuchungen zur späthethitischen Kunst*, Saarbrücker Beiträge zur Altertumskunde 8. Bonn: Habelt.

OTTO, A.

2006 *Alltag und Gesellschaft zur Spätbronzezeit: eine Fallstudie aus Tall Bazi*, Subartu 19. Turnhout: Brepols.

PALMIERI, A.
1973 "Scavi nell'area sud-occidentale di Arslantepe. Ritrovamento di una struttura templare dell'Antica Età del Bronzo," *Origini* VII: 55–228.
1978 "Scavi ad Arslantepe (Malatya)," *Quaderni de "La Ricerca Scientifica"* 100, CNR: 311–352.
1983 "Arslantepe excavations, 1982", in *V Kazi Sonuçlari Toplantisi*, pp. 97–101, 383–385. Ankara: Ministry of Culture and Tourism.
PECORELLA, P. E.
1975 *Malatya.* Vol. 3. *Rapporto preliminare delle campagne 1963–1968. Il livello eteo imperiale e quelli neoetei,* Orientis Antiqui Collectio 12. Roma: Centro per le Antichità e la Storia dell'Arte del Vicino Oriente.
2004 "Arslantepe ittita: architettura pubblica e iconografia del potere," in *Alle Origini del Potere. Arslantepe, la collina dei leoni,* edited by M. Frangipane, pp. 167–171. Milano: Mondadori/Electa.
PUGLISI, S. and MERIGGI, P., ed.
1964 *Malatya.* Vol. 1. *Rapporto preliminare delle campagne 1961 e 1962,* Orientis Antiqui Collectio 3. Roma: Centro per le Antichità e la Storia dell'Arte del Vicino Oriente.
SADER, H.
1992 "The 12th Century B.C. in Syria: The Problem of the Rise of the Aramaeans," in *The Crisis Years: The 12th Century B.C.*, edited by E. W. Ward and M. Sharp Joukowsky, pp. 157–162. Dubuque Iowa: Kendal / Hall Publishing Company.
SASS, B.
2010a "Four Notes on Taita King of Palistin with an Excursus on King Solomon's Empire," *Tel Aviv* 37: 169–174.
2010b *Taita, King of Palistin: ca. 950–900 BCE?*, http://www.bu/edu/asor/pubs/nea/dig-ital-nea.html.
SCHAEFFER, CL.
1948 "Fouilles à Enkomi (Chypre) et à Arslan-Tépé", *Académie des Inscriptions et Belles-Lettres, Comptes-rendus* 1948: 338–345.
1951 [Note de Cl. Schaeffer], *Académie des Inscriptions et Belles-Lettres, Comptes-rendus* 1951: 325–326.
STONE, E. C. and ZIMANSKI, P. E.
1999 *The Iron Age Settlement at 'Ain Dara, Syria. Survey and Soundings*, BAR Intern. 786. Oxford: BAR.
SUMMERS, G. D.
1990 "1988 Tille Höyük kazısı", in *XI Kazı Sonuçları Toplantısı (1989)*, Vol. I, pp. 305–316. Ankara: Ankara Üniversitesi Basimevi.
1993 *Tille Höyük 4. The Late Bronze Age and the Iron Age Transition*, Ankara: British Institute of Archaeology at Ankara.
2010 "Revisiting the End of the Late Bronze Age and the Transition to the Early Iron Age at Tille Höyük," *Iraq* 72: 193–200.
2013 "Some Implications of Revised C14 and Dendrochronological Dating for the 'Late Bronze Levels' at Tille Höyük on the Euphrates," this volume, pp. 311–328.
VENTURI, F.
2007 *La Siria nell'età delle trasformazioni (XIII-X sec. a.C.). Nuovi contributi dallo scavo di Tell Afis.* Bologna: CLUEB.
WEIDNER, E.
1952-53 "[Ausgrabungen in] Arslan Tepe," *Archiv für Orientforschung* 16: 151–152.

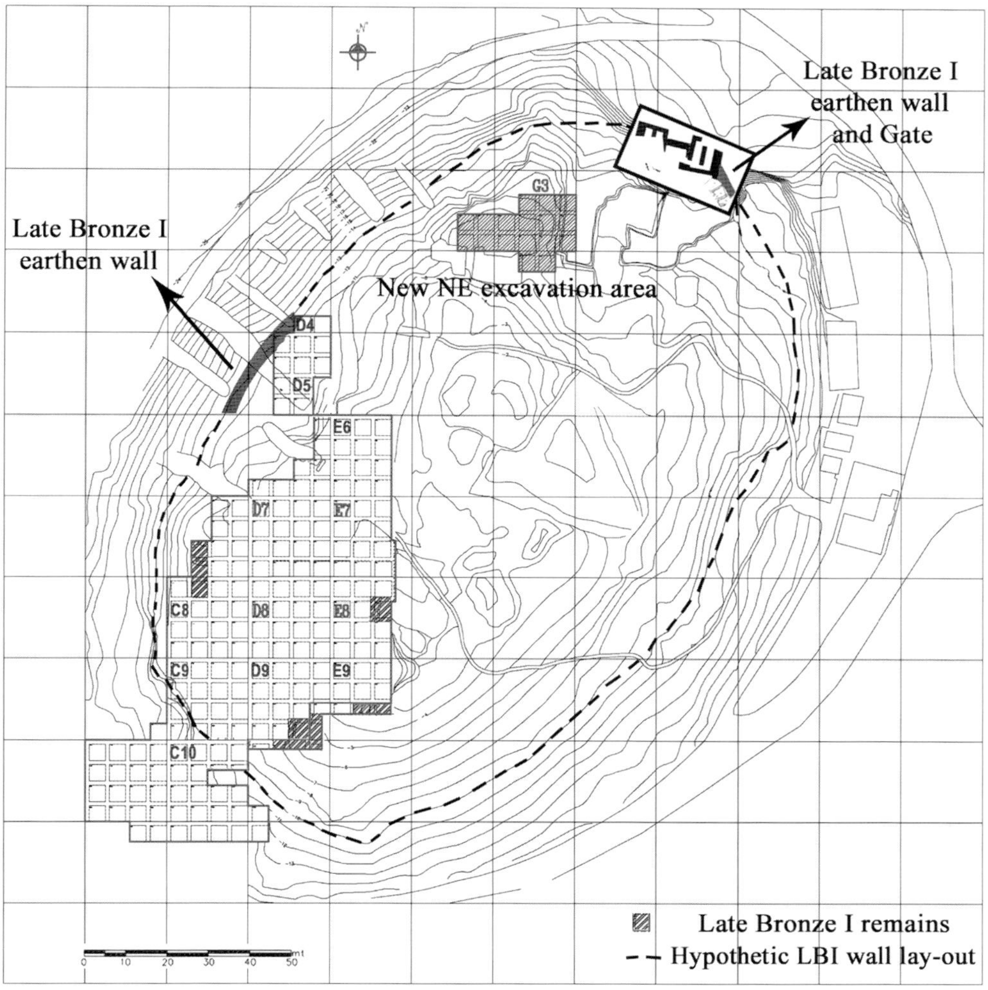

Fig. 1 Arslantepe. General plan of the tell with the indication of the new NE excavated area. The uncovered remains of the Late Bronze I earthen wall and town gate and its hypothetic minimum extension are also shown. The striped squares, in the SW part of the mound, are those where LBI structures have been found.

Fig. 2 Arslantepe-Melid. The 8th century pillared hall A1142, general view from east.

Fig. 3 Arslantepe-Melid. The "Green Building" A1279 (on the left), adjacent to the city wall M159 (in the centre), and above the Imperial Gate (on the right), general view from east.

Fig. 4 Arslantepe-Melid. The Assyrian building A1139+, general view from south-west.

Fig. 5 Arslantepe-Melid. Map of the 8th century pillared hall A1142.

Fig. 6 Arslantepe-Melid. The 9th century columned hall A1168, general view from south.

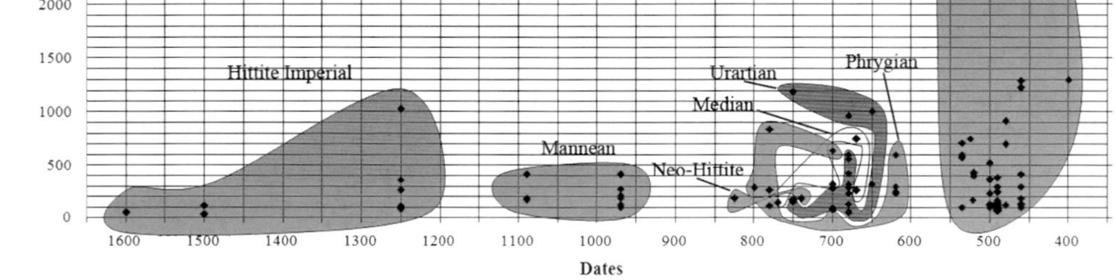

Fig. 7 The comparative size of the pillared halls, from Hittite Anatolia to Achaemenid Persia.

Fig. 8 a Arslantepe-Melid. Large plastered pits in the squatters' occupation in the 10th century.

Fig. 8 b Arslantepe-Melid. Fireplace and bin in the squatters' occupation in the 10th century.

Level	Date	Stratigraphic Units	Description	Interpretation	Local kings	Outer sources
1	710-650	A1139+	terraced building	Neo-Assyrian palace	Assyrian governors	Sargon II to Esarhaddon
2	710	M156	mud-brick platform	Neo-Assyrian platform	Tarkhunazi, Mutallu	
3	750-710	A1142	pillared hall	Neo-Hittite ceremonial hall	Sulumal, Gunzinanu	Tiglath-pileser III to Sargon II
4	830-750	A1168	columned hall	Neo-Hittie guard-post	Khilaruata	Urartian inscriptions (Menua, Argishti, Sarduri)
5 and 6	860-830	several pits		"late squatters"		no textual information
7	900-850	A1210+ M170/188	building, terrace wall	first orthogonal building	Lalli	Ashurnasirpal II
8a	1000-900	several pits, large "silos"		"early squatters"		no textual information
8b	1070-1000	several pits				
9	1070	burnt collapse of city wall		fire, destruction		Ashur-bel-kala
10	1150-1070	M159 A1278	city wall	Post-Imperial city wall	"Sulumal I"	Tiglath-pileser I
11	1180	fill above A1279		abandonment		
12	1180-1150	A1279	"green building"	ephemeral city wall	Runtiya, Arnuwanti	
13	1180	burnt collapse of city wall/gate		fire, destruction		Mushki invaders?
14	1400-1180	(old excavation)	city wall and gate	Hittite Imperial Gate	Hittite governors	Maldiya in Hittie texts

Fig. 9 The sequence of Arslantepe (northern area) after the 2010 campaign.

Fig. 10 Arslantepe-Melid. The "Green Building" A1279, view from south-west; on the left the city wall M159.

CHAPTER 16

POTTERY AS AN INDICATOR OF CHANGING INTERREGIONAL RELATIONS IN THE UPPER EUPHRATES VALLEY. THE CASE OF THE LATE BRONZE-IRON AGE ASSEMBLAGES FROM ARSLANTEPE/MALATYA

Federico MANUELLI
Arslantepe Project
Italian Archaeological Expedition in Eastern Anatolia
Sapienza University of Rome
Via Palestro 63, 00185
Rome
Italy
E-mail: fedemannu@inwind.it

Abstract

Different cultural worlds tend to converge in the Upper Euphrates Basin. The archaeological evidence for this area shows that throughout the Late Bronze Age, connections with Central Anatolia prevailed, while during the Iron Age a set of wide-ranging influences had a noticeable impact. There is a long history of investigation on these periods at the site of Arslantepe. Louis Delaporte was the first to work on the Neo-Hittite levels, discovering the famous "Lions' Gate." Subsequently Italian excavations in the northeastern sectors of the mound brought to light a sequence of occupation spanning from the Old Hittite Kingdom to Neo-Hittite phases. Recent investigations carried out since 2008 in the same area unearthed a monumental building connected with the use of the "Lion's Gate" and a series of previous occupation levels. This paper will focus on the analysis of the pottery inventories from the Imperial Hittite and Neo-Hittite phases in order to clarify the changing patterns of relations between Arslantepe and its neighbouring regions during the Late Bronze and Iron Ages. *

* I thank and congratulate Aslıhan Yener for having organized this stimulating workshop. I also express my thanks to Marcella Frangipane and Mario Liverani for their help and kindness. I am grateful to Sarah Wolferstan for the assistance with the English text. The drawings were realized by T. D'Este and A. Siracusano.

Late Bronze-Iron Age Cultural Dynamics in the Upper Euphrates Valley

Our knowledge of political changes occurring between the Late Bronze and Iron Ages in Anatolia and its neighbouring regions has largely been based on the analysis of historical sources. However, there is sparse textual evidence at our disposition for the task of reconstructing the history of these territories, especially during the centuries following the fall of the Hittite Empire. Yet the presence of monumental sculptures from these periods has allowed us to make some very interesting observations, even though these often lack contextual information.[1]

Recent analysis of material culture, especially the ceramic sequences, has led to progress in the development of a more coherent chronology. It is, above all, our understanding of pottery production and its use in clarifying the relationship between distant areas and in the identification of cultural change, that is central to this paper. Ceramic analysis can be used to improve our understanding of "centre-periphery" relations, as well as the degree of influence that the Hittite Empire had on these so-called "peripheral" areas. It also allows us to examine through the perspective of "everyday" material culture,[2] the interregional contacts that went on between the flourishing new political entities which were to emerge from the Hittite Empire tradition.

The Upper Euphrates valley is perfect for analyzing and understanding the nature of the contact between Anatolia and the northeastern Mediterranean world during the Late Bronze and Iron Age periods. Over the centuries the region was influenced by the cultures of several Near Eastern territories, many of whose elements merged with local traditions.

These lands formed a sort of cultural and political border between Hittite territories and the eastern plains during the later phases of the Late Bronze Age and were to emerge as the core of the new centres of power, laying a direct claim to the legacy of the Empire during the early Iron Age.[3]

Investigations of Late Bronze and Iron Age Arslantepe

The recent resumption of studies and excavations of Hittite and Post-Hittite levels at Arslantepe have shed more light on changes occurring in the upper Euphrates region due to increasing Hittite pressures on the settlement and the subsequent establishment of new decentralized kingdoms. The pottery assemblages from Arslantepe provide an ideal source of information by observing change in local production related to both the influence of central Anatolian material culture during the imperial period, as well as the wide range of influences during the phase when new political systems developed in the area.

[1] Sagona and Zimansky 2009, p. 295.
[2] See Sinopoli 1991 for a general discussion of these topics.
[3] Liverani 2004, p. 162.

Comparing the pottery from Arslantepe 2nd and 1st millennium stratigraphic sequences allows us to connect the settlement's production with the sequences that have been developed by scholars for eastern and central Anatolia (**Fig. 1**). The use of stratigraphic information from the main mounds of the upper Euphrates territories in general and radiocarbon dating from Korucutepe in particular, has allowed us to equate the Old Kingdom Hittite phases with eastern Anatolia's Late Bronze I and the Hittite imperial period with eastern Anatolia's Late Bronze II.[4] The period between the collapse of the Hittite Empire and the establishment of Urartian power has generally been referred to as the Early Iron Age, while the phase stretching across the 8th century BC has been defined as the Middle Iron Age.[5]

Arslantepe's Period VB roughly coincides with the Late Bronze I and Period IV with the Late Bronze II. With regards to the Iron Age, Period III is associated with the Early Iron Age levels, while Period II belongs to the beginning of the Middle Iron Age.[6] Given that absolute dating for these phases is currently limited at Arslantepe, this chronological sequence has been developed through the interpretation of both stratigraphic sequences and the evolution of ceramic traditions. A brief summary of the long history of investigations of Late Bronze and Iron Age settlements at Arslantepe is essential in order to introduce and contextualize the observations made of the pottery in the following sections of this paper.[7]

The first excavations by Louis Delaporte in the northern part of the mound uncovered massive ruins dated to the Neo-Hittite period.[8] The early years of the Italian Archaeological Expedition also concentrated on the monumental Hittite imperial and Post-Hittite levels in this northern area of the mound where excavations have continued until1971.[9] This work uncovered a remarkable sequence stretching from the beginning of the Late Bronze to the first Neo-Hittite phases.[10]

In 1971 the area under investigation included the south western part of the mound, where a very interesting series of residential quarters, mainly dated to the Late Bronze Age I, were uncovered.[11] The excavations of the residential quarter were also resumed during the 2009 season.[12]

[4] For Korucutepe dating see Van Loon 1980, pp. 276–277.

[5] See the chronological synthesis quoted by Köroğlu 2003, p. 231.

[6] The decision to define the Middle Iron Age levels as belonging to Period II was recently reached through a review of stratigraphical sequence. This is important to stress, seeing in previous preliminary publications Middle Iron Age levels were identified with the later phases of Period III, see Manuelli 2010b.

[7] For a thorough description see the paper presented in this volume by Frangipane and Liverani.

[8] Delaporte 1939, 1940.

[9] See the preliminary results in Puglisi and Meriggi 1964 and Puglisi 1968, pp. 128–129 and the final report quoted by Pecorella 1975. See also a synthesis in Pecorella 2004.

[10] See Palmieri 1969, pp. 7–12, 60–65; 1978, pp. 3–4, 37–41.

[11] See Palmieri 1973, pp. 57–72 and a synthesis in Frangipane and Palmieri 1983, pp. 289–290. See also Frangipane 1993, pp. 48–50 with the previous bibliography.

[12] For a preliminary discussion on the Late Bronze pottery production see Manuelli 2010.

The subject of this paper also focuses on the observations that can be made as a result of the new project investigating Arslantepe's Post-Hittite levels, which has provided a sequence covering the advanced phases of the Early Iron Age and the beginning of the Middle Iron Age in a large area contiguous to the "Lions' Gate."[13]

Arslantepe Period IV, III and II Pottery Descriptions

Moving our attention to the Late Bronze II to Iron Age period pottery sequences, only the most ancient assemblages, dated to Late Bronze Age I, and the already published inventories will be included within this analysis for comparative purposes. Instead, this analysis will focus on the development of the most important technical and typological characteristics of three ceramic assemblages excavated in the northern areas that have been categorised into three chronological horizons.

The first of these is the Period IV horizon, excavated between 1969 and 1971 comprising the patchy remains of a stone defensive wall dated to the Late Bronze II. The second horizon, termed Period III, was brought to light during the 2009 season, which uncovered the so-called 'squatters' occupations. That is, the levels underneath the pillared hall and the re-use of a massive mud brick fortification wall that had burned down in the later phases of the Early Iron Age. The third horizon, or Period II, was investigated during the 2008 season and comprises the fill between the pebble floors of the pillared buildings. This fill is structurally connected to the final phases of use of the "Lions' Gate" i.e. the beginning of the Middle Iron Age.

The Late Bronze Age assemblage does not have any direct stratigraphic relationship to the Iron Age. Furthermore, this analysis will not consider the "transitional phase," although the 2010 excavations reached these levels in a limited part of the investigated area; the material brought to light will be analyzed in upcoming years. Hence, this paper will examine and compare the main features of the Late Bronze II and Early/Middle Iron Age production separately in advance of a more extensive investigation of the transitional period forthcoming in the near future.[14]

Turning to a description of the pottery, the first horizons from Arslantepe's Period IV are characterized by relatively high numbers of medium and large plates with a curved or straight profile and internally thickened rims (**Fig. 2: 1–3**). Fabrics are medium-coarse with a high percentage of mineral inclusions. A high frequency of string impressions around the rims is also noticeable. This production seems to be almost entirely wheel-made.

[13] For the new excavation project see the paper presented by Frangipane and Liverani in this volume. See also Alvaro 2010 and Liverani 2009. For preliminary analyses and interpretations see Liverani 2011; 2012. For the pottery production see Manuelli 2010b.

[14] See a short report on the 2010 campaign in the paper presented by Frangipane and Liverani in this volume.

Curved profile bowls with internally thickened rims and concave or rounded bases are quite frequent (**Fig. 2: 4–6**). The pastes are buff in colour with a quite dense medium-coarse fabric and grit tempering. Occasionally, a red-painted decoration on the rim is visible. The most common shape of the assemblage is a small, shallow bowl with an internally pointed rim and rounded base (**Fig. 2: 7–11**). The fabric is medium-coarse with some irregular cavities and mineral inclusions.

Curved profile bowls with high eversible or straight carinated walls are widespread (**Fig. 3: 1–4**). The fabrics are medium-coarse with some mineral inclusions and buff pastes. Carinated bowls occasionally have a dense layer of red-painted decoration over the rim. There are also large bowls and large deep bowls with straight walls and internally thickened rims (**Fig. 3: 5–8**). Fabrics are non-dense and medium-coarse with a high percentage of mineral inclusions and cavities, while pastes are usually pale in shade.

Generally all the bowls described above are wheel-thrown and roughly smoothed. The kraters with thickened rims and vertical wall profiles are also quite common (**Fig. 3: 9–11**). Comparisons with other sites tend to associate this shape with a pair of vertical handles. Fabrics are non-dense and medium-coarse with grit tempering and brown paste, while surfaces are usually smoothed.

The most common of the necked jars is the 'funnel-high-necked' type (**Fig. 4: 1–4**). The rims are everted and the bodies are globular or ovoid. Two handles run vertically from the shoulder to the lower body. There is an interesting variability in rim shape and grooved rims also occur. The dimensions of the vessels vary as does the choice of pastes used, while grit tempering is prevalent.

Medium and large high and narrow necked bottles are also very common (**Fig. 4: 5–8**). They have an everted or thickened out rim, ovoid body, probably associated with rounded or ring bases, and a vertical handle. Pastes are pale in shade and tempers are mineral. Jars and bottle surfaces are usually smoothed. These shapes are also wheel-made but probably composed of separate sections joined together on the wheel.

The range of cooking pots includes some medium-sized, short-necked pots, and small necked-pots with a globular body, rounded base, rounded exterior rim and vertical handle (**Fig. 4: 9–10**). Their fabric is generally medium-coarse with a high amount of mineral inclusions. The paste is red or reddish-brown and surfaces are often smoothed. As with the jars and bottles above, the vessels seem to be composed of two different sections subsequently joined together on the wheel.

The second of the three horizons to be described in this paper is the Period III pottery horizon, mainly characterised by small curved or straight profile shallow bowls, which make up the majority of the diagnostic sherds present (**Fig. 5: 1–5**). The rims are rounded and the bases usually string-cut. The fabric is medium-coarse with chaff tempering and buff pastes. The surfaces are untreated, even if signs of a rough smoothing or a thin slip are sometimes discernible. A dark core is also frequent and throwing marks can be distinguished on the bowls' internal surfaces.

Carinated bowls with raised external rims also occur frequently (**Fig. 5**: 6–7). The pastes are buff or orange in colour, the fabrics are medium with grit or grit and chaff tempering. Small carinated deep bowls are also widespread (**Fig. 5**: 8–9). Their profiles and their bases are usually curved, while the rims are thickened out. The tempers are mineral, the pastes are pale in shade and the fabrics are medium-coarse and non-dense with isolated cavities.

Medium and large kraters with straight profiles and thickened in and out rims also occur (**Fig. 5**: 10–11). The pastes are buff or brown in colour with medium fabric and mineral tempering. The surface treatment of the vessels described above consists of a hastily smoothed or slipped technique, while the production is clearly wheel-made.

High and narrow necked bottles with everted or externally thickened rims are also entirely wheel-made (**Fig. 5**: 12–13). Mineral tempering, pastes, and surfaces that are pale in colour prevail.

Short-necked cooking pots with rounded rims, globular bodies, and vertical handles are widely diffused (**Fig. 5**: 14). Once again pastes are pale in shade, while fabrics are medium-coarse and non-dense with a high percentage of mineral inclusions. All the closed shapes described above are also wheel-made with evidence of surface-smoothing often noticeable.

This ceramic analysis concludes with the description of Period II pottery horizon. Wheel-made deep bowls with curved profiles and thickened rims become one of the most commonly attested shapes (**Fig. 6**: 1–2). Pastes are consistently pale in shade but now, brown tones prevail. The surfaces are often slipped, while the fabrics are medium with mineral temper. Shallow and carinated bowls are replaced by examples with curved or straight profiles and thickened rims (**Fig. 6**: 3–4). Tempers are mineral and pastes are dark in shade. Slipped and burnished surfaces are also seen in the assemblage.

Shallow bowls with chaff tempering and buff pastes occur in small numbers; these are small in size and have low carination (**Fig. 6**: 5–6). Smoothed or red-slipped surfaces are occasionally found.

Closed shapes are the most typical element of the horizon of this pottery tradition. Medium kraters, high-necked bottle and short-necked cooking pots continue to occur. A limited number of carinated deep bowls, also known as "groovy pottery" is also present[15] (**Fig. 6**: 7). Coarse fabrics with an abundance of mineral inclusions and dark pastes characterize this production. Evidence of the use of the wheel is also noted. In addition, sherds of incised ware with buff pastes and grit and chaff tempering occur quite frequently (**Fig. 6**: 8–12). The association between incised and red-painted decorations has also been noted.

[15] The term "groovy pottery" was discussed and agreed to during the 5th *Anatolian Iron Ages Colloquium* held in Van in 2001 and is also adopted here, see Roaf and Schachner 2005, p. 116.

Alongside these wheel-made productions, a limited amount of hand-made pottery is also present. Fragments of neckless, globular body pots with rounded rims and with features such as handles, lugs or spouts, and deep bowls with curved profiles, thickened rims and looped feet occur, although these are infrequent (**Fig.** 7: 1–3). Tempers are mineral, fabrics coarse or medium-coarse, and pastes are dark in colour. The pots are entirely hand-made, while the bowls seems to be wheel-finished.

A small amount of red coated sherds is present. This bright "Red Polished" ware is similar to Urartian types and is found intermittently along the Euphrates River. Curved profile bowls with looped feet have been identified (**Fig.** 7: 4). Also sherds with a thin red-orange slip are present and could be associated with Syrian "Red-Slip" ware production.

Sherds of painted jars with internally grooved rims, which are slipped in white and decorated with brown linear paint, are present (**Fig.** 7: 5–8). Shaping and decorating techniques, typical of the "Early Phrygian" period of central Anatolia also occur occasionally along the upper Euphrates valley.

A small assortment of bichrome Phrygian sherds has also been identified (**Fig.** 7: 9–12). Pastes are pale, covered with a white slip and a red and black-brown paint. Patterns typical of the production of Early and Middle Iron Age Anatolian sites under Phrygian influence recur in the sherds analysed.

A sizeable amount of monochrome and bichrome painted sherds linked to Cypro-Phoenician traditions have also been found (**Fig.** 7: 13–15). Jars with brown linear painted decoration on white slip, globular jars with red and black-brown circular or linear decorations on brown-orange paste, and also sherds with black paint on red slip surfaces seem similar to "White Painted," "Bichrome," and "Black-on-Red" wares respectively.

Arslantepe Pottery Analyses as a Tool for Understanding Patterns in Interregional Relations in the Upper Euphrates Valley from the Late Bronze to the Iron Age

In summary, by identifying the main characteristics of the three horizons described above, it is possible to describe the different cultural influences affecting the site of Arslantepe during the historical periods taken into account.

During Period IV it is possible to note a clear involvement of Arslantepe with central Anatolian cultures. A gradual detachment of the local pottery tradition is notable during the development of Late Bronze Age assemblages. Indeed, Arslantepe's Late Bronze I (Period VB) was characterized by the combination of local pottery forms, deriving from either the Middle Bronze Age or from the development of new local styles with the forms developed in central Anatolia.

In Period IV the impact of Hittite material culture became more marked. Local shapes almost disappeared; pottery production underwent a process of general simplification, with a clear decrease in the number of the ceramic wares and a tendency toward standardization. The large variety of shapes such as plates with string impressions, shallow bowls with internally thickened rims, large-deep bowls, kraters, necked bottles, and high-necked jars are typical of the Hittite imperial period in central Anatolia.[16]

There are similarities in the pottery production of Arslantepe Period IV with Late Bronze II assemblages found at the main settlements of the upper Euphrates, especially sites in the Keban area such as Norşuntepe and Korucutepe[17] (**Fig. 8**).

Some elements of continuity from Late Bronze II production are clearly evident during Arslantepe's Period III. Necked bottles, for example, clearly resemble Late Bronze Age forms. Chaff-tempered shallow bowls also seem to have developed from Hittite "drab-ware" traditions. Generally, even if the use of mineral tempers is still prevalent, there are also examples of the use of chaff temper. There are also a higher percentage of sherds with dark cores or dark surfaces, both indicators of poorer control during the firing process.

At Boğazköy, links can be inferred mainly during the middle and the later phases of the Early Iron Age and subsequently during the early Middle Iron Age.[18] Interesting comparisons can be made between Arslantepe and the Iron Age levels at İmamoğlu, Köşkerbaba and Değirmentepe in the Karakaya area.[19] In contrast, there is little to show that the settlement had links with sites in the Keban, save for a few specific forms such as the small deep bowls from Norşuntepe.[20]

Characteristic elements of Arslantepe's ceramic culture can be noted in many of the main sites in a widespread area stretching from south eastern Anatolia to northern Syria, especially along the middle Euphrates river and are especially marked at Lidar Höyük 6e–6c and Tille Höyük IV–V[21] (**Fig. 9**). Closed shapes show continuity with the forms seen in this horizon during Period II, whereas open shapes show an interesting development from shallow to deep and from carinated to curved profile bowls. Hand-made cooking pots and looped feet bowls are also quite frequent, especially in the Keban area as well as in the Karakaya region.[22]

[16] See Müller-Karpe 1988, p. 162 and Mielke 2006, pp. 158–171.

[17] For Norşuntepe see Korbel 1985 and for Korucutepe see Griffin 1980. See also Umurtak 1988.

[18] See comparisons with Genz 2004. See also Matsumura 2005 for interesting parallels with Kaman-Kalehöyük.

[19] For comparisons with these sites see Ökse 1992, 1988.

[20] See Bartl 1988, taf. 3–4, 30, 51.

[21] For Lidar Höyük see Müller 1999 and for Tille Höyük see Blaylock 1999.

[22] See comparisons with Norşuntepe in Bartl 1988, with Köşkerbaba in Ökse 1988, abb. 105, 126 and with Değirmentepe Karakaya in Ökse 1988, abb. 127–128. See also comparisons with central and south eastern Anatolian sites with Lidar Höyük in Müller 1999, abb. 5, with Tille Höyük in Blaylock

"Groovy-pottery" is very uncommon west of the Euphrates with a few examples appearing only later than in the Keban region and are wheel-made in production.[23] In contrast, "Incised" sherds are quite frequent both west and east of the Euphrates River and are found in the Iron Age levels at Norşuntepe and Korucutepe and at level III at Kaleköy and Köşkerbaba.[24]

As mentioned above, there are a wide range of elements present of non-local production in Arslantepe's assemblage. Among these, 'Red-polished' ware is one of the most useful indicators of Urartian expansion. Examples from İmamoğlu and Korucutepe attest to the expansion of this influence into western territories as early as the 8th century BC.[25] At the same time "Red-slip" ware, which diffused from the Syrian coast, can be attested from the end of the 9th century.[26]

"Early Phrygian" painted jars are found at Boğazköy in Middle Iron Age levels at Büyükkaya and in IIb levels at Büyükkale. They are also occasionally found along the upper Euphrates River.[27] "Phrygian Bichrome" sherds are also occasionally seen in the Karakaya region, for example at İmamoğlu and Değirmentepe.[28] This kind of production is typical of the Early Phrygian assemblages at Gordion. It is also seen at Boğazköy in Middle Iron Age levels of Büyükkaya and in level II of Büyükkale, at Kaman-Kalehöyük in level IIc, and at Porsuk in level III.[29]

"Cypro-Phoenician" wares appeared during the Cypro-Geometric II–III and Cypro-Archaic I periods in Cyprus and in Iron Age II levels in The Levant.[30] In the Karakaya area these wares are occasionally found in Iron Age levels at Değirmentepe and in level III of Koşkerbaba[31] (**Fig. 10**).

1999, fig. 4, with Boğazköy in Genz 2004, taf. 10, 18, with Kaman-Kalehöyük in Matsumura 2005, taf. 69, 116 and with Gordion in Sams 1994, pl. 24.

[23] Köroğlu 2003, 233. See also Bartl 2001.

[24] For "groovy pottery" see comparisons with İmikuşağı in Sevin 1995, res. 15, with Köşkerbaba in Ökse 1988, abb. 870 with Norşuntepe in Bartl 1988, taf. 7, 12 and with Tille Höyük in Blaylock 1999, fig. 3. As for "Incised wares" see comparisons with İmamoğlu in Ökse 1992, abb. 3, 6, with Norşuntepe in Bartl 1988, taf. 6, 34, 37 and with Tille Höyük in Blaylock 1999, fig. 3.

[25] See Ökse 1992, p. 61 and Winn 1980, p. 161.

[26] Braemer 1986.

[27] For Boğazköy see comparisons in Bossert 2000, taf. 2, 6–7, 11 and Genz 2004, taf. 68. For İmikuşağı see Sevin 1995, res. 18, for Değirmentepe Karakaya see Ökse 1988, abb. 593, 66, for Norşuntepe see Bartl 1988, taf. 34, and for Değirmentepe Keban see Esin 1983, r. 5. See also comparisons with the level 7 of Gordion in Sams 1994, pl. 133.

[28] See Ökse 1992, abb. 6; 1988, abb. 636.

[29] For Gordion see comparisons with Sams 1994, pl. 38, 62, 90, 97, for Boğazköy see Genz 2004, taf. 42, 56, 62, 68 and Bossert 2000, taf. 2, 9, 16, 32, 45, for Kaman-Kalehöyük see Matsumura 2005, taf. 119, 132 and for Porsuk see Dupré 1983, pl. 84, 126, 224, 233.

[30] Comparisons are widely diffuse in Cyprus and Levant. See examples in Doumet-Serhal 2004 and Gilboa 1999 with the previous bibliography.

[31] See Ökse 1988, abb. 594–595, 604–611.

In conclusion, the analyses of the three pottery horizons excavated in the northern slope of the mound show interesting changes in the pattern of Arslantepe's inter-regional relations. The ceramic horizon of Period IV is associated with layers dated to the 14–13th centuries BC. Observations about these assemblages lend further support to the hypothesis that a clearly distinguishable area existed, extending across the whole of the upper Euphrates valley, including the Malatya and Elazığ provinces. Here the influence of Hittite material culture is very evident, although it is found alongside occasional examples of local production types.

The Period III assemblage, linked to the area of the site where the so-called 'squatters' re-used levels of a mud-brick fortification wall, dated between the latter 11th and the 9th century, belonged to a settlement that had strong links to the territories in the middle Euphrates valley, and with important ties to the central Anatolian area. In contrast, the region east of the Euphrates valley was more influenced by the eastern Anatolian sphere.

The interpretation of the pottery horizon from the Period II assemblage associated with the fill between the floors of the pillared building and dated to the late 9th–early 8th century would seem to point to a position of international importance for Arslantepe, a central site where influences from central and eastern Anatolia, Syria, The Levant and the Mediterranean tended to converge.

Bibliography

Alvaro, C.

2010 "Malatya-Melid. A New Look on the 20th Century Archaeological Research. Some Remarks on the Topographical and Architectural Evidence," in *Proceeding of the 6th International Congress on the Archaeology of the Ancient Near East. May, 5th–10th 2008, "Sapienza" – Università di Roma,* edited by P. Matthiae, F. Pinnock, L. Nigro and N. Marchetti, pp. 273–278. Wiesbaden: Harrasowitz.

Bartl, K.

1988 "Norşun-Tepe. Die frühe Eisenzeit." Unpublished PhD diss. Freie Universität Berlin.

2001 "Eastern Anatolia in the Early Iron Age," in *Migration und Kulturtransfer. Der Wandel vorder und zentralasiatischer Kulturen im Umbruch vom 2. zum 1. vorchristlichen Jahrtausend. Akten des Internationalen Kolloquiums, Berlin 23. bis 26. November 1999*, edited by R. Eichmann and H. Parzinger, pp. 383–410. Bonn: Habelt.

Blaylock, S. R.

1999 "Iron Age Pottery from Tille Höyük, South-Eastern Turkey," in *Iron Age Pottery in Northern Mesopotamia, Northern Syria and South-Eastern Anatolia. Papers presented at the meeting of the international "table ronde" at Heidelberg (1995) and Nieborów (1997) and other contributions,* edited by A. Hausleiter and A. Reiche, pp. 163–286. Münster: Ugarit-Verlag.

BOSSERT, E.-M.
2000 *Die Keramik phrygischer Zeit von Bogazkoy: Funde aus den Grabungskampagnen 1906, 1907, 1911, 1912, 1931–1939 und 1952–1960*. Mainz am Rhein: Philip von Zabern.
BRAEMER, F.
1986 "La céramique à engobe rouge de l'âge du Fer à Bassit," *Syria* 63: 221–246.
DELAPORTE, L.
1939 "La troisième campagne de fouilles à Malatya," *Revue Hittite et Asianique* 5: 43–56.
1940 *Malatya I: fouilles de la mission archéologique française. Arslantepe, La Porte des Lions*. Paris: De Boccard.
DOUMET-SERHAL, C.
2004 "Jars from the First Millennium BC at Tell Rachidieh: Phoenician Cinerary Urns and Grave Goods," in *Decade. A decade of archaeology and history in the Lebanon*, edited by C. Doumet-Serhal, A. Rabate and A. Resek, pp. 70–80. Beirut: Lebanes British Friends of the National Museum.
DUPRÉ, S.
1983 *Porsuk I. La céramique de l'age du Bronze et de l'age du Fer*. Paris: Editions Recherche sur les civilisations.
ESIN, U.
1983 "Değirmentepe Kazisi," *Kazı Sonuçları Toplantısı 5*, pp. 71–80. Ankara: Ministry of Culture and Tourism.
GENZ, H.
2004 *Büyükkaya I: Die Keramik der Eisenzeit*. Mainz and Rhein: Philip von Zabern.
GILBOA, A.
1999 "The Dynamics of Phoenician Bichrome Pottery: A view from Tel Dor," *Bulletin of the American Schools of Oriental Research* 316: 1–22.
GRIFFIN, E. E.
1980 "The Middle and Late Bronze Age Pottery," in *Korucutepe. Final Report on the Excavations of the Universities of Chicago, California (Los Angeles) and Amsterdam in the Keban Reservoir, Eastern Anatolia 1968–1970. Volume 3*, edited by M.N. van Loon, pp. 3–119. Amsterdam-New York-Oxford: North-Holland.
FRANGIPANE, M.
1993 "Melid. B. Archäologisch," *Reallexicon der Assyriologie und Vorderasiatischen Archäologie* 8: 42–52.
FRANGIPANE, M. and PALMIERI, A.
1983 "A Protourban Centre of the Late Uruk Period," in *Perspectives on Protourbanization in Eastern Anatolia: Arslantepe (Malatya). An Interim Report on 1975–1983 Campaigns*, Origini XII, edited by M. Frangipane and A. Palmieri, pp. 287–454.
KORBEL, G.
1985 *Die spätbronzezeitliche Keramik vom Norşuntepe*. Hannover: Mitteilungen der Institute für Bauen und Planen in Entwicklungsländern.
KÖROĞLU, K.
2003 "The Transition from Bronze Age to Iron Age in Eastern Anatolia," in *Identifying Changes. The Transition from Bronze to Iron Age in Anatolia and its Neighbouring Regions. Proceedings of the International Workshop, Istanbul, November 8-9, 2002*, edited by B. Fischer, H. Genz, É. Jean and K. Köroğlu, pp. 271–282. Istanbul: Türk Eskiçağ Bilimleri Enstitüsü Yayınları.

LIVERANI, M.
2004 "Gli Ittiti sulle rive dell'Eufrate," in *Alle origini del potere. Arslantepe, la collina dei leoni*, edited by M. Frangipane, pp. 160–165. Milan: Mondadori/Electa.
2009 "Il salone a pilastri della Melid neo-hittita," *Scienze dell'Antichità* 15: 649–675.
2011 "The Pillared Hall of Neo-Hittite Melid: a New Link in the Development of an Architectural Type," in *Un impaziente desiderio di scorrete il mondo. Studi in onore di Antonio Invernizzi per il suo settantesimo compleanno*, edited by C. Lippolis, S. de Martino, pp. 91–112. Firenze: Le Lettere.
2012 "From Melid through Bastam to Megiddo. Stables and Horses in Iron Age II", in *Leggo! Studies Presented to Frederick Mario Fales on the Occasion of His 65th Birthday*, edited by G. B. Lanfranchi, D. Morandi Bonacossi, C. Pappi, S. Ponchia, pp. 443–458. Wiesbaden: Harrasowitz.

MANUELLI, F.
2010a "Malatya-Melid: a new look at the twenty century's archaeological researches. Some remarks on the Late Bronze Age pottery assemblages from Arslantepe," in *Proceeding of the 6th International Congress on the Archaeology of the Ancient Near East. May, 5th–10th 2008, "Sapienza" – Università di Roma,* edited by P. Matthiae, F. Pinnock, L. Nigro and N. Marchetti, pp. 399–409. Wiesbaden: Harrasowitz.
2010b "Foreign influences and local tradition in the Iron Age pottery production from Arslantepe. Evidence from the new excavations of the Neo-Hittite levels," *Mesopotamia XLV*: 71–84

MATSUMURA, K.
2005 "Die eiseinzeitliche Keramik in Zentralanatolien – auf der Grundlage der Ausgrabung von Kaman-Kalehöyük." Unpublished PhD diss. Freie Universität Berlin.

MIELKE, D. P.
2006 *Die Keramik vom Westhang. Kuşaklı-Sarissa 2*. Rahden/Westf: Leidorf.

MÜLLER, U.
1999 "Die eseinzeitliche Keramik des Lidar Höyük," in *Iron Age Pottery in Northern Mesopotamia, Northern Syria and South-Eastern Anatolia. Papers presented at the meeting of the international "table ronde" at Heidelberg (1995) and Nieborów (1997) and other contributions,* edited by A. Hausleiter and A. Reiche, pp. 403–434. Münster: Ugarit-Verlag.

MÜLLER-KARPE, A.
1988 *Hethitische Töpferei der Oberstadt von Hattuša. Ein Beitrag zur Kenntnis spätgrossreichszeitlicher Keramik und Töpferbetriebe*. Marburg/Lahn: Hitzeroth.

ÖKSE, A. T.
1988 *Mitteleisenzeitliche Keramik Zentral-Ostanatoliens mit dem Schwerpunkt Karakaya-Staudammgebiet am Euphrat*. Berlin: D. Reimer Verlag.
1992 "İmamoğlu in der Eisenzeit: Keramik," *Istanbuler Mitteilungen* 42: 31–66.

PALMIERI, A.
1969 "Recenti dati sulla stratigrafia di Arslantepe," *Origini* III: 7–66.
1973 "Scavi nell'area sud-occidentale di Arslantepe. Ritrovamento di una struttura templare dell'Antica Età del Bronzo," *Origini* VII: 55–182.
1978 "Scavi ad Arslantepe (Malatya)," *Quaderni de "La ricerca scientifica"* 100: 311–352.

PECORELLA, P. E.
1975 *Malatya – III. Rapporto preliminare delle campagne 1963–1968. Il livello eteo imperiale e quelli neoetei*. Rome: Centro per le Antichità e la Storia dell'Arte del Vicino Oriente.

2004 "Arslantepe ittita: architettura pubblica e iconografia del potere," in *Alle origini del potere. Arslantepe, la collina dei leoni*, edited by M. Frangipane, pp. 166–171. Milan: Mondadori/Electa.

PUGLISI, S. M.
1968 "Missione archeologica italiana a Malatya," *Oriens Antiquus* VII: 127–132.

PUGLISI, S. M. and MERIGGI, P.
1964 *Malatya – I. Rapporto Preliminare delle Campagne 1961 e 1962*. Rome: Centro per le Antichità e la Storia dell'Arte del Vicino Oriente.

ROAF, M. and SCHACHNER, A.
2005 "The Bronze Age to Iron Age transition in the upper Tigris region: new information from Ziyaret Tepe and Giricano," in *Anatolian Iron Ages 5: Proceedings of the Fifth Anatolian Iron Ages Colloquium, Van, 6–10 August* 2001, edited by A. Çilingiroğlu and G. Darbyshire, pp. 115–123. London: British Institute at Ankara.

SAGONA, A. and ZIMANSKY, P.
2009 *Ancient Turkey*, London and New York: Routledge.

SAMS, G. K.
1994 *The Gordion Excavations, 1950–1973: Final Reports IV. The Early Phrygian Pottery*. Philadelphia: The University Museum, University of Pennsylvania.

SEVIN, V.
1995 *Imikuşağı I (6.–1. Yapı Katları)*, Ankara: Türk Tarıh Kumuru Basımevi.

SINOPOLI, C. M.
1991 *Approaches to archaeological ceramics*. New York: Plenum Press.

UMURTAK, N. G.
1988 "Hitit İmparatorluk Çağında İšuwa Ülkesi Çanak Çömleği Üzerine Bir Araştırma." Unpublished PhD diss. Üniversitesi Edibiyat Fakültesi İstanbul.

VAN LOON, M. N.
1980 "Conclusions," in *Korocutepe. Final Report on the Excavations of the Universities of Chicago, California (Los Angeles) and Amsterdam in the Keban Reservoir, Eastern Anatolia 1968–1970. Volume 3*, edited by M.N. van Loon, pp. 271–277. Amsterdam-New York-Oxford: North-Holland.

WINN, M. M.
1980 "The Early Iron Age pottery," in *Korocutepe. Final Report on the Excavations of the Universities of Chicago, California (Los Angeles) and Amsterdam in the Keban Reservoir, Eastern Anatolia 1968–1970. Volume 3*, edited by M.N. van Loon, pp. 155–175. Amsterdam-New York-Oxford: North-Holland.

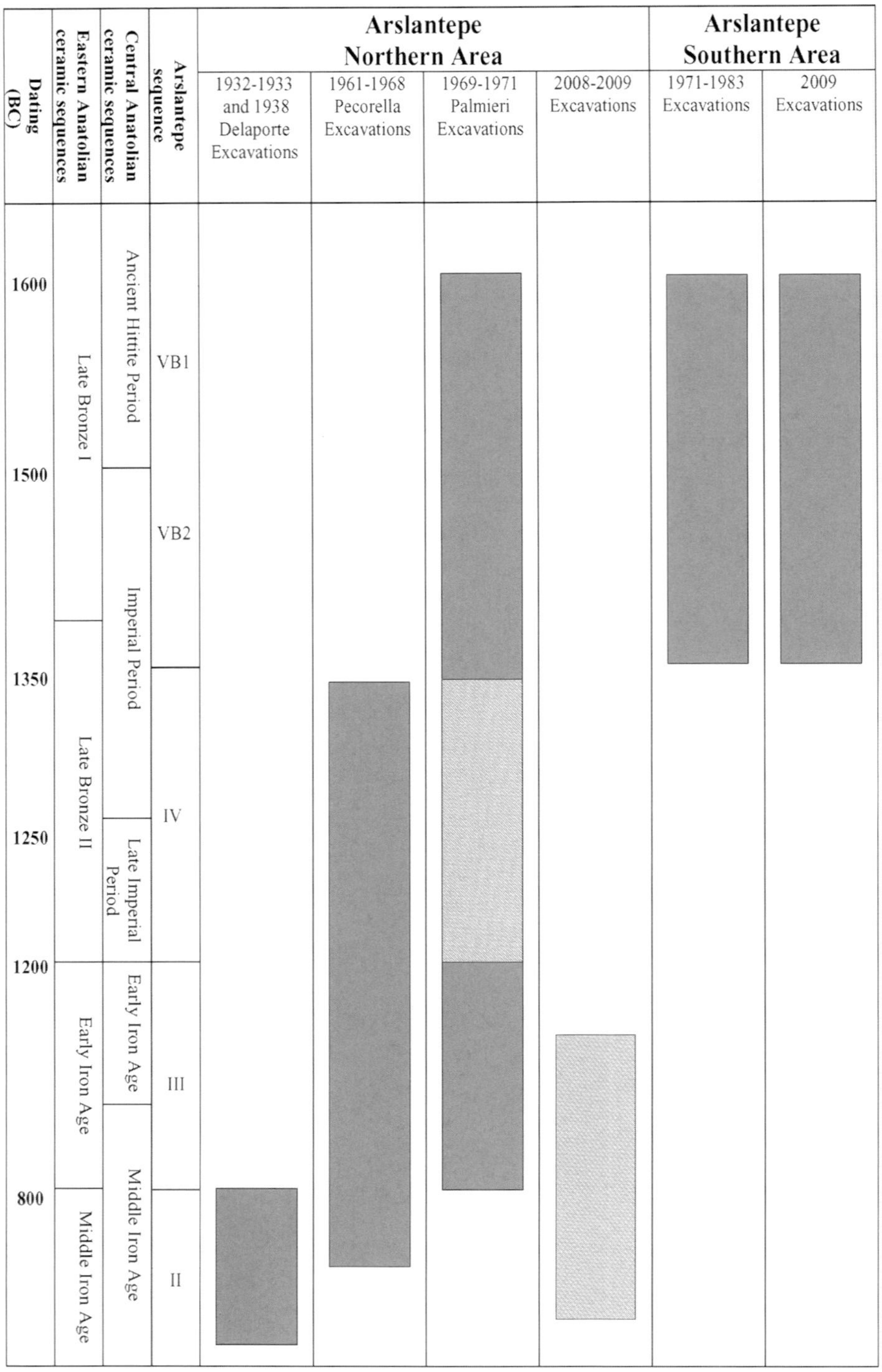

Fig. 1 Late Bronze and Iron Age sequences at Arslantepe compared to the eastern and the central Anatolian periodizations (light-gray columns indicate the horizons discussed in the paper).

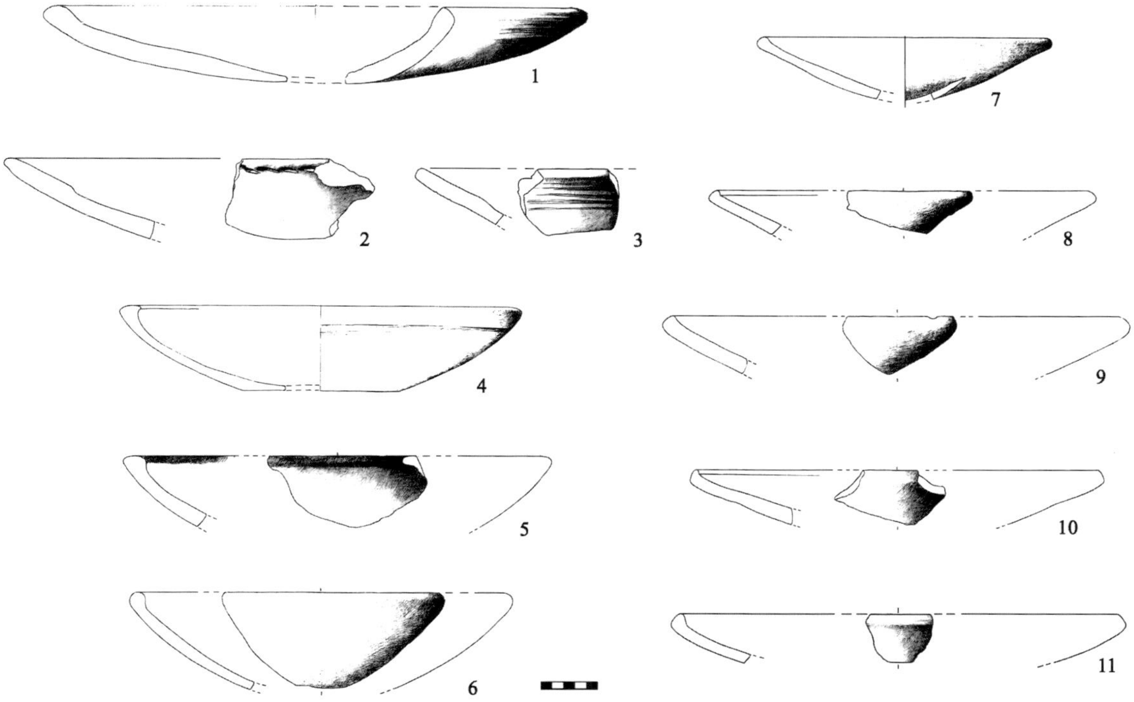

Fig. 2 Arslantepe Period IV pottery horizon
(Drawing by A. Siracusano. Archivio Missione Archeologica in Anatolia Orientale).

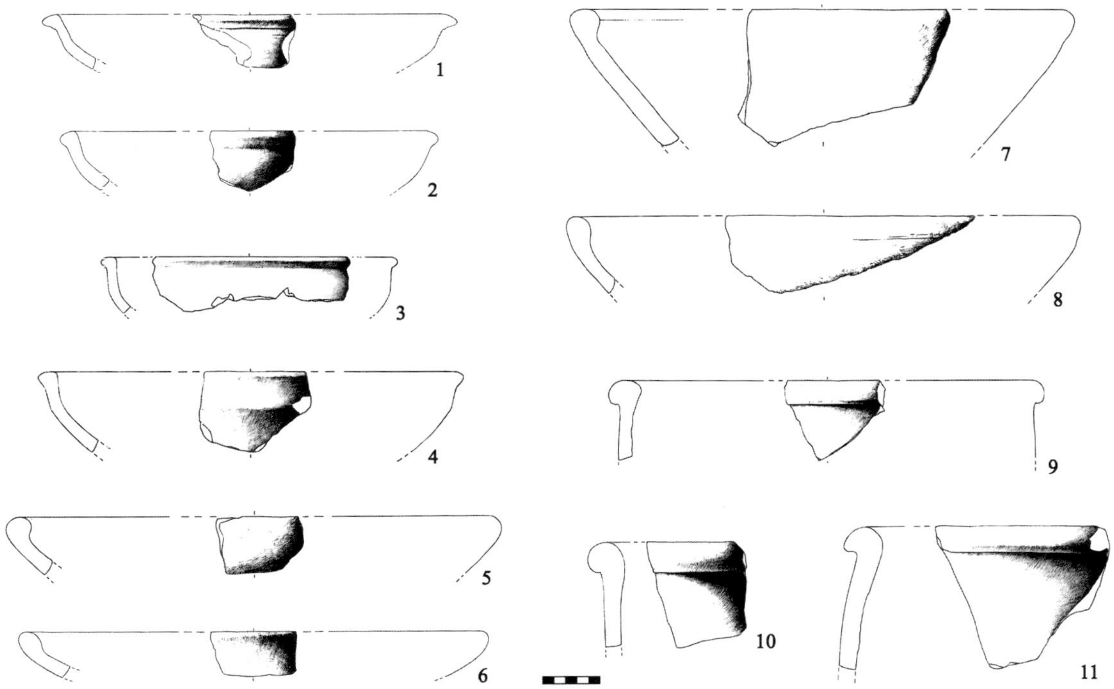

Fig. 3 Arslantepe Period IV pottery horizon
(Drawing by A. Siracusano. Archivio Missione Archeologica in Anatolia Orientale).

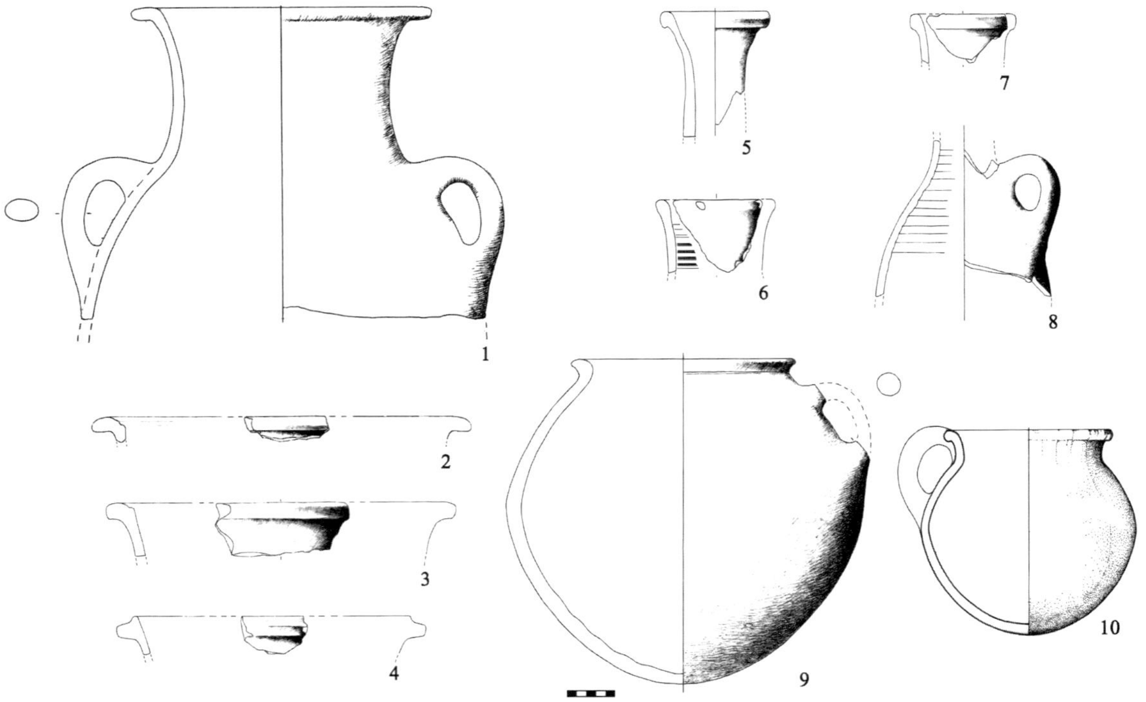

Fig. 4 Arslantepe Period IV pottery horizon
(Drawing by A. Siracusano. Archivio Missione Archeologica in Anatolia Orientale).

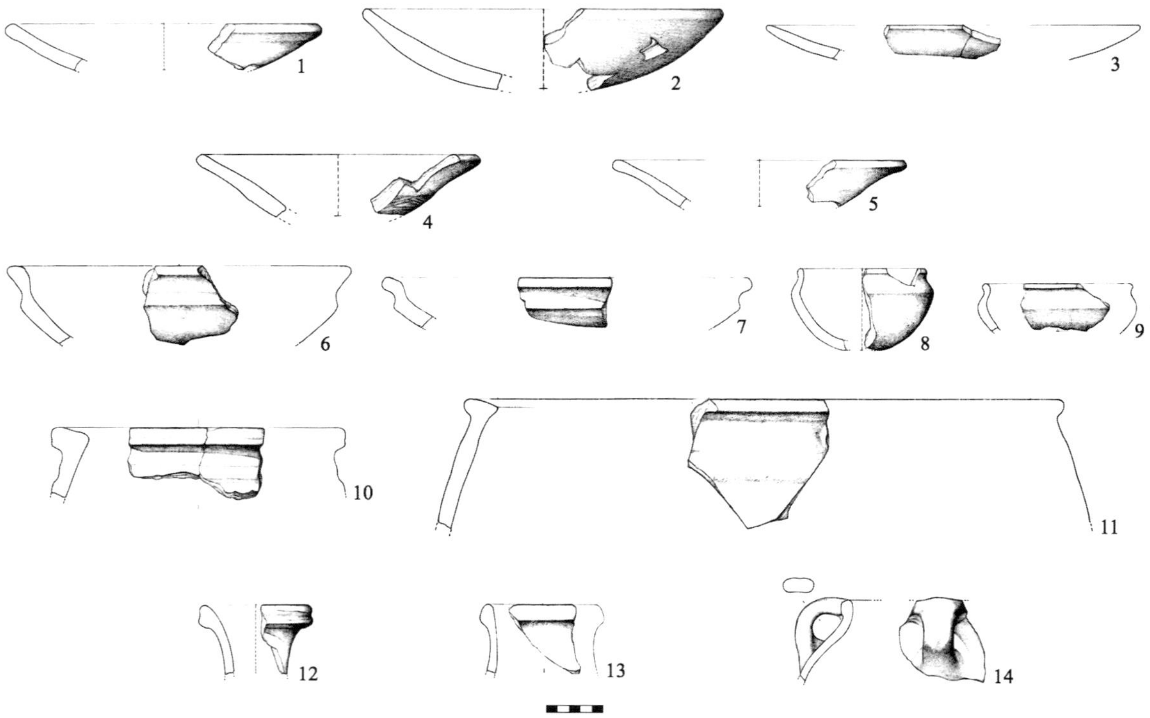

Fig. 5 Arslantepe Period III pottery horizon
(Drawing by T. D'Este. Archivio Missione Archeologica in Anatolia Orientale).

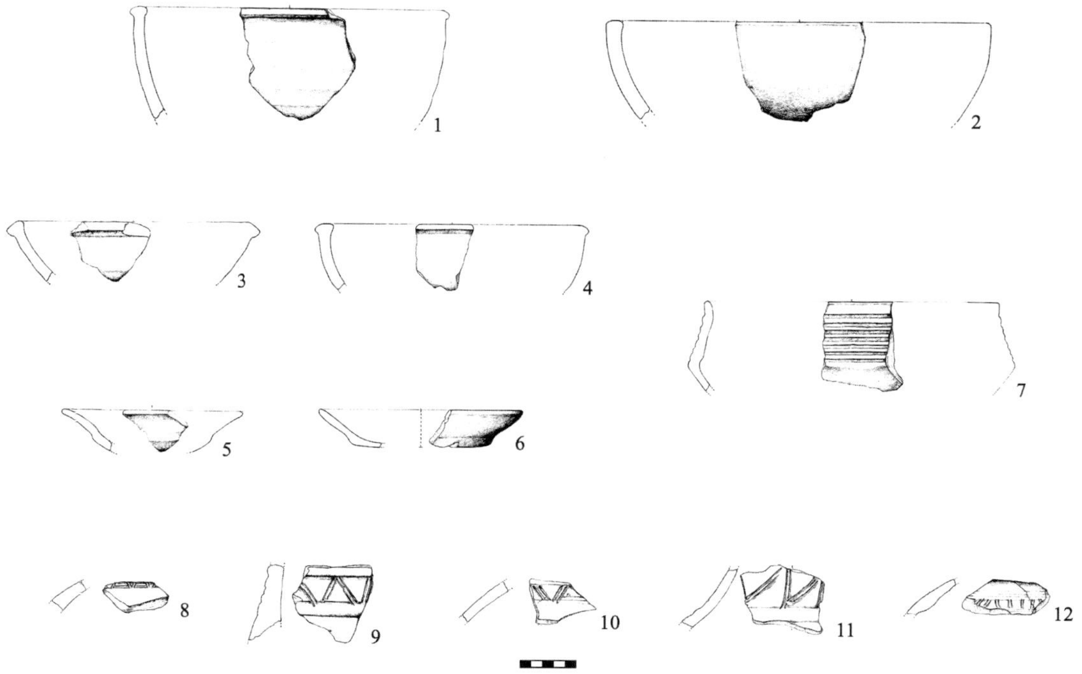

Fig. 6 Arslantepe Period II pottery horizon
(Drawing by T. D'Este. Archivio Missione Archeologica in Anatolia Orientale).

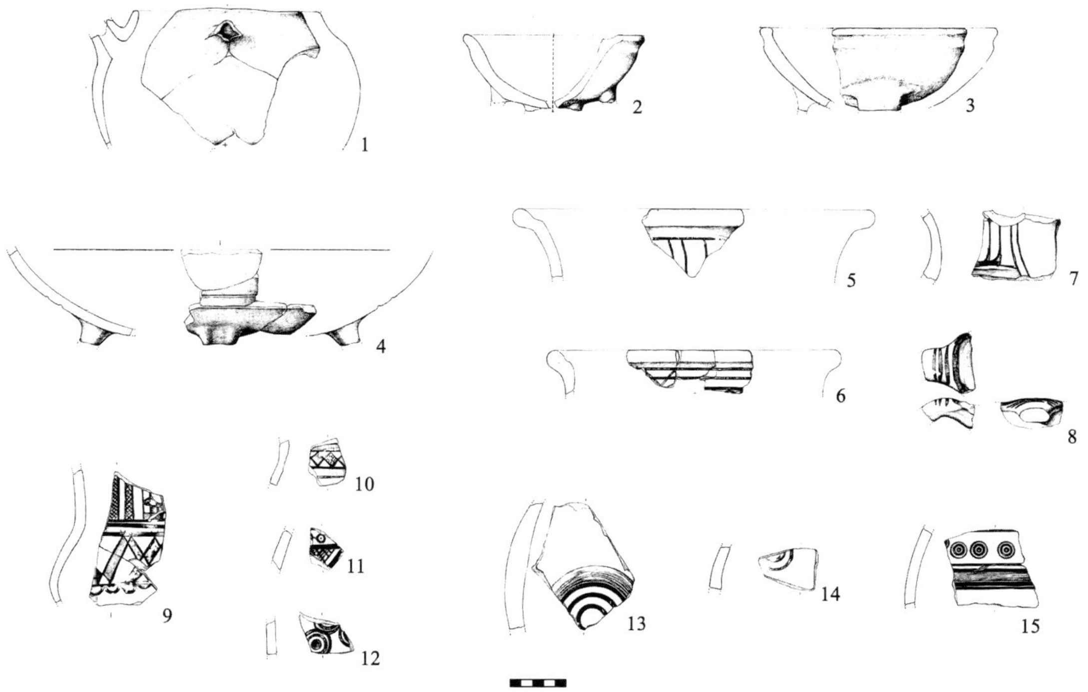

Fig. 7 Arslantepe Period II pottery horizon
(Drawing by T. D'Este. Archivio Missione Archeologica in Anatolia Orientale).

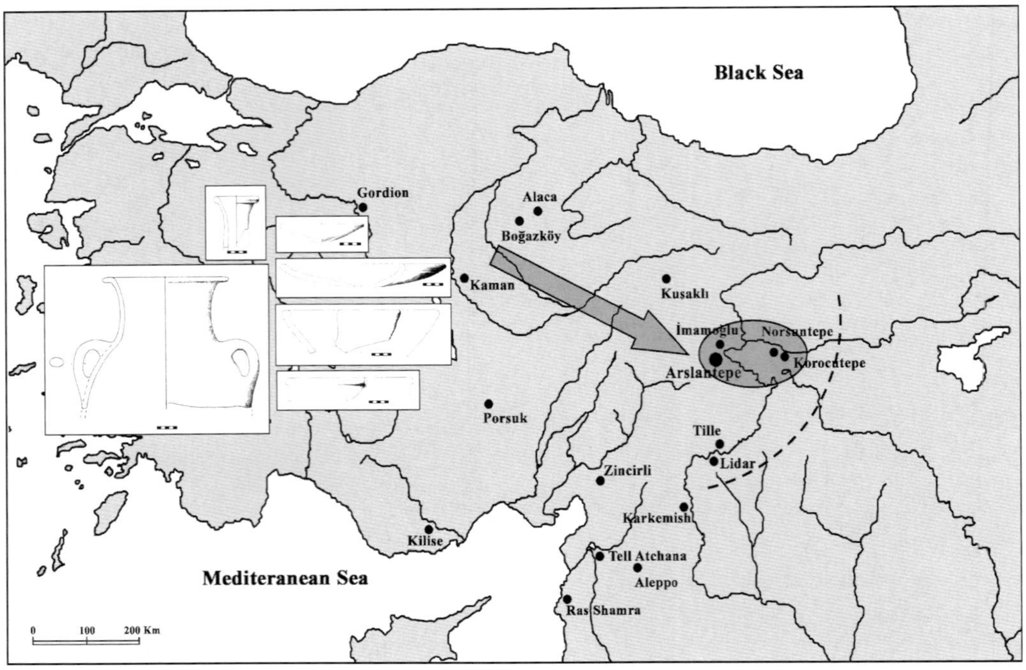

Fig. 8 Upper Euphrates valley interregional relations during the Late Bronze Age II (Arslantepe Period IV).

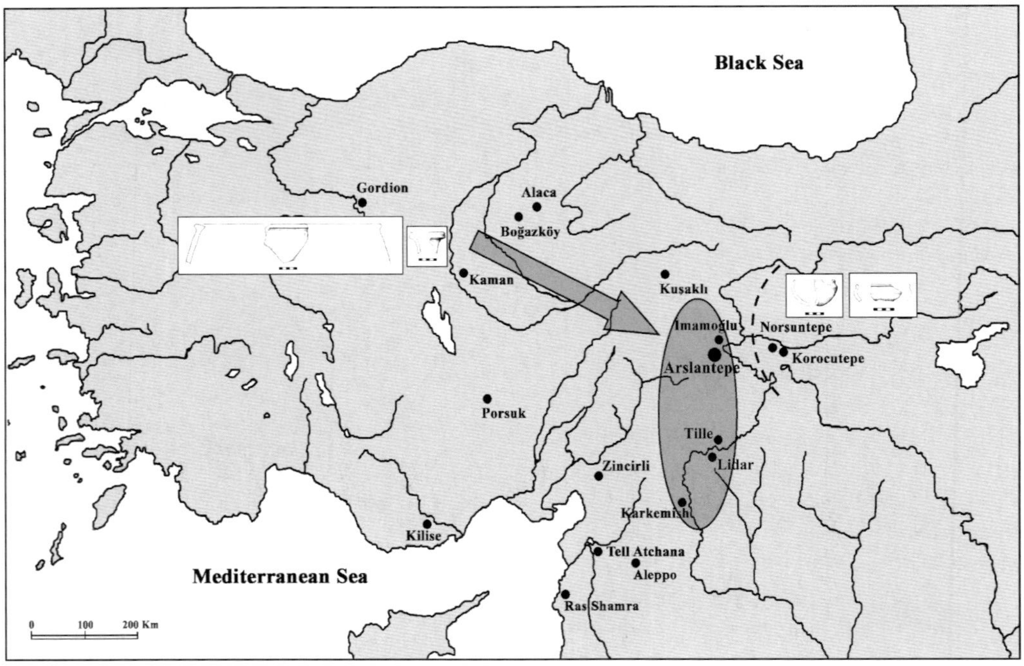

Fig. 9 Upper Euphrates valley interregional relations during the later Early Iron Age (Arslantepe Period III).

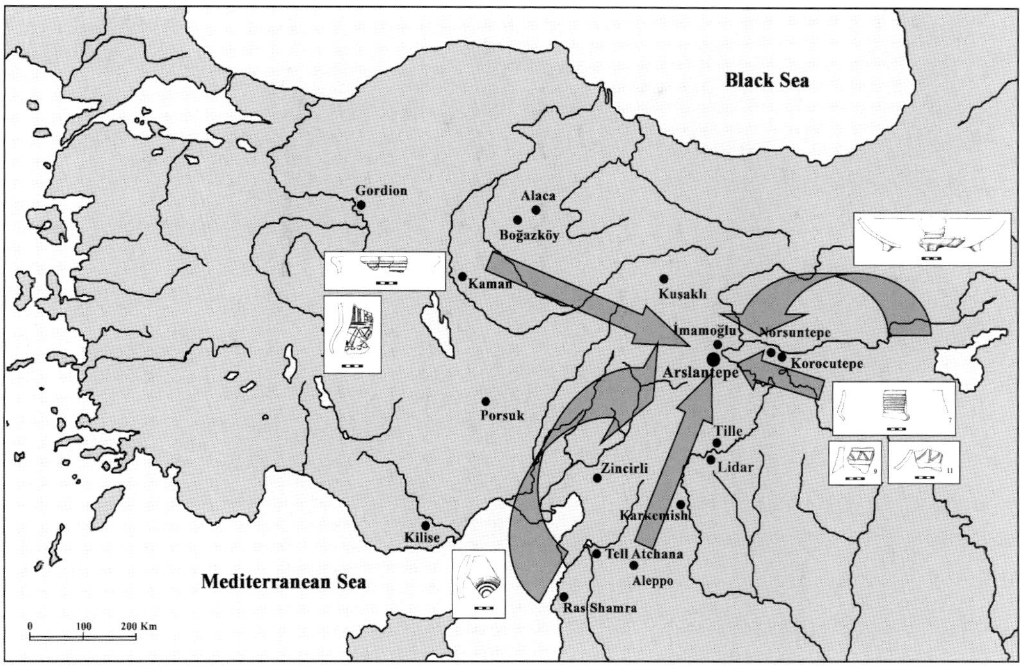

Fig. 10 Upper Euphrates valley interregional relations during the early Middle Iron Age (Arslantepe Period II horizon).

CHAPTER 17

NEW EXCAVATIONS AT THE LATE BRONZE AGE AND IRON AGE SITE OF GRE AMER ON THE GARZAN RIVER, BATMAN PROVINCE

Gül PULHAN
Assistant Professor
Department of Archaeology and History of Art, Rumelifeneri Yolu
Sarıyer, 34450. Istanbul, Turkey
E-mail: gulpulhan@gmail.com

and

Stuart R. BLAYLOCK
Independent Scholar
1 Colebrooke Lane, Cullompton
Devon, EX15 1EB,
U.K.
E-mail: stuart.blaylock@btinternet.com

ABSTRACT

After setting the scene of the larger Tigris area, and the Garzan valley in its historical, geographical and archaeological context, the site of Gre Amer, as it is known after one season of excavation in 2009, is described. The site has a closely stratified sequence spanning the second and first millennia, with well-preserved architecture over at least four building levels of the period, two of which are burned, and all of which are yielding reliable (in situ) *pottery in significant quantities. It thus has the capacity to provide a closely defined sequence of stratification, architecture and ceramics in this little known area of the Near East in the Mitannian, Middle Assyrian and Neo-Assyrian periods, and to act as an exemplar in defining the material culture of the wider region. Comparisons are drawn between the finds from the Garzan and those from other sites in the Upper Tigris region, and then with the wider area of north Mesopotamia as far as the Euphrates.**

* We are grateful to Melik Ayaz, Director of Excavations in the General Directorate of Cultural Assets and Museums, and Nilüfer Babacan of the Ilısu-HES Projects Unit of the General Directorate, who encouraged and helped to start the salvage excavations at Gre Amer. To Nihat Erdoğan, Director

Introduction

Among the eastern tributaries of the Tigris, the Garzan river is possibly the most unassuming, and is usually neglected on the maps (**Figs 1, 2, 3**). From its source between Bitlis (at the foot of the pass from the Lake Van basin) and Muş (on the upper Euphrates) the river valley cuts through the east–west mountain chains of the eastern Taurus in a broadly south-west direction before turning south-east for some 40km to join the Tigris downstream of Hasankeyf. Since the resumption of work on the Ilısu dam scheme in the late 1990s numerous rescue excavations have been carried out in the region centred on the town of Bismil, between Batman and Diyarbakır, an area that has come to be described as the 'Upper Tigris' by excavators working in that area, but the Garzan river is some 50–60 km east of this and thus represents a new area virtually unexplored by archaeological excavation. This part of the Tigris valley is separated from the Syrian plain by the Tur Abdin mountains and is generally referred to as a marginal, scarcely populated area. It has often been assumed that this isolated area with limited agricultural potential was therefore spared from the political and economic interests of the dominating powers of the region in the second and first millennia, namely Mitanni and Assyria. The site of Gre Amer begins to illustrate a different picture by revealing complex architecture, seal impressions, and a rich ceramic repertoire, including some Assyrian-type ceramics.

Separated from Urartu and the Upper Euphrates valley by virtually impassable mountain ranges, the focus of the region was firmly to the south, namely to Assyria and before that to Mitanni. The region on the east (north) bank of the Tigris was of long-standing interest to the Assyrians as the location of the source of the river, thought by them to be in the spectacular cave system through which a tributary flows at Birkleyn, north of Lice in Diyarbakır province. Here are reliefs and inscriptions marking visits to the source by Tiglath-pileser I (1114–1076 BC) and Shalmaneser III (858–824 BC).[1] Among the key sources for the topography of the region in the Neo-Assyrian period are the accounts of Ashurnasirpal II's (883–859 BC) fifth campaign in 879 BC, as recorded in the annals and the Kurkh monolith.[2]

of the Mardin Museum, Assistant Professor Haluk Sağlamtimur, of Ege University, and Batman-Siirt Co-ordinator of the Ilısu project, and Zeynep İsen, of Batman İl Kültür Müdürlüğü, representative in the 2009 season, we are deeply grateful for much support and kindness. We are also grateful to Associate Professor Aslı Erim-Özdoğan our neighbour and fellow-excavator in Garzan; to Dr Diana Stein for comments on the sealings; and all the team members and workmen whose work contributed so much to the results described here. The photographs are by Caner Şenyuva, Hakkı Uncu, and the authors; the photographs of sherd groups are by Murat Akar. The maps (figs 1–2) are by Tony Ives.

[1] Grayson 1991, p. 61; Grayson 1996, pp. 92–96; Schachner 2009, p. 13; table 1; pp. 172–223.

[2] Liverani 1992, pp. 57–62 and fig. 6; Grayson 1991, pp. 191–223; 256–262.

Evidence for the historical geography of the immediate region is complex and contradictory, and modern scholars have had various (and not always compatible) attempts to interpret the evidence.[3] Some sort of a consensus emerges, albeit with many outstanding uncertainties. Šubria and Dirru were the two entities on the north bank of the Tigris, opposite Tushan, whose capital lay at a city of the same name, now known to be Ziyaret Tepe. Dirru is generally accepted to have lain west of Šubria (although it is placed to the east by Parker).[4] In 673 BC, during the reign of Esarhaddon (680–669 BC), Šubria was annexed and subdivided into two Neo-Assyrian 'provinces', Uppumu and Kullimeri. Uppumu is convincingly located at modern Fum, near Lice, by Kessler,[5] although this too has not passed without question.[6] The location of Kullimeri is still more problematic: some scholars have favoured a location on the Batman Su (river),[7] but any attempt to locate Kullimeri has also to take into account the equation of this place with Byzantine Chlomaron, itself persuasively located at Arzen (alternatively Arzan, or Erzen), the great Hellenistic-to-medieval city on the Garzan Çayı (river), just east of modern İkiköprü.[8] If this holds, then Šubria/Kullimeri must be taken to have extended east of the Batman Su at least as far as the Garzan Çayı, and thus Gre Amer may have fallen within Kullimeri. If Šubria did not extend east of the Batman Su, then the Garzan area must have lain in Habhu *ša bītanī*, an even less-well defined topographical entity, to the east of the Tigris and probably centred on the Bohtan Su,[9] although this has also sometimes been placed further south and east.[10]

The Garzan valley was first surveyed in the 1960s by archaeologists of the Joint Istanbul-Chicago Universities' Prehistoric Research Expedition in South-East Anatolia.[11] Detailed survey in response to the threat of flooding took place in the early 1990s by a team led by Guillermo Algaze and the mound of Gre Amer was first identified at this time.[12] Further survey work was carried out in the early 2000s by Aslı Erim-Özdoğan and Jale Velibeyoğlu.[13] Based on surface collections Parker proposed a two period chronology for Gre Amer: with early second millennium and Iron Age material represented, whereas Aslı Erim-Özdoğan reported the presence of fourth and third millennium material as well.

[3] Kessler 1980; Kessler 1995; Liverani 1992; Parpola and Porter 2001; Parker 2001, chapter 4.2.
[4] Parker 2001, pp. 106–109.
[5] Kessler 1995, pp. 56–57.
[6] *cf.* Karg 1999, p. 279, citing Whitby 1983, pp. 208–211.
[7] *inter alia* Kessler 1995, pp. 57–58; Karg 1999, p. 278.
[8] Kessler 1995, p. 57; Sinclair 1989, p. 381; Whitby 1983, p. 211.
[9] Liverani 1992, pp. 25–27; 43.
[10] *e.g.* Parpola and Porter 2001, map 4.
[11] Çambel and Braidwood 1980, pp. 41–43; Benedict 1980, p. 152; figs 7–8.
[12] Algaze *et al.* 1991; Parker 2001, ch. 4.
[13] Erim-Özdoğan and Sarıaltun 2011, pp. 1073; 1099.

THE SITE OF GRE AMER

The first season of excavations at Gre Amer Höyük commenced in the summer of 2009 as part of the Ilısu Dam Salvage projects. The excavation has been funded by the General Directorate of Cultural Assets and Museums (*Kültür Varlıkları ve Müzeler Genel Müdürlüğü*) through grants provided for the Ilısu salvage projects by the General Directorate of State Waterworks (*Devlet Su İşleri*). Administratively it is a joint effort of Mardin Museum and Koç University's Department of Archaeology and History of Art under the scientific direction of one of the authors (GP).

Gre Amer Höyük is a site of approximately four hectares in area on the east bank of the Garzan Çayı (**Figs 2, 4**). The base of the Garzan valley at this point is broad with considerable agricultural potential, although it narrows both upstream, in the vicinity of Beşiri, and downstream, towards its confluence with the Tigris. The site lies within the boundaries of Işıkveren village (old name Dusadek), in the Beşiri district (*ilçe*) of Batman province (*il*) containing the richest oil fields of Turkey. By the standards of most Mesopotamian mounds, the site is small, but nevertheless it remains one of the largest ancient sites in the Garzan valley.

The confluence of the Garzan Çayı with the Tigris is a distance of 26km downstream from Gre Amer Höyük; as the crow flies the site is just 18km north of Hasankeyf (**Fig. 2**). The site is positioned on the bank of the Gre Amer stream, now a dry valley (wadi), a tributary of the Garzan Çayı, on the shoulder of a natural hill and extends to the south-west above a natural rock terrace above the river bank (**Fig. 4**). The summit of the mound lies at around 545m above sea level (rising to just above 550m at the summit of the hill), with the river terrace lying at a level of 520–30m. The site is one of the few under excavation that will be almost wholly submerged by waters of the Ilısu lake: only the summit will remain above the water line.[14]

In the course of the preliminary survey by the current team in 2008 a sherd with part of a cuneiform sign was found on the mound (**Fig. 5**). This was a fine red ware resembling the Middle or Neo-Assyrian ceramics of the area, with the sign inscribed before the piece was fired. Such inscriptions sometimes indicate the volume of the vessel, or what was stored in it, but sometimes also can imply an association with a special ceremony or function. For example, it is known from Middle and Late Assyrian tablets that Assyrian officials entertained local notables at meals (*naptanu*) and gave gifts of the drinking vessels from the dinner; and some of these cups had inscriptions on them.[15] The nearest similar examples of such inscribed cups have been found in North Syria at Tell Sabi Abyad, where one carinated bowl and two large jars

[14] According to the latest information of the *Devlet Su İşleri* final water levels will be between 530–540 m.

[15] Duistermaat 2008, pp. 561; 563.

bearing cuneiform signs dating to the Middle Assyrian period are known.[16] Middle Assyrian Tell Sabi Abyad was a farming settlement surrounded by a defensive wall.[17] There is another example of this 'official farm', termed *dunnu* in Assyrian, at Giricano Höyük excavated on the upper Tigris, near Bismil.[18] This find demonstrated the possibility before excavation that there was an official building at the site, dating to the Middle and/or Neo-Assyrian period.

Occupation has been identified on the summit of the hill (where it is very eroded and poorly preserved), on the shoulder of the hill to the south-west, and over a wide area of the flat plain still further to the south-west, extending possibly as far as the river cliff. The core of the site appears to stretch from the shoulder of the hill some 100m through to a visible terrace (**Fig.** 7). Elsewhere test trenching so far has shown traces of occupation but fewer structures in the peripheral areas of the site. The main part of the site is now bisected by the cutting for a modern road. Sections at the road cutting show that the depth of occupation is in the region of 4–5m, although there are also signs that it may be deeper in places (potentially with earlier levels so-far unattested in the excavated sequence).

Summary of the Excavated Sequence

The stratigraphic sequence of the mound was best represented in the road cutting, termed Operation 1 (**Fig. 8**). In this sector seven (10 x 10m) trenches were excavated. Two burnt levels were visible in the section with two further structural levels identified above the upper burnt level. At the end of the first season we have provisionally dated the levels as follows:

— Level 4 (the lower burnt level) to the Middle-to-Late Bronze Age (*c.*1800–1200 BC);
— Level 3 (the upper burnt level) to the Early Iron Age (*c.*1100–900 BC);
— Level 2 to the Middle or Late Iron Age (*c.*900–500 BC);
— Level 1 to the later first millennium BC, perhaps in the Hellenistic or Parthian periods.

Level 1 was confirmed as the latest on the site, found immediately beneath the topsoil. In the area excavated so far, the most likely interpretation of Levels 1 and 2 emerged as store rooms and workshops. In these places we found *in situ* storage pots, spindle whorls (indicating the presence of textile production), and iron and bronze metal fragments. In the road cutting, a section of some 22 m of external (defensive?) retaining wall belonging to Level 4 was exposed, standing at its highest to up to 3 m

[16] Duistermaat 2008, figs 4.43, 4.67, p. 563.
[17] Duistermaat 2008, pp. 25; 44–46.
[18] Schachner 2002, pp. 26–27; Radner 2004, p. 138.

(**Fig. 9**). From the fills against this wall a potsherd with a cylinder seal impression was recovered (**Fig. 6**), one of four found in 2009. The seal design shows hunters bearing spears in a style typical of the late 3rd and 2nd millennia. Also from within the same fills came ceramic zoomorphic figurines, numerous horn cores, and various obsidian objects, including arrow heads and other lithic tools (these are not residual finds, as obsidian continued to be used in these periods in the Ilısu region).

Trenches on the summit of the mound, and in the area immediately to the south-west, were known as Operation 2 (**Fig. 10**). This part of the site has wide views of the Garzan valley. The natural conditions on the summit of the mound were such that a combination of erosion, deep pit digging and recent military operations had jeopardised survival. Nevertheless, the summit trenches are distinctive for the frequency of finewares of probable Neo-Assyrian type, also seen elsewhere on the site, but in significantly-smaller quantities. One of the deep pits in the summit trenches yielded a polychrome decorated glass vessel fragment of Mitannian or Assyrian type (very similar to examples from Tell al Rimah and Tell Brak, and a bottle from North Mesopotamia displayed in the Istanbul Archaeology Museum).[19] On the south side of the road, Operation 3 consisted of a single trench in which the sequence observed in Operation 1 appeared to continue (**Fig. 11**). Further south the river terrace was sampled by means of five small 5 × 5 m trenches (Operation 4), which showed some occupation but few structures.

After one season of excavation the architecture (well-planned, stone-walled buildings) and artifacts (large storage jars with sealings, glass fragment and cuneiform inscribed sherd), indicate a site of economic administration/organization related nature. What this represents in terms of control on a local or regional basis, and the nature of its broader cultural affiliation is yet to be determined.

THE POTTERY

One of the most striking aspects of the first season was the quantity and the variety of the ceramics excavated at Gre Amer. Among other things some 44 whole or reconstructable vessels were recovered in 2009 (another 33 in 2010).

The pottery shows a number of strong traits. In giving an overview of the pottery, we will attempt some first impressions of material from the Garzan and thus from the Tigris area in general; then to look at similar material from the Euphrates and elsewhere in northern Mesopotamia, and perhaps to clarify some misconceptions about dating and associations.

[19] Oates 1968, p. 134; pl. 35c; Oates *et al.* 1997, p. 85; Istanbul Archaeological Museums, Ancient Orient section, inventory no. 2260.

Colour-washed and colour coated traditions

This material, referred to as 'Red-Brown Wash Ware' (RBWW) has been reported from numerous sites in the upper Tigris region.[20] Although there is broad agreement that it belongs to the early-to-middle second millennium, the detailed attribution varies greatly on a site-by-site basis. And the question of how late this tradition continues is still to be satisfactorily answered. At Gre Amer this material characterises Level 4 above all (**Fig. 12, rows 1–4**); we are not yet able to say exactly how late it continues, and thus whether there is a hiatus in the occupation of the site between Level 4 and Level 3 (the lower and upper burnt levels), although the very clear differences in the pottery assemblages between these two levels suggest that there might be such a hiatus. A common detail of this RBWW at Gre Amer that does not seem to have been noted elsewhere is the deep combed-incised ornament on the interior surface of some open jar and bowl forms (**Fig. 12, row 4**). Another widely-reported colour-coated type, the so-called 'Dark-Rimmed Orange Ware' (DROW), is sometimes dated to the 3rd millennium, sometimes to the 2nd millennium.[21] This appears to us to be a variant of the same tradition, occurring in similar forms alongside the RBWW (**Fig. 12, row 5**). The differential surface colouring is probably a product of kiln conditions rather than potting or finishing technique, a suggestion that appears to be supported by preliminary analysis of similar material from Hirbemerdon Tepe, near Batman.[22]

Painted pottery traditions

Numerous separate painted pottery traditions are represented in the material from Gre Amer as individual sherds alongside the colour washed wares, including Nuzi Ware and Khabur Ware pieces (and derivatives) (**Figs 13, 14**). Although this is encouraging for the future in showing that these types are present on the site, they appear in too small a quantity to tell us much that is certain for the present.

From later levels come various exotic slipped and painted pieces (**Fig. 14, rows 1–2**), and a variety of other painted sherds akin to the Early Iron Age pottery familiar from the Euphrates and Upper Tigris (**Fig. 14, rows 3–4**). Some of these are paralleled closely at Tille Höyük on the Euphrates, now flooded by the Atatürk Dam, which provides a well defined stratigraphic and ceramic sequence for comparative purposes as well as a number of significant differences and inconsistencies.[23] The painted wares typical of the earliest part of the Early Iron Age sequence at Tille, Levels I-III, show some striking similarities with the Gre Amer material: decoration with dots and circles

[20] For example, Laneri *et al.* 2006, p. 156; Parker and Dodd 2003, pp. 39–40.
[21] Kozbe *et al.* 2004, p. 500; Özfırat 2005, pp. 48; 52–3.
[22] Laneri *et al.* 2006, pp. 167–168.
[23] Blaylock 2009; Blaylock forthcoming.

(**Fig. 14, row 4**), hatched triangles, and the like,[24] but none of the red-triangle painted ware that is so typical of the Tigris and Garzan (below).

Predominant however, both in the sherd material but also as numerous complete vessels, are painted jars and jugs bearing zones of hatched or wavy-line decoration on the shoulder with long hachure-like triangles falling from them (**Figs 15, 16**). This material, called by excavators 'red-triangular ware' or 'red-triangle painted ware' (the term preferred here) is coming to be seen as one of the most typical pottery types of the Tigris region, and now characterises the pottery assemblage of the Garzan valley as well. The triangles can be painted out, or can be hatched or filled by further motifs and show considerable variation in character and complexity of decoration. The salient fact about this material is that it appears to be present throughout the Gre Amer sequence in one form or another: there are complete or near complete examples from the bottom of Level 4 (**Fig. 15, left**) to a group of pots from the very end of the sequence, in or above Level 1 (**Fig. 15, centre and right**). Here, as well as among the sherd material mentioned already there appear to be generic links to Iranian and other eastern painted pottery traditions of the second and first millennia.[25]

Ribbed or grooved pottery traditions

This material is among the most distinctive and readily recognisable of all Iron Age pottery in Eastern Anatolia and adjacent areas. It occurs at Gre Amer in some quantity throughout the upper three levels (Levels 3–1), although so far mainly as sherd material, with all the attendant hazards of interpretation that follow from this. So far there are whole vessels from Level 3 alone, and it may be that this proves to be the point of origin of much, if not all, of the material working its way up into the later levels. The grooved pottery at Gre Amer is predominantly buff, pale brown or pale grey and is unburnished (**Fig. 17, top row**). Many vessels are decorated with additional incised or applied decoration (**Fig. 17, rows 2–4**). Some also display sub-triangular lugged rims, with one, two, or three finger-impressions on their upper surface, a feature not (so far as we have seen) previously identified on this pottery, but one that has more than an echo in the Late Bronze Age pottery of the Euphrates.[26]

At Gre Amer the collection of grooved pottery contains relatively few examples of the dark red-brown-black vessels, generally heavily burnished, and typified by hole-mouthed forms often with spouts on the shoulder, which is the type widely familiar from elsewhere on the Euphrates, in the Keban, Karakaya and Atatürk lake areas.[27] We have termed this 'classic ribbed ware' (**Fig. 17, bottom row**) in contrast to the

[24] Blaylock 1999, fig. 1.
[25] Dyson 1999, pp. 116–9; Goff 1978, pp. 30–36; figs 1, 5–6, 8–9.
[26] Summers 1993, p. 44, figs 32–3.
[27] Blaylock 1999, p. 267; fig. 3.

buff and mostly unburnished 'common' ware that dominates the collection (above). The broad division into two types may provide the beginnings of an explanation for the evident variety of dating that has been applied to this material.[28] So far as it is possible to tell, the handful of 'classic' sherds so far identified at Gre Amer tend to come from later rather than earlier levels; the majority of the buff, unburnished and lug-handled sherds are spread more evenly through the three upper levels, although this may be the result of residuality. Nevertheless it seems likely that (a) the differences in manufacture and surface appearance show that more than one type is represented within this larger class of material, and that (b) there may well be a chronological implication to the difference between the 'classic' and the plain, or 'common', types.

At Tille nearly all of the grooved pottery is identifiable as the 'classic' type just described; there, it demonstrably belongs to the Middle Iron Age levels, Levels IV and V, the main structural levels relating to the heyday of the Neo-Hittite kingdom of Kummuh (**Fig. 18**). Although this is not definitively dated, it is suggested that a date of late 10th and early 9th century for Level IV and thus 9th century for Level V (with Levels VI and VII in the 8th century) cannot be too far wrong.[29] Although there is room for some manouevre in this dating, there is limited potential for radical re-dating (especially to any earlier period), given the presence of three or more structural levels beneath Level IV to be fitted into a period in the 11th and/or 10th centuries. This is a period that will shrink still further, if the redating that Summers proposed for the earlier (erstwhile Late Bronze Age) levels at Tille at the *Across the Border* conference is sustainable.[30]

This is the position when seen from the point of view of a site on the Euphrates, yet from a Tigris perspective, the explanation must be more complicated. A distribution map of ribbed or grooved pottery prepared for the second volume of the Tille final report (**Fig. 19**), shows the wide distribution of the pottery, but makes no distinction between the different types. Were such a distinction to be made, it is possible that the focus of the 'classic' grooved pottery would appear more to the north and west and the buff unburnished wares would be concentrated to the south and east; the nature of the outlying groups in Armenia and north-west Iran is more uncertain; these may belong to still more different (if related) groups.

We therefore propose that the extended span over which this grooved pottery appears to have been used can be accounted for by separate ware types within a larger tradition. As we have said, the material from Tille is largely homogeneous in appearance: Handmade, gritty, dark fabric with red, brown or black burnished surfaces, and

[28] Summarised, for example, by Roaf and Schachner 2005, pp. 120–1; Blaylock forthcoming, chapter 9.
[29] Blaylock 2009, pp. 124–5.
[30] Summers, this volume (Chp. 13 pp. 311–328).

with a preponderance of hole-mouthed forms. The material widely seen in the upper Tigris and now the Garzan, although clearly closely related, is generally much more variable; the greatest part of the collection is often very crude, with pale brown, or buff surfaces, is rarely burnished, and displays a much higher incidence of decorated vessels and open forms than seen elsewhere. Although we suspect a chronological difference as well as a spatial one, it is too early to say certainly whether these types will be distinguishable stratigraphically at Gre Amer, and thus whether they should be interpreted as parallel or serial trends within the larger tradition of grooved pottery.

The distribution map (**Fig. 19**) shows a southern limit to the use of grooved pottery broadly coincident with the present Turkish-Syrian border. Although it was found at Tell Halaf, and there are odd occurrences elsewhere in the extreme north of Syria, this material is not routinely found at Iron Age sites in the Khabur, the Euphrates, or further west in the Aleppo-Orontes-coastal regions. As with all distribution maps this really shows the distribution of archaeological endeavour rather than the true area over which this pottery was used. One suspects that outlying sites (for example in the Hatay and Gaziantep regions to the west, or the Khabur to the south) may indicate a wider distribution, as well as perhaps a failure to recognise this material elsewhere.

It may be significant that the grooved pottery (dated to the Early–Middle Iron Age) sees its heyday between periods where southern influence is demonstrable and strong, namely between the Middle Assyrian and Neo-Assyrian periods. So it may reflect in some way the period of Assyrian weakness between the 11th and 9th centuries.

An additional point worth making is that at Gre Amer we are finding this material in association with good-quality architecture rather than from pits and ephemeral structures, with a number of whole vessels *in situ* on floors that demonstrate this association unequivocally. This suggests that for us in the Garzan, at least, the thesis of semi-nomadic occupation of sites of this period proposed for the Bismil area by Timothy Matney at the conference does not apply.[31]

Pottery of Level 1

Of the pottery associated with Level 1, the latest level of the site, several observations can be made. One group of 14 whole vessels from Operation 1 included four red-triangle painted vessels (two of which are shown in **Fig. 15**, **centre and right**), three small lentoid flasks, a turquoise-glazed jar with two barley-twist handles (**Fig. 20**), an open trefoil lamp as well as numerous plain jars and jugs. Alongside this as sherd material are numerous incised pieces reminiscent of Hellenistic mould-made ceramics, and possibly imitating these (**Fig. 21**). The glazed and incised ceramics

[31] Matney, this volume (Chp. 14 pp. 329–347).

seem to suggest that this assemblage dates to the end of the first millennium BC, and might belong to the Hellenistic or Parthian period. But many familiar aspects of Hellenistic material culture are not present at Gre Amer (neither sigillata and colour-coated wares, lamps, terracottas, etc., nor coins) and this means we remain hesitant about attributing this level to a specific period at present, preferring to express a provisional dating in the mid-late first millennium. The most significant aspect of this group to be emphasised at present is the continuation of the red-triangle painted tradition into this late period, whatever its exact dating.

Other pottery

Other exotic ceramics include a number of wasters, especially in Level 4 (suggesting there was a kiln on the site at this period); many fine-ware sherds, mostly of Middle Assyrian or Neo-Assyrian date where they can be identified (**Fig. 22**); a small number of wedge-decorated pieces termed by us 'pseudo cuneiform' decoration; a variety of sherd material with incised, impressed and applied decoration; plus large quantities of plain ceramics and large storage jars and pithoi. As yet there is little else that we can identify as Late Bronze Age; Middle Assyrian; or other. A small number of combed-decorated pieces from Gre Amer have a resonance with the LBA material from Tille (**Fig. 23**).[32] We hope that more will become apparent as we explore the site further.

CONCLUSION

If there is anything to be drawn by way of a general conclusion at this point, we would suggest that everything we have seen emphasises the continuity of pottery traditions in the Garzan in the second and first millennia. With dating very far from certain, the best that can be said at the moment is that the variety within the painted and grooved ceramic traditions, and possibly the colour-washed tradition as well, is best accounted for by their production extending over a wide area and lengthy chronological span. The restricted sequence of occupation and the well-defined ceramic assemblage associated with the architecture and stratification at Gre Amer, has the potential to enable us to clarify this continuity in the seasons to come, and provide an exemplar for defining the material culture of the upper Tigris and its tributaries.

Our continuing targets for work at Gre Amer are to understand the complete chronology of the site, to define the architecture and the nature of the settlement in the second and first millennia BC, to reveal the local components of the culture and its associations within the cultural sphere of Mitanni, Assyria and with other neighbouring areas, on both sides of the border.

[32] *Cf.* Summers 1993, pp. 43–4, figs 27–31.

BIBLIOGRAPHY

ALGAZE, G., BREUNINGER, R., LIGHTFOOT, C. and ROSENBERG, M.
1991 "The Tigris-Euphrates Archaeological Reconnaissance Project: A Preliminary Report of the 1989–1990 Seasons," *Anatolica* 17: 175–240.

BARTL, K.
1995 "Some remarks on Early Iron Age in Eastern Anatolia," *Anatolica* 21: 205–212.
2001 "Eastern Anatolia in the Early Iron Age," in *Migration und Kulturtransfer: Der Wandel vorder- und zentralasiatischer Kulteren im Umbruch vom 2 zum 1 vorchristlicher Jahrtausend*, R-GK/DAI Kolloquium zur Vor- und Frügeshichte, Band 6, edited by R. Eichmann and H. Parzinger, pp. 383–410. Bonn: Habelt.

BENEDICT, P.
1980 "Survey work in Southeastern Anatolia," in *Istanbul ve Chicago Universiteleri Karma Projesi Güneydoğu Anadolu Tarihöncesi Araştırmaları/The Joint Istanbul-Chicago Universities' Prehistoric Research in Southeastern Anatolia*, Istanbul Universitesi Edebiyat Fakültesi yayınları, no. 2589, edited by H. Çambel and R. J. Braidwood, pp. 151–191 and pls 1–23. Istanbul: Edebiyat Fakültesi Basımevi.

BLAYLOCK, S. R.
1999 "Iron Age pottery from Tille Höyük, South-Eastern Turkey," in *Iron Age Pottery in Northern Mesopotamia, Northern Syria, and South-Eastern Anatolia* (Altertumskunde des Vorderen Orients), edited by A. Hausleiter and A. Reiche, pp. 263–286. Münster: Ugarit-Verlag.
2009 *Tille Höyük 3: The Iron Age, Part 1: Introduction, Stratification, and Architecture*, British Institute of Archaeology at Ankara Monograph 41. London: British Institute at Ankara.
forthcoming *Tille Höyük 3: The Iron Age, Part 2: Pottery, Objects and Conclusions* (British Institute of Archaeology at Ankara monograph).

ÇAMBEL, H. and BRAIDWOOD, R. J.
1980 "The Joint Istanbul-Chicago Universities' Prehistoric Research in South Eastern Anatolia, Comprehensive view: The work to date, 1963–1972," in *Istanbul ve Chicago Universiteleri Karma Projesi Güneydoğu Anadolu Tarihöncesi Araştırmaları/The Joint Istanbul-Chicago Universities' Prehistoric Research in Southeastern Anatolia*, Istanbul Universitesi Edebiyat Fakültesi yayınları, no. 2589, edited by H. Çambel and R. J. Braidwood, pp. 33–64. Istanbul: Edebiyat Fakültesi Basımevi.

DUISTERMAAT, K.
2008 *The Pots and Potters of Assyria: Technology and Organisaton of Production, Ceramic Sequence and Vessel Function at Late Bronze Age Tell Sabi Abyad, Syria,* Papers on Archaeology of the Leiden Museum of Antiquties 4. Turnhout: Brepols.

DYSON, R. H.
1999 "Triangle-Festoon Ware Reconsidered," *Iranica Antiqua* 34: 115–141.

ERIM-ÖZDOĞAN, A. and SARIALTUN, S.
2011 "Inventory of cultural heritage in the environs of Garzan Valley and Batman Stream, Ilısu Dam Area," in *Salvage Project of the Archaeological Heritage of the Ilısu and Carchemish Dam Reservoirs, Activities in 2002* (two volumes), edited by N. Tuna and O. Doonan, pp. 945–1146. Ankara: Orta Doğu Teknik Üniversitesi (ODTÜ)/Tarihsel Çevre Araştırma ve Değerlendirme Merkezi (TAÇDAM).

GOFF, C.
1978 "Excavations at Baba Jan, The pottery and metals from levels III and II," *Iran* 16: 29–67.
GRAYSON, A. K.
1991 *Assyrian Rulers of the Early First Millennium B.C., I (1114–859 BC),* Royal Inscriptions of Mesopotamia 2. Toronto: University of Toronto Press.
1996 *Assyrian Rulers of the Early First Millennium B.C., II (858–745 B.C.),* Royal Inscriptions of Mesopotamia 2. Toronto: University of Toronto Press.
KARG, N.
1999 "Gre Dimse 1998: Preliminary report," in *Salvage Project of the Archaeological Heritage of the Ilısu and Carchemish Dam Reservoirs, Activities in 1998,* edited by N. Tuna and J. Öztürk, pp. 271–96. Ankara: Orta Doğu Teknik Üniversitesi (ODTÜ)/Tarihsel Çevre Araştırma ve Değerlendirme Merkezi (TAÇDAM).
KESSLER, K.
1980 *Untersuchungen zur historischen Topographie Nordmesopotamiens.* Wiesbaden: Dr Ludwig Reichart Verlag.
1995 "Šubria, Urartu and Aššur: Topographical questions around the Tigris sources" in *Neo-Assyrian Geography,* edited by M. Liverani, pp. 55–67. Rome: Università di Roma "La Sapienza".
KOZBE, G., KÖROĞLU, K., and SAĞLAMTEMIR, H.
2004 "2001 Excavations at Kavuşan Höyük," in *Salvage Project of the Archaeological Heritage of the Ilısu and Carchemish Dam Reservoirs, Activities in 2001,* edited by N. Tuna, J. Greenhalgh and J. Velibeyoğlu, pp. 463–503. Ankara: Orta Doğu Teknik Üniversitesi (ODTÜ)/Tarihsel Çevre Araştırma ve Değerlendirme Merkezi (TAÇDAM).
KÖROĞLU, K.
1998 *Üctepe I.* Ankara: Türk Tarihi Kurumu Yayınları.
LANERI, N., D'AGOSTINO, A., SCHWARTZ, M., VALENTINI, S. and PAPPALARDO, G.
2006 "A preliminary report of the archaeological excavations at Hirbemerdon Tepe, Southeastern Turkey, 2005," *Anatolica* 32: 153–88.
LIVERANI, M,
1992 *Studies on the Annals of Ashurnasirpal II, 2 Topographical Analysis.* Rome: Università di Roma "La Sapienza".
OATES, D.
1968 "The excavations at Tell al Rimah, 1967," *Iraq* 30: 115–38.
OATES, D., OATES, J., and MCDONALD, H.
1997 *Excavations at Tell Brak. Vol. 1: The Mitanni and Old Babylonian periods* (McDonald Institute Monograph). Cambridge/London: The McDonald Institute for Archaeological Research/The British School of Archaeology in Iraq.
ÖZFIRAT, A.
2005 *Üçtepe II: Tunç Çağları, Kazı ve Yüzey Araştırması Işığında.* Istanbul: Ege Yayınları.
PARKER, B. J.
2001 *The Mechanics of Empire: The Northern Frontier of Assyria as a Case Study in Imperial Dynamics.* Helsinki: Neo Assyrian Text Corpus Project.
PARKER, B. J. and DODD, L. S.
2003 "The early second millennium ceramic assemblage from Kenan Tepe, southeastern Turkey. A preliminary assessment," *Anatolian Studies* 53: 33–69.

PARPOLA, S. and PORTER, M., eds
2001 *The Helsinki Atlas of the Near East in the Neo-Assyrian Period.* Helsinki: The Casco Bay Assyriological Institute/The Neo-Assyrian Text Corpus Project.

RADNER, K.
2004 *Das Mittelassyrische Tontafelarchiv von Giricano/Dunnu-sa-Uzibi: Ausgrabungen in Giricano 1*, Subartu 14. Turnhout: Brepols.

ROAF, M. and SCHACHNER, A.
2005 "The Bronze Age to Iron Age transition in the upper Tigris region: new information from Ziyaret Tepe and Giricano," *Anatolian Iron Ages 5: Proceedings of the Fifth Anatolian Iron Ages Colloquium held at Van, 6-10 August 2001*, British Institute of Archaeology at Ankara Monograph 31, edited by A. Çilingiroğlu and G. Darbyshire, pp. 115–123. London: British Institute of Archaeology at Ankara.

SCHACHNER, A.
2002 "Ausgrabungen in Giricano (2000–2001), Neue Forschungen an der Nordgrenze des Mesopotamischen Kulturraums," *Istanbuler Mitteilungen* 52: 9–57.
2009 *Assyriens Könige an Einer der Quellen des Tigris: Archäologische Forschungen im Höhlensystem von Bırkleyn und am sogenannten Tigris-Tunnel*, Istanbuler Forschungen 51. Tubingen: Ernst Wasmuth Verlag.

SINCLAIR, T. A.
1989 *Eastern Turkey: An Architectural and Archaeological Survey, Vol. III.* London: Pindar Press.

SUMMERS, G. D.
1993 *Tille Höyük 4: The Late Bronze Age and the Iron Age Transition*, British Institute of Archaeology at Ankara Monograph 15. London: British Institute of Archaeology at Ankara.

WHITBY, M.
1983 "Arzanene in the late sixth century," in *Armies and Frontiers in Roman and Byzantine Anatolia*, British Institute of Archaeology at Ankara Monograph 5/ BAR Int. Ser. 156, edited by S. Mitchell, pp. 205–218. Oxford: British Archaeological Reports.

Postscript: Further seasons of work in 2010–2012, after this article was written, have refined our understanding of the site in a number of important ways, and a brief statement of these is desirable here. There is a fragmentary uppermost level, post-dating Level 1 ('Level 0'), which dates to the Hellenistic period, but Level 1 as described here is now known to date to the Achaemenid period rather than the Hellenistic, possibly the 5th or early 4th centuries B.C. A cemetery of stone cist graves dating to Level 1 (based on the stratigraphy and associated objects) has been excavated in 2011–2012. Although our statements above about the continuity of painted ceramic traditions remain correct, it now seems that the red-painted triangle ware is also more definitely to be associated with Level 1. Levels 3 and 4 are proving to be significantly more extensive than expected, spreading across the eastern slope of the site. Level 3, of the early Iron Age, is proving to have massive and well-preserved stone and mudbrick architecture in association with a varied and plentiful ceramic repertoire, including, but by no means limited to, grooved pottery and its relations. Level 4 is buried to a great depth by colluvial soils towards the east of the site. From the incidence of wasters, it is now clear that pottery, including late Khabur type painted wares, was made on the site in the second millennium, although the kilns have not yet been located.

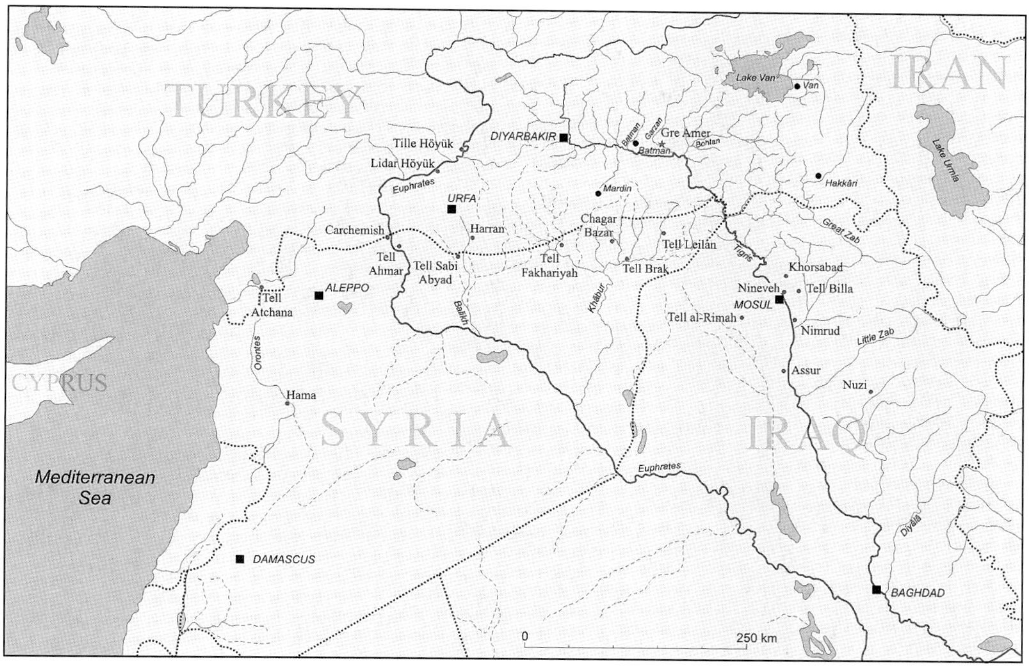

Fig. 1 North Mesopotamia showing the location of Gre Amer in its regional setting in South-East Turkey and North Syria.

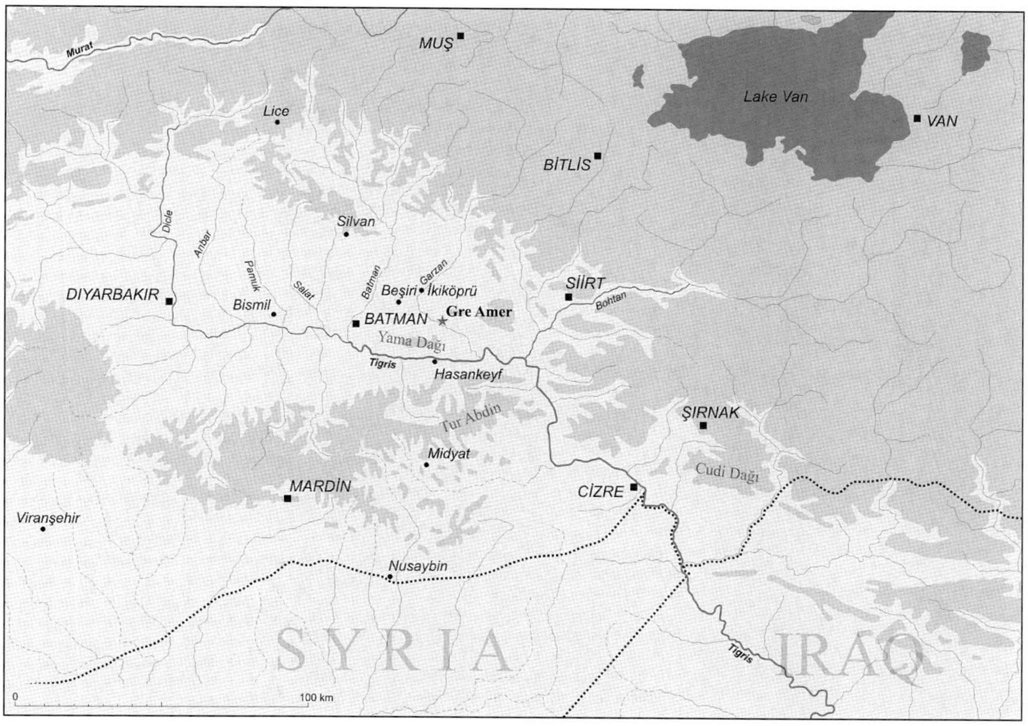

Fig. 2 South-East Turkey, showing the location of Gre Amer in relation to modern settlements.

Fig. 3 General view of the Garzan valley, looking south-east, downstream from Gre Amer.

Fig. 4 General view of the site (centre), looking east across the river.

Fig. 5 Sherd incised with part of a cuneiform sign found in the preliminary survey of Gre Amer in summer 2008.

Fig. 6 Sherd of Red-Brown Wash Ware with seal impression depicting hunters.

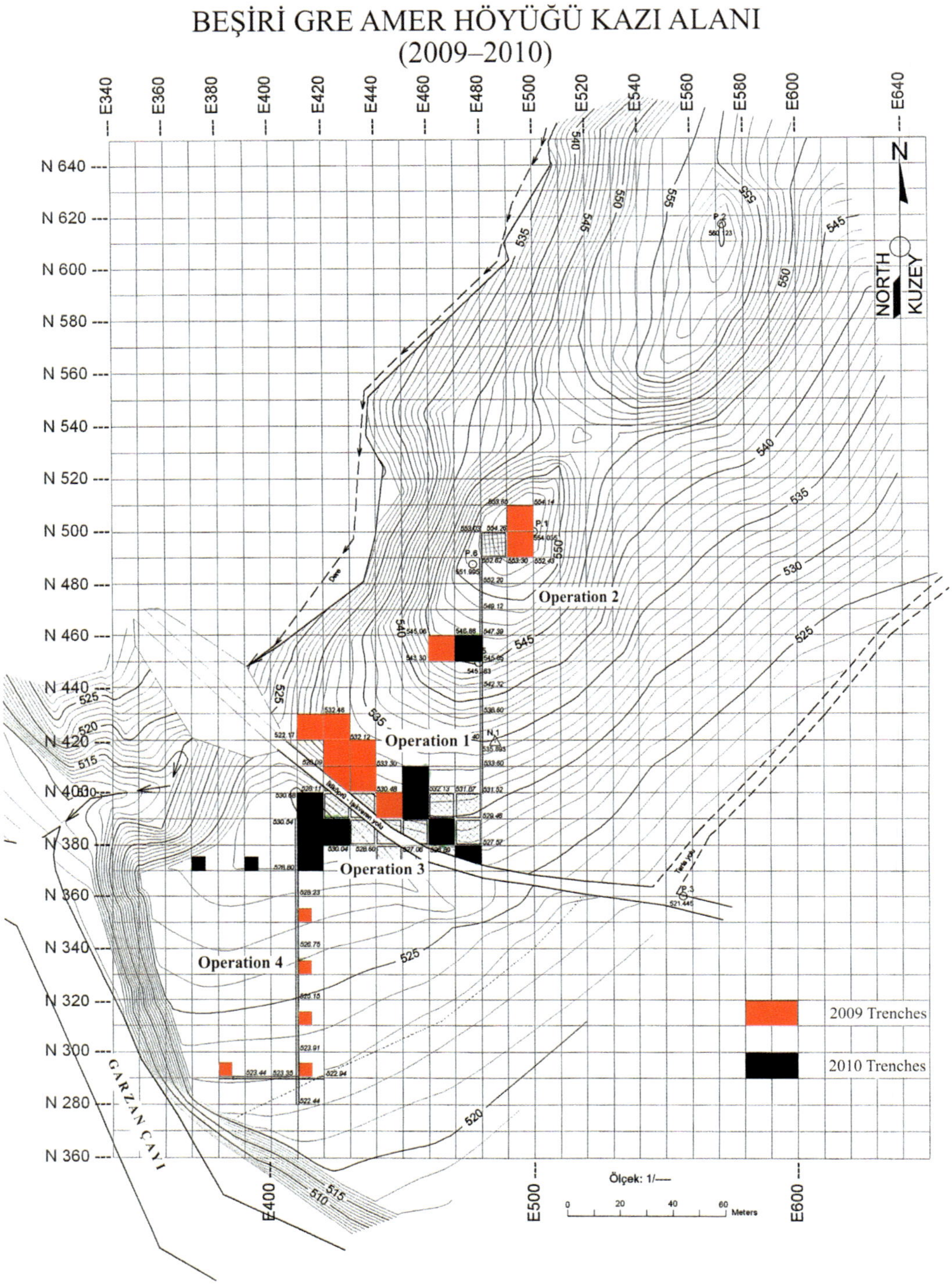

Fig. 7 Contour plan of Gre Amer,
showing operation numbers and trenches excavated in 2009–2010.

Fig. 8 Panoramic view of the Operation 1 trenches along the road cutting, looking north-east.

Fig. 9 The Level 4 retaining wall, looking north.

Fig. 10 View over Operation 2 from the shoulder of the mound, with Operations 3 and 4 in the background.

Fig. 11 The site from the south looking over Operation 3 on the south side of the road cutting to Operation 1 and to the summit of the site (rear), showing buildings of Level 3 in the foreground.

Fig. 12 Selected sherds of Red-Brown Wash Ware showing typical rim forms and surface finishes (rows 1 and 2), exterior cordon and combed decoration (row 3), and interior combed decoration (row 4); selected sherds of Dark-Rimmed Orange Ware (row 5).

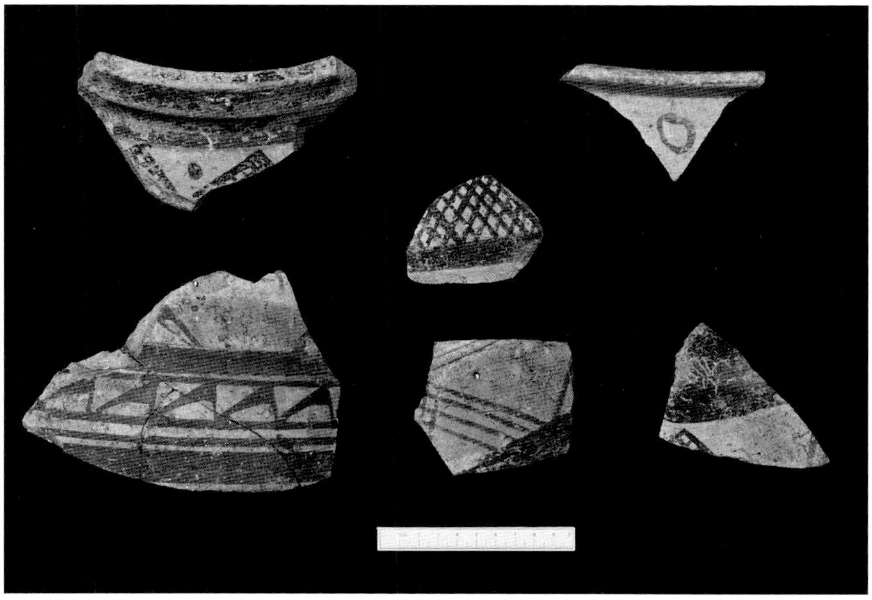

Fig. 13 Selected painted sherds associated with Level 4.

Fig. 14 Selected painted sherds, including Nuzi Ware, bichrome pieces (row 1); slipped and painted pieces (row 2); Early Iron Age painted pieces (rows 3–4); and miscellaneous painted rims (row 5).

Fig. 15 Selected vessels of red-triangle painted ware from Level 4 (left) and Level 1 (centre and right).

Fig. 16 Selected sherds of Red-Triangle Painted Ware showing the variety of designs.

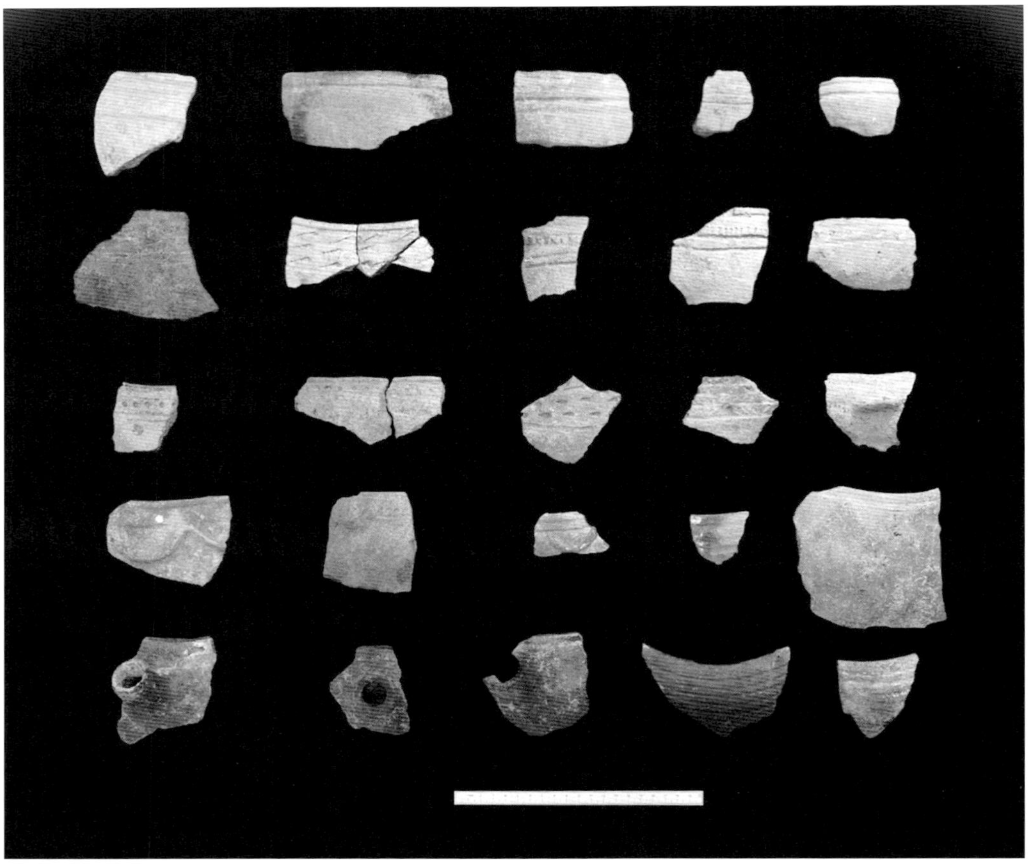

Fig. 17 Selected sherds of grooved pottery, showing sherds of the typical 'common' plain variety (top row), sherds illustrating the range of incised, impressed and applied decoration (rows 2–4), and typical sherds of the 'classic' variety (bottom row).

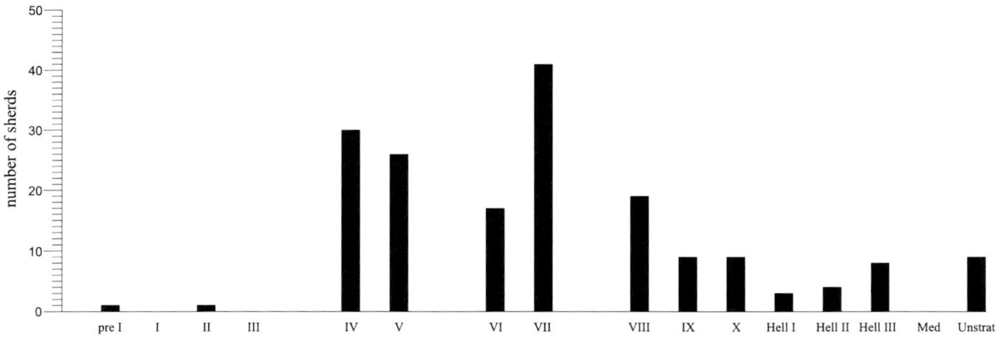

Fig. 18 Histogram showing the incidence of grooved sherds by level at Iron Age Tille Höyük (Blaylock forthcoming, table 9.3).

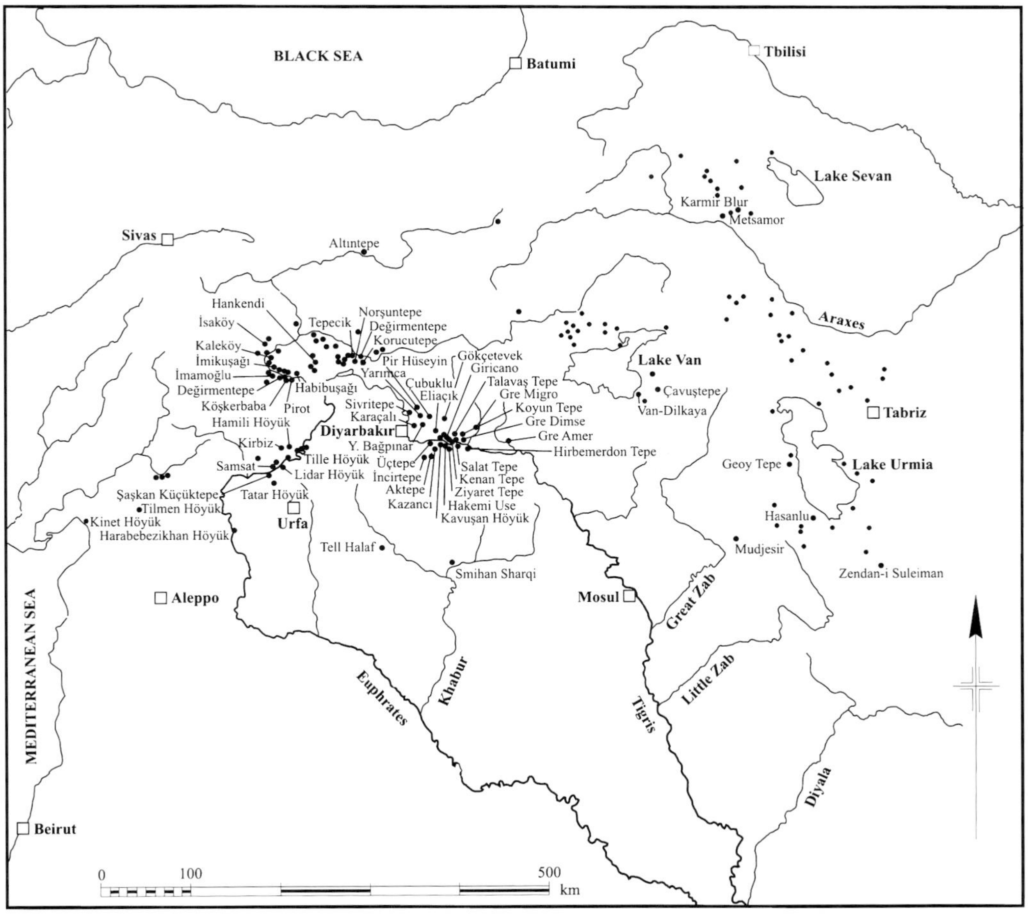

Fig. 19 Distribution map of ribbed or grooved pottery prepared for the second volume of the Tille final report (Blaylock forthcoming, fig. 9.13), drawing on similar maps by Karin Bartl (1995, 212; 2001, figs 1; 6–10), Kemalettin Köroğlu (1998, figs 11, 16, 17), Michael Roaf and Andreas Schachner (Roaf and Schachner 2005, fig. 4), among others, and other material assembled by the authors.

Fig. 20 A turquoise-glazed jar from a group of pots associated with Level 1.

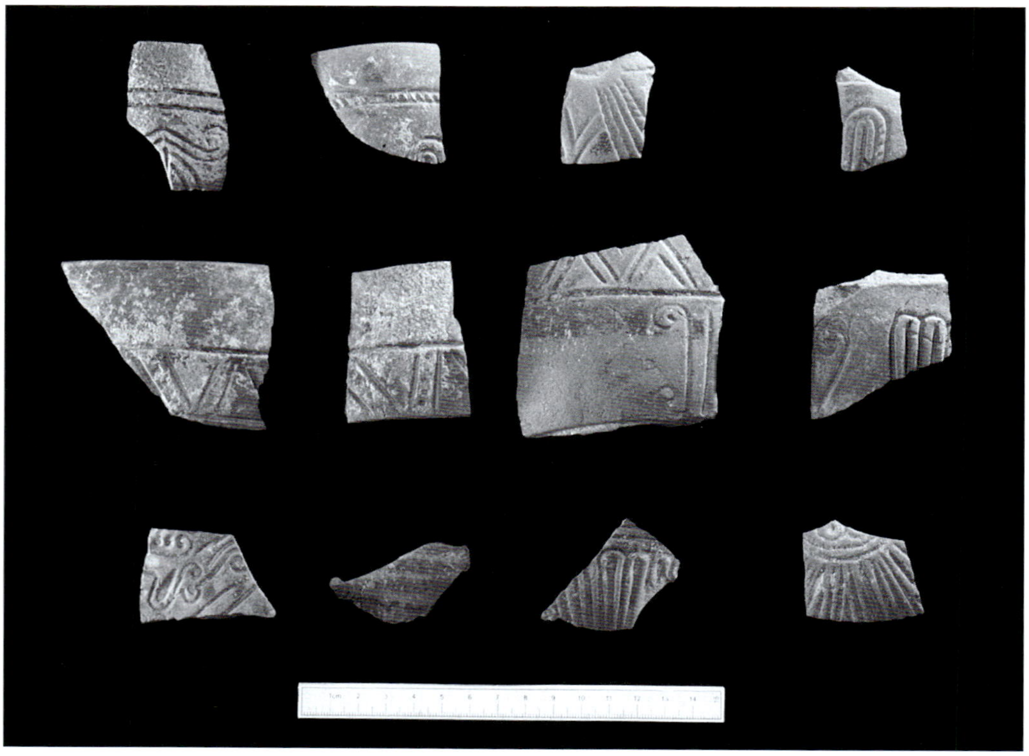

Fig. 21 Selected sherds of incised-decorated finewares from Level 1, possibly imitating late first-millennium mould-made ceramics.

Fig. 22 Selected rims and bases of finewares of Middle- and/or Neo-Assyrian date.

Fig. 23 Sherd of a comb-decorated vessel, potentially of late-second millennium date.

Section C

FUNERARY PRACTICES, TEXTS AND THE ARTS

CHAPTER 18

FUNERARY PRACTICES AND SOCIETY AT THE LATE BRONZE-IRON AGE TRANSITION. A VIEW FROM TELL SHIUKH FAWQÂNI AND TELL AN-NASRIYAH (SYRIA)

Aline TENU
CNRS - UMR 7041 (équipe HAROC)
Maison René-Ginouvès Archéologie et Ethnologie
Boîte 17
21 allée de l'Université
92023 Nanterre cedex
France
E-mail: aline.tenu@mae.cnrs.fr

ABTRACT

In 1997 and 2008 two cremation graveyards were discovered in Syria at Tell Shiukh Fawqâni in the Euphrates valley a few kilometres south of Karkemiš and at Tell an-Nasriyah on the eastern bank of the Orontes downstream of Hama. As yet about 150 and 50 graves were recognised there respectively. The careful excavation of the cemeteries and of the cinerary urns provides valuable information concerning the internal organisation of the necropolis, the composition of the tombs, the choice of grave goods, and the deceased themselves. These data combined together allow us to better reconstitute the funerary sequence from the pyre until the burying of the cremation jars. Work is still in progress at both sites, but first results may indicate that these societies managed their dead collectively and death became a matter for the entire group. More generally these discoveries convey new data pertaining to the cremation practice, which remains ill known due to its rarity. *

This paper aims to present some reflections raised by the discovery in Syria of two new cremation cemeteries since the end of the 1990's at Tell Shiukh Fawqâni, a few

* First of all I wish to thank Pr Dr Aslıhan Yener for her invitation to participate to this very stimulating symposium. I am also really indebted to Dr L. Bachelot (CNRS, UMR 7041) and to Pr Dr Dominique Parayre (Université Lille 3, UMR 8164) who gave me the opportunity to excavate and to study the two cemeteries of Tell Shiukh Fawqâni and Tell an-Nasriyah. I also would like to thank very warmly the anthropologists of these two missions with whom I work in complete cooperation. May Dr I. Le Goff, Dr S. Lenorzer, Dr S. Rottier, and A. André find here the expression of my gratitude for their help and above all for their competence!

kilometres downstream of Karkemiš and at Tell an-Nasriyah about 15 km north-west of Hama (**see map**). The first one was discovered in 1997 due to a chance find and has yielded until now about 150 graves excavated in 1998,[1] 2000,[2] 2003,[3] and studied in the Aleppo Museum between 2000 and 2006.[4] More than 50 burials were identified at the cemetery of Tell an-Nasriyah between 2008 and 2010.[5] The dating of the two cemeteries is still being discussed; pottery parallels indicate a time span from the end of the Late Bronze Age to Iron Age I for Tell an-Nasriyah.[6] For Tell Shiukh Fawqâni, we have at our disposal four radiocarbon dates.[7] Due to the complete absence of Assyrian material attributable to the 7th century BC, the cemetery must have been in use from the very end of the Late Bronze Age to the 8th century BC. Further investigations and especially radiocarbon dating are in progress to give a more precise assessment of the date of each tomb and thus a reliable internal chronology of the cemeteries.

These discoveries are all the more interesting since important cremation graveyards were already excavated around the tell of Karkemiš in the beginning of the last century and at Hama in the 1930s. At both sites, necropoleis were located at the outskirts of the city, outside the inhabited area. The main graveyard of Karkemiš, located north of the tell at Nebi Yunus, provided at least 128 graves.[8] Unfortunately, an important part of the material excavated there was lost at the end of the First World War and only preliminary remarks and observations were published in 1939 by Sir Leonard Woolley.[9] At the base of the citadel of Hama, more than 1600 cremation burials were found by a Danish team, who published the results in 1948.[10] Other cremation graves have been excavated since that time at Ras el-Bassit,[11] Tell Sukas,[12] Tell Arqa,[13] and

[1] Al-Bahloul, Barro and d'Alfonso 2005; Canci 2005.

[2] Bachelot *et al.* 2001; Le Goff 2001.

[3] Tenu and Bachelot 2005.

[4] Bachelot, Le Goff, and Tenu 2002, 2003; Lenorzer 2006a, 2006b.

[5] Al-Maqdissi, Parayre and Sauvage in press; Tenu and Rottier in press; Rottier and Tenu in press.

[6] Faivre in press.

[7] Grave 2592: 1367–1124 BC or 1395–1041 BC; Grave 2528: 1251–1051 BC or 1306–981 BC; Grave 2584: 1192–1008 BC or 1260–936 BC; and Grave 2503: 1306–1094 BC or 1383–1016 BC.

[8] Two other cemeteries were recognised by Woolley during these campaigns: the first one at Merj Khamis 6 km north of Karkemiš, and the second one west of the West Gate. Merj Khamis was widely plundered, but Woolley could identify 30 graves, 8 of which he excavated. However, only one has been published see Woolley 1939, p. 12 and p. 20. No archaeological excavations were conducted on the West Gate Cemetery, which is therefore only known by objects (unpublished) brought by villagers to Woolley and Lawrence, Woolley 1939, p. 12. According to Woolley 1939, p. 19, the Nebi Yunus graveyard was in use from *ca.* 1200 BC to the end of the 7th century BC. Two other cemeteries more distant from Karkemiš were also located at Deve Höyük and Kefrik, see Moorey 1980.

[9] Woolley 1939; see also Woolley 1914, pp. 94–98.

[10] Riis 1948.

[11] Courbin 1993.

[12] The preliminary attribution of the discoveries to the Late Bronze Age/Early Iron Age was abandoned in 1996 (Riis 1996, pp. 5–6).

[13] Thalmann 1978, pp. 73–78 and pp. 88–89.

Tyr,[14] in the northern Levant, for example; but they are in all likelihood later than those of Tell an-Nasriyah, Tell Shiukh Fawqâni, Hama[15] and Nebi Yunus.

As a result of these recent discoveries, we can propose new approaches to place funerary practices linked to those graveyards in a wider social and historical context during the transition from the Late Bronze Age to the Iron Age in north Syria and southeast Anatolia.[16] We can also tackle the significance of the practice of cremation,[17] which is in itself intriguing because of its relative rarity, by conveying precise data concerning the cremation process, the choice of funerary gifts mainly according to the sex of the deceased, and the human remains.

The Funerary Space

The cemetery of Tell Shiukh Fawqâni lies about 70 m from the tell base. It was, therefore, clearly separated from the inhabited space. The main funerary practice is cremation, but five (maybe six) residual inhumation graves were recognised and a burial (2592) associating a non-cremated skeleton with burnt remains on his legs was found in 2000.[18] The coexistence of the two treatments is also attested at Nebi Yunus, where Sir Leonard Woolley also found at least one inhumation grave (YC 72).[19] At Tell Shiukh Fawqâni, except for the last case, all inhumations were probably damaged by the digging of pits for cremation urns. It could be interpreted as a hint for a succession of the two practices, cremation gradually replacing inhumation. This hypothesis is reinforced by the older dating of the bi-ritual grave (2592).[20]

At Tell Shiukh Fawqâni, the nature of the burial ground, which constitutes the Holocene terrace of the Euphrates, precludes any micro-stratigraphic analysis to identify occupation floors associated with cemetery use. But it is, no doubt, that the burials were interred. We can then wonder how the cemetery looked like in antiquity and more precisely, whether the upper part of the tombs was visible or somehow marked on the surface, as suggested at Hama.[21] One remarkable feature is, indeed, that no deposit smashed another, even if they were very close. The precise location of graves was thus certainly known.

[14] Aubet 2004. The cemetery comprises now about 320 cremation urns dating from the end of the 10th century to the end of the 7th century, Aubet 2010, p. 145.

[15] The cremation graveyards of Hama were in use between 1200 and 720 BC see Riis 1948, p. 202.

[16] For a presentation of Iron Age Syria and southeast Anatolia, the bibliography is too vast to be wholly quoted, but see *inter alia* Bunnens (ed.) 2000, Venturi 2007 and Whincop 2009.

[17] See for the cremation in Orient, see, *e.g.*, Bienkowski 1982, Tenu 2005 with bibliography and for a study of the archaeology of cremation, Williams 2008.

[18] Le Goff in press and 2001, p. 20.

[19] Woolley 1939, p. 34.

[20] Grave 2592: 1367–1124 BC or 1395–1041 BC.

[21] Riis 1948, p. 28, fig 18.

At Tell an-Nasriyah the necropolis is also located at the outskirts of the site, in the lower city, and once again, not connected to dwelling quarters. Furthermore, no levels contemporary with the graveyard have been as yet identified elsewhere on the site. The cemetery has been severely damaged by an important medieval installation, and intact burials are thus rarer than at Tell Shiukh Fawqâni. More striking, field observations and taphonomic analysis led us to think that some cinerary urns may not have been buried, but simply placed on the bedrock, which outcrops on the surface almost everywhere in that area (**Fig. 1**).[22] Some jars were then perhaps completely apparent. If we are correct, the ancient site must have been very impressive; the sloping burial ground showed painted urns standing on natural terraces arranged purposely. This organization does not imply that access was not restricted to specific people or to special events such as funerals, of course, but also for various mortuary cultic activities.[23] Other graves were, however, clearly buried in natural holes in the bedrock. These small cavities were dug and widened to allow a complete burial of the jars (**Fig. 2**). Urns were afterwards surrounded by stones roughly squared or by fragmentary mudbricks. The holes were then filled, and probably sealed (**Fig. 3**).[24]

One of the most intriguing issues concerning mortuary practices during the Iron Age lies in the diffusion of funerary monuments studied extensively by Dominik Bonatz.[25] Although the archaeological context of the monuments is not always known, the connection of these monuments with the remains of the deceased seems to be not systematic,[26] and therefore their location in association to graves or more widely to cemeteries is not obvious. The cemeteries of Tell Shiukh Fawqâni and Tell an-Nasriyah did not yield any monument of the kind studied by Bonatz, but at Tell an-Nasriyah we found a large slab roughly worked with cup hollows. The work is still in progress and the slab has not yet been lifted, but this discovery sheds a new light on rituals performed at the cemeteries themselves. To my knowledge it is the only slab of that type found in association with graves, the rather different squared offering tables found in the Yunus graveyard excluded.[27]

[22] Tenu and Rottier in press.

[23] For the use of the terms "funerary" and "mortuary," I follow Denis Pardee's 1996, p. 273 suggestion who associates "funerary" to funerals proper and "mortuary" to other cultic activity linked to the death.

[24] Rottier and Tenu in press.

[25] Bonatz 2000a, 2000b.

[26] Bonatz 2000b, p. 189.

[27] Woolley 1939, p. 14 and pl. III, 1. Similar limestone slabs with cup-like hollows were also found in the inner town, Woolley 1921, pp. 93–94. These 'tables of offerings' have certainly a ritual or cultic function, but not necessarily linked to mortuary activities. More generally "cup-marks" are well attested on Hittite Stone monuments, in particular at Yazilikaya where one was curved on a rock in the open air sanctuary, see Ussishkin 1975.

Graves Organisation

At both sites, cremated remains are deposited in urns,[28] but the general composition of the graves differs radically. At Tell Shiukh Fawqâni, jars are subsequently closed by a cup or, more rarely, by a potsherd. Larger vessels and kraters are sometimes inverted above the cinerary urn, and in six cases, a bath tub covered the entire grave (**Fig.** 4).[29] Grave goods such as small vessels (**Fig.** 5), animal figurines, a zoomorphic object, or basalt mortars often completed the tomb.[30] No traces of firing were visible; consequently, these different components of the grave were not placed with the dead on the pyre.

At Tell an-Nasriyah, grave architecture is much plainer. In only two cases, a kind of lid, a stone for the grave 404 and a sherd for the grave 407 (**Fig.** 6), has been found *in situ* and the question of a possible closing system (maybe in perishable material) is still under consideration. However at Tell an-Nasriyah, as yet no krater, no bath tub, no material placed against the jar has ever been found.[31]

Painted pottery is almost completely absent at Tell Shiukh Fawqâni, whereas almost all the jars were decorated with red bands and geometrical motifs at Tell an-Nasriyah (**Fig.** 7 **and** 8).[32] This kind of decoration, even if not exactly similar, is paralleled by urns discovered at Hama.[33] We also identified traces of fabric around three jars (2528, 4026–2 and 4026–4), all of them being protected by a bath tub at Tell Shiukh Fawqâni. Consequently, we wonder whether the use of fabric was restricted to that type of burial (maybe the most important) or whether its presence is rather due to differential taphonomic conditions, direct contact with soil having been completely avoided. Residual textile was also discovered directly upon the ossuary in grave 2644 indicating there may have been a wider employ of fabric than was preserved to date.

As extensive levels contemporary with the necropolis were found neither at Tell Shiukh Fawqâni nor at Tell an-Nasriyah, it is not easy to know if pottery, and more generally material, was made for funerary use; but several clues indicate this was not the case. For instance, similar plates with a very low carination were discovered at the cemetery[34] and at Area G excavated by M. Luciani.[35] This attestation is not sufficient in itself, but the same observation can be made at Hama[36] or Karkemiš,[37] where

[28] See for possible exceptions, Tenu and Bachelot 2005, p. 163.
[29] See *e.g.* Tenu 2007, p. 269.
[30] Bachelot, Le Goff and Tenu 2002, pp. 17–18.
[31] Tenu and Rottier in press, Tenu 2010.
[32] Faivre in press.
[33] Riis 1948, p. 87 and p. 91, fig. 122–127. All illustrated painted jars are here dated to the Period I (1200–1075 BC) except for the one on fig. 122 which belongs to the Period II (1075–925 BC).
[34] See Tenu 2009, p. 95, fig. 13.
[35] Luciani 2005, fig. 2: 22–24 (Period IX, level B). See also Tenu 2007, pp. 270–271.
[36] Riis 1948, pp. 192–204.
[37] Woolley and Barnett 1952, p. 234.

identical pottery was found on the tell and at the cemeteries as well. In addition, some jars at Tell Shiukh Fawqâni were obviously repaired and their use as cinerary urns seems to have been a secondary one. The only exception is certainly the huge bath tubs found only at Tell Shiukh Fawqâni (six cases: 2442, 2438–1, 2635–1, 2528, 4026 and 4036) and in a greater numbers at Nebi Yunus (32 cases).[38] Those vessels measure about 1 m high and 1 m in diameter and are not only large, but also really heavy (at least six men are necessary to move them). To my knowledge, none has been ever found outside funerary contexts.

Human Remains: Individual and Plural Graves

Even if burnt bones do not allow a systematic sexual diagnosis, an important contribution of new excavations to the study of funerary practices lies in the osteological analysis of the dead. In older excavations no real attention was paid to the human remains in themselves and sexual determination was only based on funeral gifts. As a consequence, no plural burials[39] could be identified, for instance. At Tell Shiukh Fawqâni and at Tell an-Nasriyah, the treatment of the cremation urns was conducted according to the methodology of the "*Anthropologie de terrain*" as proposed by Henri Duday and his colleagues;[40] jars are considered as genuine archaeological micro-sites, and as a result excavated with a precise 3D recording of each piece in order to understand the sequence of the deposit of each bone and each object.

On both sites, bones are usually well burnt[41] then carefully, and extensively, deposited in urns.[42] Bone fragmentation is also rather limited and no selection was made on the pyre; skull, or small bones from the hand or the foot were found.[43] At Tell an-Nasriyah the work has just begun, but first observations, made by Stéphane Rottier, indicate an absence of children under four years old.[44]

The situation is different at Tell Shiukh Fawqâni, where Isabelle Le Goff and Sandrine Lenorzer, identified men, women, and children. Their study shows that children above 2/3 years of age could have their own grave,[45] indicating that age was

[38] YB 1, YB 3, YB 13, YB 14, YB 19, YB 20, YB 21, YB 23, YB 30, YB 32, YB 46, YB 47, YC 1, YC 12, YC 26, YC 27, YC 28, YC 29, YC 30, YC 46, YC 50, YC 52, YC 53, YC 57, YC 58, YC 63, YC 71, YC 73, YD 3, YH 4, YJ 2, YJ 3 (Woolley 1939, pp. 21–37).

[39] The term "plural burials" has been proposed by J. Leclerc and J. Tarrête (1988) to designate graves where more than one individual is buried without precision concerning the sequence of the deposit, contemporary (multiple burials) or successive (collective burials).

[40] Duday *et al.* 1992, 2000.

[41] Exceptions exist, see Bachelot, Le Goff and Tenu 2002, pp. 18–19; Le Goff 2007, p. 280.

[42] Bachelot, Le Goff and Tenu 2003, p. 100; Le Goff 2005, p. 25, 2007, p. 281; Tenu and Rottier in press.

[43] Le Goff 2007, in press; Tenu and Rottier in press.

[44] Tenu and Rottier in press. On the determination of age, see Lenorzer 2009, pp. 75–79.

[45] Bachelot, Le Goff and Tenu 2003, pp. 101–102; Lenorzer 2006a, p. 4 and p. 6, 2006b, p. 29.

certainly an important step in the community integration. The treatment of children is different at Tell Shiukh Fawqâni and Tell an-Nasriyah, where they would have been buried elsewhere. A special treatment for them is not really surprising; at Hama for instance, babies were not systematically cremated,[46] even if buried in the same jar with a burnt adult.[47] At Tell Shiukh Fawqâni another very interesting feature is the presence of at least eight plural graves (the complete analysis is not yet completed and therefore the data are still preliminary).[48] Isabelle Le Goff identified in four of them (2584, 2635–6, 2589 and 2591) the remains of a child and of an adult, which are all covered by a krater. Surprisingly, the adult is usually rather "robust"[49] and in some cases shows clear masculine traits. In another burial (4042), an adult male was buried with two children, one under a year old and the other one under three years old.[50] Only one tomb (2448) provided evidence for the association of a woman and children; two adults, one more strongly built than the other, were found buried with two children, the first one between four and eight years old, and the second a foetus. According to Sandrine Lenorzer, this grave actually contained the remains of three individuals, including a "robust" individual and a "gracile" one, certainly a woman who was pregnant or who just died in childbirth.[51]

The Tell Shiukh Fawqâni cemetery also yielded at least two double burials with adults: the first one (4026) was covered by a bath tub and comprised of two jars. In the first one (4026–2) the bones showed a lesser robustness than those in the second one (4026–4) (**Fig. 9**). In another grave (which belongs to the simplest type), the bones of two individuals (2502), once again a "robust" and a "gracile" were gathered. This association with two adults is very rare until now and is all the more interesting since the bones of the two people were mixed; whereas, usually in other plural graves burnt bones of each individual were kept together in the urn, betraying an obvious intentional individualisation.

Those plural graves raise the question of the simultaneity of death and of the performance of cremation, for no field or taphonomic observation indicates successive burials. All deceased were apparently burnt when still flesh covered, therefore, people buried together may have died more or less at the same moment. An alternative explanation would involve temporary waiting structures, however, we did not find these or identify them as yet. One may also suggest urns were buried only after all "scheduled deceased" died and were burnt. In the graves with two adults, it is very tempting to imagine they were kept together in death because they were, for instance, husband

[46] Riis 1948, p. 4.
[47] Riis 1948, 30 (Graves GVIII 184 and G VIII 629).
[48] Bachelot, Le Goff and Tenu 2002, p. 18, 2003, p. 99.
[49] On this osteological criterium see Lenorzer 2009, pp. 79–80.
[50] Lenorzer 2006b, pp. 22–24.
[51] Lenorzer 2006a, p. 7.

and wife. No clue allows us to confirm this speculative idea, but one may notice that no gathering of two "robusts" or two "graciles" has ever been identified. Until now, no correlation has been isolated between the burial type and the gender, but the collection on the pyre seems more complete for the burials covered by a krater,[52] or a bath tub.[53]

Grave Goods

At Tell Shiukh Fawqâni and at Tell an-Nasriyah, about half the jars contained items directly associated to the ossuary. Generally speaking, grave good categories are rather limited. At Tell Shiukh Fawqâni we discovered a small vessel, animal figurines, bone objects, spindle whorls, astragals, iron tools or weapons (such as arrow heads, axes, or knives), bronze rings and beads in the jars themselves.[54] At Tell an-Nasriyah the range is even more restricted; beads mainly in vitreous material, astragals, iron implements, and bone plaques (**Fig. 10**).[55] The choice of the funeral equipment seems clearly related to the sex and to the age of the deceased. For instance, arrow heads are reserved for "robust" or male individuals and spindle whorls for "gracile" or female individuals on the basis of their physical criteria. Similar observations can be made at Hama.[56] No sexual diagnoses were made based on skeletons,[57] but associations of different object types betray the same categories as shown at Tell Shiukh Fawqâni or at Tell an-Nasriyah. The age is also an essential factor; children were usually buried with jewellery pieces; beads, small bracelets, or rings.

All these items were found in urns, but they certainly pertain to different phases of the funerary process, revealing strong differences in their meaning. We should first distinguish objects associated with the dead, such as pieces sewn on the shroud in which they were burnt, for example. We also may consider separately burnt and non-burnt objects, even if their state of preservation does not allow us to frequently know it. Moreover, Isabelle Le Goff underlines the specific way iron weapons were placed in the urn.[58] Their limited oxidation and the kind of blisters they show on the surface may indicate they were highly heated; they were, however, not mixed with the bones, but deposited before or after them, which does contrast with other objects such as astragals or spindle whorls, which were apparently retrieved from the pyre with the bones without distinction and put into the ossuary. Weapons in iron seem thus to

[52] Bachelot, Le Goff and Tenu 2003, p. 100.
[53] On the basis of weighing made by I. Le Goff and S. Lenorzer.
[54] Bachelot, Le Goff and Tenu 2002, pp. 19–20; 2003, pp. 99–100; Tenu 2007, p. 271, Tenu 2009.
[55] Tenu and Rottier in press.
[56] For male grave goods see Riis 1948, pp. 31–33 and for female grave goods, pp. 33–36.
[57] Riis 1948, p. 31.
[58] Le Goff 2005, p. 25.

have a specific significance because they are clearly not treated as other objects. Sometimes, items normally cremated with the dead were deposited unburnt in the urn and in that case, they were more numerous than usual. According to Isabelle Le Goff, it may reveal a shift in their symbolic meaning, betraying a new will to express abundance of goods and as a result, wealth.[59]

Interestingly in plural graves, grave goods of each person were deposited with his or her remains (**Fig. 11**). As has been especially shown by Sandrine Lenorzer for grave 4042, the grave goods, 38 beads and a disc-shaped pendant, were found with the bones of the two immature individuals.[60]

Faunal Remains

Animal bones, commonly cremated, were also found mixed in some ossuaries. The data analysis is still in progress at Tell Shiukh Fawqâni, but preliminary observations indicate faunal remains from Tell an-Nasriyah consist of portions of sheep and ox. No complete skeleton has been found and on both sites, fauna was not separated from human bones, showing that it was certainly not distinguished from them when collected on the pyre. It might suggest animals were not to be intentionally buried with the deceased and their presence in urns is intrusive. Determination of bones (species, but also anatomical parts of animals) may reveal possible prevalence in the choice of animals and maybe butchery traces. Afterwards we may perhaps be able to tackle the question of the meaning of such discoveries; were they food offerings perhaps linked to meat consumption during funerals or were they "real" animal sacrifices? On that issue, grave 4033 of Tell Shiukh Fawqâni is certainly unique; burnt bones of an (?) animal were carefully placed around the neck of the jar after it was interred and then covered by the plate, which also closed the cinerary urn.[61] Similar observations were made at Hama; burnt bones of sheep or goat were found in 18 burials. Cremated remains of an ox and a dog or jackal were also identified. An important exception lies in the remains of sheep or goat and of horse or donkey deposited unburnt in a grave.[62]

Some General Trends in Funerary Practices

Generally speaking, the relatively poor funerary equipment of cremation graves previously excavated at Karkemiš or at Hama, for instance, has been stressed by many scholars, including Riis himself.[63] More precisely, he found an evolution in the social

[59] Le Goff 2005, p. 27.

[60] Lenorzer 2006b, p. 22.

[61] Tenu and Bachelot 2005, p. 163, and fig. 4.

[62] Riis 1948, p. 30.

[63] Riis 1948, p. 37 and p. 203; Struble and Hermann 2009, p. 40. K. Bittel 1958, pp. 23–24 reached the same conclusion at Osmankayesı.

status of people buried in the cemeteries; during period I (*ca.* 1200–1075 BC) rich and poor individuals were interred side by side, but by the end only middle and lower class people were buried there.[64] The apparent poverty of graves led some scholars to consider that wealthy people were probably buried elsewhere and still recently, have drawn attention to the presence of graves outside cemeteries like the "golden tomb" at Karkemiš or at Tell Halaf,[65] which may have been high ranking people tombs. In addition to those relevant remarks, we might also suggest changing our way in considering the tombs. First, cremation is, in itself, not the easiest and simplest funerary treatment. It requires wood, or at least fuel, and the care given to the complete cremation of bones associated with the careful and often extensive deposit in jars may indicate cremation was performed by specialists. In addition, even if jars used as cinerary urns were not made purposely, bath tubs are in all likelihood reserved for that specific use; and due to their dimensions, we can imagine how complicated it must have been to produce them, as well as to fire and to carry them to the cemetery. Furthermore, some graves provided iron weapons or tools, and due to their early date,[66] they cannot be simply considered as "poor."[67] More generally, the main point is that, by definition, we only find what has been transferred into the tomb and not what has been used or utilized during the complete funerary performance. For example, royal Hittite ritual texts[68] indicate that only a few pieces such as those used during the funeral are finally deposited in the tomb itself during the twelfth and the thirteenth day.[69] The ceremony is also characterized by its duration (14 days), its complexity, sacrifice of animals, and so on. All those components of the funeral can hardly be identified by archaeologists. The very careful way we excavated each urn allows us to identify tiny bits of metal in some urns of Tell Shiukh Fawqâni, whereas no complete metal object was found, indicating such artefacts were certainly present on the pyre, but not deposited in the urns.[70] They may have been part of a display of goods, which precedes the cremation and were afterwards given to mourners or placed in cenotaphs or memorials.[71]

At Tell an-Nasriyah the same situation occurs; shapeless residues of melted vitreous material, sometimes very small (diameter inferior to 0, 1 cm) were recognised. They probably belong to fragile objects almost completely destroyed by fire, not meant for the grave itself. If freestanding mortuary chapels have existed independently to actual

[64] Riis 1948, p. 203.
[65] Struble and Hermann 2009, p. 40.
[66] Graves 2528 and 2584, see note 1.
[67] Tenu 2009, pp. 89–90.
[68] Christmann-Franck 1971.
[69] Christmann-Franck 1971, pp. 75–76; Van den Hout 1994, pp. 48–49.
[70] Bachelot, Le Goff and Tenu 2002, p. 20.
[71] See for memorials in Hittite world, Van den Hout 2002.

graves,[72] hints of the social status of the deceased could also be searched for in such places. Anyway, the "poverty" of the graves needs further investigations to be better interpreted.

The composition of funerary equipment proper also raises interesting questions. First, larger graves did not necessarily contain the most significant or remarkable objects; for instance in the bath tub burial (4026), one urn (4026–4) was empty and the other one (4026–2), only contained two spindle whorls. On the contrary, a grave of the simplest type (2445–1) provided 33 iron weapons and implements, including 25 arrowheads of different types. Similar observations were made for the Hama graves; Riis was very astonished by the fact that rich equipment was often deposited in plain urns, whereas a beautiful, decorated jar may contain only poor items or be completely empty.[73]

At Tell Shiukh Fawqâni, the choice of funerary gifts is clearly related to the sex of the deceased, and the most common artefacts are spindle whorls (total: 49) usually associated with women or "gracile" subjects and arrow heads (total: 60)[74] to men or "robust" subjects (**Fig. 12**). 39 graves contained spindle whorls at Hama,[75] and 23 at Nebi Yunus[76] (among which one with 24,)[77] 56 burials at Hama yielded arrowheads.[78]

The discovery of arrowheads and spindle whorls is reminiscent of the royal Hittite ritual. Seated effigies of the deceased king and queen indeed received such objects, respectively, bow and arrows and distaff and spindle.[79] Unfortunately contemporary Hittite burial customs are very ill known because almost of the graves discovered so far are mostly dated to the Old Hittite period except for the latest burials of the Osmankayası cemetery that belong to the 14th century.[80] Syro-hittite funerary art apparently continues similar conceptions, since women are often represented holding spindles and men with arrows and bow on their shoulder.[81] The strong tie between spindle whorls and femininity is well attested and studied,[82] but its increasing association to mortuary contexts seems new and especially important in cremation graveyards. Comparisons are not easy due to the lack of data for the Late Bronze Age, but at Mari for instance, only one grave (307) yielded two spindle whorls[83] and at Alalakh

[72] Struble and Hermann 2009, pp. 36–39.

[73] Riis 1948, p. 37, note 1.

[74] This number is still preliminary because cleaning and study of the objects, which are sometimes badly corrupted, are not yet achieved.

[75] Riis 1948, p. 35 and pp. 171–172.

[76] YB 6, YB 9, YB 13, YB 28, YB 41, YB 49, YB 52, YC 2, YC 12, YC 13, YC 33A, YC 47, YC 50, YC 51, YC 53, YC 59, YC 62, YC 67, YC 79, YC 81 and YJ 5 see Woolley 1939, pp. 21–37.

[77] YB 25 see Woolley 1939, p. 23.

[78] Riis 1948, p. 32.

[79] Bonatz 2000b, p. 201; Van den Hout 1994, p. 63.

[80] Seeher 2011, pp. 388–389.

[81] Bonatz 2000b, p. 201; 2000a, pp. 78–82.

[82] See Rova 2008 with bibliography.

[83] Jean-Marie 1999, p. 135: pl. 49 (M 1527).

only three provided such items.[84] D. Bonatz suggests the representation of women holding a spindle and distaff on Syro-Hittite funerary monuments has not only a "gender" meaning but also an eschatological one linked somehow to the belief in life everlasting.[85]

Another trend we can stress is the deposit of astragals, apparently only in "female" or children's tombs (**Fig. 12**). At Tell Shiukh Fawqâni a single grave yielded 35 astragals probably from sheep or goats, among which 34 are non-burnt (grave 2642). At Nasriyah seven astragals from sheep[86] were found in a burial belonging to a "gracile" individual (grave 201). At Merj Khamis, a cremation cemetery close to Karkemiš, one burial provided 20 astragals.[87] Analysis made at Hama reveals that they belong to sheep or to gazelles[88] and were also predominantly attributed to "female" or children graves. Following the discovery of astragals as building deposits at Tell Afis,[89] Giorgio Affani, in a recent paper, summed up the different functions we may attribute to them: gaming, amulet, divination, and even primitive money. He also underlines their place in cultic and funerary contexts and interprets their conservation and collection in the sacrificial context of meat consumption. They were kept as proof of wealth and pious activity, and therefore they should have apotropaic power. The proposition of the use of astragals as a gaming piece is reinforced by a relief from Karkemiš studied by G. Affani,[90] and explains their association with children's graves very well,[91] but the reasons for their presence in female burials remain obscure.[92] The symbolic meaning of this kind of deposit still escapes us. In the next campaigns special attention will be paid to this question, keeping in mind that a peculiar relationship could have existed between women and flock possession in the context of an economy maybe mainly based on pastoralism.

More generally, we may suggest that rather than personal belongings, items found in graves more probably pertain at least partly to funerals themselves and to rituals

[84] Grave ATG 37/1: cremation burial, level I (1273–1194) Woolley 1955, p. 204; Grave ATG 38/6: inhumation burial level I Woolley 1955, p. 205; Grave 03–3017 ("Plastered tomb"): Yener and Yazıcıoğlu 2010a, p. 28; Yener 2010, p. 249 (A03–R2044).

[85] Bonatz 2000a, pp. 81–82.

[86] I thank Marie Renard for this information.

[87] Woolley 1939, p. 20.

[88] Riis 1948, p. 176. 11 graves provided 39 astragals.

[89] Venturi 2006.

[90] Affani 2008, fig. 7.

[91] At Alalakh too, astragals were found in children graves: 4 in ATG 46/3 (level III 1370–1350 Woolley 1955, pp. 208–209) and 2 in ATG 49/4 (level V 1595–1527 or 1527–1447 Woolley 1955, p. 218). During 2004 excavation season, a knucklebone (A04–R664) was found in the cemetery matrix, apparently not connected to a precise tomb (Yener 2010, p. 251).

[92] One grave (2520) from Tell Shiukh Fawqâni constitutes an important exception: a masculine individual quite robust, according to Sandrine Lenorzer, has been buried with two astragals and a bone spatula, which are commonly associated with women. This striking choice is not unparalleled and a discrepancy between the biological and "social" sex is attested in other contexts, see for instance Knüsel and Ripley 2000. This case is, however, not yet well understood and explained.

what could explain the limited diversity of funerary outfits. In addition to geographical factors, variations in deposits may have depended on age, on social status, which is, of course, slightly different from wealth, on death circumstances, and on intra-chronology of the cemeteries.

Conclusions

Preliminary comparisons to archaeological material and radiocarbon dates indicate that the cemeteries of Tell an-Nasriyah and Tell Shiukh Fawqâni date back to the end of the Late Bronze Age and continue to be used until the 8th century, underlining how mortuary practices revealed by them are deeply rooted in the local Syro-Anatolian culture, beyond historical events and political entities.

Nevertheless, one may also stress the originality of the funerary practices of this period; the cremation of the cadaver itself,[93] but also the gathering of the dead in places reserved for them and the increase of normative funerary gifts.[94] All these features appear maybe in a complex emerging context (well defined by Guy Bunnens, for instance)[95] in which the group, the kinship, or even the clan and the tribe are the basis of the social fabric, replacing or completing the "traditional" administrative structure. Group cohesion is largely provided by common rituals for the dead. The loss of a person is collectively mourned and the funeral is certainly performed by specialized people on the behalf of the group from the construction of the pyre to the end of the grieving period. The cemetery is then, not to be conceived only as a burial ground, but also as a "*complexe funéraire,*" where all the aspects linked to the death are dealt with.[96] It constitutes the privileged place where the passage from the world of the living to that of the dead took place and where contact is kept with the community of the dead.

That context may have lead to a complete "depersonalisation" of the dead. Rejected from the space inhabited by the living, their corpses are completely burnt and then no longer recognizable, no stele allows the location, or identification of their graves. In

[93] The diffusion of cremation is very difficult to explain. Foreign origins linked to Hittites or "Sea Peoples" put to one side, we may suggest, for instance, shifts in religious or cosmological beliefs leading to a new conception of fire as a privileged means to reach the Afterlife, or to a greater fear of the dead. Another explanation lies in the necessity to bury the dead together in a special space even if they died far away: burning the cadavers allowed them to carry the remains in good condition until the appropriate place was reached. This latter proposition may be particularly accurate in a context widely characterized by pastoralism. Eventually cremation was perhaps performed to avoid decomposition of the body, perceived as unbearable. These hypotheses represent only possible themes of research among others, and are still to be discussed. In the Anatolian world, inhumation is attested as well as cremation, supposedly introduced in the beginning of the 2nd Millennium BC (Seeher 1993, p. 226).

[94] The same phenomenon has been noticed at Tyre al-Bass, see Aubet 2010, p. 153.

[95] Bunnens 2000, 2009.

[96] Depierre *et al.* 2000.

addition, Syro-Hittite funerary monuments are rarely inscribed,[97] certainly indicating that they were not systematically erected for a special person, but rather for the dead in general; and at Tell an-Nasriyah the slab with cupules is apparently not associated with a precise burial. But paradoxically, human remains were very well preserved there, extensively collected, and in plural burials with the remaining bones of an individual gathered in the urn. Even if the flesh has gone with fire, corpses kept a kind of integrity because bones were never (with the exception of grave 2502 at Tell Shiukh Fawqâni) mixed together. We can also suggest that at Tell an-Nasriyah, as no jar was identical to another, the choice of painting patterns may have reinforced the personalisation of the deceased. Giving spindle whorls or arrow heads to the dead on the pyre was maybe a way to avoid complete erasing of identity, and personhood with fire. The dead buried together, separated from the living, do not constitute, however, a confused and ill defined group, but a whole composed by each deceased of the community.

At the end of the Late Bronze Age and at the onset of the Iron Age, burial practices betray radical shifts in the relationship to the dead by the use of cremation, by the separation of the dead and the living, by probable normative rites of funeral, and perhaps by the reshaping of the cult of the dead and of the ancestors. Unfortunately this last, so fascinating aspect of mortuary practices, almost completely escapes archaeologists.[98] We may, however, infer from discrete traits some hints to tackle this issue. The funerary monuments reflect the central role of family in the cult of the dead,[99] which already prevailed in the Late Bronze Age,[100] but the gathering of the dead may mirror a new way to "create" common ancestors who participate in the community strategy of remembrance and by this way, in community identity and cohesion.

BIBLIOGRAPHY

AFFANI, G.

2008 "Astragalus bone in Ancient Near East: Ritual depositions in Iron Age I in Tell Afis," in *Proceedings of the 5th International Congress on the archaeology of the Ancient Near East: Madrid, April 3-8 2006*, edited by J. Ma. Córdoba, M. Molist and Ma. C. Pérez-Die, pp. 77–92. Madrid: Ediciones Universidad Autónoma de Madrid.

AL-BAHLOUL, KH., BARRO, A. and D'ALFONSO L.

2005 "Area H. The Iron Age Cremation Cemetery," in *Tell Shiukh Fawqâni 1994–1998*, edited by L. Bachelot and F. M. Fales, pp. 997–1048. Padova: Sargon.

[97] Out of 100 monuments only 14 were inscribed see Bonatz 2000a, p. 13 and pp. 66–68.
[98] See nevertheless Pfälzner 2001 or Porter 2002 for instance.
[99] Bonatz 2000a, pp. 162–163.
[100] See *inter alia*, Pitard 1996, Schmidt 1996, Pardee 1996.

AL-MAQDISSI, M., PARAYRE, D. and SAUVAGE, M.

In press "Mission archéologique syro-française de l'Oronte. Tell an-Nasriyah and Tell Masin: les sites quadrangulaires, nouveau regard. Rapport préliminaire sur les opérations des campagnes de 2007 et 2008," *Akkadica*.

AUBET, M. E.

2004 *The Phoenician cemetery of Tyre-Al Bass: excavations 1997–1999*, BAAL Hors-série 1. Beyrouth: Ministère de la Culture, Direction générale des Antiquités.

2010 "The Phoenician Cemetery of Tyre," *Near Eastern Archaeology* 73: 144–155.

BACHELOT, L., LE GOFF, I. and TENU A.

2002 "La nécropole de l'âge du Fer de Tell Shioukh Faouqâni," *Orient-Express* 2002/1: 17–20.

2003 "La nécropole de l'âge du Fer de Tell Shioukh Faouqâni (Syrie) – Campagne 2002," *Orient-Express* 2003/4: 97–103.

2005 "La nécropole de Tell Shiukh Fawqâni," in *Entre mondes orientaux et classiques: la place de la crémation. Actes du colloque international de Nanterre, 26-28 février 2004*, Ktema 30, edited by L. Bachelot and A. Tenu, pp. 11–14. Strasbourg: Université de Strasbourg.

BACHELOT, L., BODET, C., GAILHARD, N., QUENET, PH. and TENU, A.

2001 "Tell Shioukh Faouqâni: campagne 2000," *Orient-Express* 2001/1: 9–15.

BIENKOWSKI, P.

1982 "Some Remarks on the Practice of Cremation in the Levant," *Levant* 14: 80–89.

BITTEL K.

1958 *Bogazköy-Hattusa II. Die Hethitischen Grabfunde von Osmankayası*. Berlin: Gebr. Mann Verlag.

BONATZ, D.

2000a *Das syro-hethitische Grabdenkmal: Untersuchungen zur Entstehung einer neuen Bildgattung in der Eisenzeit in nordsyrisch-südanatolischen Raum*. Mainz: Verlag Philipp von Zabern.

2000b "Syro-hittite Funerary monuments. A Phenomenon of Tradition or Innovation?," in *Essays on Syria in the Iron Age*, Ancient Near Eastern Studies Supplement 7, edited by G. Bunnens, pp. 189–210. Louvain: Peeters Press.

BUNNENS, G.

2000 "Syria in the Iron Age. Problems of definition", in *Essays on Syria in the Iron Age*, Ancient Near Eastern Studies Supplement 7, edited by G. Bunnens, pp. 3–19. Louvain: Peeters Press.

2009 "Assyrian Empire Building and Aramization of Culture as seen from Tell Ahmar/Til Barsib," in *Assyrian and Aramaean Interaction, Actes de la Table Ronde tenue au 6ICAANE, Rome, 5-11 mai 2008, Syria* 86, edited by C. Kepinski and A. Tenu, pp. 67–82. Beyrouth: Institut Français du Proche-Orient.

BUNNENS, G., ed.

2000 *Essays on Syria in the Iron Age*, Ancient Near Eastern Studies Supplement 7. Louvain: Peeters Press.

CANCI, A.

2005 "The Human Remains from Tell Shiukh Fawqâni: Anthropological Report," in *Tell Shiukh Fawqâni 1994–1998*, edited by L. Bachelot and F. M. Fales, pp. 1109–1118. Padova: Sargon.

COURBIN, P.
1993 *Fouilles de Bassit. Tombes du Fer.* Paris: Editions Recherche sur les Civilisations.

CHRISTMANN-FRANCK, L.
1971 "Le rituel des funérailles royales hittites," *Revue hittite et asianique* 29: 61–111.

DEPIERRE, G., JACQUEMIN, M., MORDANT C., and MÜLLER, J.
2000 "Propositions pour une nouvelle lecture des pratiques funéraires au Bronze final. La nécropole de Passy-Véron, « Les Prés pendus » (Yonne)," in *Archéologie de la mort, archéologie de la tombe au premier âge du fer: thème spécialisé: actes du XXIe Colloque international de l'Association française pour l'étude de l'Age du fer, Conques-Montrozier 8-11 mai 1997,* Monographies d'archéologie méditerranéenne 5, edited by B. Dedet, Ph. Gruat, G. Marchand, M. Py and M. Schwaller, pp. 179–193. Lattes: Association pour la recherche archéologique en Languedoc oriental.

DUDAY, H., DEPIERRE, G. and JANIN, T.
2000 "Validation des paramètres de quantification, protocoles et stratégies dans l'étude anthropologique des sépultures secondaires à incinération. L'exemple des nécropoles préhistoriques du Midi de la France," in *Archéologie de la mort, archéologie de la tombe au premier âge du fer: thème spécialisé: actes du XXIe Colloque international de l'Association française pour l'étude de l'Age du fer, Conques-Montrozier 8-11 mai 1997,* Monographies d'archéologie méditerranéenne 5, edited by B. Dedet, Ph. Gruat, G. Marchand, M. Py and M. Schwaller, pp. 7–29. Lattes: Association pour la recherche archéologique en Languedoc oriental.

DUDAY, H., COURTAUD, P., CRUBÉZY, É., SELLIER, P. and TILLIER A.-M.
1992 "L'anthropologie « de terrain »: reconnaissance et interprétation des gestes funéraires," in *Anthropologie et archéologie: dialogue sur les ensembles funéraires,* Bulletins et mémoires de la société d'anthropologie de Paris tome 2, edited by É. Crubézy, H. Duday, P. Sellier and A.-M. Tiller, pp. 29–50. Paris: Société d'anthropologie de Paris.

FAIVRE, X.
In press "Les jarres cinéraires de Tell al-Nasriyah, Syrie (Mission syro-française de l'Oronte)," *Studia Orontica* VII.

KNÜSEL, C. and RIPLEY, K.
2000 "The *Berdache* or Man-woman in Anglo-Saxon England and Early Medieval Europe," in *Social Identity in Early Medieval Britain,* edited by W. O. Frazer and A. Tyrrel, pp. 157–192. London, New York: Leicester University Press.

JEAN-MARIE, M.
1999 *Tombes et nécropoles de Mari,* Bibliothèque Archéologique et Historique CLIII, Beyrouth: IFAPO.

LECLERC, J. and TARRÊTE, J.
1998 "sépulture," in *Dictionnaire de la Préhistoire,* edited by A. Leroi-Gourhan, pp. 963–964. Paris: Presses Universitaires de France.

LE GOFF, I.
2001 "Premiers éléments sur les ossements humains brûlés de la nécropole du chantier H de Tell Shioukh Faouqâni," *Orient-Express* 2001/1: 19–21.
2005 "À propos de la nécropole à incinération de Tell Shioukh Faouqâni (Syrie): recherche des séquences temporelles du protocole funéraire," in *Entre mondes orientaux et classiques: la place de la crémation. Actes du colloque international de Nanterre, 26-28 février 2004,* Ktema 30, edited by L. Bachelot and A. Tenu, pp. 21–27. Strasbourg: Université de Strasbourg.

2007 "Lecture sociale des vestiges humains de la crémation: l'exemple de Tell Shiukh Fawqâni," in *Actes du colloque Pratiques funéraires et sociétés, tenu à Sens, 12-14 juin 2003*, edited by L. Baray, P. Brun and A. Testart, pp. 277–284. Dijon: Éditions Universitaires de Dijon.

In press "La nécropole à incinération de Tell Shioukh Faouqâni: premiers éléments du protocole funéraire," in *Actes du 3ICAANE, Paris, 15-19 avril 2002*, edited by J.-Cl. Margueron, P. de Miroschedji and J.-P. Thalmann. Winonna Lake: Eisenbrauns.

LENORZER, S.

2006a *Rapport sur la campagne de janvier-février 2006*. Un-published report for the Ministère des Affaires étrangères (France).

2006b *Rapport sur la campagne de décembre 2006*. Unpublished report for the Ministère des Affaires étrangères (France).

2009 *La crémation dans les sociétés protohistoriques du Sud de la France*, Monographies d'Archéologie Méditerranéenne 25. Lattes: Édition de l'Association pour le développement de l'Archéologie en Languedoc-Roussillon.

LUCIANI, M.

2005 "Area G. The Iron Productive Area (Period IX) and the Inhumation Cemetery (Period X)", in *Tell Shiukh Fawqâni 1994–1998*, edited by L. Bachelot and F. M. Fales, pp. 719–993. Padova: Sargon.

MOOREY, P. R. S.

1980 *Cemeteries of the First Millennium B.C. at Deve Hüyük*, BAR International Series 87. Oxford: British Archaeological Reports.

PARDEE, D.

1996 "*Marzihu*, *Kispu*, and the Ugarit Funerary Cult: A Minimalist View," in *Ugarit, religion and culture: proceedings of the International Colloquium on Ugarit, religion and culture, Edinburgh, July 1994: essays presented in honour of Professor John C.L. Gibson*, Ugaritisch-Biblische Literatur 12, edited by N. Wyatt, W. G. E. Watson and J. B. Lloyd, pp. 273–287. Münster: Ugarit-Verlag.

PFÄLZNER, P.

2001 "Auf den Spuren der Ahnen. Überlegungen zur Nachweisbarkeit der Ahnenverehrung in Vorderasien vom Neolithikum bis in die Bronzezeit," in *Beiträge zur vorderasiatischen Archäologie: Winfried Orthmann gewidmet*, edited by J.-W. Meyer, M. Novák and A. Pruss, pp. 390–409. Frankfurt am Main: Johann Wolfgang Goethe-Universität, Archäologisches Institut.

PITARD, W. T.

1996 "Care of the Dead at Emar," in *Emar. The History, Religion, and Culture of a Syrian Town in the Late Bronze Age*, edited by M. W. Chavalas, pp. 123–140. Bethesda, Maryland: CDL Press.

PORTER A.

2002 "The Dynamics of the Death: Ancestors, Pastoralism, and the Origins of a Third-Millennium City in Syria," *Bulletin of American Schools for Oriental Research* 325: 1–34.

RIIS, P. J.

1948 *Hama. Fouilles et Recherches de la fondation Carlsberg 1931-1938. Les cimetières à crémation*, Nationalmuseets Skrifter Større Beretninger I. Kobenhaven: Gyldendalske Boghandel, Nordisk Forlag.

1996 *Sukas X: The Bronze and early Iron Age remains at the Southern Harbour*, Publications of the Carlsberg expedition to Phoenicia 12 and Historisk-filosofiske Skrifter 17. Kobenhaven: Munksgaard.

ROTTIER, S. and TENU A.

In press "The cremation graveyard of Tell an-Nasriyah (Syria): first data for the interpretation of mortuary practices."

ROVA, E.

2008 "Mirror, distaff, pomegranate, and poppy capsule: on the ambiguity of some attributes of women and goddesses," in *4th ICAANE. Proceedings of the 4th International Congress of the Archaeology of the Ancient Near East*, edited by H. Kühne, R. M. Czichon, and F. J. Kreppner, vol. 1., pp. 557–570. Wiesbaden: Harrassowitz Verlag.

SCHMIDT, B. B.

1996 "The Gods and the Dead of the Domestic Cult at Emar: A Reassessment," in *Emar. The History, Religion, and Culture of a Syrian Town in the Late Bronze Age*, edited by M. W. Chavalas, pp. 141–161. Bethesda, Maryland: CDL Press.

SCHMIDT, C. W. and SYMES, S. A., ed.

2008 *The Analysis of Burned Human Remains*. Amsterdam: Academic press.

SEEHER, J.

1993 "Köperbestattung und Kremation–Ein Gegensatz?," *Istanbuler Mitteilungen* 43: 219–226.

2011 "The Plateau: The Hittites," in *The Oxford Handbook of Ancient Anatolia*, edited by S. R. Steadman and G. McMahon, pp. 376–392. Oxford: Oxford University Press.

STRUBLE, E. J. and RIMMER HERRMANN, V.

2009 "An Eternal Feast at Sam'al: The New Iron Age Mortuary Stele from Zincirli in Context," *Bulletin of the American Schools of Oriental Research* 356: 15–49.

TENU, A.

2005 "La pratique de la crémation en Syrie: un usage marginal?," in *Entre mondes orientaux et classiques: la place de la crémation. Actes du colloque international de Nanterre, 26-28 février 2004*, Ktema 30, edited by L. Bachelot and A. Tenu, pp. 37–46. Strasbourg: Université de Strasbourg.

2007 "À propos de la nécropole à incinération de Tell Shiukh Fawqâni: l'incinération dans le monde syrien à l'âge du Fer," in *Actes du colloque Pratiques funéraires et sociétés, tenu à Sens, 12-14 juin 2003*, edited by L. Baray, P. Brun and A. Testart, pp. 265–275. Dijon: Éditions Universitaires de Dijon.

2009 "Assyrians and Arameans in the Euphrates Valley viewed from the cemetery of Tell Shiukh Fawqâni," in *Assyrian and Aramaean Interaction, Actes de la Table Ronde tenue au 6ICAANE, Rome, 5-11 mai 2008, Syria* 86, edited by C. Kepinski et A. Tenu, pp. 86–93. Beyrouth: Institut Français du Proche-Orient.

2010 "Le cimetière à crémation de Tell al-Nasriyah. Premiers résultats," *Orient-Express* 2010/1-2: 9–14.

TENU, A. and BACHELOT, L.

2005 "Tell Shioukh Faouqâni (Syrie): la campagne de sondages 2003 dans la nécropole à incinération," *Akkadica* 126: 159–168.

TENU, A. and ROTTIER, S.

In press "Le cimetière à crémation de Nasriyah, Syrie (Mission syro-française de l'Oronte)," *Studia Orontica* VII.

THALMANN, J.-P.

1978 "Tell Arqa (Liban Nord) campagnes I-III (1972–1974) Chantier I. Rapport préliminaire. (Introduction d'Ernest Will)," *Syria* 55: 1–151.

USSISHKIN D.
1975 "Hollows, "Cup-Marks", and Hittite Stone Monuments," *Anatolian Studies* 25: 85–103.
VENTURI, F.
2006 "Deux dépôts de fondation d'astragales à Tell Afis (Syrie)," *Orient-Express* 2006/1: 26–29.
2007 *La Siria nell'età delle trasformazioni, XIII-X sec. a. C.: nuovi contributi dallo scavo di Tell Afis,* Studi e testi orientali Serie Archeologica 18. Bologna: Cooperativa Libraria Universitaria Editrice Bologna.
VAN DEN HOUT, T. P. J.
1994 "Death as a Privilege. The Hittite Royal Funerary Ritual," in *Hidden Futures: Death and Immortality in Ancient Egypt, Anatolia, the Classical, Biblical and Arabic-Islamic World*, edited by J. M. Bremer, T. P. J. Van Den Hout, and R. Peters, pp. 37–75. Amsterdam: Amsterdam University Press.
2002 "Tombs and Memorials: The (Divine) Stone-House and ḫegur Reconsidered," in *Recent developments in Hittite archaeology and history: papers in memory of Hans G. Güterbock*, edited by K. A. Yener and H. A. Hoffner Jr., with the assistance of S. Dhesi, pp. 73–91. Winona Lake, Ind.: Eisenbrauns
WHINCOP M. R.
2009 *Pots, people, and politics: a reconsideration of the role of ceramics in reconstructions of the Iron age Northern Levant*, BAR International series 1902. Oxford: Archaeopress.
WILLIAMS, H.
2008 "Towards an archaeology of cremation," in *The Analysis of Burned Human Remains*, edited by C. W. Schmidt and S. A. Symes, pp. 239–269. Amsterdam: Academic press.
WOOLLEY, L.
1914 "Hittite burial customs," *Liverpool Annals of Archaeology and Anthropology* 6: 87–98.
1921 *Carcemish, Part II. The Town Defences*. London: The British Museum.
1939 "The Iron-Age Graves of Carchemish," *Liverpool Annals of Archaeology and Anthropology* 26: 11–37.
1955 *Alalakh; an Account of Excavations at Tell Atchana in the Hatay, 1937-1949.* Oxford: Oxford University Press.
WOOLLEY, L. and BARNETT, R. D.
1952 *Carcemish, Part III. The Excavations in the Inner Town and the Hittite Inscriptions*. London: The British Museum.
YENER, K. A.
2010 "Appendix B: Small Finds Catalogue," in *Tell Atchana, Ancient Alalakh volume 1. The 2003–2004 Excavations Seasons*, edited by K. A. Yener, pp. 215–283. Istanbul: Koç Üniversitesi Yayınları.
YENER, K. A. and YAZICIOĞLU, G. B.
2010 "Chapter 2: Excavation results," in *Tell Atchana, Ancient Alalakh volume 1. The 2003–2004 Excavations Seasons*, edited by K. A. Yener, pp. 11–49. Istanbul: Koç Üniversitesi Yayınları.

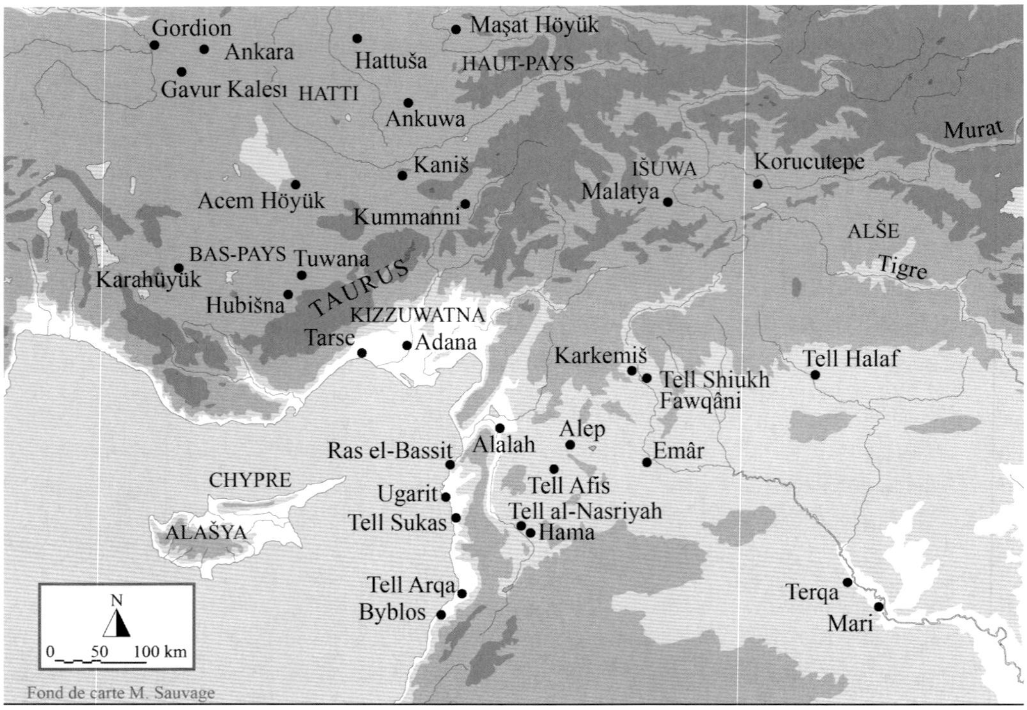

Map: Map showing location of sites
(A. Tenu after F. Joannès (dir), 2001, *Dictionnaire de la civilisation mésopotamienne*, p. 392. Paris: Robert Laffont).

Fig. 1 Tell an-Nasriyah: General view of the cemetery from the South-East in 2010 (© Aline Tenu).

Fig. 2 Tell an-Nasriyah: Grave 429: the natural hole has been widened: traces of the tool are clearly visible (© Stéphane Rottier).

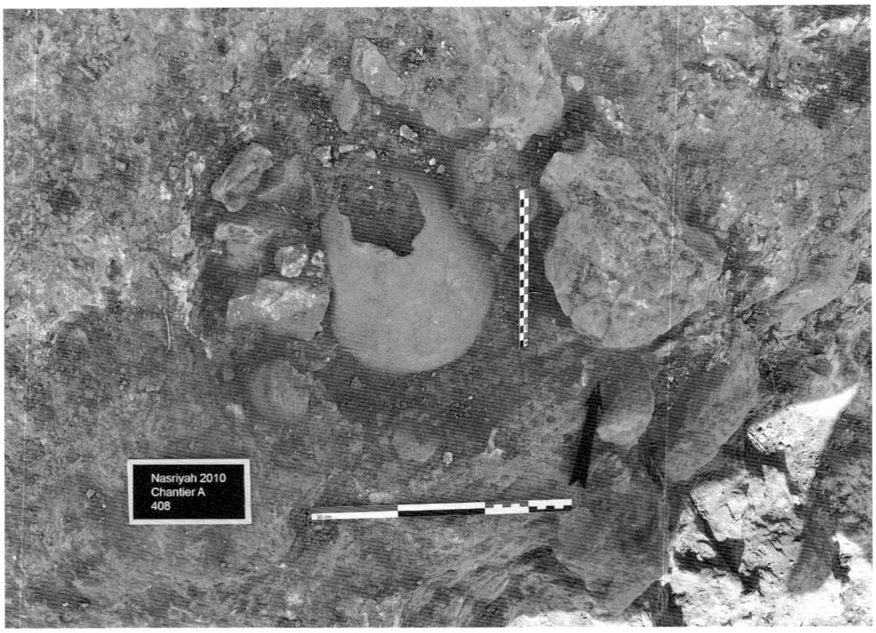

Fig. 3 Tell an-Nasriyah: Blocks surrounding cremation grave 408 buried in the bedrock (© Aline Tenu).

Fig. 4 Tell Shiukh Fawqâni:
Bath tube 4026 (© Aline Tenu).

Fig. 5 Tell Shiukh Fawqâni: Cinerary urn 4052 with two vessels (© Aline Tenu).

Fig. 6 Tell an-Nasriyah: Three graves among which 407 closed by a potsherd (© Stéphane Rottier).

Fig. 7 Tell an-Nasriyah: Cinerary urn 233 (© Gilbert Naessens).

Fig. 8 Tell an-Nasriyah: Cinerary urn 215 (© Gilbert Naessens).

Fig. 9 Tell Shiukh Fawqâni: Grave 4026
with two cinerary urns 4026-4 (on the left) and 4026-2 (on the right)
(© Aline Tenu).

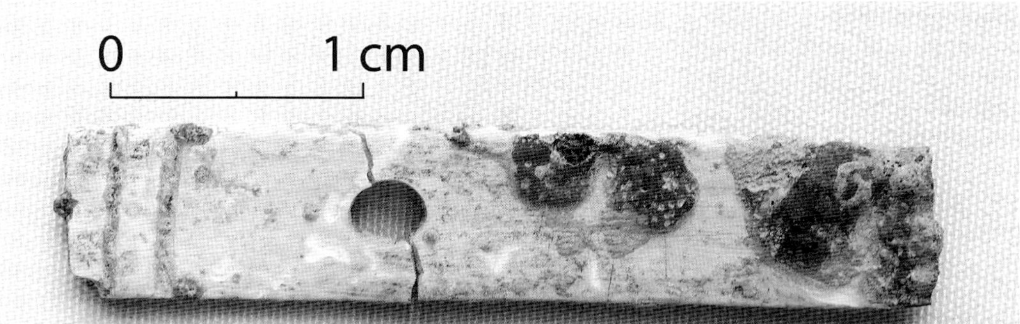

Fig. 10 Tell an-Nasriyah: Bone plaque with melted beads in vitreous material
(© Gilbert Naessens).

Fig. 11 Tell Shiukh Fawqâni: Grave goods from the plural grave 2591: bronze ring was associated to the child, the iron tools and weapons to the adult (© André Pelle).

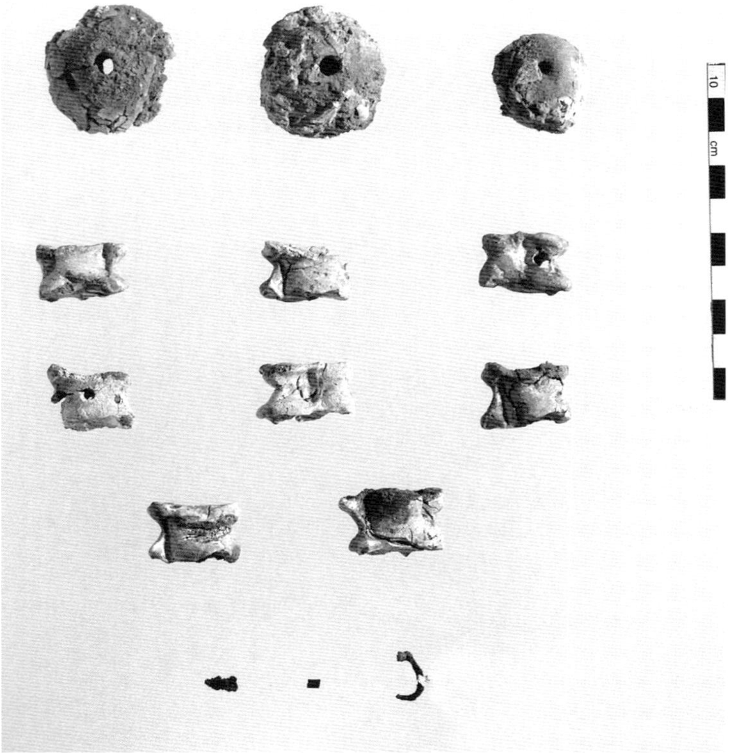

Fig. 12 Tell Shiukh Fawqâni: Grave goods associated to the grave 2529 which belongs to a gracile individual 15-20 years old (© André Pelle).

CHAPTER 19

WORKING IVORY IN SYRIA AND ANATOLIA DURING THE LATE BRONZE-IRON AGE

Annie CAUBET
Conservateur general honoraire, Musée du Louvre
3 rue Therese, 75001 Paris, France
E-mail: annie.caubet@free.fr

RÉSUMÉ

Le renouveau de la recherche concernant l'art de l'ivoire et des découvertes archéologiques récentes modifient notre vision de ces productions en Syrie et en Anatolie à la fin de l'âge du Bronze et au début du Ier millénaire. Après avoir abordé les questions d'identification, d'origine, et de circulation du matériau, l'étude du répertoire des formes et des décors permet de mettre en évidence des contrastes et des affinités entre ces deux régions limitrophes. Une certaine continuité entre l'âge du Bronze et celui du Fer peut être observée, notamment dans les types d'objets; mais une rupture marquée se produit dans le choix des matériaux (disparition de l'hippopotame à la fin du 2e millénaire) et dans la recherche de styles individuels propres à chaque centre artistique, qui contraste avec le style interchangeable de la culture internationale du Bronze récent.

ABSTRACT

New approach on the art of ivory and recent archaeological finds have influenced our understanding of what was a significant medium of elite societies in Syria and Anatolia during the LB and Iron Age. The questions of species identification, origin, circulation of raw materials, the repertoire of types and decors are evidence for affinities and contrasts between the two regions considered. Despite aspects of continuity (notably in the types of artifacts), there is a sharp distinction between Late Bronze Age and Iron Age production, in the choice of raw material; the quest for individual identity of style among the various artistic centers contrasts with the Late Bronze Age international ubiquitous style.

This paper is based on observations made through macroscopic examination of Ancient Near Eastern ivories conducted over many years in cooperation with François Poplin.[1] In view of the issues addressed by this conference, it is an attempt

[1] For the identification of ivory from different animal species, see Penniman 1952; Caubet, Poplin 1987. For a general overview of ivory production in antiquity, see Barnett 1982; Caubet, Gaborit-Chopin, Poplin 2004.

at sketching the evolution of ivory working over the *longue durée* in Syria and Anatolia, notably at sites such as Acemhöyük (ca 1800 BC)[2], Ugarit (Late Bronze Age)[3] and Arslan Tash (early first millennium).[4] Affinity and contrast between Anatolia and North Syria are especially apparent during the three periods represented by those sites. Their origins during the Late Bronze Age and the Iron Age I are based upon the evidence from the choice of material (hippopotamus versus elephant ivory, henceforward H. and E. ivory); this evidence is tentatively set in conjunction with other considerations such as the circulation and origin of the raw material, the techniques used for working it, the types of artifacts produced, the styles and motives of the iconography, the literary and epigraphic sources.

PART I — THE ORIGINS

Ivory artifacts appeared as early as the IVth millennium BC in Syria and Anatolia. H. ivory, not E. ivory, was the preferred material used from then on until the end of the Bronze Age. At Arlsantepe,[5] an amuletic seal in the shape of a bird comes from a palatial and cultic complex of ca 3800. At Umm al Marra, east of Aleppo, a tomb of the mid IIIrd millennium included forked pseudo "combs" and a handle decorated with incrustations.[6] At both sites, the artifacts came from high status contexts.

During the Middle Bronze Age, ivory working developed progressively but on a limited scale in North Syria and Cappadocia; it was entirely based on the use of H. ivory. At Ebla, ca 1800 BC, locally worked ivories depict Egyptian motifs, such as the sphinx or the *pschent* crown. They have been considered evidence for long distance trade with Egypt and the south Levant, due to the active policy on the part of Middle Kingdom pharaohs.[7] The categories of artifacts consist mainly of inlays and plaques designed to be applied on wood, and of one small figure in the round. According to our observations, all the Ebla pieces were carved out of H. tusks.

In Cappadocia, H. ivory working was active ca 1800 BC, as evidenced from the material discovered at Alaca Höyük, Kültepe[8] and Acemhöyük.[9] The kneeling youth from the royal tomb of Alaca Höyük must have formed part of a composite object:

[2] Mellink 1969; Harper 1969; Orthmann 1975, fig. 366 a–c; Barnett 1982, pl. 26.

[3] Gachet-Bizollon 2007.

[4] Thureau-Dangin, Barrois, Dossin, Dunand 1931.

[5] Frangipane 2004, n° 25 identification as H. ivory made from the photography, the fine parallel lines typical of this material are clearly visible.

[6] Examination of the material in Aleppo Museum, 2008, by courtesy of prof. G. Schwartz. See Schwartz, Curvers, Dunham, Stuart 2003 for the context of the artifacts.

[7] Scandone Matthiae 2002.

[8] The identification of the material was made possible in New York on the occasion of the exhibition at the MMA, see Aruz, Bendel, Evans 2008.

[9] Identification Caubet 1991, after examination at the Metropolitan Museum of Art, New York, courtesy of Dr. P.O. Harper; Bourgeois 1992.

the head is pierced with a mortise for attachment.[10] The craftsmen of Acemhöyük made the best use of the anatomic possibilities of their material, working with the parts of the H. tusks which are often neglected because they are difficult to exploit; the plaques, such as the kneeling lion-headed genies, are taken from the lower part of the H. canine, where the natural cavity leaves only a thin, curved wall of workable material. Other pieces are carved out from the solid part of H. incisors, which allows three dimensional volumes; the figures were made to fit into the narrow, vertical shape of the tooth (**Fig. 1**). The Acemhöyük assemblage seems to have consisted of pieces of furniture, using in-the-round elements, and appliqué decoration. With its combination of Egyptian, Aegean, and Hittite motifs, the style of this group may be "seen as an early manifestation of Hittite art, partly still under strong Egyptian Middle Kingdom influence, partly modified by Syrian transmissions and adaptations."[11] While worked pieces seemed to have been carved from H. ivory, there is evidence at Acemhöyük for the presence of unworked E. tusk. [12] Why should craftsmen who had access to E. ivory chose instead to use H. is a question also raised by the finds from other sites. At Alalakh, notably, several massive E. tusks had been uncovered in the Middle Bronze age palace. [13]

The production of ivory working in eastern Anatolia and north Syria, closely comparable in their iconographic development and their choice of material (H. ivory), contrasts sharply with the situation observed in southern and northern Mesopotamia. At sites such as Mari, Tell Brak or Assur, ivory production was restricted to a small number of miniature female figurines carved out of elephant tusks. Contacts with the east, via the Euphrates and the Gulf or via Central Asia, may account for the importation of elephant tusks from the Indus, alongside other eastern precious materials such as lapis-lazuli and carnelian.[14]

Part II — The Late Bronze period

During the LB period, the extension of the new Hittite Empire reached as far as the north of the Levant and inner Syria, while Egypt maintained its political and cultural domination over the south of the region. One might expect those political divisions to be reflected in the cultural identities and for our purpose, on ivory production. This is only partially true and the differences observed between the geographic areas in their choice of material, techniques, types of artifacts, and

[10] Barnett 1982, pl. 27 a–b.
[11] Mellink 1969.
[12] Yener 2007, p. 158.
[13] Woolley 1955, p. 288. For the worked pieces, the identification of the ivory specie is under progress (Yener personal comm. 02.02. 2010).
[14] Caubet, Poplin 2010; Francfort, Tremblay 2010.

iconography do not coincide with the political situation; the territories of north Syria and the Euphrates placed under Hittite rule rarely adopted the artistic traditions of the Hittites and on the contrary, adhered to "international art." That denomination is used by a number of scholars (including the present writer)[15] to designate the appearance of a large number of comparable artifacts over a large geographic area (the Levant in the largest sense, including coastal Syria and Palestine, Cyprus and inner Syria). There, city-states were linked by "international" diplomatic correspondence over a specific period of time between the Amarna letters and the letters from Ugarit. Although not fully justified historically, the term international art will be used here, for lack of anything better.

The Levantine ivory production of the LB Age has been the subject of recent studies.[16] Two major changes took place during that period; the number of artifacts increased spectacularly, and the use of E. ivory was introduced on a large scale, although without ever replacing H. as a choice material. The provenance of the material is a matter of discussion. E. and H. tusks could be transported and shipped over long distance, as shown from the cargo of the LB ship sunk off the coast of Uluburun.[17] H. ivory may have come from the Nile and the Palestinian shore. Elephant tusks may have been imported from Africa or India; or they may come from Syria; although the hypothesis of a Syrian breed of E. surviving from prehistoric times may be ruled out.[18] It seems possible that live E. had been imported (from India?), acclimated by man in the course of the Bronze Age, and were maintained in royal zoological reserves. Bone remains of Indian E. (*elephas maximus*) are found in a number of sites,and their number grows significantly during the LB period.[19] Easy access to E. and H. ivory may thus explain the increase in the production during the LB age. There is scant material evidence for local workshops, apart from Qatna, where hundreds of debitage of E. ivory plaques have been discovered.[20] At Ugarit, only one piece of H. ivory debitage has survived.[21] Nevertheless, it can be safely assumed that local craftsmen worked in most of the major centers of the Levant. At Ugarit, when making such luxurious items as the circular table of the bed in the royal palace,[22] they skillfully cut off plaques at the maximum of the possibilities of the E. tusk; two large pairs of tusks might have been enough to account for this tour de force.[23] Craftsmen of the

[15] Caubet 1998; Feldman 2006.

[16] Gachet-Bizollon 2007; Fischer 2007; Wicke 2008; Aruz, Benzel Evans 2008; Caubet 2009.

[17] Pulak in Aruz et alii 2008.

[18] Caubet, Poplin 2010.

[19] List in Fischer 2007, to which must be added recent finds at Qatna, see Pfälzner, Dohmann-Pfälzner 2010.

[20] Al-Maqdissi, Morandi-Bonacossi, Canci, Luciani 2005, p. 30.

[21] Caubet, Poplin 1987, fig. 14 for a H. ivory pre-form.

[22] Gachet-Bizollon 2007, n° 272 (table) and 268 (bed).

[23] Caubet, Poplin 1987, figs. 16, 20.

Iron Age were not so proficient in sparing the material at their disposal (see *infra).* The specific use made of the H. canine to produce duck boxes is also indicative of a local tradition; the various elements of the object, receptacle, neck, head, lid, ducklings. and pedestal are each carved out from different parts of the tooth, leaving very little of the canine unused.[24]

The repertoire of the Levantine production includes a few unique pieces, such as the horn (or vessel) as well as the bed and table from Ugarit. But in the main, the repertoire is "international," in the sense that the same types of artifacts, chest, gaming box, cylindrical, lenticular and duck-shaped pyxis, musical instruments, and toilet implements were found at many different sites. The ubiquitous duck box produced in a number of variants appears on sites situated as far as Greece to the West, and North Syria and the Euphrates to the East.[25] It is probable that the nucleus of production centers was situated on the coastal sites of Syria/Palestine. From there, the goods would be redistributed to far away destinations. At Emar, lenticular and duck boxes were made of bone as well as H. ivory;[26] this example was possibly a repair at a site in the Middle Euphrates far removed from the major creative centers of the international style with no easy access to raw material.

The iconography of Levantine production, with its blend of local, Egyptian, Minoan, and Mesopotamian traditions, has been much discussed.[27] For the present purpose, the emphasis will be put on the parallels with Hittite iconography and Anatolian traditions in general. As was mentioned above, a few statuettes and reliefs found at Megiddo and Nuzi display purely Hittite iconography and are probably imports. It is a question whether Hittite iconography really had an impact on the creation of images in the Levant. At Ugarit, alongside the Egyptianising flavor of most of the major pieces, discreet Hittite details may be noticed; one instance is the thunderbolt symbol depicted on the head of a winged goddess shown on an ivory bed from Ugarit (**Fig. 2**).[28] Other iconographic details such as the sphinxes with multiple ringlets are common traits between the Levant and Hittite art; one may compare the sphinxes flanking the naked goddess on the Ugarit horn[29] with the monumental sphinxes from the gate at Hattusa, although such details may derive from a common Aegean origin. Other Anatolian traits to be observed in Levantine art are the images of stags. Often depicted on monumental reliefs from the Bronze and Iron Age in the Anatolian plateau at such sites as Alaca Höyük, stags appear more rarely in the Levant: one interesting exception is the ivory bed from Ugarit

[24] Caubet, Poplin 1987, figs. 9–10.
[25] Adler 1996, Di Paolo 1997.
[26] Beyer 1982, p. 123–126: Identifications by F. Poplin were made after the publication.
[27] Feldman 2006; Fischer 2007; Aruz, Bendel, Evans 2008.
[28] Gachet-Bizollon 2007, n° 269.
[29] Gachet-Bizollon 2007, n° 386.

where a stag is depicted in two different scenes (**Fig. 3**). Whether the artists meant to represent *Dama mesopotamica*, whose distinctive spotted hide is not represented, or the larger *Cervus Elaphos,* is not clear. The imagery remained very popular among first millennium ivories, as evidenced from the hoards found at Arslan Tash or Nimrud.[30]

Compared to the abundance of international ivories from the Levant, the finds from the center of the Hittite empire seem paltry.[31] A miniature (H. 3.7 cm) mountain god from Hattusa is typically Hittite in iconography.[32] The nature of the material has not been identified, although the size and shape would be compatible with H. ivory. Barnett had already commented on the contradiction between the paucity of archaeological remains and the information gathered from the epigraphic sources.[33] The Hattusa archives record the presence of a quantity of ivory artifacts at the Hittite court, some imported from Halpa (Aleppo), some from Egypt; they list a large variety of types: combs for wool, combs and other toilet instruments, statuettes of lion and eagle, musical instruments; pieces of furniture include chair, table, and bed. On the whole, the categories of artifacts thus listed seem to correspond to the repertoire of international art. These ivory objects were decorated with gold or inlays, and some are listed as being "red" or "white".[34] The terms used to designate the ivory derives from "tooth, which, as material, can in the Near East be hardly anything but ivory."[35]

Scattered examples of purely Hittite works have been found outside the heartland of the Empire; the statuette of a half naked goddess from Nuzi,[36] a plaque from Megiddo depicting a mythological composition with Hittite hieroglyphic inscriptions,[37] are evidence of the existence of a Hittite tradition of ivory working completely distinct from Levantine production. They stand out from the rest of the assemblage, as the Egyptian imports do not; unless they carry specific inscriptions, [38] Egyptian pieces blend easily in the general appearance of Levantine production.

[30] Thureau-Dangin, Barrois, Dossin, Dunand 1931, pl. XXXVI, 61–62; Mallowan 1966, fig. 435, 439.

[31] Boehmer 1979, for instance, records only a few instruments in bone from the lower city of Bogazköy.

[32] Barnett 1982, pl. 27 c–d, dates the piece to the Old Kingdom, ca 1700; Orthmann 1975 dates it ca 1300.

[33] Barnett 1982, pp. 32–34.

[34] Güterbock 1971 [reprinted 1997].

[35] Güterbock 1971, who naturally assumed that they were carved out of E. tusks and that the tusks were imported from Africa via Egypt.

[36] Barnett 1982, fig. 15.

[37] Loud 1939, p. 10; Orthmann 1975, fig. 372a; Di Paolo 1996(b).

[38] Fischer 2007.

PART II — IRON AGE

After the disappearance of the Hittite Empire and the collapse of the LB Age palace society, the precise period and conditions for the renaissance of smaller principalities of mixed cultural identities are still a matter of debate among historians and archaeologists. It is difficult to date the revival of ivory working, although it seems reasonable to link it with the reestablishment of court life, of which ivory furniture must have been an essential adornment. The chronological question is rendered even more difficult by the fact that most of the recovered ivories come from secondary contexts; they are either loot, booty or tribute, hoarded in Neo-Assyrian capitals, most notably Nimrud, over several reigns of Assyrian kings in the IXth and VIIIth centuries BC.

Recent studies concentrated on localizing the workshop centers and schools of ivory working. The work done by Georgina Herrmann on the Nimrud ivories is invaluable.[39] Attempts at defining boundaries between schools, groups, and workshops are elaborated on the basis of epigraphic evidence and stylistic comparisons, particularly with "major" arts, architectural, votive, and funerary reliefs.[40] Centers have been identified in North Syria, Eastern Anatolia, North Western Iran, the Levant, and Cyprus.

From our observation of first millennium ivories, one major change took place between the end of the LB Age and the revival of the Iron Age; H. ivory disappeared from use while there is evidence that H. survived in the Levant during the Iron Age.[41] From then on, E. ivory was worked to the exclusion of any other and on a very large scale until the end of the Assyrian period. The provenance of the ivory tusks has been often discussed[42] and the reasons for the shift in an age-old habit of H. ivory working are still unclear, as are the possible routes of circulation of those tusks. Another change may be noted in the way craftsmen interacted with the material at their disposal. Although debitage and carving techniques remained in the whole unchanged,[43] many pieces betray a lavish, careless use of the tusks, a disregard for the possibilities offered by the natural pulp cavity. Part of the intimate interplay with the natural shape and volume of the elephant tusk displayed by the LB artists seems to be lost,[44] together with the disappearance of H. ivory, which may have made more demands on the skill of the artist.

[39] Herrmann, Laidlaw, Coffey 2009 with previous bibliography; Suter, Uehlinger 2005.
[40] Winter 1989; Bonatz 2000.
[41] Haas 1953.
[42] Collon 1977; Barnett 1982; Caubet, Poplin 2009.
[43] As we can observe from our ongoing study of the Arslan Tash assemblage, undertaken by G. Affani, E. Fontan, F. Poplin.
[44] Caubet 2002.

Especially relevant to the topic of this conference are the productions which may possibly be assigned to the regions "across the border," in North Syria and Cilicia, where Luwian and Aramaean kingdoms reestablished themselves over the ruins of the Hittite Empire. A large number of ivories among the Nimrud hoard have been assigned by Herrmann to North Syrian traditions. The few remains actually discovered in north Syrian sites do not help much in refining the attributions. Ivories from tell Fekheriyeh[45] or tell Ahmar-Til Barsib[46] were in use during the time of the Assyrian occupation and probably do not reflect local production. The hoard from Arslan Tash,[47] on a smaller scale than that of Nimrud, was a loot taken over from Damascus (see infra); in the case of Sam'al – Zinjirli,[48] however, the combined evidence from the stone sculptures and the ivories destroyed by the Assyrian conquerors, may serve as the basis for the reconstruction of the production of a major North Syrian art center.

There is scant evidence from the inscribed ivories. Very few name the city or kingdom from where they originate. The best known is the fragment (of a bed?) found at Arslan Tash, naming Hazaël, in all probability the king of Aram, a contemporary of Salmaneser III,which is a good indication that the ivory hoard may have been looted from Damascus.[49] On the bottom of a pyxis from the Burnt Palace at Nimrud, an inscription reads "Bît- Gusi", ancient Arpad, a North Syrian state often recorded in the Assyrian military campaigns.[50] It is a fine piece depicting a banquet scene in honor of a seated lady, a goddess or a queen, accompanied by musicians (**Fig. 4**).[51] A second fragmentary pyxis (possibly a pair to the first) from the same room, shows a musician and a stag, an imagery inherited from the Anatolian LB Age.[52] Convincingly linked to the tribute paid by a king of Bît-Gusi, the two pyxides provide fairly solid grounds for the reconstruction of ivory working in Arpad during the IXth, or possibly the VIIIth, century.[53]

Types of artifacts and iconography show the survival of tradition with a few innovations since the LB Age. Pieces of furniture and chests, chariot and horse equipments, toilet implements, and instruments already produced in the LB age are still favorites in the Iron Age; one instance is the *longue durée* of the pyxis.[54] The wide distribution of these types among the different schools and groups show they belong to an international repertoire. The iconography, too, shows a number of themes

[45] Di Paolo 1996.
[46] Bunnens 1997.
[47] Thureau-Dangin et alii 1931.
[48] Luschan, Andrae 1943.
[49] Thureau-Dangin et alii 1931, pl. XLVIII, 112; Puech 1981.
[50] Puech 1978.
[51] Barnett 1975, S 3, pl. XVI, XVII and CXXXII.
[52] Barnett 1975, S 9, pl. XVI.
[53] The name of the owner is partly missing and may reconstructed as that of a king of Arpad contemporary with Salmaneser III (858–824) or, less probably in my view, with Tiglatpilasar III (744–727).
[54] Wicke 2008.

inherited from the second millennium and are common to production centers localized over a large geographic area. Egyptian motifs such as the sphinx or the birth of Horus, related to the expression of royal ideology are almost ubiquitous. Religious motives, such as the lady in the window, the cow and suckling calf, the genies and sacred tree are present in every artistic group as are traditional themes related to war and power, like the chariot scenes. The choice of types and imagery reflects the taste and demands of a clientele, which is recruited as in earlier ages, among the ruling elites seeking to express their status through the possession of luxurious items. There are few purely religious artifacts. The ivories are eminently of social value, if not "utilitarian." Their symbolic significance and meaning is in the material and the craftsmanship, not particularly in their function.

Stylistically, however, there is a complete shift from the Bronze Age. The many artistic groups and workshops active in the first centuries of the first millennium competed with each other to create distinctive, strongly personal styles with sharp differences in the rendering of body proportions and details of hair, fabrics, and animal hides. Each group tended to favor different decorative techniques, such as encrustation, cloisonné, à jour, as if to differentiate themselves from the others. It would be anachronistic, of course, to speak of "national" expressions. But one may wonder whether the specific stylistic rendering of a common imagery and typology is not related to the wish of expressing one's territorial and political identity. The same observation may be attempted for other artistic forms, such as the so called "Phoenician Aramaean" metal bowls.

This quest for identity through style is a major shift from the "international style" of the LB Age, when style as well as imagery and types were ubiquitous and interchangeable, advertising the will of both artists and owners to abide to a given set of standards. The individuality of each style seems to be more accentuated in the North Syrian and Cilician groups, despite (or because of?) the mixed identities of those centers, which is reflected in the adoption of either Luwian hieroglyphic or Phoenician script.[55] In the southern Levant groups, the traditional Egyptianising international style endured into the Iron Age. One wonders if the individuality of the former groups is not a trait inherited from the self-centered spirit of the Hittite culture.

Conclusion

The balance between tradition and innovation between LB/IA is difficult to assess, and regional differences are differently expressed according to each criterion; raw material, working technique, types of artifacts, and iconography. One major common trait between Anatolia and the Levant is to be found in the general use of H. ivory

[55] Winter 1979.

until its disappearance in the Iron Age. That the choice of material has little connection with local access to that material and the reasons for that choice remain a question. One major difference resides in the contrast between the respective quantity of ivory products between the Hittite and the LB city states of the Levant. Beyond mere numbers, the specific, self-centered identity of imperial Hittite art, favoring religious artifacts that displayed a particular iconography, contrasts with the eclectic international art of the Levant; types and iconography contributed to a gracious *art de vivre* developed out of marrying foreign ladies, who would come with their trousseau and their toiletry, accompanied by musicians, weavers and craftsmen; owning the last model in war chariots, carrying splendid weapons, eating and drinking out of imported vessels. Types and iconography inherited from that period endured into the Iron Age, evidence for the continuity in the way of life among the elites; but the new quest for individual identity of style, in sharp contrast with the previous period, and particularly notable among the Luwian and Aramaean states of North Syria and Cilicia is possibly an inheritance of Hittite ideology.

Bibliography

ADLER, W.
1996 "Die spätbronzezeitlichen Pyxiden in Gestalt von Wasservögeln", in *Kamid el Loz* 16. *Schatzhaus Studien*, Saarbrücken Beiträge zur Altertumskunde 59, edited by Hachmann, pp. 27–117. Bonn.

AL-MAQDISSI, M., MORANDI-BONACOSSI D., CANCI A., LUCIANI M.
2005 *The Metropolis of the Orontes. Art and Archaeology from the Ancient Kingdom of Qatna.* Damascus: DGAM.

ARUZ J., BENZEL K., EVANS J. eds.
2008 *Beyond Babylon. Art, Trade and Diplomacy in the Second Millennium.* New York: Metropolitan Museum of Art.

BARNETT, R. D.
1975 *A Catalogue of the Nimrud Ivories in the British Museum.* London: The Trustees of the British Museum.
1982 *Ancient Ivories in the Middle East*, Qedem 14. Jerusalem: The Hebrew University of Jerusalem.

BEYER, D.
1982 "Matières dures animales" in *Meskéné-Emar: Dix ans de travaux: 1972-1982: A l'occasion d'une exposition,* edited by D. Beyer, pp. 123–126, Paris: ERC.

BOEHMER, R.-M.
1972 *Die Kleinfunde von Bogazköy aus den Grabungen 1931-39 und 1952-69, Bogazköy-Hattusa 7*, WVDOG 87. Berlin: Gebrüder Man Verlag.
1979 *Die Kleinfunde aus der Unterstadt von Bogazköy. Ausgrabungenkampagnen 1970-1978.* Berlin: Gebrüder Man Verlag.

BONATZ, D.
2000 "Syro-hittite Funerary Monuments. A Phenomenon of Tradition or Innovation?", in *Essays on Syria in the Iron Age*, Ancient Near Eastern Studies Supplement 7, edited by G. Bunnens, pp. 189–210. Louvain: Peeters.

BOURGEOIS, B.
1992 "An Approach to Anatolian Techniques of Ivory Carving during the Second Millennium BC," in *Ivory in Greece and Eastern Mediterranean from the Bronze Age to the Hellenistic Period*, London: British Museum Occasional Paper 85, edited by J. L. Fitton, pp 61–66. The Trustees of the British Museum.

BUNNENS, G.
1997 "Carved ivories from Til Barsib," *American Journal of Archaeology* 101: 435–450.

CAUBET, A.,
1991 "Ivoires de Cappadoce," in *Mélanges P. Garelli*, edited by J.-M. Durand, D. Charpin, pp. 223–225. Paris: ERC.
1998 "The international Style: a point of view from the Levant and Syria," in *The Aegean and the Orient in the Second Millennium*, Aegaeum 19, edited by E. Cline and D. Harris-Cline, Proceedings of the 50th Anniversary Symposium, Cininnati, 18-0 April 1997, pp. 105–113. Liège: .
2002 "Le travail de l'ivoire au Levant, de la fin de l'âge du Bronze au début de l'âge du fer: continuité et rupture," in *Die Nahöstlichen Kulturen und Griechenland an der Wende vom 2. Zum 1. Jahrtausend v. Chr.*, edited by E. Braun-Holzinger and H. Matthäus, pp. 109–122. Bibliopolis: Möhnesee-Wamel.
2009 "L'art de l'ivoire au Levant durant la période du Bronze récent," in *Interconnectons in the Eastern Mediterranean. Lebanon in the Bronze and Iron Ages*, edited by A. M. Afeiche, pp. 375–384. Beyrouth: BAAL.

CAUBET, A. and POPLIN F.
1987 "Matières dures animales: étude du matériau," in *Ras Shamra-Ougarit III. Le centre de la ville,* edited by M. Yon, pp 273–306. Paris: ERC.
2010 " Réflexions sur la question de l'éléphant syrien," in *Dur-Katlimmu 2008 and Beyond*, Studia Chaburensia I, edited by H. Kühne, pp 1–9. Wiesbaden: Harrassowitz Verlag.

CAUBET, A., GABORIT-CHOPIN D., POPLIN F.
2004 *Ivoires, de l'Orient ancien aux Temps modernes.* Paris: RMN.

COLLON, D.
1977 "Ivory," *Iraq* 39: 219–222.

DI PAOLO, S.
1996 "Considerazioni sulla cronologia degli avori di Tell Fekheriyah," *Contributi e Materiali di Archeologia Orientale (CMAO)* 6: 191–216.
1996(b) "Gli avori di Megiddo: un esempio di arte ittita: alcune riflessioni," *Vicino Oriente* 10: 163–208.
1997 "Sulla tipologia e l'origine degli unguentari à canard nella Siria-Palestina del bronzo tardo," *Rivista degli studi orientali* 71: 25–53.

FELDMAN, M.
2006 *Diplomacy by Design: Luxury Arts and an 'International Style' in the Ancient Near East, 1400-1200 BCE.* Chicago: University of Chicago Press.

FISCHER, E.
2007 *Ägyptische und ägyptisierende Elfenbeine aus Megiddo und Lachish. Inschriftenfunde, Flaschen, Löffel*, AOAT 47. Münster: Ugarit-Verlag.

FRANGIPANE, M.
2004 *Alle origine del potere. Arslantepe, la collina dei leoni.* Milan: Electa Mondadori.

FRANCFORT, H. P., TREMBLAY X.,
2010 "Marhasi et la civilisation de l'Oxus," *Iranica Antiqua* XLV: 51–224.

GACHET-BIZOLLON, J.
2007 *Les ivoires d'Ougarit et l'art des ivoiriers du Levant au Bronze récent*, Ras Shamra Ougarit XVI, Paris: ERC.

GÜTERBOCK, H. G.
1971 [1997] "Ivory in Hittite Texts," *Anadolu/Anatolia. Journal for the Institute for Research in Near Eastern and Mediterranean Civilizations of the Faculty of Letters of the University of Ankara* 15: 1–7 (Reprinted in H. A. Hoffner and I. L. Diamlond (eds.), *Perspectives on Hittite Civilization: Selected Writings of Hans Gustav Güterbock*, The Oriental Institute of Chicago, Assyriological Studies, Chicago, 1997, pp. 147–150).

HAAS, G.
1953 "On the occurrence of Hippopotamus in the Iron Age of the coastal area of Israel (tel Qasileh)," *BASOR* 132: 30–34.

HARPER, P. O.
1969 "Dating a group of ivories from Anatolia," *The Connoisseur*: 156–162.

HERRMANN, G., LAIDLAW S., COFFEY H.
2009 *Ivories from the North West Palace (1845-1992).* Ivories from Nimrud VI. Oxford: Oxbow Books.

LOUD, G.
1939 *The Megiddo Ivories*, Oriental Institute Publications 52. Chicago: University of Chicago Press.

LUSCHAN, F. VON, ANDRAE, W. (Herausgabe und Ergänzung),
1943 *Die Kleinfunde von Sendschirli.* Staatliche Museem zu Berlin. Mitteilungen aus den Orientalischen Sammlungen XV. Ausgrabungen in Sendschirli V. Berlin: Walter De Gruyter.

MALLOWAN, M. E. L.
1966 *Nimrud and its Remains.* London: Collins.

MELLINK, M. J.
1969 "The Pratt Ivories in the Metropolitan Museum of Art," *American Journal of Archaeology* 73: 285–286.

ORTHMANN, W.,
1975 "Hethitische Kunsthandwerk," in *Der Alter Orient*, Propyläen Kunstgeschichte 14, edited by W. Orthamnn, pp. 432–436. Berlin.

PENNIMAN, T. K.
1984 *Pictures of Ivory and other Animal Teeth, Bone and Antler*, Occasional Paper on Technology 5, Oxford: Pitt Rivers Museum, (original edition 1952).

PFÄLZNER, P., DOHMANN-PFÄLZNER H.
2010 "Elefantenknochen und über 50 Schädel," *Antike Welt* 41: 75–78.

PUECH, E.
1978 "Un ivoire de Bît-Gusi (Arpad) à Nimrud," *Syria* 55: 163–168.
1981 "L'ivoire inscrit d'Arslan-Tash et les rois de Damas," *Revue Biblique* 88: 544–562.

SCANDONE, MATTHIAE G.
2002 *Gli Avori Egittizzanti dal Palazzo Settentrionale.* Missione Archeologica Italiana in Siria. Roma: Materiali Studi archeologichi di Ebla III, Universita degli Studi di Roma "La Sapienza".

SCHWARTZ, G., CURVERS H., DUNHAM S., STUART B.,
2003 "A Third-Millenium BC Elite Tomb and Other New Evidence from Tell Umm el-Marra, Syria," *American Journal of Archaeology* 107: 325–361.

SUTER, C. E, UEHLINGER C. ed.
2005 *Craft and Images in Contact: Studies on Eastern Mediterranean Art of the First Millennium B.C.E.* Fribourg: University Press.

THUREAU-DANGIN, F., BARROIS A., DOSSIN G., DUNAND M.
1931 *Arslan Tash*. Paris: Paul Geuthner.
WINTER, I.
1979 "On the Problems of Karatepe: the Reliefs and their Context," *Anatolian Studies* 29: 115–151 (reprinted in *On Art in the Ancient Near East I. On the First Millennium BC*. Leiden-Boston: Brill, 2010, p. 467–524).
1989 "North Syrian Ivories and Tell Halaf Reliefs: The Impact of Luxury Goods upon "Major" arts," in *Essays in Ancient Civilization Presented to Helen J. Kantor*, edited by A. Leonard Jr and B. B. Williams, pp. 321–332. Chicago: Chicago University Press (reprinted in *On Art in the Ancient Near East I. On the First Millennium BC*, Leiden-Boston: Brill, 2010, p. 381–430).
WICKE, D.
2008 *Vorderasiatische Pyxiden der Spätbronzezeit und der Früheisenzeit*, AOAT 45. Münster: Ugarit-Verlag.
WOOLLEY, L. C.
1955 *Alalakh. An Account of the Excavations at Tell Atchana in the Hatay, 1937–1949*. Reports of the Research Committee of the Society of Antiquaries of London, XVIII. London: Printed at the University Press, Oxford, for The Society of Antiquaries.
YENER, A.
2007 "The Anatolian Middle Bronze Age Kingdoms and Alalakh: Mukish, Kanesh and trade," *Anatolian Studies* 57: 151-160.

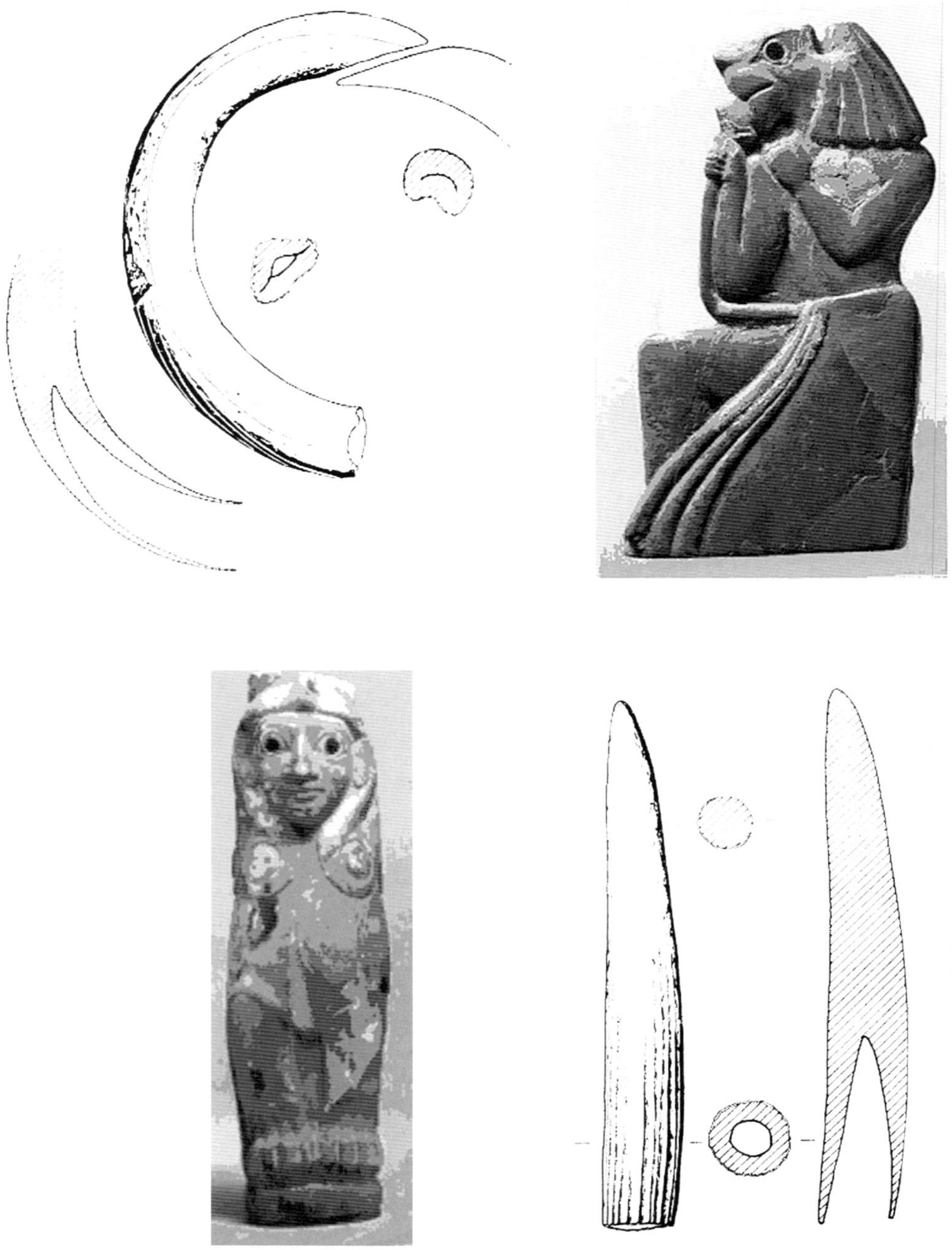

Fig. 1 Inscription of Acemhöyük sphinx and plaque in H. incisor and canine (drawing C. Florimont).

Fig. 2 Winged goddess with thunderbolt symbol from an Ugarit bed (photo A. Caubet).

Fig. 3 Stag from Ugarit bed (photo A. Caubet).

Fig. 4 Pyxis from Nimrud, after Barnett 1975.

CHAPTER 20

ARTS AND CROSS-CULTURAL COMMUNICATION IN THE EARLY 1ST MILLENNIUM: THE SYRO-ANATOLIAN CONTACT

Stefania MAZZONI
University of Florence
E-mail: smazzoni@uni.net
stefania.mazzoni@unifi.it
Via Montevideo 2A, 00198 Roma, Italy

ABSTRACT

The cultural regeneration that marks northern Syria and southern Anatolia in Iron I cannot be disconnected from the political and social changes following the 12th century collapse. The emergence of new social and political forces and the renovated expansion of traditional powers were important factors of renewal, prompting competition and conflicts but also encouraging reciprocal cultural interplay. This is documented precisely by the emergence of many artistic centres characterised by distinct origins and different lingering and innovative traits and styles.

Two stages can be actually defined for the early Syro-Hittite art, and they both give evidence of a flourishing and dynamic period of artistic creativity. A first stage (Iron I: 12th–10th cent. BC) is documented by the diffusion of monumental stone sculpture in architecture. A second stage (Iron II: 9th–8th cent.) attests to a notable increase of production and diffusion especially of minor arts.

The first stage comprises two distinct phases of development. A first phase (Iron Age IA-B: 12th–11th cent. BC) is characterised by the continuation and gradual renewal of Hittite artistic techniques, genres and traditions. Monumental stone sculpture for the architectural decoration of open-air spaces, gates and façades of temples and palaces was the prevailing artistic genre; traditional religious and dynastic celebrative themes were consequently resumed and renovated. The second phase (Iron Age IC: 10th cent. BC) was marked by an unprecedented intensity of production and spread of different genres thanks to the activity of many new and old art centres encouraged by the local rulers. Monumental sculpture was regenerated with the introduction of a new repertory of images for dynastic propaganda, and new stylistic and figurative traits. The reappraisal and intensification of the production of minor arts and particularly ivory manufacture has to be situated in the same active phase of renewal in the arts and promotion of workshops documented by monumental sculpture.

THE LATE BRONZE-IRON I TRANSITION: CONTINUITY, CHANGE AND INTERCULTURALITY

The cultural regeneration that marks northern Syria and southern Anatolia in Iron I cannot be disconnected from the political and social changes emerging thereafter, or from the 12th century collapse. The breakdown of empires, the formation of small regional kingdoms, the emergence of exogenous ethnic components and the taking of power by endogenous groups were certainly the major factors involved in, first the destabilisation and then the renewal of the geo-political and cultural scenario of the area. Both processes, destabilisation and renewal, underwent various timings, stages and scales and experienced various dynamics of development in the different regions according to the nature of the events and their agents.[1] The political and cultural landscape emerging from this turning point was consequently marked by a great variety of manifestations, with new or renewed towns and capitals, new political entities in search of a place and rank in a multifaceted scenario, powerful, previously established states in search of economic and military achievements, and tribal aggregations claiming distinct social, territorial, and eventually ethnic affiliation.

This was a variegated process that entailed different mechanisms and cases of cultural continuity and transformation; change and continuity represent one of the most hotly debated arguments in archaeology and are central to theoretical discussion, beginning with the seminal "Explanation of Culture Change " by Renfrew 1973[2] and continuing with the subject of the 57th RAI in Rome in 2011: "Tradition and Innovation in the ancient Near East."

The development of the crisis and post-crisis years is now evaluated as a multifaceted process that involved a great interplay among the many interacting political and social spheres. These were often in opposition and at war for the control of nodal routes and lands whose borders became unstable and flexible, this being a further factor accelerating changes in the political setting. Furthermore, the many interrelating new and old components in this scenario both possessed and introduced different systems of verbal, visual and spatial communication in order to express their proper identity, affiliation as well as their cultural and social origin. In recent years the debate about transitional periods and especially the Late Bronze-Iron Age transition has developed along different lines, focussing on the investigation of ethnicity as an important factor of the transformation.[3] Archaeological materials, mainly pottery,

[1] On the argument see now a copious literature mostly from international symposia: Ward, Sharp Joukowski 1992; Gitin, Mazar, Stern 1998; Braun-Holzinger and Matthäus 2002; Fischer, Genz, Jean, Köroğlu 2003; Harrison 2006–2007; Bachhuber, Roberts 2009. On economy and trade in the transitional period: Bell 2006; Pedrazzi 2007. More recently, for the coast of south Levant, see Jasmin 2006; Gadot 2008; Yasur-Landau 2010. For northern Levant see Venturi 2007, pp. 381–426 and Venturi 2009.

[2] Renfrew 1973.

[3] As an example, Killebrew 2005.

have been credited as reliable documents for detecting elements of change or continuity, mirroring ethnicity and social identity, and this is now reflected in a vast literature. In the case of the southern Levant, the research has investigated material in order to understand the role of different peoples (Philistines, Israelites, Phoenicians) in shaping the Iron Age culture and society. Similarly, for the northern Levant attention has now been given to the role of different peoples and their cultural identities as well as their occasions for contact and exchange. Pottery is also evaluated within this framework and is, in fact, a direct source which enables us to understand the distinct social dynamics of the period, not according to the old "pots and peoples" paradigm but according to a model of shared, and not exclusive to, cultural affiliation. In fact, despite the many mechanisms of differentiation, distinctiveness and seclusion that are apparently visible in the historical sources of the period, material culture, as well as the arts, attests instead to a quite dynamic process of mutual assimilation and communication.[4]

ARTS: REGENERATION AND INTERCULTURALITY

We are more used to recognising the very composite crowd of components of the Iron Age societies by their languages; Assyrians, Luwians, Aramaeans, Phoenicians, Hebrews, Ammonites and Moabites, Arabs and Iranians, Urartians, Phrygians and Ionians. Visual and spatial communication bring us to less perceptible fields of investigation; they can, however, supply other cultural evidence, images, solid volumes and built spaces that can positively help to understand the cultural dynamics of this period. They furnish, ultimately, the picture of a Levant marked by two parallel trends; a substantial renewal of lingering traits of the former local regional traditions and an increasing intercultural communication that eventually resulted in stimulating reciprocal acculturation. This second process culminated with the Assyrian expansion and the cultural *koiné* that emerged in the 8th–7th cent. BC when factors of emulation and appropriation substantially homogenized the distinct cultural *facies* of the area; it is to this scenario that the rise of Orientalizing art is now related.[5] Interculturality was, however, an evolving trend already emerging in the post-crisis years and at the beginning of the millennium when the relations between the many actors on the stage, native and intruders, became necessarily more direct and interactive, generating, besides competition and cultural distinction, mutual knowledge and eventually assimilation. The visual arts especially, with their many traditions, genres, techniques and

[4] Two cases seem to be paradigmatic of this model, cooking wares see Birney 2008 and LH IIIC style painted ceramics see Lehmann 2007 and related bibliography, which have been both interpreted as a document of exogenous components intruding in the Levant and eventually prompting local cases of assimilation and imitation by the endogenous components.

[5] Gunter 2009, especially pp. 28–40, 178.

media give us a vivid picture of a flourishing creativity that can illustrate the manifold social and cultural forces emerging and confronting each other in this period.

The documentation offered by the visual arts, architectural decoration, decorative arts for furniture and luxury objects during the early Iron Age gives, in fact, a clear illustration of a flourishing and dynamic phase of regeneration and development. Different media conveyed communication to quite a differentiated audience, adopting a large choice of images from many sources and iconographic repertories, as well as of different formal and aesthetic values. To this aim, precious materials were more often employed and luxurious objects produced, and a number of specialised techniques were accordingly mastered. This variety was certainly not a new characteristic; the luxury arts of the Late Bronze Age furnish evidence of a plurality of genres, techniques and styles for the purpose of institutional exchanges and gifts,[6] but they are more often documented by single pieces for each class or genre. This is clear with ivory production. To cite only the rich collection of ivories from Ugarit,[7] they display different styles, artistic traditions and techniques used for objects of different functions. Each ivory was a single masterpiece with no direct comparisons. A similar consideration can be made in relation to monumental art even in Hittite Anatolia, where we can cite different monuments celebrating different occasions and then showing distinct iconographies in different locations and visual spaces;[8] each monument was a single unparalleled masterpiece.

The transformation from the Late Bronze to the Iron Age was in fact of both a qualitative and quantitative nature. During the Iron Age artistic production substantially increased and many art centres emerged. Several distinct workshops of stone and ivory working can be easily recognised. We cannot identify the centres of production of the ivories that are documented mostly from the Assyrian capitals as a result of looting or tribute.[9] We can, instead, attribute the workshops of monumental art to the same towns where monuments were erected and decorated with sculpture. Only a scenario of single regional and even city workshops can, in fact, account for the plurality of styles and iconographies displayed by Syro-Hittite art.

It is well known that this intensification of art production and plurality of art centres was not an abrupt event but, instead, gradually developed over the course of five centuries (12th–8th) and was closely related to the political fragmentation of the local kingdoms and principalities and the consequent competition for exerting and communicating their power. Local rulers could patronize artists and artisans and promote the choice of a repertoire of attractive and significant images; a visual language was

[6] Feldman 2002, 2006. Liverani 2008, pp. 163–168.

[7] Gachet-Bizollon 2007, pp. 231–234; Caubet 2008; Feldman 2008, pp. 446–447; Feldman 2008; Feldman 2009, pp. 346–348.

[8] Kohlmeyer 1983; Emre 2002; Ehringhaus 2005.

[9] See now the conference edited by Cecchini, Mazzoni, Scigliuzzo 2009.

accordingly shaped to be appealing and easily appreciated on a local as well as external level.[10] With this aim, regional traditions were resumed and successfully regenerated, but also a number of new trends were prompted and foreign elements were adopted. Art and power competition efficiently encouraged emulation and the circulation of models and styles among the different centres; this eventually resulted in the diffusion of common trends and cross-cultural, occasionally symbiotic, traits.

It is also well known that the dynamics of a less ephemeral intercultural interplay had already emerged in the Late Bronze Age, in the so-called "International Period"; this is when direct contacts among peoples began to play a nodal role in the economic and commercial life of the Levantine states, i.e. when borders also became steadily permeable to traders as well as to goods.[11] This process was accelerated in the crisis years and the immediate post-crisis period thanks to the increased mobility consequent to instability and a more direct interaction that involved the many actors on the stage. In the end, the trend culminated with the creation of a shared cultural and visual language of communication and propaganda encouraged by the dominant powers but expressed in a large variety of dialects which ultimately reflected different regional traditions and origins.

Arts in the early Iron Age: a diachronic perspective

A few aspects and genres may be taken into consideration as they can give better evidence of the composite nature of the traditions involved with their geographic and technical implications. There is also a chronological sequence to be considered which attests to the many regional and cultural routes followed and borders crossed in the course of the emergence of the new Iron Age art tradition. A first stage (Iron I: 12th–10th cent. BC) is documented by the diffusion of monumental stone sculpture in basalt, especially in architecture, with religious and dynastic celebration themes for the decoration of open-air spaces, gates and façades of temples and palaces and processional/ceremonial passages. This was certainly the most creative phase in sculpture, which reveals itself over the course of three centuries as being rooted in a distinct Anatolian artistic and technical background. A second stage (Iron II: 9th–8th cent.) is documented by an unparalleled increase in the number of artistic genres. Stone sculpture then included both monumental (carved relief for architecture and isolated monuments, such as stelae and statues) and minor arts (pyxides and lion/hand bowls). Ivory and metal minor arts comprised an unprecedented selection of luxury and precious objects, furniture and vessels, bridle-harnesses for cavalry and a variety of instruments for ritual and ceremonial use. All these genres were patronised by the élites and

[10] Herrmann 2000, pp. 268; Harmanşah 2011, pp. 639–640.
[11] Collins 2008, pp. 20–89; Feldman 2002, 2006.

destined to the restricted circuit of the palaces for display and used in ceremonial and ritual court occasions, *symposia* and funerary celebrations. They consequently show a choice of subjects connected with the symbolic and practical function of the objects decorated; thus we find court themes, religious and magic images, funerary portraits. Moreover, "they attest to the wealth and artistic vigour of life in the area at the time."[12]

A wide variety of techniques and materials were employed, and there was a selected choice of iconographies restricted to the different genres and media. They can apparently be distinguished according to regional sources and traditions and provide evidence of an active regeneration of old traditions performed by local old and new components. A Levantine and Syrian orientation can be recognised more easily in bronze and ivory production, as well as a Phoenician tradition of Canaanite origin. In glyptics and decorative arts, Assyrian characteristics and style began to penetrate, possibly earlier than is usually believed in the 12th–11th cent. BC, following the activities of the Assyrian kings along the western frontier.[13] A Late Hittite style and technique prevailed in stone sculpture and monumental art. Therefore, the artistic scenario was apparently quite composite and characterised by a certain amount of cross-culturality from the beginning of the early Iron Age. This might have been a further element of attraction to foreign, especially Aegean components, already acquainted with the Levant since the middle of the 2nd millennium BC After a period of intense relations culminating in the Late Bronze Age and documented by an active circulation of oriental goods in Greece (Thebes, Kadmeion) and especially Mycenaean pottery along the Levantine coasts, a new flow of exotic and precious goods started again to circulate in both directions probably beginning in the late 10th cent. BC (Toumba cemetery, Lefkandi) and culminating in the 9th cent. BC.[14] Direct interactions between peoples became more intense and stable, encouraging reciprocal communication; whether this might have also stimulated a direct knowledge and fruition of the eastern monuments in their setting by Greek and Aegean components is certainly a more speculative issue but not to be dismissed.

For the first stage, we can isolate two phases, a first one (Iron Age IA-B: 12th–11th cent. BC) characterised by the continuation and gradual renewal of the Hittite artistic techniques, genres and traditions in monumental stone sculpture, and a second phase of active regeneration (Iron Age IC: 10th cent.).[15]

[12] Herrmann 2000, p. 267.

[13] See now the reappraisal of the question of the Assyrian and Syro-Hittite artistic interaction by Gilibert 2004 and Aro 2009.

[14] On the chronology of the materials from the single graves of the cemeteries of Lefkandi, see Kourou 2008.

[15] For the Iron IA-C periodization grounded on an evaluation of archaeological, artistic and historical data, see Mazzoni 2000a; Gilibert 2011, pp. 115–131, has now proposed a different phasing: an

Iron IA-B: a phase of continuity and renewal

The 12th–11th centuries, i.e., the post-crisis years, attest to a process of diffused urbanization consisting of activities of re-planning of the old centres and traditional monuments as well as new foundations in a vast area stretching from northern inner Syria, including the Amuq, and south-eastern Anatolia, where a few kings of Hittite dynastic origin resumed, at different levels and extension, territorial control of their regions (**Fig. 1**).[16] We know from the documentation that rebuilding operations also included architectural decoration; this was not a new trait but was not apparently exploited during the Hittite period with the same intensity and with the same variety of formal languages that we find in the post-Hittite phase.

Moreover, we also have to admit that an embarrassing absence of documentation for the final phase of the empire prevents any speculation on the real diffusion and amount of production of stone reliefs on the eve of the crisis years. In this scenario we can certainly produce the rather unique documentation of the quarry of Yesemek even with its questions of date, destination, reasons and time of final use and dismissal.[17] As a general comment, we can undoubtedly emphasize the fact that during the 13th cent. Hittite stone sculpture was a flourishing art in different contexts and genres as rock-cut monumental sculpture, architectural reliefs in urban gates and façades of buildings and in a variety of open-air settings vividly attest. We can also argue that in southern Anatolia (Yesemek) (**Fig. 2**) and northern Syria (Sikizlar) (**Fig. 3**), a distinct workshop was able to produce an impressive number of sculpted blocks for the decoration of gates with a high level of standardization.[18] Carving hard stones such as granitic rocks or basalts was, in fact, a genre mastered by Hittite artists and stonecutters, who adopted specialised metal instruments to this aim. We know of at least two other granite quarries in central Anatolia documenting for an earlier period the adoption of procedures for cutting the stone and preparing the rough relief, like those found in Yesemek.[19] Moving from the central plateau to the south and the Taurus regions, basalt was available and was currently exploited. This stone was also used in Syria in the Middle and Late Bronze periods to carve statues, stelae and a variety of reliefs. Basalt plain orthostats were also employed to protect the lower sections of the walls, occasionally alternated with white limestone orthostats to obtain a decorative effect.[20]

"archaic transitional period (12th to mid 10th cent.), an age of civic ritual (late 10th–early 9th) and a mature transitional period (870–790 BC.).

[16] Giusfredi 2010, pp. 37–44.

[17] Alkım 1974, Duru 2004, 2011.

[18] Mazzoni 1984, 1986–87, 2011, pp. 141–143.

[19] Summers 2007; Summers and Özen 2012.

[20] Harmanşah 2007.

Besides carving techniques and style, a further trait characterising Hittite monumental art was its setting in distinct open air landscapes in connection with the rituals performed therein. Three famous cases illustrate this tradition with their different styles, settings and functional and ideological intents; Yazılıkaya, Eflatun Pınar and Alaca Höyük.[21] In these three cases, the decoration consisted of carving solid walls and rock surfaces, resulting in a physical and ideological shaping of the urban and natural environment in a scenic landscape of strong visual and spatial impact. Decorated spaces were, therefore, the stage where the ritual acts were performed; sculptures and natural or urban environments with their spatial relations came to play a substantial role in visual communication.

Building and decorating special open-air settings for ritual activities represent a distinct architectural and artistic trait that apparently flourished towards the end of the imperial period, in the course of the 13th century and we can recognize the activity of specialised ateliers exploiting different stone quarries. The sculpture workshops operated under the patronage of the palace, sharing a common standardized repertory of images but maintaining individual styles. Alaca Höyük and Eflatun Pınar show quite distinct styles, probably to be recognized as regional variants more than chronological ones. Despite the trend towards centralising the artistic language on an institutional scale, regionalism must, in fact, have played a significant role in the development of the Hittite art, and local artistic traditions could emerge with their mastery of different genres according to the materials and media adopted.

This same regionalism in the style of stone sculpture played an even greater role at the beginning of Iron I (Iron IA-B: 12–11th cent.) when we can document different cases of architectural decoration of outer façades (Ain Dara), gates (Water Gate at Karkemish, Lion Gate at Malatya), as well as the innermost spaces of temples (Ain Dara, Aleppo).[22] We can, in fact, distinguish easily between the style of the reliefs of Malatya and Ain Dara despite the fact that both groups share lingering Hittite traits and again recognize as a further distinct style that seen in the older reliefs of the Aleppo cella. It is, instead, clear that the older reliefs from Karkemish show lingering Syrian traits. Exemplary of this stylistic differentiation is the case of the scene of the offering to the Storm God represented in the Malatya Lion Gate and the Karkemish Water Gate (**Fig.** 4 and **Fig.** 5):[23] they share the same scenic organisation and iconographic conventions, such as the bull carried to the sacrifice by an attendant, but differ in their style, i.e. in the formal language and figurative traits.

[21] See Emre 2002; Ehringhaus 2005, pp. 6–11, 14–31, 50–57; Sagona, Zimanski 2009, pp. 276–283, On the open-air sanctuaries, see Ökse 2011; Harmanşah 2011, pp. 634-638. For the reliefs of Alaca: Sievertsen 2008.

[22] Ain Dara: Abu 'Assaf 1990; Aleppo temple: Kohlmeyer 2008, 2009. See discussion on chronology and iconographies of the Malatya and Karkemish reliefs cited here in Mazzoni 1997a, 2000a; Orthmann 2002a, 2002b.

[23] Mazzoni 1997; Orthmann 2002a; See now Gilibert 2011, pp. 115–116.

Besides regional variants, chronological phasing, still to be assessed, also has to be considered for an evaluation of the artistic trends of this period. The Ain Dara and Aleppo temples were in use and decorated over a long period. The temple of Ain Dara reliefs can be safely attributed to the 13th (Ishtar-Shaushga; 1st style mountain gods), 12th (2nd style mountain gods) and 11th centuries (passing sphinxes and lions) (**Fig. 6**).[24] This chronology is now supported by the relevant documentation from the temple of the Storm God of Aleppo; K. Kohlmeyer has, in fact, convincingly compared the bull men of the two temples and proposed three stages of decoration for the Aleppo temple between the Late Bronze Hittite Imperial period, the 11th century (king Taita) and the 10th–9th centuries BC[25]

In the context of the transmission of artistic traditions and workmanship from the Hittite to the Syro-Hittite period and area, as noted earlier, the role of the sculpture workshop documented at Yesemek and operating also in Sikizlar is nodal. In both quarries we can document the same types of sculptures, the sphinx protome, the lion portal slab, and the same figurative conventions such as the sphinx headdress; similar also are the techniques for cutting the basalt and drafting the figures. In these quarries we may recognize the work of a single, possibly itinerant workshop, adopting Hittite conventions and style for the Hittite patrons on the eve of the crisis years. After the fall of the Hittite kingdom sculptors of this *atelier* might have moved towards the south where other patrons could have supplied new occasions for monumental decoration. The isolated case of Sikizlar can document this relocation to northern Syria.

Unfortunately, we ignore the role of Karkemish in this phase. The golden inlays indicate the circulation of Hittite pieces with their icons, which may have been imported or produced *in situ*.[26] The date Karkemish supplies its important artistic materials would be in the 12th/11th century, a period during which this capital was certainly a main centre of artistic revival and political and economic regeneration in northern Syria. The Water Gate was probably decorated over a fairly long span of time during this period, beginning with the older single orthostats with composite figures and the Storm God relief paralleling, as said above, the Malatya reliefs.

In the same phase we have the renewed decoration of the temple of Aleppo, which has been confidently dated to the 11th cent. by K. Kohlmeyer and D. Hawkins, thanks to the hieroglyphic inscription of Taitas, king of Palistin.[27] It is noteworthy that the architectural decoration was aptly adapted joining a new slab with the relief and inscription of Taitas adjacent to the older relief of the Storm god of Aleppo. Taitas had himself represented as paying homage to the god with the gesture of the

[24] Orthmann 1993; Mazzoni 2000b.
[25] Kohlmeyer 2008, 2009 and this volume.
[26] Seidl 1972.
[27] See now Hawkins 2009; 2011.

closed hand (**Fig.** 7), usually a praying enactment performed by Hittite kings.[28] The adoption of this gesture and the related protocol was clearly aimed at reinforcing the legitimacy of the king. Moreover, it is important that the performance and the gesture act as a strong visual reference to the old Imperial Hittite tradition.

Iron IC: a phase of regeneration and innovation

The second phase of the first stage belongs to the 10th century (Iron IC) and is better represented by the decorative friezes of the Suhis-Katuwas dynasty showing a new repertory of scenes and new stylistic and figurative conventions. The most notable innovation among the iconographies is the subject of the military triumph; this is depicted in the Long Wall of Sculpture in a continuous scene introduced by king Suhis, who leads his victorious army and follows the gods marching to the entrance of the Storm God temple. A variegated parade of worshippers, gods and composite monsters is also displayed on the walls which face the central *plaza* of the citadel and its gate, decorated by Katuwas in the late 10th cent. This same crowd of divinities can also be seen performing its visually appealing and protective role in the gates of Zincirli.

This phase attests to an efficacious renewal of the Syro-Hittite figurative language. Especially at Karkemish the images of the triumph in war with the parades of chariots and soldiers were a convincing form of visual propaganda employed by the local kings. It is noteworthy that the inscription of Suhis II (A1a), who probably led the triumphant parade (but whose image is not documented), refers precisely to the military victories of the ruler. This was, as D. Hawkins wrote:[29] "a building inscription with passages of historical narrative, the deeds of the ruler. It formed the text to the divine and military scenes portrayed on the Long Wall of Sculpture ". We can raise the question as to whether this was a Syrian trait and a reappraisal of a local Late Bronze Age subject documented in seals, such as in Emar, also deriving from older traditions,[30] or instead an Assyrian oriented element without direct comparisons in Assyria but not without references in literary sources of the time of Tiglath-pileser I and Tukulti-Ninurta II.[31] Whilst I find the first hypothesis more convincing, I am aware of the fact that the second cannot be ruled out simply because the Karkemish reliefs are chronologically antecedent to the Ashurnasirpal II freizes; only in these last reliefs,

[28] See comparison with the gesture by Muwatalli at Sirkeli, Ehringhaus 2005, fig. 175, p. 98.

[29] Hawkins 2000, pp. 87–91, Pls. 6-7. Denel 2007, pp. 189–191 and Gilibert 2011, p. 32. The procession of gods corresponds to the formula found the inscription (Hawkins 2000, p. 88, 3, §17–18): "and when I came forth, all these gods came forth with me" as suggested in Mazzoni 1997b, p. 297.

[30] As argued in Mazzoni 2005.

[31] The decoration of the palace of Tiglath-pileser I with his "royal deed " is alluded to in his inscriptions: Grayson 1991, pp. 55, 71–88, A.O.87.10. On the argument see Matthiae 1998, pp. 44–56; see the reconsideration by Aro 2009, pp. 15–17.

in fact, were narrative war scenes displayed with a variety and complexity unparalleled before and elsewhere.

We can, however, better perceive the original role of the contribution of the sculptors of Karkemish to the artistic language of their time by looking at the way they created new conventions for a direct and efficacious visual communication. Apparently Katuwas was the first ruler to be depicted in the attitude of speaking with the gesture of the hand folded at the mouth in full-length as an introductory *amu*-figure in the relief A13d (**Fig. 8**).[32] This gesture is, in fact, nothing more than the gesture represented in the hieroglyphic sign for EGO, *amu*, "I am,"[33] which opens the inscriptions of Katuwas of the portal orthostats A11a (A8), A11b+c (A9,10), A2+3 and the stele A12.[34] This hieroglyphic sign is present in with the inscription of Suhis on the left flank of portal lion A14a and of the stele of Kelekli, attributed by D. Hawkins to Suhis II (Fig. 9).[35] The sign is also present in the inscription of the funerary stele from Sheizar of Kupapiyas, wife of Taitas, probably the same person who dedicated the stele from Meharde.[36] This Taitas is now recognized by D. Hawkins as a later (hence Taitas II) successor, perhaps grandson, of Taitas (I) of the Aleppo Storm-God temple.[37] Moreover, it is in the Aleppo inscription of Taitas (I) that we find: "the archaic EGO-sign at the beginning of the text, which resembles that of the Hittite Empire period (bald-headed, ear below eye) rather than those of Iron Age inscriptions (cf. especially the EGO signs of the inscriptions of Suhis and Katuwas at Karkemish)," as Hawkins noted.[38]

However, we do not apparently have full images of the king in the gesture of the hand folded at the mouth before Katuwas; in inscriptions of later date, we have, instead, the small icon of the introductory *amu*-figure in full-length inside the inscription (**Fig. 10**).[39]

This image, therefore, has to be considered as an important innovation for representing the figure of the ruler. Being an adaptation from writing to visual imagery, it was intended to emphasize the communicative power of the image, i.e. the personage

32 Hawkins 2000, pp. 115–116, no. II.16, Pls. 24–25.

33 Laroche 1960, no. 1, pp. 1–2; Meriggi 1967, nos. 5, Restan, 6, Apamea, 8.1–3, Hama, pp. 14–18. Hawkins 2000, nos. IX.1, Hama 4; Hama 5–6 IX.3–4, Restan, Qal'at el Mudiq, pp. 403–409, Pls. 221–224.

34 Hawkins 2000, pp. 94–116, nos. II.9–15, Pls. 10–12, 14–15, 18–19.

35 Hawkins 2000, pp. 83–87, no. II. 4, Pls. 4–5 (A14a); pp.77, 92–93, Pl. 9. Giusfredi 2010, p. 49 has also argued for an attribution of the inscription of Kelekli to Suhis I.

36 Hawkins 2000, nos. IX.13–14, Pls. 225–228, pp. 415–419.

37 Hawkins 2011, pp. 51–53. The attribution of the stele of Meharde with the image of the «Goddess of the Heaven» under the winged sun to the same period as the Aleppo reliefs seems rather unconvincing to me for stylistic reasons. Also taking into consideration some degree of regionalism, a later date seems more adequate for the soft carving, and the images of the goddess and the lion.

38 Hawkins 2009, p. 171.

39 Laroche 1960, no. 2, p. 2. See the reliefs of Marash, Sheizar, Tuleil: Orthmann 1971, Pls. 44c, 54f.

represented. The gesture here becomes the visual expression of the act of the ruler speaking and telling his deeds to the audience; it makes his physical presence alive and purposeful. Moreover, the ruler is represented in full scale as a single distinct image and this is a further innovative trait. He is not worshipping a god, but is standing alone near his inscription.

Taitas was depicted in front of the Storm-god in the Aleppo temple in the gesture of adoration and respect, raising his fist before his face. He had himself represented adoring his god in his temple, as an act of due homage and legitimization. He then performed the same gesture of devotion adopted by the Hittite kings facing their gods. The royal personages in front of the bull and the altar and the Storm-God seated on his throne in the gate reliefs of Alaca Höyük, the personage facing an altar in a relief from Hattusha (**Fig. 11**), and the high ranking couple in the Tudhalija relief from Alalakh are all portrayed raising their closed hand with the thumb lifted up, as does Tudhalija embraced by Sharruma in Kammer B at Yazılıkaya.[40] In the relief at Sirkeli, king Muwatalli II is represented in this same gesture as if standing in worship of the gods.[41]

We can compare this gesture to the Assyrian *ubāna tarāṣu* gesture "stretching the finger",[42] known since the Old-Babylonian period in textual sources but whose visual representation is documented at the time of Tiglath-pileser I as a gesture of addressing the gods.[43] This conventional gesture was adopted by Ashurnasirpal II in his reliefs and stelae and also by the Aramaean king Kilamuwa, portrayed in his stela before the symbols of his gods and his inscription, and therefore emulating the Assyrian ritual protocols (**Fig. 12**).[44] The *ubāna tarāṣu* shown by a later king in his probably funerary stela, followed by his son, is then assumed as an indication of the act of adoration performed to the gods.[45]

In this context, the gesture performed by the kings of Karkemish assumes a special character of dignity and distinctiveness. It is an innovating trait of visual imagery intended to illustrate clearly, with an easily understandable image, the act of verbal communication as a real and individual performance but also as an act of self representation. The fact that the gesture refers to the author as addressing his story to the audience as a personal exaltation and monumental celebration, assumes, therefore,

[40] Bittel 1976, figs. 212, 214, 229, 231, 253; Ehringhaus 2005, figs. 3, 44.
[41] Ibidem, fig. 175.
[42] Magen 1986, pp. 45–55, 94–104.
[43] Magen 1986, p. 50; Pl. 21: 3.
[44] Orthmann 1971, p. 66, no. Zincirli E2, Pl. 63a. Brown 2008 for the political role of the image. Gilibert 2011, pp. 79–84, fig. 43; at p. 82 she argues for a derivation of this image from the hieroglyphic sign *amu*. Bunnens 2005 had already suggested that the small panels with the Assyrian king in the *ubāna tarāṣu* gesture joining the inscriptions in the stelae might have been modelled on the Luwian *amu* figures.
[45] Orthmann 1971, pp. 67–68, no. J/2, Pl. 66b.

a significance of great social and cultural transformation. While the Aramaean lords adopted imagery and protocols from their Assyrian kings and patrons for both emulation and submission, the Luwian-speaking lords could promote the creation of a distinct visual language of visual communication; this had the aim of offering an immediate perception and fruition of the portrayed personage and his ceremonial performance.

To this same purpose, figurative conventions were accordingly transformed in order to underline the physical and real appearance of the figures, gods, humans and composite monsters. Elsewhere we have noted that a few transformations for the rendering of the mane and the muscles of the legs were in progress in the front façade reliefs of Ain Dara, to be dated to the local third and last decorative phase.[46] The spade-shaped mane-hair rendering was changed to a flame-shaped rendering while a geometric stylization apparently seems to have been introduced for the leg muscles. The spiral rendering of the lion claws is a further stylistic marker of 12th–11th cent. Syro-Hittite sculpture. It is maintained in the Suhis and Astuwatimanzas portal lions, while the Herald's Wall, Processional Entry and King's Gate reliefs attest to the presence of a new convention.[47] It is, however, noteworthy that the lions represented at the sides of the base of the statue and grasped by their manes by a kneeling hero, found at corner of the Royal Buttress with the Processional Entry[48] and the lions grasped at the mane by the griffin-headed man of the base of Atarluhas in the inner side of the King's Gate[49] do present minor variations in the rendering of the claws, which are incised in the first case and, instead, well carved in the second example. It is also interesting to note that the first base presents minor inner inconsistencies in the rendering of the paws between the two lions represented, which can be fully appreciated only by direct examination in the Museum of Anatolian Civilization in Ankara. The left lion (when looking at) has in fact a paw with the spiral rendering, while the right one has the convention found in the Katuwas relief. This variation can be found exactly in the rendering of the paws of the lions on the base of the standing king which was buried outside the gate of the inner palace compound at Zincirli[50] and that can be recognized only by direct examination of the statue in the Archaeological Museum in Istanbul.

The variants in the rendering of the details of the animals' bodies would appear to attest that changes were in progress in the same workshop and a renewal of figurative conventions and physical details also accompanied the transformation of the

[46] Mazzoni 2000b, pp. 1046–1048.

[47] This might suggest an attribution of the Herald's Wall to the same time as the King's Gate and Processional Entry reliefs, i.e. the time of Katuwas. See Gilibert 2011, pp. 117–118.

[48] Orthmann 1971, pp. 40–41, 508, no. Karkemis F/17, Pl. 32d; see Akurgal 1949, Pl. 10a.

[49] Orthmann 1971, pp. 41, 512, no. Karkemis H/11 Pl. 32c,e; Akurgal 1949, Pl. 10b.

[50] Orthmann 1971, pp. 69, 545, no. Zincirli E/1, Pl. 62c,d,e. Gilibert 2011, pp. 76–79.

iconographic repertoire; style and formal values were gradually developing to suit the ideological goals of the visual representation.

A further element of innovation during this period consisted of the emergence of other media, minor arts and especially ivory working. Although we can actually attribute to the 9th century BC, i.e. Iron IIA in our terminology, the first *floruit* of ivory production with the so-called "Flame and Frond" group belonging to the north-Syrian tradition;[51] a 10th cent. BC date has also been proposed for the reappearance of this craft in the Levant. Comparisons between the Karkemish monumental sculpture and groups of ivories of this tradition have also supported the assumption that the city was a major centre of production of ivories as well as other minor and major arts.[52] A crucial problem concerning the appearance of ivory production is apparently the lack of documentation for the 12th–10th century period[53] which attests instead to the continuity of monumental stone sculpture. Different reasons may be argued for the disappearance or crisis of ivory working during the early Iron Age and the post-crisis years.

Shortage of the raw material and difficult access to the sources of supply due to unstable conditions might have been a further factor contributing to the decline of this luxury genre of art. We know in fact that during the Late Bronze Age hippopotamus tusks were mainly used for small objects of daily use while elephant ivory was instead destined for precious objects.[54] Whether the Syrian elephant, in the course of the Iron Age, was going to disappear in the region because of both deforestation and human exploitation is, however, a matter of debate;[55] references in the Assyrian sources indicate, in fact, that elephants were hunted in the period from Tiglath-Pileser I to Shalmaneser III in northern Syria, while after the reign of this king no more elephant hunts but only tusks are mentioned in the texts. If elephant hunting was not a mere narrative device but responded to actual events, no shortage of the material would have apparently affected northern Syria in Iron I. The reasons for the gap may be consequently searched for in other causes.

A principal motive was probably related to the economic and political downfall of the Levantine coastal centres patronising ivory manufacture, such as Ugarit with its palaces, which was one of the main centres of accumulation and possibly manufacture of ivories in the Late Bronze Age.[56] Even though historical sources provide the picture of a stable political scenario around 1100 BC, at least in the case of the Phoenician

[51] For the attribution, see Herrmann 1989; Winter 1989. See the re-evaluation by Gunter 2009, pp. 98–100. More recently the conference on ivories held at Pisa, Cecchini, Mazzoni, Scigliuzzo 2009.

[52] Winter 1983, pp. 186–187.

[53] Only the ivories from Tel Miqne.Ekron and from other Iron I Philistine sites (Ashdod, Ashkelon) apparently fill this gap: Ben-Shlomo, Dothan 2006.

[54] Caubet 2002, p. 108.

[55] A synthesis of this debate in Moorey 1994, pp. 117–118.

[56] Gachet-Bizollon 2007; Feldman 2009.

cities such as Byblos,[57] archaeological documents and objects of reliable dating are lacking for this period for northern Levant. This is unfortunate especially for ivory manufacture, which in the Phoenician, Intermediate and north Syrian styles shows many lingering traits of the Late Bronze Levantine productions, including distinct iconographies (the hero and griffin combat), figurative details (stylization of animal bodies, flames on the hindquarters), and typologies of objects decorated (furniture, pyxides), as H. J. Kantor first and more recently, A. Caubet have pointed out.[58] It is certainly true that the Philistine Iron I ivories can furnish a reliable missing link, but they offer a quite contradictory picture. A few ivories were probably residual from Late Bronze II, others show lingering Cananaean traits or instead a strong Egyptian orientation.[59] Noteworthy for our purposes is the lid with the row of bulls attacking winged griffins; iconography, posture of the animals in the combat and figurative conventions for the body details, such as the flames on the hindquarters, can be more easily compared with the Kantor's Mycenaeanizing Late Bronze production[60] than illustrate a regenerated Iron I production. The comparison with the ivory plaque from the tomb of Ahiram at Byblos with a lion and a griffin attacking a bull, characterized by similar style and conventions, is also contradictory in this case; this ivory shares, in fact, with the famous sarcophagus, the problem of the chronological attribution between a 13th or a 10th century BC date.[61]

Despite the many similarities that link the Late Bronze and the Iron Age ivories, it has been noted that a number of differences separate them in the sphere of the system of production. The diffusion of serial objects and classes of materials and stylistic groups in the Iron Age, resulting from a plurality of workshops and artistic centres, may reflect the change from a centralized, palace-based to a more decentralized production which might have also responded to the demands of a larger and foreign clientele.[62]

However, as stressed at the beginning, intensification of art production and plurality of art workshops were profoundly linked to the political fragmentation and the individual search by the art centres for a distinctive visual language of propaganda. This ideological and political intent can be evaluated more easily in monumental stone sculpture than in the minor arts, but the many subjects characterising minor objects such as ivory pyxides, horse-harnesses and furniture do belong to a symbolic

[57] Markoe 2000, pp. 26–29.

[58] Kantor 1956 emphasized the Aegean and Mycenaean stylistic and iconographic traits and the continuity from the Late Bronze to the Iron Age productions. See Caubet now 2008, pp. 411–412.

[59] Ben-Shlomo, Dothan 2006, pp. 27–31. Dothan 2003.

[60] Kantor 1956, pp. 166–167; Barnett 1982, p. 43.

[61] Barnett 1982, pp. 46–47, dates the plaque to the 10th cent. also on the base of its "*fin de siècle* manner, rather lifeless and uninspired".

[62] Feldman 2008, p. 447. For the commercial role of Phoenician ivories and arts, see Herrmann 2000, p. 269, quoting the interpretation of Barnett.

and ritual sphere of protection that was associated with the beneficial role of kingship.[63] The plurality of ivory workshops corresponds well to the plurality of stone sculpture ateliers. Differences in the iconographic repertories might have reflected the different finalities of the media and their use in different occasions and rituals, but they also responded to the distinct specialization of craftmanship between the genres, each provided with a proper repertory of images and figurative conventions.

To conclude, the reappraisal of ivory manufacture in the probably late 10th century[64] can be situated within a common artistic scenario characterized by an increase of genres, media and workshops which is better documented by the reliefs of the dynasty of Suhis-Katuwas at Karkemish, the contemporaneous reliefs at Zincirli, and the emergence of a distinct atelier in Guzana/Tell Halaf, each site and workshop being characterized by different artistic languages and styles.

The 10th century was, therefore, a period of major regeneration of the artistic language of Syro-Hittite monumental arts thanks to the active role of a few workshops, and especially the one documented at Karkemish. As a centre of art production and craftsmen, it was the place where it was possible "to forge an appropriate visual vocabulary ", as I. J. Winter has well pointed out,[65] absorbing external elements, and translating them into a distinctive style and language. Moreover, as a major trading centre, by exporting goods and craftsmen it was able to spread the new trends, thus exerting a seminal role and shaping a new Syro-Hittite art. The political and ideological intent and economic occasions of this development were certainly provided by the coming to power of the Suhis-Katuwas dynasty. Competition and emulation by the coeval partners of the fragmented political scenario of the area permitted a wide diffusion of this artistic language and its adaptation in new forms of expression of probably minor formal coherence but often vivid creativity.

Bibliography

Abu 'Assaf, 'A.
1990 *Der Tempel von 'Ain Dara*, Damaszener Forschungen 3. Mainz am Rhein: Verlag Philipp von Zabern.

Akurgal, E.
1949 *Spaethethitische Bildkunst*, Ankara Üniversitesi dil ve Tarih-Cografya Fakültesi Yayımları No. 60. Arkeoloji Enstitüsü No. 4. Ankara.

Alkim, B.
1975 *Yesemek Taşocagi ve Heykel Atelyesinde Yapilan Kazi ve Araştirmalar*, Türk Tarih Kurumu Yayınlarından V.Seri – Sa. 32, Ankara: Türk Tarih Kurumu.

[63] Protective and beneficial aspects of Assyrian kings have recently been investigated for the iconography of the Assyrian king and the sacred tree: Nevling Porter 2003, pp. 11–37; Giovino 2007, pp. 61–76.

[64] On the 10th cent. revival of ivory production see Barnett 1982, pp. 46–47.

[65] Winter 1983, pp. 195–197.

ARO, S.
2009 "The Origins of the artistic interactions between the Assyrian Empire and North Syria revisited", in *Of God(s), Trees, Kings, and Scholars. Neo-Assyrian and Related Studies in Honour of Simo Parpola*, Studia Orientalia 106, edited by M. Luukko, S. Svärd and R. Mattila, pp. 9–17. Helsinki:

BACHHUBER, CH. and ROBERTS, G. R., eds.
2009 *Forces of Transformation. The End of the Bronze Age in the Mediterranean. Proceedings of an international symposium held at St. John's College, University of Oxford 25–26th March 2006.* Oxford: Oxbow Books.

BELL, C.
2006 *The Evolution of Long Distance Trading Relationships across the LBA/Iron Age Transition on the Northern Levantine Coast. Crisis, Continuity and Change*, BAR International Series 1574. Oxford: Archaeopress.

BEN-SHLOMO, D., DOTHAN, T.
2006 "Ivories from Philistia: Filling the Iron Age Gap," *Israel Exploration Journal* 56/1: 1–38.

BIRNEY, K.
2008 "Tracking the Cooking Pot à la stéatite: Signs of Cyprus in Iron Age Syria," *American Journal of Archaeology* 112: 565–580.

BITTEL, K.
1976 *Les Hittites*. Paris: Editions Gallimard.

BRAUN-HOLZINGER, E. A. and MATTHÄUS, H., eds.
2002 *Die nahöstlichen Kulturen und Griechenland and der Wende vom 2. zum 1. Jahrtausend v. Chr. Kontinuität und Wandel von Strukturen und Mechanismen kultureller Interaktion*. Paderborn: Bibliopolis.

BROWN, B.
2008 "The Kilamuwa Relief: Ethnicity, class and power in Iron Age North Syria", in *Proceedings of the 5th International Congress on the Archaeology of the Ancient Near East*, edited by J. M. Cordoba et al., pp. 339–355, Madrid: Universidad Autonoma Ediciones.

BUNNENS, G.
2005 "From Carchemish to Nimrud. Between visual writing and textual illustration", in *Si un homme... Textes offerts en hommage à André Finet*, Subartu 16, edited by Ph. Talon and V. Van der Stede, pp. 21–23. Turnhout: Brepols.

CAUBET, A.
2002 "Le travail de l'ivoire au Levant, de la fin de l'Âge du Bronze au début de l'Âge du Fer: Continuité et rupture," in *Die nahöstlichen Kulturen und Griechenland and der Wende vom 2. zum 1. Jahrtausend v. Chr. Kontinuität und Wandel von Strukturen und Mechanismen kultureller Interaktion*, edited by E. Braun-Holzinger and H. Matthäus, pp. 109–116. Paderborn: Bibliopolis.
2008 "Ivory, Shell, and Bone," in *Beyond Babylon. Art, Trade, and Diplomacy in the Second Millennium BC*, edited by J. Aruz, K. Benzel, and J. M. Evans, pp. 406–418. New Haven and London: Yale University Press.

CECCHINI, S. M., MAZZONI, S., SCIGLIUZZO, E., eds.
2009 *Syrian and Phoenician Ivories of the Early First Millennium BCE: Chronology, Regional Styles and Iconographic Repertories, Patterns of Interregional Distribution*, Ricerche di Archeologia del Vicino Oriente 3. Pisa: Edizioni ETS.

COLLINS, P.
2008 *From Egypt to Babylon. The International Age 1550-500 BC*. London: The British Museum Press.

DENEL, E.
2007 "Ceremony and Kingship at Carchemish", in *Ancient Near Eastern art in context. Studies in honor of Irene J. Winter by her students,* Culture and History in the Ancient Near East 26, edited by J. Cheng and M. H. Feldman, pp. 179–204. Leiden – Boston: Brill.

DOTHAN, T.
2003 "A Decorated Ivory Lid from Tel Miqne-Ekron," *Eretz Israel* 27: 83–90.

DURU, R.
2004 *Yesemek. The largest sculpture workshop of the Ancient Near East.* Istanbul: Tursab.
2011 "Yesemek heykel atelyesi ile ilgili iki bulgu", in *Karadeniz'den Fırat'a bilgi üretimleri. Önder Bilgi'ye armağan yazılar / From the Black Sea to the Euphrates Knowledge Production. Studies Presented in honour of Önder Bilgi,* edited by A. Öztan, Ş. Dönmez, pp. 147–150, Ankara: Bilgin Kültür Sanat Yayinlari.

EHRINGHAUS, H.
2005 *Götter Herrscher Inschriften. Die Felsreliefs der hethitischen Großreichszeit in der Türkei,* Mainz am Rhein: Philipp von Zabern.

EMRE, K.
2002 "Felsreliefs, Stelen, Orthostaten," in *Die Hethiter und ihr Reich. Das Volk der 1000 Götter,* edited by Kunst- und Ausstellungshalle der Bundesrepublik Deutschland, pp. 218–233. Stuttgart: Konrad Theiss Verlag GmbH.

FELDMAN, M. H.
2002 "Luxurious Forms: Redefining a Mediterranean "International Style," ca. 1400–1200 BCE.," *Art Bulletin* 84: 6–29.
2006 *Diplomacy by Design: Luxury Arts and an "International Style" in the Ancient Near East, 1400–1200 BCE.* Chicago: University of Chicago Press.
2008 "The Legacy of Ivory-Working Traditions in the Early First Millennium BC," in *Beyond Babylon. Art, Trade, and Diplomacy in the Second Millennium BC,* edited by J. Aruz, K. Benzel, and J. M. Evans, pp. 445–448. New Haven and London: Yale University Press.
2009 "Classification and Contextualization of 2nd Millennium Ivories: The Case of Ugarit," in *Syrian and Phoenician Ivories of the Early First Millennium BCE: Chronology, Regional Styles and Iconographic Repertories, Patterns of Interregional Distribution,* Ricerche di Archeologia del Vicino Oriente 3, edited by S. M. Cecchini, S. Mazzoni, E. Scigliuzzo, pp. 337–352. Pisa: Edizioni ETS.

FISCHER, B., GENZ, H., JEAN, É., KÖROĞLU, K. , eds.
2003 *Identifying Changes: The Transition from Bronze to Iron Ages in Anatolia and its Neighbouring Regions. Proceedings of the International Workshop Istanbul, November 8-9, 2002, Istanbul.*

GADOT, Y.
2008 "Continuity and Change in the Late Bronze to Iron Age Transition in Israel's Coastal Plain: a Long Term Perspective," in *Bene Israel. Studies in the Archaeology of Israel and the Levant during the Bronze and Iron Ages in Honour of Israel Finkelstein,* Culture and History in the Ancient Near East 31, edited by A. Fantalkin and A. Yasur-Landau, pp. 55–73. Leiden-Boston: Brill.

GACHET-BIZOLLON, J.
2007 *Les ivoires d'Ougarit et l'art des ivoriers du Levant au Bronze Récent,* Ras Shamra-Ougarit XVI. Paris: Éditions Recherche sur les Civilisations.

GILIBERT, A.
2004 "Jenseits von Stil und Ikonographie. Späthethitische Einflüsse auf das assyrische Wandrelief," *Die Außenwirkung des späthethitischen Kulturraumes. Güteraustausch - Kulturkontakt - Kulturtransfer*, Alter Orient und Altes Testament 323, edited by M. Novak, F. Prayon, A.-M. Wittke, pp. 373–385. Münster: Ugarit Verlag.
2011 *Syro-Hittite monumental art and the archaeology of performance: The stone reliefs at Carchemish and Zincirli in the earlier First Millennium BCE*, Topoi. Berlin Studies of the Ancient World 2. Berlin - New York: De Gruyter.

GIOVINO, M.
2007 *The Assyrian Sacred Tree. A History of Interpretations*, Orbis Biblicus et Orientalis 230. Fribourg and Göttingen: Academic Press Fribourg and Vandenhoeck & Ruprecht.

GITIN, S., MAZAR, A., STERN, E., eds.
1998 *Mediterranean Peoples in Transition. Thirteenth to Early Tenth Centuries BCE. In Honor of Professor Trude Dothan.* Jerusalem: Keterpresses Enterprises Ltd.

GRAYSON, A. K.
1991 *Assyrian Rulers of the Early First Millennium BC 1 (1114-859 BC),* Royal Iscriptions of Mesopotamia, Assyrian Periods 2. Toronto: University of Toronto Press.

GIUSFREDI, F.
2010 *Sources for a Socio-Economic History of the Neo-Hittite States*, Texte der Hethiter 28. Heidelberg: Universitätsverlag Winter.

GUNTER, A. G.
2009 *Greek Art and the Orient.* Cambridge: Cambridge University Press.

HARMANŞAH, Ö.
2007 "Upright Stones and Building Narratives: Formation of a Shared Architectural Practice in the Ancient Near East," in *Ancient Near Eastern Art in Context. Studies in Honor of Irene J. Winter by Her Students*, Culture and History in the Ancient Near East 26, edited by J. Cheng, M. H. Feldman, pp. 69–95. Leiden, Boston: Brill.
2011 "Monuments and Memory: Architecture and Visual Culture in Ancient Anatolian History", in *Cambridge Handbook of the Bronze Age – Iron Age Mediterranean World*, edited by Sh. R. Steadman, G. McMahon, pp. 623–651. Cambridge: Cambridge University Press.

HARRISON, T. P. (ed.)
2006–2007 *Cyprus, the Sea Peoples and the Eastern Mediterranean: Regional Perspectives of Continuity and Change*, Scripta Mediterranea XXVII-XXVIII: Canadian Institute for Mediterranean Studies.

HAWKINS, J. D.
2000 *Corpus of Hieroglyphic Luwian Inscriptions. I. Inscriptions of the Iron Age.* Berlin-New York.
2009 "Cilicia, the Amuq, and Aleppo. New Light in a Dark Age," *Near Eastern Archaeology* 72/4: 164–173.
2011 "The inscriptions of the Aleppo temple", *Anatolian Studies* 61: 35–54.

HERRMANN, G.
1989 "The Nimrud Ivories, 1: The Flame and Frond School," *Iraq* LI: 85–109.

2000 "Ivory Carving of first millennium workshops, traditions and diffusion", in *Images as Media. Sources for the cultural history of the Near East and the Eastern Mediterranean (1st millennium BCE)*, Orbis Biblicus et Orientalis 175, edited by Ch. Uehlinger, pp. 267–282. Fribourg and Göttingen: Academie Press Fribourg and Vandenhoeck & Ruprecht.

JASMIN, M.
2006 *L'étude de la transition du Bronze récent II au Fer I en Palestine méridionale*, BAR International Series 1495. Oxford: Archaeopress.

KANTOR, H. J.
1956 "Syro-Palestinian Ivories," *Journal of Near Eastern Studies* XV: 153–174.

KILLEBREW, A. E.
2005 *Biblical Peoples and Ethnicity. An Archaeological Study of Egyptians, Canaanites, Philistines, and Early Israel, 1300-1100 BCE.*, Archaeology and Biblical Studies, n. 9. Atlanta.

KOHLMEYER, K.
1983 "Felsbilder der hethitischen Großreichszeit," *Acta Praehistorica et Archaeologica* 15: 7–153.

2008 "Zur Datierung der Skulpturen von 'Ain Dara," in *Fundstellen. Gesammelte Schriften zur Archäologie und Geschichte Altvorderasiens ad honorem Hartmut Kühne*, edited by D. Bonatz, R. M. Czichon and F. Janoscha Kreppner, pp. 119–130. Wiesbaden.

2009 "The Temple of the Storm God in Aleppo during the Late Bronze and Early Iron Ages," *Near Eastern Archaeology* 72/4: 190–202.

KOUROU, N.
2008 "The Evidence from the Aegean," in *Beyond the Homeland: Markers in Phoenician Chronology*, Ancient Near Eastern Studies, Supplement 28, edited by in C. Sagona, pp. 305–364. Leuven-Paris-Dudley, Ma: Peeters.

LAROCHE, E.
1960 *Les hiéroglyphes Hittites*. Paris: Éditions du Centre Nationale de la Recherche Scientifique.

LEHMANN, G.
2007 "Decorated Pottery Styles in the Northern Levant during the Early Iron Age and their Relationship with Cyprus and the Aegean," *Ugarit Forschungen* 39: 487–550.

LIVERANI, M.
2008 "The Late Bronze Age: Materials and Mechanisms of Trade and Cultural Exchange," in *Beyond Babylon. Art, Trade, and Diplomacy in the Second Millennium BC*, edited by J. Aruz, K. Benzel, and J. M. Evans, pp. 161–168. New Haven and London: Yale University Press.

MAGEN, U.
1986 *Assyrische Königdarstellungen – Aspekte der Herrschaft*, Baghdader Forschungen 9. Mainz am Rhein: Verlag Philipp von Zabern.

MARKOE, G. E.
2000 *Phoenicians*. Berkeley-Los Angeles: University of California Press.

MATTHIAE, P.
1998 *Ninive*. Milano: Electa.

MAZZONI, S.
1984 "Sikizlar: una cava d'età siro-ittita," *Studi Micenei ed Egeo-Anatolici* XXIV: 233–243.

1986-87 "A Sculptures Quarry at Sikizlar," *Annales Archéologiques Arabes Syriennes* XXXVI–XXXVII: 268–272.

1997a "The Gate and the City: Change and Continuity in Syro-Hittite Urban Ideology," in *Die Orientalische Stadt: Kontinuität-Wandel-Bruch*, Kolloquien der Deutschen Orient-Gesellschaft 1, edited by G. Wilhelm, pp. 307–338. Halle: SDV Saarbrücker Druckerei und Verlag.

1997b "L'arte siro-ittita nel suo contesto archeologico," *Contributi e Materiali di Archeologia Orientale* 7, pp. 287–327.

2000a "Syria and the Periodization of the Iron Age. A Cross-Cultural Perspective," in *Essays on Syria in the Iron Age*, Ancient Near Eastern Studies Supplement 7, edited by G. Bunnens, pp. 31–59. Louvain: Peeters.

2000b "Crisis and Change: The Beginning of the Iron Age in Syria," in *Proceedings of the First International Congress on the Archaeology of the Ancient Near East,* edited by P. Matthiae, A. Enea, L. Peyronel, F. Pinnock, pp. 1043–1055. Roma: Università di Roma La Sapienza.

2005 "Narrare il trionfo nell'arte siro-ittita," in *Narrare gli Eventi,* Studia Asiana 3, edited by F. Pecchioli Daddi and M. C. Guidotti, pp. 233–243. Roma: Herder.

2006 "Réflexion sur l'espace architectural de la période syro-hittite," in *Les espaces syro-mésopotamiens. Dimensions de l'expérience humaine au Proche-Orient ancien. Volume d'hommage offert à Jean-Claude Margueron*, Subartu 17, pp. 231–251. Turnhout: Brepols.

2011 "Urban Landscapes of the Syro-Hittites Capitals", *Mesopotamia* XLVI: 137–156.

MERIGGI, P.

1967 *Manuale di Eteo Geroglifico, Parte II: Testi -1° Serie*, Incunabula Graeca XIV, Roma: Edizioni dell'Ateneo.

MOOREY, P. R. S.

1994 *Ancient Mesopotamian Materials and Industries. The Archaeological Evidence.* Oxford: Oxford University Press.

NEVLING PORTER, B.

2003 *Trees, Kings, and Politics. Studies in Assyrian Iconography*, Orbis Biblicus et Orientalis 197. Fribourg and Göttingen: Academic Press Fribourg and Vandenhoeck & Ruprecht.

ÖKSE, T.

2011 "Open-Air Sanctuaries of the Hittites", in *Insights into Hittite History and Archaeology*, Colloquia Antiqua 2, edited by H. Genz, D. P. Mielke, pp. 218–240. Leuven: Peeters.

ORTHMANN, W.

1971 *Untersuchungen zur Späthethitischen Kunst,* Saarbrücker Beiträge zur Altertumskunde 8. Bonn.

1993 "Zur Datierung des Ištar-Reliefs aus Tell 'Ain Dara," *Istanbuler Mitteilungen* 43: 245–251.

2002a "Die Bildkunst im Übergang von der Großreichszeit zur späthethitischen Periode", in *Die nahöstlichen Kulturen und Griechenland and der Wende vom 2. zum 1. Jahrtausend v. Chr. Kontinuität und Wandel von Strukturen und Mechanismen kultureller Interaktion*, edited by E.A. Braun-Holzinger and H. Matthäus, pp. 153–159. Paderborn: Bibliopolis,

2002b "Kontinuität und Einflüsse. Die Entwicklung der späthethischen Kunst zwischen 1200 und 700 v. Chr.," in *Die Hethiter und ihr Reich. Das Volk der 1000 Götter*, pp. 274–279. Stuttgart: Konrad Theiss Verlag GmbH.

PEDRAZZI, T.

2007 *Le giare da conservazione e trasporto del Levante. Uno studio archeologico dell'economia fra Bronzo Tardo II e Ferro I (ca. 1400-900 a.C.,* Ricerche di Archeologia del Vicino Oriente 2. Pisa: Edizioni ETS.

RENFREW, C. ed.
1973 *The explanation of culture change: models in prehistory*. London: Gerald Duckworth and Co. Ltd.

SAGONA, A. and ZIMANSKY, P.
2009 *Ancient Turkey*. New York: Routledge.

SEIDL, U.
1972 "Lapisreliefs und ihre Goldfassungen aus Karkamiş," *Istanbuler Mitteilungen* 22: 15–43.

SCHLOEN, D. and FINK A. S.
2009 "Searching for Ancient Sam'al: New Excavations at Zincirli in Turkey," *Near Eastern Archaeology* 72/4: 203–219.

SIEVERTSEN, U.
2008 "Visual images of the Sphinx Gate at Alaca Höyük," in *Proceedings of the 4th International Congress of the Archaeology of the Ancient Near East*, Volume 1, edited by H. Kühne, R. M. Czichon, and F. Janoscha Kreppner, pp. 571–582. Wiesbaden: Harrassowitz Verlag.

SUMMERS, G.
2007 "A Hittite Quarry and Sculpture Workshop at Karaziz Kasabasi," *Kerkenes* 10: 8–11.

SUMMERS, G. D. and ÖZEN E.
2012 "The Hittite Stone and Sculpture Quarry at Karakiz Kasabası and Hapis Boğazı in the District of Sorgun, Yozgat, Central Anatolia", *American Journal of Archaeology* 116: 507–519.

WARD, W. A., SHARP JOUKOWSKI, M., eds.
1992 *The Crisis Years: The 12th Century BC From Beyond the Danube to the Tigris*, Dubuque, Iowa: Kendall/Hunt Publishing Company.

VENTURI, F.
2007 *La Siria nell'età delle trasformazioni (XIII-X sec. a.C.). Nuovi contributi dallo scavo di Tell Afis*, Studi e Testi Orientali 8, Serie Archeologica 1, Bologna: CLUEB.
2009 *Societies in Transition in the Northern Levant between Late Bronze Age II and Early Iron Age. Papers Presented on the Occasion of the 20th Anniversary of the New Excavations in Tell Afis, Bologna 15th November 2007*, Studi e Testi Orientali 9, Serie Archeologica 2. Bologna: CLUEB.

WARD, W. A., SHARP JOUKOWSKI, M. eds.
1992 *The Crisis Years: The 12th Century B.C. From Beyond the Danube to the Tigris*, Dubuque, Iowa: Kendall/Hunt Publishing Company.

WINTER, I. J.
1983 "Carchemish *Ša Kišad Puratti*," *Anatolian Studies* XXXIII: 177–197.
1989 "North Syrian Ivories and Tell Halaf Reliefs: the Impact of Luxury Goods upon "Major' Arts," in *Essays in Ancient Civilization presented to H. J. Kantor*, SAOC 47, edited by A. Leonard Jr., B. Beyer Williams, pp. 321–332. Chicago: The Oriental Institute of the University of Chicago.

WOOLLEY, C. L.
1921 *Carchemish Vol. II: The Town Defenses*. London: The Trustees of the British Museum.

YASUR-LANDAU, A.
2010 *The Philistines and Aegean Migration at the End of the Bronze Age*. Cambridge: Cambridge University Press.

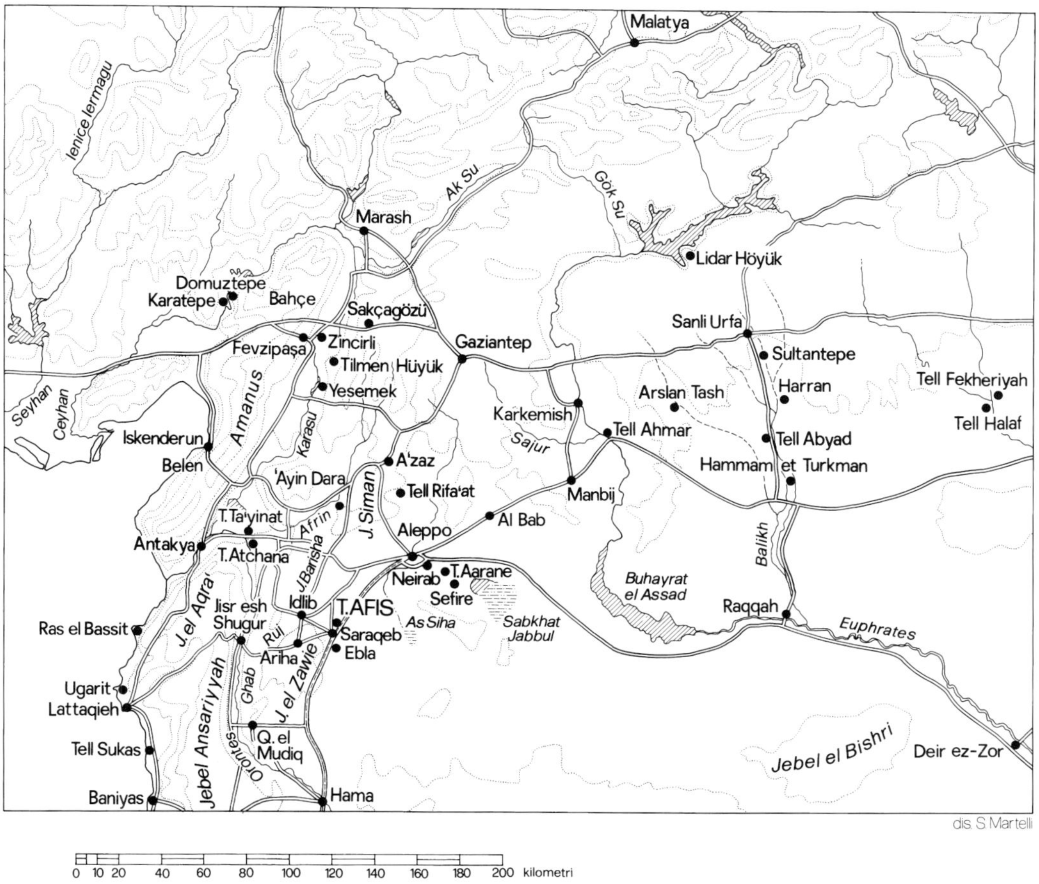

Fig. 1 Map of Syria and Anatolia in Iron Age, drawn by S. Martelli.

Fig. 2 Sphinx at Yesemek, after Alkim 1975, Fig. 88.

Fig. 3 Sphinx at Sikizlar, photo 1978 by the author.

Fig. 4 Melid, Lion Gate, relief, after Orthmann 1971, Fig. 41f.

Fig. 5 Karkemish, Water Gate, relief, after C.L. Woolley, *Carchemish. Report on the Excavations at Jerablus on Behalf of the British Museum. Part II. The Town Defences*, London 1921, Pl. B30a.

Fig. 6 Ain Dara, decoration of the outer podium, photo by the author.

Fig. 7 Aleppo, relief of Taita, after Gonnella, Khayyata, Kohlmeyer 2005, Fig. 126.

Fig. 8 Karkemish, relief A13d, after Woolley 1921, Pl. A 13d.

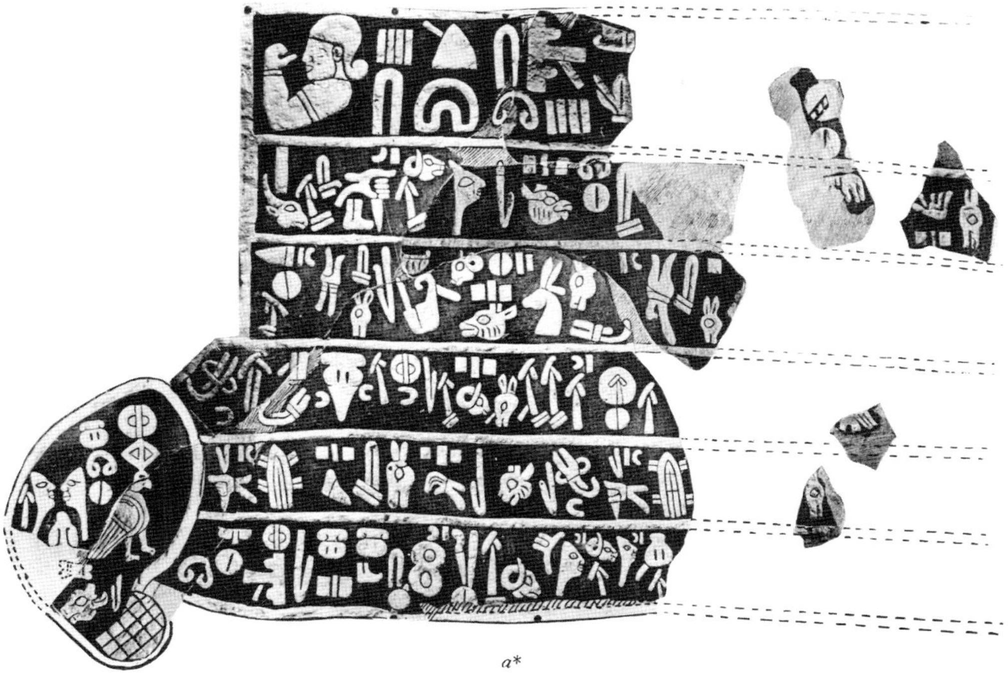

Fig. 9 Karkemish, inscription A14a, after Woolley 1921, Pl. A 14a*.

Fig. 10 Marash,
inscription on a statue,
after Orthmann 1971, Pl. 44c.

Fig. 11 Relief from Alalakh,
after Bittel 1976, Fig. 231.

Fig. 12 Relief and inscription of Kilamuwa, Zincirli, after F. von Luschan, *Ausgrabungen in Sendschirli. IV*, Berlin 1911, Fig. 273.

CHAPTER 21

THE LUWIAN INSCRIPTIONS FROM THE TEMPLE OF THE STORM-GOD OF ALEPPO

J. David HAWKINS
School of Oriental and African Studies,
University of London, London WC1H 0XG, U.K.

Excavations begun on the Citadel of Aleppo in 1996 rapidly began to uncover the famous Temple of the Storm-God[1]. In 2003–2005 two substantial Hieroglyphic Luwian inscriptions were excavated: a complete one accompanying the figure of a king in the east wall (ALEPPO 6), and a broken one on a lion and a sphinx from the south entrance (ALEPPO 7). The author of the inscriptions was Taita King of Palistin (as now read), who was also responsible for a recognizable phase of remodelling the Temple interior.

ALEPPO 6 consists of the dedication of the Temple, and ALEPPO 7, mentioning Karkamiš and Egypt, would have been more important, but not enough of it has yet been recovered to yield connected sense. Palaeographically the inscriptions date to the 11th century BC approximately and constitute important documentation for an otherwise "dark age". Taita's kingdom Palistin, probably based in the Amuq at Tell Tayinat (Harrison, this volume), is revealed as a major power of the period. A possible link with the Philistines and the spread of Mycenaean IIIC pottery is suggested.

Our Symposium focuses on the period between the collapse of the Late Bronze Age kingdoms of south-east Anatolia and north Syria and the subsequent emergence of the Iron Age states in this area. The key events of the period are the dissolution of the Hittite Empire, the destruction of its imperial vassals in Syria, and the retreat of Assyria and Egypt from regional involvement. The totality of the collapse is suggested by the disappearance of written records for the period c. 1200–1000 BC: the end of the cuneiform tablet archives of the imperial capital Hattusa and the subsidiary archives of its Syrian dependencies such as Ugarit and Emar, and the silence of Assyrian and Egyptian annals recording their military incursions. Only the stray shaft of light from Assyria or Egypt hints at conditions in these years: Tiglath-pileser I's campaign(s) in the West and the Wen-Amun narrative.

[1] Kohlmeyer, 2009; This paper is a shortened and updated version of J. D. Hawkins, "Cilicia, the Amuq and Aleppo" (*Near Eastern Archaeology* 72/4 (2009), pp. 164–173), where more detailed references may be found; and for cited inscriptions see my *Corpus of Hieroglyphic Luwian Inscriptions*.

Thus the period has been regarded as a "dark age" lasting until the reviving states known as Neo-Hittite begin to provide documentation in the form of Hieroglyphic Luwian inscriptions. The dating of this revival has been difficult to establish, and it has been considered to be not earlier than c. 900 BC, but it is probable that the inscriptions of Karkamiš with neighbouring Tell Ahmar and of Maraş, recording several generations of rulers, do extend well back into the 10th century BC.

A unique document showing unmistakably archaic features is the stele KARAHÖYÜK (Elbistan), and its original dating to the 12th century BC, thus to the heart of the Dark Age, has been generally accepted. It records the visit of a "Great King" to Elbistan, who, finding the city "empty" (devastated), undertook, insofar as we can understand the text, restoration works. The stele was set up by a subordinate, who was likewise active in the land, building, setting up the cult and administering. The king and his minister seem to have come from outside Elbistan, probably from Tabal. A similar record of finding devastation and proceeding with restoration can be read on MARAŞ 8, an archaic-looking stele which was probably the foundation monument of the Maraş dynasty, dating c. 1000–950 BC. The two documents must refer to actual conditions obtaining at the time in Elbistan and Maraş.

Quite unconnected with the KARAHÖYÜK stele is the group of inscriptions of the rulers of Malatya from the site of Arslantepe and its environs. These have been securely dated and contextualized by the discovery of impressions of the seal of Kuzi-Teššub, king of Karkamiš, a fifth-generation descendant of Suppiluliuma I, and the subsequent recognition of his name as grandfather in inscriptions of two Malatya rulers, brothers (the inscriptions of one grandson were set up by his own grandson, the fourth-generation descendant of Kuzi-Teššub). These rulers' inscriptions record their building of cities (GÜRÜN, DARENDE) and a road (KÖTÜKALE). The king whose name appears on the sculptures of the Lion Gate is a namesake of Kuzi-Teššub's son and great-grandson, so may be identified as either of these or yet another ruler of a further generation.

The Malatya Lion Hunt stele with inscription MALATYA 1 names three more generations of rulers, in which the grandfather was the author of the IZGIN stele, recording the colonization of the plain of Elbistan by Malatya. We thus have a minimum of seven generations descending from Kuzi-Teššub, which must extend down well into the 11th century BC. We also gather that the Malatya dynasty, bearing the title "Country Lords" rather than kings, though claiming descent from Kuzi-Teššub, must have split from the kingdom of Karkamiš.

Tiglath-pileser I (1114–1076 BC), the only Assyrian king before Assurnaşirpal II to record campaigns across the Euphrates, encountered Milidia (Malatya) in his fourth year and again later in his reign under a king Allumari, whose name does not appear in the MALATYA inscriptions. Tiglath-pileser regarded Milidia as being in the "great land Hatti". On his return from an expedition to the Mediterranean, he took tribute from Ini-Teššub, king of Hatti, i.e. of Karkamiš, who bearing the famous name of Kuzi-Teššub's grandfather was probably himself descended from those two kings. Beyond this we have no information of events in Karkamiš until the earliest group of the city's inscriptions begin, the work of a four-generation line of "Country-Lords", the "house of Suhi", not precisely datable but as noted above probably falling within the 10th century BC. From their inscriptions we see that these Country-Lords coexisted in the city with a line of "Great Kings", perhaps late descendants of Kuzi-Teššub, but to judge from the inscriptions and associated sculpture, it must have been the Country-Lords who exercised the actual power.

On the Anatolian plateau the recent discovery of two inscriptions of Tudhaliya IV, the Bronze Tablet treaty and the Hieroglyphic Luwian inscription of YALBURT (both published in 1988) have provided dating criteria and content for later monuments, specifically the KARADAĞ-KIZILDAĞ group of inscriptions (including BURUNKAYA) and the KARAHÖYÜK (Elbistan) stele. The treaty's revelation of the size and importance of the LBA kingdom of Tarhuntassa suggests that Great King Hartapu, son of Great King Mursili, of KARADAĞ-KIZILDAĞ, may have ruled a successor state to Tarhuntassa as a surviving descendant of the dynasty of Hattusa at a date not long after its disappearance (12th century BC?). The Great King of KARAHÖYÜK who came to Elbistan also seems likely to have belonged in this Tabalian dynastic and epigraphic tradition.

No further historical reference for Tabal is known, until Shalmaneser III in 836 BC passing through the land, north to south (Kayseri-Niğde) encountered the king Tuatti and twenty other kings. No native inscriptions from the country however have been found until the quite extensive group from the later 8th century BC. Among these is the long rock inscription of Wasusarma Great King, son of Tuwati Great King (TOPADA), and inscriptions of servants of both from the neighbourhood of Kululu (KULULU 1, SULTANHAN, KAYSERİ). Whence comes this claim of Great Kingship? We may perhaps envisage some dynastic continuity, real or pretended, between LBA Tarhuntassa and Iron Age Tabal across the blank centuries.

Another recent discovery may suggest a similar sequence and continuity in Cilicia. The ÇİNEKÖY bilingual[2] permits the identification of its author Warika king of Hiyawa with KARATEPE's Awariku king of Adanawa, and with Urikki king of Que named in the inscriptions of Tiglath-pileser III and Sargon II in the period c. 738–710 BC. He claims descent from Muksa (MPŠ). The derivation of the toponym Hiyawa/Que from Hittite Ahhiyawa on the one hand, and its association on the other with Herodotus' statement that the Cilicians were earlier known as the Hypachaeoi, suggests a degree of historicity to the classical tradition that after the Trojan War (12th century BC) Mopsos (Moxos) led his followers from western Anatolia to

[2] Tekoğlu and Lemaire 2000.

Pamphylia and Cilicia founding cities *en route*. That the 8th century royal house of Cilicia should remember this figure as the founder of their line suggests the preservation of historical tradition here too in Cilicia as in Tabal.

Thus we see that in the main centres of the Early Iron Age, Malatya, Karkamiš, Tabal and Cilicia, sparse pieces of evidence hint at some form of dynastic continuity and tradition from the LBA Hittite Empire across largely undocumented centuries. It is entirely possible however that new Hieroglyphic Luwian inscriptions of this period parallel to the KARAHÖYÜK stele may in future appear, either from regular excavation or by chance discovery. Indeed just such a group of inscriptions with momentous information relating to the Amuq and north Syria as far as the Euphrates and south to the area of Hama has recently been found, namely the Aleppo Temple inscriptions, excavated in 2003–2005, as documented by Kohlmeyer.[3]

Of these inscriptions ALEPPO 4 (discovered earlier) is the epigraph identifying the Storm- and Stag-God figures in the middle of the row of reliefs adorning the north wall of the cella, and ALEPPO 5 the epigraph attached to the Storm-God of Aleppo in the middle of the east wall. The main inscriptions are ALEPPO 6, a complete inscription accompanying the King facing the God in the middle of the east wall; and ALEPPO 7, two parts of a broken inscription on a lion (frag. A) and a sphinx (frag. B) on the west side of the monumental south entrance of the cella.

ALEPPO 5. This relief epigraph identifying the figure of the Storm-God must be contemporary with the figure, which is dated by the excavator to the Hittite Empire period. The same writing is found on two other Empire period monuments, both times identifying the Storm-God in his eagle-chariot drawn by bulls: (1) the great seal of Mursili III (Urhi-Teššub), *Bo.-Ha.* XXIII, no. 57.; (2) the IMAMKULU rock-relief. This icon of the Storm-God in his bull-drawn eagle-chariot is found also in the Aleppo Temple in the middle of the north wall accompanied by the epigraph ALEPPO 4 (1), "GOD.MACE". The epigraph ALEPPO 5 was already interpreted from the other occurrences as "Storm-God of Aleppo", to be read in Hittite *Tarhunna Halpuma* [4] and the fact that this is only attested as a Hittite Empire writing supports the excavator's dating of the piece. The Luwian equivalent *Tarhunza Halpawani* appears in the post-Empire Hieroglyphic Luwian inscriptions, including now ALEPPO 6.

ALEPPO 6. This incised 11-line inscription is placed on the slab with the King's figure, beginning in the space in front of his head and continuing behind it, and then on the doubly-rebated slab behind him, running boustrophedon and terminating a short distance into line 11. Among its peculiarities are some clear dating criteria: (1) the consistent use of the graphic practice known as initial-*a*-final; (2) the clear

[3] Kohlmeyer 2009.
[4] Hawkins 2003, pp. 169ff.

use of *zi+a* for *za* and *i(a)* for *ia* as well as *i*; (3) the use of the "*crampon*" (L.386) not as word-divider but as determinative. All these practices originate as Empire period usage and persist only into the early part of the Late period, the 10th century BC at latest.

A detailed discussion of the dating, with transliteration, translation and commentary, also copy and photographs appears in *Anatolian Studies* 61 (2011). Here I give only a translation, with a note on the toponym.

§1. I (am) King Taita, the Hero, Palistin-ean King.
§2. For my lord, Halabean Tarhunza, I honoured the image,
§3. Halabean Tarhunza made me [...].
§4. (He) who comes to this Temple to celebrate the god,
§5. if he (is) a king,
§6. let him sacrifice an ox and a sheep.
§7. On the other hand if he is a ... king's son,
§8. or he (is) a country-lord,
§9. or he (is) a river-country lord,
§10. let him too sacrifice a sheep.
§11. On the other hand if he (is) an inferior man,
§12. (there shall be) bread, oblation and ....

Note. Palistin-ean (*pa-lá/í-sà-ti-*[*ní*]*-za-sa*): the sign *lá/í*, formerly read ta_5, has now been convincingly re-read.[5] Note also ALEPPO 7, §1, ...]*-sà-ti-ní-za-sa*, where the name of Taita with the same titulary may be restored.

ALEPPO 7. In the Temple's south entrance the preserved west side of the portal was decorated with figures: from the interior outwards, a row consisting of a fish-man relief, and a lion protome and a sphinx protome both facing across the entrance passage, then a lion now in fragments facing outwards. The base slabs show that this lion and the sphinx protome abutted each other at a right angle. The lion's right side and the sphinx's left side show inscribed areas which must have combined to make a single inscription. The sphinx's 12-line inscription is almost complete. Its right edge, ll.4-12, is formed by a rosette of the sphinx's cap and its hair-lock and ear; ll.1-2 were extended rightwards on to the sphinx's cap and survive as a still detached fragment; its left edge is formed by an incised vertical ridge where the lion figure would have butted in. What survives of the left part of the inscription is on the lion's neck and shoulder, its preserved left edge formed by the curls of the lion's mane, ll.3, 4+5, 6+7, 8, 10, 12+15. The amount of text lost on the still missing body of the lion can be estimated with reasonable accuracy.

[5] See Rieken and Yakubovich 2010, pp. 199–219, esp. 216.

The text began on the lost (lion) A l.1, running dextroverse on to (sphinx) B l.1, continuing boustrophedon, and ending on A l.13 (B l.13 is uninscribed). No obvious sense or context between the two preserved sides of the text can be observed, and it is broken into short, largely unintelligible fragments by the loss. Additionally some unknown words obscure the sense.

The text shows the same graphic features and peculiarities as ALEPPO 6, and is clearly the same date. The preservation of the end part of the same titulary as ALEPPO 6 indicates that its author was also Taita, though his name is lost.

The text is fully published with ALEPPO 6 in *Anatolian Studies* 61 (2011). Here only the translation and some explanatory notes are given.

§1. [I (am) Taita …Pali]stin-ean Hero, King.
§2. […] from the city Karkamiš from the bed-chamber (?)/treasury (?) forth […] I went (?)
§3. The god(dess) Ku[baba(?) …
…
§4. and him/her […
…
§5. (to) me …[…
§6. But if the scribe
…
§7. …] he/they brought mule(s) (to/from) the land Egypt
§8. and (to) me(?) …
…
§9. …] I will make run.
§10. These my last […
…
§11.] to his lord and to his … […
…
§12. …] to the land.
§13. That scribe […
…
§14. …] let him/them run.
§15. […
…
§16. …] … […
…
§17. …] forth […
…
§18. …] ninety … child (and) man Halpa […

...

§19. ...

Notes. As may be seen, apart from the restorable titulary, only §§2 and 7 preserve anything approaching intelligible sense.

§2. As noted ll.1-2 were extended rightwards on to the sphinx's cap and this survives as a fragment separated by a short gap from the main text, where what is probably the verb of the clause is preserved.

"from the city Karkamis" ([*k*]*ar-ka-mi-sà-ti* (U[RBS]), is clear enough, preceded by a gap sufficient for a single word.

"from the bed-chamber(?)/treasury" ((DOMUS) sa_5-sa_5-*tà-ti*): this word, also in the ablative case, bears a striking resemblance to Hitt. É.ŠÀ *sastas*, "bed-chamber". If this sense be thought improbable in the context, the double use of the "seal" sign (sa_5) might suggest the recognition of a word *sasa*(*n*)*ta*-, "seal-house, treasury" (Hitt. É.^{NA4}KIŠIB/*siyannas per*).

"forth" (PRAE ...), followed by a gap for 1-2 words

pa-zi/*a-i*(*a*)-*ha*, probably the verb of the clause, perhaps the same as the known ("PES_2")*paza*-, "go".

§3. DEUS.*ku*[...]: the collocation of those signs in the context of *Karkamis* suggests a restoration [+AVIS-*pa-pa*], "Kubaba".

§7. "the land Egypt" (*MÍ*.REGIO): the understanding of this writing thus is based on the writing ("*MÍ*.REGIO")*mi-za+ra*/*i*(URBS), "Mizri", i.e. Egypt (KARKAMIŠ A6, §4).

"mule(s)", $ASINUS_{2A}$-*ni*: the equid head appears in the form usual on Empire inscriptions (YALBURT blocks 2 and 13) and seals, read *tarkasni*-. A case ending is expected (acc. plur. MF) but absent.

"he/they brought" ((PES)*u-sa-tá*), attested in Late inscriptions.

The Aleppo Temple inscriptions, ALEPPO 6 and 7, may be dated by the archaic features of their palaeography to the 11th century BC (±), falling thus squarely into the period considered a dark age. Their author, Taita Palistin-ean King, has the same name and titles as Taita author of the MEHARDE stele, attested also on his wife's stele SHEIZAR, where his kingdom appears as Walistin. The toponym was also known from a fragment of inscription found at Tell Tayinat in the Amuq, thus assumed to be the Hieroglyphic Luwian name of that city and kingdom. Recently it has reappeared on the two ARSUZ stelae (see A. and B. Dinçol, paper read at this symposium).

ALEPPO 6 and 7 show striking palaeographic similarities with MEHARDE-SHEIZAR indicating a close connection, yet a recent observation has noted one significant difference. The use of the Hieroglyphic sign "crampon" (L.386) as a determinative was cited above as an archaic feature of ALEPPO 6 and 7, as against the Late usage as word-divider as seen in KARKAMIŠ inscriptions from the 10th century onwards. Both MEHARDE and SHEIZAR show the latter usage, which must alert us to the possibility that Taita of these inscriptions may not be the same king as Taita of ALEPPO 6, as I had assumed, but a later ruler, perhaps his grandson.

However this may be, the discovery of ALEPPO 6 and 7 suggests the existence of a powerful kingdom based in the Amuq and controlling Aleppo, perhaps even Karkamiš, in the 11th century B.C. A notable feature of the archaeology of the area, 12th–11th centuries B.C. is the spread of Mycenaean IIIC pottery from the Aegean, through Cilicia, Cyprus and the Amuq down the coast to the south Levant, which has been associated with the movement of the Sea-Peoples, especially the Philistines[6]. In this context, the designation of Taita's kingdom Palistin (with variant Walistin) cannot but be considered: can it be linked to the archaeological evidence and even to the name of the Philistines and their hypothesized origin in the Aegean area? The suggestion is made to inaugurate rather than to preempt discussion. However the argument may go, one thing is clear: a highly significant new piece of information has become available to suggest the shape of events in a previously unknown period of the area.

BIBLIOGRAPHY

HAWKINS, J. D.

2000 *Corpus of Hieroglyphic Luwian Inscriptions I/1-3.* Berlin, New York: de Gruyter.

2003 "The Storm God Seal of Mursili III," in *Studies in Honor of Harry A. Hoffner*, edited by G. Beckman, R. Beal and G. McMahon, pp. 169–175. Winona Lake IN: Eisenbrauns.

2009 "Cilicia, the Amuq and Aleppo," *Near Eastern Archaeology* 72/4: 164–173.

2011 "The inscriptions of the Aleppo temple," *Anatolian Studies* 61: 35–54.

KOHLMEYER, K.

2009 "The Temple of the Storm God in Aleppo during the Late Bronze and Early Iron Ages," *Near Eastern Archaeology* 72/4: 190–202.

RIEKEN, E. and YAKUBOVICH, I.

2010 "The New Values of Luwian Signs L319 and L 172," *Luwian and Hieroglyphic Studies presented to J. David Hawkins*, pp. 199–219. Tel Aviv: Emery and Clair Yass Publications.

TEKOĞLU, R. and LEMAIRE, A.

2000 "La bilingue royale louvito-phenicienne de Çineköy," *Comptes rendus, Academie des inscriptions et belles-lettres:* 961–1007.

6 See *Reallexikon der Assyriologie X/7-8, s.v.* Philister, Philister-Keramik.

CHAPTER 22

QADESH, SEA PEOPLES, AND ANATOLIAN-LEVANTINE INTERACTIONS

Karl STROBEL
Abt. f. Alte Geschichte, Altertumskunde und Archäologie
Universität Klagenfurt
Universitätsstraße 65-67
A-9020 Klagenfurt, Austria

ABSTRACT

The 13th c. BC appears as the zenith of the international Late Bronze Age political and economic systems. At the same time, the conflict between the Anatolian great power, the Hittite Empire, and Egypt over influence and control in the Middle Levant culminated in the battle of Qadesh during the 5th year of Ramses II, in May 1274 BC. For the first time, troops of nearly all parts of Anatolia marched into southern Syria and thus brought Syria until the demarcation line which was later fixed in the Hittite-Egyptian peace and friendship treaty in direct connection with the destiny of the Hittite Empire. But only a century after the battle of Qadesh several far reaching events changed 'global' players and caused the transition into a world of smaller political entities and new commercial and seafaring networks in the Mediterranean, in Anatolia and in the Levant. In this context, the so called Sea Peoples were thought in a traditional picture to have been the central element in a disaster of the 'old world' of Late Bronze age. The so called Sea Peoples should have come from the Aegean world, the Balkans and from parts of western or south-western Anatolia, and they should have destroyed the cities and Bronze Age civilization of the Levant down to the Nile Delta. A detailed analysis of the propaganda-inscriptions of Ramses II and Ramses III can demonstrate if such interactions between the Aegean-Anatolian and Levantine world happened and what we really can say about the 'Sea Peoples' in the context of these developments, which not only crossed borders but also changed the frontiers around the north-eastern Mediterranean into the system of Neo-Hittite states and civilization.

The analysis of the Anatolian troops at Qadesh shows us the Hittite vassal states and minor partners under Hittite overlordship whose treaties with Ḫattuša included military obligations in the case of a conflict with another great power and so gives us a clear picture of Hittite control in Anatolia under Muršili II and Muwattalli II. Hittite texts demonstrate that this control was still dominating Anatolia at the end of the 13th c. BC and that

Šuppiluliuma II was still able to reconquer Cyprus with a powerful fleet. However, is it possible to gain information for 'Sea People-Problem' already from the texts of Ramses II? At least they give us important evidence for the region around the Gulf of Iskenderun.

Anatolian Vassals of the Hittites in the battle of Qadesh (12.5.1274 BC)

Important information concerning the extent of the rule and power of the Hittite Empire under Muwattalli II and for the forces he was able to mobilize during the confrontation with Egypt is provided by the different lists of the enemies in the records of Ramses II given for his 'overwhelming' victory in the battle of Qadesh.[1] The first list in the *Poem Text or Literary Record* (sigl. P) records the following countries which were hostile to Egypt and were the enemies who were 'defeated' by Ramses (P 1)[2]: against the Land of Hatti, Naharina (traditional name for Mitanni, now for Ḫanigalbat), and against the Land of Arzawa;[3] against Pidassa, against Dardanaya; against the Land of Masa, against the Land of Qarqisha (Karia) Lukku (Lukka/Lycia); against Karkemish, *Qdy* (translitt. as Qode, Qedi, Qadi; East Cilicia), the Land of Qadesh; against the Land of Ugarit, Mushnatu. The second list (P 2), which is also in the *Poem Text*, gives the following names of all the troops and allies of the Hittite king, who "had gathered round himself all foreign countries to (the furthest) limits of the Sea"[4]: the entire land of Hatti, of Naharina, of Arzawa; Dardanaya, that of Gasgas (Kškš; Kaška Lands), that/those of Masa (The denomination of Masa changes between singular and plural); those of Piddassa, that of Arwanna, that of Qarqisha (and) Lukku; Qizuwadna (Kizzuwatna), Karkemish, Ugarit; *Qdy*, the entire land of Nuhasse,[5] Mushnatu, Qadesh. Later in the third list (P 3),[6] when the Hittite chariots attacked, chariot-spans from Arzawa, Masa, and Pidassa, and *in rasura*, "from Gasgas, Arwanna and Qizuwatna" were mentioned.

Kizzuwatna no longer existed as a separate state after Šuppiluliuma I's annexation of the country, but was still in use as a politico-geographical term. It is very important that both parts of Cilicia (without Rough Cilicia/Tarḫuntašša) are mentioned separately side by side in these paragraphs, i.e. Qizuwadna and *Qdy*. Kizzuwatna comprises the Cilician Plain with Tarša/Tarsus and Adaniya/Adana, and inner and north-eastern

[1] Kitchen 1996, pp. 2–26 and Addenda p. 606; notes and comments in Kitchen 1999, pp. 3–55. See in addition Edel 1994, Nr. 24.25 and KUB XXI 17. The spelling of the names is in most cases taken from Kitchen's translation to avoid complications. However, some alterations have been made for clarity.

[2] Kitchen 1996, p. 2, 3:1–4:1, ll. 2–6; cf. Kitchen 1999, pp. 50–52.

[3] This is a traditional denomination too, now the Hittite vassal kingdom of Mira-Kuwaliya with the capital Apaša/Ephesos, being the central authority in Hittite western Anatolia.

[4] Kitchen 1996, p. 4, 16: 1–18:1, ll. 41–47.

[5] Nuhasse or Niya is the area of the middle Orontes valley and the inner Syrian plateau between the territories of Aleppo and Hama.

[6] Kitchen 1996, p. 5, 32:1, ll. 86 and 86'–86".

Cilicia, i.e. the Seyhan and Çeyhan regions up into southern Cappadocia with the important religious centres of Kummanni-Kizzwatna, very probably Hierapolis-Kastabala,[7] and La(ḫu)wazantiya, most probably Sirkeli Höyük.[8] The geographical term *Qdy*,[9] however, was used in Egyptian texts since Thutmosis III for East Cilicia, i.e. the coastal plain round the Gulf of Iskenderun; the country was also separated in Egyptian terminology from the kingdom of Danuna/Adaniya (Luw. Adanuwa) and numbered among the Syrian states. The poetic record of the Hittite king's personal visit to Ramses II in P. Anastasi III shows that QDY was still a vassal state in the mid-13th c. BC with its own king. *Qdy* probably was the Egyptian transliteration of the elder pre-Luwian, Hurrian name of the country. Hurrians were present in the pre-Luwian population of the whole area, which was under direct influence of the Mitanni kingdom in the 15th c. BC. An important centre of *Qdy*, eastern Cilicia up to the Anamus, was Kinet Höyük (ancient Issos).

A further part of the *Poem Text* provides the following list of the Hittite vassal rulers who were on the battlefield with their chariot troops (P 4)[10]: the rulers of Arzawa, Masa, Arwanna, Lukku, Dardanaya, Karkemish, Quarqisha, and Aleppo together with the brothers of Muwattalli II. This list seems to be the most reliable. We know from the inscription that the king of Aleppo fell into the Orontes River when he retreated because of Ramses' counterattack and was saved by his men (R. 40). The counter-attack forced the Hittite charioteers back to the Orontes where they had to cross the river, a manoeuvre causing severe casualties (R. 19). The names in the list of the Hittite casualties of higher ranks (R. 23–40) seem to contain a series of errors from the hasty reports of the Egyptian scribes on the battlefield.[11] However two troop commanders from Alshe (Alzi/Alši) were registered as being killed (R. 33.37). The lists of prisoners of war comprises foot soldiers of Dardanaya, Pidassa, Karkemish, Masa, Lukku, Arwanna, Arzawa, Ugarit, and *maryannu*-warriors, i.e. elite-soldiers,[12]

[7] Cf. Casabonne 2009. However, the site of Kastabala only started in Achaemenid times. The regional centre from Middle Bronze Age to Iron Age was the nearby Tartarlı Höyük; it later shifted to classic Kastabala.

[8] Shalmaneser III conquered the cities of Lusanda and Kisuatni in 839/838 BC after having crossed the Anamus; cf. Yamada 2000, pp. 200–202 with the right location, but still discussing the older equation of Kummanni with the later Komana in Kataonia.

[9] Cf. Astour 1967, pp. 28–30, 36–37; H. M. Kümmel, *RlA* 5, 1976–80, p. 627, s.v. Kizzuwatna. For the linguistic analysis of the Kizzuwtna dialect of Luwian and its Hurrian substrate cf. Yakubovich 2010, pp. 272–283, 301.

[10] Kitchen 1996, p. 8, 49:1–51:1, ll. 147–153.

[11] Kitchen 1999, pp. 53–55. R. 26 mentions the troop commander of the Qabusu (or people of Qabusu?). All geographic proposals (see Kitchen 1999, p. 52) for this term are not convincing. It could be a special troop of the Hittite army in Egyptian (mis?–)spelling.

[12] Cf. G. Wilhelm, *RlA* 1978–1990, pp. 419–421 s.v. Marijannu. These soldiers are partly mounted on chariots and recruited from social and military elites in northern Mesopotamia and Syria.

of Naharina (Ḫanigalbat/former Mitanni), Aleppo, Gasgas, Alshe, Nuhasse, and Dardanaya.[13] Only Dardanaya is mentioned twice.

The *Bulletin Text* (sigl. B) of year 5 gives a more detailed and less panegyric report for Ramses' second campaign in Syria. In contrast to the *Poem Text* which contains extensive poetical and semi-poetic sections, this text is mostly characterized by narrative prose. The list of the Hittite "allies from all the foreign land" who belong to the area of Hatti and delivered infantry and chariots (B 1)[14] starts (l. 43) in the Ramesseum and Abu Simbel version (omitted by mistake in Luxor) with the Land of Dardanaya, followed by the land of Naharina (Mitanni/Ḫanigalbat). In the next line (L. 44) the land of Gasgas and the lands of Masa and the land of Pidassa are mentioned, followed by the land of Qarqisha and Lukku and the land of Karkemish (l. 45). It is difficult to understand the order of this list, because Arzawa, Arwanna and *Qdy* were written within the geographic context of Syria (l. 46: the land of Arzawa, the land of Ugarit, that of Arwanna; l. 47: the land of Alshe (Alzi/Alši in northernmost Mesopotamia), Mushnatu, and Qadesh; l. 48: Aleppo and the entire land of *Qdy*.

Mushnatu is not known in Hittite texts; its identification is uncertain.[15] However, this list is the most reliable for the empire of Muwattalli in 1275 BC and his vassal states. It shows the extant of the Great King's rule after the successes of his father Muršili II in the north and after his brother Hattušili had again defeated the so-called Kashka-people and had reorganized the appanage kingdom of Hakmiš; thus Muwattalli's rule extended widely over north central Anatolia.[16] As a result, major parts of the Kashkaeans were under Hittite overlordship and provided contingents of infantry together with charioteers (!) to the army of Muwattalli in 1275 BC (P 3). It is probable that these contingents were under the command of Muwattallis' brother Hattušili as well. To provide chariotry is not very likely for a population who were thought to be only North-Pontic mountain pastoralists and semi nomadic societies, which is the traditional picture of the Kashkaeans in modern research. However, Hittite texts mention cities and kings in the Kashka lands too, thus showing a higher degree of political organisation, small fortified cities at least, for important parts of the Kashkaeans.[17] The mountain population itself surely lived in Alpine forms of transhumance. In addition, the former land of Zalpuwa ("rich in cities"), known as the

[13] R. 64.65.70.72.78.80.82 (cf. Kitchen 1999, p. 50).86.90.

[14] Kitchen 1996, pp. 16–17, 111:1–112:1, ll. 41–49.

[15] Syrian Mušunipa? Cf. Kitchen 1999, p. 52.

[16] Cf. Klengel 1999, pp. 180–188, 255–256; now Klinger 2002; 2005; 2008; 2009. The newest archaeological research demonstrates that after the mid-13th c. BC monumental buildings were still erected in Nerik (Oymaağaç) and Hittite correspondence was constantly written. It is important that the latest Late Bronze Age Level of Nerik extended into the transitional phase between Hittite Final and Early Iron Age especially known at Büyükkaya in Ḫattuša. Cf. excavation reports from the Nerik-Project Website, Berlin (http://www.nerik.de).

[17] Cf. Klinger 2008, pp. 286–287.

early dominating power in northern Hattian heartlands, was an integral part of the Kashka lands on both sides of the lower Halys. From the inscription (P 2; 3, 4) it is known that from Ar(a)wanna[18], the other Hittite vassal state in northern Anatolia, the ruler himself was present with his contingents of infantry and chariotry at Qadesh. Ar(a)wanna can be identified with the original western part of Paphlagonia (i.e. the Palaean region of Anatolia) including the plains of Düzce, Bolu and Gerede and the region of Mudurnu; the centre of Ar(a)wanna was very probably the large prehistoric mound in the city centre of Bolu. Muršili II had subdued the country in his 5th year after an aggressive act of Arawanna-troops against Hittite Kaššiya. Muršili II named Arawanna at the beginning of his reign in his prayer to the Sun-Goddess of Arinna in a list of countries (Arawanna, Kalašma, Lukka, and Pitašša) which had deserted Ḫatti during the severe epidemic crisis which caused the death of Šuppiluliuma I and of his son and successor Arnuwanda II.[19]

One stereotypical combination is present in all the lists; Qarqisha - Lukka.[20] This gives a hint that both countries were seen by the Egyptians as a sort of combined area between Arzawa in the west and *Qdy* and Kizzuwatna, i.e. Eastern Cilicia and Cilicia Pedias, in the East. It seems that the Egyptians did not use the term Tarḫuntašša for the country between the territory of Ura and the Lukka Lands, i.e. Rough Cilicia. The coast of Rough Cilicia between Ura and Lukka was obviously of no interest for Egypt and without greater importance prior to the formation of the vassal kingdom of Tarḫuntašša by Ḫattušili III. The important harbour city of Ura must be located in the area of the Göksu delta and was long known in Egypt. Amenemes II (1914–1879/76 BC) had even sent a naval expedition against Alashiya on Cyprus and Ura.[21]

As a result of the victories of Muršili II in western Anatolia,[22] army contingents, infantry and chariot troops, from the vassal state of Mira-Kuwaliya were fighting under the direct command of the King of Mira (P 4 and P 3; P 1, P 2, B). The Šeha-Riverland is not explicitly mentioned, but should be still included in the Egyptian use of the term Arzawa. The Masa-Lands,[23] in the 13th c. BC comprising Mysia, Hellespontic Phrygia and probably Bithynia west of the lower Sangarios, were present with infantry and chariotry. They were fighting under a prince as a Hittite vassal (P 4 and P 3; P 1, P 2, B). The list P 4 gives us a summary of the vassal kings and princes who commanded their contingents in person at Qadesh. After the campaigns of Muršili II and Muwattalli II, the Masa-Lands were a Hittite vassal state. However, we do not know the identity of this prince, who must have represented a centralized power in

18 Cf. Strobel 2008a, pp. 29–30.
19 Klengel 1999, p. 173, A 14.
20 Cf. Strobel 2008a, pp. 21–23, 38–40; Yakubovich 2010, pp. 157–158.
21 Kitchen 2009, pp. 2–3.
22 For the geography of West Anatolia cf. Strobel 2008a.
23 Cf. Strobel 2008a, pp. 27, 28–29.

Masa in some way, being a partner and addressee of the Hittite king; nor do we know where his residence was. He was not only the commander of infantry troops but of a contingent of chariotry too. Thus his army was not only a levy of tribal warriors from the mountainous areas of north western Anatolia as often thought. However this is not the only the problem provided by the information of the Qadesh text; we also do not know who were the princes of Lukka and Karkisha present at Qadesh, because these countries seem to have no single monarchic centre. However, somebody from these countries must have been recognized by the Hittite overlord and bound by a Hittite vassal treaty.

The next question arises because Dardanaya is so prominently mentioned in the texts (P1, P2, P4, B1) while this name does not appear in Hittite sources. On the other hand, the name Wilusa is completely missing in Egyptian texts.[24] Dardanaya has quite a prominent place in Ramses' II lists; fifth place in P 1, fourth place in P2, even first in B 1 and also in the prisoners' list twice. Because of the list P 4 there is no doubt that the prince of Dardanaya himself was on the battlefield with chariots and infantry as part of Muwattalli's army. Therefore, it is obvious that Dardanaya cannot be the Egyptian name of a geographic and political entity within the Mycenaean world. It was a vassal-state of the Hittite empire and its prince was leading his troops in the battle of Qadesh. We know from the treaty (§ 13) between Muwattalli II and Alaksandu of Wilusa[25] that the ruler of Wilusa had to send infantry and chariotry troops for the army of his Hittite overlord: "But from Ḫatti, these are the obligations for you: The Kings who are the equals of My Majesty — the king of Egypt, the king of Babylonia, the king of Ḫanigalbat, or the king of Assyria — if someone in this group comes in battle, or if domestically someone carries out a revolt against My Majesty, and I, My Majesty, write to you for infantry and chariotry, then send infantry and chariotry to my aid immediately." Therefore no doubts can be raised against the identification of Hittite Wilusa with Egyptian Dardanaya in the context of the battle of Qadesh. Dardanaya was also previously mentioned in Amenophis' III geographical list ETL XIId.[26] In Greek tradition, Dardania is an old name of the Troas.[27] According to Greek myth and epic, Dardanos was the founder of the Trojan royal dynasty. We are told that the dynasty of the Dardanids split into two branches, one of the kings of Troy, one of the Aineads, the rulers in the more southern part of the Troas. The historical dynasty of the Aineads is known in Dardania in the 8th c. BC; their residence was the old mountain city of Palaio-Skepsis. Homer tells us that the Dardanoi are first of all the people ruled by the Aineads in the inner part of the Troas round Mount Ida (Strabo 13, 1, 24) and that they were allies of the Trojans who are

[24] Cf. for a summary of the whole question Strobel 2008a, pp. 10–19.
[25] Beckman 1999, pp. 87–93 no. 13. Translation after Beckman l. c.
[26] Cf. Edel and Görg 2005, pp. 25–26, 34–36.
[27] Cf. Strobel 2008a, pp. 11–19 with all references.

the people of Ilios, the city of the Trojans, and its surrounding region. The city of Dardanos, founded by the legendary king Dardanos, is very probably not only a mythological site, but was the political centre of the more southern and south-eastern region of the Troas before Troy VI gained overlordship of the whole region and became the Hittite vassal kingdom of Wilusa. It had already recognized the Hittites as overlords for the first time when Labarna I (ca. 1670–1640 BC), successor of Huzziya I, established a great Anatolian empire.[28] This fact is recorded in the historical introduction (§2) of the Alaksandu treaty; furthermore the text says that the land of Wilusa later defected from Ḫatti, probably during the dynastic crisis in the early reign of the successor Labarna II/Ḫattušili I. The region of the Troas had an important role in controlling naval traffic to the Propontis (Marmara Sea) and the Black Sea, regions with which contact and knowledge was provided to the Egyptians by Arzawa. The name Dardania, i. e. Dardaniya, for the Troas must have been in use in Arzawa in the 16/15th to 14th c. BC. Knowledge of the north-western Anatolian regions was surely brought to Egypt through close contacts between Arzawa and Egypt since the time of Thutmosis III when Arzawitian craftsmen were working in the dockyard of Perunefer and people from Arzawa could get posts in the pharaonic administration under Amenophis II.[29]

The other Egyptian geographic term Danaya or Tanaya/u is to be identified with the Peloponnese.[30] D/Tanaya/u was already mentioned in the annals of Thutmosis III during his 42nd year when the pharaoh got diplomatic gifts, 'tribute,' from the prince of the D/Tanaya foreign land.[31] On the contrary, Aḫḫiyawa does not appear in Egyptian sources; the often repeated interpretation that the Eqwesh or Aqawash(a), the allies of the Libyans in 1209/8 BC, should represent the Achaioi is incorrect. [32] The lists of fallen enemies during the victory of year 5 in Merenptah's triumphal inscription show that these warriors were circumcised, something improbable for Mycenaean culture. Good arguments are available that Aḫḫiyawa should be identified with Thebes which now emerges as the great rival of Mycenae for power and international relations.[33] Still in Greek epic tradition, Aulis, the harbour of Thebes, is the place where

[28] Cf. Forlanini 2007; 2010.

[29] Cf. Glanville 1931; 1933; Helck 1971, 280; Haider 1999; the scepticism of Schneider 1992, p. 40 is not convincing.

[30] Cf. Haider 1988, pp. 2–15; 1999; 2000; 2004; 2008a.b; Niemeier 2008, 2009; misleading Oettinger 2010.

[31] Cf. Haider 2000, p. 156 and n. 23.

[32] Against an early Aegean settlement or invasion in the Cyrenaica cf. Haider 1988, pp. 83–127.

[33] Cf. Niemeier 2008; Dakouri-Hild 2010. The theory of Carruba 1995, p. 157 that the ethnic names of the Ionians (Iáones) and Aeolians (Aiolées) can be deduced from *Aḫḫiyawa-li- and *Aḫḫia(wa)-wanni- must be rejected since Anatolian inner /ḫḫ/ corresponds with Greek K/Γ and vice-versa and cannot disappear. For the storage depot of lapis lazuli cylinder seals (already partially reworked in Cyprus; including Kassite seals of the 14th c. BC) which were reworked at Thebes for inlays and beads, cf. Cline 2009, pp. 154–160. The storage of these seals, raw material imported via Cyprus together with

the Greek fleet gathered and from where the Greeks, the Danaoi and Achaioi, sailed against Troy at the beginning of the Trojan War. There must have been a tradition that Aulis had been a central point for naval presence in the central and northern Aegean.

Of great importance is the extraordinary geographical list E_N found on a statue base of Amenophis III located in the northern part of the column court of his funerary temple.[34] E_N obviously records the destinations of itineraries, most probably of diplomatic missions from Egypt to Crete and to the Peloponnese. Although M. Görg opposes the idea of a strict itinerary with good arguments and sees more parallels to the lists A_N-D_N, the differences to other geographical lists can be explained because of the novelty of such diplomatic and commercial contacts by Egyptian missions in parallel to the intensified relations to Arzawa under Amenophis III. It seems that the Egyptians did not enter the sphere dominated by Arzawa and Aḫḫiyawa, i.e. the central and northern Aegean and the Southern Sporades. They obviously had to address Arzawa directly in such 'northernmatters' as the request for Kashaean specialists in the correspondence between Amenophis III and king Tarḫundaradu of Arzawa (EA 31.32) demonstrates.[35] The right front-side of the statue base has only two general geographical terms ("Leitnamen"); Kaftu (Crete) and Tanaya/u (Peloponnese); the right lateral side of the base is empty. The left side starts on the front with Amnisos, Phaistos and Kydonia (Chania) on Crete, then follow the Peloponnesian place names Mykene, D/Tikaias (Tegea?), Messene, Nauplia (probably the major harbour town of Ayios Stephanos[36]), Kythera, then back to Crete to Wayur/layi or Wayur/lia(i) (no. 9; probably a harbour on Crete, Melos perhaps possible too), Knossos, Amnisos, Lyktos, Sētaia (in eastern Crete); then two toponyms are missing, one was very probably Kommos (but not Kato Zakros as often proposed), the other might be Palaikastro.[37] The first three toponyms on the left side of the front are written into the cartouches where three names are erased: Amukla/Amyklai, Pisaia (?) and probably again Amukla/Amyklai.[38] Then a redactor changed the list and replaced the first three names by Cretan ones, thus adding Phaistos and Kydonia and doubling Amnisos as the first destination. Therefore central Laconia, where the new Mycenaean palace at Ayios Vasilios/Xirokampi with its archive of Linear B-tablets is found, i.e. Bronze Age

Cypriot cylinder seals, is not dated by pottery; sherds of LH III B Early and Middle under the floor give only a terminus post quem.

[34] Basic edition by Edel and Görg 2005; Görg, in Edel and Görg 2005, pp. 192–213. For the discussion of E_N including the new fragments F_N and G_N cf. Haider 2008a.b; for the geographical lists of the funerary temple of Sethos I at Gourna, the temple of Ramses II in Aksha, on the columns of Amenophis III in the temple of Amun at Soleb and at Karnak cf. Grimal 2009. Cf. also Cline 1987.

[35] For the Arzawa letters cf. Hawkins 2009b.

[36] Cf. Taylour and Janko 2008.

[37] Cf. Shaw 2006; MacGillivray and Sackett 2010.

[38] Görg, in Edel and Görg 2005, pp. 199–203, 209–213. Seven Peloponnesian toponyms, then the island of Kythera, and then seven places on Crete as the original order of the list.

Amyklai, had lost its importance for Egypt, and Crete gained the primary position for the Egyptian diplomacy again. This might indicate a power shift within the Mycenaean world during the 1st half of the 14th c. BC. Although supposed by several studies, Ilion is not mentioned in this list on place no. 9[39], neither can be identified a toponym "Great-Ionia" in the newly found fragment G_N (cartouche no. 3) for western Asia Minor.[40]

In conclusion, during the 1st half of the 13th c. BC all coastal areas of Anatolia from the (more western) area of Pontus to Ugarit were under Hittite control; only Milawanda/Miletus with its strong connections to Aḫḫiyawa was a base of unrest. An important result is the Egypt differentiation between *Qdy* and Kizzuwatna and between *Qdy* and Danuna, i.e. Adaniya or Adanuwa, the Central Cilician plain west of the Nur Dağı.

Anatolians as part of the Sea Peoples?

In 1278 BC, his second regnal year, Ramses II had achieved a triumphant victory in a naval battle against the Sherden or Shardana (*Šrdn*)[41]: He had defeated the Sherden who came on their ships from the midst of the Sea and brought them to Egypt. Up to now nobody had been able to fight or to resist the Sherden, when they came and were sailing in their war-ships on the sea. Now he had defeated and captured these powerful warriors of the Sea when he engaged them with his fleet, and Lower Egypt could sleep again without fear. Therefore, the Egyptian fleet must already have been strengthened under Sethos I. The pirates seem to have used the time of the transition of power to Ramses II for attacks on the Egyptian coast. Ramses II expressed pride that his powerful fleet dominated the south-eastern part of the Mediterranean. The Sherden are portrayed with long swords of Central European and Adriatic-Italian Naue II-type (see below) and with a specific form of horned helmets (horns on both

39 Supposed by Kitchen, Edel and especially Cline 1987, p. 28. Cf. Görg, in Edel and Görg 2005, pp. 208–209.

40 Cf. Haider 2008 a.b, but the Kizzuwatnian city of Luwana on the middle Seyhan cannot be identified with Assyrian Lamenash (Lamiya in East Cilicia, cf. Astour 1967, p. 26; Yamada 2000, p. 220 and n. 493–494 who still follows the vague supposition of Garstang and Gurney 1959, p. 60) and not with the 2nd toponym in G_N which should be identified as Ruwano on Crete. The identification of the 4th toponym with Madunašša on the eastern frontier of the Šeha-Riverland near Sarıgöl is implausible. It is possible that the fragmentary list contains toponyms from Crete and from Attica (cf. Medon/ Medontidai).Very problematic is the contribution of Duhoux 2008. Contra Görg 2008 (G_N Arawanna – Great-Ionia – Maša) cf. Adrom 2008; however his reading of *Mdn* as Maeonia (cf. Yakubovich 2010, 91.92) is not convincing because it is based on the supposed appearance of a Great-Ionia. In fragment F_N Görg 2008 reads Adana and Tarša, but contrary to him and Haider l.c. the fragment F_N should belong to another detail list of Aegean toponyms.

41 Rhetoric stela II from Tanis KRI II 290 see Kitchen 1996, pp. 118–122 No. 73, l. 13. Rock-stela from Assuan KRI II 345 see Kitchen 1996, pp. 181–183 Nr. 121, l. 8; 2nd year: He has annihilated the warriors of the Sea, now the Nile-Delta can sleep again. Cf. Kitchen 1999, p. 174.

sides and a sort of ball on the top).[42] The Sherden of the Sea, "who plundered the foreign countries", had become Egyptian elite soldiers.[43] It is probable that more Sherden were hired as mercenaries in the following years. The Sherden-warriors, now military colonists, were gathered as Ramses' II elite troops when he started his march to Syria in Pi-Ramesse on the 1st of April 1274 to confront Muwattalli II.[44] However, Sherden were already used as mercenary soldiers in Byblos in the times of Amenophis III and Amenophis IV/Akhenaton[45], and in the mid-13th c. BC, Sherden had been "men of the king" in Ugarit for at least two generations.[46]

Raids of pirates on the coast of Lower Egypt already happened under Amenophis III and IV when Amenophis, the son of Hapu, was in charge of fortifying the coast of the Nile delta. [47] The Pharaoh wrote a letter to the king of Alashiya because of the raids of pirates from Lukka who were joined by men from Alashiya. The king of Alashiya answered in a letter that Lukka-pirates make raids against the villages of his own country year by year too (EA 38). If men from Alashiya were together with the Lukka pirates, the Pharaoh should send them back to the king of Alashiya for punishment. Actions of smaller groups of pirates and raids led by smaller dynasts were not only endemic in the Mediterranean during the late 2nd and the 1st half of the 1st c. BC, but also in the 2nd half of the 2nd millennium BC, only to mention the joint and repeated raids on Alashiya, over which the Hittite king claimed sovereignty, by Maduwatta and Attariššiya/Attaršiya, the man/prince of Aḫḫiya, together with the "man of Piggaya"[48] during the time of Arnuwanda I[49] as well as the military actions of Piyamaradu[50] in the East Aegean and in West and Southwest Anatolia. Naval warfare became an important motif in LH III C painted pottery. On Crete, during the

[42] Cf. for example warrior-statuettes from Sardinia with a similar type.
[43] Cf. P. Anastasi II verso 5, 3; 7–8.
[44] Kitchen 1996, p. 3, 11:1.
[45] EA 81, 16; 122, 55.
[46] Heltzer 1983.
[47] Cf. Helck 1979, p. 133.
[48] S. De Martino, *RlA* 10, 2003–2005, pp. 562–563 s.v. Pikkaja.
[49] Indictment of Madduwatta; Beckman 1999, pp. 153–160 no. 27. Madduwatta was first attacked by Attariššiya who chased him out of his land; he fled to Arnuwanda's father Tutḫaliya I/II and became his disloyal vassal. The clashes in the reign of Tutḫaliya I/II between Hittite armies and the troops of Attariššiya on behalf of Maduwatta happened without doubt in western Anatolia. The territory of Mount Zippasla in the Hittite border zone against Arzawa, which was given to Madduwatta by the Hittite king, must have been the mountain area southeast of Denizli. The first conflict between Madduwatta and Attariššiya was most probably in Caria which was already a Mycenaean outpost at the end of the 15th c. BC. Madduwatta seems to have been the neighbour of Milawanda. There is little doubt that Aḫḫiya and Aḫḫiyawa are the same. But contra Yakubovich 2010, pp. 150–151, there is no hint that Attariššiya had possessions in southern Anatolia. After making an alliance with Kupanta-Kurunta of Arzawa, Madduwatta took the Land of Ḫapalla in the north and several cities in Central Caria, so Ialanta/Alabanda and Wallarima/Hyllarima; then he reached the southern coast where he took the land of Attarimma, the region of the northern and western side of the original gulf of Carian Kaunos (Xbide) to the former Indos-delta (Strobel 2008a, pp. 20–22).
[50] S. Heinhold-Kramer, *RlA* 10, 2003–2005, pp. 561–562.

period of LM III C Early, the population left the coastal plain and settled in places with good natural defences, and short-lived fortifications were built by organized military groups.[51] Just at the beginning of the reign of Ammurapi, the last king of Ugarit (after 1210/before 1205 to sometime before 1184 or 1179 BC, depending on the accession date of Ramses III), Šuppiluliuma II wrote to the governor of Ugarit (RSO 7, 12)[52], because, in the words of Šuppiluliuma, the king himself was young and did not know anything. A certain Ibnaduša had been captured by the Ši-ka-la-iu-ú and was later freed by the Ugaritians. This man should be brought to the Great King; the matter was important, therefore the Hittite *kartappu,* prince Nerikkaili, would be sent to get the man. It is obvious that the Hittite Great King wanted information about the Šikalaju "who live on their ships." It is very probable that this happened during the preparations of the naval expedition against Cyprus.

The date of this episode shows us the presence of one of the so-called Sea Peoples around 1210/1205 BC in the north eastern part of the Mediterranean. Nearly at the same time, warrior-groups of "Sea Peoples" were mercenaries of the Libyan prince Mariyu, Son of Didi, and his tribal federation when attacking the western frontier of Lower Egypt in the 5th year of Merenptah.[53] In this year, 1209/08, Mariyu called upon all tribes of his alliance and gathered an impressive army strengthened by the mercenary contingents of the "Northerners". Families and cattle followed the army; Mariyu took his own family with him. At the beginning of March 1208 the pharaoh got the information that Mariyu had left his country and had reached the frontier of Lower Egypt in the area of Pi-Iru[54]. Merenptah ordered the mobilization of the army to be ready for battle within 14 days and marched to the neighbourhood of the provincial district Pi-Iru where the battle was fought during six hours on the 29th of March 1208 (Gregorian calender).[55] The fighting ended with the flight of Mariyu and a crushing defeat of his forces. 6,111 Libyans and 2,362 Northerners were killed; 9,376 prisoners and a rich booty were brought to Egypt.

These "Northerners, wanderers of all lands," were the *3kwš*, vowelized as Eqwesh or Aqawasha[56], *Twrw/yš.w* (*Twrš3*) or *Trš.w*, the Turush (or Teresh or Tursha), the Lukka, the Sherden and the *Škr/l(w)š*, the Shekelesh or Shakalusha — the Šikalayu of the Hittite letter. The list of fallen enemies shows that the Eqwesh had the greatest

51 Cf. Nowicki 2000; 2008.

52 Lehmann 1979; Singer 1999, p. 722; Strobel 2008b, pp. 649–650.

53 Great Lybian War Inscription Karnak: Kitchen 2003, pp. 2–10 No. 2; Athribis-Stela: Kitchen 2003, pp. 16–19 no. 4. For an analysis of the Karnak inscription cf. Manassa 2003.

54 The identification with Letopolis north of Memphis (thus Grandet II, p. 250) is not proven and not probable.

55 Cf. Meeus 2002, 362. Merenptah's accession to the throne dates between 23rd of July and 3rd of August 1213 BC, cf. Beckerath 1997, 104.

56 Kitchen, Great Libyan War Inscription: Aqawasha; Athribis-Stela: Aqawasha (Kitchen 2003, pp. 2, 4, 19); Great Libyan War Inscription, list of fallen enemies Aqaywasha (l. c., p. 7). Not to be identified with Aḫḫiyawa and not to be reconstructed with vowels after his model.

number of casualties, followed by the Turush. However, on the 'Israel'-stela and its parallel texts,[57] Merenptah only mentions the Libyan enemy; the Sea People do not appear in this triumphal monument. They seemed not so important within the triumph of the pharaoh. From these 'Sea Peoples' only the Shekelesh later appeared again as enemies of Ramses III.

There is a huge amount of discussion about the possible origins of these Sea Peoples.[58] In the case of Merenptah's war against the Libyan aggression, they must be seen as *symmachoi*, as real mercenaries. The campaign of Tutḫaliya III/IV into the Lukka Lands and the inner dynastic conflict between Arnuwanda III and Šuppiluliuma II on one side and the successor of Great King Kurunta of Tarḫuntašša on the other, together with the military actions against Tarḫuntassa and its supporters by Šuppiluliuma II (Südburg-Inscription), could have destabilized the situation in southern Anatolia at that time.[59] The expeditions of Tutḫaliya III/IV and Šuppiluliuma II against Alashiya to gain or regain control over Cyprus might have had the same effect. However, only the Lukku can be attributed with certainty. They are warriors from the Lukka lands (later Lycia), the region west of the Kastraya/Kestros to the area of Carian Kaunos. On the contrary, there is no evidence that the Turush were warriors coming from somewhere in western Asia Minor. Susan Sherratt[60] poses the question whether the Sherden or Shekelesh are real ethnic groups or parts of a cosmopolitan mobile mariner society based on the increased volume of sea traffic in the 13th c. BC. The ethnicity of these groups should be considered as a construct of the Egyptian description. She also emphasizes the importance of Cyprus within the growing maritime activity of the 13th and 12th c. BC.[61] Therefore, the 'Sea Peoples' should be considered as a type of "aggressively open economy" in the eastern Mediterranean, who were subversive competitors to the centralized and controlled exchange economy. They could be seen as small mobile groups of multi-ethnic mariners acting as merchants and pirates in the same way as it is later known for the so called Phoenicians, also a pseudo-ethnicity, or for the Greeks[62] in Submycenaean to Archaic times as merchants, pirates and mercenaries. The appearance of the Sherden or Shardana in the eastern Mediterranean in the 14th c. BC must be considered in this context of seafarers and mercenaries, including the Central Mediterranean (see below). Assaf Yasur-Landau is still too focussed on the theory of larger scale migrations starting in the Mycenaean

[57] Kitchen 2003, pp. 10–15, no. 3 A.B. In the Cairo Column and the Heliopolis texts Libya and only the Shekelesh and every foreign land are mentioned.

[58] Much too optimistic Helck 1979 and still in the 2ndedition 1995; Haider 1988, pp. 71–82. Cline and O'Connor 2003 with a summary of the different theories.

[59] Cf. Strobel 2008b, pp. 639–649.

[60] Sherratt 1998.

[61] Cf. also Hirschfeld 1996. Groups of Cypriot origin were still living in Tiryns in LH III C; see below.

[62] Cf. also Rollinger 2001.

Aegean, especially in the Eastern Aegean or Mycenaeanized East Aegean — West Anatolian interface; key formulations are "Aegean behaviour patterns," "a trail of sites from western Anatolia to Syria, which were filled by newcomers," "large numbers of migrants along the land routes," "more than one region of the Aegean involved". [63] His assumption that the "migrants" used land routes from western Anatolia to the Levant, through the Cilician Gates into Cilicia and through the Anamus Gates to the Amuq must be rejected; there is no evidence at all. A major point of criticism against Yasur-Landau is that he does not recognize the stereotypes in the Egyptian pictorial language which was used in the Medinet Habu reliefs, i.e. the uniformity of the enemies or the topic depiction of hostile chariot forces in the 'land battle.' The ideological aspects and a critical discussion of these sources are missing in his reasoning. He even believes that Hittites participate because of their traditional and ideological (!) depiction in the reliefs. The general uniformity of several patterns, especially modes of painted pottery, in the LH III C period from the central Mediterranean to the Levant cannot be used as an indicator for similar ethnic or cultural origin. Yasur-Landau sees his "migrants" as peoples from different locations along the coasts of the Aegean and various groups of non-Aegean-Mycenaean origins joining as minorities the different actions. However, neither Bademgediği Tepe nor Çine Tepecik, the last continuously settled from Middle Bronze Age to Early Geometric, are new Mycenaean foundations because of imported or imitated pottery. Yasur-Landau postulates "raids and maritime colonization of any maritime power surviving in the Aegean in the twelfth century, or of any coastal settlement with an Aegean cultural background" on the one side, and on the other that "any group of people from virtually any community in mainland Greece or western Anatolia could have used the newly opened land routes to the Levant."[64] But there is no evidence of such migrations on land routes through Anatolia, and his historical picture drawn for the Anatolian states in the early 12th c. BC is incorrect too;[65] therefore, a major part of his theories collapses. Yasur-Landau furthermore emphasizes the parallels between the 'Sea Peoples'-ships in Medinet Habu and the Aegean depictions of 12th-century ships on LH III C pottery. However, these ships represent a 'northern' type which was already commonly known during the 13th c. BC.[66]

[63] Yasur-Landau 2010, especially pp. 189–193.

[64] Yasur-Landau 2010, p. 193.

[65] Cf. for the historical background Strobel 2008b.c; 2010. The history of Rhodos and of Chios together with Psara are much more complicated too; cf. Marketou 2010; Merouses 2002.

[66] The sherd from Ashkelon showing a bird-head ship prow, on which a warrior is standing, is now proved to be an import from the Argolis (Mycenae-Berbati group) during LH III A 2 or III B and not a local Philistine or LH III C product of the 12th c. BC. Cf. now P. A. Mountjoy, A Bronze Age Ship from Askelon with Particular Reference to the Bronze Age Ship from Bademgediği Tepe, AJA 115, 2011, 483–488, where the Bademgediği-krater is presented with the new fragment found in 2005.

An important phenomenon of the 13th c. BC is the spread of new weapons of central Mediterranean origin to Mycenaean Greece, the Aegean and Cyprus. The spread of the Naue II-type swords,[67] which originated in Northern Italy, introduced a new fighting technique (thrusting and slashing) in the Aegean and eastern Mediterranean and finally became the new standard weapon in LH III C. This phenomenon was combined with the spread of spearheads with a cast socket, daggers of the Pertosa-type, fibulae, knives and axe-types, all belonging to the central European and (North) Italian Urnfield traditions.[68] The transfer evidently happened along the Adriatic coasts and from the South Italian complex to the east using the Ionian Sea as a bridge. The earliest examples belong to the Naue II A type or Cetona-type in Italy and even reached the region of Halikarnassos; other relevant finds came from Kos, from Ialysos (necropolis) on Rhodos and from Panaztepe.[69] Of specific importance is, as Jung demonstrates, the inhumation burial of a warrior in the Langada necropolis on Kos (LH III B 2 Final or LH III C Early, i.e. at the end of the 13th c. BC[70]) connected with the major Late Bronze Age town of Seraya existing from LBA IA to LH III C Middle and fortified in LH III B.[71] It includes a Cetona-type sword and a spearhead with parallels in northern Italy and Achaia. In contrast to Achaia, where Naue II swords were combined in warrior burials with Mycenaean spearheads, the grave in Langada had both weapons of Italian type. That points to a possible non-Aegean origin of the warrior; it is no surprise that Mycenaean Rhodian pottery was found in Apulia. At Enkomi on Cyprus, the rich elite tomb no. 18 has three warrior burials dated to LC II C or LH III B2, one with a Naue II sword of the Cetona-type.[72] Other burials show objects with parallels in western Greece and southern Italy. The burials are earlier than the Enkomi level IIIA with its characteristic locally produced pottery of LH III C Early and Advanced types.[73] After the destruction of stratum LC II C in Enkomi, the city flourished with its typical ashlar architecture in LC III A; now weapons of central Mediterranean type were used much more frequently from the beginning. However, the younger Allerona-type of the Naue II swords of the period LH III C Advanced does not appear in Cyprus.[74] Thus, already in the 1st half of the 13th c. BC, the new combat technology was of great interest in the Aegean and on Cyprus for the Mycenaean elite as for the ruling class in Enkomi.[75]

67 Cf. Kilian-Dirlmeier 1993, pp. 94–106; Bietti-Sestrieri 1973.
68 Cf. for a summary of the different aspects Jung 2009; Jung and Mehofer 2005/2008.
69 Jung 2009a, pp. 73–74 and fig. 1.2–4.
70 Cf. Strobel 2008c.
71 Cf. Marketou 2010, pp. 762–766.
72 Jung 2009a, pp. 75–77.
73 Cf. Mountjoy 2009.
74 Jung 2009a, p. 77.
75 Cf. Jung 2009b. However Jung 2009a, p. 79 is wrong in identifying the Hittite Hijawa soldiers in Lukka with Mycenaeans from Aḫḫijawa (see below). The Mycenaean counterparts of the Hittites

Another weapon type also came from the central Mediterranean, the so-called feathered hat or hat-helmet[76] of the second stereotype for Sea Peoples' warriors in the reliefs of Medinet Habu. This is figured also on two LC II objects from Enkomi, a warrior with a beard who has a battle-ax, a kilt and a feather hat-helmet on a game board, and a warrior with such a helmet on a seal.[77] The finds from Pórtes and Praisos make a reconstruction possible. It is a thick woven straw-cap which forms the domed calotte; the lower part consists of bronze strips and rows of rivets applied onto the cap. The strips of organic material projecting above the cylindrical lower part which was made of bronze have been added on top of the cap or between the metal part and the straw calotte. We can assume that the 'feather crown' should make the appearance of the warrior more frightening and should protect the straw calotte. The forerunners of this helmet type can be found in Middle Bronze Age Italy (parallel to LH II-III A) from the Veneto to Apulia.[78] This originally non-Aegean type of helmet is found on Crete, in Achaia and on Cephalonia too. It is most probably that this type was transferred by warriors from northern and southern Italy to Mycenaean Greece and might be further developed there. Since the 17th c. BC, a network of trade and exchange existed between the Mycenaean Aegean, western Peloponnese plus Ionian Islands and the Adriatic, Apulia, Calabria, Sicily, the Aeolian Islands, Malta, Pantelleria and North Africa.[79] The Thapsos culture of costal Sicily provides a dense presence of Mycenaean objects and cultural influence.[80] The 12th and earlier 11th c. BC in Italy is characterized by locally produced Mycenaean-like pottery which was found in a large distribution. Production centres were even established in the Marche and in the Veneto. Sea traffic from and to the Levant reached Sicily and Sardinia. We must consider that seafarers from Italy, Sicily and Sardinia and other Central Mediterranean islands also played a major role; their importance seems to increase in the 12th c. BC. But people of South Italian origin were already present in Mycenaean centres and coastal places in central and southern Greece and western/central Crete in LH III B2 and still after the end of the palaces in LH III C. The marker, however only present in low percentage, is the locally produced handmade burnished pottery ('Barbarian Ware') which is connected with handmade pottery in the central Mediterranean in general and especially in central and southern Italy (impasto ware).[81] Therefore the presence of armed

never miss the first syllable with the starting vowel (Aḫḫijawa, Aḫḫija); cf. Strobel 2010, p. 47–48 and n. 47.

[76] Cf. Jung 2009a, pp. 78–79, 82–83, fig. 2.

[77] Dothan 1982, p. 277, fig. 13.14.

[78] Salzani 2005, pp. 124–127, 298–300, 391–448.

[79] Cf. Belardelli 1994; Bettelli 2002; Jones et al. 2002; Eder and Jung 2005; Eder 2006; Borgna and Cassola Guida 2009; for Monkodonja Hänsel 2007. A summary is given in Cazzella and Recchia 2009; Vagnetti 2010.

[80] Cf. Albertini 2005; 2007; 2008.

[81] Cf. Bettelli 2002; Kilian 2007; especially Jung 2006a, pp. 24–39.

seafaring people from the central Mediterranean, especially from the southern Italian complex and its Adriatic coasts, and very probably of foreign mercenaries incorporated into the armies of the Mycenaean rulers and also of the post-palatial elites must be taken into consideration.[82]

Ramses III: the evidence of P. Harris I

The papyrus Harris I (BM 9999)[83] was written after the unsuccessful coup d'état, the so-called Harem-Conspiracy, and the death of Ramses III and by the order of his son and legitimate successor Ramses IV. The conspiracy had tried to replace Ramses IV, who was already in charge of the empire during the final period of his father's reign, with a half-brother born by a secondary wife of the old pharaoh. The report of the *res gestae* of his father in war and peace, including a detailed catalogue of the benefactions to gods and temples was part of the measures of Ramses IV to stabilize his own reign. In contrast to the triumphal propaganda-inscriptions of Ramses III, the P. Harris I gives a realistic account of his deeds because there is no reason why his son and successor should not have mentioned all the successful campaigns of his father to embellish his own legitimacy and hereditary charisma. In the first part, the "discours aux dieux" the important information is given that Ramses III has built warships equipped with armed troops and military commanders and with captains for maritime actions on the open sea (7, 8).[84] He strengthened the Egyptian fleet first to secure the sea routes between the land of Djahi (Djahy), i.e. Canaan and Lebanon south of Amurru as the Egyptian southern part of Retjenu (Canaan and Syria from the Negev to the north of the Orontes river), first of all for the import of timber from the Lebanon, but also to make long distance trade on the Sea safe. Ramses III also strengthened the Egyptian fleet on the Red Sea (77, 8–9) and ordered an expedition to the land of Punt sometime after the 2nd Libyan war (77, 9-78, 1). The record of his deeds in war starts with the reorganisation of the Egyptian army at the beginning of the reign; the foreign elite troops of the Sherden and the Libyan *Ḳhḳ.w* (Qehequ) were explicitly mentioned (76, 5–6). The Qeheq had participated in the attack on Egypt in the 5th year of Merenptah and were now settled as military colonists in Egypt.

[82] The handmade burnished pottery from Emporio on Chios and from Bademgediği (LH III C context) has no parallels in the Italian impasto or in the Handmade Burnished Ware of Greece; cf. Jung 2009a, p. 78. Handmade Burnished Ware in Cyprus is of western origin, but much more restricted, and most types cannot be related to the material known in Greece. It dates only to LC III A and III B and even CG I. Jung 2009a, pp. 80–82 gives a summary of the results of the relevant research. Cf. also Matthäus 2009.

[83] Edition by Grandet I–III, 1994–1999 with commentary (For the war against the Northerners in several parts out of date, also Grandet 1993, pp. 185–218). For the text and the scribes cf. Grandet I, pp. 19–42.43–84, for the historical context of the papyrus Grandet I, pp. 101–127.

[84] Cf. for the different types of ships for costal guard, costal traffic and open sea cf. the literature Grandet I, p. 40 n. 156.

The report of the wars of Ramses III has three parts: the campaigns against the Sea People, then against the Shasu-Bedouins (76, 9–11) and third the Libyan War, obviously a combined record of year 5 and 11 (76, 11–77, 6).[85] It is of great importance that neither the Nubian War nor the Asiatic War, both part of the propaganda-reliefs of Ramses III himself, are mentioned. Both wars are fictitious copies of the deeds of Ramses II and of Merenptah. The only real 'Asiatic War' was the campaign against the Shasu-nomads in Egyptian Palestine and Sinai, here especially against the Sâru in the area of Edom.[86] As a result of the new golden age of the second half of Ramses' III long reign from the 12th to the 32nd year, the Egyptian army was not needed for action and the troops of the Sherden and the Libyan Qeheq stayed quiet in the villages in which they were settled and lived with their families (78, 9–12). P. Harris I reports only one war against the so-called Sea People (76, 7–9) and makes no differentiation between a naval battle and the Djahi-campaign as in Medinet Habu. Ramses III is praised to have annihilated the *D3nwn3*[87] (who came from) their isles, i.e. the Danuna, the *Ṯkr.w* and *Plst.w*, the Tjekker and Peleset, also the Sherden — this is an obvious mistake for the *Škl*š*.w*, the Shekelesh — and the *Wšš.w* of the Sea, the Washash (or Weshesh). Ramses III had taken many prisoners and settled them in his fortresses where the young men became soldiers and got their annual provision from the pharaoh.[88] However such military colonists were not settled by the pharaohs in outer provinces but in central areas of Egypt as it is documented for the Sherden as mercenaries and military colonists. One example of such a fortress is located at the entrance to the Fayûm.[89]

THE TRIUMPHAL PROPAGANDA INSCRIPTIONS AND RELIEFS IN MEDINET HABU

Ramses III started his triumphal report[90] on the walls of the temple in Medinet Habu, which was finished in his year 12, with the "Nubian War." However this war never happened. The same is true for the "Asiatic or Syrian War,"[91] the last of the reported military deeds.[92] Ramses' ideological invention of these wars should bring his

[85] There is a discussion whether P. Harris reports only one Libyan war, but is seems plausible that the record consists of two paragraphs, one the fighting back of an invasion, second the decisive offensive of year 11, combined by the construct of a great Libyan conspiracy (77, 3). Cf. Grandet II, pp. 246–251, for the exact date of the Libyan victory of year 11 Grandet II, p. 249.

[86] Grandet II, pp. 244–245.

[87] Cf. Edel 1983, p. 96. Grandet I, p. 336 "Dénénu"; III p. 309 Danuna, Danunim.

[88] The same is reported for the young warriors under the captives of the 2nd Libyan war (77, 5).

[89] Cf. Grandet II, n. 833, p. 244. The new chronology for the settlement of the Philistines in the coastal area of Palestine excludes a settlement there under Ramses III.

[90] The German translations of Schachermeyr, Helck and Hölbl are corrected by Edel 1985 who correctly analyses the structure of the text.

[91] Kitchen 2008, pp. 60–67.

[92] The topographic list of the Medinet Habu pylon, southern and northern triumphal scene, is second-hand, a careless copying from earlier lists through hieratic copies, especially from the lists of Ramses II, Thutmosis III and Sethos I. Cf. Egerton — Wilson 1936, p. 108.

deeds on the same level as the triumphs of Ramses II and Merenptah, especially Merenptah's Asiatic war. The texts and reliefs of Ramses III are no 'war journal' or realistic picture of his military campaigns, but a triumphal self-representation on a highly ideological degree.[93] The texts are first of all rhetorical and formulaic; the events are presented and described in a fixed ideological scheme.[94] The pharaoh on his chariot dominates the scenes on a superhuman scale; there are no real battles, the enemy is just collapsing before the pharaoh. The emphatic laudatory inscriptions are carefully constructed, but highly propagandistic, illustrations of victory; triumphal stelae are encomia devoted to the praise of the pharaoh as a divine hero. The enemies are always in an evil rebellion or conspiracy against Egypt; they always act in great coalitions or conspiracies. Direct parallels are the Sea Peoples' conspiracy and the conspiracy of the Libyans against Egypt (inscriptions of year 8, ll. 17–18 and year 5, ll. 26–28). However, Ramses III was a "plagiarizer and self-aggrandizer of the first order."[95] He ordered direct copies from the records and illustrations of the Ramesseum and without doubt, from the today destroyed funerary temple of Merenptah in his direct neighbourhood. He even took a quite important amount of blocks, recuts and not recuts, by quarrying other temples, especially those of his predecessors.[96] Ramses III copied topographic lists from their monuments,[97] but he omitted Naharina/Ḫanigalbat mentioned in the Qadesh-lists of Ramses II, which was meanwhile finally conquered by Shalmaneser I ca. 1259/58 BC.[98]

The Great Inscription of Year 5[99], i.e. March 1184 to March 1183 BC,[100] starts with the victory of Ramses III in the 1st Libyan War and the praise of the pharaoh

[93] Cf. Heinz 2001, especially pp. 19–20, 53–58, 298–322. Models: Nubian campaign of Sethos I, Qadesh/Amurru campaign of Sethos I, Ramses II campaigns in Palestine and Syria, Asiatic campaign of Merenptah (conquest of Gezer and Ashkelon). The locations are interchangeable. Misleading is Redford 2000 when trying to defend the trustworthiness of the Medinet Habu depictions and texts.

[94] Cf. Cifola 1988; 1991. The texts (and pictures!) are part of the 'King's Novel' as a narrative focussing on the pharaoh's deeds with specific structures and elements; cf. Loprieno 1996.

[95] Cf. Lesko 1992; Drews 2000, pp. 167–168.

[96] Cf. Nims 1976; Lesko 1992.

[97] Cf. in general Stockfisch 2008.

[98] Cancik-Kirschbaum 2008, especially pp. 210–213.

[99] Kitchen 2008, p. 19; Egerton – Wilson 1936, pp. 19–34.

[100] The most probable dates are Ramses II 1279–1213 (convincing date for the accession 31.5.1279) and Merenptah 1213 (accession between 23rd July and 3rd August) — 1204 BC. The last documented date for Merenptah is in his 10th year (24.9.1204); he died before the end of this regnal year (Beckerath 1997, 105 and n. 429) 1204. Sethos II was the son and crown prince of Merenptah (Seti-Merenptah) and followed his father very probably in December 1204 BC. Amenmesse, a younger half-brother of Sethos II, usurped the royal power obviously first in Nubia with the support of the viceroy in office, and then gained control over Thebes and Upper Egypt in Sethos' 2nd year. Amenmesse's 3rd and 4th year are attested in Thebes, but also the 1st year of Sethos II when he already built his tomb in the Valley of the Kings (KV 13; cf. for the evidence of the ostraca and of P. Salt 124 also Janssen 1997). Amenmesse was defeated in his 4th year and removed by Sethos II who died in October of his 6th or 7th year, i.e. 1198 or 1197 BC; the earlier date seems more plausible. His young son Siptah was under the tutorship of the chief-chancellor Baya, the real ruler of the country, although Sethos' II widow Tewosret, Siptah's

(ll. 1–51). However, the text changes in ll. 13–17 to events in Amurru; the prince of Amurru is destroyed, his people are taken captives, scattered and humiliated, the surviving people had all fled to the Egyptian territory. The war against the Sea Peoples filled ll. 51–59; it is noteworthy that only the Tjekker and the Peleset are here presented by name. The text clearly distinguished between the enemies on land and the raiders on Sea. However, there is a major problem. The fact that Ramses III gives a record of the Sea Peoples' war in his year 5 together with his 1st Libyan war can very well be explained by the fact that Merenptah was fighting in his 5th year against Libyans and Sea Peoples too. Ramses' aim of self-aggrandizing in the composition of this stela was to be victorious at the same level in his 5th year as Merenptah was in the same year of his reign.[101] There are more problems about the 1st Libyan War, because Ramses III integrated names of tribes and chiefs from Merenptah's records, and we can assume that he at least partially copied the lost illustrated records of Merenptah's Libyan campaign too. The aimed parallelization of both campaigns even in the description of the locations is obvious. But the record of Ramses III for this campaign had no relevant dating and no precise list of booty in contrast to the records for his 2nd Lybian war in year 11. Therefore it is a plausible assumption that, despite the battle scene presented in Medinet Habu, the fighting against Libyan tribes was in reality a series of clearing actions against penetrating nomadic and semi nomadic Libyan groups and happened not only in year 5, but during the early years of Ramses III, and that he launched a minor campaign led by himself into the troubled zone west of the Nile delta of Lower Egypt in his year 5 to compete ideologically with Merenptah's great victory. The whole fighting on the north-western frontier was styled into a single great victory of the pharaoh which in reality never happened in that way.

On the outer side of the temple the pictorial report is composed in a continuous *narratio:* Nubian War, 1st Libyan war, Sea Peoples campaign (Djahi — Lion's hunt — naval battle) and triumph, 2nd Libyan war of year 11. The 'Asiatic war' is given neither in a continuous textual account nor in a continuous series of pictures; there are three separate pictures of conquest: a city of the Canaanites "in Amurru" (Sherden as

stepmother, claimed the first place for herself. After Siptah's death Tewosret proclaimed herself pharaoh and is still documented in her 8th year (after January 1190 or 1189 BC; she continued counting the years of Siptah). Obviously Sethnacht removed Tewosret from the Throne by force and liquidated the partisans of the already executed Baya (O. IFAO 1864). He took the title Pharaoh in March 1190 or 1189; 1190 is more plausible. In his first year, Sethnacht had to fight to gain control over the whole country. He died in his third regnal year. His son Ramses III climbed the throne on the 7th of March, i.e. in 1188 BC; his 5th year is March 1184 to March 1183 BC. Cf. Beckerath 1997, pp. 103–108, 127–129; however Amenmesse was not the successor of Merenptah, but a rival king (Kraus 1997). Cf. for the historical context Drenkhahn 1980; Seidlmayer 1991; Maderna-Sieben 1991. The assumption of Krauss that Amenmesse was first Messuwy, viceroy of Kush, and usurped the royal power in Upper Egypt (Krauss even tries to identify him with Moses) is not possible; cf. Yurco 1997. Grandet 1993, p. 47f. dates the accession of Ramses III into January 1184.

[101] Cf. Lesko 1992. I do not follow him in the assumption that there was no first Libyan campaign at all. Cf. above for P. Harris, for the locations Grandet II, pp. 249–250.

Egyptian elite soldiers with Naue II-sword, round shield and typical helmet), the storm on Tunip, the conquest of two cities of the Hittites, one of them should be the city of "Arzi"[102]. However, Ramses III never marched for conquest into Syria. In the outer closing scene Hittites are missing, in the inner a whole summary of his represented deeds is given: defeated Libyans, Hittites, Bedouins (!), Sea People, Asiatic population. The Southern and Northern Triumphal Scene in Medinet Habu pylon, l. 9 and 11 (Kitchen 2008, p. 72 and 75) is the only place where the victory over the Bedouins is mentioned. The uniformity of the ethnic characterisation of the enemies is a fundamental element for the narrative structures of the pictorial reports of Sethos I, Ramses II or Ramses III.[103] It cannot be seen as reality.

The Great Inscription of Year 8 (March 1181 to March 1180) is devoted to the Sea Peoples' campaign.[104] In the general praise of the pharaoh (ll. 1–12), a specific accent is laid on the defeat of the Asiatics who were forced in battle to retreat (ll. 1, 4 and 28). In the speech of the pharaoh praising himself as the saviour of Egypt, the central passage became the starting point for the construct of an all devastating 'Sea Peoples catastrophe' in Anatolia, the Eastern Mediterranean and the Levant as a single event ending the world of Late Bronze Age. "The foreign countries, they made a conspiracy on their isles. Removed and scattered in battle were the countries at one time [i.e. the attackers by the Pharao, then follow the mention of the earlier attacked:[105]] No land could stand up against their arms and (the lands) from Hatti on — Qode (*Qdy*), Karkemish, Arzawa and Alashia — were cut off at one time. A camp was set up in one place in Amurru; they devastated its people and its land was like what had never existed. They came on towards Egypt although the fire was prepared before them [i.e. the Egyptian defence was ready]. Their alliance was the Peleset, Tjekker, Shakalusha, Dꜣnwnꜣ/Danuna,[106] and Washash. The lands united[107] laid their hands on the land to the outer circuit of the world, their hearts trusting and confident" (ll. 16–18). "I organized my frontier in Djahi, prepared the (local) chiefs, garrison-commanders and maryannu-warriors. I caused the Nile mouth(s) to be prepared, like a strong rampart, with warships, (large) vessels and boats, (all) prepared; and they are manned completely from bow to stern with valiant warriors bearing their weapons" (ll. 19–20). The report of the fighting seems to mix the events on land and sea into one event; however it is only a summary: "Those who reached my frontier, their seed no (longer) exists, and their heart and soul is finished eternally and forever. Those who came on together by sea, the full flame was before them, at the Nile mouth, while a stockade

102 Cf. Kitchen 2008, p. 61 n. 1.
103 Cf. Heinz 2001, 204.
104 Kitchen 2008, pp. 32–36; Egerton – Wilson 1936, pp. 49–58; Edel 1985 for the linguistic analysis of the central passage ll. 16–20.
105 Edel 1985, pp. 225–226.
106 Cf. Edel 1983, pp. 96–97.
107 Edel 1985, pp. 228–230.

of lances surrounded them on the shore — (they were) dragged in, capsized and laid prostrate on the beach, slain and made into heaps from tail to head; their ships and property were as fallen into the water. I made the lands turn back from (even) mentioning Egypt; (when) they pronounce my name in their lands, then they are burned down" (ll. 23–25).

There is no doubt that this passage is full of propaganda and ideology. The great coalition and its united action are stereotypes, as said before, and the list of "fallen lands up to the very circuit of the world" should emphasize the greatness of Ramses' victory. We can assume with good reason that Hatti, Arzawa and Karkemish are mentioned because they are prominent enemies in the Qadesh-records of Ramses II. It is not possible to use this propagandistic formulation as real historical evidence, neither for Karkemish or Hatti nor for the contemporary states in Western Anatolia, Mira-Kuwalija or Šeha-Riverland. The only historical information is given for Amurru in a combination of both inscriptions. Amurru, i.e. the rich coastal plain north of today Lebanon with the capital at Ṣumur, probably Tell Kazel, was invaded and conquered, the royal dynasty vanished and a lot of fugitives fled to the south into the territory under Egyptian control. The invaders were only classified as coming from the North, somewhere beyond the Sea in Egyptian perspective. This might have happened shortly before or in the 5th year of Ramses III and the pharaoh promptly reacted by alarming and strengthening the Egyptian garrisons and the local lords in Djahi because of the threatening turmoil. However, the attackers of coastal cities and areas were operating on ship, most probably not in large pirate flotillas; against possible raids, Ramses III activated the coastal defence of Egypt, especially of the Nile delta. Ramses III had started his reign with a reorganisation of the administration, army and fleet and with the building of his temple complex in Medinet Habu.[108] His naval policy was probably a reaction to the growing insecurity on the Levantine Sea. Now the reorganisation and strengthening of the Egyptian fleet at the beginning of his reign paid well. It seems quite possible that the collapse of Ugarit had already happened around the beginning of his reign, thus in the early eighties. It is not necessary that this event should be dated close to the turmoil in Amurru or Ramses' year 8.

The narration of the Sea Peoples' war report starts when the king issued weapons to his army (Medinet Habu I, pl. 29), followed by the march of Pharaoh and his army to Djahi ("His Majesty sets out for Djahi, just like Montu, to trample down every foreign country that has infringed his frontier"; pl. 31). The battle scene on land comes next (pl. 32–34).[109] The text to the first scene, the issue of weapons, gives an important marker: "the heart of the land of the Libyans is removed, and the Peleset

[108] Cf. also Grandet 1993, pp. 70–153, 164–175.
[109] Texts Kitchen 2008, pp. 24–26; Egerton – Wilson 1936, pp. 35–39.

are in suspense (i. e. anxious), hidden in their towns" (ll. 20/24). This is not a description of a population living on ships and coming by ship from far away over the Sea. As elite troops of the Egyptian army, Sherden and Nubians are mentioned here separately (ll. 37/40).The narration of the Sea Peoples' war is interrupted by the scene of Pharaoh's lions' hunt (pl. 35) as the symbol of his victorious might. After the lions' hunt follows the naval battle in the mouths of the Nile (pl. 37–39).[110] "Now indeed, the northern foreign countries that were in their isles were restless in their bodies; they penetrated the channels of the Nile mouths. Their nostrils have ceased (to work), so that they would (even) desire to breathe air ... (they are) overturned and destroyed in their place(s) ... their weapons were scattered in the sea ... and the fugitive ends up fallen in the water" (ll. 8–18). In the celebration scene of the victory, which is related to the whole war, not only to the naval battle, Ramses III receives captives and spoil and addresses his soldiers and entourage: "The foreign countries that came from their land, from their isles in the midst of the Great Sea, they were bound straight for the Nile-land, their hearts relying on their arms; (but) a net was laid ready for them to ensnare them. Caught was who(ever) entered the Nile mouths, falling into its midst, pinioned on the spot and butchered, and their chests hacked up" (ll. 2–7). It is surprising that in the final presentation scene (pl. 43) the captive (fallen) chiefs of the Tjekker and those of the Libyans (!) are presented in picture and text; his is an ideological construct. The same is true for the topographical list at base including Naharina, Tunip, Qatna, Asiya, Artug(ga) and mixing up traditional 'Nine Bows' with Syrian and other geographic names by using careless copying of elder lists. Captives on the statue bases in the first court of the temple are also ahistoric:, "the wretched chief of Qode, the wretched chief of Hatti," but then "the lands of the Peleset" is mentioned alone.[111] In the "South Rhetorical Stela" of Year 12, the building inscription of the temple,[112] Ramses III praised himself when summarizing his successes: "I laid down the Tjekker, the land of the Peleset, the Danuna, the Weshesh, and the Shakalusha" (ll. 7–8). In the Rhetoric Stela of Chapel C, Deir-el Medina,[113] the praise of is very fragmentary and its restoration not sure (ll. 7–9); the Turush and their characterization are clearly taken from the inscriptions of Merenptah; here, the Peleset are not mentioned as coming from the midst of the Sea. In the presentation scene of pylon II for the Sea Peoples' campaign[114], first the Asiatic enemy is emphasized, only later the Peleset, Danuna and Shakalusha (ll. 14–15). Presented were only captives of the Danuna and Peleset (l. 23 and 24).

[110] Five ships of the enemies pressed by four Egyptian ships, on the shore the shooting Egyptian archers. Text Kitchen 2008, pp. 27–30; Egerton – Wilson 1936, pp. 41–42.

[111] Egerton – Wilson 1936, 118C, e, 119A.

[112] Kitchen 2008, pp. 56–57. For the reading cf. Cifola 1994, p. 5 n. 18.

[113] Kitchen 2008, pp. 68–70.

[114] Kitchen 2008, pp. 30–32; Egerton – Wilson 1936, pp. 46–48.

In contrast to the 2nd and even to the 1st Libyan war the report on the Sea Peoples campaign is much less detailed and little attention is paid to the narrative structure of the record.[115] There is no scene of Ramses' triumphal return, the text is only vague and imprecise, no concrete place names and no date are given and furthermore the campaign is mentioned twice, in year 5 and in year 8 as obvious doublets. The picture of a united military coalition of the enemies making a combined attack on land and sea at the same time is an ideological fiction;[116] the reality shows two different events and places. One group of enemies are migrating people, the other are warriors or better bands of pirates on ships. No concrete description of single decisive battles is given; instead we find only stereotype and rhetoric formulas. There are no precise numbers of fallen enemies, captives and booty as in the 2nd Libyan war. The reasonable conclusion is that quite varying and multifarious military events were transformed into the traditional model of military self-representation.[117] Turush, Scherden and Hatti as defeated enemies in the triumphal relief of the eastern pylon are anachronistic additions and even contradictory. Sherden warriors are marching against the 'Sea Peoples' to Djahi and are fighting against the 'Sea Peoples' at the frontier of Djahi.[118] Sherden troops are a prominent contingent of the Egyptian army in the lion's hunt scene (Medinet Habu I, pl. 35), on the march into the 2nd Libyan War and in the 'Asiatic war' (Medinet Habu I, pl. 62; 94–95). They are also fighting with spears and Naue II swords in the battle of the 2nd Libyan war (Medinet Habu I, pl. 72); in this scene, warriors with the typical 'feather hat-helmets' are also fighting with spears and long swords against the Libyans (Medinet Habu I, pl. 71–72). Furthermore Sherden troops are already marching into the first Libyan war and even Sea Peoples' (!) warriors with the typical 'feather hat-helmets' are fighting with spears and long swords against the Libyans in this war too![119] The 'feather hat-helmet' soldiers are also shown in the relief of the fictional Nubian war as a part of the Egyptian army (Medinet Habu I, pl. 8).They are very probably copied from Merentptah's former prisoners of war who were now military colonists in Egypt.

In the Sea Peoples' reliefs of Ramses III we have two stereotypical depictions of hostile warriors, one with Naue II sword, horned helmet, cuirass, round shield and short kilt, the second with the famous 'feathered hat', a helmet type of central Mediterranean origin as already discussed above. The first stereotype is present in the naval battle together with the second; the second is the only type in the land battle. There is no possibility to distinguish the combatants of the different groups of Sea Peoples

[115] Cf. Cifola 1991, especially pp. 18–20.

[116] Cf. Cifola 1988, pp. 284, 302–303; 1991, pp. 51–55; Heinz 2001, pp. 53–57.

[117] Cf. Cifola 1991, p. 55.

[118] Medinet Habu I, pl. 30–31; 32–33: fighting against ox-cart no. 1 with spears and killing the warrior in ox-cart no. 4 with the sword.

[119] Medinet Habu I, pl. 17 and 19–20; cf. also Grandet 1993, pp. 180–181.

mentioned in the texts. The horned helmet-men are similar to the Sherden, but at the same time clearly distinguishable from them because of the missing ball on top of the helmet. The other type of Sea Peoples' warriors characterizes the Italian-Aegean straw cap with bronze lamellas and 'feathers', neck-guard and chin-belt, a short kilt with tassels and a breast-cuirass. This warrior-type had reached Cyprus already in the 13th c. BC (LC II). However the civilians, women, children and non-combatant men, partially whole families, depicted in heavy ox-carts with one ax-disc wheels, in the great fighting scene at the frontier of Djahi (Medinet Habu I, pl. 32.34) represent different 'ethnic' stereotypes in hairstyle and costume, Canaanite and Syrian, Bedouin and even Libyan types, but no Aegean one.[120] In the presentation scene of the Sea Peoples war, only captives with feathered hat-helmets are shown (Medinet Habu I, pl. 44). However, they are also shown as captives in the victorious return from the Asiatic campaign (Medinet Habu I, pl. 98). Therefore it is obvious that the reliefs are no realistic documentation. We can even assume with good arguments that the two types of Sea Peoples' warriors, apart from the long known Sherden soldiers, were already depicted in Merenptah's lost funerary temple in the triumphal illustration of his victory of year 5. 'Feather-hat' warriors were obviously since then part of the Egyptian army as mercenaries or military colonists, perhaps mostly former captives of Merenptah's Libyan campaign. The use of a stereotype depiction of the different actors in historical reliefs was necessary to make a reading of the pictures by themselves possible. This technique was in permanent use not only in Egypt but also in Greek and Roman propaganda art; a well-known example is Trajan's column in Rome.[121] Therefore we cannot deduce from the reliefs that all enemies of Ramses III in his campaigns against 'Northerners' really had only these two forms of appearance. The 'feather-hat' as the dominating appearance of Sea Peoples' warriors in the fighting and especially in the depiction of captives might only be a copy of Merenptah's pictorial language. And if it might not be a copy from his predecessor, it is a formula of the pictorial language developed for the reliefs of Ramses III. However the first solution is more probable. The uniformity of the military equipment of the Sea Peoples cannot be realistic too. Metal cuirass and metal helmet were without doubt only the equipment of the upper social stratum, not of all the common fighters. Furthermore helmets with horns on both sides might be disadvantageous in real close combat; they are only of great value for aggrandizing the physical power and threatening outfit of military leaders and heroic elite warriors. In the panels of captives (Tjekker, Danuna, Peleset, chiefs of all foreign lands) who were presented to Amun and Mut (Medinet

[120] Thus not convincing Sweeney and Yasur-Landau 1999 based on an extensive migration theory.

[121] Other elements of the traditional pictorial language are fortified towers or migdols, an emblem of royal power, not a real topographic definition. Cf. Heinz 2001; also Cline and O'Connor 2003, pp. 127–130, especially p. 130.

Habu, 1st court)[122] only one unified type of 'Sea Peoples' appears, the type with the feathered hat-helmet. The triumphal reliefs were not intended to provide historical information, but to present the pharaoh being victorious over the whole world and to enact in a magic way the defeat of the foreign foes/peoples and places named by the pharaoh.[123] Thus we cannot expect any naturalistic picture of the Sea Peoples in the reliefs of Ramses III, but stereotypes of that pictorial language which was especially developed under Ramses II and Merenptah in Egyptian art. No real hint is given for the homelands of the so-called second Sea Peoples'wave. However it is evident that the fighting on the frontier of Djahi had a totally different nature in contrast to the defeat of pirate raids against the Nile delta.

Conclusion

There is no question that "the dramatic historical account, based almost entirely on a handful of Egyptian inscriptions" that the Sea Peoples came sweeping across the Mediterranean and causing the collapse of the Hittite Empire, the downfall of Cyprus, "the very collapse of Bronze Age civilization in the Aegean and eastern Mediterranean"[124] needs dramatic revision. No real evidence exists that combined military and migratory forces moved along the southern coast of Anatolia or even through Anatolia; the attack of pirate flotillas into the Nile mouths does not indicate that they intended to penetrate and settle into Egypt or that the land and sea battle took place side by side just beyond the mouth of the Pelusinian Nile.[125] O'Connor even postulates a "well organized, centralized and relatively short-term program" of the Sea Peoples under a core leadership of perhaps a supreme chief, a program highly successful until the confrontation with Egypt.[126] It is obvious from the depiction of the battle in the frontier zone of Egyptian Djahi that Ramses III was confronted with nomadic or semi nomadic squatters and moving rural population with their heavy oxcarts and their families, not with an army of Sea Peoples attacking Egypt and followed by a long migration trek.[127] The texts given to comment the Djahi campaign mention at the very beginning "the Peleset are in suspense, hidden in their towns"[128], and the Great Inscription of year 8 emphasizes "I have overthrown the Asiatics [--] in their lands ... No land could stand firm, at hearing my name; they abandoned their settlements,

[122] Medinet Habu I, pl. 44.
[123] Cf. also Wilson 2005.
[124] See Cline and O'Connor 2003, p. 107, 109 for a summary.
[125] Thus Redford 2000, especially pp. 12–13; not convincing also Cline and O'Connor 2003, p. 120.
[126] O'Connor 2000, p. 100. In Cline and O'Connor 2003 he no longer defends the great historical trustworthiness of the royal narrations.
[127] Rightly emphasized by Drews 2000.
[128] Kitchen 2008, p. 24, 28:1.

deserting their place(s), scattered [--]" (ll. 28–30). The punitive action against the Sâru, missing in Medinet Habu war reliefs, must be summarized under the Djahi campaign because it was of greater importance as documented in P. Harris I. The whole campaign should be seen as a series of minor fighting and punitive actions against Bedouins and moving groups of rural or pastoral population who had caused disturbances in the Egyptian northern and eastern frontier zones of Djahi. All such events at the frontiers of Djahi were condensed and styled into one monumental battle scene connected with the expedition of Ramses III into Canaan and southern Syria in his year 8 ("His Majesty sets out for Djahi just like Montu, to trample down every foreign country that has infringed his frontier"[129]) which obviously was the final Egyptian action to annihilate turmoil in the northern frontiers of the empire. Such a royal counter actions had also happened in year 5 in an expedition to the Libyan frontier zone and later in year 11 when the final major offensive against the Libyans was launched.

Today the discussion about the Peleset must be based on the new evidence of the Taita-inscriptions. However, this is the subject David Hawkin's contribution. The city of Dor is connected with the Tjekker in the Wenamun-tale, while the later, so-called Onomasticon of Amenemope[130] copied elder topographic lists. The historical situation during the 1st half of the 21st dynasty is well reflected in the literary story of Wenamun;[131] it is a historical novel varying between historical report, literary fiction and religious and political intentions, but based on a realistic knowledge of the international situation when Egypt had lost its control in Syria and Palestine. The date given for the beginning of the story is the 5th year of Smendes I in Tanis, i.e. 1070/69 or 1066/65 BC; the hero of the tale should have left Egypt by ship in the following year with the order to bring timber for the god Amun to Thebes. He was confronted with problems in Dor, the city of the Tjekker and ruled by their prince, because his silver was robbed and not replaced by the ruler of the city; therefore Wenamun robbed silver from a ship of the Tjekker on his way to Byblos. Later eleven ships of the Tjekker blocked him in Byblos. The story gives us the information that the Tjekker had established their rule in the city-state of Dor, far north from the centre of Philistine settlement in the southern coastal plain, and played a role in the maritime traffic and trade along the Levantine coast in the 1st half of the 11th c. BC. But no Philistine-type material was found in Dor, instead

[129] Kitchen 2008, p. 26, 30:5.

[130] Under no. 238–252 foreign peoples and lands in the west and the Hittite Empire and its allies in the battle of Qadesh, under no. 253–294 peoples, foreigners and foreign lands from Syria to Nubia; no. 268–270 are Sherden, Shekelesh, Peleset, obviously a copy from a Sea Peoples list; no. 257–267 cities in Palestine and Phoenicia. The list is neither an itinerary nor is there a recognizable logic behind the order of the presentation. The Onomasticon is a scribal product and dates probably to the time of Sheshonq I or to the middle of the 21st Dynasty. Cf. Wilson 2005, especially pp. 44, 63.

[131] Cf. Schipper 2005.

evidence for a large and stable local population mixed up with a small group of migrants from Syria and Cyprus.[132] This is the evidence for a city ruled by one of the Sea Peoples!

It is surprising that Yasur-Landau (2010) does not discuss the term Danuna, which can be identified with the land and kingdom of Danuna, akkad. ^{KUR}Da-nu-na. Except the Lukka warriors, the only other possible identification for one of the Sea Peoples are the *Dȝnwnȝ*/Danuna. They provide evidence that people from the Central Cilician plain and coastal zone participated in the actions. The name cannot be identified with the Danaoi, the people of T/Danaya, a different and since long fixed term as discussed above. Speculations in that direction fail. The country was already in the mid-14th c. BC within the interests of Egypt. In his report to Amenophis IV, Abi-Milku, the Egyptian vassal king of Tyre, answered the question of the pharaoh about new information (EA 151, ll. 49–58) that the king of Danuna had died and his brother had followed him on the throne and that his land is in peace. His second information was that one half of the palace of Ugarit had burnt down. The land of Danuna, Phoen. DNN, and its people, Phoen. DNNYM, are known as the land and kingdom of Que in the 10th to 8th c. BC, later an Assyrian province. The name is written in cuneiform texts as Quaia, Qawa, Quwe, Que etc. or in Babylonian terminology as Ḫume.[133] Urikki, known in the Assyrian sources as king of Que ca. 738–709 BC, can be identified with king Warika/Awariku in the two Luwian-Phoenician bilingual inscriptions of Karatepe[134] and Çineköy.[135] From these texts it is evident that DNNYM means the same as Luw. Adanawannis, the people of (the kingdom of) Adana (Luw. Adanuwa, Hitt. At/daniya). The author of the Çineköy inscription, Awariku, is the king of the DNNYM, the Adanaeans, in the Phoenician version and of Ḫiyawa in the Luwian version of the inscription. He mentioned Mu-ka-sa as his ancestor. In the Karatepe-bilingual the dynasty of Adana is the "House of Mukasa."[136] In both Phoenician versions the name of the ancestor is written MPŠ, in Greek *Mopsos*. Yakubovich postulates in an axiomatic way that "Mok^{w}so constituted a common dynastic name in the Greek Colonies in Asia Minor in Late Bronze Age and Early Iron Age;"[137] however, there is no proof or convincing argument for such an assumption.[138] The name

[132] Cf. Gilboa 2006/2007; also Yassur-Landau 2010, pp. 171, 304. It is evident that the interpretation of the finds by E. Stern was based on axiomatic suggestions developed on the Wenamun tale and Biblical traditions.

[133] Hawkins, *RlA* 11, 2007, pp. 191–195. Cf. Strobel 2010, pp. 47–48.

[134] Hawkins 2000, I/1 pp. 45–68 Cilicia no. 1.

[135] Tekoğlu and Lemaire 2000.

[136] Hawkins, *RlA* 8, 1993–1997, p. 413.

[137] Yakubovich 2010, p. 156.

[138] Jasink and Marino 2007 try to demonstrate that the names of the Mukasa/Muksa-, Phoen. Mpš-Dynasty is of Aegean, of Cretan origin, but their arguments and linguistic combinations are neither compelling nor convincing as many of the other combination proposed by Jasink and Yakubovich, for example *Wrikios > *Wrakios > Rhakios, the legendary father of the Greek Mopsos, or Awariku

mo-qo-so in Linear B-tablets from Knossos (De 1381) and Pylos (Sa 774) is not proven to be Greek. That confirms the appearance of Mukšuš[139] in the Indictment of Madduwatta in a purely Anatolian context. The obviously wide spread name can be seen as Luwian, a name used in Luwian speaking western and southern Anatolia. Xanthos the Lydian (FGrHist 765 F 17) gives the name Moksos, not Mopsos, and makes him a Lydian; he obviously follows a non-Greek and non-Phoenician spelling of the name.

The Hittite and Luwian name of Adana and its kingdom/land, i.e. Adaniya, Adanuwa or Adanawannis, was obviously never truncated by the aphaeresis of the initial /a/. This initial vowel was not accentuated and could be slurred over when the name was transferred into the Semitic Canaanite language of the Levant and its Akkadian writing as in EA 151. This truncated form was used by the Egyptians and continued into the Phoenician language and script. Jasink, Yakubovich and Hajnal[140] think that Ḫiyawa should be a truncated variant of Aḫḫiyawa. However, the aphaeresis of initial /a/ is only a phenomenon of Luwian dialects during the 1st millennium BC, known in Lycia, Pamphylia and Pisidia. It does not appear in Hittite and there is a clear linguistic distinction between the two terms in Hittite writing. Of great importance is that the *res gestae* of Arnuwanda I has this name already in a list of cities/city states including Adaniya.[141] Ḫijawa-soldiers ("men of Ḫiyawa") were garrisoned by Šuppiluliuma II in Lukka, and the king of Ugarit had to deliver the food supply for them using his own ships; this was a strict order of the Hittite Great King.[142] The city-state KUR^{URU} Adaniya came under Hittite control first in the time of Labarna I; later it was part of Kizzuwatna (treaty of KBo I 5, ll. IV 53–61). Tarša and Adaniya were the central cities of southern Kizzuwatna, the Danuna being the population of

< Evarkhos > Euarchos. The name of the Cypriot king of Amathus Wo-ro-i-ko is no argument for the Greek nature of the name Warika/Awariku, especially because Cilicia and Cyprus had a dense network of connections in the north-eastern Levant. *Vanassa* and ΔIϜIA as epithets (regularly used in Homeric language!) of the Artemis of Perge, the Lady of Perge, do not point to a Mycenaean colonization of Pamphylia, but to common elements in the later Greek dialects of Pamphylia and Cyprus, as Yakubovich says himself. Cf. for Mopsos Strobel 2010, p. 48 n. 48.

[139] Hawkins, *RlA* 8, 1993–1997, p. 413.

[140] Jasink and Maroni 2007; Yakubovic 2010, pp. 150–156; quite problematic I. Hajnal, Namen und ihre Etymologien — als Beweisstücke nur bedingt tauglich? (http://www.uibk.ac.at/sprachen-literaturen/sprawi/pdf/Hajnal_Cilicia._namen.pdf). Yakubovich 2010, pp. 151–152 supposes that the Achaeans initiated the colonization of Pamphylia and Cilicia and that the name Ḫiyawa shows that the "memory of Greek settlers" probably lived in the name of the kingdom centred in Adana still in a time when its population was only speaking Luwian and Phoenician.

[141] ^{URU}ḫi-ja-w[a-an?] KUB XXIII 21 Vs. 6'; CTH 143; Carruba 2008, p. 66. However this is not an argument for the presence of Mycenaean Greeks in Cilicia in the 15th c. BC.

[142] ^{LÚ} hi-ia-ú-wi-i; ^{LÚ} Hi-ia-a-ú; $^{LÚ.MEŠ}$ Hi-ia-ú-wi-i RS 94.2523; 94.2530. Lackenbacher and Malbran-Labat 2005; however, starting from the assumption that these must be Aḫḫijawa-people, they translate "(Ah)hiyawa". The two letters, showing business as usual between the Hittite sovereign and his vassal kings of Amurru and Ugarit are close to ca. 1190/1185 BC because the son of Ammurapi, who himself came to the throne quite young in 1210/1205 BC, was already in the age to act as an ambassador of his father at the Hittite court.

the Central Cilician Plain (Phoen. ʿMQ ʿDN) west of the Nur Dağı. Therefore we can convincingly assume that Ḫiyawa was already in the 2nd millennium the Luwian, non-Hurrian denomination of the coastal plain of East Cilicia round the Gulf of Iskenderun with Kinet Höyük as one centre. The Egyptians used for this area the non-Luwian geographical term *Qdy*. In the Iron Age, this country was united with the kingdom of Adana under the rule of the Luwian Mukasa/Muksus-Dynasty. Our analysis provides a real hint of Anatolian-Levantine interaction in the transformation in the 12th c. BC. That such groups of the population in the Central Cilician Plain and coastal zone were able to be part of Ramses' III 'Sea Peoples' must be connected with a breakdown of the control of the Hittite Empire over this region, a breakdown which could not be compensated by the king of Karkemish. The Danuna had the possibility to move on land and sea into *Qdy*, Mukiš and Ugarit and even Amurru in short distance. The Early Iron Age culture of the area from Cilicia to the Amuq Plain and beyond shows us close connections in many aspects, especially in its painted ware and local production of LH III C style pottery.

The death of Šuppiluliuma II perhaps around 1190 BC might have stimulated further dynastic instability and centrifugal activities. But without the archives of Karkemish, the historical reconstruction of the events remains vague. However, we must take into consideration another major player, the Aḫlamu, Aramaic pastoral tribes who became a dangerous problem for Ḫatti/Karkemish and Assur by the end of the 13th c. BC., especially when a quite abrupt climate deterioration worsened the situation in northern Mesopotamia and inner Syria. The living conditions in the dry farming zones and for the seminomadic or pastoralist population became precarious. The massive pressure of the Aḫlamu must have caused the fall of Emar, the important outpost of Karkemish, sometime after 1185 BC. After the breakdown of political and military authority in Ugarit and Amurru and their Syrian hinterland, population groups and pastoralist elements of the Syrian population became mobile and regional and interregional habitation tracking and short-distance migration developed as shown in the depiction of Ramses' III Djahi-campaign. However, the details will be discussed in a future article.

BIBLIOGRAPHY

ADROM, F.

2008 "Mappa mundi. Neue Facetten einer spätbronzezeitlichen Weltkarte," in *Altägyptische Weltsichten,* Ägypten und Altes Testament 68, edited by F. Adrom and K. and A. Schlüter, pp. 11–18. Wiesbaden: Harrassowitz.

ALBERTINI, G.

2005 "The Earliest Contacts between Southeastern Sicily and Cyprus in Late Bronze Age," *Aegaeum* 25: 343–351.

2007 "Minima Thapsiana. Riflessioni sulla cronologia dell'abitato di Thapsos," *Rivista di Science Preistoriche* 57: 363–376.

2008 "There is something Cypriot in the Air. Some Thoughts on the Problem of the Base Ring Pottery and other Cyprus-Related Items from (Local) Middle Bronze Age Contexts in Sicily," in *Islands Dialogue: Proceedings of the Postgraduate Cypriot Archaeology Conference (POCA) 2006*, pp. 130–153. Edinburgh: University of Edinburgh.

ALPARSLAN, M.
2002 "Artukka: Das Land Assuwa und seine Lokalisation," *Anadolu Araştırmaları/ Jahrbuch für Kleinasiatische Forschung* 16: 28–34.

ASTOUR, M. C.
1967 *Hellenosemitica*. Leiden: Brill.

BECKERATH, J. VON
1997 *Chronologie des pharaonischen Ägypten*. Mainz: von Zabern.

BECKMAN, G.
1999 *Hittite Diplomatic Texts*, 2nd ed. Atlanta: Scholars Press.

BELARDELLI, C.
1994 "La ceracica grigia," in *Enotri e Micenei nella Sibarite I*, edited by R. Peroni and F. Trucco, pp. 265–346. Taranto: Istituto per la storia e l'archeologia della Magna Grecia.

BETTELLI, M.
2002 *Italia meridionale e mondo miceneo: ricerche su dinamiche di acculturazione e aspetti archeologici, con perticolare riferimento ai versanti adriatio e ionico della penisola Italiana.* Firenze: All'insegna del giglio.

BIETTI-SESTRIERI, A. M.
1973 "The Metal Industry of Continental Italy, 13th to 11th cent. B.C., and its Connection with the Aegean," *Proceedings of the Prehistoric Society* 39: 383–424.

BORGNA, E. and CÀSSOLA GUIDA, P., ed.
2009 *Dall'Egeo all'Adriatico. Organizzazioni sociali, modi di scambio e interazione in età postpalaziale (XII-XI sec. a.C.).* Roma: Edizioni Quasar.

CANCIK-KIRSCHBAUM, E.
2008 "Assur und Hatti — zwischen Allianz und Konflikt," in *Ḫattuša – Boğazköy. Das Hethiterreich im Spannungsfeld der Alten Orients,* CDOG 6, edited by G. Wilhelm, pp. 205–222. Wiesbaden: Harrassowitz.

CARRUBA, O.
1995 "La Grecia e l'Egitto nel II millennio," *Istituto Lombardo (Rend. Lett.)* 129: 141–160.
2008 *Annali Eetei del Medio Regno*. Pavia: Italian University Press.

CASABONNE, O.
2009 "Kataonia, Melitene, Kummanni, and the Problem of Komana," in *Vin, bière et ivresse dans les civilisations orientales. René Lebrun in honorem*, Acta orientalia Belgica 22, edited by C. Cannuyer *et al.*, pp. 181–188. Louvain-la-Neuve: Société belge d'études orientales.

CAZZELLA, A. and RECCHIA, G.
2009 "The 'Mycenaeans' in the Central Mediterranean: A Comparison between the Adriatic and the Tyrrhenian Seaways," *Pasiphae* 3: 27–40.

CIFOLA, B.
1988 "Ramses III and the Sea Peoples: A Structural Analysis of the Medinet Habu Inscriptions," *Orientalia* NS 57: 275–306.
1991 "The Terminology of Ramses III's Historical Records with a Formal Analysis of War Scenes," *Orientalia* NS 60: 9–57.

1994 "The Role of the Sea Peoples at the End of the Late Bronze Age: A Reassessment of Textual and Archaeological Evidence," *Orientis Antiqui Miscellanea* 1: 1–22.

CLINE, E. H.
1987 "Amenhotep III and the Aegean: A Reassessment of Egypto-Aegean Relations in the 14th Century," *Orientalia* NS 56: 1–36.
2009 *Sailing the Wine-Dark Sea: International Trade and the Late Bronze Age Aegean*, BAR International Series 591 (reprint of the 1994 edition, with additions). Oxford: British Archaeological Reports.

CLINE, E. H., ed.
2010 *The Oxford Handbook of the Bronze Age Aegean (ca. 3000-1000 BC).* Oxford: Oxford University Press.

CLINE, E. and O'CONNOR, D.
2003 "The Mystery of the 'Sea Peoples'," in *Mysterious Lands*, edited by D. O'Connor and S. Quirke, pp. 107–138. London: Institute of Archaeology.

DAKOURI-HILD, A.
2010 "Boeotia. Thebes," in *The Oxford Handbook of the Bronze Age Aegean (ca. 3000-1000 BC),* edited by E. Cline, pp. 614–630, 690–711. Oxford: Oxford University Press.

DOTHAN, T.
1982 *The Philistines and their Material Culture.* Jerusalem: Israel Exploration Society.

DRENKHAHN, R.
1980 *Die Elephantinestele des Sethnacht und ihr historischer Hintergrund*, Ägyptologische Abhandlungen 36. Wiesbaden: Harrassowitz.

DREWS, R.
2000 "Medinet Habu: Oxcarts, Ships, and Migration Theories," *Journal of Near Eastern Studies* 59: 161–190.

DUHOUX, Y.
2008 "Les relations égypto-égéennes au Nouvel Empire: que nous apprend la toponymie?" in *Altägyptische Weltsichten,* Ägypten und Altes Testament 68, edited by F. Adrom and K. and A. Schlüter, pp. 19–34. Wiesbaden: Harrassowitz.

EDEL, E.
1983 "Kleinasiatische und semitische Namen und Wörter aus den Texten der Qadešschlacht in hieroglyphischer Umschrift," in *Fontes atque Pontes. Festgabe Hellmut Brunner*, Ägypten und Altes Testament 5, edited by M. Görg, pp. 90–105. Wiesbaden: Harrassowitz.
1985 "Der Seevölkerbericht aus dem 8. Jahre Ramses' III. (MH II, pl. 46, 15-18)," in *Mélanges Gamal Eddin Mokhtar*, vol. I, edited by P. Posener-Kriéger, pp. 223–237. Kairo: Institut français d'archéologie orientale.
1994 *Die ägyptisch-hethitische Korrespondenz aus Boghazköi in babylonischer und hethitischer Sprache I-II.* Opladen: Westdeutscher Verlag.

EDEL, E. and GÖRG, M.
2005 *Die Ortsnamenslisten im nördlichen Säulenhof des Totentempels Amenophis' III.*, Ägypten und Altes Testament 50. Wiesbaden: Harrassowitz.

EDER, B.
2006 "The World of Telemachos: Western Greece 1200–700 B.C.," in *Ancient Greece from the Mycenaean Palaces to the Age of Homer*, edited by S. Deger-Jalkotzy and I. S. Lemosse, pp. 549–580. Edinburgh: Edinburgh University Press.

EDER, B. and JUNG, R.
2005 "On the Character of Social Relations between Greece and Italy in the 12th/11th c. B.C.," *Aegaeum* 25: 485–497.

EGERTON, W. F. and WILSON, J. A.
1936 *Historical Records of Ramses III. The Texts in Medinet Habu Volumes I and II,* OIP 12. Chicago: Chicago University Press.

FORLANINI, M.
2007 "The Offering List of KBo 4.13 (I 17'–49') to the Local Gods of the Kingdom, Known as Sacrifice List, and the History of the Formation of the Early Hittite State and Its Initial Growing beyond Central Anatolia," in *VI Congresso Internazionale di Ittitologia,* SMEA 49, edited by A. Archi and R. Francia, pp. 259–280. Roma: Istituto di studi sulle Civiltà dell'Egeo e del Vicino Oriente.
2010 "An Attempt at Reconstructing the Branches of the Hittite Royal Family of the Early Kingdom Period," in *Pax Hethitica. Studies on the Hittites and their Neighbours in Honour of Itamar Singer,* StBo 51, edited by Y. Cohen *et al.,* pp. 115–135. Wiesbaden: Harrassowitz.

GARSTANG, J. and GURNEY, O. R.
1959 *The Geography of the Hittite Empire*, London: British Institute of Archaeology at Ankara.

GILBOA, A.
2006/2007 "Fragmenting the Sea Peoples, with an Emphasis on Cyprus, Syria and Egypt: A Tel Dor Perspective," *Scripta Mediterranea* 27–28: 209–244.

GLANVILLE, S. R. K.
1931/1933 "Records of a Royal Dockyard of the Time of Tuthmosis III. Papyrus British Museum 10056 I–II," *Zeitschrift für Ägyptische Sprache und Altertumskunde* 66: 105–122; 68: 7–41.

GÖRG, M.
2008 "Zu einigen kleinasiatischen Toponymen in hieroglyphischer Bezeugung," in *Altägyptische Weltsichten,* Ägypten und Altes Testament 68, edited by F. Adrom and K. and A. Schlüter, pp. 50–55. Wiesbaden: Harrassowitz.

GRANDET, P.
1993 *Ramsès III. Histoire d'un règne.* Paris: Pygmalion.
1994/1999 *Le papyrus Harris I (BM 9999),* vols. I–III. Kairo: Institut français d'archéologie orientale.

GRIMAL, N.
2009 "Peuples, États et cites. Enquête sur la cartographie géopolitique égyptienne," in *Egypt and Cyprus in Antiquity,* edited by D. Michaelides, V. Kassianidou and R. S. Merrillees, pp. 9–22. Oxford and Oakville: Oxbow.

HAIDER, P. W.
1988 *Griechenland – Nordafrika. Ihre Beziehungen zwischen 1500 und 600 v. Chr.* Darmstadt: Wissenschaftliche Buchgesellschaft.
1999 "Vom Nil zum Mäander. Die Beziehungen zwischen dem Pharaonenhof und dem Königreich Arzawa in Westkleinasien," in *Steine und Wege. Festschrift Dieter Knibbe,* edited by P. Scherrer, H. Täuber and H. Thür, pp. 205–219. Wien.
2000 "Die Peloponnes in ägyptischen Quellen des 15. Und 14. Jhs. v. Chr.," in *Österreichische Forschungen zur Ägäischen Bronzezeit 1998,* edited by F. Blakolmer, pp. 149–158. Wien: Phoibos Verlag.

2004 "Westkleinasien nach ägyptischen Quellen des Neuen Reiches," in *Der neue Streit um Troia – Eine Bilanz*, edited by C. Ulf, pp. 174–192, 2nd ed. München: Beck.

2008a "Existierte ein "Groß-Ionien" um 1360 v. Chr.? Zu neuen Fremdvölkerlisten im „Millionenjahrhaus" Amenophis' III. in Theben-West," in *Antike Lebenswelten. Konstanz – Wandel – Wirkungsmacht. Festschrift Igomar Weiler*, edited by P. Mauritsch, W. Petermandl, R. Rollinger and C. Ulf, pp. 667–681. Wiesbaden: Harrassowitz.

2008b "War ein „Groß-Ionien" tatsächlich um 1360 v. Chr. in Westkleinasien existent? Eine kritische Analyse zu den Lesungen und Identifizierungen der jüngst entdeckten topographischen Namenslisten aus der Regierungszeit Amenophis' III.," *Klio* 90: 291–306.

HÄNSEL, B.

2007 "Kreta, Istrien, Alpenvorland – Kontaktwege in der Bronzezeit," in *Von Noricum nach Ägypten. Eine Reise durch die Welt der Antike. Aktuelle Forschungen*, Altertumswissenschaftliche Studien Klagenfurt 3, edited by K. Strobel, pp. 23–37. Klagenfurt: Hermagoras.

HAWKINS, J. D.

2000 *Corpus of Hieroglyphic Luwian Inscriptions I. Inscriptions of the Iron Age*. Berlin and New York: De Gruyter.

2009a "Cilicia, the Amuq, and Aleppo. New Light in a Dark Age," *Near Eastern Archaeology* 74/4: 164–173.

2009b "The Arzawa Letters in Recent Perspective," *British Museum Studies in Ancient Egypt and Sudan* 14: 73–83.

HEINHOLD-KRAMER, S.

1977 *Arzawa. Untersuchungen zu seiner Geschichte nach den hethitischen Quellen*. Heidelberg: Winter.

HEINZ, S. C.

2001 *Die Feldzugsdarstellungen des Neuen Reiches. Eine Bildanalyse*, Österreichische Akademie der Wissenschaften. Denkschriften der Gesamtakademie 18. Wien: Österreichische Akademie der Wissenschaften.

HELCK, W.

1971 *Die Beziehungen Ägyptens zu Vorderasien im 3. Und 2. Jahrtausend v. Chr.*, 2nd ed. Wiesbaden: Harrassowitz.

1979 *Die Beziehungen Ägyptens und Vorderasiens zur Ägäis bis ins 7. Jahrhundert v. Chr.* Darmstadt: Wissenschaftliche Buchgesellschaft (2nd edition 1995).

HELTZER, M.

1983 "Some Questions Concerning the Sherdana in Ugarit," *Israel Oriental Studies* 9: 9–16.

HIRSCHFELD, N.

1996 "Cypriots in Mycenaean Aegean," in *Atti del Secondo Congresso di Micenologia*, vol. I, edited by E. De Miro *et al.*, pp. 289–297. Roma: Grupo editorial internazionale.

HÖLBL, G.

"Die historischen Aussagen der ägyptischen Seevölkerinschriften," in *Griechenland, die Ägäis und die Levante während der »Dark Ages« vom 12. bis zum 9. Jh. v. Chr.*, Sitzungsberichte Wien, Philosophisch-Historische Klasse 418, edited by S. Deger-Jalkotzy, pp. 121–138. Wien: Österreichische Akademie der Wissenschaften.

JANSSEN, J. J.
1997 "Amenmesse and After: The Chronology of the Late Nineteenth Dynasty Ostraca," in *Village Varia. Ten Studies on the History and Administration of Deir El-Medina*, edited by J. J. Janssen, pp. 99–109. Leiden: NINO.

JASINK, A. M. and MARINO, M.
2007 "The West-Anatolian Origins of the Que Kingdom Dynasty," in *VI Congresso Internazionale di Ittitologia*, SMEA 49, edited by A. Archi and R. Francia, pp. 407–426. Roma: Istituto di studi sulle Civiltà dell'Egeo e del Vicino Oriente.

JONES, R., VAGNETTI, L., LEVI, S. T., WILLIAM, J., JENKINS, D. and DE GUIO, A.
2002 "Mycenaean Pottery from Northern Italy. Archaeological and Archaeometric Studies," *SMEA* 44: 221–261.

JUNG, R.
2006 *Chronologia comparata. Vergleichende Chronologie von Südgriechenland und Süditalien von ca. 1700/1600 bis 1000 v. u. Z.*, Veröffentlichung der Mykenischen Kommission 26, Wien: Österreichische Akademie der Wissenschaften.
2009a "Pirates in the Aegean: Italy – the East Aegean – Cyprus and the End of Second Millennium BC," in *Cyprus and the East Aegean: Intercultural contacts from 3000 to 500 B.C.*, edited by V. Karageorghis and O. Kouka, pp. 72–93. Nicosia: A.G. Leventis Foundation.
2009b "I "bronzi internazionali" ed il lore contest sociale fra Adriatico, Penisola balcanica e coste Levantine," in *Dall'Egeo all'Adriatico. Organizzazioni sociali, modi di scambio e interazione in età postpalaziale (XII–XI sec. a.C.),* edited by E. Borgna and P. Càssola Guida, pp. 129–139. Roma: Edizioni Quasar.

JUNG, R. and MEHOFER, M.
2005/2008 "A Sword of the Naue II Type from Ugarit and the Historical Significance of Italian-type Weaponry in the Eastern Mediterranean," *Aegean Archaeology* 8: 111–135.

KILIAN, K.
2007 *Tiryns XV. Die Handgemachte Keramik mykenischer Zeitstellung.* Wiesbaden: Harrassowitz.

KILIAN-DIRLMEIER, I.
1994 *Die Schwerter in Griechenland (außerhalb der Peloponnes), Bulgarien und Albanien*, Prähistorische Bronzefunde IV 12. Stuttgart: Steiner.

KITCHEN, K. A.
1996/1999 *Ramesside Inscriptions. Translated and Annotated II. Ramesses II, Royal Inscriptions*, vol. 1 *Translations*, vol. 2 *Notes and Comments*. Oxford: Oxbow.
2003 *Ramesside Inscriptions IV. Merenptah and the Late Nineteenth Dynasty. Translations*. Oxford: Oxbow.
2008 *Ramesside Inscriptions. Translations V. Setnakht, Ramses III and Contemporaries*. Oxford: Oxbow.
2009 "Alas(h)i(y)a (Irs) and Asiya (Isy) in Ancient Egyptian Sources", in *Egypt and Cyprus in Antiquity*, edited by D. Michaelides, V. Kassianidou and R. S. Merrillees, pp. 1–8. Oxford and Oakville: Oxbow.

KLENGEL, H.
1999 *Geschichte des Hethitischen Reiches*, HdO I 34. Leiden, Boston and Köln: Brill.

KLINGER, J.
2002 "Die hethitisch-kaskäische Geschichte bis zum Beginn der Großreichszeit," in *Anatolia antica. Studi in memoria di Fiorella Imparati*, Eothen 11, edited by S. De Martino and F. Pecchioli Daddi, pp. 437–451. Firenze: LoGisma.
2005 "Das Korpus der Kaskäer-Texte," *Altorientalische Forschungen* 32: 347–359.
2008 "Zalpa, Nerik und Ḫakmiš. Die Bedeutung der nördlichen Peripherie Zentralanatoliens in hethitischer Zeit," in *Ḫattuša – Boğazköy. Das Hethiterreich im Spannungsfeld der Alten Orients,* CDOG 6, edited by G. Wilhelm, pp. 277–290. Wiesbaden: Harrassowitz.
2009 "The Cult of Nerick – Revisited," in *Central-North Anatolia in the Hittite Period. New Perspectives in the Light of Recent Research*, Studia Asiana 5, edited by F. Pecchioli Daddi, G. Torri and C. Corti, pp. 97–107. Roma: Herder.

KRAUSS, R.
1997 "Untersuchungen zu König Amenmesse: Nachträge," *Studien zur Altägyptischen Kultur* 24: 161–184.

LACKENBACHER, S. and MALBRAN-LABAT, F.
2005 "Ugarit et les Hittites dans les archives de la „Maison d'Urtenu"," *SMEA* 47: 227–240.

LEBRUN R.
2004 "Le monde Hittite et les îles de la Méditerranée orientale: le cas chypriote", *Res Antiquae* 1: 359–364.

LEHMANN, G. A.
1979 "Die Šikalāju — ein neues Zeugnis zu den ‚Seevölker'-Heerfahrten im späten 13. Jh. v. Chr.," *Ugarit-Forschungen* 11: 481–494.

LESKO, L. H.
1992 "Egypt in the 12th Century B.C.," in *The Crisis Years: The 12th Century B.C.*, edited by W. A. Ward and M. Sharp Joukowsky, pp. 151–156. Dubuque/Iowa: Kendall/Hunt Publishing.

LOPRIENO, A.
1996 "The "King's Novel," in *Ancient Egyptian Literature. History and Forms*, edited by A. Loprieno, pp. 277–295. Leiden *et al.*: Brill.

MACGILLIVRAY, J. A. and SACKETT, L. H.
"Palaikastro," in *The Oxford Handbook of the Bronze Age Aegean (ca. 3000–1000 BC),* edited by E. Cline, pp. 571–581. Oxford: Oxford University Press.

MADERNA-SIEBEN, C.
1991 "Der historische Abschnitt des Papyrus Harris I," *Göttinger Miszellen* 123: 57–90.

MALBRANT-LABAT, F.
2004 "Alashiya et Ougarit," *Res Antiquae* 1: 365–377.

MANASSA, C.
2003 *The Great Karnak Inscription of Merenptah: Grand Strategy in the 13th c. BC*, New Haven: Yale University Press.

MARKETOU, T.
2010 "Dodecanese," "Rhodos," in *The Oxford Handbook of the Bronze Age Aegean (ca. 3000–1000 BC),* edited by E. Cline, pp. 762–774,775–793. Oxford: Oxford University Press.

MARAN, J. and PAPADIMITRIOU, A.
2006 "Forschungen im Stadtgebiet von Tiryns 1999–2002. Bericht zu den Ausgrabungen im Stadtgebiet Nordost," *Archäologischer Anzeiger* 2006/1: 99–133.

MATTHÄUS, H.
2005 "Handel, Kulturaustausch und Seefahrt im Mittelmeerraum während der Spätbronzezeit," in *Das Schiff von Uluburun. Welthandel vor 3000 Jahren*, edited by Ü. Yalcın, C. Pulak and R. Slotta, pp. 333–366. Bochum: Veröffentlichungen aus dem Deutschen Bergbaumuseum Bochum 138.
2009 "Zeitenwenden im Mittelmeergebiet. Kunst und Kultur Zyperns zwischen 1100 und 750 v. Chr.," in *Zypern — Insel im Schnittpunkt interkultureller Kontakte. Adaption und Abgrenzung von der Spätbronzezeit bis zum 5. Jahrhundert v. Chr.*, edited by R. Bohl, K. Kleibl and S. Rogge, pp. 139–190. Münster: Waxmann-Verlag.

MEDINET HABU I
Medinet Habu I (Plates 1-54): Earlier Historical Records of Ramses III, OIP 8, Chicago 1930. Chicago University Press.

MEDINET HABU II
Medinet Habu II (Plates 55-130): Later Historical Records of Ramses III, OIP 9, Chicago 1932. Chicago University Press.

MEDINET HABU VIII
Medinet Habu VIII, The Eastern High Gate, OIP 94, Chicago 1970. Chicago University Press.

MEEUS, J.
2002 *More Mathematical Astronomy Morsels*. Richmond: Willmann-Bell.

MEROUSES, N.
2002 *Xíos [Chios. Physiko periballos kai katoikese apo te neolithike epoche mechri to telos tes achaiotas]*. Chios: Papyros.

MORAN, W. L.
The Amarna Letters. Baltimore: The John Hopkins University Press.

MOUNTJOY, P. A.
2009 "Cyprus and the East Aegean: LH IIIC pottery connections," in *Cyprus and the East Aegean: Intercultural contacts from 3000 to 500 B.C.*, edited by V. Karageorghis and O. Kouka, pp. 59–71. Nicosia: A.G. Leventis Foundation.

NELSON, H. H. *et al.*
1936 *Reliefs and Inscriptions at Karnak I-II. Ramses' III Temple within the Great Inclosure of Amon and Ramses' III Temple in the Precinct of Mut*, OIP 35. Chicago: Chicago University Press.

NIEMEIER, W.-D.
2008 "Ḫattušas Beziehungen zu West-Kleinasien und zum mykenischen Griechenland (Aḫḫijawa)," in *Ḫattuša – Boğazköy. Das Hethiterreich im Spannungsfeld der Alten Orients,* CDOG 6, edited by G. Wilhelm, pp. 291–349. Wiesbaden: Harrassowitz.
2009 "Milet und Karien vom Neolithikum bis zu den 'Dunklen Jahrhunderten'. Mythos und Archäologie," in *Die Karer und die Anderen,* edited by F. Rumscheid, pp. 7–25. Bonn: Habelt.

NIMS, C. F.
1976 "Ramesseum Sources of Medinet Habu Reliefs," in *Studies in Honor of George R. Hughes,* edited by J. H. Johnson and E. F. Wente, pp. 169–175. Chicago: The Oriental Institute of the University of Chicago.

NOWICKI, K.
2000 *Defensible Sites in Crete c. 1200–800 B.C.: LM IIIB/IIIC through Early Geometric*, Aegaeum 21. Liège: Université de Liège.
2008 *Monastiraki Katalimata: Excavation of a Cretan Refuge Site, 1993–2000.* Philadelphia: Instap Academic Press.

O'CONNOR, D.
2000 "The Sea Peoples and the Egyptian Sources," in *The Sea Peoples and Their World: A Reassessment*, edited by E. D. Oren, pp. 85–102. Philadelphia: The University of Pennsylvania Museum.
OETTINGER, N.
2010 "Seevölker und Etrusker," in *Pax Hethitica. Studies on the Hittites and their Neighbours in Honour of Itamar Singer*, StBo 51, edited by Y. Cohen *et al.*, pp. 233–246. Wiesbaden: Harrassowitz.
REDFORD, D. B.
2000 "Egypt and Western Asia in the Late New kingdom: An Overview," in *The Sea Peoples and Their World: A Reassessment*, edited by E. D. Oren, pp. 1–20. Philadelphia: The University of Pennsylvania Museum.
ROLLINGER, R.
2001 "The Ancient Greeks and the Impact of the Ancient Near East: Textual Evidence and Historical Perspective," in *Mythology and Mythologies: Methodological Approaches to Intercultural Influences*, edited by R. M. Whiting, pp. 233–264. Helsinki: The Neo-Assyrian Text Corpus Project.
RUMSCHEID, F., ed.
2009 *Die Karer und die Anderen*. Bonn: Habelt.
SALZANI, L., ed.
2005 *La necropoli dell'età del Bronzo all'Olmo di Nogara*. Verona: Museo Civico di Storia Naturale di Verona.
SCHIPPER, B. U.
2005 *Die Erzählung des Wenamun. Ein Literaturwerk im Spannungsfeld von Politik, Geschichte und Religion*, Orbis Biblicus et Orientalis 209. Fribourg and Göttingen: Academic Press Fribourg and Vandenhoeck & Rupprecht.
SCHNEIDER, T.
1992 *Asiatische Personennamen in ägyptischen Quellen des Neuen Reiches*, Orbis Biblicus et Orientalis 114. Fribourg and Göttingen: Academic Press Fribourg and Vandenhoeck & Rupprecht.
SEIDLMAYER, ST. J.
1998 "Epigraphische Bemerkungen zur Stele des Sethnachte," in *Stationen: Beiträge zur Kulturgeschichte Ägyptens (Festschrift R. Stadelmann)*, edited by H. Guksch and D. Polz, pp. 363–386. Mainz: von Zabern.
SHAW, J. W.
2006 *Kommos. A Minoan Harbour Town and Greek Sanctuary in Southern Crete*. Athens: American School of Classical Studies at Athens.
SHERRATT, S.
1998 "«Sea Peoples» and the Economic Structure of Late Second Millennium in the Eastern Mediterranean," in *Mediterranean Peoples in Transition. Thirteenth to Early Tenth Centuries BCE*, edited by S. Gitin, A. Mazar and E. Stern, pp. 292–313. Jerusalem: Israel Exploration Society.
SINGER, I.
1999 "A Political History of Ugarit," in *Handbook of Ugarit Studies*, HdO I 39, edited by G. W. E. Watson and N. Wyatt, pp. 603–733. Leiden, Boston and Köln: Brill.
STOCKFISCH, D.
2008 "Original und Kopie – ein Aspekt in den Untersuchungen zu den Fremdvölkerlisten," in *Altägyptische Weltsichten*, Ägypten und Altes Testament 68, edited by F. Adrom and K. and A. Schlüter, pp. 168–182. Wiesbaden: Harrassowitz.

STROBEL, K.
2008a "Neues zur Geographie und Geschichte des Alten Anatolien. Eine Einführung mit einem Beitrag zur hethitischen Geographie des westlichen Anatolien," in *New Perspectives on the Historical Geography and topography of Anatolia in the II and I Millenium B.C.*, Eothen 16, edited by K. Strobel, pp. 9–61. Firenze: LoGisma.
2008b "Die kulturelle und religiöse Entwicklung Altphrygiens II: Von Hattuša nach Gordion. Mit einem Anhang zum Kızıl Dağ," in *Vom Euphrat bis zum Bosporus. Kleinasien in der Antike. Festschrift Elmar Schwertheim*, Asia Minor Studien 65, edited by E. Winter, pp. 639–671. Bonn: Habelt.
2008c "The 13th to 11th Centuries BC: Questions of Chronology and History in Central and Western Anatolia," in *Bati Anadolu ve Doğu Akdeniz Geç Tunç Çağı Kültürleri Üzerine Yeni Araştırmalar*, edited by A. Erkanal-Öktü, S. Günel and U. Deniz, pp. 193–208. Ankara: Hacettepe Üniversitesi Yaınları.
2010 "Althethitische Religion und Königsideologie — Eine weitere Brücke zur hethitischen Großreichszeit?," *Colloquium Anatolicum* 9: 29–85.
SWEENEY, D. and YASUR-LANDAU, A.
1999 "Following the Path of the Sea Persons: The Women in Medinet Habu Reliefs," *Tel Aviv* 26: 116–145.
TANSANI, D.
2003 "Mycenaean Influence on the Pottery of North Pantalica culture (Sicily)," in *The Periphery of the Mycenaean World*, edited by N. Kyparissi and M. Papakonstantinou, pp. 599–611. Athens: Greek Ministry of Culture.
2008 *La Sicilia e l'arcipelago maltese nell' età del Bronzo Medio*. Palermo: Officina di Studi Medievali.
TAYLOUR, W. D. and JANKO, R.
2008 *Ayios Stephanos: Excavations at a Bronze Age and Medieval Settlement in Southern Laconia*, BSA Suppl. 44. Athens: British School at Athens.
TEKOĞLU, R. and LEMAIRE, A.
2000 "La bilingue royale louvito-phénicienne de Çineköy," *CRAI* 2000/3: 961–1006.
VAGNETTI, L.
2010 "Western Mediterranean," in *The Oxford Handbook of the Bronze Age Aegean (ca. 3000–1000 BC)*, edited by E. Cline, pp. 890–905. Oxford: Oxford University Press.
WILSON, A.
2005 *The Campaign of Pharao Shoshenq I into Palestine*. Tübingen: J. C. B. Mohr.
YAKUBOVICH, I.
2010 *Sociolinguistics of the Luvian Language*. Leiden and Boston: Brill.
YAMADA, SH.
2000 *The Construction of the Assyrian Empire. A Historical Study of the Inscriptions of Shalmaneser III (859–824 BC) to the West*. Leiden, Boston and Köln: Brill.
YASUR-LANDAU, A.
2010 *The Philistines and Aegean Migration at the End of the Bronze Age*. Cambridge: Cambridge University Press.
YURCO, F. J.
1997 "Was Amenmesse the Viceroy of Kush, Messuwy?" *The Journal of the American Research Center in Egypt* 34: 49–56.

CHAPTER 23

AN AMULET WITH THE NAMES OF RAMESSES II FROM THE ROMAN BATHS AT ANKARA

Hasan PEKER

In Memory of Professor Ali Dinçol

During the 2009 season of the archaeological excavations in the Roman Baths at Ankara, a plaque (measuring 24 × 18 × 6.3 mm) made of white faience was unearthed[1] in the earliest layer together with Phrygian pottery. Two names of the pharaoh of the 19th dynasty, Ramesses II (1279–1213 BC) were inscribed on the object, which functioned as an amulet. The amulet was perforated through the perpendicular axis, and a groove for the string to hang it encircled the whole object (**Fig. 3**).

On the side which we designated as side A (**Fig. 1** and **Fig. 4**), the birth name (*nomen,* Son of Ra) of Ramesses II was placed twice in the double cartouche. The double cartouche was decorated by double ostrich plumes with a sun disc in between. The *nomen* of the pharaoh is written with Egyptian hieroglyphs as *mr(y) ꜣImn Rꜥ-ms-sw*, which means "Born of Ra (Ramesses), Beloved of Amun."

On side B (**Fig. 2** and **Fig. 5**) the throne name (*praenomen*) is repeated twice as *wsr-mꜣꜥt-Rꜥ stp n Rꜥ*, which means "The Justice of Ra is Powerful, Chosen of Ra." The double cartouche and the decoration is identical with side A.

On the Ankara example, the birth name of the Ramesses II is written twice side by side on one side, and the throne name is also repeated on the other side. On the other hand, similar objects found elsewhere, bear the birth and the throne name side by side on one face[2] (**Fig. 6**, **Fig.** 7 and **Fig. 8**). Futhermore, on the examples in Petrie[3] (**Fig. 9** and **Fig. 10**) and Ashmolean Museums[4] there is no sun disc between the ostrich plumes and their rear rectangular sides contain an inscription mentioning "daughter of the ruler of Kheta" and her name *Maaherneferura* in a cartouche (**Fig. 10**).

[1] I would like to thank to the Dr. Melih Arslan, Director of the Ankara Museum of Anatolian Civilisations who published the first report of my readings in Arslan *et al.* 2011.

[2] Petrie 1917, XL 45 and Petrie 1917, XLII 117 (the same inscription on the gemma); Petrie 1889, 1580; Hall 1913, 2096.

[3] Petrie Museum, UC61395; Petrie Museum, UC61296 (Petrie Museum Online Catalogue: http://petriecat.museums.ucl.ac.uk/, accessed 13 April 2012).

[4] Ashmolean Museum, Ashm. AN 1925.638.

The names of Ramesses II, who is one of the most powerful pharaohs of the 19th dynasty, and the magical symbols around them should be considered as a strengthening effect of the protective power of the amulet. This find in central Anatolia centuries after the death of Ramesses II is proof of the strength of the lasting tradition of his fame. The amulets of this shape, cartouches with double ostrich plumes bearing royal names, are found in non-royal burials of the 26th Dynasty and later[5], and with this find and similar examples,[6] we may date the production of them to the 25th Dynasty and later, in the beginning of the Late Egyptian Period. In addition to that, the find of this amulet in an archaeological context, although bearing the names of Ramesses II, could also support the dating of the other similar objects.

Bibliography

Andrews, C.,
1994 *Amulets of Ancient Egypt*. London: British Museum Press.

Arslan, M., Akalin, M., Talaakar, A.
2011 "Roma Hamamı 2009 Yılı Kazı Çalışmaları," *19. Müze Çalışmaları ve Kurtarma Kazıları Sempozyumu*: 341-362.

Budge, E. A. W.,
1925 *The Mummy: A Handbook of Egyptian Funerary Archaeology*, 2nd ed. Cambridge: Cambridge University Press

Hall, H. R. H.
1913 *Catalogue of Egyptian Scarabs etc. in the British Museum. Volume 1: Royal Scarabs*. London: British Museum.

Petrie, W. M. F.,
1889 *Historical Scarabs: A Series of Drawings from the Principal Collections Arranged Chronologically*. London: D. Nutt Publisher.
1917 *Scarabs and Cylinders with Names*. London: British School of Archaeology in Egypt.

[5] Andrews 1994, pp. 77 and 80.
[6] Budge 1925, p. 451: BM EA 55564.

Fig. 1 Photograph of the side A.

Fig. 2 Photograph of the side B.

Fig. 3 Left, right, top and bottom edges.

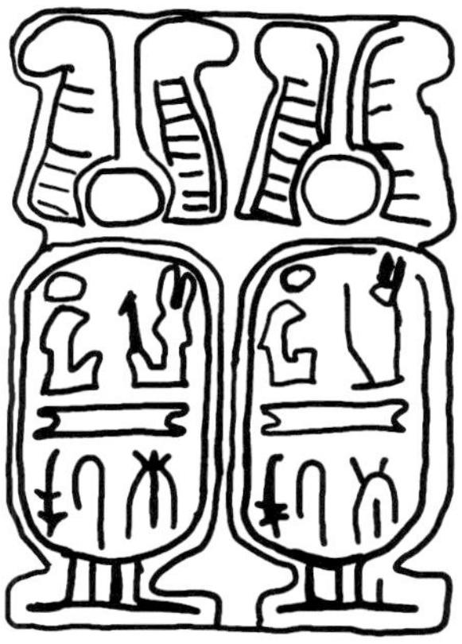

Fig. 4 Drawing of the side A.

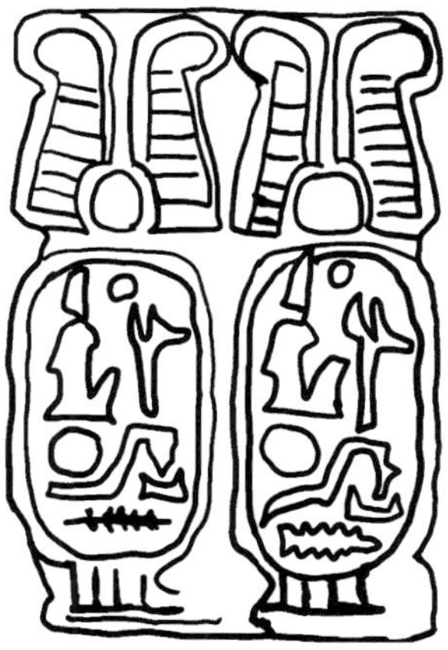

Fig. 5 Drawing of the side B.

Fig. 6 Petrie 1917, XL, 45.

Fig. 7 Petrie 1917, XLII, 117.

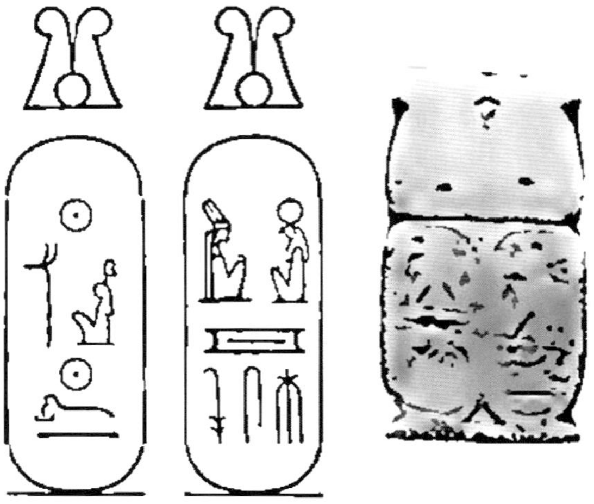

Fig. 8 British Museum (Hall 1913: 2096).

Fig. 9 Petrie Museum, UC61395.

Fig. 10 Petrie Museum, UC61296.

ANCIENT NEAR EASTERN STUDIES

(FORMERLY ABR-NAHRAIN)

Supplement Series

Series Editors: Antonio & Claudia Sagona

1. **Mayer L.A.**, *Bibliography of the Samaritans*, 1964, 50 p. — 30 EURO
2. **Bunnens G.**, *Tell Ahmar, 1988 Season*, 1990, 151 p. — 38 EURO
3. **Muraoka T.**, *Studies in Qumran Aramaic*, 1992, 167 p. — 45 EURO
4. **Muraoka T.**, *Studies in Ancient Hebrew Semantics*, 1995, VIII — 107 p. — 35 EURO
5. **Bunnens G.**, *Cultural Interaction in the Ancient Near East. Papers Read at a Symposium Held at the University of Melbourne, Department of Classics and Archaeology (29-30 September 1994)*, 1996, VIII — 155 p. — 40 EURO
6. **Muraoka T.**, *Semantics of Ancient Hebrew*, 1998, 151 p. — 35 EURO
7. **Bunnens G.**, *Essays on Syria in the Iron Age*, 2000, X — 557 p. — 105 EURO
8. **Adamthwaite M.R.**, *Late Hittite Emar. The Chronology, Synchronisms and Socio-Political Aspects of a Late Bronze Age Fortress Town*, 2001, XXIV — 294 p. — 70 EURO
9. **Sagona C.**, *The Archaeology of Punic Malta*, 2002, XIV — 1165 p. — 160 EURO
10. **Sagona C.**, *Punic Antiquities of Malta and Other Ancient Artefacts Held in Ecclesiastic and Private Collections*, 2003, XXII — 374 p. — 105 EURO
11. **Hopkins L.**, *Archaeology at the North-East Anatolian Frontier, VI. An Ethno-archaeological Study of Sos Höyük and Yigittasi Village*, 2003, XXVII — 184 p. — 90 EURO
12. **Sagona A.**, *A View from the Highlands: Archaeological Studies in Honour of Charles Burney*, 2004, XX — 743 p. — 120 EURO
13. **McConchie M.**, *Archaeology at the North-East Anatolian Frontier, V. Iron Technology and Iron-making Communities of the First Millennium BC*, 2004, XXIV — 393 p. — 90 EURO
14. **Sagona A., Sagona C.**, *Archaeology at the North-East Anatolian Frontier, I. An Historical Geography and a Field Survey of the Bayburt Province*, 2004, XXIV — 600 p. — 110 EURO
15. **Çilingiroğlu A., Derin Z., Abay E., Sağlamtimur H., Kayan İ.**, *Ulucak Höyük. Excavations Conducted between 1995 and 2002*, 2004, XII — 162 p. — 60 EURO
16. **Payne M.**, *Urartian Measures of Volume*, 2005, XX — 387 p. — 95 EURO
17. **Stoop-van Paridon P.W.T.**, *The Song of Songs. A Philological Analysis of the the Hebrew Book* **שיר השירים**, 2005, XVI — 540 p. — 90 EURO

18. **Sagona C., Vella Gregory I., Bugeja A.**, *Punic Antiquities of Malta and Other Ancient Artefacts Held in Private Collections*, 2, 2006, XXII — 276 p. 77 EURO
19. **Sagona A., Abramishvili M.**, *Archaeology in Southern Caucasus: Perspectives from Georgia*, 2008, VIII — 477 p. 94 EURO
20. **Çilingiroğlu A., Sagona A.**, *Anatolian Iron Ages 6: The Proceedings of the Sixth Anatolian Iron Ages Colloquium Held at Eskişehir, 16-20 August 2004*, 2007, X — 348 p. 85 EURO
21. **Azize J., Weeks N.**, *Gilgameš and the World of Assyria. Proceedings of the Conference Held at the Mandelbaum House, The University of Sydney, 21-23 July 2004*, 2007, VIII — 240 p. 84 EURO
22. **Wightman G.**, *Sacred Spaces. Religious Architecture in the Ancient World*, 2007, XX — 1156 p. 120 EURO
23. **Aitken J.K.**, *The Semantics of Blessing and Cursing in Ancient Hebrew*, 2007, XVI — 306 p. 85 EURO
24. **Steiner M., van der Steen E.J.**, *Sacred and Sweet. Studies on the Material Culture of Tell Deir ʿAlla and Tell Abu Sarbut*, 2008, VIII — 286 p. 85 EURO
25. **Yagodin V.N., Betts A.V.G., Blau S.**, *Ancient Nomads of the Aralo-Caspian Region. The Duana Archaeological Complex*, 2007, VIII — 138 p. 65 EURO
26. **McGeough K.**, *Exchange Relationships at Ugarit*, 2007, XVIII — 438 p. 95 EURO
27. **Rubinson K.S., Sagona A.**, *Ceramics in Transitions. Chalcolithic Through Iron Age in the Highlands of the Southern Caucasus and Anatolia*, 2008, VI — 364 p. 90 EURO
28. **Sagona C.**, *Beyond the Homeland: Markers in Phoenician Chronology*, 2008, VIII — 655 p. 98 EURO
29. **Bienkowski P.**, *Studies on Iron Age Moab and Neighbouring Areas in Honour of Michèle Daviau*, 2009, XIV — 273 p. 87 EURO
30. **Kuty R.J.**, *Studies in the Syntax of Targums Jonathan to Samuel*, 2010, XIV — 285 p. 85 EURO
31. **Redford S., Ergin N.**, *Perceptions of the Past in the Turkish Republic: Classical and Byzantine Periods*, 2010, X — 236 p. 79 EURO
32. **McGeough K., Smith M.S.**, *Ugaritic Economic Tablets. Text, Translation and Notes*, 2011, XXVI — 625 p. 98 EURO
33. **Hartley J.E.**, *The Semantics of Ancient Hebrew Colour Lexemes*, 2010, XVI — 247 p. 78 EURO
34. **Connor S.E.**, *A Promethean Legacy: Late Quaternary Vegetation History of Southern Georgia, the Caucasus*, 2011, XII — 419 p. 94 EURO
35. **Jamieson A.**, *Tell Ahmar III. Neo-Assyrian Pottery from Area C*, 2012, XVIII — 385 p. 105 EURO
36. **Sagona C.**, *Ceramics of the Phoenician-Punic World: Collected Essays*, 2011, X — 450 p. 95 EURO

37. **Ergin N.**, *Bathing Culture of Anatolian Civilizations: Architecture, History, and Imagination*, 2011, X — 329 p. 84 EURO
38. **Muraoka T.**, *A Grammar of Qumran Aramaic*, 2011, XLVI — 285 p. 70 EURO
39. **Çilingiroğlu A., Sagona A.**, *Anatolian Iron Ages 7: The Proceedings of the Seventh Anatolian Iron Ages Colloquium Held at Edirne, 19-24 April 2010*, 2012, X — 332 p. 87 EURO
40. **Redford S., Ergin N.**, *Cities and Citadels in Turkey: From the Iron Age to the Seljuks*, 2013, X — 346 p.

PRINTED ON PERMANENT PAPER • IMPRIME SUR PAPIER PERMANENT • GEDRUKT OP DUURZAAM PAPIER - ISO 9706
N.V. PEETERS S.A., WAROTSTRAAT 50, B-3020 HERENT